CUBA IN TRANSITION

Volume 6

Papers and Proceedings of the

**Sixth Annual Meeting
of the
Association for the Study of the Cuban Economy (ASCE)**

Miami, Florida
August 8-10, 1996

(ISBN 0-9649082-5-5)

Cuba in Transition volumes may be ordered from:

Association for the Study of the Cuban Economy
Attention: Treasurer
1629 K Street, N.W., Suite 1000
Washington, D.C. 20006
Tel. 202-296-8849
Fax 202-296-4884

PREFACE

The Proceedings from the Sixth Annual Meeting of the Association for the Study of the Cuban Economy contain a large selection of essays and commentaries presented in Miami, on August 8-10, 1996. We are very grateful for the co-sponsorship and support ASCE received from the North-South Center of the University of Miami and for the financial contributions to the meeting by several corporate sponsors.

As in the past, the essays contained herein represent a valiant effort at understanding current Cuban economic and legal reality. They also explore the possibilities and obstacles which exist for a rapid transition to economic and political democracy in Cuba. In particular, these studies identify many key parameters that a Cuban leadership seeking transition should consider in making important policy decisions for the future. The authors have focused on macro economic and legal framework issues, agricultural development, expropriation and privatization, foreign investment, sociological factors currently at play, United States policy toward Cuba, tourism, and the environment.

The Association is deeply in debt to those members who contributed to make the Sixth Annual meetings successful. I want to be particularly thankful to Armando Lago, our past president, for the continuous efforts and personal sacrifice that characterized his tenure. Special thanks are due to Jorge Pérez-López and José F. Alonso for the enormous volume of work they undertook to make these Proceedings possible. The high quality of this publication is due, largely, to their commitment to the Association.

Antonio Gayoso
President

TABLE OF CONTENTS

ASSOCIATION FOR THE STUDY OF THE CUBAN ECONOMY (ASCE)

Sixth Annual Meeting
University of Miami, James L. Knight Center, Hyatt Hotel
August 8-10, 1996

Conference Program

Panel Discussion: The Current Situation

Carmelo Mesa-Lago (University of Pittsburgh)

Pablo Alfonso (El Nuevo Herald)

Gerardo González Núñez (former Senior Researcher, Centro de Estudios de América)

Roundtable: Non-Sugar Agriculture — Current Situation and Prospects

William Messina (University of Florida)

José Alvarez (University of Florida)

Thomas H. Spreen (University of Florida)

Anne E. Moseley (University of Florida)

Charles M. Adams (University of Florida)

Macroeconomic and Debt Issues

The External Debt and the Principle of Solidarity: The Cuban Case

Alberto Martínez-Piedra (Catholic University) and Lorenzo L. Pérez (International Monetary Fund)

Discussant: Armando Ribas (Consultant, Argentina)

Cuba's Hard Currency Debt

Gabriel Fernández (Leonard N. Stern School of Business, New York University)

Discussant: Alberto Luzárraga (Amerinvest Corporation)

Cuba: A Shockless Stabilization and Financial Recovery

Rolando Castañeda and George Plinio Montalván (Inter-American Development Bank)

Discussant: Evaldo Cabarrouy (University of Puerto Rico)

Labor Markets

The Minimum Wage and Employment in Poland: Lessons for Cuba

Andrew M. Melnyk (University of Miami)

Discussant: Ernesto Hernández-Catá (International Monetary Fund)

Alternative Policies to Deal With Labor Surpluses During the Cuban Transition

Joseph M. Perry (University of North Florida)

Transition Strategies

Cuba: Five Key Policy Options for the Transition
Rolando Castañeda and George Plinio Montalván (Inter-American Development Bank)
Discussant: Ricardo Martínez (Inter-American Development Bank)
Post-Cold War Transition in Cuba and Vietnam
Julie Bunck (University of Louisville)
Discussant: Carlos Quijano (World Bank)
International Monetary Fund and World Bank Conditionalities and Cuba's Economic Reforms of the 1990s: A Comparison
Ramón Barquín III (B&B Importers)
Discussant: Joaquín Pujol (International Monetary Fund)

Roundtable: The 1995-96 Sugar Zafra — Results and Implications

Juan Tomás Sánchez (Agricultural Consultant)
Alfredo Blanco, Jr. (Productores de Azúcar de Cuba, Inc.)
Rafael Núñez (North-South Center, University of Miami)
Judy Ganes (Merrill Lynch)

Governance

Decentralization, Local Government and Citizen Participation in Cuba
Nelson R. Amaro (Universidad del Valle, Guatemala)
Discussant: Alfred Cuzán (University of West Florida)
Civil Society, Social Control and the Structure of Power in Cuba
Maida Donate (Sociologist)
Discussant: Guillermo Cueto (Cuba Consultants Corporation)
El dólar, la crisis y el hombre nuevo: Homo Economicus and Civil Society in Cuba
Juan Carlos Espinosa (University of Miami)
Discussant: Ricardo A. Puerta (International Development Consultant)

Special Topics

The Future Faces of the Cuban Economy: A Bayesian Forecast
Barton Bernales
Discussant: Jorge L. Romeu (State University of New York at Cortland)
The Effect of Socialism on the Entrepreneurial Abilities of Cuban Americans
Luis Locay (University of Miami) and Jorge Sanguinetty (DevTech Systems)
Discussant: Silvia Pedraza (University of Michigan)
Teoría de Contratos y Privatización: Insinuaciones para el Análisis del "Problema Cubano"
José Antonio Herrero (Consultant)
Discussant: Francisco León Delgado (ECLA, Santiago de Chile)

Roundtable: Economic Information on Cuba

Guillermo Cueto (CUBAWORLD)
Isabel Ezquerra (Richter Library, University of Miami)
Laurence I. Press (University of California, Dominguez Hills)
Jaime Suchlicki (Cuba On-Line)
Oscar Visiedo (Consultant)

Alberto Luzárraga (Cuban American Research Group and Instituto Internacional de Abogados Cubanos)

Law and International Economic Relations

Foreign Investment in Cuba: The Limits of "Commercial Engagement"

María C. Werlau (Orbis)

Discussant: Jorge Sanguinetty (DevTech Systems)

Helms-Burton: Checkmate or Challenge for Canadian Firms Doing Business in Cuba

Julia Sagebien (Dalhousie University); presentation by Beverly Campbell (Journalist)

Discussant: George Harper (Steel, Hector & Davis)

Graph Theory Modeling of U.S.-Cuban and Coalitional Conflicts Around Implementation of the Helms-Burton Legislation

Mario A. Rivera (University of New Mexico)

Discussant: Enrique S. Pumar (American University)

The Continued Good Standing of Legal Entities Organized in Cuba Through 1959-1960

Agustín de Goytisolo (Katz, Barron, Squitero & Faust)

Discussant: Juan Consuegra-Barquín (Attorney at Law)

IN HONOR OF FELIPE PAZOS

Roberto González Cofiño

It is a real pleasure, and an honor, for me to have this opportunity to say a few words about Felipe Pazos. Rather than being an introduction—which is not needed in the case of Felipe—they are aimed at highlighting some aspects of Felipe's personal history—as an economist, as a Cuban patriot, and as an exceptional human being—which make this recognition of his achievements particularly well deserved.

Felipe's work as an **economist** and in **managing economic policy** has had a profound impact, in Cuba and internationally. Within Cuba, or abroad as a Cuban Government official, he:

- Was a member of the Cuban delegation to the Bretton Woods Conference, which founded the World Bank and the International Monetary Fund.

- Founded, and was the first President of, Cuba's Central Bank (the *Banco Nacional de Cuba*), in 1950-52.

- Was a pioneer in the teaching of modern economics in Cuba, as Professor of Economic Development in the *Universidad de Santo Tomás de Villanueva* in 1954-55, and as Director of the Department of Economics of the *Universidad de Oriente* in 1955-57.

- Became again President of the Central Bank, from January to October of 1959.

- Held several diplomatic positions, including Commercial Attaché in the Cuban Embassy in Washington D.C. (1942-1946), and Ambassa-

dor-at-Large for Economic Affairs in Europe (1959).

At the Latin American and broader international levels, Dr. Pazos has been:

- A founding staff member of the IMF, holding the positions of Assistant Chief, and subsequently Chief, of the Fund's Western Hemisphere Department (1946-1948), and Assistant Director of its Research Department (1948-1949).

- Senior Economist in the World Bank (1952-1953).

- Research Director of the Center for Latin American Monetary Studies-CEMLA (1954-1957).

- Member of the top coordinating body of the Alliance for Progress, the Committee of Nine (*"the Nine Wise Men"*) of the Organization of American States (1961-1966).

- Senior Economist in the Inter-American Development Bank (1966-1975).

- A participant in numerous seminars and international meetings on economic development, inflation and other economic policy issues.

Since 1975, when he moved his residence to Caracas, Dr. Pazos has been Economic Advisor to the President of the Central Bank of Venezuela, while also serving during several years as member of the Bank's Board of Directors, and continuing his intensive participation in Latin America's intellectual activities

I would like to note also the impact of Felipe's articles and books over the last 50 years. His writings on

1

economic development were an important part of the emerging Latin American economics from the 1940s to the 1960s. His works on inflation—including his *Notas para un Estudio de la Espiral Inflacionaria* (1963), and *Chronic Inflation in Latin America* (Praeger Books, 1972)—are recognized today—in Latin America and in U.S. and European academic circles—as very important contributions to the understanding of the mechanics of inflation and to the design of stabilization policies. The list of his writings on diverse aspects of the economies of Cuba and Venezuela, and of the history of Latin American economic thought, would be too long to be mentioned here in detail.

There is, however, one contribution of Felipe that I believe should be pointed out with particular emphasis before this forum: his outline of the main economic problems likely to be encountered by the Cuban economy during the period of transition, which he included in his remarks for the first ASCE "Carlos Díaz-Alejandro Lecture," in 1991. Such problems were:

1. How to handle the reconversion of the economy from a centrally planned to a market determined system? In this context, one of the main issues will be how to bring about the privatization of the existing publicly-owned enterprises?

2. How to manage the country's international trade policy during the period of transition?

3. How to prevent economic activity from declining sharply in the initial stages of the transition and how to mobilize external economic and financial assistance?

4. How to implement a realignment of domestic prices, to bring them in line with costs of production, without depressing further the low levels of income of the population or giving rise to inflationary pressures?

5. How to keep the fiscal deficit under control and prevent the development of hyperinflation?

6. How to reestablish the work ethic of the population?

7. How to create the necessary institutions (financial and other) required for the proper functioning of a market economy?

8. How to encourage external private capital inflows without selling off existing assets at bargain prices?

9. How to reincorporate into the Cuban economy those entrepreneurs, administrators, technical personnel, and professionals now living in exile without creating undue friction and resentment in the population?

Dr. Pazos explored the implications of these issues in his Lecture, and suggested that they be studied in depth, in anticipation of the transition. As the records of the five subsequent ASCE annual meetings, and the agenda of the present one, clearly show, the issues raised by Felipe five years ago have been at the center of ASCE's analysis of the situation and prospects of the Cuban economy.

I would not like to finish these remarks without mentioning other facets of Felipe's life which are, to my mind, not less important than his professional achievements. His fidelity to democratic ideals took him to adopt difficult and risky positions more than once. As a young student, in the early 1930s, he was already active in the opposition to the dictatorship of Gerardo Machado. Years later, when Fulgencio Batista's coup interrupted Cuba's democratic process on March 10, 1952, Felipe Pazos resigned as President of the *Banco Nacional*. When Batista closed all doors to the possible peaceful resolution of the Cuban crisis, Pazos went to the Sierra Maestra in 1958, and signed a Document of Revolutionary Unity with Raúl Chibás and Fidel Castro. And when Castro jailed Hubert Matos in October 1959 because of his denunciation of communism, Felipe left, once more, the Presidency of the *Banco Nacional*. Shortly afterwards, he was involved anew in another revolutionary movement against the then-new and now very old dictatorship.

Throughout his whole life, Felipe Pazos has maintained moral and ethical standards which, I believe, should serve as an example for the Governments of the future Cuba. In 1950-52, for example, the *Banco*

Nacional was created and operated by Felipe in a clean and transparent way, in the midst of the corruption affecting much of Cuban political life at that time. And in 1959, Felipe again managed the same *Banco Nacional* in a fully independent and transparent manner, until it became clear that such independence and transparency were not virtues to be respected under Castro.

Last, but not least, I am sure that I am far from being the only one in this room who has an eternal debt of gratitude to Felipe because of the way he and his family helped us when we left Cuba. I believe that you would not be able to count how many of us you helped to find professional jobs, and how many of our families were assisted in many ways by you and your family.

Because of your many professional achievements... because of your contributions to Cuba and to Latin America...because of your moral and ethical standards...and because of your enduring friendship to so many....all of us wish to say to you: **Thank you, Felipe Pazos!**

THE STATE OF THE CUBAN ECONOMY: 1995-96

Carmelo Mesa-Lago

This essay deals with three important issues on the Cuban economy in 1995-96: (1) the rate of economic growth; (2) the net effect of the sugar harvest; and (3) faulty reporting by serious publications on Cuba's economic recovery. The following analysis is mostly based on official Cuban data.

THE RATE OF ECONOMIC GROWTH IN 1995-96

Until 1989, Cuba's State Committee on Statistics (CEE) published a series on the Global Social Product (GSP) based on the Soviet-style "material product system," not comparable with the Gross Domestic Product (GDP) based on the Western "national accounts system." A few Cuban scholars estimated GSP in 1990-93. The combination of these two sets of data show that GSP in constant (1981) prices suffered a cumulative decline of 45 percent in 1989-93 (CEE 1991; Carranza 1993; Carranza, Gutiérrez and Monreal 1995). A series of GDP (also in constant prices), published by the most popular Cuban magazine, indicated a decrease of 48 percent over the same period (Terrero 1994). In 1995 Cuba's National Bank (BNC) released a different series on GDP at constant prices exhibiting a decline of only 35 percent over the same period (10 percentage points lower than the decline in GSP and 13 points lower than in the previous GDP series). The Bank, nevertheless, revealed that the GDP decline in 1986-90 (during the anti-market "Rectification Process") was 6.7 percent, more than twice the previously reported fall of 3.1 percent in GSP (CEE 1991; BNC 1995). Be it deliberate or not, the reduction of the growth rate in 1986-89 resulted in a smaller decline of the rate in 1990-93. These changes and contradictions cast a

doubt on the reliability of Cuban economic growth data, aggravated by the absolute absence of information on how the new GDP series is calculated, the deflator used, and so forth (Mesa-Lago 1997).

The National Bank's GDP official growth rate for 1994 was 0.7 percent, or 0.2 percent per capita (the population growth rate that year was only 0.5 percent due to the raft-exodus of 35,000 Cubans) and the Bank projected a 2 percent growth rate for 1995, but the Minister of Economics later reported a rate of 2.5 percent, or 1.6 percent per capita (BNC 1995; Rodríguez 1996a). These figures suggested that the four-year decline in the Cuban economy had been halted and a modest recovery had begun. The 1996 target was set at 5 percent, or 4.1 percent per capita, but in June the Minister of Economics reported a 7 percent growth rate for the first half of the year (Rodríguez 1996b). Less than a month later, Vice-President of the Council of State Carlos Lage raised that rate to 9.6 percent; he added, however, that such a high rate was the result of the increase in sugar output which was entirely credited to the first semester, and that growth in the second semester would be "smaller" but enough to fulfill the annual target rate of 5 percent (Lage 1996). A simple mathematical calculation reveals that to achieve an annual rate of 5 percent, the rate in the second semester would be only 0. 4 percent, or -0. 6 percent per capita.

The stagnation/decline in the second semester could have two explanations: (a) the very high growth in the first semester makes more difficult a strong performance in the second (still this does not justify stagnation/decline, particularly in view of official reports of recovery in part of the non-sugar sector); and (b) payment of loans taken by the Cubans to finance 1996 sugar output has reduced import capacity in the second half of the year (this point is developed in the next section).

Even assuming that the Cuban economy indeed grows at an annual rate of 5 percent in 1996 (4 percent per capita) and that the Cuban economy is able to sustain such a rate in the future, it would take 9 years to recover the absolute GDP peak of 1985 or 14 years (until 2,009) to match the GDP per capita peak of 1985. The latter was 2,006 Cuban pesos. The official exchange rate of the peso for the U.S. dollar was par at the time (one peso for one U.S. dollar) but such rate was arbitrarily set by the government and did not reflect the real value of the peso in the domestic market (the peso is not traded in the world market). If the more realistic Cuban black-market exchange rate of 6 pesos per dollar prevailing in 1985 is used, Cuba's GDP per capita that year was US$334 similar to that of Haiti (World Bank 1987). In September of 1996, the exchange rate in official exchange agencies was 20 pesos per one dollar; hence the projected GDP annual per capita of 1,228 pesos for 1996 was equivalent to US$61, the lowest in the world (World Bank 1996).The above projection of GDP per capita to the year 2009 was done in pesos; hence, the recovery of the 1985 level in dollar terms would depend on the market peso-dollar exchange rate in 2,009 remaining at the same level as in 1985.

THE NET EFFECT OF THE SUGAR HARVEST

The official figure of sugar production in the 1995-96 harvest is 4.445 million tons (Lage 1996). This was 1.115 million tons more than the 3.3 million tons of the previous harvest (the lowest in 50 years). Domestic consumption in 1995 was reported as 800,000 tons (ECLAC 1995); assuming that a similar consumption occurs in 1996, the increase of sugar available for export would increase from 2.5 million tons in 1995 to 3.645 in 1996, for a net gain of 1.145 million tons. The sugar price in the world market averaged 13.28 U.S. cents in 1995, but fell to an average of 12.46 U.S. cents in the first eight months of 1996, with a tendency to decline. Based

on those prices, the value of sugar exports in 1995 was US$730 million and would be about US$1,000 million in 1996, for a net export value increase of US$270 million.

In order to increase sugar production in 1996, Cuba had to take substantial loans from foreign banks at a very high interest rate and repayable in one year. There are no accurate statistics on the amounts of those loans; published figures range from US$130 to $300 million, with a mid-point figure of US$228 million (*The Economist* 1996). The most quoted interest rate is 14 percent, but rates as high as 18 percent have been published. Based on loan values of US$228 million at an interest rate of 14 percent (US$32 million), the total to be paid back would be US$260 million, that is, a net gain of only US$10 million based in the US$270 million net increase in export value in 1995-96. In spite of the physical increase in sugar output, accounted in the GDP for the first semester of 1996, the net gain in hard currency revenue was very small and the payment of the loans will reduce Cuba's capacity to import in the second semester of 1996. The reported oil shortages in September reflect that problem, and the cut in imports could then explain the stagnation/decline in the growth rate in the second semester.

The lasting effects of the loans obtained to finance the sugar crop should be very small or nil because most of them were used to import fertilizers, herbicides, pesticides and fuel for the 1995-96 harvest, and those inputs will not have any effect on the next harvest. Part of the loan proceeds, nevertheless, was allocated to import spare parts for the sugar mills and should have more lasting effects; and yet the poor state of the Cuban mills is likely to provoke increasing break downs and need for spare parts. The long harvest of 1996 (there were mills still grinding in June) probably will have an adverse impact on the next crop, because unripe cane planted for 1996-97

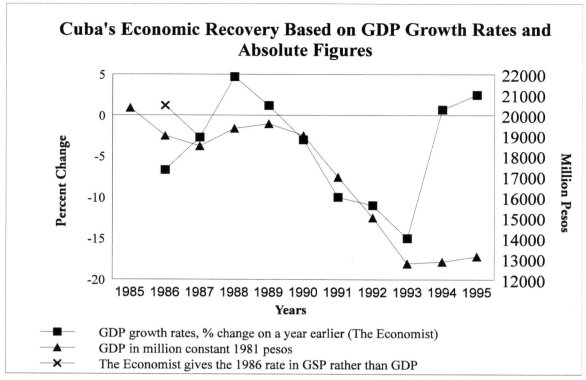

Cuba's Economic Recovery Based on GDP Growth Rates and Absolute Figures

Legend:
- ■— GDP growth rates, % change on a year earlier (The Economist)
- ▲— GDP in million constant 1981 pesos
- ✕— The Economist gives the 1986 rate in GSP rather than GDP

was cut and the time for replanting and preparing for the next harvest was reduced (Lage 1996).

Conversely, paying the loan should have a positive effect on Cuba's credit ranking, but the Helms-Burton Law seems to be playing a negative role. For instance, a Dutch bank that provided one of the 1995 loans to Cuba has announced that it will not do it again in 1996. In any case, to maintain sugar production at the same level as in 1995-96, Cuba would have to borrow a similar amount, with prospects of minimal gains and high risks (e.g., sugar world market prices may decline further, bad weather may harm the crop). Increasing sugar production over the 1995-96 level would require bigger loans and stakes would be higher.

FAULTY REPORTING ON CUBA'S ECONOMIC RECOVERY

The first section of this essay made clear that Cuban macro statistics should be subject to careful scrutiny, while the second section showed that even unquestionable improvements in physical output, such as sugar, must be seriously analyzed to assess their net impact on growth. This author believes that the dramatic decline in the Cuban economy was halted in

1995-96, at least temporarily, but the recovery has been sluggish to say the least. Part of the problem is that the Cuban leadership has been reluctant and hesitant on market-oriented reforms and there have been setbacks as well as lack of an integrated, coherent reform package. Furthermore, the reform seems to have been halted or at least is proceeding at a very slow pace since mid-1995. Raúl Castro's speech of March 1996 criticized both the adverse effects of the reforms and some institutions (e.g., the Center for the Study of the Americas, CEA) which had played a positive role in it. The speech prompted the demotion of, or admonition to, some scholars who had been leaders in the reform process and urged the government to accelerate and deepen it (CEA scholars have been prohibited to conduct research on Cuba's domestic economy, unless doing so is necessary to tackle an international topic).

Prestigious international organizations and publications have not always been serious in the analysis of Cuban data and even distorted them. A recent example is *The Economist*'s (1996) handling of the economic recovery. The graph above shows that such publication used the GDP **rate** of growth in 1986-95 to depict the recovery, "demonstrating" that, in 1995, Cuba had almost matched a 1988 "peak"(which actually occurred in 1985--not shown by *The Economist*) and was well above the 1986 level (which incorrectly was given in GSP). A miraculous recovery indeed! But if the **absolute** GDP figures published by the BNC had been used (the proper procedure to plot the trend), the results would have been dramatically different: In 1995 Cuba's GDP was well below its 1988 level as well as its 1985 peak, and the recovery was extremely weak. The gap in 1995 between *The Economist* rate and the absolute GDP is astonishingly wide. Unfortunately, such distortion confused readers of the prestigious publication and gave credit to the old saying "there are small lies, big lies and statistics."

BIBLIOGRAPHY

"A Survey of Cuba," *The Economist* (April 6, 1996), 16 pp.

Banco Nacional de Cuba (BNC), *Economic Report 1994*. La Habana, August 1995.

Carranza, Julio, "Cuba: los retos de la economía," *Cuadernos de Nuestra América*, no. 19 (1993), pp. 131-159.

Carranza, Julio, Luis Gutiérrez and Pedro Monreal, *Cuba: la Restructuración de la Economía: Una Propuesta para el Debate*. La Habana: Editorial de Ciencias Sociales, 1995.

Castro, Raúl, "Informe del Buró Político sobre la situación política y social del país...," *Granma* (March 27, 1996), pp. 2-6.

Comité Estatal de Estadísticas (CEE), *Anuario Estadístico de Cuba 1989*. La Habana, 1991.

Economic Commission for Latin America and the Caribbean (ECLAC), "Cuba: Evolución económica durante 1994," Santiago, 1995.

Lage, Carlos, "Informe del Ministerio de Economía y Planificación," La Habana: EFE, July 23, 1996.

Mesa-Lago, Carmelo, "Assessing Cuban Socio-Economic Statistics in the 1990s," paper to be presented at the Meetings of the American Economic Association, ASCE Panel, New Orleans, January 1997.

Rodríguez, José Luis, "Discurso en la V Feria Comercial del Caribe," La Habana, June 30, 1996a.

Rodríguez, José Luis. "Perspectivas Económicas de Cuba 1996." Davos: World Economic Forum, February 1-6, 1996b.

Terrero, Ariel, "Tendencias de un ajuste," *Bohemia* (October 28, 1994).

World Bank, *World Development Report 1987* and 1996. New York: Oxford University Press, 1987, 1996.

APUNTES SOBRE LA SITUACION SOCIO-ECONOMICA DE CUBA

Pablo Alfonso

El proceso de reformas económicas que el gobierno de Cuba comenzó a implementar en 1993, a partir de la llamada "dolarización," se ha visto prácticamente detenido en lo que va de año.

La causa de este *"congelamiento"* parece ser, en esencia, la voluntad política del gobierno de impedir el surgimiento de una economía de mercado que conduzca a una apertura política.

El signo ideológico y político del gobierno cubano ha puesto un límite al proceso de reformas económicas. Su profundización o ampliación no depende de su propia dinámica, sino que está sometido al marco político definido por los que gobiernan.

Un ejemplo que puede ilustrar esta afirmación es el proyecto de ley que permitiría a los cubanos ser propietarios de pequeñas o medianas empresas y que desde hace más de un año circula por distintas instancias del gobierno. Su promulgación parece ahora definitivamente pospuesta para un indefinido futuro.

Durante 1996 el gobierno ha aprobado varias medidas económicas que no profundizan las reformas, sino que más bien son consecuencia de otras aprobadas anteriormente.

- El primero de enero de 1996 entró en vigor el impuesto sobre ingresos personales en divisas, con excepción de las remesas familiares que se envían desde el exterior.

- En mayo fue aprobada la Resolución Conjunta No.1 de los Ministerios de Trabajo y Seguridad Social y de Finanzas y Precios, que regula el ejercicio del trabajo por cuenta propia.

- En junio se aprobó el decreto que regula el funcionamiento de las zonas francas. Las primeras áreas donde se instalarán estas zonas son en el puerto del Mariel, en la bahía de Cienfuegos, y en Wajay, localidad próxima al Aeropuerto Internacional de Rancho Boyeros.

- La Ley 73, que creó el actual Sistema Tributario y que fue aprobada en agosto de 1994, ha venido aplicándose gradualmente. Este año, según esa legislación se establecieron 11 tipos diferentes de impuestos; una contribución de las empresas a la Seguridad Social y tres tasas impositivas: servicio de aeropuertos a pasajeros; peaje; y anuncios y/o propaganda comercial.

Atendiendo a los límites de esta panorámica informativa de la situación socio-económica cubana, quiero centrar la atención en tres aspectos que considero relevantes: 1) la política impositiva; 2) la estructura agrícola y mercados agropecuarios; y 3) la distribución de la fuerza laboral.

LA POLITICA IMPOSITIVA

La aplicación de la nueva política impositiva ha tenido repercusiones negativas en una población que, como la de Cuba, no conoció esta modalidad en las últimas tres décadas. A esa comprensible reacción de la población, hay que sumar el criterio negativo con que el gobierno está aplicando la política impositiva. El pago de los impuestos ha sido planteado como un castigo a los productores independientes y a los trabajadores por cuenta propia. Como una manera de evitar el enriquecimiento.

Estos conceptos, expresados reiteradamente por los más altos dirigentes del gobierno, fueron recogidos en un reciente editorial del semanario *Trabajadores*, órgano oficial de la Central de Trabajadores de Cuba, que arremetió contra los denominados "*nuevos ricos*," refiriéndose a los intermediarios en los mercados agrícolas y, en general, a todos aquellos "que se aprovechan de las necesidades para ganar más y más dinero."

> Nada mejor contra ellos que un buen impuesto que les sustraiga al menos una parte del dinero que, abusivamente, ganan a montones.[1]

Aunque el año fiscal comenzó el primero de enero, y los cubanos con ingresos en dólares empezaron a pagar un mes después, la resolución que estableció los procedimientos de recaudación fiscal para el resto de los afectados, no entró en vigor hasta el 11 de abril.

En el primer cuatrimestre de 1996, las arcas del Estado captaron $4,325.3 millones de pesos por concepto de diferentes impuestos y otros ingresos. De ese total sólo 63 millones —el 1.5%— correspondió al pago de impuestos por los ingresos personales de los trabajadores por cuenta propia. Aún así, la contribución global de los trabajadores por cuenta propia, más que duplicó en ese cuatrimestre la de igual período del pasado año.[2]

Para aplicar la política fiscal se creó la Oficina Nacional de Administración Tributaria (ONAT), con representación en cada uno de los municipios del país.

La recaudación fiscal depende del sistema de honor, con frecuentes visitas de los inspectores fiscales. Aunque los trabajadores por cuenta propia deben llevar registros de sus ganancias y gastos, no se requiere que sus libros sean auditados. Pero además resulta que, legalmente, nadie puede hacerlo. Los contadores privados no existen en las categorías aprobadas de

trabajadores por cuenta propia y no hay oficinas de contabilidad del gobierno para prestar esos servicios.

El considerable aumento de las nuevas normas impositivas sobre el ingreso a trabajadores por cuenta propia ha obligado a un buen número de ellos a cancelar sus licencias y pasar a la ilegalidad, según informes de diversas fuentes.

La cuota que debe pagar un conductor de taxi, por ejemplo, subió de 100 a 400 pesos mensuales, mientras que el aumento para un manicurista implicó un alza de 60 a 100 pesos mensuales.

En La Habana había en junio 30, un total de 900 restaurantes o paladares. Hasta el día primero de ese mes sus dueños pagaban una licencia mensual equivalente a $40.00 dólares en pesos cubanos y otros $100.00 dólares por el derecho de aceptar pagos en divisas.

Sin embargo, bajo las nuevas reglas la licencia subió a $750.00 dólares (con igual paridad peso-dólar); una cuota por cada miembro de la familia empleado y deben pagar, además, impuestos por ingresos personales.

A pesar de estos drásticos aumentos, no hay informes de que se haya producido, hasta ahora, un aumento correspondiente de los precios en los servicios privados y/o en los productos que se comercializan en los mercados agropecuarios.

ESTRUCTURA AGRICOLA Y MERCADOS AGROPECUARIOS

En septiembre de 1993 comenzó en Cuba un reordenamiento del uso y tenencia de las tierras agrícolas que algunos especialistas han calificado como la Tercera Reforma Agraria llevada a cabo por el régimen que mantiene el poder desde hace 37 años.

A partir de esta última reforma la estructura agrícola cubana ha cambiado radicalmente. Hasta hace tres años se podía hablar, en términos generales, de empresas agrícolas estatales y pequeños campesinos.

---

1. *Trabajadores* (27 de mayo 1996), p. 2.

2. "Aumenta la captación de impuestos," *Juventud Rebelde* (26 de mayo 1996), p. 2.

Hoy la situación es diferente. Las antiguas empresas agrícolas estatales se han convertido en empresas cooperativas de diversas modalidades y distritos agrícolas militares, que coexisten con productores privados.

La estructura agrícola actual se compone de:

- Unidades Básicas de Producción Cooperativa
- Cooperativas de Producción Agropecuaria
- Cooperativas de Crédito y Servicio
- Productores Privados
- Distritos Agrícolas Militares
- Granjas Estatales

El 42.3 % de la tierra explotable de la isla está ocupado hoy por las UBPC, en tanto que las Cooperativas de Producción Agropecuaria, ocupan el 10 %; las de Créditos y Servicios el 11.5 % y los campesinos independientes el 3.4%.[3] El resto del área disponible corresponde a las granjas estatales y a los distritos agrícolas militares.

Unidades Básicas de Producción Cooperativa (UBPC)

Constituídas a partir de las antiguas granjas estatales, las UBPC poseen la mayor cantidad de tierras cultivables, que fueron entregadas en usufructo a sus miembros.

Un total de 1,556 UBPC están dedicadas al cultivo de la caña de azúcar en tanto otras 1,577 corresponden al sector no cañero con un importante peso en la producción de viandas y vegetales.

La escasa participación de las UBPC no cañeras en los mercados agropecuarios es atribuída a su baja producción que apenas alcanza a cubrir sus compromisos con los organismos estatales de acopio que abastecen la red oficial minorista.

En opinión de los analistas del gobierno los altos precios del mercado agropecuario obedecen, precisa-

mente, a esa baja presencia de las UBPC y otras empresas agrícolas estatales en estos mercados que son abastecidos por lo general, por cooperativistas y productores privados.

En un seminario organizado por la Asociación de Economistas de la Ciudad de La Habana, a mediados de noviembre se concluyó que "tras el impacto inicial, el mercado agropecuario muestra síntomas de estancamiento al no lograr los efectos esperados en la incentivación de la oferta."

Las causas son los altos precios que impone una participación mayoritoria del sector privado.

Un reciente estudio del Instituto Nacional de Investigaciones Económicas titulado *¿Mercado: apertura o limitación?* advirtió que "de continuar ese monopolio, las ventas descenderían a pesar de existir una demanda insatisfecha, por la vigencia de altos precios y la cada vez más limitada posibilidad de acceso a la población."

El mismo estudio concluyó que la mayor parte de las ganancias, el 87 %, han ido a parar a mano de los productores privados que, por otra parte, no tienen muchas alternativas para invertir ese dinero.

Cooperativas de Producción Agropecuaria (CPA)

Las CPA están integradas por pequeños agricultores privadores que entregaron sus tierras a estas cooperativas. Existen en la actualidad 771 CPA que ocupan el 10% de las tierra agrícola del país, a pesar de lo cual producen el 51 % de las hortalizas y el 30 % de las viandas que consume el país. Este año alcanzaron, además, el 20 % de la producción total de caña.[4]

En 1995, el 90% de las CPA fueron rentables y obtuvieron una ganancia de 97 millones de pesos según datos del Buró Nacional de la Asociación Nacional de Agricultores Pequeños. En contraste, ese mismo año, sólo el 36% de las UBPC no cañeras fueron rentables.[5]

---

3. "Agricultura no cañera," Revista *Tips* (mayo 1996).

4. "En la vinculación al área también está la fuerza," *Trabajadores* (22 de abril 1996).

5. "Hay que pensar en ellos," *Juventud Rebelde* (21 de abril 1996).

Cooperativas de Créditos y Servicios (CCS)

A diferencia de las CPA, en las Cooperativas de Créditos y Servicios los campesinos mantienen la propiedad individual sobre sus tierras y de sus medios de trabajo.

Existen 2,260 CCS que abarcan el 11.5% de la tierra cultivable y que se han revitalizado en los últimos años con las entregas de pequeñas áreas de tierra a particulares para desarrollar el cultivo de café, tabaco y cacao.

Distritos Agrícolas Militares

Existe muy poca información de las áreas agrícolas que administran las Fuerzas Armadas y cuya producción va mucho más allá de un simple programa de autoconsumo para las tropas.

Dos datos recientes pueden dar una idea de la importancia de estos distritos agrícolas militares.

- En 1995 el Ejército Juvenil del Trabajo administraba 119 granjas dedicadas a cultivos varios, cítricos, café, caña y frutales, según el informe presentado en abril de este año al Consejo Militar del MINFAR, por el general de brigada Alvaro López Niera, subjefe del Estado Mayor General.

- Por su parte, el Ejército Oriental cuya jurisdicción abarca las cinco provincias orientales y la actual provincia de Camagüey cuenta con 70 granjas agrícolas, 65 de las cuales han sido rentables en el primer semestre de este año.[6]

Granjas Estatales

Las Granjas Estatales (GE), llamadas de nuevo tipo, comenzaron a constituirse con un concepción y estructura diferente a las que tenían antes de la restructuración agrícola de 1993.

Hasta el 30 de abril de 1996, el Ministerio de Agricultura había aprobado la creación de 36 nuevas granjas estatales.[7] En general estas granjas se están creando en la ganadería vacuna de ceba y genética, granjas de semillas para cultivos varios, granjas forestales y frutales.

Las GE reciben la tierra en usufructo, son autofinanciadas, con personalidad jurídica independiente y patrimonio propio, pero al igual que las UBPC y las CPA, su plan de producción dependerá de los volúmenes y destinos que determine el Estado.

A diferencia de las UBPC y las CPA los trabajadores de las GE tienen un salario fijado por el Estado, aunque pueden participar hasta del 50% de las utilidades, las cuales se distribuirán en proporción directa a la cantidad y calidad del trabajo aportado. Del otro 50%, la mitad engrosará el presupuesto estatal y el resto se destinará al desarrollo social y contingencias de cualquier índole.

DISTRIBUCION DE LA FUERZA LABORAL

Según las más recientes cifras del Ministerio del Trabajo, Cuba tiene una población laboral activa de 4.6 millones de habitantes.[8] Esa fuerza laboral, que hasta las reformas económicas iniciadas hace tres años dependía abrumadoramente del Estado, tiene ahora una composición diferente.

El trabajo por cuenta propia

Desde su aprobación en 1993, las normas del trabajo por cuenta propia han sido enmendadas en varias oportunidades.

Los trabajadores por cuenta propia tuvieron que reinscribirse el pasado mes de junio tras la aprobación de las nuevas normas que regulan esa actividad. De acuerdo con las cifras obtenidas al concluir ese proceso existían en todo el país, 208,500 personas autorizadas a trabajar por cuenta propia en 160 actividades aprobadas por la ley. Cálculos de fuentes independientes aseguran que aproximadamente otras 190,000 trabajan por su cuenta, sin la correspondiente autorización del gobierno.

Los servicios más populares que ofrecen los trabajadores por cuenta propia continúan siendo los "*pala-*

---

6. "Reportaje de Miosoti Fabelo, Noticiero Haciendo Radio," *Radio Rebelde* (5 de agosto 1996).

7. "Van surgiendo las Granjas Estatales de nuevo tipo," *Trabajadores* (13 de mayo 1996), p. 2.

8. "Intensifican guerra contra los nuevos ricos." *El Nuevo Herald* (28 de mayo 1996), p. 1B.

dares" (cafeterías y restaurantes) los taxis, salones de belleza y los talleres de artesanía y mecánica.

El Ministro de Trabajo y Seguridad Social, Salvador Valdés, afirmó recientemente que más del 50 % de los trabajadores por cuenta propia registrados eran personas sin vínculo laboral, es decir, desempleados.[9]

Sector de empresas mixtas

El sector de empresas mixtas en el que participa capital extranjero empleó en 1995 a 53,000 trabajadores cubanos, "lo que representa un 5 % de la fuerza laboral en la esfera productiva."[10] Como dato adicional vale la pena señalar que en un comentario editorial publicado por el semanario *Trabajadores*—a propósito de lo que calificó como errónea consideración de la Ley Helms-Burton, de que "Cuba vive exclusivamente por el impulso de las inversiones extranjeras"—se afirmó:

> Las empresas o asociaciones con el capital extranjero aportaron el año pasado (1995) *"entradas netas"* que no pasan de 114 millones de dólares, "apenas un 3% de los ingresos nacionales en el período."

Sector campesino privado y cooperativo

Las cifras de integrantes de este sector no han podido ser muy bien definidas. Las informaciones publicadas presentan casi siempre imprecisiones, respecto a lo que se entiende por sector cooperativo. No siempre queda claro si las referencias al sector cooperativo, incluyen a las UBPC o únicamente a los campesinos privados.

Las más recientes de estas referencias señalaron que "el sector campesino y cooperativo tiene hoy unos 30,500 jóvenes, el 14 % del total."[11] Es decir que, a partir de esa cifras, el sector campesino y cooperativo estaría integrado por 217,857 personas.

En esta cifra habría que incluir a los 33,768 integrantes de las Cooperativas de Producción Agrope-

cuaria (CPA), y a miles de personas que en los últimos meses han recibido en usufructo pequeñas áreas de tierra, en las zonas montañosas, dedicadas al cultivo de café y tabaco. En el caso del tabaco, hasta marzo 31 de 1996, se habían entregado 1,871 caballerías a 11,986 personas.[12]

Un resumen de la distribución de la fuerza laboral en el sector no estatal ofrece el siguiente cuadro:

Trabajadores por cuenta propia con licencia	208,500
Trabajadores por cuenta propia sin licencia	190,000
Trabajadores del sector mixto	53,000
Sector campesino y cooperativo	217,857
Total sector no estatal	669,357

Añado un dato de interés acerca de la fuerza de trabajo empleada en el sector estatal: el 12 por ciento de la fuerza laboral en el sector civil estatal se compone de trabajadores contratados a tiempo parcial.[13]

Por último hay un aspecto muy importante relacionado con la Seguridad Social que representa un serio problema actual, con implicaciones futuras.

Cuba, con un promedio de vida de 75 años, es un país con un alto porcentaje de jubilados por incapacidad de trabajar. De enero a agosto de 1995, de cada 1,000 trabajadores que se jubilaron 388 lo hicieron por incapacidad laboral, es decir, sin llegar a la edad establecida.

Cada año unos 100,000 trabajadores acuden a las comisiones de peritaje buscando retiro por incapacidad. Hay en total 1,200,000 jubilados en el país. En 1990 la invalidez total representaba el 25.9% de las jubilaciones concedidas. En 1995 ascendió a 37.3% Lo más grave aún es que la mayoría de estos *"jubilados por incapacidad"* cuya edad promedio es de 45 años, además de cobrar sus pensiones vitalicias, vuelven a emplearse en áreas estatales o se convierten en trabajadores por cuenta propia. Este año los ingresos a la Seguridad Social no llegarán a los 900

---

9. "El cuenta propia también es cuenta nuestra," *Trabajadores* (22 de abril 1996), p. 5.

10. "Con nuestras propias fuerzas," *Trabajadores* (8 de abril 1996), p. 2.

11. "Rejuvenece el sector campesino? *Juventud Rebelde* (5 de mayo 1996), p. 3.

12. "En la vinculación al área también está la fuerza," *Trabajadores* (22 de abril 1996), p. 7.

13. "Uso y abuso del contrato por tiempo determinado," *Trabajadores* (3 de junio 1996), p. 10.

millones de pesos, pero los gastos sobrepasarán los 1,600 millones.[14]

Todos estos cambios en la estructura laboral han tenido a su vez un impacto en la sociedad cubana cuyas repercusiones más significativas se reflejan desde la organización sindical hasta las sociedad en general. Algo que abre un amplio campo a la investigación de los sociólogos y políticos.

---

14. "Una paradoja que debemos resolver". *Trabajadores* (25 de marzo 1996) p. 2.

REMARKS ON THE CURRENT CUBAN ECONOMIC SITUATION

Gerardo González

I would like to give my point of view on Cuba's recent economic results. By that I mean the economic results for 1995 and the first part of 1996.

I am going to assume for purposes of these remarks that the official information of the economic results that has been reported is reliable. So, if the economy is finally growing, where eventually will it head? Do the economic results imply the beginning of an economic recovery? Are the "soft" economic reforms enough to guarantee sustained economic recovery?

The recovery of the nation's economy is only possible under two conditions: 1) economic stabilization; and 2) deep economic reform. I do not see either of them in the current situation.

ECONOMIC STABILIZATION

Economic stabilization requires the solution of the problem of inflation. The results attained in this area in 1995 and the first part of 1996 indicate that this problem has not been solved.

It is true that during 1995 the monetary growth was limited. In fact, the monetary overhang was reduced in this year from around 12,000 million pesos to 9,000 million pesos. But a monetary overhang of such magnitude is still an inflation factor.

To achieve stabilization, the level of monetary flow should be around 3,000-4,000 million pesos. This means that there are excess currency holdings of around 5,000-6,000 million pesos. So, it is necessary to remove the excess currency holdings and at the same time to avoid the reproduction of the inflation again.

The problem is that the current mechanisms are not sufficient to remove the necessary levels of excess currency. For example, the design and implementation of the new tax system approved by the Cuban Parliament in 1994 are irrelevant in relation to the magnitude of the excess currency. The new tax system responds to political considerations, focusing on the self-employment sector, the "new rich," according to Cuban official speech.

In order to avoid the return of inflation, it is necessary to attack its source: the budget deficit. Let's take a look at the composition of the budget:

- On the spending side, the solution of the budget deficit problem is in cutting the subsidies to state enterprises. This item alone comprises 27 percent of overall spending

- On the revenue side, the solution is changing the composition of the sources of revenue. Right now, the principal source of revenue feeding the state budget is taxes on cigarettes, tobacco, and alcoholic beverages (raising 45 percent of revenue). These taxes are not a reliable source, especially as the demand for these products is dropping. Only 10-15 percent of revenues are from profits of state enterprises. This number is logical because around 70 percent of the enterprises are unprofitable. Taxes on profits should be the principal source of budget revenue. The only way for this to happen is to make the enterprises profitable.

So, in our opinion, economic stabilization should begin with a daring reform of the enterprise system that should include privatization of some enterprises or sectors and real autonomy for state enterprises.

ECONOMIC REFORM

But the reform of the enterprise system should occur in the context of a deep transformation of the economy, the second condition for sustained economic recovery.

Essentially, economic reform should guarantee a decentralized market economy with some degree of state participation. State and private enterprises alike would operate according to a market dynamic that would demand a high level of efficiency and profit.

In the economic reform scenario, the state would have three fundamental characteristics:

- It would have participation in the control of the fundamental means of production.

- It would retain the capacity to set the strategic lines of development through direct and indirect mechanisms.

- It would have the capacity to produce the necessary resources to guarantee social spending.

And, of course, one important condition of this transformation is to put the relation between economy and policy in the right way: let the economy work with autonomy.

CUBA'S NON-SUGAR AGRICULTURE: CURRENT SITUATION AND PROSPECTS[1]

William A. Messina, Jr., Thomas H. Spreen, Anne E. Moseley and Charles M. Adams

OVERVIEW[2]

The International Agricultural Trade and Development Center at the University of Florida has been conducting research on Cuba's agricultural sector since 1992 with the financial support of the John D. and Catherine T. MacArthur Foundation. I would like to point out that our research has never been intended to suggest any change in U.S. policy. Rather, it has been designed to provide objective and current data and information on Cuban agriculture for Federal and State legislators, government agencies, private sector agribusiness firms, consumer groups and others to incorporate into the discussion and debate regarding the embargo.

The question then may arise, why should we be interested in Cuban agriculture? There is a tremendous similarity between Cuba's traditional agricultural production patterns and those of Florida and there was a great deal of agricultural trade between the U.S. and Cuba prior to the embargo. On the basis of this information, it becomes very clear that a resumption of trade between the U.S. and Cuba, whenever it occurs, will have important implications for Florida and for U.S. agriculture.

As most of you know, the most recent year for which the Cuban government released its official, detailed statistical yearbook was 1989. To obtain more current information we have been collaborating with the Centro de Investigaciones de la Economía Internacional (CIEI) at the University of Havana. For this Roundtable Session, we have brought together a group of commodity specialists from our faculty at the University of Florida who have been working with our collaborators at CIEI on the project and have traveled to Cuba on a number of occasions studying the citrus, vegetable, tropical fruit, rice and fisheries sub-sectors.

Prior to these commodity presentations, I want to take a few moments to present a bit of background information on Cuba's agricultural sector. The agricultural sector has historically been a fundamentally important segment of the Cuban economy. For the past 40 years, agriculture has consistently represented over two-thirds of Cuba's export earnings. During the 1980s, that figure actually averaged over 80 percent. Despite the dramatic decline in Cuba's export earnings since 1989, agriculture continues to represent over 75 percent of the country's net export earnings.

These statistics may appear to contradict what you might hear about foreign currency earnings from the tourist sector. However, the problem with tourism for Cuba is that, for every dollar that tourism brings in, an estimated 75 to 80 cents go out of the country

---

1. Summary of a roundtable session organized and chaired by William A. Messina, Jr., with participation by José Alvarez, Thomas H. Spreen, Anne E. Moseley, and Charles M. Adams. Contributions by individual participants are identified in the paper.

2. Remarks by William A. Messina, Jr.

again to purchase imported supplies and products. My purpose here is not to trivialize the importance of the tourist sector, because I believe it will continue to grow in importance to Cuba. Rather, the point I am trying to make is that agriculture has been, and will continue to be, an important sector of the Cuban economy for the foreseeable future.

I also believe that agriculture holds a unique position in Cuba's economy today because policy changes in this sector are leading the way in terms of movement toward a market economy. Here I am speaking of the breaking up of state farms into Basic Units of Cooperative Production (UBPCs) and the opening of farmers markets. Another important policy change that is not unique to agriculture is the allowance of foreign investment into the Cuban economy.

We do not have time to present information on these subjects in this session. However, for those of you who might be interested in more detail on these topics I will unabashedly recommend a paper being presented in this conference on foreign investment in Cuba's agricultural sector by Jim Ross of our faculty,[3] and a paper on the UBPCs and the agricultural markets that José Alvarez and I will also be presenting here.[4] With this introduction, I would like to turn like to the commodity presentations.

THE CITRUS INDUSTRY IN CUBA[5]

After the Castro regime took power in 1959, citrus was designated as an agricultural crop with export potential. The production area expanded rapidly, reaching 300,000 acres by the 1974-75 season. Since the dissolution of the Soviet Bloc in 1989, however, the production area has contracted. The production area devoted to citrus in the 1994-95 season (called the "net tree acres") is estimated at approximately 238,000 acres.

Oranges are the most important citrus crop produced in Cuba. In the 1992-93 season, approximately 350,000 metric tons (MT) of oranges were produced. Over 64 percent of the orange crop was utilized in the fresh domestic market, with nearly 13 percent sent to the fresh export market, and the remaining 23 percent processed into orange juice. Nearly all orange juice production is exported. At this level of production, Cuba is a small supplier of both fresh and processed orange products as total world production of oranges is approximately 50 million MT.

The second most important citrus crop in Cuba is grapefruit. In the 1992-93 season, total production was 250,000 MT; 34 percent of the grapefruit crop was utilized in the fresh domestic market, 21 percent was sent to the fresh export market, and 44 percent was processed. Unlike oranges, Cuba has been a significant force in the world grapefruit market. Before the decline in production area, Cuba and Israel followed the United States as the leading grapefruit production areas.

Cuba is a small producer of other citrus fruits such as limes, sour oranges, and tangerines. These varieties are mostly utilized in the domestic market.

In an attempt to stem the decline in citrus production, which fell from 1 million MT in 1989 to 620,000 MT in 1993, the Cuban government has instituted several changes. The first major change was to encourage foreign companies to enter into marketing agreements with Cuban state farms. Four companies entered the citrus business in Cuba over the 1991-93 period.

• BM Corporation, an Israeli company, entered into a foreign economic association with Cuba's largest citrus state farm at Jagüey Grande, in the province of Matanzas.

• Pole, S.A., a Chilean company, established an economic association at the Isle of Youth, the major grapefruit production area.

---

3. See James E. Ross, "Agribusiness Investment in Cuba in the Post-Embargo Period" in this volume.

4. José Alvarez and William A. Messina, Jr., "Cuba's New Agricultural Markets: Antecedents, Organization, Early Performance, and Prospects" in this volume.

5. Remarks by Thomas H. Spreen.

- Lola Fruit, S.A., a Greek company, formed a joint venture with the state farm located near Ciego de Avila.

- I.N.G., another Chilean company, is involved in an economic association dealing in juice products produced by the processing plant located at Jagüey Grande.

The fresh fruit companies are marketing Cuban citrus in Europe and Latin America. The juice company is marketing juice products in the Caribbean region.

The other recent development is the formation of UBPCs. In selected areas, the state farms have been divided into several smaller farms or UBPCs. In the case of citrus, some equipment has been sold to the UBPCs financed by loans from the government. Each UBPC is managed autonomously with regard to grove care-taking. The UBPC is obligated to purchase its inputs from the state and sell a portion of its output to the state. The basic idea behind the UBPC is to decentralize decision-making and create smaller, more manageable units. To export fruit, the UBPC must deal with a state company or one of the joint ventures.

At this time, the Cuban government has not released information on the 1994-95 or 1995-96 seasons. Unofficial reports are that the decline in citrus production has stopped, but a dramatic turn-around in output has not occurred. Given the recent expansion of citrus production in Florida—which competes with Cuba and Israel in the European market—it will be difficult for Cuba to successfully gain market share.

THE CUBAN VEGETABLE AND TROPICAL FRUIT INDUSTRIES[6]
Vegetables
Cuba produces the following vegetable crops: calabaza, tomato, cucumber, onion, garlic, sweet pepper, melon, cabbage, and a wide variety of other vegetables grown in smaller quantities. Approximately 25 percent of Cuban vegetables are produced in La Habana province and Pinar del Río province supplies

approximately 14 percent. About 382,000 acres of vegetables were planted in Cuba in 1992, with the largest crop acreage devoted to calabaza (110,000 acres), tomato (90,000 acres), cucumber (58,000 acres), and melon (21,000 acres). Average annual vegetable production in the late 1980s was 572,000 tons. During the 1990s, annual vegetable production declined, with 392,000 tons produced in 1993—approximately 30 percent less than average annual production in the late 1980s.

In 1989, Cuba had almost twice as much tomato and cucumber acreage as Florida. Cuba had 105,000 acres while Florida had only 62,500 acres of tomatoes and Cuban cucumber acreage was approximately 34,000 acres compared to less than 18,000 acres in Florida. With respect to crop yields, Cuban tomato yields decreased approximately 20 percent between 1975 and 1989, but Florida's tomato yields increased approximately 15 percent over the same time period.

Tuber and Root Crops
The tuber and root crops produced in Cuba include cassava, boniato, potato, malanga, and tropical yam. Approximately 490,000 acres of tuber and root crops were planted in 1992. This acreage was primarily devoted to cassava (260,000 acres), boniato (161,000 acres), potato (37,000 acres), and malanga (24,000 acres). Production of these crops steadily increased, more than doubling between 1975 and 1981, but production from 1982 through 1992 was relatively stable.

For purposes of comparison, boniato acreage in Cuba was approximately 131,000 acres in 1989 while boniato acreage in Florida totaled approximately 6,000 acres. Cuban malanga acreage in 1989 was 31,000 acres compared to approximately 5,100 acres in Florida. Although Cuba had significantly more boniato and malanga acreage, Cuban crop yields were generally much lower than Florida's yields. Boniato yields during the 1980s in Cuba were from two to four times less than Florida's yields. Cuban malanga yields during the 1980s were at times as

---

6. Remarks by Anne E. Moseley.

high as Florida's, but generally were about half as large.

Since the late 1980s, usage of fertilizers and other agricultural inputs has been changing. While certain crop yields have historically been lower in Cuba than in South Florida, Cuban producers now appear to be making efforts to increase productivity and yields, despite limited quantities of agricultural inputs.

Tropical Fruit

Cuban tropical fruit crops include mango, guava, papaya, pineapple, and coconut. For statistical purposes, bananas are a separate category and include both sweet bananas and plantains. Tropical fruit acreage in 1989 totaled approximately 220,000 acres, including 118,000 acres of papaya and 32,000 acres of pineapple. By 1992, however, the tropical fruit industry had virtually disappeared. Only 14,000 acres of tropical fruit crops, of which 9,800 acres were papayas, existed in 1992.

Tropical fruit production in 1975 totaled 138,000 tons and production peaked in 1985 at 240,000 tons. By 1992, however, tropical fruit production had fallen to only 68,000 tons. Tropical fruit yields also declined over time. Mango yields decreased by more than 20 percent between 1975 and 1992. During the same period, guava yields fell about 35 percent, and papaya yields were decreased by half.

Unlike other tropical fruit crops, banana acreage increased between 1989 and 1992. Total banana acreage—for both sweet bananas and plantains—increased from 106,000 acres in 1989 to 140,000 acres in 1992. Banana acreage consisted primarily of plantain plantings (73,000 acres in 1989 and 117,000 acres in 1992). Although acreage increased between 1989 and 1992, banana yields declined. Sweet banana yields decreased by about 9 percent while plantain yields decreased by about 20 percent.

Investment

The 1989 Food Program focused on banana, tuber, and root and vegetable crops but did not address tropical fruit, which has not been targeted by any specific development programs. As part of the Program, investments were made in irrigation equipment to be used in vegetable and tuber and root crops. These investments primarily included center pivot and semi-stationary irrigation machinery. Since the Program, investments have also been made in micro-jet irrigation equipment for banana production.

With the exception of reduced fertilizer deliveries between 1991 and 1993, the last three decades in Cuban agriculture have been characterized by intensive input use, that is, high availability and usage of tractors and high fertilizer usage. While certain crop yields have historically been lower in Cuba than in South Florida, Cuban producers now appear to be making efforts to increase productivity and yield despite limited quantities of agricultural inputs. The formation of agricultural markets has created a favorable environment for increased productivity, and changes in the structure of agriculture appear to be affecting farmers' incentives in a positive way.

THE CUBAN COMMERCIAL FISHING INDUSTRY[7]

Prior to the Revolution, the commercial fishing industry in Cuba was characterized by a fleet of small boats and vessels that plied the nearshore waters. These craft, which were typically low capacity and technically unsophisticated, primarily targeted a complement of reeffish, spiny lobster, sponge, and a few pelagic finfish species. The landings were handled by small-scale processing facilities and were then primarily directed into the local tourist and domestic markets. Following the Revolution, much attention was given to further development of the commercial fishing fleet. A viable, modern Cuban fishing fleet would not only provide a badly needed source of domestic protein and export revenue, but would also enhance coastal surveillance capabilities, provide training opportunities for naval recruits, and re-establish relations with neighboring Latin American nations via fishery access agreements. Modernization of the Cuban commercial fishing industry would, however, require considerable investment funds,

---

7. Remarks by Charles M. Adams.

which unfortunately were in short supply as a result of the then-recently imposed U.S. trade embargo.

The Soviet Union sought deepwater port access in the Westem Hemisphere. In an attempt to establish an alliance, the Cuban government agreed to provide such strategic access in return for Soviet financing of the much needed modernization of existing port facilities, the commercial fishing fleet, and the seafood processing sector, as well as access to relatively cheap fuel oil. During the next two decades, the modernization program entailed the construction of port facilities which not only satisfied the strategic needs of the Soviet Navy but also provided for expansion of the Cuban fishing fleet, the seafood processing sector, and various service-related industries. The Cuban fleet that emerged from this program was characterized by a level of technical sophistication and capacity unrivaled in Caribbean and Central American regions. Annual commercial fishery landings had averaged about 20,000 metric tons before the Revolution; by 1970, landings exceeded 100,000 metric tons per annum and by 1976 surpassed 200,000 metric tons.

While the pre-revolutionary fleet had primarily operated in near shore waters, the new Cuban fleet had four distinct components, each operating in a different region.

- The Flota Cubana de Pesca (FCP) was a distant-water fleet composed of purse seiners and mid-water trawlers that engaged in a different form of fishing activity than the Cuban fleet had traditionally done. The FCP developed into the largest distant-water fleet in all of Latin America and targeted low-valued species such as mackerels, herring, and hake. These fish, harvested from southern Atlantic and Pacific regions, were destined primarily for the domestic market

- The Flota Atunera de Cuba (FAC) was composed of tuna and swordfish longliners that operated in the Gulf of Mexico and Mid-Atlantic regions.

- The Flota del Golfo (FG) was composed of bottom-longliners and other hook and line vessels

that targeted bottom fish and reeffish in the nearshore waters

- The Flota de Plataforma (FP) was comprised of nearshore vessels that possessed a wide variety of gear types, such as traps, hooks and lines, trawls, grappling hooks, and others. The FP targeted a complement of high-value, nearshore species, such as shrimp, spiny lobster, sponge, reeffish and crab.

The catch of the FCP (the fleet most highly subsidized by the Soviets) was primarily intended for domestic consumption, whereas the high-value catches of the FAC, FG, and FP were destined for lucrative export markets and represented an important source of revenue.

The development of the modern Cuban commercial fishing fleet was fraught with bad timing. This was particularly true for the FCP, FAC, and FG. Virtually all coastal nations in the Americas imposed 200-mile limits for their territorial waters in the late 1970s. The exclusive rights claimed by these coastal nations excluded all other countries from accessing the fisheries resources in their territorial seas. Cuba's fleets, especially the distant-water fleet, were designed to access these coastal resources throughout Latin America. Unfortunately, with only few exceptions, this access was soon denied throughout the region; thus, Cuba was left with a fleet of large, operationally expensive vessels that were only able to operate in the open-ocean regions where operating was even more costly. The FCP's operation was almost totally dependent on inexpensive Soviet fuel oil and additional subsidization. Soviet subsidization allowed the FCP to continue operations for a number of years, even as the aging and costly fleet continued, by necessity, to target low-value species for domestic markets, instead of concentrating on export revenue generation.

The breakup of the Soviet Union in 1992 and the subsequent end of subsidization has caused the virtual shutdown of the FCP and reduced operations of the FAC and FG. Cuban landings decreased from 230,000 metric tons in 1988 to 90,000 metric tons in 1993. The FP continues to operate in the near-shore waters and produces a wide variety of high-valued species, the most important of which is spiny lobster. The distant-water trawlers of the FCP are currently tied up in Havana harbor because the Cubans have been unable to generate the revenue required for fuel oil and badly needed repairs. The Cuban government is attempting to develop joint-venture agreements or to find buyers for the aging vessels, many of which are now about 30 years old. A few FCP trawlers are currently targeting hake in Canadian waters under a longstanding fisheries agreement with Canada that provides access to the Cuban fleet; however, the much publicized state of overexploitation that exists in Canadian groundfish fisheries may jeopardize that agreement.

The state of flux in Cuba's commercial fishing fleet is reflected in the Cuban fisheries management infrastructure. The Fishing Industry Ministry (MIP) is currently undergoing substantial changes in its structure and its goals. Most strikingly, it is trying to dramatically reduce governmental oversight in the day-to-day management of fishing operations. The MIP formerly managed 42 companies or enterprises. Within the FP, all nearshore landings had to be sold through one of 18 enterprises. Two enterprises administered seafood processing, and one enterprise administered the FCP, FG, and FAC fleets. Other enterprises oversaw vessel construction, export operations (CARIBEX), training, research, and other activities. The MIP exercised tight controls over virtually all aspects of fishing operations.

The restructured MIP will contain only 21 associations (formerly enterprises) and FP will be administered through 15 provincial production associations. In many ways these associations resemble cooperatives. Each association will contain a number of vessels, with each vessel operating within a prescribed budget. Production over the predetermined vessel quota will generate a profit percentage in the form of monthly bonuses paid in dollars; thus, cost control is a new incentive. Captains, crew members, and mechanics are paid a salary which can now be augmented by bonuses awarded from profit-maximizing behavior. Conversely, poor production history can result in expulsion from the association. Six additional specialized associations will administer the follow-

ing functions: export activities (ACEPEX); domestic sales (Pesca Caribe); inputs, supplies, and imports (APROPES); processing (INIPES); vessel construction (ARGUS); and offshore fleet operations (FCP, FAC, and FG combined).

The likely consequences of renewed trade between the United States and Cuba have sparked much interest. Those consequences could be substantial for Florida.

• The primary species that Cuba would probably export to Florida would be spiny lobster, pink shrimp, reeffish, and fresh tuna. Currently, most Cuban spiny lobster is exported to Japan and the European Union (EU). Cuba has received preferential duty treatment when accessing the EU market with spiny lobster (for example, lobster from the United States is assessed a 25 percent duty while lobster from Cuba is assessed a 5 percent duty). Given the close proximity of the U.S. market and the existing price structure, Cuba would likely attempt to divert significant quantities of lobster into Florida and the United States in general. Because of the existing U. S. dependence on imported spiny lobster, only a slight downward pressure on ex-vessel prices in Florida would result. Interestingly, 40 percent of Cuban spiny lobster landings occur during the Florida closed season. This may provide a window of opportunity for Cuban lobster.

• Imports from Cuba of reeffish, such as snapper and grouper, would likely generate downward pressure on ex-vessel prices for these species in Florida.

• The same would likely be true for imports of pink shrimp from Cuba. However, Cuban trawlers would be required to utilize turtle excluder devices (as mandated by the U.S. Endangered Species Act) to avoid a U.S. ban on imported shrimp.

• Cuba could likely find markets for fresh tuna, which has been characterized by a growing market in the United States for several years. The impact on ex-vessel tuna price is less clear.

It should be noted that Cuban seafood exporters will be required to meet the quality and safety standards established by the new FDA Hazardous Awareness at Critical Control Points (HACCP) program. This program is designed to improve the quality and safety of seafoods processed by the U.S. seafood industry. U.S. importers will be required to ensure that foreign exporters meet these new standards.

EXTERNAL DEBT PROBLEMS AND THE PRINCIPLE OF SOLIDARITY: THE CUBAN CASE

Alberto Martínez-Piedra and Lorenzo L. Pérez[1]

As the planet earth advances rapidly towards the twenty-first century, people are becoming more aware that the various problems affecting contemporary society cannot be solved exclusively at the national level. Increasingly the world is shrinking in size as distances are shortened and technology advances at a rapid pace. Isolationist policies have no alternative but to fade into the background if real progress with justice is to be attained. No satisfactory and just solution of the numerous problems affecting contemporary society can be achieved without the collaboration of all individuals and nations alike, in particular, the international community. The problems posed by the high level of indebtedness of certain developing countries and their inability to comply with their external obligations after the effective resolution of most of the problems associated with the debt crisis of the 1980s is a prime example of the need for further international cooperation.

This paper will discuss the ethical implications of the external debt burden of the developing countries with special emphasis on Latin America and Cuba. The study is divided into seven parts: First, a general discussion of the challenge of the debt crisis and its ethical implications. Second, a review of the origins and magnitude of the debt problems of developing countries. This will be followed with a third part that discusses the steps taken by the international community to address the debt crisis. The fourth part examines Cuba's external debt service burden. The ethical dimension of the debt crisis and its relationship to development will be discussed in the fifth part. The sixth part analyzes the future implications of the external debt service burden for a free and democratic Cuban government within the context of social justice and in accordance with the principle of solidarity.[2] The last section has the conclusions.

THE CHALLENGE OF THE DEBT CRISIS

The debt crisis of the eighties was of international proportions. It threatened not only the political and socioeconomic well-being of many developing countries but also endangered the very stability of the international financial system. Being a source of concern for the world community, it required the immediate attention of international policy makers. The mere magnitude of its size entailed political, so-

---

1. The views expressed here are those of the author and in no way represent the official views of the International Monetary Fund.

2. As defined by Pope Paul VI in his encyclical *Populorum Progressio*, solidarity is a broad ethical concept that states that there can be no progress towards the complete development of man without the simultaneous development of humanity in the spirit of cooperation. There are no specific norms arising from the teaching of the Church regarding the principle of solidarity, but in the same encyclical it is stressed that the duty of solidarity is the concern especially of better-off nations. Their obligations take on a threefold aspect: the duty of human solidarity—the aid that the rich nations must give to developing countries; the duty of social justice—the rectification of equitable trade relations between powerful nations and weak nations; and the duty of universal charity—the efforts to bring about a world that is more human towards all men, where all will be able to give and receive, without any group making progress at the expense of the other.

cial, and economic implications that could not be brushed aside easily.

Politicians and economists, just as well as social and religious leaders and the public in general, realized that the debt problem had also implications of an ethical nature. Citizens of debtor and creditor countries alike around the globe would be affected negatively if certain countries would default in their international obligations and were forced to declare themselves in a state of bankruptcy. As Ved P. Nanda wrote recently:

> During the 1980s world attention was appropriately drawn to the challenge of overcoming global debt. The total debt level worldwide rose from US$650 billion in 1980 to US$1,035 billion in 1986. Many countries in Africa and Latin America were hit especially hard by the debt crisis. Economic development remained an illusory goal for these countries.[3]

There was a general consensus that relief from the debt burden was a must, if development was to proceed in an orderly and equitable way.

It was generally recognized that the debt crisis concerned not only the authorities of the creditor and debtor nations but, in a particular way, the most neglected sectors of society. A just solution had to be reached; a solution that respected the dignity of the persons affected and minimized the negative consequences of a debt burden that imperiled the development and growth of many a country in both the northern and southern hemispheres.

Perhaps few persons have expressed these concerns more clearly than Pope John Paul II. On October 14, 1985, Pope John Paul II, in his message to the 40th General Assembly of the United Nations, called the attention of international leaders about the ethical aspects of the problems raised by the international debt. As a result of this concern, the Roman Pontiff asked the Pontifical Commission *Justitia et Pax* to reflect on the topic and propose to the affected

parties—creditor and debtor countries, financial institutions and commercial banks—discerning criteria and methods of analysis that approach the problem from an ethical perspective.[4]

The Pontifical Commission *Justitia et Pax* issued in December 1986 a set of reflections which called upon all parties concerned with the debt question "to examine the ethical implications of the question of the external debt of developing countries in order to arrive at just solutions that respect the dignity of those who would be most strongly affected by its consequences." The reflections included in the Commission's publication, "An Ethical Approach to the International Debt Question," were the result of John Paul II's personal involvement with the international debt crisis. The Roman Pontiff advocated for the formulation of criteria to analyze the situation in the light of ethical standards. He insisted that decision makers could not disregard ethical principles in their plans of action to solve the crisis and stressed the need for a greater degree of solidarity between all countries in the international community. The Pope stressed that the debt problem could not be analyzed exclusively in economic, political and technological terms. It must take into account also the need for international collaboration and the pursuit of the common good. However, the final document of the Papal Commission did not recommend any specific program of action because it was felt that this would fall outside the Church's field of competence.

The world community did not face the gravity of the situation until it was forced in 1982 with the near default of Mexico. As the world concentrated on the Mexican crisis, little attention was given to the developments that were taking place in Castro's Cuba. The island's poor economic performance, caused primarily by the inefficient socialist policies of the Castro regime, was threatened with even greater problems as a result of the significant changes that were

---

3. Ved P. Nanda, "World Debt and the Right to Development," in *World Debt and the Human Condition* (Westport, Connecticut: Greenwood Press), p. 3.

4. See: "An Ethical Approach to the International Debt Question," Report of the Pontifical Justice and Peace Commission, *Origins*, Vol. 16, No. 34, (February 5, 1987).

rapidly taking place in the former Soviet Union. For many years Castro, following a policy of economic dependence on the Soviet Union and its communist satellites, became increasingly indebted towards his communist partners. It was not until the advent of Gorbachev that the Soviets cut back their economic assistance programs and curtailed their large subsidies to the Cuban economy.

After the fall of communism, Cuba's need for increased economic and financial relations with the industrialized free market economies became quite evident. But, this also meant a correspondent increase in the islands foreign debt in freely convertible currency. Already by 1982, Cuba's debt in freely convertible currency had reached $2.9 billion, not counting Castro's high level of indebtedness towards the former Soviet empire. Mexico, among others, was not the only country on the verge of bankruptcy. Cuba was another heavily indebted countries at the brink of bankruptcy.

ORIGINS AND MAGNITUDE OF THE DEBT CRISIS

Up to the early 1970s, the external debt of developing countries was relatively small and Latin America and Caribbean nations were no exception. The majority of creditors were foreign governments and international financial institutions and most loans were on concessional terms that were extended primarily for development purposes. The economic performance of Latin America had been satisfactory in the decade and a half preceding the early 1970s. The region benefitted from economic growth, low inflation together with low interest rates, and an expanding trade sector.[5]

The Organization of Petroleum Exporting Countries (OPEC) price cartel triggered a series of events in 1973 that led eventually to the debt crisis. The massive oil surpluses of the oil producing countries, which were deposited in European and American banks, were recycled and lent to developing countries to provide balance of payments support and help ex-

pand their import level. The abundance of liquidity held by the international capital market, together with the prevailing low interest rates, fueled the continuous economic expansion that took place during the early and mid-seventies. The commercial banks were more than willing to lend their excess funds to the eager borrowers from Latin America and other developing countries. The developing countries constituted an ideal loan clientele for the international capital market, in particular those with a growing industrial sector.

The Latin American countries, many hard hit by the sharp increase in oil prices and excessive government spending, resorted to financing their external disequilibrium by borrowing in the international capital market. On the other hand, the industrialized countries and some developing countries outside Latin America reacted to the "oil shock" by adjusting their economies and reducing their current account deficits promptly even at the price of lower growth rates. The recession in the industrialized countries resulted in a drop in the demand for the exports of developing countries which was reflected in a decline in the prices of raw materials. The problems of developing countries were compounded by a drying up of commercial credit which they had enjoyed for many years and soaring interest rates.

While negative external factors such as the world recession and the high interest rates contributed to the development of the debt crisis, economic mismanagement in developing countries also played a major role in the debt crisis. Excessive spending, together with lax monetary policies that included the monetary financing of fiscal deficits, increased price pressures, eroded competitiveness, and widened balance of payments deficits to unsustainable levels. The only way out of the crisis was a major tightening of fiscal and monetary policies accompanied by a program of structural reforms to establish the basis for stability and sustainable economic growth.

---

5. For a comprehensive account of the Latin American debt crisis see Pedro-Pablo Kuczynski, *Latin American Debt* (Baltimore: The Johns Hopkins University Press, 1988).

The long-term debt of developing countries (including public, publicly-guaranteed and private nonguaranteed debt) amounted to US$62 billion in 1970, and for Latin American and Caribbean countries it was US$26 billion.[6] By 1980, long-term debt of developing countries had increased to US$480 billion, an almost eight-fold increase, and short-term debt amounted to US$165 billion (the comparable figures for Latin American and Caribbean countries were US$187 billion and US$69 billion, respectively). Total debt service as a percentage of exports of goods and services for Latin American and Caribbean countries had reached almost 36 percent by 1980 (compared to only 13.3 percent for all developing countries). This ratio peaked at 38 percent in 1988.

STEPS TAKEN TO ADDRESS THE DEBT CRISIS

An international debt strategy was developed over time by the governments of major creditor countries and multilateral organizations to address the external debt problems that erupted with the 1982 Mexican crisis. Actions were taken to address the problems associated with the servicing of the debt to commercial bank creditors as well as with the debt to official creditors. The strategy to deal with the debt to commercial bank creditors had three goals: avoidance of a collapse of the international banking and financial systems, minimization of economic dislocation in debtor countries, and restoration of the access of heavily indebted countries to capital markets. William Cline has argued that, overall, the strategy succeeded well on the first and third objectives. In his opinion the results on the second objective were more disappointing, but he acknowledges that the strategy encouraged domestic policy reforms that eventually paid-off in terms of stability and economic growth. Many of the structural reforms that were initiated would have need to be carried out even without the debt crisis.

With regard to the international debt strategy to address the problems associated with debt to private

banks, there were three distinct phases to the strategy: emergency lending to Mexico and subsequent coordinated lending to other individual countries (1982-85); the indicative Baker Plan, which set targets for bank and official lending and called for structural reform in debtor economies (1986-88); and the Brady Plan, emphasizing debt reduction agreements (1989-1994).

The first phase consisted of involuntary lending by banks, orchestrated by the International Monetary Fund (IMF), with the central premise being that the debt problem was not one of insolvency, so that further lending was appropriate. Multiyear rescheduling agreements (MYRAs) were initiated at this time. By 1985, however, it became apparent that voluntary lending was not returning. Imports had been compressed severely and the return to civilian governments in Argentina and Brazil increased the political urgency of addressing more adequately the debt crisis. In late 1985, the Baker Plan was announced. The plan, named after the Secretary of the Treasury of the United States, established indicative targets for lending from commercial banks and multilateral banks in exchange for policy reforms to improve fiscal balances, liberalize import regimes and direct investment, and privatize public sector assets. Some experimentation was done with market based debt reduction. Moreover, the amount of financing made available under the plan did not reach the levels envisaged.

The situation was complicated with the collapse of oil prices in 1986. As a result, prospects for key debtors such as Mexico and Venezuela changed from solvency to potential solvency. By 1987 there had been a widespread provisioning by banks against possible losses on their loans to developing countries. This influenced secondary market prices of developing countries debt which fell from about 70 cent on the dollar to about 35 cents by 1989. The combination of these two factors provided an opportunity to implement financial workouts that involved a trade of some portion of the face value of bank claims in ex-

---

6. World Bank, *World Debt Tables, External Finance for Developing Countries, 1994-95*. No information was available in 1970 about the short-term debt of developing countries.

change for increased security through officially aided collateralization.

A growing divergence of interest among the banks, and the increasing reluctance of European, Japanese and regional U.S. banks to lend new money also compromised the Baker Plan. To address these problems, by 1988 a menu approach was being offered to banks under which banks would exit by converting claims to concessional bonds, while others would continue the new-money strategy with the aid of such devices as new-money bonds. There also was a growing frustration among policy makers of creditor countries that the public share of debt was rising and that of the banks was failing, even though the trend was a return to patterns predating the unusual petro-dollar recycling of the 1970s and still left the bank exposure far higher than that of the public sector.

In March 1989 the new U.S. Treasury Secretary Nicholas Brady announced the next phase of the debt strategy which emphasized debt and debt service reduction. The Brady Plan introduced public sector collateral as the catalyst to convince banks to reduce their existing claims on debtor countries. The plan also envisaged additional new money lending by those banks that preferred this option. An additional inducement to the plan was that the IMF was willing to lend to countries that had arrears to banks. Previously, the IMF had not lent to countries until they had reached an agreement with the respective banks. The Brady Plan was quasi-voluntary as the previous plan because it incorporated the alternative of new money and it was market oriented in that the depth of debt reduction typically negotiated was commensurate with the existing secondary market price on the one hand and the extent of collateralization of the replacement claims on the other. Moreover, the Brady Plan had a case-by-case approach and was conditional on policy reform.

Information compiled by IMF staff shows that by the end of June 1995, 21 countries had completed deals that restructured commercial bank debts with a face value of US$170 billion, obtaining roughly US$76 billion in total debt and debt service reduction in present value terms at a cost of US$25 billion (Table 1).[7] Allocation to the options in the various debt packages have differed, reflecting in some cases explicit limits and the views of the holders of the debt regarding the expected future values of the debt instruments issued in exchange for the old bank claims. The cost per unit of debt reduction achieved (the buyback equivalent price) has been roughly in line with the secondary market price of the bank claims at the time of the agreement in principle, and thus as a whole have been cost efficient.

Net capital inflows to Latin America, which had fallen from an average of about US$55 billion in 1980-81 to approximately an average of US$5 billion annually during the period 1983-89, rebounded to nearly US$55 billion during the early 1990s. This turnaround in capital inflows reflected a more favorable domestic environment for foreign investment. As a result, the size of debt relief associated with the Brady Plan became less urgent and relatively smaller. Particularly noteworthy has been the improvement in direct and portfolio investment in the early 1990s. The adoption of a quasi-voluntary, market-oriented approach to debt forgiveness was important in generating this positive market perception of Brady countries and other developing countries.

The second prong of the international community debt strategy dealt with the debt to official bilateral creditors. Since 1980, 65 countries have rescheduled their official bilateral debt under the aegis of the Paris Club (Table 2). The Club has neither a fixed membership nor an institutional structure; rather it represents a set of practices and procedures that has evolved since the first ad hoc meeting for Argentina

---

7. *Private Market Financing for Developing Countries*, World Economic and Financial Surveys (Washington: International Monetary Fund, November 1995). The US$170 billion of face value of the debt excludes past due interest and includes debt restructured under new money option for certain countries.

Table 1. Comercial Bank Debt and Debt-Service Reduction Operations[a]: Concluded Agreements
(In millions of U.S Dollars)

	Debt and Debt-Service-Reduction (DSSR)[b]						Total Debt and Debt-Service Reduction	
Debt Restructured Under DDSR Operation[c]	Debt Reduction		Debt-Service Reduction		Prepayments Through Collateralization	Total	Debt Restructured	Cost of Reduction[e]
	Buy-Back	Discount Exchange	Principal Collateralized par Bond[d]	Other par Bond[d]				
(1)	(2)	(3)	(4)	(5)	(6)	(7) = 2+..(6)	(8) = (7)/(1)	
Argentina (1992) 19,397	—	2356	4291	—	2739	9386	48.4	3059
Bolivia 643	331	232	29	—	20	612	95.2	61
(1987) 473	253	182	—	—	7	442	93.5	35
(1993) 170	78	50	29	—	13	170	100.0	26
Brazil (1992) 40600	—	4974	3996	337	3891	13189	32.5	3900
Bulgaria (1993) 6186	798	1865	—	421	443	3527	57.0	652
Chile (1988) 439	439	—	—	—	—	439	100.0	248
Costa Rica (1989)[f] 1456	991	—	—	101	36	1128	77.5	196
Dom. Republic (1993) 776	272	177	—	—	63	511	65.8	149
Ecuador (1994) 4522	—	1180	826	—	596	2602	57.5	583
Guyana (1992) 69	69	—	—	—	—	69	100.0	10
Jordan (1993) 736	—	84	111	—	117	312	42.5	118
Mexico[f] 51902	—	7953	6484	—	7777	22214	42.8	7677
(1988) 3671	—	1115	—	—	555	1670	45.5	555
(1989) 48231	—	6838	6484	—	7222	20544	42.6	7122
Mozambique (1991) 124	124	—	—	—	—	124	100.0	12
Niger (1991) 111	111	—	—	—	—	111	100.0	23
Nigeria (1991)[f] 5811	3390	—	651	—	352	4393	75.6	1708
Philippines 5812	2602	—	516	116	467	3701	63.7	1795
(1989) 1339	1339	—	—	—	—	1339	100.0	670
(1992) 4473	1263	—	516	116	467	2362	52.8	1125
Poland (1994) 9989	2424	2427	796	74	611	6332	63.4	1933
Sao Tome and Principe (1994) 10	10	—	—	—	—	10	100.0	1
Uganda (1993) 152	152	—	—	—	—	152	100.0	18
Uruguay (1991) 1608	633	—	—	—	—	888	55.2	463
Venezuela (1990) 19700	1411	511	2012	471	1639	6043	30.7	2585
Zambia (1994) 200	200	—	—	—	—	200	100.0	22
Total 170,243	13,956	21,759	19,872	1,520	18,845	75,951	44.6	25,212

a. Debt and debt-service reduction are estimated by comparing the present value of the old debt with the present value of the new claim, and adjusting for prepayments made by the debtor. The methodology is described in detail in Annex I of *Private Market Financing for Developing Countries* (Washington, International Monetary Fund, December 1992). The amounts of debt reduction contained in this table exclude debt extinguished through debt conversions. Years in parenthesis refers to the date of the agreement in principle.

b. The figure for debt-service reduction represents the expected present value of the reduction in future interest payments arising from the below-market fixed interest rate path on the new instruments relative to expected future market rates. The calculation is based on the estimated term structure of interest rates for U.S. Treasury bond at the time of agreement in principle.

c. Excludes past due interest and includes debt restructured under new money options for Mexico (1989), Uruguay (1991), Venezuela (1989), the Philippines (1992), Poland (1994) and Panama (1995); the Philippines (1989) new money option was not tied to a specific value of existing debt.

d. Excludes prepayment of principal and interest through guarantees.

e. Cost at the time of operations closing. Includes principal and interest guarantees, buy-back costs, and for Venezuela, resources used to provide comparable collateral for bonds issued prior to 1990. Excludes cash downpayments rekated to past due interest.

f. Includes estimated value recovery clauses.

Table 2. Paris Club Rescheduling[a]

Low - Income		Lower - Middle Income[b]		Other Middle-Income		Total
Countries that have graduated from rescheduling						
Gambia, The	9/87	Dominican Republic	3/93	Argentina	3/95	
Malawi	5/89	Ecuador	12/94	Bulgaria	4/95	
**Uganda	2/95	Egypt	5/91	Brazil	8/93	
* Vietnam	12/93	El Salvador	9/91	Chile	12/88	
		Guatemala	3/94	CostaRica	6/93	
		Kenya	1/96	Mexico	5/92	
		Morocco	12/92	Panama	3/92	
		Philippines	7/94	Romania	12/83	
		Poland	4/91	Trinidad & Tobago	3/91	
				Turkey	6/83	
Subtotal	*4*		*9*		*10*	*23*
Countries with rescheduling agreements in effect						
* Benin	12/95	Jamaica	9/95	Algeria	5/98	
** Bolivia	12/97	Jordan	5/97	Croatia	12/95	
* Burkina Faso	12/95	Peru	3/96	Form. Yugoslav Rep Macedonia	6/97	
** Cambodia	3/97			Russian Federetion	12/95	
* Cote d'Ivoire	3/97					
* Ethiopia	10/95					
* Eq, Guinea	2/96					
Guinea	12/95					
** Guinea-Bissau	12/97					
** Haiti	3/96					
* Honduras	7/95					
* Mali	8/95					
** Mauritania	12/97					
** Nicaragua	6/97					
** Senegal	8/97					
* Sierra Leone	12/95					
** Togo	9/97					
Subtotal`	*17*		*3*		*4*	*24*
Countries with previous rescheduling agreements but without current rescheduling agreements which have not graduated from rescheduling						
Angola	9/ 90	Congo	5/95	Gabon	3/9	
* Cameroon	9/ 95	Nigeria	3/ 92	Yugoslavia	6/9	
Cent. African Republic	3/95					
** Chad	3/95					
* Guyana	12/ 94					
Liberia	6/ 85					
Madagascar	6/ 91					
* Mozambique	6/ 95					
* Niger	3/ 95					
Somalia	12/88					
Sudan	12/ 84					
* Tanzania	6/ 94					
Zaire	6/90					
Zambia	3/95					
Subtotal	*14*		*2*		*2*	*18*
All countries	*35*		*14*		*16*	*65*

Note: Dates refer to end of current or last consolidation period. In the case of stock-of-debt operation, canceled agreement, or arrears only rescheduling, date shown is that of relevant agreement. An * denotes rescheduling on London terms, and ** denotes rescheduling on Naples terms (stock treatment in italics).

Source: International Monetary Fund, *Official Financial for Developing Countries*, December 1995.

a.   Includes agreements of the Russian Federation and Turkey with official bilateral creditors

b.   Defined here as countries that obtained lower middle-income but not concessional terms with Paris Club reschedulings; stock treatment in italics.

in 1956. Meetings are open to all official creditors that accept those practices and procedures.[8] Official creditors require two preconditions for the initiation of a debt renegotiation: First, that the debtor country will be unable to meet its external payments obligations unless it receives debt relief and, second, that the debtor country will take the steps necessary to eliminate the causes of its payments difficulties and to achieve a durable improvement in its external payments position. Creditors have relied on the IMF to help member countries design appropriate adjustment measures and generally require that a Fund program be in place before the debt renegotiations are initiated.

Official debt reschedulings typically cover both principal and interest payments on medium- and long-term debt falling due during a given period (the consolidation period); where necessary, creditors may also cover payments already in arrears at the beginning of the consolidation period, especially with countries undertaking reschedulings with official creditors for the first time.

Paris Club reschedulings have generally paralleled the sharp rise in commercial bank restructuring but were less concentrated at the onset of the debt crisis in 1982. This reflected the more diversified experience of countries largely indebted to official creditors, in part because these creditors did not abruptly change their lending practices. Fifteen countries had approached the Paris Club already during the 1976-82 period, prior to the emergence of more widespread debt-servicing difficulties. During the following three years, 1983-85, nineteen other countries obtained Paris Club reschedulings, mostly middle-income countries with large debts to private creditors. From 1986 through 1993 another twenty-four countries required reschedulings in the Paris Club.

Most of the rescheduling countries have returned to the Paris Club several times and progress in resolving debt servicing difficulties to official creditors through successive reschedulings has remained slow. Less than half of the 65 countries that have required reschedulings have resumed normal relations with bilateral creditors. Successful graduates from the Paris Club reschedulings process have been mostly those middle-income countries that had been predominantly indebted to private creditors. Their success has been based on the sustained implementation of macroeconomic and structural reform policies, often accompanied by comprehensive commercial bank debt restructurings. However, for the other middle income countries that currently continue to require cash-flow relief from Paris Club creditors, prospects are presently generally favorable.

The debt situation of the low income rescheduling countries (most of which are in sub-Saharan Africa) has remained more difficult. This has led them to rely on protracted debt reschedulings. The difficulties have been associated with a sharp deterioration in their terms of trade. Difficulties in adjusting to the deterioration to the terms of trade were usually accompanied by the accumulation of external arrears which undermined the efforts of these countries to re-establish creditworthiness and reduced their access to new financing from official sources. As countries found themselves unable to meet the obligations arising from previous reschedulings, they required increasingly comprehensive cash-flow relief.

In late 1988, creditors took a first step toward reducing the future debt-service burden resulting from successive reschedulings. Agreement was reached to implement a menu of options (the Toronto terms) which included elements of debt and debt-service reduction. Rescheduling under Toronto terms provided an average grant element of well over 20 percent for nonconcessional debt. However, it was soon clear to creditors that the vast majority of low-income rescheduling countries required more far reaching concessions for a sustained improvement in their debt situation. In December 1991, Paris Club creditors reached agreement in the modalities of implementing deeper concessions for the low-income countries.

---

8. For a comprehensive description of the Paris Club procedures see Appendix I of *Official Financing for Developing Countries* (Washington: International Monetary Fund, April 1994).

The new approach combined the flexibility of the flow approach during the adjustment period with the possibility of a later stock-of-debt operation that could provide a definitive resolution of the debt problem . The new menu of enhanced concessions identified as the London terms provided for 50 percent reduction (in net present value terms) of debt service consolidated on non-official development assistance debts. The rescheduling agreements based on the new menu contained the provision that Paris Club creditors would be willing to consider the matter of the stock of debt after a period of 3-4 years. Some 17 low-income countries concluded agreements during 1992-94 with the Paris Club creditors with enhanced concessions.

During 1994 and 1995 more progress was made in graduating countries from Paris Club reschedulings. Seven middle-income countries did so, bringing to 23 the countries which have graduated from the Paris Club out of a total of 65 countries that have required Paris Club reschedulings (Table 2). A majority of the remaining middle-income countries with agreements now in force are expected to graduate at the end of their current consolidation period. The debt situation for of the very low-income rescheduling countries remains difficult despite repeated reschedulings over the past several years.In recognition of their heavy debt service burden, Paris Club creditors adopted the Naples terms in December 1994. According to these terms, the level of concessionality was increased to 67 percent in net present value terms compared with 50 percent under London terms. As under the previous reschedulings on London terms, agreements under Naples terms also feature a goodwill clause referring to a stock-of-debt operation after a period of three years of good performance under both IMF arrangements and the rescheduling agreement.

As a result of these efforts to reduce the debt and the debt service obligations on external debt to private and official creditors, the debt service pressures on Latin America have been alleviated. World Bank debt data show that for Latin America and the Caribbean the ratio of total external debt to GNP, which had risen from 36 percent in 1980 to 66 percent of GNP in 1987, began to decline in 1988.[9] By 1994 the ratio was back to the level of 1980: 36 percent of GNP.[10] The ratio of total debt service for Latin America and the Caribbean as a percent of exports of goods and services also peaked in 1988 at 38 percent and it declined to less than 29 percent in 1994, reflecting in part the restructuring of the debt.

By 1994 the public and publicly-guaranteed external debt of Latin America and the Caribbean was US$380 billion or about 87 percent of the total long-term debt of the region. About 18 percent of the US$380 billion debt was owed to multilateral creditors and about 26 percent was owed to foreign governments. Debt to private creditors accounted for the remaining 56 percent of the public and publicly-guaranteed debt of Latin American and the Caribbean in 1994.

The newly adopted measures taken by the international community, together with the significant changes in economic policy that have taken place within Latin America, are likely to continue to have positive effects and permit the countries of the region to attain higher levels of sustained economic growth. However, as a recent report of the Inter-American Development Bank notes, Latin America still exhibits an excessive dependency upon external savings, which should be replaced by the use of private internal savings in order to raise investment. At the same time, the regions new openness to world trade must be accompanied by a major effort to increase exports in order to ensure the viability of this important process. This will require the elimination of legal, insti-

---

9. World Bank, *World Debt Tables: External Finance for Developing Countries, 1994-95,* Vol. 1.

10. For all developing countries, on the other hand, the ratio of external debt to GNP was about 40 percent of GDP or the same ratio as in 1987, but the ratio of debt service to exports of good and services amounted to only 17 percent because the debt to many of these developing countries has been given at more concessional terms.

tutional, and tax-related limitations that hamper exports.[11]

Notwithstanding the progress made in recent years, there is a group of heavily-indebted-countries (mostly outside Latin America) which are likely to continue to experience serious debt-servicing problems and they face the challenging task of formulating a satisfactory adjustment policy. They must achieve a significant improvement in their external current accounts balance while at the same time reviving the confidence of domestic and foreign investors in the viability of their economies. Access to Naples terms to reschedule their debt to bilateral official creditors would no doubt help them, but they still need to adopt domestic measures to attain sustained economic growth together with political and social stability. Otherwise they will find it extremely difficult, if not impossible, to overcome the vicious circle in which they now find themselves.

It is possible that a country, such as Cuba, after many years of inefficient economic policies, will face such a large external debt service burden that it will be very painful (and politically impossible) to apply the adjustment measures necessary to service fully its debt. The debt outstanding may be so large that the repayment of arrears and debt service obligations would make it impossible for the country to invest and grow. Under such circumstances it would be in the interest of both creditors and Cuba to restructure the debt in a way that would permit the countrys required long-term growth. Once Cuba reinserts itself in the international economy, it would also be able to reduce its debt service burden through export expansion to markets reopened to it.

CUBA'S EXTERNAL DEBT SERVICE BURDEN

Ever since the very early stages of the revolution, the Cuban government embraced the principles of Marxism-Leninism and embarked on a policy of total political and economic centralization. It rejected all the basic postulates of the market economy and forced the country into a new era of "real" socialism,[12] in accordance with the former Soviet model. In the international arena, Havana's totalitarian regime turned its back on its former allies and friends—in particular the United States—and initiated a policy of alliances and economic agreements with Moscow, Eastern Europe and other communist bloc countries. The Government's increasing dependence on the common market of the socialist economies, the Council for Mutual Economic Assistance (COMECON), together with its dismal record on human rights violations and external military adventures, contributed in no small matter to its gradual isolation from the western democracies and the major international financial institutions. Havana's major and almost exclusive source of financial assistance was reduced to Moscow and its communist allies. This misguided policy of dependence proved to be disastrous with the collapse of the Soviet Union. It was only then that Castro was forced to look for new sources of financial assistance in the western capitalist democracies in order to find relief from his outstanding external obligations, primarily a consequence of the inefficient economic policies of his failed socialist experiment.

Cuba's external debt in freely convertible currency in 1969 amounted to only 291 million pesos, but as noted earlier, by 1982 it had reached 2.9 billion pesos.[13] During the 1980s Cuba also tried to reschedule its external debt. In 1982, Cuba requested from its creditors the renegotiation of the medium-term debts

---

11. Inter-American Development Bank, *Economic and Social Progress in Latin America, 1994 Report* (Washington, IDB, 1994).

12. See John Paul II, *Centesimus Anno*, #13, #35 and #56.

13. Banco Nacional de Cuba, *Economic Report 1994* (La Habana, August 1994). The data that follow are all taken from this report and do not include Cuba's debt to the former Soviet Union and other communist bloc countries. As will be indicated later, little reliable information exists on Cuba's debt to Russia. Cuba's official exchange rate is Peso 1=US$1 and, presumably, for purposes of its 1994 report, the Banco Nacional converted the foreign exchange denominated debt at the official exchange rate. In reality, Cuba's peso is heavily overvalued as indicated by the exchange rate prevailing in the unofficial parallel market.

maturing between September 1982 and December 1985, and the postponement of these payments for a period of 10 years, including a three-year grace period.[14] During the following years further negotiations took place between the Cuban government and its foreign creditors, but with mixed results. The economic situation continued to deteriorate and in 1986 the conditions for paying the debt service worsened to such a degree that Cuba was no longer able to meet its international obligations. Since 1986, the Cuban government has not been able to normalize its financial relations with bilateral creditors and foreign banks.

According to an August 1994 report of the Banco Nacional de Cuba, foreign debt in freely convertible currency grew to 9.1 billion pesos by the end of 1994, including principal and arrears on interest payments. No information is provided by the mentioned report on how the debt trebled from 1982 to 1994; undoubtedly part of the growth was due to the accumulation of interest arrears but this factor cannot explain the total growth. About 4 billion pesos of the debt of Cuba at end-1994 was to official bilateral creditors (almost all export credits with government guarantee) and 500 million pesos to multilateral institutions. Debt owed to suppliers amounted to 2 billion pesos (it is not clear whether these credits have the guarantee of foreign governments), while the debt to commercial banks was 2.5 billion pesos. Of Cuba's total external debt of 9.1 billion pesos in 1994, 77.6 percent (7.1 billion pesos) corresponded to principal and 22.4 percent (2.0 billion pesos) to interest arrears.[15]

No estimate is available of Cuba's GNP in 1994 in current market prices and, because of this, it is difficult to assess the relative size of the countrys external debt in freely convertible currency. In the report of the Banco Nacional de Cuba, the 1994 GDP is reported at 12.9 billion pesos (in 1981 prices). This represents a drastic fall from the GDPs of the years 1989 and 1990 which were approximately 19.6 and 19.0 billion pesos, respectively. However, it is clear that the relative size of the external debt of Cuba is quite large. Assuming that the official GDP estimate for 1994 in 1981 prices was a reliable one, and that the GDP in current market prices increased by 50 percent between 1981 and 1994 (an average price increase of 3 percent per year during this period), the amount of freely convertible debt of 9.1 billion pesos would have been equivalent to 50 percent of GDP, significantly higher than the ratio of 36 percent of GNP for Latin American countries and the Caribbean.

The poor showing of Cuba's exports in recent years also has made it more difficult for the country to service its external debt. Cuban exports (fob) fell from 5.4 billion pesos in 1989 to 1.1 billion pesos in 1993 and to an estimated 1.3 billion and 1.5 billion pesos in 1994 and 1995, respectively.[16] For illustrative purposes, if one assumes that about 1/10 of the principal of the freely convertible debt would have fallen due in 1994 and that Cuba would have had to pay an interest rate of about 7.5 percent on its debt (one-year LIBOR averaged about 5.5 percent in 1994), the total debt service payments would have been about US$1.5 billion, equivalent to almost 70 percent of

---

14. Banco Nacional de Cuba, *Economic Report 1994*, p.22.

15. According to Banco Nacional de Cuba, *Economic Report 1994*, the structure of Cuba's foreign debt by individual creditor country was as follows: Japan (25 percent), Spain (13 percent), France (12 percent), Argentina (9 percent), United Kingdom (8 percent), Italy (5 percent), Switzerland (2 percent), Germany (2 percent), Austria (2 percent) and others (22 percent). The denomination of the foreign debt in hard currencies was as follows: Deutsche marks (27 percent), Japanese yens (25 percent), U.S. dollars (13 percent), Swiss francs (8 percent), Spanish pesetas (6 percent), Canadian dollars (6 percent), French francs (5 percent), British pounds (3 percent) and others (7 percent). In accordance to previous agreements, the U.S. dollar debts are payable in other currencies.

16. Raw sugar production decreased from around 8 million tons in 1989-90 to approximately 4 million tons in 1993-1994. In 1994-95 production fell even more to 3.2 million tons. It is expected that it will increase to 4.5 million tons in 1995-96. (See Banco Nacional de Cuba, *Economic Report 1994*, p. 8). According to the Directorate of Intelligence of the Central Intelligence Agency (CIA) of the United States, Cuba's sugar exports (f.o.b.) amounted to 5.4 billion dollars in 1989 and fell to 2.0 billion dollars in 1992 and even lower in the following years. See *Handbook of International Statistics*, Directorate of Intelligence, Central Intelligence Agency, September 1993.

exports of goods and services of Cuba in 1994 as reported by the Banco Nacional de Cuba. This is a debt service ratio more than twice the average for Latin America and the Caribbean.

The official statistics presented by the Banco Nacional de Cuba, leave no ground but to conclude that the country is experiencing extremely serious economic and financial difficulties. The Cuban economy has shown a constant downward trend between 1989 and 1993, and meeting the debt service payments would pose enormous additional strains on an already precarious economy. In these circumstances, Cuba needs urgently foreign assistance and external debt relief to meet its external obligations but, what is even more important, the country also needs a change in its centralist economic policies if it is to recover from its present lamentable situation and restore its international creditworthiness.[17]

Castro's communist regime realizes perfectly well the heavy burden that Cuba's huge external debt is imposing on the countrys economy but refuses to admit its own policy errors. It tries to justify its present chaotic economic situation by placing the blame on external factors, such as the U.S. economic blockade, over which it has no control. For example, the Cuban government claims that during the seventies and up to 1982, the flow of financial resources into the country was "a consequence of the islands international prestige and authority and the sustained economic and social development achieved."[18] It also alleges that Cuba's level of indebtedness during that period "was in correspondence with the countrys real possibilities of facing these obligations and with the reasonable expectations as to how the international financial situation would behave."[19] The Castro gov-

ernment keeps stressing that the dramatic withdrawal of external credits to Cuba has no justification whatsoever. The crisis is perceived as one arising primarily from pressures exerted by the United States to isolate the island. But the crisis was also worsened by other exogenous factors such as: "the cyclical evolution of sugar prices with a bearish trend, the inflation prevailing in market-economy developed countries, the inordinate increase of interest rates and other effects of the economic blockade imposed by the U.S. government."[20]

Obviously, no mention is made in official Cuban documents of the disastrous socialist economic policies followed by the Castro government. Neither is there any reference made of the government's total rejection of market forces nor of the inefficiency of bureaucratic management and other misdirected government expenditures. Without the incentive of profits, production will almost inevitably tend to decrease and the potential for economic growth stifled, as the Soviet experience has amply demonstrated. The recognition of the right to private property, including the right of ownership of the means of production, is a necessary prerequisite for a sustained and integral development.

With respect to the present Cuban debt to the former Soviet Union and the communist bloc countries, the partial information available tend to indicate that the Cuban government owes Russia approximately Rub. 21.5 billion. Credit agreements between the former Soviet Union and developing countries provided for the debtor country to service its debt mainly with exports of goods. It was only in the more recent agreements that the Russian government stipulated that the service debt payments

---

17. According to London's *The Economist*, the Cuban authorities believe that economic growth could be spurred if medium- and long-term financing were to be available. But, this could only happen if Cuba could show itself to be an orderly and disciplined society. Unfortunately for Castro, *The Economist* adds: "Cuba has a history to live down. In the early days of the revolution, when Che Guevara ran the National Bank, paying back international debts was seen as a wimpish thing to do. Since 1986, when it stopped making payments on its debt to western banks and institutions, Cuba has been shut out of the international credit markets." See *The Economist*, Cuba Survey I (April 6, 1996), p. 11.

18. Banco Nacional de Cuba, *Economic Report 1994*, p. 22.

19. Banco Nacional de Cuba, *Economic Report 1994*, p. 22.

20. Banco Nacional de Cuba, *Economic Report 1994*, p. 22.

should be made in convertible currency. Its value was to be determined based on the corresponding exchange rate of the State Bank of the USSR (the Gosbank).[21] Although a Rub 21.5 billion debt may have seemed a huge sum in the past, today, at Russia's official exchange rate, Cuba's debt to Russia is much reduced.[22]

THE ETHICAL DIMENSIONS OF THE DEBT PROBLEM AND THE PRINCIPLE OF SOLIDARITY

Since the end of the Second World War, the growing awareness of the tremendous economic differences that exist between the developed and developing countries have shifted, to a certain extent, the center of the social question from the national level to the international level. The debt crisis of the 1980s was the most recent indication of the interdependence between developed and developing countries and the need for a greater degree of cooperation and understanding within the world community.

The centers of economic and social power gradually began to realize that a just and sustained development in the poverty stricken nations of the world would contribute not only to their own economic growth and development but also to the moral, cultural, and economic growth of the entire human race. The Mexican crisis reinforced this realization when the more developed countries had to intervene and take emergency measures to avoid a possible collapse of the international financial system with its negative consequences on growth and development.

The complexity of the debt crisis of the 1980s has demonstrated the need for solutions that go beyond temporary agreements between creditor and debtor nations. The solution cannot be limited to a simple debate as to whom or how the payment or non-payment of the debt should be made. A deeper analysis of the very roots of the crisis is required in order to prevent the recurrence of some of the economic problems that led to the lamentable events of the 1970s and 1980s. This leads us directly to the concept of development and the need for international cooperation.

The response to the debt crisis cannot be separated from every nations right to development, a right that is defined by the United Nations as "an inalienable human right by virtue of which every human person and all peoples are entitled to participate in, contribute to and enjoy economic, social, cultural, and political development, in which all human rights and fundamental freedoms can be fully realized."[23] To achieve this inalienable right to development, the less endowed nations of the world need the support and cooperation of the more privileged countries which

---

21. According to Russian sources, Moscows official claims on all developing nations amounted to US$173 billion at the end of 1993. Russia acquired all the external claims of the former Soviet Union as a result of the Zero Option Agreement which covered all pre-1991 claims, both commercial and state credits. In accordance with these agreements, provisions were made for the conversion into freely convertible currencies the debt service payments on Soviet ruble denominated claims. Russia insists that the appropriate exchange rate at which to value its claims is the U.S.S.R. Gosbank ruble exchange rate. There are many debtor countries that disagree with the valuation method claimed by the Russians. They contend that the valuation for calculating the value of the outstanding claims and debt service should take into account recent developments in the ruble foreign exchange market. The estimate of US$173 billion was made by the IMF staff on the basis of the ruble denominated claims of Russia and converted into dollars at the official exchange rate of Rub 0.5854/US$1 prevailing at the end of 1993. See International Monetary Fund, *Official Financing for Developing Countries*, 1994, pp. 93-99. *The Economist* claims that Cuba's debt owed to Russia stands at about US$20 billion. But when Russia inquired last year about the servicing of Cuba's debt to Russia it received a cheeky response: "Why, the figure happened to be exactly the same as that for the damage Armageddon had inflicted on the Cuban economy." See *The Economist* (April 6, 1996), p. 11.

22. Russia reached an agreement with Nicaragua concerning Managuas US$3 billion plus debt to the former Soviet Union. According to a newspaper report, Mikhail Sarafanov, Deputy Foreign Economic Relations Minister of Russia, claimed that both sides had agreed that Nicaragua owed Russia US$3.4 billion. This amount, said Sarafanov, "was computed from the official exchange rate Gosbank USSR, which will be quoted by the Bank of Russia. This debt will be paid in hard currency with a *discount of 90 percent* over 15 years, with the refinancing rate calculated at a market rate." In addition, the Russians claim that "the entire consolidated debt has to be settled without writing off a large part of it because of the political factors involved in the formation of the debt, something other debtor countries press for." See *Journal of Commerce* (April 25, 1996), p. 41A.

23. United Nations: Declaration of Human Rights.

are the ones that have the resources to make it possible; an achievement that requires a concerted worldwide effort that is based on a genuine spirit of solidarity. Dana W. Wilbanks has expressed it this way: the debt crisis must be regarded "as a vivid disclosure of the distressing vulnerability of particular peoples in the world and the urgent need for international, regional and national cooperation to correct injustices."[24]

The need for development becomes paramount if peace with justice is to prevail. And this requires a collective effort on the part of the world community. John Paul II has stated that there is a collective responsibility to promote development and to overcome poverty. If peace with justice is to prevail in todays world, development must be promoted through closer international cooperation—condition *sine qua non* for a durable peace. The very concept of interdependence must be raised to the moral level and this cannot be done without a greater degree of solidarity at both the national and international levels. As John Paul II has declared in his encyclical *Sollicitudo Rei Socialis*:

> ... in a world divided and beset by every type of conflict, the conviction is growing of a radical interdependence and consequently of the need for a solidarity which will take up interdependence and transfer it to the moral plane.[25]

Pope John Paul II clarifies the principle of solidarity when he states that the very reality of interdependence "must be transformed into solidarity, based upon the principle that the goods of creation are meant for all."[26] In other words, solidarity "helps us to see the other—whether a person, people or nation—not just as some kind of instrument, with a work capacity and physical strength to be exploited at low cost and then discarded when no longer useful, but as our "neighbor," a "helper" to be made a sharer, on a par with ourselves..."[27] The validity of the principle of solidarity, both in the internal and in the international order, is one of the fundamental principles of the Christian view of social and political organization. It should not be viewed as being in contradiction with a market economy which in the social justice tradition of the Church is viewed as the most efficient economic system and in line with the respect to the right of private property.[28] The principle of solidarity, does call, however, to take action to help the disadvantaged and to ensure that the poor have the means for participating in the process of development.

The Pope also stresses the need "for effective international agencies which will oversee and direct the economy toward the common good, something that an individual State, even if it were the most powerful on earth, would not be in a position to do."[29] Decision makers, both at the national and international levels, cannot ignore the phenomenon of globalization and the obligation it entails if the common good of all nations is to be attained.

As part of these efforts, the Pontifical Justice and Peace Commission set the following preconditions as necessary for a satisfactory and durable solution to the debt problem: 1) interdependence should give rise to expressions of solidarity which respect the equal dignity of all peoples; 2) acceptability of co-responsibility for the causes and the solutions relative to the problems associated with external debt; 3) create or restore relations based on trust between nations (creditors and debtors) and between the various

---

24. Wilbanks, Dana W., "Religious Ethics, Human Rights, and the Debt Problem", in *World Debt and the Human Condition*, edited by Ved P. Nanda, George W. Shepherd Jr., and Eileen McCarthy-Arnolds (Westport, Connecticut: Greenwood Press, 1995), p. 74.

25. John Paul II, *Sollicitudo Rei Socialis*, #26.

26. John Paul II, *Sollicitudo Rei Socialis*, #39.

27. John Paul II, *Sollicitudo Rei Socialis*, #26.

28. John Paul II has clearly stated that capitalism can be efficient and just. An economic system which recognizes the fundamental and positive role of business, the market, private property and the resulting responsibility for the means of production, as well as free human creativity in the economic sector can be a very positive element for development (*Centesimus Anno*).

29. John Paul II, *Centesimus Anno*, # 58.

agents (political authorities, commercial banks, international organizations) for cooperation in the search for solutions; 4) an equitable sharing of the adjustment efforts and the necessary sacrifices, taking into account the priority to be given to the needs of the most deprived peoples; 5) financial and monetary officials have the prime responsibility for finding solutions to the debt crisis, but they share this responsibility with political and economic leaders; and 6) a reform of the financial and monetary institutions needs to be studied.[30]

What needs to be stressed is that the external debt of the developing countries cannot be analyzed exclusively in economic and political terms. The analysis must broaden its content so as to include also the ethical dimension, so necessary if solidarity is to prevail among nations. For justice to triumph "interdependence should give rise to new and broader expressions of solidarity which respect the equal dignity of all peoples, rather than lead to domination by the strongest, to national egoism, to inequalities and injustices."[31]

Solidarity requires an awareness and acceptance of co-responsibility for the causes and solutions of the debt question; solutions that must be found if every nations right to development is to be respected. With respect to the causes, they can be either external or internal or both, depending on each specific case. Very often, the problem is the result of internal conditions, caused by inefficient economic or political systems which hamper economic growth and development. Other times, the cause can be traced to international market factors or protectionist policies carried out by the industrialized nations. The important lesson that can be learned from the debt crisis is the need for an agreement on an equitable sharing of the adjustment efforts and of the sacrifices that must be made in order to solve the problem.

But, above all, the international community must realize that peoples and nations have a right to develop. As long as large sections of the world population live in abject poverty and suffer the scourge of under development, no durable solution will be found to the debt problem. The severe affliction of underdevelopment cannot be treated with small doses of aspirin. It demands a more profound cure that requires painful adjustments and sacrifices on the part of both the creditor and debtor nations. Fortunately, as it has been described in the third section of this paper, the steps taken by the international community to address the debt crisis reflect the spirit of solidarity and a realization of the interdependence of creditors and debtors. Faced with the reality that debtors could not meet their obligations, creditors have provided debt relief in exchange for the adoption of meaningful economic reforms in debtor countries.

In the particular case of Cuba, what type of cure will the new government have to apply once freedom and the rule of law are restored on the island? Will a free Cuba need the cooperation and assistance of the international community in order to reduce the burden of its debt and help reconstruct the countrys devastated economy after years of inefficient marxist-socialist policies? Does the international community have a shared responsibility in the reconstruction of Cuba in accordance with the principle of solidarity? An attempt will be made to answer these questions in the section that follows.

IMPLICATIONS FOR THE FUTURE OF THE EXTERNAL DEBT SERVICE BURDEN OF CUBA

Cuba's debt problems and their possible solutions cannot be separated from the economic policies pursued by the Castro government. What is even more disturbing than Cuba's economic failures is the way that, in such a type of totalitarian regime, man is compelled to submit to a concept of reality that is imposed on him by coercion, and not reached by virtue of his own reason and the exercise of his own freedom. This practice, insists John Paul II,

> must be overturned and total recognition must be given to the rights of the human conscience, which is

---

30. "An Ethical Approach to the International Debt Question," pp. 604-605.

31. "An Ethical Approach to the International Debt Question," p. 604.

bound only to the truth, both natural and revealed. The recognition of these rights represents the primary foundation of every authentically free political order.[32]

Hopefully, with the end of Castro's Marxist-Leninist regime, a new era of political and economic freedoms will begin. It is highly probable that Cuba's centralized socialist economy will be replaced by a more liberal economy where the market system will prevail and the right to private property and human rights respected. However, the newly installed government will have to face the inherited formidable burden of an external debt in freely convertible currency which, as already indicated, amounts to over US$9 billion without counting the debt to Russia.

The new Cuban government will have to confront the important task of determining how to deal with its large external debt. This is a matter of importance for both Cuba and its creditors. Given its very large debt, Cuba will need all the cooperation it can get from the international community so that the transition period to a market economy can result in a process of genuine development as quickly as possible. To renegotiate and reschedule in the best possible terms the islands debt to its foreign creditors will be among the governments top priority goals.

Total repudiation of the external debt that has not been serviced for approximately 10 years is probably not a realistic option for a new Cuban government. The costs of a default would be great in both economic and ethical terms. Defaulting, as Professor Gerald M. Meier of Stanford University has stated, "entails the cost of losing future access to international markets, not being able to receive trade credits, having its assets possibly subject to assessment by the

creditors, and suffering in general a loss of reputation."[33] Cuba's new democratic government could ill afford to begin a new era of respectability by defaulting or refusing to pay its debts, even though they were incurred by the previous Marxist regime.

It is highly probable that a democratic government committed to carry out economic reforms would be likely to receive a sympathetic treatment from its foreign creditors. Creditors may conclude that if debt and debt-servicing reduction, as well as new financing, are given to Cuba, the island's economy will prosper and will become creditworthy in the future. Countries that have embarked on adjustment programs and implemented structural reforms with the support of multilateral institutions have had substantial debt relief. However, given its debt service burden, the extent of debt relief that Cuba would need to receive would be extensive if it is going to restore its relations with foreign creditors, even if new sources of financing such as from multilateral institutions, are opened again to Cuba.

A reduction of Cuba's large external debt would give the country a greater incentive to service the smaller debt and to implement measures to stimulate the domestic economy. The debt and debt service reduction should be sufficient to enable Cuba to bring the stock of its debt down to a level that is manageable given the size of the economy and export capacity. In addition, it should be sufficient to permit part of Cuba's future income growth to accrue to domestic residents and not just to foreign creditors, and sufficient to permit trade lines and interbank lines to be maintained on a voluntary basis.

There is always, of course, the unlikely possibility that the creditors may decide to forgive in its totality

---

32. John Paul II, *Centesimus Anno*, #29. It is appropriate to mention that the Papal encyclicals have stressed repeatedly that certain nations must reform their unjust structures and, in particular, their political institutions, "in order to replace corrupt, dictatorial and authoritarian forms of government by democratic and participatory ones" (John Paul II, *Sollicitudo Rei Socialis*, #45). A development "that does not respect and promote human rights—personal and social, economic and political, including the rights of nations and of peoples—is not worthy of man (John Paul II, *Sollicitudo Rei Socialis*, #33). Any type of economic assistance to a totalitarian system, that does not permit free and responsible participation of all citizens in public affairs, in the rule of law and in respect for the promotion of human rights, will only serve to strengthen and perpetuate the evils of the regime. Humanitarian aid to oppressed populations would be the only exception.

33. Gerald M. Meier, *Leading Issues in Economic Development* (New York: Oxford University Press, 1995), p. 245.

the debt burden of a debtor country. However, concerning total forgiveness there is the more crucial question, apart from economic consideration, of how just or ethical it would be to forgive the debt of certain countries and not of others. In addition, a dangerous precedent would be established whereby any country would be inclined to borrow with the near conviction that sooner or later its debts would be forgiven in order to avoid, for example, an international crisis.

In the final analysis, how the creditor nations will react once Cuba enters a new democratic phase in its history is impossible to predict with absolute certainty. It seems fair to state that Cuba will be able to overcome many of its present difficulties and reinitiate a path of economic growth and development if it endorses the basic principles of the free enterprise system and fosters the common good and accepts democratic principles. Cuba is endowed with good natural and human resources that could be used in a more efficient manner once the proper incentives are provided in an environment of freedom and justice. As soon as confidence in the future of Cuba is reestablished and the countrys trustworthiness restored, the international community is likely to come to its assistance. In particular, the inflow of private foreign capital could be significant and more than willing to take advantage of the multiple opportunities that the Cuban market will offer foreign investors.

During Cuba's difficult transition period the new government will need the full cooperation and assistance of the world community. It is precisely during the transition period that multilateral institutions can and should play a significant role in the countrys economic recovery. They should come to the assistance of the new Cuban government and help it to renegotiate and/or reschedule many of the debts owed by the Castro regime. Neither can the wealthier nations shy away from their responsibility to help a free Cuba in its efforts to recover from the deprivations of the past. To do otherwise would be to ignore the principle of international solidarity. Cuba suffered too much under Marxism to be ignored by the world community.

Obviously, such a favorable outcome might be deemed too optimistic. Other countries that have endured Marxist policies for many years have found it very difficult to pass from economic collectivism to economic freedom without serious economic problems. The period of transition, as the Russian example clearly demonstrates, is full of perils. A long tradition of dependence on government can very easily wither away the incipient desire for freedom.

History tends to indicate that there is an inverse relationship between freedom and dependence. The greater the level of dependence, the lesser the degree of freedom and vice versa. That is why the transition from total dependence on the state to individual freedom can be extremely hazardous if the latter is not accompanied with a large dose of personal responsibility on the part of all sectors of society: public and private. It is a proven fact that the abuse of freedom can destroy the chances for success of even the best political or economic systems.

Ironically, it is precisely in this area of political and economic freedom that lies the greatest danger facing Cuba's post communist era. The changes that will have to be introduced if Cuba's ills are to be cured will require many painful adjustments that all sectors of Cuban society will have to accept and endure, not only the less privileged groups. This may not be easy to carry out in a democratic and free environment unless everyone - rich and poor- are willing to accept the changes and act in a responsible manner. The new Cuban society must be built on responsible freedom and with a great dose of solidarity; a solidarity that will bind all Cubans together in a continuous search for the common good of the country. Otherwise Cuba could fall back into chaos and some other type of totalitarianism, whether of the right or of the left.

It is to be hoped that Cubans, with their long history of private initiative and love of freedom, will not be led astray by a false sense of dependence on government, so characteristic of the Castro years, and use instead their newly acquired freedom in a responsible and constructive way. The Cuban people will surely accept and support the long awaited economic changes of the post communist era as long as they are carried out with justice and provide the necessary safeguards for the underprivileged sectors of society.

SUMMARY AND CONCLUSIONS

There is a growing interdependence between peoples and nations which should be used to pursue the objectives of the common good and not limited to individual or collective vested interests. Interdependence can give rise to new and broader expressions of solidarity; a solidarity which respects the dignity of the human person and fosters the development of both individuals and nations. A clear manifestation of the interdependence between developed and developing countries are the problems associated with the growth of the external debt of developing countries. In many cases, their solution requires genuine cooperation at the international level which can provide for an efficient management of debt problems and help foster the economic recovery of the indebted countries. But, for authentic development to take place all the nations of the world must participate; not only the more wealthy ones. Fortunately, as demonstrated in this paper, important steps are already being taken to alleviate the external debt service burden of heavily indebted countries.

What will happen to Cuba in the post socialist era cannot be predicted with any degree of certainty. The probability weighs heavily in favor of the post-Castro government dismantling the entire apparatus of Marxism-Leninism, responsible for the penury that has afflicted the Cuban population for so many years. The apparent heirs are democratic pluralism and the free market system. The fall of Marxism in the former Soviet Union contributed in no small manner to the reality of interdependence among peoples and intensified the free flow of ideas, not to mention the flow of capital and other factors of production. The flow of capital into Russia after the fall of the Berlin wall in 1989 set the example for future types of assistance to former communist countries that have endorsed political and economic freedoms.

Renegotiation and rescheduling of its foreign debt in equitable terms similar to those received by other countries of similar level of development and debt indebtedness will be among the top priorities of the incoming authorities. Cuba must become once again a trustworthy nation, gain the respect of the world community and meets its international obligations. But, at the same time, both the creditor nations and the international financial institutions must show a deep understanding of Cuba's needs and help the country to recover from the dismal policies of communism. Such a willingness to cooperate in the reconstruction of Cuba's devastated economy would be proof enough that the international community takes the principle of solidarity seriously.

Undoubtedly, international financial assistance can help solve many of the problems accompanying the reordering of Cuba's previously collectivized economic system. But, the solution to Cuba's problems and its future well-being in the post Marxist era do not depend exclusively or even primarily on foreign assistance and, much less, on the renegotiation of its external debt, no matter how important they might be. The future of Cuba lies with the Cubans themselves. Cuba must carry the major economic and financial burden of the islands reconstruction with all the sacrifices and hardships that this may entail. This in spite of the fact that Cuba's present condition, as in the case of other victims of communism, "is not the result of free choice or mistakes which were made, but as a consequence of tragic historical events which were violently imposed on them, and which prevented them from following the path of economic and social development."[34]

While it is true that the free market system can achieve a higher standard of living than collectivism in any of its forms, it is false to assume that economic and political freedoms per se will contribute also to a better and more humane society. There is little doubt that the capitalist model is by far more efficient and productive than socialism but there is no guarantee that the former will not exclude also all spiritual principles and deny an autonomous existence and value to morality, law, culture and religion. If it does, the

---

34. John Paul II, *Sollicitudo Rei Socialis*, #28.

difference between capitalism and Marxism tends to fade away because both systems would reduce man to the sphere of economics and the satisfaction of material goods.

Cuba has to be rebuilt morally and economically and, as in the case of all former communist dominated countries, will need to go through a patient material and moral reconstruction, even as people, exhausted by longstanding privation will be asking the new government for tangible and immediate results in the form of material benefits and an adequate fulfillment of their legitimate aspirations.

Cuba's long suffering people will some day experience the fall of Marxism-Leninism and, hopefully, experience a new era of peace and justice for all Cubans of goodwill. But Cubans should not expect the immediate improvement in living standards after the long night of Castro's dictatorial experiment. Recent experience has demonstrated that the simple overthrow of prevailing socioeconomic structures have not necessarily brought about the "panaceas" that their sponsors had predicted. Progress does not always follow change "per se." Change will be successful only if the economic and technical aspects of the change are accompanied by a proper ethical foundation. Without such a foundation, the needed political and economic changes will falter and the problems will only intensify to the detriment of the Cuban people. Cubans should look to the future with optimism. As the bonds of solidarity increase, both at the national and international levels, the problems related with the foreign debt will fade into the background and finally the Cuban people will be able to enjoy a well deserved integral development.

COMMENTS ON

"External Debt Problems and the Principle of Solidarity: The Cuban Case" by Alberto Martínez-Piedra And Lorenzo L. Pérez

Armando P. Ribas

In their paper "External Debt Problems and the Principle of Solidarity: The Cuban Case," Alberto Martínez-Piedra and Lorenzo Pérez have given a thorough account of the historical process of the debt of less developed countries (LDCs) and the present situation. At the same time, the authors try to frame the possible solution of the LDCs external debt on the basis of the principle of solidarity. It is to their ethical approach that I am going to direct my comments.

There is no doubt that the debt problem has deep ethical implications, but I do believe that the solidarity approach adds to the confusion instead of providing a needed solution. In that sense, I do think that it is a mistake to believe that the debt is a problem for the LDCs when the truth is that at the end it was the international financial system the one that at least for a time was really threatened, and with it the industrial world. Then, my main contention is that the solution of the debt problem should not come out of compassion of the industrial world for the well being of the LDCs, but on account of the correct understanding of the nature of the problem. In that sense, we should acknowledge that ethical questions not always imply an alternative between ethical and non-ethical solutions. In many instances, the real issue is which ethical principles should be applied. It is in this respect that I think that the Martínez-Piedra and Pérez paper, when trying to apply the so-called principle of solidarity, really misses this point.

There is no ethical problem which could be addressed without due regard to rights and responsibility. It is in this area where major differences could arise notably when we try to apply the principle of solidarity. Allow me to say, then, that such principle is based on the assumption that there is someone in a privileged position, with respect to another, and for that very reason has a moral duty to the latter. But can we expect that international financial markets operate under that assumption? What would be the meaning of risks? I would say, then, that solidarity is the contradiction of the market economy.

Now, we have entered the realm of ideology and I dare to say that the so-called principle of solidarity implies the acceptance of the Marxist view according to which the rich are the exploiters of the poor, and that a similar situation arises in the international field, as explained by Lenin in his "Imperialism: The Last Stage of Capitalism." But if we accept this approach, no international lending should take place since in fact what is challenged is precisely the property rights of the lender. If, on the other hand, we recognize the property rights of the lender, what are the implications of solidarity?

The problem is even more complicated, because the lender in this particular case is an institution, whose capital belongs to the stockholders, and the loaned money to the depositors. Do the banks have the right—out of the principle of solidarity—to relinquish the rights of collecting moneys owed, at the expense of the stockholders and the depositors? I would say that the authors would never accept that proposition, but in fact to some extent it is implied in their approach, and the quotations of the Pope.

But there is another relevant question. Why did the banks loan money to the LDCs when they knew, or should have known, that those countries and their governments were unwilling or unable to repay the debt? The origin of the debt problem was the quadrupling of the oil prices. I do think that out of the solidarity principle, the industrial countries, through the IMF, decided to help the LDCs to "finance" the oil bill. This decision took form in the so called "Oil Facility" created by the IMF in 1974 and extended a year later. This was the basis of the so called recycling process, according to which the international banks loaned the surplus petrodollars to the LDCs. Obviously the impact of this expanding bubble was to produce another increase in the price of oil in 1979. The decision to finance the oil price increases was based on the wrong assumption: that the demand for oil was completely inelastic, because there was not any other energy substitute available. The fact was the other way around. It was the availability of financing that permitted the price of oil to appear to have no ceiling. This was the prevailing wisdom which determined the evolution of the LDC external debt from 1973 onwards.

In 1979, however, there was another factor which determined a further increase in the debt as well as the potential bankruptcy of the international financial system. That was the decision of the president of the U.S. Federal Reserve System, Mr. Volker, to raise interest rates in order to stem the United States inflation. When the prime rate skyrocketed to close to 23 percent on account of this "wise" decision, the problem of the international debt worsened. From then on, it was no longer the problem of the debtor countries but of the international banking system, and for that very reason of the industrial countries as a whole.

Even though the problem of the debt may be perceived as a conflict of interest between the debtor countries and the international banks, there is another factor which is affecting the whole situation and it is necessary to take into account. On the one hand, the level of international interest rates which result form the expansion of government expenditures in the industrial countries and, on the other, the protectionist policies of those countries. In this respect it should be remembered the collapse of the international payments system in 1932, as a result of the U.S. Smoot-Hawley Tariff Act, which hindered all possibilities of European countries to pay their debt to the United States. In that sense the words of the economist Seligman are still valid: "It is not they who do not want to pay, we are the ones who do not want to collect the debts."

Hence it is obvious that the plans to solve the problem of the debt, for example the recent bailout of the Mexican economy, has not come out of compassion, but of enlightened self interest. But it is important that a new approach should be followed with respect to the recurrent banking crisis, and try to avoid to indulge in practices that finally end up with a bubble. In that sense, it should be now evident that such crisis rather than resulting from the moral hazard of the bankers are caused by "moral hazard" involving the welfare expenditures of governments acting on the basis of the principle of solidarity.

Even though I have not touched upon the Cuban external debt, there is no doubt that the major considerations which I have explained above are, and should be, applicable to the Cuban case. I am sure that the possibility of resolution of the Cuban external debt problem will not come about as a result of compassion and solidarity. The solution, if there is any, will come about through the wisdom of the Cuban government and the international creditors to find their common interests.

CUBA'S HARD CURRENCY DEBT

Gabriel Fernández[1]

This paper focuses on Cuba's hard currency debt with Western creditors and not on debt in non-convertible currencies with the former Eastern bloc countries. It also provides an overview of the island nation's political and economic history over the past 37 years.

Information on Cuba's hard currency debt is hard to come by, particularly for United States citizens. This is because Cuban debt is not traded in New York and is only thinly traded abroad, primarily in London and Madrid. My first goal in writing this report was to gather information on Cuba's hard currency debt. My second goal relates to the notion that the bond market represents a consensus of investor's expectations. If this is true, what can the bond market, through its historical prices, tell us about prospects for reform in Cuba?

In November of 1995, the Economist Intelligence Unit ran a report on Cuba with the headline, "Cuba: Caribbean Tiger or Basket Case?" The title aptly describes Cuba's current paradoxical situation. As an emerging market, Cuba has as much long-term growth potential as any of the Asian tiger nations. It is rich in natural resources such as nickel, has the climate and soil fertility to become an agricultural powerhouse, is rich in human capital (with a literacy rate

over 90 percent), and is only 90 miles from the vast U.S. markets.

Why, then, is Cuba so poor? The three reasons most often given by analysts are: 1) Cuba's hugely inefficient thirty-seven year old statist economy; 2) the thirty-five-year old U.S. trade embargo; and 3) the blow the Cuban economy received from the loss of its largest trading partner, the Soviet Union, in 1990. Today, the island nation faces a dire economic outlook. Given the slow pace of reform, little relief is in sight.

Expectations about Cuba as a Caribbean tiger or basket case are reflected in the bond market's price of Cuba's hard currency debt. When investors are encouraged about the prospects for change in Cuba, Cuban debt prices rise. Conversely, prices fall along with investors' pessimism.

Cuban debt instruments, all of which are in default, are grouped in a class of debt instruments known as "the exotics." Here, Cuba keeps company with debt from Nicaragua, North Korea, Yemen, Iran and Laos. Exotics are highly speculative, and not for the risk averse. Their price movements are sudden and dramatic, and their liquidity is low.

From 1800-1992, Cuba has defaulted three times on its debt.[2] In 1994, according to Institutional Inves-

1. No work is ever done in a vacuum, and this paper is no exception. Thanks to Professor Abraham Ravid of NYU's Stern School of Business, Anna Szterenfeld of the Economist Intelligence Unit, Mark Siebel of the Miami Herald, and Leo Guzman of Leo Guzman and Associates for their thoughts on the subject. Special thanks go to Dr. Jerome Booth of London's ANZ Grindlays Bank whose input and comments were invaluable.

2. *Institutional Investors 1994 Country Risk Ratings.*

44

tors Country Risk Ratings, Cuba had one of the lowest country ratings in the world, barely ahead of Iraq, Sudan, and Haiti. The September, 1994 edition of the magazine *Euromoney* concurred with this finding, rating Cuba as the riskiest country to invest in out of the 167 countries it surveyed. To aggravate this already dismal credit history, the investment situation is complicated by unpredictable political factors.

HISTORICAL OVERVIEW

In January 1959, Fidel Castro, a guerrilla leader, assumed power from General Fulgencio Batista after waging a six-year-long military struggle. Castro proceeded to transform the existing market-oriented Cuban economy to one based on collective ownership of the means of production and centralized control.

The United States severed relations with Cuba in 1961 following the expropriation of assets belonging to U.S. enterprises then worth over $1 billion.[3] (At 6 percent compounded interest, these assets are today worth approximately $7.7 billion). A full trade embargo, which is still in effect, was imposed on Cuba by the United States in 1962. The embargo prohibits U.S. citizens from having direct commercial dealings with Cuba. Prior to 1959, the U.S. was Cuba's largest trading partner and its largest source of foreign investment. In defiance of the U.S., Cuba aligned itself with the Soviet Union. Cuba retained a close relationship with the Soviet Union until the latter's demise in 1990.[4]

For three decades, the Soviet Union subsidized Cuba, primarily by bartering oil for sugar at below world market prices. In exchange for this and other economic subsidies, estimated to be worth $4 billion per year, Cuba acted as the Soviet Union's surrogate, fomenting communism in Africa and Latin America.

By 1990, due to the deteriorating domestic situation, the Soviet Union was unable to maintain its high level of aid to Cuba.

The Cuban economy took a direct hit in 1990, plunging by 40 percent since then.[5] The privileged trading relations with the Soviet Union which Cuba enjoyed abruptly ceased. Trade between Russia and Cuba fell from a high of $9 billion in 1990 to $506 million in 1994.[6] Until 1988, 85 percent of Cuban two-way trade was with the former Soviet Union; by 1993, the eastern bloc accounted for 20 percent of Cuban trade. In 1991, Cuba was the world's largest exporter of sugar, producing 6.7 percent of total world output.[7] In 1993, sugar production dropped to 50 percent of its 1991 levels. The collapse of the socialist bloc barter system starved the sugar sector of key inputs and contributed to poor sugar harvests.

A SEARCH FOR SOLUTIONS

Since the collapse of the Soviet Union, Cuba has been trying to re-orient its economy. Efforts have been directed at encouraging direct foreign investment, implementing modest market reforms, and finding new trading partners.[8] The tourism, telecommunications, and agricultural sectors have been targeted for foreign participation. The health, defense, and sugar industries remain closed to foreign activity, as these sectors are seen as vital to Cuba's national interests.

Reforms from 1993 include legalization of the dollar, the allowance of independent workers, and the establishment of agricultural cooperatives. In May 1994, Cuba's National Assembly approved a far-reaching austerity package. It was designed to cut subsidies to unprofitable state-owned companies, make cuts in

---

3. The Economist Intelligence Unit, *Country Profile: Cuba,* 1995-96.

4. Archibald Ritter, ed., *Cuba in the International System.* New York: St. Martin's Press, 1995.

5. According to the Economist Intelligence Unit, Cuban GDP fell by 2.9 percent in 1990, 10.7 percent in 1991, 11.6 percent in 1992, and 14.9 percent in 1993; in 1994 and 1995, GDP experienced positive growth rates of 0.7 and 2.0 percent, respectively.

6. *The Reuters Business Report* (October 9, 1995).

7. The Economist Intelligence Unit, *Country Profile: Cuba,* 1995-96.

8. Jaime Suchlicki and Antonio Jorge, editors, *Investing in Cuba: Problems and Prospects.* New Brunswick: Transaction Publishers, 1994.

the bloated government bureaucracy, and reinstate income taxes.

Throughout 1994, representatives from nearly one hundred U.S. businesses, including Radisson Hotels, the Ford Motor Company, Archer-Daniels, and General Motors, visited Cuba on business exploration trips.[9] They came to Cuba on the heels of business representatives from Canada, Spain, Italy, France, Great Britain, Mexico, Japan, and Argentina.

In response to these developments, prospects for economic recovery brightened. The Cuban peso, the exchange rate of which is officially pegged at par with the U.S. dollar, increased in value on the Cuban black market from a low of 120 pesos to the U.S. dollar in July, 1994, to 35 pesos to the dollar by December of that same year. The modest economic growth of 0.7 percent in 1994 and 2 percent in 1995 indicated that the economy was starting to respond positively to the reforms after having hit bottom in 1993.

However, Cuban debt speculators should not be too buoyed by this news. Talk of reform in Cuba needs to be taken with a grain of salt. Statements in the press by Cuban officials speak of their ambivalence towards change. Roberto Robaina, Cuba's foreign Minister, says that although Cuba is making market-oriented reforms, "still, Cuba doesn't plan to create a stock exchange and has not focused on bonds."[10]

Fidel Castro stresses that "Cuba won't give up socialism just because it is entering into joint ventures, and allowing foreign investment, self-employment and agricultural cooperatives."[11] In a decree that must create expropriation anxiety for foreign investors, the Cuban government retains the right to nationalize any company that goes against "the national interest."[12]

Because of the collapse of its economy and the decline in foreign trade, Cuba has little hard currency. The level of foreign reserves in the *Banco Nacional de Cuba*, Cuba's central bank, were estimated to be about US$100 million in 1994.[13] Roberto Robaina, Cuba's foreign minister, says: "Cuba simply doesn't have the money to pay," its defaulted debt.[14]

Cuba has been holding bilateral talks with Mexico, Argentina, and Brazil aimed at negotiating repayment terms on official debt. Because of the weakness of the Cuban economy, negotiations revolve around when Cuba can afford to start making payments. The form of commercial debt restructuring is still open to question. Because Cuba is not a member of either the International Monetary Fund (IMF) or the World Bank, guarantees normally available to foreign investors are not available in Cuba.

With small amounts of hard currency reserves, and low export revenues from an ailing economy, the Cuban government has tried getting out of its debt problem by offering debt-for-equity swaps in state-owned companies that are being privatized. In a swap, a buyer purchases debt at a discount, offering to cancel the debt in exchange for an ownership stake in the government company. Debt-equity swaps are also attractive to Cuba, because they reduce the amount of debt trading on the market, increasing prices.

A highly visible debt-for-equity case involved Cuba's telephone company, *Empresa de Telecomunicaciones de Cuba*, or Emtel. In 1994, forty-nine percent of Emtel was purchased for $1.5 billion by *Grupo Domos* of Mexico.[15] In late 1995, this deal collapsed, a

---

9. *Bloomberg Business News* (June 14, 1995).

10. *American Banker-Bond Buyer* (April 18, 1994).

11. *American Banker-Bond Buyer* (April 18, 1994).

12. *American Banker-Bond Buyer* (October 2, 1995).

13. *Moody's International Manual*, Volume 1, 1994.

14. *American Banker-Bond Buyer* (October 2, 1995).

15. *Business Week* (March 4, 1996).

victim of the Mexican financial crisis, when Domos failed to make a $320 million installment to the Cuban government. Domos, under financial distress, subsequently sold 25 percent of its share of Emtel at a deep discount to Stet, an Italian telecommunications concern.[16] Because Emtel was the flagship sale in Cuba's privatization program, it was very important to the country symbolically. Domos' default was a major setback for the reform program.

Another debt-for-equity swap case, currently in negotiation, involves Argentine creditors. Instead of a cash settlement, Argentine businesses would use Cuban debt as credit to invest in Cuba.[17] In April of 1995, the Banco Nacional de Cuba recognized $1.28 billion in principal, interest, and arrears owed to the Argentine government.[18]

In June of 1994, Cuba and Brazil reached an agreement to settle Brazil's debt claim totaling $40 million.[19] In the deal, Cuba agreed to a debt repayment plan through the export of Cuban medicines to Brazil.

Cuban officials met with Paris Club members on the subject of Cuban debt in October 1995. Cuba owes the Paris Club group of creditors US $2.9 billion.[20] The last time Cuba spoke with the Paris Club was in 1986. While investors were encouraged by Cuba's interest in resuming talks, expectations for debt resolution were not high. The Paris Club can only deal officially with countries which are members of the International Monetary Fund, to which Cuba does not belong. Any attempt to hold formal talks between Cuba and the Paris Club would almost certainly be blocked by the United States.

CUBAN DEBT

For the purposes of this paper, Cuban debt is divided into pre-Castro government and Castro government debt. The Castro government debt, in turn, is broken down into hard and soft currency debt. Exact debt amounts are difficult to come by because the quality of financial reporting out of Cuba is poor. The figures for the London and Paris Clubs, and the commercial trade debt, are based from the last official figures published in June, 1990 by the Banco Nacional de Cuba. Arrears owed to the London and Paris Clubs are estimated to be $2.5 billion. An additional $1.6 billion in arrears is owed on the commercial trade debt.[21]

Table 1.   Cuba's Hard Currency Debt

Creditor	$ Billions
Pre-Castro Government	$0.052
Paris Club	$2.900
London Club	$2.100
Commercial Trade Debt	$1.400
Subtotal	$6.452
London and Paris Club Arrears	$2.500
Commercial Trade Debt Arrears	$1.600
Total Debt	$10.552

Cuba's debt to the former Soviet Union is estimated at Rb 15 billion.[22] Russia, which assumed the Soviet Union's debt burden, granted Cuba a moratorium on its debt in 1991, knowing that its debt is unlikely to be repaid in the near future.[23]

Pre-Castro Government Debt

During the 1950's, Cuba maintained good fiscal accounts. Its average total debt/GNP ratio was under

16. *The Financial Times* (February 8, 1996).

17. *Reuters Money Report* (April 9, 1994).

18. *Bloomberg Business News* (April 25, 1995).

19. *Bloomberg Business News* (June 2, 1994).

20. *Bloomberg Business News* (June 26, 1995).

21. *Bloomberg Business News* (October 20, 1995).

22. The Economist Intelligence Unit, *Country Profile: Cuba, 1995-96*.

23. The Economist Intelligence Unit, *Country Profile: Cuba, 1995-96*.

30 percent.[24] Foreign debt averaged 10 percent of total debt and about 3 percent of GNP. In Latin America, Cuba's foreign exchange reserves of $505 million were second only to Venezuela's.

For U.S. citizens wishing to speculate on Cuban debt, the U.S. trade embargo makes it legally impossible. Until recently, the loophole in the law was to buy pre-Castro Cuban government bonds. In 1994, Moody's International Manual described two pre-Castro government dollar bonds totaling $52 million in default.

In June, 1937, the Republic of Cuba floated a $44.4 million note with a forty-year maturity and a 4½ percent coupon. It is noteworthy that Cuba was able to issue a note with a forty year maturity, reflecting the bond market's faith in the long term stability of the Cuban Republic. The 4½ percent coupon, which is low by today's standards, was offered at 175 basis points above the current twenty-year U.S. Treasury note.[25] My sense is that with the 1937 Republic of Cuba debt, implied in the price is the backing of the United States government, if not financially then through military intervention.

In March of 1953, the Republic of Cuba floated a $39 million note with a thirty-year maturity and a 4 percent coupon. Again, it is significant that Cuba was able to issue a note with a thirty-year maturity. The 4 percent coupon, also low by today's standards, was offered at 150 basis points above the current twenty-year U.S. Treasury note.[26]

On Wall Street, pre-Castro government notes are referred to as "Batista bonds." This is a misnomer because the 4½s issued in 1937 pre-date the Batista regime. Both the Republic of Cuba 4½s of 1937 and the 4 percent bonds of 1953 have been in continuous default since the 1959 Cuban revolution. A total of $640,098 had been paid into the defaulted notes' sinking fund before 1960. In 1988, a bondholder was unsuccessful at accessing the sinking fund's money, and that account remains frozen.[27]

Trading in pre-Castro bonds on the New York Stock Exchange was halted on July 6, 1995 pending regulatory review by the U.S. Treasury concerning the "appropriateness of the continued listing of the notes."[28] The trading halt appeared to have been linked to a sudden rise in the price of the bonds in late June, 1995 from 41.5 to 54 percent on the dollar. The price increase surrounded speculation that Cuba was entering into debt restructuring negotiations as a way to access fresh credit. The suspension of trading, which destroys a note's value through illiquidity, thus pre-empts Cuba's re-entry into the debt markets. In 1995, a total of 803 trades occurred prior to the suspension of trading worth $803,000 in face value.

Castro Government Hard Currency Debt

Cuba's hard currency debt is with Western governments and commercial banks from Japan, Germany, Italy, France, Spain, United Kingdom, Canada, Argentina and Mexico. These loans originated during the 1970's, when Cuba took advantage of a wave of bank lending to Latin America.[29]

Castro government debt instruments are traded abroad in low volume. In 1995, the Emerging Markets Traders Association recorded $1.2 billion face value in trades of Cuban instruments in only 12 debt markets. Fifty-four percent, or $652 million of that amount, was in trades that averaged less than $2 million each.[30] In 1994, $652 million in Cuban debt

---

24. Philip Newman, *Cuba Before Castro*. New Delhi: Foreign Studies Institute, 1965.
25. *The Wall Street Journal* (March 1, 1953).
26. *The Wall Street Journal* (March 1, 1953).
27. *Bloomberg Business News* (August 28, 1995).
28. *The Financial Times* (August 25, 1995).
29. The Economist Intelligence Unit, *Country Profile: Cuba, 1995-96*.
30. *American Banker-Bond Buyer* (January 15, 1996).

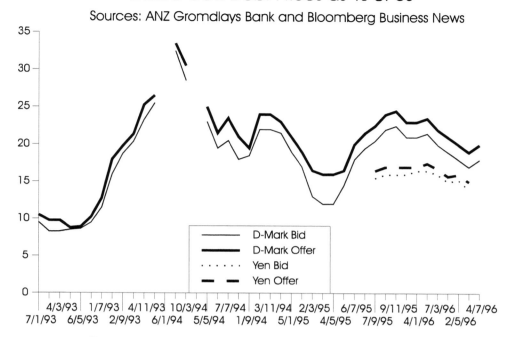

Castro Gov. Debt Prices as % of US

Sources: ANZ Gromdlays Bank and Bloomberg Business News

- D-Mark Bid
- D-Mark Offer
- Yen Bid
- Yen Offer

was traded in 384 trades.[31] Buyers include the Standard Bank Group of South Africa, Banque Indosuez and ANZ Grindlays Bank.

The benchmark price of Cuban debt is set by trades in deutsche mark denominated loans totaling U.S. $1 billion that were refinanced in the early 1980's, with Credit Lyonnais as the agent bank.[32] Under the refinancing agreement, semi-annual installments were to commence on January, 1986 at the contractual interest rate of LIBOR +2.25 percent. To date, no interest payments have been made on the refinanced notes.

Other syndicates of Cuban debt include Barclays and the Bank of Tokyo. The notes of the latter creditor, denominated in Yen, are small relative to the Credit Lyonnais debt, have not been refinanced, and trade far less frequently. Because of these factors, the debt with Japanese creditors tends to be valued at a discount of 200 to 400 basis points to the refinanced Credit Lyonnais notes.

Hard Currency Debt Timeline: January 1993-July 1996

The following chart, describing Cuba's monthly European debt prices, looks like a roller coaster. Prices as a percent of face value go from a low of 8.25 bid 9.75 offer in February of 1993 to a high of 32.5 bid 33.5 offer in February of 1994. In July 1996, the debt was trading at 18 bid 20 offer. It should be noted that all exotics, despite the improbability of repayment, exhibit a price level floor, meaning a point below which the debt price will not fall. In Cuba's case, 8 percent of face value appears to be the lowest point that the debt will trade. Prices have clearly been influenced by historical events (see also the appendix):

- In January 1993, Cuban debt was trading at 9.5 bid 10.5 offer. This low price reflects the market's low expectations that the debt will be repaid since the contraction of the Cuban economy following the collapse of the Soviet Union.

- July 1993 marks the beginning of a six-month-long surge in prices. The start of this increase co-

---

31. *American Banker-Bond Buyer* (October 2, 1995).

32. *Bloomberg Business News* (October 20, 1995).

incides with the announcement in Cuba of the Dollarization Plan. Prices increased further in October 1993—to 20.375 bid 21.375 offer—following the announcement that individuals could open private businesses and work for themselves.

- The increases culminated at 32.5 bid 33.5 offer in February 1994 after President Clinton normalized trade relations with Vietnam. Cuban debt prices rose following expectations that Clinton would, in turn, normalize U.S./Cuba relations. Vietnamese debt increased from 15 to 80 percent of face value in the months prior to U.S./Vietnam trade normalization. Today, Vietnamese debt trades at 66 percent of face value.

- During the first six months of 1994, Cuban debt fell, bottoming at 18 bid 21 offer in August 1994. This fall is coincident with the rise in U.S. interest rates beginning in January 1994 and the subsequent flight to quality. The price decrease occurred despite Grupo Domos' purchase of 49 percent of Emtel in March, the passage of an austerity package by the Cuban National Assembly in May, and Cuba's agreement in June to settle Brazil's bilateral debt.

- Cuban debt prices troughed in August 1994, reflecting the uncertainty surrounding that month's large anti-government demonstration in Havana and the subsequent two-week-long "balsero" or rafter crisis. Prices increased modestly in the last quarter of 1994—to 22 bid 24 offer—as the "balsero" crisis stabilized and a new immigration agreement between the U.S. and Cuba was reached. This modest price increase was followed by a plunge during the first six months of 1995 to 14.5 bid 16.5 offer in June of 1995. This fall is coincident with the 1994 Mexican meltdown.

- In the second half of 1995, debt prices began to steadily increase again. On June 26, 1995, *Bloomberg Business News* reported that Cuba was looking to restructure its $6.4 billion hard currency debt.

- During the week of September 5, 1995, prices climbed to 20.5 bid 22.5 offer as a new foreign investment law was passed in Cuba. The new law allows 100 percent foreign ownership of enterprises except in health, education and defense, and permits investment in property and free trade zones.

- On September 22, 1995, the U.S. House of Representatives passed a bill allowing Americans to sue third parties for trafficking expropriated property and preventing traffickers from entering the U.S. The new legislation did not affect Cuban debt prices however, apparently because the bond market expected the bill to be vetoed by President Clinton.

- On October 6, 1995, Cuban debt prices climbed to 22 bid 24 offer as President Clinton announced a change in U.S./Cuba policy. The new policy allowed U.S. media to set up in Cuba, and charities and other non-governmental organizations to operate in the country.

- During November 1995, the price of debt continued to increase—to 22.5 bid 24.5—offer as Castro visited China and Vietnam. The purpose of the trip was to see what Cuba could learn from those two nations, which had revitalized their economies by making a transition from a command economy to market socialism.

- Debt prices peaked during the week of February 22, 1996—at 21 bid 23 offer—after Patrick Buchanan won the New Hampshire Republican primary. Buchanan's victory increased the market's expectations that President Clinton would be re-elected and that the embargo would be lifted.

- Debt prices fell to 20 bid 22 offer during the week of February 27, 1996, when Cuba shot down two planes belonging to the humanitarian group "Brothers to the Rescue." President Clinton responded to the shooting by restricting entry of Cuban diplomats into the United States and halting direct charter flights.

- During the week of March 12, 1996, prices fell to 19 bid 21 offer in response to President Clinton's signing of the Helms-Burton legislation.

Hopes in Cuba for progress through liberalizing reforms were squashed later in the month. Fearing that they were losing control over the economic activity unleashed through liberalization, the Cuban government expressed strong opposition to change and began a crackdown on dissent and reforms.[33]

• During the week of May 30, 1996 debt prices continued to fall—to 18 bid 20 offer—as the U.S. State Department issued its first letters under Helms-Burton, warning foreign firms investing in or doing business with Cuba about the possibility of U.S. sanctions.

A Debt Timeline Analysis

Because prices in July 1996 were 10 percent of face value higher than in January 1993, the bond market does believe that Cuba is making internal progress, that Cuba's integration into the world economy is forthcoming, and that rapprochement with the U.S. is possible. High, stable prices, which we have not seen, would indicate that the market is willing to believe in Cuba's recovery, even with Fidel Castro in power. The dramatic volatility of prices reflects the bond market's assessment of Cuba as a high risk creditor.

Based on the evidence, the market is able to respond quickly to new internal and external developments. The sudden price increases in 1993 and 1995 indicate that the market believes that once the process of change begins in earnest, significant change in Cuba will happen quickly. However, the fact that Cuban debt today trades at a deep discount says that the market thinks Cuba still has a long way to go on the road towards meaningful reform.

The differences in trading prices between pre-Castro government and Castro government debt are of interest. When trading of pre-Castro debt was halted on July 6, 1995 by the New York Stock Exchange, it was trading at 54 percent of par. This is a significant premium over the 18 bid 20 offer price of Castro government debt trading on the same day in Europe.

One possible explanation for the differences in prices is a difference in liquidity. Because U.S. citizens are by law prohibited from trading in Castro government debt, these instruments are shut out of the large U.S. capital market, and their liquidity is low relative to pre-Castro debt.

The changes in the bid-asked spread are also worthy of note. A narrow bid-asked spread indicates high liquidity and continuity of pricing between sellers, while a wide spread indicates the exact opposite. Unlike highly liquid U.S. Treasury notes, where it is common to see bid-asked spreads of a fraction of a point, a two point bid-asked spread is not uncommon with exotic debt issues. The wide bid-asked spread encourages long-term speculation of exotics and discourages in-and-out trading. This is because large pricing gains must occur to offset transaction costs.

When Cuban debt prices climbed rapidly during the second half of 1993, the bid-asked spread narrowed to under one percent of face value, indicating increased demand. The spread opened up to its widest point—four percent of face value—following the 1994 Mexican financial meltdown as investors worldwide panicked and sold emerging market debt. Throughout 1996, the bid-asked spread has maintained a constant two percent of face value.

WHY DO INVESTORS BUY CUBAN DEBT?

Due to the lack of a Cuban stock market, direct equity investment is not possible in Cuba. Cuban debt thus offers investors the potential to enjoy significant capital appreciation as an equity-proxy. Cuban debt is usually a long-term hold position, held in the context of an emerging market debt portfolio.

Other reasons why investors buy Cuban paper include the possibility of a debt-equity swap, increased debt price through a successful debt restructuring, and price appreciation following rapprochement with the U.S. and a lifting of the embargo.

---

33. *The New York Times* (March 31, 1996).

RECENT FINANCINGS

Cuba currently has a modest short-term credit line with France of $150 million.[34] French banks and trade houses agreed to prefinance inputs for the 1995/96 sugar crop. This deal, which is worth over $100 million, must be repaid with proceeds from sugar sales.[35] The Dutch ING Bank, Britain's ED&F Man Sugar, and Vitol, the Anglo-Dutch company, also helped fund Cuba's 1995-96 sugar crop and are expected to provide credits for the 1996-97 harvest.[36] Short-term financing to Cuba is not without risks. On September 19, 1995, *The Financial Times* reported that most of Cuba's hard currency earnings from its sugar harvest were targeted to pay off its short-term debt payments, leaving Cuba with a shortage of hard currency to pay for imported fuel and basic foods.

FINAL THOUGHTS

As to Cuba's future, at least this much is known: relations between the United States and Cuba remain the key to positive change on the island. This is because of the proximity of the U.S. to Cuba, the vast size of its markets, and its influence on world affairs. Pressure is being exerted now, by the U.S. government and by prominent groups within the Cuban-American community, for Cuba to go the way of a free-market democracy.

When will a major change will occur in Cuba? No one can say for sure. In the late 1980's, as the regimes of eastern Europe toppled like dominoes, it was popularly believed that the regime in Cuba too would fall. This seemed sensible, given the importance of the Soviet Union's subsidies to Cuba's economy.

The Berlin Wall fell in 1989. Seven years later, in 1996, and Fidel Castro is still in power. One current joke is that the Cuban government has already fallen—its demise is tied up in the Cuban bureaucracy. So much for sensible predictions. Certainly the bond market is a good way to monitor future expectations, but when it comes to predictions, it is not infallible. Cuban debt speculators, beware!

BIBLIOGRAPHY

Cline, William R. *International Debt Reexamined.* Washington: Institute for International Economics, 1995.

Mesa-Lago, Carmelo, ed. *Cuba After the Cold War.* Pittsburgh: University of Pittsburgh Press, 1993.

Newman, Philip C. *Cuba Before Castro: An Economic Appraisal.* New Delhi: Foreign Studies Institute, 1965.

Ritter, Archibald, ed. *Cuba in the International System.* New York: St. Martin's Press, 1995.

Suchlicki, Jaime, and Antonio Jorge, eds. *Investing in Cuba: Problems and Prospects.* New Brunswick: Transaction Publishers, 1994.

---

34. *Columbia Journal of World Business* (March 22, 1995).
35. The Economist Intelligence Unit, Country Profile: Cuba, 1995-96.
36. Bloomberg Business News, June 5, 1996.

Appendix—Castro Government Cuban Debt Prices as a Percent of US$

Date	D Mark Bid	D Mark Offer	Yen Bid	Yen Offer
7-Jan-93	9.500	10.500		
4-Feb-93	8.250	9.750		
4-Mar-93	8.250	9.750		
1-Apr-93	8.500	8.750		
6-May-93	8.625	8.875		
3-Jun-93	9.500	10.250		
1-Jul-93	11.500	12.750		
5-Aug-93	16.000	18.000		
2-Sep-93	18.750	19.750		
7-Oct-93	20.375	21.375		
4-Nov-93	23.250	25.250		
2-Dec-93	25.500	26.500		
6-Jan-94				
3-Feb-94	32.500	33.500		
10-Mar-94	28.500	30.500		
7-Apr-94				
5-May-94	23.000	25.000		
2-Jun-94	19.500	21.500		
7-Jul-94	20.500	23.500		
4-Aug-94	18.000	21.000		
1-Sep-94	18.500	19.500		
6-Oct-94	22.000	24.000		
3-Nov-94	22.000	24.000		
1-Dec-94	21.500	23.000		
5-Jan-95	19.000	21.000		
2-Feb-95	17.000	19.000		
2-Mar-95	13.000	16.500		
6-Apr-95	12.000	16.000		
4-May-95	12.000	16.000		
1-Jun-95	14.500	16.500		
6-Jul-95	18.000	20.000		
3-Aug-95	19.500	21.500		
7-Sep-95	20.500	22.500	15.500	16.500
5-Oct-95	22.000	24.000	16.000	17.000
9-Nov-95	22.500	24.500	16.000	17.000
14-Dec-95	21.000	23.000	16.000	17.000
4-Jan-96	21.000	23.000	16.500	17.000
1-Feb-96	21.500	23.500	16.500	17.500
7-Mar-96	20.000	22.000	16.000	16.750
4-Apr-96	19.000	21.000	15.000	15.750
2-May-96	18.000	20.000	15.250	16.000
6-Jun-96	17.000	19.000	14.000	15.000
4-Jul-96	18.000	20.000		

COMMENTS ON

"Cuba's Hard Currency Debt" by Gabriel Fernández

Alberto Luzárraga

There is no question that Cuba is one of the most heavily indebted countries in the world and that its capacity to pay even a fraction of what it owes is severely impaired. Fernández puts this amount at 10.552 billion U.S. dollars and notes that a further 15 billion rubles are owed to Russia, as that country assumed the debt burden of the former Soviet Union.

Given the gyrations of the ruble, converting the latter figure into U.S. dollars is difficult. Suffice it to say that the October 10, 1996, quotation in the *Wall Street Journal* was 5422 rubles per U.S. dollar. Further, the nature of this debt is in question. Much of it can be justly named "politico-military" and is a remnant of the Cold War. Whether a part of it constitutes legitimate trade debt is an issue that will have to be proven. In any case, a free Cuban Government will in all probability be compelled to repudiate any Russian debt that stems from the financing of Cuba's proxy role in Africa and elsewhere.

If we accept that the Russian debt has special characteristics and exclude it for calculation purposes, we can then focus on the "Western Debt." At 10.5 billion U.S. dollars, it amounts to 2 times the Cuban gross domestic product (GDP) of 5 billion U.S. dollars for a 2 to 1 ratio of debt to GDP. This is surely one of the highest ratios anywhere.

The Western countries' debt is essentially commercial and includes a small amount of pre-Castro debt that is not significant. It has been erroneously named "Batista Debt" by the debt traders whose forte is not

history. The trading in Cuba's debt and the wild price gyrations attached to it do not reflect any rational assessment of what it is worth in terms of the economic and political constraints that a free Cuban government may face. Rather, it is a mere reflection of a market that operates in a speculative mode and bases its pricing on rumors, news, and hope that the paper will be renegotiated at favorable terms To a great extent, it bases its expectations on the Latin American restructuring model. The traders are hoping for a Brady Bond solution, again extrapolating the past into the future without examining the situation and its particular circumstances.

The Latin American debt was contracted by countries that were part of the Western World and had not "enjoyed" the "benefits" of a 37-year rule by an international adventurer that almost provoked a nuclear catastrophe in 1962, not to speak of innumerable other episodes of Castro's export of his revolution. In this sense, the commercial credits granted to the Castro Government were a subsidy to a policy contrary to the interests of the Western Alliance and a direct challenge to its leader, the United States. (All of which proves Lenin's assertion that the "capitalists will sell us the rope with which to hang them.")

Although some will scoff at moral arguments when applied to commerce, there is a commercial conclusion to be derived from the above. The level of risk assumed when engaging in transactions with this type of regime egregiously exceeded the dictates of what a prudent lending policy dictates. A cursory examination of the loans will show that Cuba's Government started to default and roll-over principal and interest **before** the Russian collapse. The lack of viability of the Cuban economy is not a new phenomenon and neither is the irreflexive cupidity of those who will sell to anybody who signs a piece of paper without pausing to think that there are people who sign anything simply because they do not have the slightest intention of honoring it. It is a mentality that is not much impressed by contract law, as it has succeeded precisely by acting against what it considers "bourgeois weaknesses."

The issue was not lost on the official creditors who hold the bulk of the debt. They have sought to improve their position by subscribing trade treaties with Castro and by the sale of the paper to their respective private sectors. At the same time they have encouraged debt-to-equity conversions. In this way it was thought that some of the losses could be recovered. Further, from the official point of view, this scheme transferred the risk to the private sector, who is notoriously more adept at getting its "money out" by engaging in transactions that offer a very quick pay back of principal.

Enter the Helms law that suddenly complicated this scheme in a way that was not anticipated. Whatever the outcome of the ensuing Helms battle, there is no question that the Castro debt has been tainted as it now has been used for a purpose deemed illegal by the U.S. Congress.

In conclusion, Cuba's creditors face two problems. A classical one related to inability to pay and a political-legal situation that will not be easily resolved. The markets will eventually focus on this latter issue and realize that the Cuban situation is indeed different. Brady Bonds to pay Canadian, Mexican, etc. investors? They had better wait in a comfortable chair.

A free Cuba will have two arguments to pose to its creditors. First, it certainly can claim dire circumstances and demand the preferential treatment recently agreed by the Paris Club (80 percent discount), while at the same time asking for additional concessions taking advantage of the characteristics of the debt and the fact that it will inevitably be subject to legal and political entanglements. And second, the issue of conditionality demanded by the Paris Club is moot. It pertains to privatization, dismantling of the Socialist state, etc., things that Cuba has to do as there is no other choice or alternative.

The settlement will be modest. A free Cuba will have to do something, because after all it has to live in the community of nations and must trade. But it cannot afford a traditional or generous settlement. It simply does not have the resources. This applies to all types of debt, including the certified debt to U.S. nationals under the U.S. Foreign Claims Commission, although we would predict that here a Brady-type solution may well be proposed and implemented as there is no legal taint. As to the aspirations of compensation by Cuban nationals (now U.S. citizens) that lost their properties, the most probable outcome is that said matter inevitably will be transferred by U.S. courts to Cuban jurisdiction once Cuba is free. The Helms law contains the mechanism to produce that result and the U.S. interest will lean in that direction.

CUBA: ESTABILIZACION RAPIDA SIN RECESION NI CHOQUE MONETARIO

Rolando H. Castañeda y George Plinio Montalván[1]

"Una importante enseñanza de la reforma, tanto económica como política, es que las fuerzas del mercado, por sí solas, no siempre son capaces de llevar adelante el proceso de reestructuración".

— Banco Mundial (1996, p. 91)

"Is stabilization from high inflation contractionary, neutral or expansionary? Traditional wisdom used to say the first; conventional wisdom has drifted partially towards the second; recent theory and events may suggest the third."

— William Easterly (1996, p. 67)

"Almost every country in the region succumbed to an extreme financial crisis during the reform period."

—Jeffrey Sachs (1996b, p. 129)

En la actualidad Cuba enfrenta los demandantes retos de estabilizar su economía y alcanzar pronto altas tasas de crecimiento económico. Para lograr la estabilización, deberá eliminar el excedente monetario y la dolarización, que determinan fuertes presiones inflacionarias ("inflación reprimida") dados los niveles de actividad económica real y de precios del país. En contraste, para lograr la recuperación y la consolidación del crecimiento económico sustentable, estimular el ahorro y canalizarlo a las inversiones de alta productividad, así como para ampliar el papel del sector privado en la economía (privatización) y reintegrarse plenamente a la economía internacional, Cuba deberá monetizar la economía como preludio a las necesarias ampliación, profundización y diversificación financieras.

Este ensayo presenta una propuesta concreta con medidas monetarias y cambiarias coherentes y efectivas, dentro de un paquete de reformas más amplio, encaminadas a eliminar el excedente monetario y la dolarización de la economía que impiden la estabilización económica al crear fuertes presiones inflacionarias e incertidumbres generalizadas, situación reconocida por los propios académicos y autoridades del país. Asimismo, la propuesta contempla medidas monetarias y cambiarias orientadas a lograr y consolidar la monetización mediante la liberalización y desregulación graduales e incrementales que contrarrestarían las imperfecciones iniciales de los mercados financieros no acostumbrados a hacer evaluación de préstamos ni de riesgos y alentarían mayores niveles de ahorro, tanto nacional como del exterior, y harían más eficiente la intermediación financiera.

La propuesta está diseñada para evitar una recesión como resultado del programa de estabilización y se fundamenta en las ideas de Dornbusch/Wolf y Sachs, en el análisis de que los instrumentos que se necesita aplicar están dirigidos a tratar adecuadamente los desequilibrios de los acervos ("stocks") monetarios, así como en las experiencias de los antiguos países socialistas europeos en 1989-1995 y de Chile en 1973-1995.

---

1. Las opiniones aquí expresadas son de exclusiva responsabilidad de los autores y de ninguna manera reflejan sus vínculos institucionales.

El ensayo está organizado de la forma siguiente. En la primera sección se analiza el excedente monetario y la dolarización existentes en la economía cubana, así como el escaso desarrollo institucional y la segmentación financiera. La segunda sección resume la experiencia de los antiguos países socialistas europeos y de Chile en cuanto al papel del sector financiero en los procesos de estabilización y recuperación económicas y presenta algunas consideraciones sobre las reformas financieras aún pendientes. La tercera sección resume la literatura económica reciente sobre la importancia de la ampliación, profundización y diversificación financieras, destacando algunos estudios empíricos. La cuarta sección analiza en detalle los objetivos, la estrategia, los instrumentos y los posibles efectos de la propuesta para lograr una pronta y efectiva estabilización sin recesión y compara sus posibles efectos con la liberalización inicial de precios y la flotación cambiaria seguida del "choque monetario" (una política monetaria/crediticia reactiva y muy restrictiva para estabilizar). La quinta sección indica cómo se podría implantar la propuesta y sus posibles implicaciones para el futuro. La última sección presenta el resumen de las principales conclusiones del ensayo.

LAS CONDICIONES INICIALES DE CUBA. EL EXCEDENTE MONETARIO Y LA DOLARIZACION EXISTENTES. EL ESCASO DESARROLLO INSTITUCIONAL Y LA SEGMENTACION FINANCIERAS

De acuerdo con estudios recientes (Carranza, Monreal y Gutiérrez, 1995 y 1996), así como la información proporcionada por el Vicepresidente Carlos Lage del 23 de julio de 1996, la economía cubana se caracteriza por un considerable excedente monetario y una dolarización, los cuales deberán ser eliminados para que el país se estabilice y comience a crecer. El excedente monetario básicamente es un fenómeno de consumo postergado y no de ahorro debido al exceso de demanda agregada a los precios vigentes. Es de esperar que se desate una fuerte inflación en Cuba una vez que los precios se liberalicen, a menos que ambos fenómenos se atiendan adecuadamente al inicio de la transición.

Dichos fenómenos se intensificaron significativamente en la década de los noventa cuando la economía experimentó una severa contracción de la producción nacional a la vez que el gobierno incurrió, por lo menos hasta 1994, en un creciente déficit fiscal financiado principalmente con emisión monetaria. El déficit aumentó de CU$1,400 millones (CU$=pesos cubanos) en 1989, o el 7 por ciento del producto interno bruto (PIB) a CU$5,100 millones en 1993, o el 40 por ciento del PIB. Desde ese año, el gobierno parece haber controlado y reducido el déficit fiscal con el aumento de algunos precios (cigarrillos, tabaco, bebidas alcohólicas) y la reducción de los subsidios a las empresas estatales;[2] no obstante, todavía es similar en términos relativos a los que tenían los antiguos países socialistas europeos antes de comenzar sus procesos de ajuste. El déficit se redujo a CU$1,400 millones en 1994, o el 11 por ciento del PIB.

La dolarización (o la tendencia a utilizar dólares como medio de intercambio, unidad de cuenta e instrumento para conservar valor) y la tendencia a adquirir activos reales se produjeron endógenamente como resultado de las políticas macroeconómicas aplicadas. Así, la población se protegió de la creciente inflación y depreciación de la moneda nacional en el mercado negro, las que se acentuaron cuando el gobierno despenalizó la libre tenencia de divisas para estimular las remesas del exterior en agosto de 1993. O sea la dolarización es resultado de deficientes

---

2. La zafra azucarera de 1996 establece dudas sobre la reducción del déficit de las empresas públicas y el logro de un crecimiento en el producto interno real de casi el 10 por ciento en el primer semestre de 1996. El gobierno incurrió en un financiamiento de US$300 millones para comprar insumos importados y expandir la producción sobre los niveles de 1995 (3,300,000 t.m.), pero el aumento de producción logrado (1,200,000 toneladas métricas) apenas alcanza para financiar el principal y los intereses del financiamiento (US$350 millones). Asimismo, el crecimiento del PIB con base en la expansión del azúcar no parece correcto, porque el PIB generado por el azúcar es la diferencia entre las exportaciones e importaciones, o sea sólo US$50 millones y el PNB es cercano a cero debido al pago de intereses.

políticas macroeconómicas, la represión financiera y los factores institucionales existentes.

Según el Informe del Banco Nacional de Cuba (BNC) de 1994, la circulación monetaria, definida como el efectivo en circulación y los depósitos en las cuentas de ahorro, aumentó de CU$4,152.5 millones en 1989 a CU$9,939.7 millones en 1994, es decir, una expansión del 139.4 por ciento, mientras que la producción real a precios de 1981 se contrajo de CU$19,585.5 millones en 1989 a CU$12,868.3 millones en 1994, o sea una disminución del 34.3 por ciento. La relación entre dichos activos monetarios y la producción real pasó del 21.2 por ciento en 1989 al 77.2 por ciento en 1994 (ver Gráfica 1). Dado que los precios oficiales o controlados se han mantenido virtualmente fijos, es explicable la fuerte presión inflacionaria reprimida o el exceso de circulante a los precios oficiales vigentes. El Informe del BNC de 1994 no presentó cifras sobre el nivel de precios en los años recientes, ni sobre el efectivo en circulación y las cuentas de ahorro denominadas en "pesos convertibles" que se inició en diciembre de 1994.

Una vez que comenzó el proceso de ajuste económico en agosto de 1993, el gobierno adoptó medidas para reducir el déficit fiscal; sin embargo, sólo ha adoptado medidas administrativas para eliminar el excedente monetario y la dolarización de la economía.

El sistema financiero cubano es muy rudimentario y pasivo. Los instrumentos monetarios se limitan básicamente al dinero en circulación y los depósitos en cuentas de ahorro con tasas de interés reales negativas en moneda nacional, así como cuentas de ahorro en divisas en la banca comercial. En 1995 sólo existían el BNC, que realizaba algunas funciones de banca central y comercial y el Banco Popular de Ahorro, que realizaba las funciones de caja de ahorro para captar el ahorro personal y brindar pequeños créditos personales. El Informe del BNC de 1994 es más amplio sobre las diversas instituciones financieras que se planeaban establecer que sobre las instituciones existentes.

Grafica 1. Cuba Indice de Monetizacion 1989-1995

◆ PIB-precios constantes 1981   ✳ Dinero y Cuentas de Ahorro
▲ Indice de Monetización

Fuente: Banco Nacional de Cuba, Economic Report 1994

La intermediación financiera legal entre ahorristas e inversionistas privados no existe, ya que el gobierno sólo permite la actividad privada de los pequeños agricultores y los trabajadores por cuenta propia. Además, el sector financiero está segmentado entre servicios rudimentarios para el sector externo—7 bancos comerciales extranjeros operaban en 1995 vinculados con el turismo y la inversión extranjera— mientras sólo hay servicios muy limitados para el sector privado nacional que realiza el BNC.

LA EXPERIENCIA DE LOS ANTIGUOS PAISES SOCIALISTAS EUROPEOS EN 1989-1995 Y LA POSTERGACION DE LAS REFORMAS FINANCIERAS. LA EXPERIENCIA CHILENA EN LA LIBERALIZACION Y PROFUNDIZACION FINANCIERAS EN 1973-1995

Las experiencias de los antiguos países socialistas europeos en 1989-1995 y de Chile en 1973-1995 son bastante ricas en aciertos y errores cometidos de política económica en la estabilización, liberalización y desregulación financieras. Por ello hay un conjunto de lecciones útiles para Cuba en el establecimiento de un sistema financiero y de un mercado de capitales sanos y desarrollados para evitar incurrir en errores de política y en los consecuentes costos innecesarios.

Diseño del programa ejecutado en Europa y Chile

La política de liberalización inicial de precios y de restricciones al comercio internacional como elemento fundamental del programa de estabilización que se ha aplicado en los antiguos países socialistas europeos ha sido muy similar y mecánico. No obstante, inicialmente hubo una amplia discusión y diferentes puntos de vista sobre el alcance y el ritmo de la liberalización de precios o de la reforma monetaria y sobre las posibles dinámicas de sus respectivos efectos, así como sobre el papel que le correspondía, si alguno, a la política de precios e ingresos como instrumento de estabilización, o sea, a los elementos heterodoxos en dicha política. En cambio, en cuanto a la política cambiaria ha habido marcadas diferencias entre los países que devaluaron y mantuvieron, al menos temporalmente, un régimen de cambio fijo y los que desde el comienzo flotaron su moneda, así como entre los que adoptaron una convertibilidad parcial de la moneda, principalmente para la cuenta corriente, y los que adoptaron una convertibilidad más amplia y generalizada.

En un régimen acostumbrado a los presupuestos y créditos suaves, la liberalización de precios para eliminar el excedente monetario y el déficit fiscal acompañada de la liberalización del sistema financiero se convirtió en una trampa de la transición al desatar una dinámica espiral inflacionaria, que en más de la mitad de los países superó niveles del 5 por ciento mensual por más de dos años y como tal se pueden considerar alta inflación de acuerdo con la definición clásica de Cagan o la nueva de Bruno y Easterly (1995). Asimismo, creó incertidumbres sobre la validez y credibilidad de la política aplicada, estimuló la demanda por bienes extranjeros y la fuga de capitales, y expectativas perversas e inercias, caracterizadas por ajustes más frecuentes en los precios y por la indexación para proteger a los grupos más vulnerables, que hicieron muy volátil e insostenible el proceso y tendieron a erosionar la liberalización inicial.[3] Ello obligó a los países a adoptar, en general, entre otras, severas medidas

monetarias restrictivas —altas tasas de interés real, entre el 10 por ciento y el 15 por ciento,[4] limitado crédito bancario y medidas de esterilización por los bancos centrales— para estabilizar el nivel de precios y fortalecer el uso de las monedas nacionales, lo que a su vez desató un significativa recesión que ha tenido efectos perversos sobre el sector financiero, pues debilitó la disciplina financiera y extendió el uso de los créditos suaves por las empresas.[5] En algunos países los objetivos de acumulación de reservas *internacionales* y de crédito reprimido generaron fuertes contradicciones en las políticas macroeconómicas.

Calvo y Coricelli (1992) y Calvo y Kumar (1994) consideran que la falta de capital de trabajo desempeñó un papel importante en la reducción de la producción, aún en las empresas viables, la cual fue mayor y más persistente de lo esperado, llegándose a tasas de desempleo de dos dígitos. El crédito real a las empresas fue menor que antes del inicio de la transición, especialmente para las pequeñas y medianas empresas, los agentes más dinámicos de la economía, que generalmente se han tenido que autofinanciar. El crédito es muy necesario a las empresas para que puedan realizar su proceso de ajuste y reformas (reestructuración) y para la reasignación de recursos en la economía. A su vez, la fuerte recesión influyó que no se fuera tan estricto con la solvencia de las empresas y con los préstamos incobrables, dándoles préstamos revolventes o preferencias a determinados clientes, lo que determinó un marcado debilitamiento de la calidad de la cartera, la disciplina y la solvencia de los bancos comerciales en particular y del sistema financiero y del mercado de capitales en general, con serias

---

3. En general los países en transición no experimentaron crecimiento hasta dos años después que lograron reducir la inflación por debajo del 50 por ciento anual (Bruno el al, 1996, p. 230).

4. ECE, *Economic Survey of Europe in 1994-1995*, p. 167.

5. En general las recesiones fueron amplias y profundas con una reducción acumulada del producto del 33.6 por ciento (Fischer, et al, 1996, p. 229). El Informe del Banco Mundial de 1996 sobre las economías en transición considera que la severa reducción se debió a otros factores "En algunos de los primeros análisis, que se concentraban principalmente en ECO, se culpaba del decrecimiento inicial de la producción a una estabilización demasiado entusiasta. Pero los datos actualmente disponibles revelan la existencia de tres factores: los cambios en la demanda promovidos por la liberalización, el colapso del CAME y la Unión Soviética y las perturbaciones provocadas en la oferta por la desaparición de las instituciones, o su ausencia, y por unos incentivos distorsionados" (Banco Mundial, 1996, p. 32). Sin embargo, ni en el texto ni en la amplia bibliografía de apoyo que presenta hay una sustentación de esta interesante posición.

implicaciones generales, fiscales y de confianza sobre la credibilidad del paquete de reformas financieras y de las reformas en su conjunto y sobre el programa de privatización (Rapaczynski, 1996). Asimismo, influyó en que el nuevo crédito bancario se dirigiera a los instrumentos sin riesgos del sector público o créditos al sector privado de corto plazo, dado los bajos niveles de capitalización de los bancos, su consecuente aversión al riesgo y su escasa práctica evaluando riesgos (así se determinaron las fallas del mercado por el lado de la oferta en el sector financiero).[6] Con base en la situación descrita, Calvo y Kumar (1993) recomendaron no aplicar la "gran explosión" en el sector financiero en las economías en transición.

Galbis (1994) considera que es necesario tener mecanismos de regulación y supervisión[7] prudentes establecidos durante la liberalización que eviten la selección adversa de préstamos y eviten la crisis financiera con su secuela de efectos negativos y de *histéresis*. Algunas de las crisis financieras han sido sistémicas y no sólo de algunas instituciones individuales. Por ejemplo, el 40 por ciento de los activos del sistema bancario de Latvia se perdió en 1995 (Fleming y Talley, 1996).

En el contexto anterior, los procesos de liberalización, desregulación y privatización financieros se vieron detenidos y postergados. El sector financiero tiene una gran fragilidad y vulnerabilidad y es un flanco débil en las reformas (Berthelot, 1996), aún en los países donde se redujo la inflación y no había presiones cambiarias significativas. En general, no se ha removido una serie de restricciones y obstáculos sectoriales, ni se ha

creado un marco jurídico-institucional para orientar y regular un mercado financiero eficiente, competitivo y seguro, y se ha hecho más lento el proceso de privatizaciones.

El diseño de la política aplicada no tuvo en consideración la situación muy especial de los antiguos países socialistas en la cual el excedente monetario era muy significativo en relación con otros países en desarrollo, en los cuales se ha aplicado una política inicial de liberalización de precios y de restricciones al comercio internacional para efectuar la estabilización de la economía. La espiral inflacionaria que desata la liberalización inicial de precios y de restricciones al comercio internacional en una economía con excedente monetario no es fácil de controlar y hace imprescindible el choque monetario a pesar de que muchas empresas rentables necesitan crédito para mantener sus actividades y para reformarse y ajustarse a una economía de mercado. Además, el diseño utilizado parece haberse basado en un modelo monetario muy simplista o en el supuesto de expectativas racionales que ignoró algunas características estructurales o distorsiones diferenciales de estas economías (la elevada concentración industrial y los mercados monopólicos), los efectos perversos e inerciales de altas tasas de inflación (histéresis y deseconomías externas), y los efectos sobre los costos y la oferta agregada del choque monetario a corto plazo.

El aumento de precios que es necesario para eliminar el déficit fiscal es menor, y tal vez mucho menor, que el que se requiere para eliminar el excedente monetario, ya que en el caso de las economías socialistas este último es el resultado de la

---

6. En las economías en transición el sistema financiero debe realizar el papel muy importante de imponer la disciplina financiera a las empresas acostumbradas a operar con presupuestos y créditos blandos.

7. *Regulaciones* son el conjunto de leyes, normas y reglamentos para brindar información y hacer transparente el riesgo asumido por los inversionistas, los depositantes y las instituciones financieras y para asegurar la seguridad y sanidad tanto de las instituciones individuales como del sistema en su conjunto, o sea, para evitar malas prácticas, corrupción, fraudes y estafas. Las regulaciones incluyen criterios y requisitos para la entrada de instituciones en el sistema, normas de contabilidad y sobre estados financieros, límites para concentraciones de préstamos y exposiciones a individuos o grupos relacionados, prohibiciones o límites de préstamos a propietarios, estándares de capital mínimo, proporciones de liquidez, colaterales, clasificación y provisión de reservas para liquidez y para pérdidas por activos, frecuencia y contenido de las auditorías. *Supervisión* se refiere al seguimiento y monitoreo de las instituciones financieras por las respectivas autoridades (superintendencias), así como hacerles cumplir las regulaciones y las políticas vigentes para evitar incompetencia gerencial y la toma de riesgos excesivos para evitar quiebras.

acumulación de déficits fiscales por varios años. Consecuentemente, se requieren aumentos de precios diferentes para atender el déficit fiscal y el excedente monetario. En el caso de Cuba, el excedente monetario era aproximadamente el 55 por ciento del producto, mientras que el déficit fiscal era aproximadamente el 8 por ciento del producto en 1995.[8]

Con base en las experiencias de estabilización en Europa en la posguerra en general y de Alemania Occidental en particular, Dornbusch y Wolf (1990) señalaron que era mejor seguir alguna forma de reforma monetaria decisiva e inmediata en el proceso de estabilización para eliminar los excedentes monetarios, que la estrategia de liberalización de precios para eliminar los fuertes desequilibrios monetarios existentes determinaría situaciones de inestabilidad que podrían degenerar en una hiperinflación, y que los países (Hungría y Grecia) que la habían utilizado en la posguerra habían terminado desatando un fuerte proceso inflacionario. Calvo y Frenkel (1991, p. 291) también consideraron la reforma monetaria y su posible combinación con la privatización, como instrumentos efectivos para eliminar el excedente monetario.[9] Dornbusch (1992) señaló los significativos costos de la inflación en la innovación institucional en el sector financiero.

Sachs (1995, 1996b) considera que una vez que se liberan los precios, y la tasa de cambio se devalúa adecuadamente, el régimen cambiario debería ser fijo, al menos temporalmente, respecto a una moneda internacional y no basado en la flotación de la moneda nacional. Esto permitiría una remonetización más rápida sin la espiral inflacionaria, las inercias y las conductas especulativas que desata la flotación cambiaria. Sachs compara el ajuste exitoso y más rápido realizado por Estonia, que también otros antiguos países socialistas (Checoslovaquia, Polonia, Hungría) utilizaron exitosamente, en contraste con

Latvia que flotó la moneda y tuvo un proceso de ajuste más inflacionario y depresivo al igual que otros países que utilizaron el mismo régimen cambiario (Bulgaria, Rumania, Ucrania y en general los países de la antigua Unión Soviética). Fischer, et. al. (1996, pp. 61-63) encontraron que el régimen cambiario fijo o de ajustes periódicos tiene efectos positivos sobre la detención de la inflación y la recuperación económica más rápida, mientras la flotación cambiaria tiene los efectos contrarios. La flotación cambiaria acentúa los riesgos cambiarios de los proyectos y hace más difícil el proceso de privatización con participación externa. Los hallazgos de Sachs y Fischer, et. al. son consistentes con los anteriores de Sargent (1982), Végh (1992) y Rebelo y Végh (1995). El Informe del Banco Mundial de 1996 sobre los países en transición si bien sostiene que Albania, Latvia, Moldovia, Eslovenia y Vietnam han logrado estabilizar bajo un régimen cambiario flexible, reconoce que un régimen cambiario fijo podría lograr la estabilización más rápidamente y a un menor costo de crecimiento (Banco Mundial, 1996, p. 46, 47).

Chile acumuló un significativo excedente monetario en los tres años del gobierno de la Unidad Popular (1970-1973). El gobierno militar que lo sucedió, decidió eliminarlo con un proceso de liberalización de precios y de restricciones al comercio internacional acompañado de la liberalización, desregulación y privatización financieras. Dentro de una política monetaria restrictiva, se eliminaron los controles sobre la tasa de interés y se eliminaron todos los controles cuantitativos del crédito, se redujeron significativamente las reservas bancarias, se promovió la competencia y la libre entrada al sector financiero. Después de una contracción económica en 1973-1974, se desató una inercia inflacionaria en 1975-1981 que se trató de controlar mediante la revaluación y la congelación cambiarias, lo cual tuvo un decidido impacto en la crisis subsiguiente, junto con el débil marco regulador de las instituciones

---

8. El BNC estimó el déficit fiscal en $1,000 millones en 1995, mientras que la producción era del orden de $13,000 millones.

9. Dado que los agricultores han acumulado una parte importante del excedente monetario en Cuba, una forma interesante de eliminarlo y desarrollar la agricultura privada en el país sería vendiéndoles tierras.

financieras que se basó en prácticas contables y no en la regulación y supervisión del riesgo de la cartera ni en la solvencia de las instituciones y determinó que el sistema financiero fuese muy vulnerable (Le-Fort, 1993, p. 118). En 1981-1983 se desató una significativa crisis financiera con la insolvencia generalizada del sistema bancario que influyó al menos parcialmente en una contracción del PIB real superior al 15 por ciento.[10] El gobierno adquirió, a través del Banco Central, gran parte de la cartera incobrable con serias implicaciones fiscales y de limitaciones a la flexibilidad del Banco Central. Esto generó un déficit cuasi-fiscal del orden del 1.5 por ciento en 1993.

A partir de 1984 Chile reinició una liberalización y desregulación graduales, pero incrementales y progresivas, del sistema financiero y del mercado de capitales que han sustentado mayores tasas de ahorro, una mejor eficiencia en la asignación de recursos y altas tasas de crecimiento económico.[11] Esto se ha realizado dentro del contexto de un marco regulador bicontrolado, es decir, sometido al escrutinio y a la presentación de información, tanto al público como a las entidades estatales especializadas, orientado a hacer transparente el riesgo de la cartera, los niveles de capitalización y de reservas. Las actividades de los bancos comerciales se separaron entre actividades primarias propias de la banca comercial tradicional y secundarias que cubren una amplia gama de instrumentos financieros y que no están tan reguladas. Es intención declarada de las autoridades chilenas ir transfiriendo las regulaciones y supervisión financieras del sector público al sector privado. El marco regulatorio y de supervisión bancario todavía es muy estricto, en tanto que el marco para otros

intermediarios no se ha desarrollo a un nivel similar, lo que hace que esos intermediarios tengan ventajas de flexibilidad *vis à vis* la banca comercial. Chile también ha desarrollado varios instrumentos para asegurar que el crédito, reforzado por asistencia técnica, alcance a la pequeña y mediana empresa.[12]

El gobierno chileno jugó un papel proactivo y pragmático muy importante en el diseño y aplicación de las políticas para tener un marco macroeconómico estable y un marco regulatorio y de supervisión financieros sanos.

Las reformas financieras todavía pendientes en los antiguos países socialistas Europeos

Como consecuencia de la dinámica creada por la liberalización inicial de precios y de restricciones al comercio internacional aplicada en los antiguos países socialistas europeos, reforzada en algunos casos por el régimen de flotación cambiaria empleado y las estructuras de mercado monopólicas, estos países no tienen todavía un sector financiero desarrollado en cuanto a instituciones e instrumentos, el cual para comenzar presentaba un significativo retraso con relación a la dotación de capital social. La incipiente estabilización y recuperación económica de algunos de esos países en 1994-1995, requiere de un pujante sector financiero que brinde información a los distintos agentes económicos (prestamistas, inversionistas), facilite mayores niveles de ahorro y los canalice a inversiones de elevada productividad para así lograr y sostener altas tasas de crecimiento. Adicionalmente, el entorno internacional, caracterizado por una creciente competencia e integración de los mercados, demanda una serie de servicios y variedad de instrumentos del sector financiero, especialmente para la pequeña y mediana

---

10. A principios de la década de los años ochenta Argentina y Uruguay tuvieron crisis financieras similares a la chilena debido a que liberalizaron y desregularon prematuramente el sistema financiero dentro de un entorno de desequilibrios financieros y sin marcos reguladores y de supervisión prudentes. Uruguay, al igual que Chile, no tenía déficit fiscal. En cambio, Corea que comenzó un proceso de liberalización y desregulación financieras similar, lo frenó y lo revirtió pragmáticamente cuando comenzó a encontrar severas dificultades. Después, continuó dicho proceso gradualmente (Bascom, pp. 34-35).

11. Según la CEPAL, Chile experimentó la mayor tasa de crecimiento del producto real (7 por ciento anual) en la región en el quinquenio 1991-1995.

12. Entre ellos se destacan los subsidios a la asistencia crediticia (SUAF), los cupones de bonificación aplicables a las primas de seguro de crédito (CUBOS), las tarjetas de crédito para la producción y apoyo a entidades no gubernamentales que trabajan con la microempresa.

empresa privada, porque tienden a encontrarse en desventaja competitiva y son importantes desde el punto de vista social. Existe bastante acuerdo entre los especialistas en la materia (ver por ejemplo, Berthelot, 1996) que sólo estableciendo marcos de regulación y de supervisión prudentes y estrictos bajo la responsabilidad de instituciones independientes, se podrá superar la fragilidad financiera existente y liberalizar y desregular gradual, pero progresivamente, de acuerdo como lo indique la experiencia, para facilitar así los servicios y la profundización del sector financiero requeridos, lo que a su vez facilitará la integración a los mercados internacionales, como lo ha logrado Chile exitosamente en el período 1984-1995.

IMPORTANCIA DEL SECTOR FINANCIERO EN EL DESARROLLO

La literatura económica comenzó a darle mayor importancia al sector financiero con los trabajos de McKinnon (1973) y Shaw (1973) referentes a la reforma financiera para establecer tasas de interés reales positivas que, por un lado, estimularan el ahorro y una más eficiente intermediación financiera y que, por otro lado, mejoraran la asignación de recursos, especialmente de la inversión. Varios estudios empíricos en los años ochenta no mostraron resultados robustos para los efectos de la reforma financiera propuesta por McKinnon y Shaw, tal vez porque como señalan De Gregorio y Guidotti (1992) no distinguieron entre las liberalizaciones financieras exitosas de las realizadas precipitadamente que crearon crisis financieras. Sin embargo, en años más recientes varios estudios de King y Levine (especialmente el de 1993) no sólo han profundizado sobre los posibles mecanismos en que la ampliación, profundización y diversificación del sector financiero pueden influir en el crecimiento económico y en el aumento de la productividad, sino que también han encontrado resultados robustos para los efectos positivos de la profundización y ampliación en el crecimiento económico y en el aumento de la productividad. Estos mecanismos son el facilitamiento de información y de una serie de transacciones, la reducción de los costos de la intermediación financiera, la contribución a la innovación y la reducción del riesgo para los empresarios y la mejor selección de éstos.

Además, King y Levine (1993) encontraron que los países que realizaron una reforma financiera al principio de su proceso de reformas han visto que el resto de las reformas económicas ha sido más exitoso. Johnson y Pazarbasioglu (1995) encontraron que una crisis financiera tiene un significativo impacto negativo sobre la economía; por lo tanto, hay que realizar la liberalización y desregulación financieras prudentemente. En general se acepta que la inestabilidad macroeconómica afecta negativamente al sector financiero y que la inestabilidad financiera perjudica a la economía, especialmente al nivel microeconómico, ya que genera severos costos y distorsiones.

En cuanto a la secuencia de la reforma financiera en la literatura, predomina el enfoque que hay que lograr la estabilización primero para entonces comenzar los procesos de recuperación y crecimiento económicos (Fischer, et. al., 1996b, p. 97 y Fischer, et. al., 1996a, p. 230). Adicionalmente, que la supresión del déficit fiscal es necesaria para superar el problema del flujo que crea las presiones inflacionarias, así como que es necesario eliminar el excedente monetario para atender el problema de acervos ("stocks") excesivos. En cambio no hay posiciones predominantes sobre qué régimen cambiario utilizar durante el proceso de estabilización. Sin embargo, recientemente los artículos mencionados de Sachs y de Fischer, et. al. muestran resultados empíricos muy favorables a un régimen cambiario fijo o de ajuste administrado. El tema de la reforma monetaria para eliminar el problema de "stocks" prácticamente no ha recibido atención en la literatura después de los ensayos de Dornbusch y Wolf y de Calvo y Frenkel, con lo cual la liberalización de precios y de restricciones al comercio internacional ha predominado como instrumento para eliminar tanto el déficit fiscal como el excedente monetario. El tema del excedente monetario no ha sido considerado en estudios empíricos recientes sobre los programas de estabilización en los antiguos países socialistas europeos (Fischer et. al, 1996).

Végh presenta evidencia de una recuperación inmediata sin recesión cuando se utiliza la tasa de cambio fija como instrumento de estabilización en economías con alta inflación. Rebelo y Végh (1995) presentan evidencia de una recuperación inmediata con recesión posterior cuando se utiliza la tasa de cambio fija como instrumento de estabilización, así como de recesiones inmediata y posterior cuando sólo se utiliza la política monetaria restrictiva como instrumento de estabilización en economías con inflación crónica (elevada y persistente inflación).

Stiglitz (1993) señala que existen siete áreas de imperfecciones en los mercados financieros (entre ellas las relacionadas con el monitoreo de la solvencia y administración de las empresas, las externalidades del monitoreo, las externalidades de la bancarrota de este tipo de instituciones, la competencia imperfecta de estos mercados). Dichas imperfecciones son más pronunciadas en las etapas iniciales del desarrollo económico y justifican una intervención reguladora potencial por parte del estado al menos temporalmente, en especial en el desarrollo de instituciones que faciliten instrumentos de largo plazo no sólo para que los mercados financieros funcionen mejor sino también la economía en su conjunto debido al papel estratégico de estos mercados. Sin embargo, considera que las intervenciones tienen que estar bien diseñadas, ya que la evidencia de los resultados de dichas intervenciones son mixtos debido a la debilidad de los gobiernos para implantarlas adecuadamente. Stiglitz menciona que, en el caso del Este de Asia, las intervenciones fueron en general beneficiosas en proveer un marco macroeconómico estable y asegurar la solvencia de las instituciones financieras. Asimismo, indica sus reservas sobre apoyar la liberalización de los mercados financieros desde las primeras etapas del desarrollo.

En lo referente al sector financiero, el Informe del Banco Mundial de 1996 sobre las economías en transición se concentra principalmente en tres temas: (1) la rehabilitación de los bancos comerciales existentes, o la nueva entrada de nuevos bancos comerciales, o una combinación entre ellos; (2) el tipo de banca comercial a adoptar: múltiple siguiendo el ejemplo de Japón y Europa Occidental o más especializada siguiendo el modelo de Estados Unidos; y (3) la conveniencia de la independencia de la banca central y de las entidades reguladoras y supervisoras. En general recomienda la entrada de nuevos bancos y la banca comercial de tipo múltiple. (Banco Mundial, 1996, pp. 118-132).

UNA PROPUESTA PARA LOGRAR UNA RAPIDA MONETIZACION DESPUES DE ELIMINAR LA DOLARIZACION Y EL EXCEDENTE MONETARIO

"In designing the sequencing of financial reforms and stabilization, the issues have to be approached in a pragmatic way, and often tactical adjustments have to be made to seize opportunities that present themselves for moving the process along as quickly as possible."

— Vicente Galbis (1994, p. 21)

Objetivos y consideraciones generales

Considerando la situación actual de Cuba, los objetivos iniciales que se pretenden son la efectiva y pronta eliminación del excedente monetario y de la dolarización existentes, o sea lograr la estabilización interna y externa, así como el establecimiento de un marco regulador y de supervisión prudentes en el sector financiero, y evitar una recesión en el sector real. Después, el libre funcionamiento de los mercados financieros y cambiarios bajo la dirección de una autoridad monetaria independiente con verdaderos poderes para lograr una rápida y sostenida monetización, intermediación y profundización financieras estimularán el crecimiento económico, el aumento de la productividad y un papel mayor del sector privado en la economía. Para ello es necesario establecer y desarrollar secuencialmente un sistema financiero y un mercado de capitales sanos, flexibles y dinámicos, con escasa ingerencia estatal y el entorno de regulaciones para que intermediarios cumplan múltiples funciones y ofrezcan múltiples instrumentos que faciliten la inversión y la expansión productiva (por ejemplo, los arrendamientos financieros ("leasings") y los "factorings") en creciente vinculación con el exterior.[13] Ello contribuirá al mejoramiento de los niveles de inversión, eficiencia y privatización de la economía, lo que constituirá un aporte sinérgico determinante al proceso de desarrollo económico en general.

Nuestra propuesta, más que tener objetivos diferentes en cuanto a la liberalización y desregulación financiera y cambiaria, es diferente y puede lucir controversial en lo referente a la utilización inicial de instrumentos como la reforma monetaria y un régimen cambiario fijo, así como en la amplitud inicial, el ritmo y la secuencia al implantar la liberalización y desregulación financieras y cambiarias. Una apertura gradual más prudente establece señales únicas y coherentes a los agentes económicos y evita la paralización de la liberalización financiera o la crisis encubierta del sistema financiero y logra resultados finales antes. Sin embargo, la propuesta plantea avanzar y consolidar varios frentes financieros y cambiarios *simultáneamente*. El diseño y aplicación de un paquete secuencial similar fue utilizado por Yugoeslavia para estabilizar con éxito y rápidamente en 1994 en condiciones de bloqueo externo y de guerra (Avramovic, 1996).

Diseño de la estrategia e instrumentos requeridos

El diseño de la estrategia se basa en las condiciones y características estructurales iniciales de Cuba ya indicadas, las experiencias recientes de Europa Oriental y Chile, y en los supuestos que una espiral inflacionaria, desatada por la dinámica de la liberalización de precios y de restricciones al comercio internacional y de la flotación cambiaria en el contexto de un significativo excedente monetario, escasos mecanismos y una estructura monopólica de mercados, no facilita la profundización financiera, como tampoco lo hace la política monetaria que caracteriza al choque monetario. Además, que las

Situación Actual y Propuesta para Superarla

Problemas Existentes

(1) Excedente Monetario, (2) Dolarización, (3) Fragmentación, (4) Carencia de Instituciones Financieras

Medidas Propuestas para Superar los Problemas
Primera Fase (Bases Fundamentales)

- Reforma Monetaria Consistente en Aumento de Precios, Salarios

- Ajuste Administrativo de Tasas de Interés Activas y Pasivas

- Devaluación del Peso, Tasa de Cambio Fija

Segunda Fase

- Liberalización de Precios y Salarios

- Convertibilidad Parcial del Peso

- Banco Central Independiente

- Marco Regulatorio y de Supervisión Financiera, y Libre Entrada de Nuevas Instituciones Financieras

reformas financieras y cambiarias deben ser parte integral de un paquete mayor de reformas coherentes para la transición hacia una economía de mercado que tengan la credibilidad, que vayan eliminando sostenida y progresivamente las distorsiones existentes en la economía y ampliando sus niveles de eficiencia. De lo contrario los efectos de las liberalizaciones financieras y cambiarias, "tipo gran explosión", podrían acentuar y verse acentuadas por las distorsiones e ineficiencias existentes y conducir a una crisis financiera.

Nuestra propuesta, para lograr los objetivos indicados, consiste en la reforma monetaria para eliminar el excedente monetario[14] y el

---

13. Los arrendamientos financieros para los bienes de capital presentan la ventaja que los bancos comerciales o las empresas prestamistas conservan la propiedad del activo hasta que el prestatario paga el activo en su totalidad y de tener ventajas tributarias debido a la depreciación y al tratamiento del IVA, para los prestatarios les permite adquirir bienes de capital que no estarían disponibles en otras condiciones. Los arrendamientos financieros han tenido bastante éxito en Europa Oriental (Banco Mundial, 1996, p. 129).

14. Los defensores de la liberalización de precios que se oponen a la reforma monetaria por razón de que es confiscatoria están errados en dos consideraciones. Tanto la reforma monetaria como la liberalización de precios eliminan el excedente monetario aumentando los precios. Sin embargo, la liberalización de precios es peor al aumentar más los precios por la espiral y las inercias inflacionarias que desata.

Dinámica de Cambio de la Propuesta

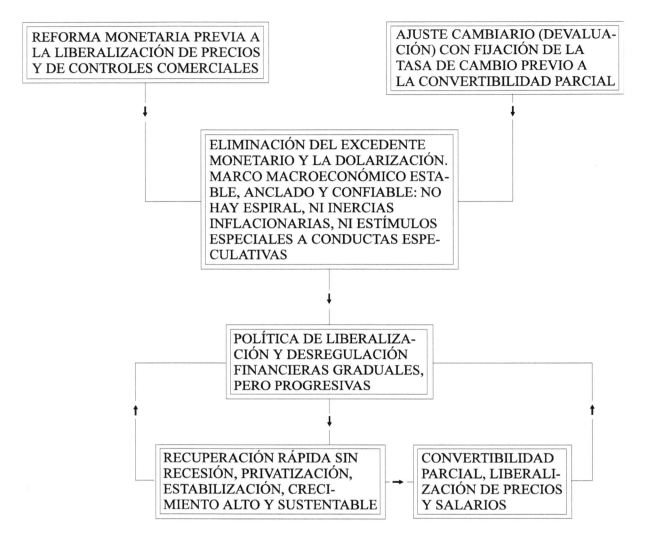

establecimiento administrativo de una tasa de interés real positiva para modificar las expectativas, aumentar la demanda por los activos financieros nacionales en relación a los activos financieros internacionales, no sólo por los residentes sino también por los no residentes y extranjeros, y sentar así las bases para la estabilización y la desdolarización. Simultáneamente, se devaluaría la moneda nacional y se establecería un régimen cambiario fijo de convertibilidad parcial, respaldado por un fondo con base en préstamos de los organismos internacionales o del sector privado y al menos temporalmente sujeto al dólar, para reforzar los efectos de las medidas

financieras para lograr la desdolarización y la consolidación de un sostenido proceso de monetización o de inducción para aumentar la tenencia de activos financieros reales nacionales y dar un punto de referencia o *ancla* al tremendo ajuste que es necesario realizar en los precios relativos internos y en relación con los precios internacionales. Posteriormente habría que ajustar la tasa de cambio para evitar presiones contraccionarias. También las medidas incluirían la liberalización y desregulación financieras y cambiarias graduales, pero incrementales y progresivas, con base en unos regímenes prudentes de administración monetaria/

Dinámica de Cambio Recesivo de Algunos Países Europeos

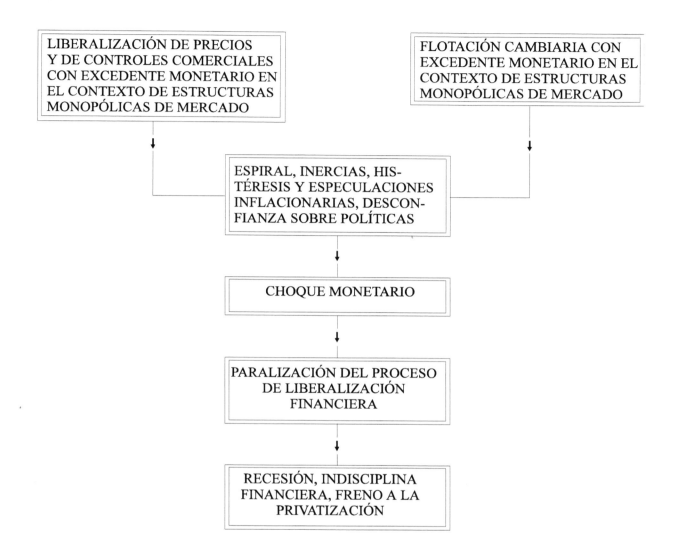

crediticia por un banco central independiente y de regulaciones y supervisión transparente por instituciones independientes, incluyendo el establecimiento de instituciones clasificadoras de riesgo.

Este paquete de medidas coherentes tenderá a aumentar la utilización de la capacidad productiva existente y a mejorar la productividad, y se basa en dos consideraciones fundamentales: (1) que el gobierno haya adoptado suficientes medidas adicionales para eliminar el déficit fiscal, o sea, la causa última de la expansión monetaria, lo cual

también disminuiría las presiones sobre la tasa de interés y la tasa de cambio; y (2) que el gobierno adopte las medidas y los incentivos para alentar la activa participación de la comunidad cubana en el exterior, que tiene amplia experiencia en la operación, administración gerencial y capitalización de instituciones financieras e, idealmente, establecería un flujo de capitales y de recursos humanos talentosos hacia Cuba. La comunidad cubana en su conjunto tiene una serie de habilidades, destrezas y experiencias en mercados e instituciones financieras que los antiguos países socialistas europeos no tuvieron.

La reforma monetaria consistiría en aumentar los precios, salarios, pensiones y otros pagos recurrentes en X veces para restaurar una relación entre activos monetarios y producción en términos monetarios similar a un año más o menos normal como 1989, acompañada del establecimiento por vía administrativa de una estructura de tasas de interés real positiva de Y puntos reales y una tasa de cambio realista de Z pesos por dólar para las principales transacciones, dirigidas a eliminar el excedente monetario, las expectativas inflacionarias y estimular la utilización de cuentas de ahorro y otros instrumentos financieros. La tasa de interés real positiva deberá ser moderada para evitar la entrada masiva de capital de corto plazo del exterior, mientras las empresas nacionales no tienen que buscar su financiamiento en el exterior y pueden enfrentar las tasas vigentes. En estas condiciones, y con un régimen cambiario de convertibilidad parcial para asegurar la disponibilidad de divisas para las principales transacciones externas requeridas (las transacciones en la cuenta corriente y en la cuenta de capital a largo plazo), se podría realizar la monetización de la economía que el país requiere para su crecimiento, ya que el ajuste propuesto de los precios, salarios y tasa de cambio no debe generar una inercia inflacionaria. (¿Para qué son necesarios ajustes frecuentes en los precios o una indexación en estas condiciones?) De hecho, habría un aumento significativo de precios, salarios y tasa de cambio *por una sola vez*, seguido de los ajustes en los precios relativos, pero no en el *nivel* de precios. Este paquete de políticas coherentes lograría una rápida estabilización y evitaría una recesión.

La liberalización y desregulación financieras, que son *un proceso y no un acontecimiento*, estarían encaminadas a alentar la entrada de nuevas instituciones financieras y la competencia entre ellas. Esto debe realizarse a partir de un prudente y estricto marco de regulaciones y supervisión básicas mínimas con entidades clasificadoras de riesgos. Así se crearán las condiciones para asegurar la capitalización, la liquidez y el establecimiento de normas sobre información transparente y pública sobre la rentabilidad, solvencia y riesgo de las instituciones financieras que alienten la ampliación,

profundización y diversificación para que el sector financiero estimule el crecimiento económico, el aumento de la productividad y facilite el proceso de privatización. El papel, autoridad y amplitud de las responsabilidades de las entidades reguladoras y supervisoras independientes y las clasificadoras de riesgos se deberán establecer para lograr los resultados indicados y definir tan pronto sea posible. Estas medidas de regulación y supervisión iniciales, que podrán liberalizarse gradual, pero incremental y progresivamente, a medida que el sector financiero se fortalezca, deberán acompañarse de otras medidas macroeconómicas que desalienten que la liberalización comercial, cambiaria y financiera se traduzcan principalmente en el aumento de consumo importado (el síndrome holandés resultado de la liberalización) o que hagan la economía muy vulnerable a los movimientos de capital de corto plazo.

Fortalezas, debilidades y posibles efectos de las políticas y medidas propuestas vis-à-vis la liberalización de precios, la flotación cambiaria y el choque monetario

La liberalización inicial de precios y de restricciones al comercio internacional y la flotación cambiaria eliminan el excedente monetario, pero desatan una espiral, inercias y conductas especulativas inflacionarias que, acentuadas por los mercados monopólicos y los débiles mecanismos de mercados existentes, tienden a disminuir la tenencia de activos monetarios, acentúan la tenencia de otras monedas, o sea la dolarización, con lo cual se agudiza la propia inflación y el problema fiscal por el efecto Olivera-Tanzi. El choque monetario que entonces es necesario para eliminar la espiral inflacionaria y la dolarización tiene efectos negativos sobre la demanda agregada y sobre la oferta agregada vía aumento de costos y desata una recesión. Adicionalmente, la estabilización basada en el choque monetario tiene efectos negativos sobre la disciplina financiera, y sobre la institucionalización, liberalización y desregulación financieras. La inconsistencia de esta política y los costos transicionales de esta forma de estabilización son muy elevados ya que están concebidos para eliminar problemas de flujos más que de "stocks" y crean fuertes ineficiencias dinámicas por actuar muy rápido si bien están orientadas a corregir las ineficiencias estáticas de actuar más lento. Además, tiene efectos perversos al desatar una espiral inflacionaria que impide los efectos positivos sobre la oferta agregada de la estabilización y la monetización, y dificulta al propio sector financiero escoger las mejores empresas. Asimismo, termina postergando la liberalización y la privatización que son tan importantes en el proceso de reformas económicas.

Hay un doble error en utilizar la liberalización de precios para eliminar el excedente monetario: (1) porque es un instrumento por excelencia para eliminar las distorsiones en los precios relativos y las ineficiencias en la asignación de recursos, y (2) porque la espiral y las inercias inflacionarias hacen que la política monetaria se utilice para frenarlas en vez de para facilitar la reestructuración y el crecimiento dentro de un marco estable. En última instancia confunde instrumentos con objetivos de política económica e ignora la secuencia necesaria en las reformas. No todo debe hacerse a la vez (Avramovic, 1996).

En contraste, la reforma monetaria y el ajuste cambiario sin flotación eliminan el excedente monetario sin crear espiral e inercias inflacionarias, pues son ajustes iniciales de una sola vez al problema de "stocks", y si son acompañados de la eliminación del déficit fiscal y del establecimiento de una tasa de interés real, crean la confianza en la moneda nacional que tiende a la desdolarización y a la monetización. Dado el caso de que la reforma monetaria fuera excesiva, esto crearía un incentivo a las empresas a desprenderse de sus inventarios para financiarse y en cualquier caso podría ser atendido mediante una expansión monetaria (Dornbusch y Wolf, p. 16). Sólo entonces es viable comenzar un robusto proceso de liberalización, desregulación, privatización e institucionalización financieras progresivas basadas en un marco inicial de regulación y supervisión prudentes orientadas a la ampliación, profundización y diversificación financieras. De esta forma el sector financiero podrá contribuir al aumento del crecimiento y la productividad desde el inicio del proceso de transición al proveer el crédito necesario para el capital de trabajo, la expansión de la inversión

y facilitar el proceso de privatización. Una de las ventajas del paquete propuesto es que es rápida, evita la recesión asociada a la estabilización y establece las condiciones para una recuperación de la actividad económica y de la inversión.

Las desventajas de la liberalización de precios y de restricciones al comercio internacional, así como la flotación cambiaria para eliminar el excedente monetario y lograr el nivel de precios y la tasa cambiaria de equilibrio en contexto de estructuras de mercado monopólicas, son la espiral, las inercias, las conductas especulativas y la histéresis transitoria o permanente que desatan cuando lo ideal es lograr anclas que tiendan a estabilizar rápidamente el sistema alrededor de los precios de equilibrio, evitar una recesión y otros costos del proceso de ajuste. Los argumentos de Sachs (1995 y 1996b) para la fijación cambiaria después de una devaluación con credibilidad, o sea que la población la perciba como permanente y estable, también son válidos para utilizar la reforma monetaria en vez de la liberalización de precios para eliminar el excedente monetario y controlar las inercias inflacionarias y conductas especulativas, tal como lo propusieron Dornbusch y Wolf (1990) y como lo consideraron Calvo y Frenkel (1991). Además, es mucho mejor mientras más pronto se logren la estabilización interna y externa y comience la recuperación dentro de un contexto de libre juego de las fuerzas de mercado. La evidencia empírica sugiere que cuando se logra exitosamente la estabilización le sigue de inmediato la recuperación (Rebelo y Végh, 1995, p 113). Uno de los peligros de no lograr la estabilización rápidamente es crear una inflación crónica que después es difícil eliminar, pues varios grupos sociales establecen mecanismos para protegerse de la inflación y tienen desconfianza del sistema financiero lo que impide la remonetización.

IMPLANTACION DE LAS MEDIDAS DE LA PROPUESTA. SECUENCIA EN LA APLICACION DE LAS MEDIDAS PROPUESTAS. IMPLICACIONES PARA EL

COMPORTAMIENTO DE LAS INSTITUCIONES FINANCIERAS Y DE LA ECONOMIA EN EL FUTURO

En la situación actual de Cuba y con base en la escasa información disponible al final del verano de 1996, la mejor forma de implantar el paquete de medidas propuesto con objeto de lograr la estabilización interna y externa es establecer simultáneamente y tan pronto sea posible lo siguiente: (1) la reforma monetaria aumentando los precios, salarios, pensiones y otros pagos recurrentes en 3 veces para reducir la oferta de activos monetarios reales y con ello las presiones inflacionarias reprimidas restableciendo la relación existente en 1989;[15] (2) fijar una tasa de interés real del 6 por ciento para los pasivos del sistema financiero (depósitos) y del 9 por ciento para los activos (préstamos) para hacer más atractiva la tenencia de activos monetarios nacionales y mejorar la asignación de recursos, bajo el supuesto que la tasa de interés real internacional es del 3 por ciento; y (3) devaluar la moneda a una tasa de 10 a 15 pesos por dólar para racionalizar el uso de los recursos externos y mejorar la competitividad de la producción nacional.

Estas medidas son fundamentalmente de saneamiento financiero básico y sentarían las bases para el funcionamiento del sistema financiero y las cuatro medidas siguientes orientadas a aumentar la eficiencia del sistema económico mediante una mejor asignación de los recursos económicos haciéndolo más flexible y dinámico y facilitando la capacidad empresarial cubana: (1) la liberalización de precios para incentivar la reacción de las empresas del sector productivo, incluyendo tanto las del sector público como del sector privado, y el ajuste de precios de las empresas de servicios públicos que por su naturaleza son monopólicas a fin de evitar sobreprecios o bajos niveles de producción con la liberalización de insumos claves para la actividad económica general; (2) la convertibilidad parcial del peso para casi todas las transacciones de la cuenta corriente y los movimientos de capital a largo plazo;[16] (3) el establecimiento de un banco central independiente que siga una politica monetaria y crediticia para la estabilización dentro de un marco de crecimiento económico; y (4) el establecimiento de los marcos regulatorio y de supervisión para la ampliación del sistema financiero que permitan la libre entrada de nuevos bancos comerciales y otras instituciones financieras, así como el desarrollo de nuevos instrumentos y funciones financieras. Este paquete de medidas serían parte de un conjunto mayor de medidas macroeconómicas (fiscales, monetarias, cambiarias, comerciales) para consolidar la estabilización interna y externa e ir reformando y liberalizando gradual, pero progresivamente, el sistema económico y sometiéndolo a la competencia externa para hacerlo más eficiente y dinámico (ver Castañeda y Montalván, 1993 y 1996).

Las tres medidas estabilizadoras se deberán implantar de inmediato para eliminar el excedente monetario y la dolarización y con ello lograr la estabilización interna y externa. Esto permitirá una rápida recuperacion de la producción sin la necesidad de grandes inversiones iniciales. Las medidas de liberalización de precios y de restricciones al comercio internacional, convertibilidad parcial, y de reformas institucionales financieras que vendrían después, tendrán un substantivo impacto en la asignación de los recursos, mejorarán la eficiencia y dinamismo de la economía y velarían porque la expansión del sistema financiero se realice sobre bases sanas que impidan una crisis financiera con un impacto que se podría sentir aún una década después de alto crecimiento y de creciente estabilización interna y externa, como pasó en Chile con la crisis de 1981-1983.

RESUMEN Y CONCLUSIONES

La literatura reciente destaca el importante papel que el sector financiero desempeña como factor

---

15. También la reforma monetaria se podría utilizar para eliminar el déficit fiscal. Así los salarios, pensiones y otros pagos recurrentes se podrían ajustar en una proporción ligeramente menor que los precios, por ejemplo 2.75 veces.

16. Calvo y Frankel (1991, p. 147) presentan razones de por qué la convertibilidad total debe establecerse al final de reformas monetarias y cambiarias.

determinante del crecimiento económico y del aumento de la productividad. La liberalización de precios y de restricciones al comercio internacional y, en varios casos, la flotación cambiaria, se utilizaron para lograr una más pronta estabilización interna y externa en los antiguos países socialistas europeos. La "liberalización prematura" creó una espiral e inercias inflacionarias e incertidumbres que fue seguida por una política de estabilización monetaria crediticia reactiva y muy restrictiva, "choque monetario". El choque tuvo efectos perversos e indujo "fallas de mercado" en la disciplina y la liberalización financiera y posteriormente la ha demorado, incluyendo el desarrollo institucional, la privatización y el proceso de reformas en su conjunto, uno de los grandes errores de política económica en los procesos de transición en los antiguos países socialistas europeos. Chile tuvo un amplio proceso de liberalización financiera en 1973-1980 que desembocó en una marcada y profunda crisis financiera en 1981-1983; después, comenzó un proceso de liberalización y desregulación financieras graduales e incrementales, así como de manejo cambiario a partir de un marco prudente de regulación y supervisión que han contribuido en forma significativa a un alto y sostenido crecimiento de la economía.

Los argumentos de Sachs (1995, 1996b) para emplear la devaluación con un régimen cambiario fijo o de ajustes periódicos en vez de la flotación cambiaria, comprobados por la evidencia de Fischer, et. al. (1996b), dan base a argumentos similares a favor de que la reforma monetaria debe preceder a la liberalización de precios, tal como Dornbusch y Wolf (1990) lo habían propuesto. Nuestra propuesta se fundamenta en dichos argumentos y en que las políticas a emplear deben estar dirigidas a eliminar específicamente los desequilibrios en los "stocks". Adicionalmente, la experiencia chilena en 1984-1996 es muy favorable a la desregulación y liberalización financiera gradual, pero incremental, a partir de un régimen de regulación y supervisión básica inicial que se puede ir relajando progresiva y sistemáticamente.

Al diseñar su política de eliminación de la dolarización y del excedente monetario, Cuba deberá evitar las experiencias negativas de los antiguos países socialistas europeos y aprovechar la experiencia chilena de profundización y diversificación financieras en 1984-1996. El paquete propuesto de reforma monetaria, ajuste en la tasa de interés real y tasa de cambio fija después de la devaluación, que debe preceder la liberalización de precios y las restricciones al comercio internacional, la convertibilidad parcial en cuenta corriente y la institucionalización financiera, será más efectivo para lograr rápidamente los resultados de la estabilización interna y externa, evitar una recesion, alcanzar una recuperación económica, y realizar los procesos de ampliación y profundización financieras que a su vez tendrán efectos positivos sobre un alto crecimiento sustentable. La experiencia de Yugoeslavia en 1994-1996 demuestra que este tipo de estabilización se puede lograr aún en condiciones de bloqueo externo.

El paquete propuesto es una autopista de alta velocidad algo apartada hacia el crecimiento sustentable vis-à-vis la liberalización de precios y la flotación cambiaria inmediatas que constituyen un largo atajo que se puede convertir en un "camino sin salida."

BIBLIOGRAFÍA

A. H. Amsden, J. Kochanowics and L. Taylor (1994). *The Market Meets Its Match*. Cambridge, Mass.: Harvard University Press.

D. Avramovic (1996). "Lessons from the Transition: The Case of Yugoslavia 1994-96." Ensayo presentado en Development Thinking and Practice Conference, auspiciada por el BID, setiembre.

Banco Mundial (1996). *Informe sobre el desarrollo mundial 1996: De la planificación centralizada a la economía de mercado* (Washington, DC: Banco Mundial).

Banco Nacional de Cuba (1994). *Economic Report*. La Habana: Banco Nacional de Cuba.

Y. Berthelot (1996). "Lessons from Countries in Transition." Ensayo presentado en Development Thinking and Practice Conference, auspiciada por el BID, setiembre.

M. Bruno y W. Easterly (1995). *Inflation Crisis and Long-Run Growth*. National Bureau of Economic Research, Working Paper 5209. Cambridge: The MIT Press.

G. Calvo and F. Corricelli (1992). "Stagflationary Effects of Stabilization Programs in Reforming Socialist Countries: Enterprise-Side and Household-Side Factors." *The World Bank Economic Review*, Vol 6, No. 1 (January) .

G. Calvo and J. Frenkel (1991). "From Centrally Planned to Market Economy." *IMF Staff Papers* 38 (June), pp. 268-299.

G. Calvo, M. Kumar, E. Borensztein and P. Masson (1993). *Financial Reforms and Exchange Arrangements in Eastern Europe*, IMF Occasional Paper No. 102.

G. Calvo and M. Kumar (1994). "Money Demand, Bank Credit, and Economic Performance in Former Socialist Economies." *IMF Staff Papers* 41 (June), pp. 314-349.

J. Carranza, L. Gutiérrez y P. Monreal (1995). *Cuba: La restructuración de la economía*. La Habana: Centro de Estudios sobre América, documento preliminar, enero.

R. H. Castañeda and G. P. Montalván (1993). "Transition in Cuba: A Comprehensive Stabilization Proposal and Some Key Issues." *Cuba in Transition—Volume 3*. Washington, D.C.: ASCE, pp. 11-72.

R. H. Castañeda and G. P. Montalván (1996). "Cinco áreas de acción estratégicas para lograr el mila-gro económico cubano: una rápida recuperación con un alto y sustentable crecimiento con equidad e inclusión social". Ensayo presentado en la 6ª reunión anual de la Asociación para el Estudio de la Economía Cubana (ASCE), agosto.

J. De Gregorio y P. Guidotti (1992). "Notas sobre Intermediación Financiera y Crecimiento Económico". *Cuadernos de Economía*, Vol 29 No. 87 (agosto de 1992), pp. 329-348.

R. Dornbusch and H. Wolf (1990). *Monetary Over-hang and Reforms in the 1940s*. Cambridge, MA: The MIT Press, National Bureau of Economic Research, Working Paper 3456, October.

R. Dornbusch (1992). "Lessons from Experiences with High Inflation." *The World Bank Economic Review*, Vol. 6, No. 1, pp. 13-31.

W. Easterly (1996). "When is Stabilization Expansionary." *Economic Policy*, No. 22, pp. 65-107.

Economic Commission for Europe, United Nations (1995). *Economic Survey of Europe in 1994-1995*.

European Bank for Reconstruction and Development (1995). *Transition Report, 1994 & 1995*.

A. Fleming and S. Talley (1996). "The Latvian Banking Crisis." The World Bank, Policy Research Working Paper 1590.

S. Fischer, R. Sahay and C. Végh (1996a). "Economies in Transition: The Beginnings of Growth." *The American Economic Review* (May , pp. 229-233.

S. Fischer, R. Sahay and C. Végh (1996b). "Stabilization and Growth in Transition Economies: The Early Experience." The Journal of Economic Perspectives (Spring), pp. 44-66.

V. Galbis (1994). *Sequencing of Financial Sector Reforms: A Review*. Washington, D.C.: International Monetary Fund, IMF Working Paper (September).

J. Greenwood and B. D. Smith (1993). "Financial Markets in Development, and the Development of Financial Markets." *Journal of Economic Dynamics and Control.*

L. Gutiérrez, P. Monreal y J. Carranza (1996). *La desmonetización de la economía cubana: una revisión de alternativas.* La Habana: Centro de Estudios sobre América, documento preliminar (enero).

R. B. Johnson y C. Pazarbasioglu (1995). *Linkages between Financial Variables, Financial Sector Reform and Economic Growth and Efficiency.* Washington, D.C.: International Monetary Fund, IMF Working Paper.

G. Le-Fort (1994). "The Financial System and macroeconomic Stability: The Chilean Experience." In Shakil Faruqi (ed). *Financial Sector Reforms, Economic Growth, and Stability.* Washington, D.C.: Economic Development Institute of the World Bank, pp. 113-138.

R. King and R. Levine (1993). "Finance, Entrepreneurship, and Growth: Theory and Evidence." *Journal of Monetary Economics,* 32 (December), pp. 513-542.

R. McKinnon (1973). *Money and Capital in Economic Development.* Washington, D.C.: The Brookings Institution.

A. Rapazczynski (1996). "The Roles of the State and the Market in Establishing Property Rights." *The Journal of Economic Perspectives* (Spring), pp. 87-103.

S. Rebelo and C. A. Végh (1995). "Real Effects of Exchange-Rate-Based Stabilization: An Analysis of Competing Theories." *Macroeconomics Annual 1995.* Cambridge, MA: The MIT Press for the National Bureau of Economic Research.

J. Sachs (1995). "Comments to Rebelo and Végh." *Macroeconomics Annual 1995.* Cambridge, MA: The MIT Press for the National Bureau of Economic Research.

J. Sachs (1996a). "The Transition at Mid Decade." *The American Economic Review* (May), pp. 128-133.

J. Sachs (1996b). "Economic Transition and the Exchange-Rate Regime." *The American Economic Review* (May), pp. 147-152.

T. Sargent (1982). "The Ends of Four Big Inflations." In R. E. Hall (ed.). *Inflation: Causes and Effects.* Chicago: University of Chicago Press, pp. 41-97.

E. Shaw (1973). *Financial Deepening in Economic Development.* New York, NY: Oxford Economic Press.

J. E. Stiglitz (1993). "The Role of the State in Financial Markets." *Proceedings of the World Bank Annual Conference on Development Economics,* pp. 19-52.

C. Végh (1992). "Stopping High Inflation." *IMF Staff Papers,* Vol 39, No. 3 (September), pp. 626-695.

THE MINIMUM WAGE AND UNEMPLOYMENT IN POLAND: LESSONS FOR CUBA'S TRANSITION

Andrew M. Melnyk[1]

Poland is one of the more successful cases of transition from a centrally planned to a market economy. Despite its relative success, it has one of the highest unemployment rates in Central and Eastern Europe. During the post-war era Poland's *official* unemployment rate was negligible. Since the introduction of the Economic Transformation Program (ETP) in January 1990, the unemployment rate has increased steadily and is currently about 15 percent. Undoubtedly, the shocks associated with the ETP and the collapse of the Council for Mutual Economic Assistance (Comecon) initially produced unemployment. However, a factor contributing to its continued increase is Poland's minimum wage system. Unlike any other previously centrally planned economy (PCPE), Poland's minimum wage has been continually revised upward throughout the transition period and has increased both in real terms and relative to the average wage. Poland's minimum wage also differs from those of other countries in that it is based on monthly earnings, rather than hourly. For these reasons Poland provides an excellent environment in which to study the effect of minimum wages on transitional labor markets and serves as an example from which to draw lessons for the Cuban economy.

According to conventional labor market theory, if a wage floor is raised above market clearing level, employment in the covered sector will fall. This has been confirmed by most empirical studies of developed market economies. Studies of the United States have also shown that this "disemployment" effect is small and limited to teenagers and youth. A comprehensive survey of the U.S. literature by Brown, Gilroy and Kohen (1982) concluded that a 10 percent increase in the minimum wage will result in only a one to three percent reduction in *teenage* employment. More recent studies by Card and Krueger (1995) have questioned the relevance and accuracy of mainstream theory and previous empirical research, concluding that an increase in the minimum wage has no effect or may actually *increase* employment. The response to this work has ranged from sharp criticism (Hamermesh 1995; Welch 1995; Kennan 1995; Deere et al. 1995) to calls for further research. More importantly, this recent line of research has led to questions regarding the role of minimum wages in the transition process (Standing 1995; Vaughan-Whitehead 1995). To date, however, there have been no detailed studies on the effects of minimum wages on transitional labor markets.

Poland's minimum wage is of great interest because, if conventional theory is correct, disemployment effects should be clearly seen. In Poland there is only one minimum wage which is continually revised upward, is high by international standards, and covers *all* labor. Most previous studies have relied on U.S. data where the magnitude of the minimum wage is small, increases are much less frequent, and coverage

---

1. This paper is based on parts of my Doctoral Dissertation at the University of Miami, tentatively entitled "Understanding the Polish Labor Market." I would like to thank John Devereux, Luis Locay, and Philip Robins for their helpful comments.

is incomplete. Additionally, because Poland's minimum wage is based on *monthly* remuneration, employers are less likely to respond to increases by simply limiting the number of hours a minimum wage earner works. They may instead limit the number of workers employed and increase the number of hours per minimum wage earner. For these reasons Poland's labor market offers a unique environment in which to determine the effects of minimum wage increases on employment.

Another way in which Poland's minimum wage is unique concerns it's relationship to unemployment benefits. It is commonly agreed that unemployment benefits which offer a high replacement rate,[2] unlimited duration, and/or few restrictions may contribute to unemployment. Poland's current unemployment benefit system[3] is related to the minimum wage. Unlike the unemployment benefit systems of most countries, where compensation is determined according to replacement rate, Poland offers four flat levels of compensation, three of which are directly pegged to the minimum wage (World Bank 1993). The fourth level of compensation, the one which most recipients qualify for, is equivalent to 36 percent of the average wage. In practice, all four benefit levels lie between 90 and 125 percent of the minimum wage. Unlike other countries, the benefit level an individual receives depends on his current status (i.e. recent university graduate, recent secondary school graduate, mass lay-off, fired, etc.) rather than his/her previous earnings.[4] Because the benefit *levels* are universal, actual *replacement rates* vary by individual. An individual with a high previous income may receive the same *level* of benefit as someone with a lower previous income, but will have a lower *replacement rate*. The drawback of this arrangement is that, given a high wage floor and a nearly equivalent level of unemployment compensation, when individuals with lower wage earning potential choose between labor and leisure, they may rationally choose unemployment over employment.

The following section of this paper further addresses these aspects of Poland's minimum wage and provides additional factual information. First, using pooled data and time-series data from individual regions, the impact of Poland's minimum wage on employment and unemployment is examined. Special emphasis is given to regional differences. Second, since employers face a monthly minimum wage, the November 1992 Polish Labor Force survey is used to examine whether employers may be lowering the *effective hourly wage* by altering the number of hours employees work. Finally, the implications of an unemployment benefits system which offers remuneration nearly equivalent to the minimum wage will be further examined. The final section discusses lessons for Cuba.

THE MINIMUM WAGE IN POLAND

Prior to reform, Poland's minimum wage had four main functions: (1) it was used by state-owned enterprises to determine pay scales; (2) the central government used it to calculate social benefits; (3) it served as an indirect form of wage control, and (4) it also had a poverty-prevention purpose. During the early part of transition the objective of the minimum wage laws became decidedly less administrative and started to focus on poverty-prevention. Rather than simply being mandated by the central government, the minimum wage is now determined jointly by trade union federations and the Ministry of Labor and Social Policy. Since October 1990 (10 months into transition) the minimum wage has been revised several times a year and, during the period from January 1989 to April 1994, it has increased 21 times (see table 1). By comparison, during this same time period, Hungary revised it's minimum wage 9 times, Russia 7, the Czech Republic 2, Romania 5, Bulgaria 10, Albania 4, Estonia 9, Moldova 10, and Ukraine 9 times.

---

2. The replacement rate is the ratio of unemployment benefits to income prior to becoming unemployed.

3. The current system was implemented in 1991.

4. There is one exception to this rule. Workers who were part of a mass lay-off and are within five years of retirement qualify for benefits which equal 75 percent of their previous earnings (World Bank 1993).

Table 1. Minimum Wage in Poland[a]

Date	Minimum Wage (in thousand zloty)	Real Minimum Wage[b]	Minimum Wage/ Average Wage[c]	Date	Minimum Wage (in thousand zloty)	Real Minimum Wage[b]	Minimum Wage/ Average Wage[c]
1981 (average)	2,400	n.a.	0.289				
1982 (average)	4,000	n.a.	0.347	May 1992	1,000,000	116.4	0.369
1987 (average)	7,000	n.a.	0.246	August 1992	1,200,000	132.0	0.403
1988 (average)	9,000	n.a.	0.169	September 1992	1,300,000	135.8	0.416
January 1989	17,800	95.9	n.a.	October 1992	1,350,000	136.9	0.408
July 1989	22,100	74.7	0.194	January 1993	1,500,000	139.8	0.450
October 1989	38,000	44.3	0.129	July 1993	1,650,000	136.5	0.412
January 1990	120,000	54.0	0.216	October 1993	1,750,000	135.5	0.405
September 1990	368,000	100.0	0.361	January 1994	1,950,000	135.0	0.420
October 1990	440,000	113.1	0.380	April 1994	2,050,000	133.8	0.385
January 1991	550,000	113.0	0.367	July 1994	2,200,000	135.9	0.393
April 1991	605,000	105.4	0.347	October 1994	2,400,000	135.6	0.397
July 1991	632,000	102.1	0.358	January 1995[d]	260	136.0	0.407
October 1991	652,000	97.3	0.352	April 1995	280	137.9	0.383
December 1991	700,000	98.1	0.331	July 1995	295	142.6	0.401
January 1992	875,000	114.1	0.352	October 1995	305	140.8	0.379

a. Minimum wage data was obtained from Vaughan-Whitehead (1995). The more recent figures were obtained from Jan Rutkowski by personal correspondence.

b. September 1990=100. The minimum wage was deflated by a consumer price index.

c. Average wage is equal to the mean wage for *all* workers in the economy.

d. In January 1995 a new currency was instituted. It is equal to (1/10,000)(Old Currency).

Perhaps because of its relatively high magnitude, Poland's minimum wage earners are not as heavily concentrated among groups which traditionally earn a low wage. Column 5 of table 2 shows the personal characteristics of those who earned the net minimum wage (1.20 million zloty per month after taxes) or less in November 1992. Also presented is the distribution of workers by age and education. These figures are compared to the distribution of three other groups: the entire labor force (column 2), all employed labor (column 3), and the unemployed (column 4). Although women, those who have not completed any higher education, and part-time workers are the most likely to earn the minimum wage, table 2 also shows that minimum wage earners are not as heavily concentrated among any one demographic group as is the case in most OECD countries where minimum wage earners tend to be disproportionately young. Mellor (1987) reports that, in the United States, teenagers between the ages of 16 and 19 were

the most heavily represented group of minimum wage earners, comprising 36.6 percent (1.85 million) of all minimum wage earners. The next largest age group were young adults between 20 and 24 who made up 22.9 percent (1.16 million). Surprisingly, this is not the case in Poland. In November 1992, almost three years into the transition process, 12.6 percent of *all* employed workers, both hourly and salaried,[5] reported earning the minimum wage or less. Of those, only 10.45 percent were between 15 and 20, and 12.59 percent were between 21 and 25. The remainder, 76.96 percent, were over age 25.

In both Poland and the United States women comprise a large percentage of minimum wage earners, 61.7 and 65.6 percent respectively. However, in Poland 16.9 percent of *all* employed women earn the minimum wage or less as opposed to only 11.9 percent of women being paid on an *hourly* basis in the United States. If salaried employees were included in the U.S. estimates, as is the case for Poland, this per-

---

5. The figure cited excludes own account workers and unpaid household workers.

Table 2.   Characteristics of Minimum Wage Earners and of the Labor Force in Poland[a]

	Unemployment Rate	Distribution of entire labor force	Distribution of all employed labor[b]	Distribution of all unemployed	Distribution of minimum wage earners (1.2 million zl. Per month or less)[c]
Education:					
Higher Degree Completed)	6.00%	8.76%	12.35%	3.52%	4.50%
Higher (Degree Not Completed)	10.06	3.58	5.11	2.43	3.00
Secondary	18.40	5.96	6.85	7.38	6.43
Technical	14.91	21.93	24.99	22.01	18.06
Vocational	18.66	32.75	33.71	41.13	33.65
Primary or Less	12.92	27.02	17.00	23.53	34.35
Age:					
15-20	37.69%	6.17%	3.59%	16.07%	10.45%
21-25	24.78	10.18	10.15	16.98	12.59
26-30	17.69	11.28	12.13	13.43	9.38
31-35	14.00	14.93	16.69	14.06	13.72
36-40	12.50	16.93	19.05	14.24	13.61
41-45	11.51	14.91	17.23	11.55	12.81
46-50	9.88	8.47	9.61	5.63	8.74
51-55	8.20	6.85	6.91	3.78	6.81
Over 55	6.14	10.28	4.64	4.26	11.89
Personal Characteristics:					
Male	13.38	53.89	54.04	48.54	38.26
Student	9.97	1.40	0.64	0.94	3.54
Part-time employee	—	—	5.31	—	30.17
Sample Size	—	25809	14852	3834	1868

a.   Based on the November 1992 Labor Force Survey.

b.   Figures for employed groups are based on full and part-time employees. Own account workers and unpaid domestic workers are excluded. Unemployed workers are defined as individuals who are not currently working but are actively seeking employment. The unemployed are not necessarily registered as such.

c.   Based on a 40 hour work week.

centage would undoubtedly fall. In general, because a larger cross-section of Poland's population is affected by the minimum wage, mainstream theory should be reflected in lower employment overall, rather than for specific groups. For this reason the empirical work described in the following section will concentrate on the entire labor force.

MINIMUM WAGE AND REGIONAL LABOR MARKETS

According to Deere et al. (1995), a minimum wage increase will have the strongest impact on employment where its effects on wages is the largest. In other words, the demographic groups and geographic regions most adversely affected by a wage floor are those which are comprised of a large percentage of low wage earners. The evidence is overwhelming that

in the United States teenagers are the lowest paid and the most adversely affected demographic group. Because both the minimum wage and unemployment benefits are uniform across the country and do not reflect regional wage or cost of living differences, a high minimum wage may have the strongest impact on Poland's low-wage regions.

Poland's 49 regions (called voivodships) exhibit large disparities in unemployment, average wage, degree of urbanization, and industrialization. For example, in February 1996 regional unemployment varied from 5.4 percent to 29.4 percent. In comparison, regional dispersion of unemployment is far lower in the United States where in 1990 it ranged from 2.2 percent to 8.3 percent. Because average wages also vary widely by region, the proposition that employment in some of Poland's regions is more adversely affected by a universal minimum wage is supported. For example, in the second quarter of 1995 the minimum wage as a percentage of local average wage ranged from 29.0 percent to 60.3 percent.[6] By comparison, in the United States in 1990 this percentage ranged from 23.1 percent to 38.1 percent.[7]

A region may become low-wage and suffer from high unemployment after experiencing an adverse shock. As mentioned, Poland experienced several shocks during the first few years of transition. As the dispersion of unemployment and wage rates indicate, some regions were more adversely affected than others. This being the case, the relevant question to address is whether the presence of an increasing and universal minimum wage worsened the shocks and/or slowed recovery. Using the United States as an example, Blanchard and Katz (1992) find that the most important factor for a state's recovery from an adverse shock is outward migration. Migration within transitional Poland has not been widely studied, but the results of all recent Labor Force Surveys indicate that only 24 to 28 percent of the unemployed are *willing* to relocate. Since individuals under 35 years of age comprise about 60 percent of the unemployed, and since early retirement forced many out of the labor force, the low willingness to relocate cannot simply be attributed to older people who are traditionally less geographically mobile. Housing shortages may offer one of the more likely explanations for geographic immobility. During central-planning Poland experienced considerable housing shortages where 15 to 20 year waiting lists for government subsidized housing were the norm (Mayo and Stein 1995). Additionally, large differences in the regional cost of living, and consequently in the value of cash

benefits, may also contribute to low internal migration.

In order to determine whether a minimum wage increase does indeed decrease employment and increase unemployment, table 3 presents the results of several regressions. Because of the importance of regional differences, the cross-sectional impact of minimum wage increases as well as changes through time must be taken into account. For this reason quarterly pooled data from each of Poland's 49 regions from the first quarter of 1991 to the second quarter of 1995 is used.

Minimum wage studies using pooled data are rare but offer several advantages. Because regions vary in the degree to which they experienced shocks, and because labor mobility is low, the minimum wage may have a stronger local impact than national-level data could reveal. Ideally, many of these differences may be captured if the minimum wage is measured in terms of local price indices. Because such indices are currently unavailable, the minimum wage is represented relative to the local average wage. Unfortunately, regional average wage data covering all sectors of the economy is also unavailable. A weighted measure of local average monthly earnings in the industrial and construction sectors was created and was used to determine the relative minimum wage. Williams (1993) uses a similar technique but relies on average wages in manufacturing rather than industry and construction. Regional dummy variables are included in each regression to control for differences in employment and unemployment between *voivodships* which are not accounted for by other variables. A variable which measures the percent of the population residing in urban areas is also included in several regressions.

---

6. For Poland, the average and minimum wages used to determine these ratios are pre-tax. Due to data limitations, the average wage is based on *all* labor in the industrial and construction sectors only. Sample includes forty nine *voivodships*.

7. For the United States, average wage is determined by considering both full- and part-time workers. Sample includes all fifty states and the District of Columbia.

Table 3. Pooled Time-Series Cross-Sectional[a]

	1	2	3	4	5	6
	Dependent Variable: Log (Regional Employment Rate)			Dependent Variable: Log (Regional Unemployment Rate)		
Constant	-5.686	-5.621	-1.502	4.247	4.196	4.542
	(-21.143)	(-20.704)	(-23.651)	(11.851)	(11.025)	(57.912)
Log(Minimum Wage/Local Average Wage)	-0.592	-0.538	-0.502	2.143	2.015	2.018
	(-11.858)	(-11.032)	(-9.071)	(32.200)	(29.457)	(29.539)
Log(Percent Residing in Urban Areas)	0.946	0.943	—	0.092	0.079	—
	(15.720)	(15.504)		(1.153)	(0.932)	
Seasonal Dummies[b]	Yes	No	No	Yes	No	No
Regional Dummies (Voivodship Level)[c]	Yes	Yes	Yes	Yes	Yes	Yes
R²	0.490	0.476	0.324	0.838	0.815	0.815
Adjusted R²	0.458	0.444	0.284	0.827	0.804	0.804
F-statistic	15.019	15.069	8.131	80.576	73.312	74.802
Observations	882	882	882	882	882	882
Dates	1991.Q1-1995.Q2	1991.Q1-1995.Q2	1991.Q1-1995.Q2	1991.Q1-1995.Q2	1991.Q1-1995.Q2	1991.Q1-1995.Q2

a.   t-statistics are in parenthesis.

b.   Winter is in the base

c.   Gdansk is in the base.

Table 3 presents regressions which assess the impact of the minimum wage on the employment rate.[8] In magnitude, the results are stronger than those of studies of the United States which rely on pooled data. Using a similar measure of relative minimum wage, Williams (1993) estimated the elasticities of teenage employment with respect to relative minimum wage ranging from -0.182 to -0.333. In the first three columns of table 3 the elasticity of employment with respect to relative minimum wages ranges from -0.502 to -0.592. All estimates of the minimum wage are significant. These results also reveal that the more urbanized regions experience a higher employment rate. The reason for this may be that urban regions have a greater mix of industries than rural areas (see Scarpetta 1995). When a particular sector suffers a shock, unemployed labor can be more easily absorbed by a growing sector when migration is not necessary.

Columns four through six of table 3 also present the results of identical least-squares regressions which use the unemployment rate as a dependent variable. In each regression the minimum wage was significant and varied in elasticity from 2.015 to 2.143. Whether an area is urban or not has no impact on unemployment. As is the case in virtually all such studies, the effect of the minimum wage appears to be stronger on unemployment than on employment.

In order to further consider the effect of the minimum wage on local labor markets, 98 separate regressions, one for each region, were run. In each case, the employment rate and the unemployment rate were alternately used as the dependent variable. The elasticities of employment with respect to the relative minimum wage varied from -0.26 to -1.23, with the 39 estimates being significant. The elasticities of unemployment varied from 1.02 to 4.15, with 43 estimates being significant. Both sets of regression results confirmed a large degree of regional disparity.

Minimum Wage and Labor Input

Most countries base minimum wages on hourly remuneration. However in Poland the stated objective of the minimum wage is to serve as a minimum level of *monthly* remuneration for full-time employment (Hagemejer 1995). Even though it is based on

---

8.   Ideally the employment rate should be measured as the ratio of employment to working age population. Due to data limitations the ratio of total employment divided by total population is considered instead.

monthly remuneration, the minimum wage law covers all labor in the formal sector and does not distinguish between hourly and salary workers or between full- and part-time workers. Of particular interest is the fact that 30.2 percent of the individuals who earned the minimum wage or less in November 1992 were part-time workers (less than 40 hours per week). During this same period, only 5.4 percent of all employed labor held a part-time job as their primary source of employment (see table 2). By comparison, 25.6 percent of U.S. hourly workers are employed part-time.[9] The fact that Poland's minimum wage is based on monthly remuneration may preclude legitimate part-time employment for all but the most skilled and may in large part explain any noncompliance. According to the most recent labor force surveys, most individuals who work part-time do so out of choice, not because of a shortage of jobs. The May 1995 Labor Force Survey reports that 83.8 percent of all part-time labor worked part-time for "non-economic" reasons.

An important point which was overlooked by Card and Krueger (1995) is that when policy makers increase an *hourly* minimum wage employers may respond by reducing the total number of hours employees work. Because Poland's minimum wage is based on *monthly* earnings, a more likely response would be to *increase* the number of worker-hours for low skilled labor as well as reducing the number of employees. By doing so employers would attempt to maintain the same *effective hourly wage* and the total labor input. Because this would primarily effect lower-skilled individuals, it should be reflected in the distribution of hours by education.

The strong negative correlation between education and hours worked shown in table 4 confirms that employees who had completed at least some higher education are more likely to work less than 40 hours per week than those with less education. This suggests that employers may indeed change effective

hourly wages by changing hours. It may also explain why 5.4 percent of those who have had at least some university level education are minimum wage earners.[10]

Table 4. Hours and Education[a]

Dependent Variable	Hours	Log(hours)
Constant	39.910	3.662
	(155.870)	(455.006)
Higher Education	-4.348	-0.160
	(-13.615)	(-15.895)
Some Higher	-4.646	-0.147
	(-11.881)	(-11.941)
Secondary	—	—
Technical	0.940	0.030
	(3.254)	(3.290)
Vocational	2.060	0.060
	(7.339)	(6.806)
Primary	0.876	0.016
	(2.883)	(1.700)
Less than Primary	0.162	-0.034
	(0.122)	(-0.815)
R^2	0.072	0.080
adjusted R^2	0.072	0.080
F-statistic	190.642	215.103
Observations	14786	14786

a. From the November 1992 Labor Force Survey.

Minimum Wage and Unemployment Benefits

Pre-reform Poland officially denied the existence of unemployment and consequently deemed unemployment insurance unnecessary. Anticipating a certain degree of joblessness the central government established a cash benefits system on December 29, 1989. This original system had several major flaws, the most prominent of which was a significant moral hazard problem. Because any jobless individual claiming to be in the labor force was eligible for benefits, and because the minimum available compensation was excessively generous, by the end of 1990 the number of unemployed applying for benefits was greater than the number of those laid off (Chilosi 1993). During this time the Public Auditing Chamber had discovered what had become common

---

9. It should be noted that U.S. surveys usually consider anything less than 35 hours part-time. If less than 40 hours were considered part-time, as is the case for Poland, the estimate would be greater.

10. When the "monthly minimum wage" is coverted into its hourly equivalent (assuming a 40 hour work-week), less than one percent of individuals who have completed university earn the minimum wage.

practice—employed individuals collecting unemployment benefits. Although estimates are not available, a significant percentage of recipients may have entered the labor force simply to claim benefits. By October 1991 new rules were implemented requiring proof of attachment to the labor force. Because of this rule 21 percent of recipients became ineligible (Chilosi 1993).

By February 1992 the old cash benefits system was abolished and the current unemployment benefits system was fully implemented. The new system includes a 12 month duration limit,[11] and four "flat-rates." The benefit level an individual receives is primarily determined by previous employment status, method of job loss, and age. Currently, the four levels of unemployment compensation are:[12] (1) 36 percent of the average national wage, (2) 95 percent of the minimum wage, (3) 110 percent of the minimum wage, and (4) 125 percent of the minimum wage. The great majority of the unemployed qualify for the first level. Because the benefit levels are nearly equivalent across individuals, the system is such that an individual who earned a high income in his/her previous job will receive a lower replacement rate than one who earned a lower previous income. Consequently, the individual who previously had a low income will experience lower job-search incentives. According to the World Bank (1995), the problem is being worsened because throughout the transition period the increase in the average wage has been driven by increases in white-collar wages—the upper tail of the earnings distribution. For this reason the average wage does not adequately represent the wages of less skilled workers. Consequently the replacement rate may approach 100 percent for many unskilled workers.

Because Poland's unemployment benefits system is based on flat-levels, it is obvious that income replacement alone is not an objective. The minimum wage and unemployment benefits create an income maintenance system which, in practice, guarantees a minimum income to most labor force participants whether or not they work. Assuming that income and leisure are both normal goods, when choosing between labor and leisure, a guaranteed minimum income may encourage an individual to rationally choose unemployment rather than employment. The objective of unemployment benefits is to restore lost income whereas the goal of income maintenance, or welfare, is to increase the income of the poorest households to a certain level. This may indeed be happening, but at a cost of greater unemployment.

Poland's minimum wage system may impede regional recovery in two ways: (1) indirectly, through unemployment benefits; and (2) directly, by preventing the wage rate from falling sufficiently. Beneficiaries in low-wage regions receive the same nominal level of compensation as those in high wage regions. If the recipient in a low-wage region does not migrate, their benefits may retain a higher value in relative terms. The incentive to migrate is further lowered because beneficiaries are technically required to reside in their own region. Second, because employment will start to recover from an adverse shock once wages fall low enough, a high minimum wage may prevent wages from falling sufficiently.

LESSONS FOR CUBA

The Polish case may offer several lessons for post-communist Cuba. First, the results and discussion in the previous section suggest that the minimum wage is not an effective poverty prevention tool. In Poland the minimum wage, coupled with unemployment benefits, creates an "absolute wage floor." This strategy may be *somewhat* effective in preventing poverty but it also creates very strong work disincentives which result in higher national unemployment, greater unemployment among the less skilled, greater dispersion in regional unemployment, and a heavier burden on government. It is also likely that, because wages are prevented from adjusting downward, regional recovery from adverse shocks may be impeded.

---

11. There are exceptions to this rule. In especially impoverished regions the duration may be extended to 18 or 24 months.

12. See World Bank (1993) for further details.

Second, when formulating minimum wage policy it is important to consider what groups are most likely to suffer employment loss. In order to minimize job loss the most adversely affected groups or industries should face a separate (lower) wage floor. For example, it has been suggested that if a nationally determined minimum wage has a detrimental effect in certain regions, or if the cost of living differs between regions, then it may be most appropriate to determine minimum wages on a more local level (OECD 1995). In effect, the United States has a similar system. The federal government sets a minimum wage and individual state governments may increase it. It has been suggested that labor mobility in Cuba may already be impeded by housing shortages (Buttari 1994). If this is indeed the case, then labor immobility may lead to regional employment disparities in post-communist Cuba. Minimum wages determined on a more local level may then be an appropriate policy.

The third issue which must be addressed is compliance with wage floors. Transitional Cuba will not only be a previously centrally planned economy, but also a developing economy. One of the most common problems with minimum wages in developing countries is noncompliance (Watanabe 1976; Gindling and Terrell 1995). It is uncertain to what degree this is a problem in Poland but, a recent study by Gindling and Terrell (1995) has shown that in the early 1980s noncompliance in Costa Rica was as high as 33 percent. This problem is more likely to occur when the laws are too complicated, as in Costa Rica where in 1980 there were 350 separate minimum wages, or when the minimum wage is especially high. Compliance may also be an issue in economies with a large agricultural sector where adequate enforcement is difficult if not impossible.

Finally, the minimum wage should be determined on an hourly basis and should eventually be set at a level closer to that of the United States, perhaps 25 percent of average hourly wage. When minimum wages are lower and regulations less stringent, the resulting employment loss is minimized and non-compliance a much less important issue.

RERERENCES

Blanchard, Olivier Jean, and Lawrence F. Katz. "Regional Evolutions," *Brookings Papers on Economic Activity*, 1: 1992, pp. 1-75.

Brown, Charles, Curtis Gilroy and Andrew Kohen. "The Effect of the Minimum Wage on Employment and Unemployment," *Journal of Economic Literature*, vol. XX, June 1982, pp. 487-528.

Buttari, Juan J. "The Labor Market and Retirement Pensions in Cuba During Transition: Reflection on the Social Safety Net Experience of Former Socialist Economies," in *Cuba in Transition — Volume 4* (Washington: Associaton for the Study of the Cuban Economy, 1994), pp. 80-88.

Card, David and Alan B. Krueger. *Myth and Measurement: The New Economics of the Minimum Wage* (Princeton: Princeton University Press, 1995).

Chilosi, Alberto. "Economic Transition and the Unemployment Issue," *Economic Systems*, vol. 17, no. 1, March 1993, pp. 63-78.

Deere, Donald, Kevin M, Murphy, and Finis Welch. "Employment and the 1990-1991 Minimum-Wage Hike," *American Economic Review*, vol. 85, no 2, May 1995, pp. 232-237.

Gindling, T.H. and Katherine Terrell. "The Nature of Minimum Wages and Their Effectiveness as a Wage Floor in Costa Rica, 1976-91," *World Development*, vol. 23, no. 8, 1995, pp. 1439-1458.

Glowny Urzad Statystyczny. *Aktywnosc Ekonomiczna Ludnosci Polski (Economic Activity of the Population of Poland)*, August 1993, November 1993,

February 1994, May 1994, August 1994, November 1994 (Warsaw).

Glowny Urzad Statystyczny. *Bezrobocie Rejestrowane W Polsce (Registered Unemployment in Poland)*, various issues, (Warsaw).

Glowny Urzad Statystyczny. *Biuletyn Statystyczny (Statistical Bulletin)*, volumes 34-39 (Warsaw 1989-1995).

Glowny Urzad Statystyczny. Polish Labor Force Survey, Warsaw (November 1992 data set).

Hagemejer, Krzysztof. "What Role for the Minimum Wage in the New Polish Labour Market?" in *Minimum Wages in Central and Eastern Europe: From Protection to Destitution*, edited by Guy Standing and Daniel Vaughan-Whitehead (Central European University Press, c1995), chapter 4, pp. 68-84.

Hamermesh, Daniel S. "Comment on: 'Myth and Measurement: The New Economics of the Minimum Wage,'" *Industrial and Labor Relations Review*, vol. 48, no 4, July 1995, pp. 835-838.

Kennan, John. "The Elusive Effects of Minimum Wages," *Journal of Economic Literature*, vol. XXXIII, December 1995, pp. 1949-1965.

Mayo, Stephen K. and James I. Stein. "Housing and Labor Market Distortions in Poland: Linkages and Policy Implications," *Journal of Housing Economics*, vol. 4, pp. 153-182, (1995).

Mellor, Earl F. "Workers at the Minimum Wage or Less: Who are They and the Jobs They Hold," *Monthly Labor Review*, 111, 1987, pp. 34-8.

Organization for Economic Cooperation and Development. *The OECD Jobs Study: Evidence and Explanations, Part II - The Adjustment Potential of the Labour Market* (Paris: OECD, 1995).

Scarpetta, Stefano. "Spatial Variations in Unemployment in Central and Eastern Europe: Underlying Reasons and Labour Market Policy Options," in *The Regional Dimension of Unemployment in Transition Countries* (Paris: Centre for Cooperation with the Economies in Transition, OECD, 1995), pp. 27-54.

Standing, Guy. "What Role for Minimum Wages in the Flexible Labour Markets of the 21st Century?" in *Minimum Wages in Central and Eastern Europe: From Protection to Destitution*, edited by Guy Standing and Daniel Vaughan-Whitehead (Central European University Press, c1995), pp. 7-14.

Vaughan-Whitehead, Daniel. "Minimum Wages in Central and Eastern Europe: Slippage of the Anchor," in *Minimum Wages in Central and Eastern Europe: from Protection to Destitution*, edited by Guy Standing and Daniel Vaughan-Whitehead (Central European University Press, c1995), chapter 2, pp. 15-48.

Watanabe, Susumu. "Minimum Wages In Developing Countries: Myth and Reality," *International Labor Review*, vol. 113, no. 3, May-June 1976, pp. 345-358.

Welch, Finis. "Comment on: 'Myth and Measurement: The New Economics of the Minimum Wage,'" *Industrial and Labor Relations Review*, vol. 48, no 4, July 1995, pp. 842-849.

Williams, Nicolas. "Regional Effects of the Minimum Wage on Teenage Employment," *Applied Economics*, 25, 1993, pp. 1517-1528.

World Bank. *Poland: Income Support and the Social Safety Net During the Transition* (Washington: World Bank, 1993).

World Bank, *Understanding Poverty in Poland* (Washington: World Bank, July 1995).

COMMENTS ON

"The Minimum Wage and Unemployment In Poland: Lessons for Cuba's Transition" by Melnyk

Ernesto Hernández-Catá[1]

This is an important paper on an important topic. The author convincingly argues, on the basis of both theory and careful empirical work, that Poland's minimum wage scheme has contributed to that country's high rate of unemployment and has hindered an otherwise successful process of transition. I agree with this conclusion. The lessons are important for Poland, and they are important for all countries in transition, present or future. Cuba, in particular, will not be able to afford labor market policies that keep unemployment high at a time when wage flexibility will be needed to smooth the transition and when budgetary resources will be scarce. Melnyk's conclusion also is important and timely because it comes at a time when the economic profession's broad consensus about the damaging effects of minimum wages on employment has been challenged as part of the debate that preceded and influenced the recent decision to raise the minimum wage in the United States.

Since I found Melnyk's technical analysis to be thorough and since I agree with his conclusions I will limit myself to some comments on the policy dimensions of minimum wage laws.

One way to start is to ask why anyone would want to impose minimum wages. In Poland, Melnyk tells us, the minimum wage had four main functions: (i) it was used by state enterprises to determine pay scales; and it was used by the government to (ii) calculate social benefits; (iii) to influence the overall level of wages; and (iv) to prevent poverty.

The first function, to assist state enterprises in setting the pay scales, should be rejected as being contradictory with the aim of reform--which is to allow relative prices and relative wages to be determined by market conditions and not by administrative formulae. The second function is unnecessary: social benefits can be targeted to specified personal income thresholds without any need to legislate a floor on wages. Indeed, Melnyk argues convincingly that the interaction between the minimum wage and the unemployment insurance system in Poland may well have induced individuals to voluntarily choose unemployment over work. The third function is to use minimum wages as an instrument of wage control, and this is an area where great damage can be inflicted.

When the process of transition to a market economy begins in earnest—in other words when prices are decontrolled—enterprises will find themselves in one of two categories: (i) those that produce goods for which demand has dropped (dramatically in those cases where prices had been kept well below equilibriumbrium levels before decontrol); and (ii)

---

1. The views expressed in this comment are those of the author and not necessarily those of the IMF.

those that produce goods for which demand has increased. In a situation in which inter-enterprise movement of labor is costly (for psycho-sociological reasons, because of imperfections in housing markets or for other reasons), rigid sectoral wages will prevent the "losing" enterprises from reducing labor costs and thus will force an unduly large fall in output. Indeed, empirical evidence recently provided by Thierry Pujol [2] strongly suggests that in Poland relative wage rigidity in the face of large changes in relative prices contributed significantly to the fall in employment and output. This is, of course, fully consistent with Melnyk's results. The fact that minimum wages in Poland were so high, applied to such a large proportion of the labor force and were revised so often suggests that these legal minima contributed significantly to *overall* wage rigidity.

It is probably not a coincidence that in countries like Russia where minimum wages were revised less frequently than in Poland and were binding for a much smaller proportion of the workforce, the fall in output was accompanied with a much more limited rise in the unemployment rate. One possible explanation may be that in Russia the largely Party-affiliated labor unions were co-victims of the collapse of communist power and, with the exception of the coal miners, played virtually no role in economic decision-making in the subsequent reform period. In contrast, Polish unions played a key role in the demise of the communist system and thus an important role in the reform process. Indeed, Melnyk tells us that the minimum wage in Poland is no longer set by the government only but is determined jointly by the Ministry of Labor and the trade unions. This, of course, is like asking the bear to guard the barrel of honey.

The process of transition unavoidably involves a temporary drop in output. This is because within the group of enterprises for which demand falls there is a sub-group that produces goods that nobody wants and under the new set of relative prices these enterprises will have negative value added. The question faced by policy-makers is not how to avoid the contraction of the junk-goods producing sector, but how to facilitate a rapid redeployment of resources from this sector to more productive enterprises, thus making the fall in aggregate output as short and shallow as possible. This will require cutting subsidies and administrative credits to the junk-producing enterprises, but also eliminating barriers to inter-enterprise and inter-regional labor mobility, and removing those factors that reduce the incentives faced by profitable enterprises to expand the supply of jobs. Here again, the Polish minimum wage law appears to be an example of what not to do.

Let me now turn to the fourth alleged reason for minimum wages, which is to help the poor. Clearly, the minimum wage is a suboptimal way to achieve that goal. There is a way to redistribute income towards the poor without introducing a distortion in the labor market and without harming employment, i.e., through the tax system. A good example of that is the earned income credit in the United States, which is really a form of negative income tax. No one in the United States denies that this is a better system. Why then, have so many voted to increase the minimum wage? One answer that has been given is that a rise in the minimum wage does not increase unemployment. That's the wrong answer. There is now a substantial body of empirical evidence—of which Melnyk's paper is an example—indicating that minimum wages have significantly negative effects on employment whenever and wherever they are imposed.

The second answer is that the effect is small. Yet, a recent study by the IMF's North American Division concludes that an increase in the U.S. minimum wage of 90 cents per hour (from $4.25 to $5.15 per hour)—as has been recently approved—would result in job losses of 100,000 to 300,000 workers. [3] This may be considered "small," but if you are one of the job losers that will not do much to comfort you.

---

2. *The Role of Labor Market Rigidities During the Transition: Lessons from Poland,* IMF Working Paper WP/96/77, June 1996.

3. Alun Thomas, *The Cyclical Position of the U.S. Economy and Its Relationship with Inflation,* IMF Working Paper (forthcoming).

So, why minimum wages? Politicians sometimes have reasons that are difficult for reason to grasp. But I suspect that one reason is income redistribution—not from the rich to the poor, but rather from the outsider to the insider, from the unemployed to the employed, from the teenage non-voter to the adult voter.

Cuba's future transition, like any process of economic transformation, will get special interest groups lobbying for privileges of all kinds, and it will be the task of economists to keep the global interests of society in mind. At some point pressures for minimum wage legislation probably will arise under the banner of social justice. Economists will then need to make it clear to politicians that they will be responsible for the increase in joblessness that will result, particularly among the youngest and less skilled members of society, and for its' social and budgetary consequences. If the idea of a minimum wage cannot be killed, economists will have to argue for a system that minimizes adverse effects on employment—in other words a system that exempts the young (or at least assigns to them a lower wage floor, like in Canada); that is based on *hourly* earnings rather than on *monthly* earnings, unlike in Poland; and that keeps the gap between legal minimum and market-determined wages as narrow as possible.

ALTERNATIVE POLICIES TO DEAL WITH LABOR SURPLUSES DURING THE CUBAN TRANSITION[1]

Joseph M. Perry, Louis A. Woods and Jeffrey W. Steagall

It is axiomatic that an aging, centrally-planned economy, such as the Castro administration has nurtured in Cuba, will suffer from underemployment or labor redundancy. Because most economic decisions are made by a central planning agency, the economic system exhibits both distributive and allocative inefficiency. Such an economy suffers from hidden unemployment as well as underemployment. The government guarantees workers lifetime jobs, regardless of the level of aggregate demand, and often places workers in positions ill-suited to their training and qualifications.

Recent changes in Cuba's international relations with other countries, including the loss of economic support from the former Communist Bloc countries and the tightening of the United States embargo, have added to the island's normal economic ills that stem from central planning. Slow economic growth, limited foreign exchange, and reduced access to markets for supplies and replacement parts have forced the Cuban government to adopt policies that have moved the economic system slightly toward a capitalist orientation. This movement has not been accompanied by a perceptible softening of central control and government intervention in the marketplace. The result is a growing number of unemployed Cubans, a labor surplus in an economy that is never supposed to suffer from this malady. The Castro administration is now confronted with the problem of finding employment for these displaced workers in an economy that cannot accommodate them.

THE CUBAN ECONOMY AND LABOR MARKET

Córdova (1994) argues that the Cuban economy has been operating under a Stalinist model. In such an economy, both employers and labor organizations, such as unions, become subservient to the state (and to the Communist Party). Córdova lists the following additional characteristics of the Stalinist model:

1. Work is a right, a duty, and a source of pride for every citizen.

2. Non-paid voluntary work for the benefit of society is regarded as an important element of the system.

3. Brigades, micro-brigades, and other forms of militarizing labor are used.

4. Self-employment is looked upon with disapproval as all production efforts are supposed to be carried out for the government.

5. Workers are constantly subjected to an intensive system of social mobilization intended to maintain the "heroic" tempo of the revolution.

---

1. This is a revised version of the longer paper presented at the 1996 ASCE Annual Meetings. Some portions of this study appeared in an earlier paper, "Planning for a Free Market Labor Force in Post-Transition Cuba," presented at the Allied Social Science Association meetings in San Francisco, California, January 4-7, 1996.

6. Strikes are prohibited and free and voluntary collective bargaining disappears (p. 145).

The only sectors of the Cuban economy that would depart from this model are the tourist industry, various joint ventures involving foreign investors, and the underground or secondary economy.

Svejnar and Pérez-López (1993) confirm the similarity of the Cuban economy to those of the former Communist Bloc nations. They identify the major features of the socialist economies of the 1980's as follows:

[T]he limited existence and functioning of domestic markets; an openness to regulated trade within the CMEA, together with isolation from other international markets; centrally controlled prices; perverse economic incentives that encouraged inefficiency; policy imperatives such as the maintenance of full employment irrespective of labor productivity in a given use; ill-defined property rights within the state or social ownership system; and the virtual absence of institutions essential to market-related activities such as banking, accounting, auditing, and taxation. These common conditions resulted in misallocated resources, little incentive to innovate and maintain infrastructure and capital equipment, low incomes and productivity, and macroeconomic instability (p. 342).

UNEMPLOYMENT AND UNDEREMPLOYMENT IN CUBA

In an ideally-planned socialist economy, only frictional unemployment should exist, as the government shifts labor resources from one employment to another. In Cuba, the 1992 Constitution unequivocally guarantees employment and income for every able-bodied worker. Section 9(b) reads as follows:

El Estado como poder del pueblo, en servicio del propio pueblo, garantiza que no haya hombre o mujer, en condiciones de trabajar, que no tenga oportunidad de obtener un empleo con el cual pueda contribuir a los fines de la sociedad y a la satisfacción de sus propias necesidades.

Full employment is clearly not the norm in real-world economies, however. Porket (1989) suggests that command socialist systems suffer from almost all of the unemployment ills of market capitalist systems (some of them not officially admitted), and com-

pound the situation by widespread overmanning (Porket's term for labor redundancy or underemployment). He observes that

. . . market capitalism is prone to the more visible open unemployment (combined with an economical use of the employed labor force), whereas command socialism is prone to the less visible hidden unemployment (combined with open unregistered unemployment and a continuous demand for additional labour). This describes the differences between them more accurately than saying . . . that while unemployment is a basic problem of capitalism, labour shortage is a basic problem of socialism (p. 19).

Based upon current news reports, it can be concluded that Cuba suffers from all of the unemployment and underemployment ills listed by Porket, but, interestingly, does not now have a labor shortage.

THE CUBAN ECONOMY BEFORE THE REVOLUTION

During the 1950's, Cuba exhibited a contradictory picture to observers. In spite of Cuba's apparently favorable economic situation, relative to its Caribbean and Central American neighbors, it suffered from serious internal socioeconomic problems. Carmelo Mesa-Lago identifies the following: (1) low rates of economic growth; (2) the dominant role of sugar as a generator of income and foreign exchange; (3) extreme dependence upon the United States for capital and markets; (4) high rates of unemployment and underemployment; and (5) extreme differences between urban and rural standards of living (cited in Azicri, 1988, 36).

Between 1953 and 1959, while the Cuban population grew at an average annual rate of 2 percent, the labor force increased at about 1.8 percent per year. Brundenius (1984, 133-134) estimates the 1960 labor force to include 2.276 million persons, of whom 86.8 percent were male. At that time, the estimated national unemployment rate was 11.8 percent. By comparison, annual unemployment rates in the United States during the 1950's ranged between 2.9 and 6.8 percent, with the higher rates occurring during the recessions of 1953-54 and 1957-58 (United States Bureau of Labor Statistics, 1975, 145).

Ritter (1974) attributes the high unemployment rates of the 1950's to rapid population growth, slow job creation, a bias toward imports in Cuban consumption patterns, inappropriate imported technology, and high barriers to entry in urban industrial labor markets. Seasonal patterns in unemployment were also evident, with rates rising after the sugar harvest had taken place. Other crop seasons, including those for tobacco, coffee, rice, and vegetables contributed to the seasonality in a less pronounced fashion (p. 50).

LABOR DURING THE REVOLUTION AND AFTERWARD

The revolution that Fidel Castro led from 1953 through 1959 brought significant changes to Cuba. Although the Castro government attempted to diversify the Cuban economy after 1959, moving away from sugar in agriculture and encouraging the development of light industry (consumer goods, in particular), the initiative failed. Governmental policies attempted to force the Cuban economy away from those goods and services in which there was a comparative advantage. The inexorable and predictable response of international markets was quite damaging. Declining earnings from sugar exports, combined with the United States embargo and Soviet trade pressure, served to move Cuba back toward a primary dependence upon sugar. Pérez-López (1991) concludes that "management of the Cuban economy by the revolutionary government over the last twenty-five years appears to have had a marginal impact in changing the structure of the economy to reduce the role of the sugar industry. . . . Moreover, Cuba's plans to increase sugar production . . . virtually assure that the industry will continue to play a predominant role in the economy" (p. 228).

It is also clear that Cuba suffered from the recessions that hit other countries in 1960-1961 and 1970-1971. A third sharp recession hit the island by mid-1979, triggering the Mariel exodus of approximately 125,000 persons. Although the Castro government had permitted some liberalization of economic activity, allowing both produce and handicraft markets to flourish, encouraging state enterprises to exercise more independence, and encouraging labor produc-

tivity through wage incentives, the economy was performing more slowly as the 1980's arrived. By the middle of the decade, Castro decided on structural reform.

In 1986, he proclaimed a rectification process (*proceso de rectificación de errores y tendencias negativas*) that was designed to move Cuba back toward a full-blown socialist system. Free markets were discouraged, personal wage incentives were abolished, and state enterprises were warned to toe the socialist line. Not surprisingly, the Cuban economy dropped into recession in 1986-1987, and has never recovered (Bethell, 1993, 107-115).

Mesa-Lago (1981) describes the path of unemployment as follows:

> Open unemployment stood at about 12 percent of the labor force in 1958, increased in 1959, and reached a peak of 20 percent early in 1960; thereafter it declined to a low of 1.3 percent in 1970. Unemployment increased in the early 1970's, peaked in 1974, declined again possibly until 1978, and increased in 1979-1980 (p. 189).

Brundenius (1984) takes a contrary view, arguing that the overall unemployment rate showed a rising trend from 1970 until 1979 (1.3 percent to 5.4 percent), largely because of rapidly increasing female unemployment. Since Marxist regimes typically encourage increased female participation in the labor force, the higher participation rate may contribute to the unemployment Brundenius identifies.

THE CUBAN ECONOMY AS IT ENTERED THE 1990'S

Ritter (1994) points out that the Fourth Congress of the Cuban Communist Party, held in 1991, ratified a new economic plan that emphasized import substitution, export promotion, energy substitution to handle the lack of petroleum, programs to encourage foreign investment, management reforms to increase efficiency, and greater decentralization of business firm decision-making. This complex of policies and programs was formulated in direct reaction to the loss of subsidization by the former Soviet Union and the debilitating effects on the economy of the United States trade embargo (pp. 69, 75-76).

Although recent events, such as the "dollarization" of the Cuban economy, and the adoption of a liberalized foreign investment law in September, 1995, suggest more than cosmetic changes in the Cuban system, the basic socialist structure has persisted. Economic policy is set by the Council of State, headed by Fidel Castro. The Central Planning Board (JUCEPLAN), together with the Banco Nacional de Cuba, administer that policy and establish specific price levels and target levels for production and trade. All of the legal industrial enterprises in Cuba are still state-owned and/or operated, with the exception of some joint ventures with foreigners. Agriculture is still largely socialized, with state farms holding 70 percent of farmland, peasant cooperatives holding 20 percent, and private farms holding the remaining 10 percent (U. S. Department of State, 1993 and 1994).

THE IMPORTANCE OF BROKEN TIES WITH EASTERN NATIONS

Two key factors dominate recent Cuban economic history. The first is the strengthened U. S. embargo, newly supported by the Helms-Burton Act. The second is the breakup of the former Communist Bloc countries, followed by the reduction or elimination of economic support from those nations.

Blasier (1993) points out that, by 1989, the Soviet Union was providing a secure and protected market for Cuban exports. The Soviets absorbed almost 60 per cent of sugar exports, and 50 to 60 percent of nickel-cobalt exports, neither of which the Soviet economy actually needed. Other CMEA countries took another 20 percent of the nickel-cobalt ore. It is reported that, in 1991, the Soviets paid Cuba 24 cents per pound for sugar, at a time when the world market price was at 9 cents (pp. 79-82). It should also be remembered that Communist countries provided Cuba $18.5 billion in economic and military aid between 1970 and 1989, and that other countries and agencies (excluding the United States) extended another $710 million in aid over the same time period.

Both of the mentioned factors have weakened the Cuban economy. Many Cuban firms have gone out of business because of the lack of spare or repair parts. Major damage has occurred in the electrical power, food processing, cigar, chemical, petroleum, textile, and metallurgy industries. As indicated above, attempts to diversify the economy have failed. The sugar industry, which has been the major producer of foreign exchange, has shown a drastic reduction in output since 1990 (Mesa-Lago, 1993, 79-82).

CUBAN ACCOMMODATIONS TO LABOR MARKET PROBLEMS DURING THE "SPECIAL PERIOD"

When Fidel Castro announced a "special period in time of peace" (*período especial en tiempo de paz*), it was in explicit recognition of the problems noted above. As noted above, the Fourth Congress of the Cuban Communist Party reaffirmed the right of Cuban workers to employment and income. From 1990 through 1992, a series of emergency laws and resolutions, most of them promulgated by the Comité Estatal de Trabajo y Seguridad Social (CETSS), provided the detailed rules and regulations to make this policy workable.

Díaz-Briquets and Pérez-López (1994) indicate that the following emergency measures were in effect in late 1992: (1) workers were eligible for retraining or reassignment in the case of permanent dislocation (factory closings or restructuring); (2) workers were eligible for reassignment in the case of temporary dislocations stemming from a shortage of fuel, raw materials, or spare parts; (3) workers who were not reassigned were eligible for full salary for one month, and 60 percent of full salary thereafter; and (4) workers were encouraged to swap jobs, so as to reduce commuting distance and time. Additional policies were aimed at changes in working hours and the retirement process (pp. 132-133).

Only fragmentary information is available concerning the success of these policies. Tourism and agriculture were the two sectors identified by the Cuban government as suitable outlets for displaced workers. Since the tourist sector has expanded since 1990, it probably absorbed a modest proportion of the total. Most displaced workers have apparently been relocated to agricultural jobs, in the *programa alimentario*, in support of Castro's policy to reduce dependence on imported foodstuffs. Reportedly, late in 1992, 85 to 87 percent of then-displaced workers had been re-employed. The remaining 13 percent were idle and receiving government support (Díaz-Briquets and Pérez-López, 1994, 136-142).

RECENT POLICY DECISIONS IN CUBA

The deepening economic crisis has forced the Castro government to make unusual recent adjustments to confront the situation. A chronology of Cuban policy actions and public pronouncements, compiled by Nancy Singer for Radio Martí, details some of the major changes:

• In February, 1995, Pedro Ross Leal, president of the Cuban Workers Union and a member of the Politburo of the Cuban Communist Party, argued for a more open, flexible, and less imperfect labor market, so that workers could become self-employed if economic conditions required it. Significantly, he stated that workers were no longer to be guaranteed lifetime employment.

• In May, 1995, the Cuban government began layoffs of certain workers, as part of an economic restructuring effort to increase economic efficiency. Governmental figures indicated that as many as 800,000 workers might be displaced, or about 20 percent of the official figure for the Cuban labor force.

• In June, 1995, reports circulated that the Cuban government intended to legalize some family-operated businesses. Many small restaurants (perhaps as many as 4,000 *paladares*) and boarding houses were then operating illegally. It was also reported that the revenues of the again-legal businesses would be taxed.

• Later in the same month, laws were passed opening another 20 job categories for private-sector employment, adding to the 130 occupations from which restrictions were lifted in September, 1993. Official estimates at this time suggested that about 500,000 workers were losing their jobs, and would need remunerative alternatives somewhere in the economy.

• On April 1, 1996, the government imposed a new income tax on private professional incomes.

• Finally, on July 1, the Cuban government announced that university graduates could legally obtain licenses to enter about 140 different trades and services, basically becoming self-employed (Singer, 1995 and 1996, *passim*).

It is important to note that these marginal movements toward a market economy aroused strong reactions in the Castro administration. Both Raúl Castro and Carlos Lage expressed reservations about the developments, and emphasized that the central government should still maintain strong control over the labor markets (The New York Times News Service, 1996, April 1).

The exact current level of unemployment in Cuba is very difficult to ascertain, since centrally-planned economies are supposed to enjoy full employment over time. If 500,000 workers have been displaced, and the economically active population is 4.6 million persons, then the *additional* unemployment created by the surplus is 10.9 percentage points. The initial government estimate of as many as 800,000 displaced workers would indicate an increase in the unemployment rate of 17.4 percentage points. Note that these figures do not reflect any of the underemployment that certainly exists in the Cuban economy today.

The National Association of Independent Economists of Cuba (ANEIC) recently argued for an unemployment rate of 51.6 percent of the labor force. They posit a labor force (*población apta para el trabajo*) of 6,213,700, out of a total population of 11 million. They argue that total employment is 3,006,000, leaving 3,207,700 unemployed. Male workers show an unemployment rate of 36.1 percent, while 66.4 percent of working force women are unemployed. According to these figures, half the Cuban work force is supporting the other half, plus the remaining Cuban population (ANEIC, 1995).

SHORT-TERM OPTIONS OPEN TO CASTRO

The consensus view of Cuban analysts is that the needed structural changes to accomplish the transition to a market economy may require an entire generation to be accomplished, in spite of probable high levels of capital inflow and possible intervention by the United States to maintain stability during the transition. Svejnar and Pérez-López (1993) point out that the state ownership of production facilities is more extensive in Cuba than in Europe; that the private sector is weak, or functional only in the underground economy; that, unlike some Eastern European nations, Cuba has not experienced any significant partial market reforms before the transition; and that Cuba has been partially isolated from world markets (pp. 336-338). In the short run, therefore, accommodation will probably take place within the existing institutional structure of Cuba, apart from any marginal changes that may be accomplished.

There are several possible eventualities or policies that may ameliorate the problem of labor surplus— apart from the abdication or displacement of the Castro government and the beginning of the true transition to a market economy. They are as follows.

Institutional Change

The latest transformations in the Cuban economy are obvious movements away from the command socialism model, and toward market capitalism. They follow earlier, grudging moves by the government to "dollarize" the system and to legalize certain private-sector business concerns.

Given the political and ideological stance of the Cuban government, any significant institutional change is unlikely in the short run. It is possible that more occupations will be added to the list for private-sector licensed employment, and that other types of small businesses will be legitimized. Full-blown acceptance of private property, free markets, a revamped financial system, and all of the other characteristics of market capitalism will not happen, however. The impact of any additional institutional change on unemployment will therefore be small.

Economic Expansion

It goes without saying that market restructuring will succeed only if the economy is in a state of expansion or of relative economic health. And without restructuring, lasting economic health is unlikely to be generated. Even without restructuring, an economic expansion could put large numbers of unemployed Cubans back to work. In its present depressed state,

the Cuban economy cannot create substantial numbers of additional jobs, even private-sector jobs that might be permitted by law. A growing private sector also requires some strength on the aggregate demand side of the market.

Even if Cuba's trading partners are able to circumvent the provisions of the Torricelli Act and the Helms-Burton Act, and continue pouring investment funds into the Cuban economy, the stimulus so generated will probably be slight, affecting only limited sectors such as tourism. Economic expansion will not solve Cuba's unemployment and underemployment problems in the short run.

The Emigration of Surplus Labor

Mesa-Lago (1981) points out that the reduction in Cuban unemployment during the 1960's was accomplished partly by the emigration of workers, opening up approximately 200,000 jobs (p. 124). Another 125,000 Cubans left the country during the Mariel boatlift of 1980. The current immigration agreement between the United States and Cuba originated in 1987. It was renegotiated in 1994. According to its provisions, 20,000 legal Cuban immigrants will be accepted into the United States each year. This outflow of labor will slightly reduce labor market pressure for jobs.

Other significant flows of emigrants appear to be unlikely at the present time. In order to achieve significant relief, an exodus of the size Cuba suffered in the 1960's would have to take place. Since population movements of this kind require not only a stimulus to emigrate but also a country or countries willing to absorb the migrants, relief through substantial migration seems unlikely.

Military Expansion

The Cuban military involvement in Africa permitted an expansion of the armed forces from about 185,000 persons in 1974, when unemployment peaked, to 230,000 in 1978. Mesa-Lago (1981) points out that the 45,000 additional troops so employed helped to lower domestic unemployment (p. 131). At the present time, Cuba's relationships with other countries do not appear to favor the export of violence or the housing of Cuban troops on foreign soil (at foreign expense). This alternative appears to be a weak one, and unlikely to provide any relief for short-term unemployment, especially since the Cuban economy cannot financially support such activities.

The Movement of Labor Into Private-Sector Employment

Over the past three decades, the Cuban government has toyed with the expansion of private-sector employment, although under the licensing control of the central government. In 1976, a law was passed legalizing employment in a variety of private-sector occupations, ranging from bootblacks and electricians to physicians and dentists. By 1979, as many as 100,000 non-agricultural workers had taken advantage of this change (Mesa-Lago, 1981, 131).

As noted above, recent governmental policy changes have expanded the list of approved private-sector occupations, have permitted university graduates to become self-employed, and have legalized many small businesses. Private-sector employment will clearly rise as a result of these changes, absorbing some displaced workers, but the extent of that increase is uncertain. There is additional uncertainty about further market reforms. More jobs can be added to the approved list, and more small business types may be legalized. At some point, however, private-sector activity becomes extensive enough that it clearly conflicts with the ruling ideology of the land. Institutional reform then becomes necessary for further private-sector expansion. Such reform, as argued above, is unlikely. The bottom line is that additional private sector jobs can and will be created, but not in numbers large enough to make a significant dent in overall unemployment.

The Movement of Labor Into the Underground or Secondary Economy

The size of the underground or informal or secondary economy in Cuba, like most informal economies around the globe, cannot be stated precisely. Pérez-López (1995) has taken the measure of Cuba's "second economy" as effectively as possible, and concludes that it is a significant part of Cuba's overall economic operation.

As long as the Castro government tolerates an underground economy in Cuba, and the U.S. dollar remains the key currency on the island, then illegal or "off-the-books" activities constitute a possible outlet for unemployed labor. Again, the state of overall economic health in Cuba will affect the ability of the underground economy to absorb displaced workers.

In the short term, then, the Cuban government faces a perhaps insoluble problem: providing employment for 500,000 workers in an economy that is depressed and constricted by both internal inefficiency and external embargo pressures. Some relief may be found through the expansion of private-sector employment and the leakages of labor into the underground economy. Without significant economic expansion in the near future, however, the outlook for many Cuban workers is bleak.

THE LONGER-TERM VIEW

The preceding analysis and discussion suggest several conclusions concerning the labor situation in the longer term, in post-transition Cuba. It is likely that the size of the labor supply will not restrict economic growth, although the number of available workers will clearly be affected by both in-migration and out-migration, as the restrictions on human movement are lifted. It is also likely that the labor force will not require extensive retraining, especially in the export industries. Given that the transition will probably be prolonged, and will be open to the forces of international trade and investment, there will be adequate signals given to the post-Castro government to permit planning for any needed job training. As the transition progresses, the development of financial and other support institutions for small business should permit the resurgence of a healthy private-sector trade and service sector. The existence of a healthy underground economy suggests that the spirit of entrepreneurship has not died out.

The major challenge faced by the new, post-Castro government will be the renewal of a free and open labor market, something that has not existed in a meaningful form in Cuba for three decades. Probably one of the most difficult tasks will be the inculcation of free market attitudes among both workers and employers. Workers are not accustomed to making their own choices in the labor marketplace, or of responding to wage signals. Two generations of Cubans have grown up under a system of controlled training and employment. By the same token, businesspersons have not had the opportunity of responding to market-determined profit or loss, but have instead tried to meet JUCEPLAN guidelines and goals. The prolonged nature of the transition may be one of its disguised blessings, as a new generation of workers and entrepreneurs experience a revived private sector, and gradually learn its workings.

CONCLUSIONS

Unemployment has been a persistent problem in the Cuban economy. According to the best estimates, perhaps 20 percent of the Cuban labor force was out of work in 1960, when the Castro administration took over. Subsequent socialist restructuring of the economic system was supposed to provide a job for every able-bodied Cuban citizen. Accordingly, official unemployment rates dropped over time, reaching a low in 1970 of about 1.3 percent of the labor force. This figure obviously does not reflect the extensive underemployment that must have existed at the time. After 1970, unemployment crept upward, with some fluctuations over time. It did not become a serious problem again until the 1986-1987 recession damaged the Cuban economy. From that time forward, the combined effects of the loss of Communist Bloc financial support and the restrictive forces of the United States trade embargo pushed the Cuban economy into depression. Today, a large percentage of Cuban workers are unemployed. Some

Cuban economists argue for a current unemployment rate as high as 50 percent or more.

Given this virtually intractable problem, the Castro administration will be forced to find some short-term policies to provide work or financial support to displaced workers. An economic expansion would clearly relieve the pressure, rejuvenate the labor market, and revive the system. The U.S. embargo, now tighter than ever, is unlikely to permit such an expansion, regardless of recent pronouncements by Cuban government officials.

In the absence of an economic expansion, the most likely outlets for Cuban displaced workers are the complex of again-legalized private sector jobs, and the jobs that can be created in the underground economy. Unfortunately, both job-creating sectors are unlikely to have the ability to absorb several hundred thousand workers. The expansion of both the private sector and the underground economy will be constrained and limited by the ruling ideology of the island, since they presage the emergence of a non-socialist, market economy.

Continued mass unemployment and underemployment are therefore likely, as long as the economy is in a depressed condition. Only in the longer-term, when the transition to a full market economy is accomplished, will the changes occur that will provide jobs for the displaced workers. Time is on the side of Cuban workers. It is also the worst enemy of the Castro administration.

BIBLIOGRAPHY

Asociación Nacional de Economistas Independientes de Cuba (ANEIC). (1995). *Documento Número 1: El Nivel de Desempleo*. Documents published on the Internet, available through Cubanet.

Azicri, Max. (1988). *Cuba: Politics, Economics and Society*. New York: Pinter Publishers.

Bethell, Leslie (Ed.). (1993). *Cuba: A Short History*. New York: Cambridge University Press.

Blasier, Cole. (1995). "The End of the Soviet-Cuban Partnership." In Carmelo Mesa-Lago (Ed.), *Cuba After the Cold War* (pp. 79-82). Pittsburgh: University of Pittsburgh Press.

Brundenius, Claes. (1984). *Revolutionary Cuba: The Challenge of Economic Growth with Equity*. Boulder: Westview Press.

Córdova, Efrén. (1994). "Legal Changes in the Area of Labor Relations." In *Cuba in Transition— Volume 3* (pp. 145-147). Miami: Association for the Study of the Cuban Economy, Florida International University.

"Cuban communists take a harder line." (1996, April 1). New York Times News Service, as reported on Nandonet (Internet).

Díaz-Briquets, Sergio, and Jorge Pérez-López. (1994). "Cuba's Labor Adjustment Policies during the Special Period." In Jorge Pérez-López (Ed.), *Cuba at a Crossroads: Politics and Economics after the Fourth Party Congress* (pp. 118-146). Gainesville: University Press of Florida.

Mesa-Lago, Carmelo (Ed.). (1993). *Cuba After the Cold War*. Pittsburgh: University of Pittsburgh Press.

Mesa-Lago, Carmelo. (1981). *The Economy of Socialist Cuba: A Two-Decade Appraisal*. Albuquerque: University of New Mexico Press.

Pérez-López, Jorge (Ed.). (1994). *Cuba at a Crossroads: Politics and Economics after the Fourth Party Congress*. Gainesville: University Press of Florida.

Pérez-López, Jorge. (1995). *Cuba's Second Economy: From Behind the Scenes to Center Stage*. New Brunswick: Transaction Publishers.

Pérez-López, Jorge. (1991). *The Economics of Cuban Sugar*. Pittsburgh: The University of Pittsburgh Press.

Perry, Joseph M., Louis A. Woods, and Jeffrey W. Steagall. (1996). "Planning for a Free Market Labor Force in Post-transition Cuba." Paper Presented at the Allied Social Sciences Association Annual Meetings, January 5-7, 1996, San Francisco, California.

Perry, Joseph M., Louis A. Woods and Jeffrey W. Steagall. (1994). "The Implications of the Privatization Movement for Post-Transition Cuba." Paper presented at the annual meetings of the American Economic Association, Boston, Mass., January 2-5, 1994. Presented in revised form at the 64th Annual Conference of the Southern Economic Association, November 20-22, 1994, Lake Buena Vista, Florida.

Porket, J. L. (1989) *Work, Employment, and Unemployment in the Soviet Union*. New York: St. Martin's Press.

Ritter, Archibald R. M. (1994). "Cuba's Economic Strategy and Alternative Futures." In Jorge Pérez-López (Ed.), *Cuba at a Crossroads: Politics and Economics after the Fourth Party Congress* (pp. 67-93). Gainesville: University Press of Florida.

Ritter, Archibald R. M. (1974). *The Economic Development of Revolutionary Cuba: Strategy and Performance*. New York: Praeger Publishers.

Singer, Nancy. (1995) *Chronology of Cuban Events, 1995*. Accessed through Radio Martí Gopher on the Internet. Washington, D. C.: Information Resources Branch, Department of Research, Radio Martí Program.

Singer, Nancy. (1996) *Chronology of Cuban Events, 1996*. Accessed through Radio Martí Gopher on the Internet. Washington, D. C.: Information Resources Branch, Department of Research, Radio Martí Program.

Svejnar, Jan, and Jorge Pérez-López. (1993). "A Strategy for Cuba's Economic Transformation." In Carmelo Mesa-Lago (Ed.), *Cuba After the Cold War*. Pittsburgh: University of Pittsburgh Press.

United States. Department of Commerce. Bureau of the Census. (1995). *Statistical Abstract of the United States: 1995*. Washington: U.S. Government Printing Office.

United States. Department of Labor. Bureau of Labor Statistics. (1975). *Handbook of Labor Statistics 1975—Reference Edition*. Washington: U.S. Government Printing Office.

United States. Department of State. (1993, 1994). *Background Notes: Cuba.* Washington: U.S. Government Printing Office.

Zimbalist, Andrew, and Claes Brundenius. (1989). *The Cuban Economy: Measurement and Analysis of Socialist Performance.* Baltimore: The Johns Hopkins University Press.

COMMENTS ON

"Alternative Policies to Deal With Labor Surpluses During The Cuban Transition" by Joseph M. Perry, Louis A. Woods, and Jeffrey W. Steagall

Ricardo L. Tejada

This well-researched paper addresses an important and very real topic which will be one of the primary foci of a Cuban economy in transition. Rather than discussing the Castro government's short-term options for dealing with surplus labor, most of which are unlikely alternatives or scenarios, I will concentrate on the section of the paper which analyzes labor surpluses in the long run and therefore are more relevant to a Cuban economy in transition.

More than presenting policy options, this paper discusses the characteristics of the Cuban labor force and how these might affect the transformation into a market economy. The authors analyze: 1) the size of the Cuban labor force; 2) the occupational structure of the labor force; and 3) attitudinal problems. The following discussion comments on these factors and attempts to offer policy alternatives to deal with labor surpluses during a Cuba in transition.

THE SIZE OF THE CUBAN LABOR FORCE

The authors assert that the size of the Cuban labor force does not present a serious problem for a transition. This is most likely an accurate observation. Low participation rates by women in the labor force may lighten the burden of open unemployment during an economic transition. However, it is unlikely that factors such as emigration will take place at rates high enough to ease the labor supply shock which would result as firms privatize and move from labor hoard-

ing to labor shedding. As I will discuss later, worker retraining will be a crucial component of economic development and an important policy tool to minimize duration of unemployment.

THE OCCUPATIONAL STRUCTURE OF THE LABOR FORCE

Despite early efforts to industrialize and a number of attempts to diversify away from dependence on sugar, the revolutionary government has indeed made a relatively small impact on the overall structure of the economy. The authors thus suggest that, given that the present composition of the Cuban economy is not likely to change significantly under a market system, vocational retraining of the labor force may not be necessary. However, this analysis may fail to take into account the existence of skill mismatch within the individual sectors of the economy. What will be the skill needs within, for example, the tourism industry? Are workers from down-sizing firms prepared to fill the demand for new positions, even if this demand lies in the same industries?

While we know that industries such as tourism are likely to remain important in the Cuban economy organized under a market system, a centrally planned tourism sector may look quite different from one built based on responses to market signals. When we look closely into the broad-sector categories, it is impossible to see where demands for labor will arise.

Therefore, it is over optimistic to state that "extensive vocational retraining of the Cuban labor market may not be necessary." This gives rise to important questions regarding the need for policies which will deal with labor surpluses and skill mismatch during the Cuban transition.

ATTITUDINAL PROBLEMS

The recent recession has played an important role in what will be Cuba's economic transition. Extreme conditions in the Cuban economy have, in a sense, "hardened" the budget constraints of state firms, forcing workers into open unemployment or some sort of self-employment activity. This situation differs dramatically from that which existed in the centrally-planned economies of Central and Eastern Europe prior to market reforms. This means that the labor shedding experienced in several of the European transition economies is already taking place in the Cuban economy and that the Cuban population has had to learn to adapt to these new challenges.

In recent years, the Cuban population has had to fend for itself in order maintain a minimum level of basic needs. The Cuban economic crisis of today has no precedent in any of the former centrally-planned economies of Central and Eastern Europe. This has promoted a culture of entrepreneurs, both in the formal and informal sector. It is unfair to say that these individuals are completely oblivious to market signals. The increase in self-employed workers is evidence of this. The true attitudinal problem will rest with the larger-scale entrepreneurs, the possible Donald Trumps of Cuba. Running a profitable hotel which employs hundreds is a far cry from running a small family restaurant. Large-scale entrepreneurs will require a great deal of assistance, technical as well as economic, from the outside.

POLICY ALTERNATIVES

The paper outlines three important elements for a successful labor transition in a post-Castro Cuba: a labor market that understands incentives, employers who understand the operation of a free market, and a government that adopts a "hands off" policy toward its labor market. Of these, I would assert that, for the labor force, the second is most important. As is the case in most of the world's economies, larger firms are likely to play the most important role in absorbing labor. Large private firms, most likely funded and managed by foreign or expatriate entrepreneurs or parent companies, will be the dominant factor in reshaping Cuba's economy and, consequently, its labor market. Because this capital will almost necessarily come from abroad, employers will be familiar with the workings of a free market; indeed, it may be the only economic environment with which they are familiar. It will be up to the Cuban labor market to adapt to them.

I am not saying anything new when I state that a post-Castro Cuba will be very dependent on foreign capital and investment for its development. A stable, post-Castro Cuba will attract foreign capital. To think otherwise is to be overly-pessimistic. None of the European transition economies, with the exception of East Germany, had such an organized group of expatriates waiting to participate in its transformation. This conference is testament to this. Many expatriates will play key roles in the Cuban transition as investors.

Policy makers in a transition economy must be shrewd yet understanding. While the best economic policy for a post-Castro government will be to take a relatively "stand-offish" approach, political considerations will make the extreme application of this policy unwise. Too radical a change, one which is considered as disregarding the working population, could cause rifts and perhaps turmoil in a post-socialist environment. It will be in everyone's interest to make the transition to a free labor market as smooth as possible, free of the jolts that could cause tension in the labor force. The government will, inevitably, have an important role to play in this transition. The challenge will be for policy makers to play a significant role yet maintain a "hands-off" approach that avoids distortions.

Policies that encourage private-sector training of workers must be emphasized in the short run. Such policies should focus, to the greatest extent possible, on active labor market policies rather than the deadly trap of passive policies. Tax incentives to firms hiring local unskilled labor should be provided in exchange for formal and on-the-job training. Given Cuba's ailing infrastructure, public works programs could well provide temporary jobs while simultaneously creating a more investment-friendly economy. Even public-sector training should not be ruled out.

Cuba's highly educated population may be an important factor in the transition process. The level of educational attainment of the labor force will play a significant role in the success and relative low cost of vocational retraining. A better educated worker more easily incorporates new skills and new technologies into the workplace thereby lowering the level of frictional unemployment, decreasing jobless spells, and promoting non-inflationary macroeconomic growth. Training policies which integrate the existing educational level of the labor force will prove important tools to dealing with labor surpluses during the Cuban transition.

To conclude, this paper examines the vital issue of the how Cuba's labor force, as it exists today, is poised for an economic transition. Clearly, the move from an inefficient centrally-planned economy, where the process of labor allocation is an artificial one, to a market determined system will make for a bumpy ride. Cuba's transition to a market economy will in many ways be unique, differing from the experience of the Central and Eastern European economies. It is crucial that works such as this one begin to examine the Cuban labor force and bring to the fore the discussion of which policies will prove most successful in guaranteeing a speedy and smooth transition of the country's labor force.

LABOR EFFECTS OF ADJUSTMENT POLICIES IN CUBA[1]

Enrique S. Pumar[2]

In the past two years, the Cuban government has devised several policy reforms in an attempt to overcome the most severe economic crisis since the revolution. These reforms have created new opportunities in several sectors of the economy for foreign investors and for self-employment by Cuban nationals. Yet, while many of these new initiatives are unprecedented, some even radical within the parameters of previous revolutionary practices, they continue to affect the basic human rights and welfare of individual citizens, particularly the three and one half million or so who actively participate in the official labor market.

In this paper, I argue that recent economic changes in Cuba are fomenting a segmented labor market which rewards allegiance to the regime. The state has managed to successfully take advantage of popular deprivation by its ability to regulate opportunities in the labor market to cultivate a new form of political acquiescence. This is done by regulating access to better paid jobs through informal networks controlled by former civilian and military high officials. Hence, those with "conecciones" or ties can bargain their history (or appearance) of revolutionary participation to improve their chances of obtaining well paid employment. In other words, structural opportunities in the labor market impose a disciplinary effect which ultimately reinforces the social order. This

might explain why in the midst of its worse economic crisis and concomitant discontent, the regime has managed to survive. My emphasis on networks and patronage also explains why the well connected fare better than the average worker even in non-skilled, yet lucrative, jobs.

To illustrate this point, I will examine five labor practices which contribute to a split labor market. I do so for two reasons. First, it is impossible to quantitatively document any evidence of segmentation and discrimination since the government does not release adequate data in this subject, and a survey of workers would be almost impossible to undertake without official approval. To substantiate my argument, then, I must rely on information I gathered following nonparticipant observation methodologies such as interviews and focus groups. All interviews were conducted in La Habana during the first three weeks of January 1995.[3]

More importantly, following Pierre Bourdieu, I view social practice as encompassing specific goals and interests of actors even when these actions are routine (Bourdieu, 1990). Thus, the practices of the regime reflect a particular agenda even if it claims otherwise. Based on the evidence I present here, one can conclude that this strategy is to only make sufficient re-

---

1. An abbreviated version of this paper was prepared as a Briefing Paper for Dr. Carl-Johan Groth, Special Rapporteur of the UN Commission on Human Rights in Geneva. Some sections were incorporated into Agenda item 112 (A/50/663) at the Fiftieth Session of the General Assembly, Fall 1995.

2. I would like to thank Carlos Seiglie and Phil Brenner for helpful comments and Laurie Meyers and Rebecca Young for editorial assistance. Of course, I am solely responsible for its contents.

3. I visited Havana as a Consultant to the Center for International Affairs at Brown University.

forms to stay in power without regard to the workers' welfare. This government goal explains the erratic nature of recent reforms. In the words of Carlos Lage, a Vice President of the Council of State, "... haremos reformas pero solo para salvar el socialismo" (*El País*, June 19, 1994, p.32).

With this in mind, I will proceed as follows. First, I will review the extent of the economic crisis and adjustment practices to demonstrate that the latter are sectoral and designed to reverse what James O'Connor (1973) calls "the fiscal crisis of the state" in Cuba. Then, I will discuss labor practices and their effects on workers.

THE EXTENT OF THE ECONOMIC CRISIS

The Cuban economy began to deteriorate in the late 1980s when economic relations with the former Soviet Union, Cuba's main trading partner, financial underwriter, and source of technical assistance, were transformed to reflect international market prices. Up to that point, the Soviet Union and its Eastern European allies accounted for about 85 percent of the island's trade and the bulk of its development financing. The economy also showed deteriorating effects from the rectification process, a development strategy designed by the government to reverse some of the tentative market reforms and economic incentives that characterized the late 1970's and early 1980s and which had improved economic performance. In addition, the Cuban economy was adversely affected by global forces beyond its control, such as the decline in the price of sugar and other traditional exports, the mounting cost of debt financing, and bottlenecks resulting from the U.S. economic embargo. To these factors one can add the regime's own highly politicized and bureaucratic decision-making process, low productivity, lack of diversification in production mechanisms, and other endemic political features of the Cuban economy.[4]

As Table 1 illustrates, at the steepest point of the "special period in time of peace," as the austerity period that began in 1989 is known in Cuba, the economic deterioration was marked by four major trends.

First, there was a decline by half of the island's gross national product between 1990 and 1993. This downward trend was only reversed in 1994 when the economy reached a growth level of 0.7 percent, according to Lage (Lage, 1995, p.1). Second, the level of production in the agricultural and nonrenewable commodity sectors also fell sharply, causing major food shortages and steep loss of export revenues. As a result, in 1993, Cuba's imports were only 20 percent of 1989 levels (Ferriol, 1995, p.17). Revenues from sugar exports, still the most important export commodity, went down by 43 percent between 1989 and 1993. In 1994, sugar production was about 4 million tons, or 5 percent less than the production level of the previous year (Pérez-López, 1995, p. 2). Drops in sugar production alone resulted in a loss of US$1.6 billion. Third, the ballooning budget deficit and external debt, estimated by economists at Havana's Center for the Research on the World Economy to be more than $8 billion, is regarded as one of the major obstacles blocking Cuba's full participation in international financial markets. Still, by 1994 very little progress was reported on debt renegotiation and rescheduling. The fiscal dimension of the crisis has also undermined investors confidence in the probability of recovery. Cuba was ranked recently by *The Economist* as the 116th out of 129 countries for investment safety.

Fourth, the magnitude of the crisis and the austerity initiatives has adversely affected employment and consumption levels as well. Economists calculate that up to 80 percent of the manufacturing sector stood idle between 1993-94 and 40 percent of the labor force is either underemployed or unemployed (Pérez-López, 1995, p. 2). To compensate for the loss of personal income, the government continues to provide 60 percent of monthly wages to the unem-

---

4. There have been many reports showing evidence of lagging economic troubles throughout the revolution. One of the most revealing was published in *The Latin American Times,* Vol. 8, No. 10 (1989). According to this publication, the Communist Party took a survey of 10,756 participants in the province of Holguín in 1988, and 87.6 percent had an unfavorable opinion of the Party's performance.

Table 1. Macroeconomics Indicators of the 1989-93 Austerity Crisis

Issue-Area	Date	Proportion
Growth levels	1989-1993	Decline by half
Sugar exports	1989-1993	Down by 43 percent
Manufacturing	1993-1994	Idle by 80 percent
Employment	1993-1994	40 percent unemployed and underemployed
Import levels	1993	20 percent of 1989 levels
Fiscal policy	1994	Ranked 116th in investment confidence

Note: Figures were taken from Centro de Investigaciones de la Economía Cubana, *Economía Cubana--Boletín Informativo*, No. 19 (Enero-Febrero 1995).

ployed. Yet since wages are generally depressed, unemployment benefits are not enough to purchase basic necessities for the average worker, inducing many to engage in illegal activities, informal markets, and unreported employment practices. These activities are periodically repressed by the regime as a demonstration effect to keep the population in line.

The rise of structural unemployment threatens to exacerbate existing social inequalities within the revolution in various ways. One indicator of these growing inequalities already generated by the crisis is in the area of savings. Official figures indicate that 70 percent of all savings is concentrated amongst 6 percent of the population and only 10 percent of all citizens account for 70 percent of the money supply (*Boletín ANEIC*, 1995, p.11).

A less quantifiable but important effect of the crisis nonetheless is evident in worker attitudes. Several people I interviewed in 1995 stated that they felt under compensated for their job productivity and that they had lost interest in, and dedication to, their work. Most of their efforts, they claimed, were directed at not antagonizing their supervisors so that they would be left alone to "resolver": meaning, to negotiate access to food and other household necessities through contacts in the informal sector while at work.

Finally, there is evidence of a burgeoning informal sector. The exact number of people engaged in this activity is difficult to estimate, but their presence is evident in all sectors of the economy, at least in the capital city. Opportunities in the informal sectors are drawing professional and skilled labor away from government services and entrenching a widespread perception of inefficiency and bottlenecks in the formal sector.

RECENT ADJUSTMENT POLICIES

In light of the extent of the economic crisis and its potential social and political repercussions, the government of Fidel Castro embarked on a series of legislative reforms starting in 1993 aimed at reversing these indicators. These changes have altered state-society relations in the realm of economics to a considerable extent. Still, as I will argue later, many of these reforms actually strengthen the authority of the state considerably.

In many cases, the new legislation has created new opportunities for foreign investment and increased participation by Cuban nationals in some economic sectors. However, as Cuba moves cautiously away from a "commando economy" towards more private initiatives and market reforms basic human rights of individual citizens, and workers in particular, continue to be adversely affected. This section discusses some of these recent economic initiatives and their social impact (see Table 2).

Fiscal Reforms

The central aim of these reforms is to achieve fiscal stability by reducing the public deficit and increasing productivity while holding back on political reforms—in short, a tropical version of the Chinese model. Finance Minister José Luis Rodríguez targeted a 4.6 percent reduction in public spending and 19.5 percent cutback in subsidies for state-owned enterprises for 1995. These cuts are likely to increase unemployment since the practice of self-employment as it stands now can not absorb jobs lost to downsizing, in effect forcing more spending on entitlement programs. According to Pedro Ross, President of the

Table 2. Summary of Austerity Measures

Policy	Social Effects
Fiscal reforms and currency devaluation	Dollarization of the economy, inflation.
Privatization	Discriminates against nationals, a split-labor market
Tourism	Exacerbates relative deprivation and discontent
Self Employment	Controls labor market

Cuban Workers Union, 500,000 out of the 2.2 million workers employed by the public enterprises will lose their jobs if restructuring policies announced by Rodríguez are carried out (Stern, 1995, p.2). Other fiscal reforms include the new license fees for business, a progressive tax on personal income,[5] and currency devaluation. In 1994, a new convertible peso pegged to the U.S. dollar was introduced, and the U.S. dollar was made legal. The new peso is accepted in all legal establishments where dollars are required for payments. This program is designed to eventually eliminate some of the problems associated with running a double currency market; however, as of this date results are mixed. The abolition of Article 140 of the Penal Code which prohibits national from trafficking with foreign currencies, has contributed to inflation and an erratic exchange rate. In 1991, the going rate was 30 pesos. However, less than five years later, the exchange rate increased by 1400 percent (FBIS, 1995, p. 8) before it recently came down to 1991 levels again. The psychological effects of this fluctuation has meant that consumers hold dollars as if they were an insured commodity, since it withstands the market fluctuation better than the peso.[6] Finally, in this regard, fees for licenses have been increased and the government is contemplating the idea of charging a nominal fee for some of its services[7]. Regarding the former, the Price Ministry set these monthly fees at between 100 and 400 pesos as of June of 1995 (FBIS, 1995, p. 5).

Privatization

The Cuban government has also aggressively engaged in privatization. These efforts, however, are sectoral, not structural, and involve promoting joint ventures, giving this program a resemblance of the passé import substitution industrialization (ISI) strategy which Latin American nations implemented during the 1960s. Much of the privatization activities cluster around the real estate, tourist (19), mining (10), energy (9), agriculture (6), manufacturing (4), and telecommunication (3) sectors. Investment in the service sector alone accounts for more than half of the 60 FDI reported in a recent study by the AFL-CIO (1995).[8] According this report, Canada, Spain, and Mexico account for the majority of foreign investment on the island. In 1993-94, foreign investment and joint ventures generated an estimated U.S. $1.5 billion, according to the Cuban Chamber of Commerce. There is a widespread perception among Cubans that the regime is gradually selling off the island to foreigners. This popular mood prompted a government official to declare recently "... all of this talk about Spain buying up Cuba piece by piece is simply not true" (The Miami Herald, April 18, 1995, p. 1A).

In March 1995, Fidel Castro announced at the Fourth Congress of the Cuban Women's Federation that the government was considering introducing "more elements of private property, capitalism, and market forces" (The Miami Herald, March 5, 1995, p. 20A). With this announcement he proceeded to say that the government was contemplating the pos-

---

5. Since I wrote the first draft of this paper in the Fall of 1995, the Cuban government has announced a progressive personal income tax for the self employed which ranges from 5 to 50 percent of earnings. In addition, self-employed workers must pay a monthly license fee. In some cases, the cost of operating a small business could reach up to 60 percent of earnings.

6. In a recent phone interview I conducted, I was told "what everyone wants is dollars."

7. During my recent trip to Cuba, officials were informally even talking about charging fees for education and health services, two of the most highly touted programs of the revolution.

8. According to Lage, as of the end of 1994, the number of joint ventures totaled 176 with capital from 36 countries (Lage, 1995, p. 1).

sibility of opening small and medium enterprises to foreign investment. During the same time there was talk among government officials of allowing foreigners to buy real estate on the island. Both measures will exclude nationals, even if they manage to accumulate enough dollars to enter this market, illustrating the discriminatory effects of many government adjustment policies.

Tourism

Tourism illustrates some of the mixed results associated with foreign investment in Cuba. In 1994, 617,000 tourists visited the island, about 13 percent more than the year before, but short of the government's goal of 700,000. Visitors contributed a mere $850 million to the national economy, with only one third of it retained by the government as profit (*The Miami Herald*, April 18, 1995, 1A). Part of the reason for the revenue shortfall is that, with the exception of Cuban exiles, the island primarily attracts middle-income tourists with a fixed budget who often do not return for further stays on the island. Moreover, tourism has not generated the spillover economic activities normally associated with leading sectors since Cuba does not have the production capacity to supply the services and products demanded by this industry. The Grupo Sol Meliá, a Spanish tourist management firm with various investments throughout the island, flies in food for its restaurants at a cost of 45 to 90 cents a pound. The food alone for a $22 buffet costs Meliá $8 (*The Miami Herald*, April 18, 1995, p. 1A).

On the other hand, these relative gains need to be weighed against growing widespread popular discontent, frustration, and a sense of relative deprivation generated by the affluence and special privileges enjoyed by foreigners. The average Cuban does not have access to the food, transportation, and recreational facilities designated by the government for tourists unless they are rewarded by the state as model workers. Here again, we see how the state has strengthening its capacity to reaffirm order and consent through incentives. Cubans nationals, for instance, are discourage from visiting the lobby of hotels in Havana, and prohibited from visiting restaurants and rooms in these hotels. Taxis rarely

pick up the average citizen in the streets. While tourists drive around the city in rented modern cars, most Cubans must be content to move around on bicycles.

There is no evidence that foreign investment has generated sufficient jobs to alleviate unemployment, either. Thus far, tourism has only generated around 54,000 jobs nationwide. In fact, one of the first decisions made by many foreign companies is to streamline the over-staffed, state-run enterprises they took over. When the Guitart Investment Group from Spain took over the management of the Habana Libre Hotel, the number of hotel employees was reduced from 1,200 to 400 without any rights to appeals. Recently, Guitart had difficulties with the government and withdrew its investments from Cuba.

Self-employment

Self-employment is another of the innovations recently introduced by the government. The initial rationale for this change was that it was needed to alleviate the growing number of workers who lost their jobs because of downsizing. Today, as these microenterprises provide essential services, not only has the number of the self employed grown, but the state seems to consider them a permanent feature of the government reform plan. Already, early in 1995, government figures estimate that more than 170,000 people, or about 5 percent of the working population, hold licenses to provide close to 100 services and trades; to this number one must add several thousand more that work full- or part-time in the informal sector (*FBIS*, March 22, 1995, p. 4). Yet the government is determined to firmly control these numbers. Besides demanding taxes and fees for those self employed, in 1995 the government issued Joint Resolution 4, restricting the number of employees private businesses can hire. For instance, in the case of home restaurants (*paladares*), no more than 12 persons can be hired. The Resolution also bars many university graduates and professionals from self employment jobs. One of the complaints I often heard with regard to self-employment was that the regime governing this practice fluctuates constantly, thus creating uncertainty and bafflement among entrepreneurs.

Farmers have been one of the primary beneficiaries of this legislation. Starting in 1993, the government turned 55 percent of state-controlled land into Basic Units of Cooperative Production (UBPC). The UBPC farmers must sell the bulk of their products at very low prices to the state in exchange for free lease of the land, and are permitted to sell their surplus in Farmers Markets. There is increasing evidence that this double-tiered pricing system is in fact contributing to shortages at local supermarkets, since it provides an incentive to the farmers to sell the same produce at highly inflated prices in the Farmers Markets.

THE SOCIAL AND POLITICAL IMPACT OF ECONOMIC REFORMS

Several theories of political economy in the social sciences assume that economic liberalization erodes the power of nondemocratic regimes and that increased economic opportunities foster individual empowerment. The current situation in Cuba contradicts these assumptions. Reforms have fostered an environment where new forms of human rights abuses related to economic rights have emerged while organized political dissent is still repressed (Amnesty International, 1996). The recent crackdown on Concilio Cubano among others, demonstrates the intolerance on the part of the government when confronted with an emerging, peaceful opposition.

In this section of the paper I will discuss four recent forms of economic rights violations that directly affect workers to demonstrate how the regime manipulates the scope and extent of reforms to its advantage. I do not consider political rights since they are more evident and have been well discussed by others.[9] These violations are: 1) lack of worker representation in joint ventures; 2) depressed worker's salaries; 3) a controlled labor market; and 4) the use of economic opportunities as a new form of political patronage.

Union Representation

Cuba's version of ISI has, as in years past in Latin America, resulted in the demobilization of labor.

This is done to offer incentives to foreign investors. In a speech at the 1994 World Economic Forum in Davos, Switzerland, Carlos Lage, Vice President of State and chief economic advisor to President Castro, said that much. He said that Cuba was "an orderly and stable nation, a society where terrorism and drug trafficking does not exist... a place where all of the labor resources are utilized rationally"(CIEM, 1995, p.2).

The other dimension of this policy is that independent labor unions are not permitted to organize. The official labor union (the Central de Trabajadores de Cuba, CTC) has little power in foreign-operated firms. The impression among many workers I interviewed is that there is a labor-management consortium of some sort that works against workers. Many were cynical in their remarks about union representation and some said they had gone as far as to stop paying their union dues. The lack of union representation and collective bargaining usually lead to abuses, exploitation, discrimination, and illegal dismissals. I was told repeatedly that employers based their hirings, promotions, compensation, and even benefits on subjective judgments regardless of what the labor legislation stated. Schemes for severance pay do not work well and seem to linger forever in court and appeals processes.

Intimidation and threats to send workers home without pay were common even by *delegados* or union representatives. Workers were also told that if they did not have discipline at work, they could lose their jobs and would have no choice but to work in the fields where there is always a need for labor. This attitude by union representatives and, in some cases even employers, results from two conditions. First, there is an excessive supply of labor coming from the under- and unemployed on the one hand, and from the intensive competition for high-paying jobs on the other. Moreover, there is no accountability in labor-management relations. These conditions undermine the value and efforts of employees.

9. The Cuba program at Freedom House, Amnesty International, and Human Rights Watch have published a newsletter and several briefing papers documenting the systematic abuses of political rights.

The lack of collective bargaining represents a serious legitimization dilemma for the regime, since it claims that its unconditional support for workers' rights is radically different from previous governments in Cuba and calls the Communist Party a workers' organization. Yet, in practice, the average worker does not see the benefit of union representation. Besides, older Cubans still reminisce about the relative high standard of living and populist policies of the various governments during the Republic.

Wages

Another problem with the government's economic plan is its depressed wages. Cuban workers are paid in Cuban pesos while the government obtains fees from investors in hard currency. Even in cases where the workers are partially compensated in dollars or paid overtime in dollars, this amount is so minimal that is not enough to pay for groceries.

Given the dollarization of the national economy, this practice has two effects on the average citizen. First, most consumer items, and increasingly most service transactions as well, are in dollars, yet Cubans do not earn hard currency legally unless they work in officially designated sectors of the economy where labor competition for the few jobs available is intensive. This practice has increased the state's power over the distribution of opportunities.

The average salary is the equivalent of about $4.50 dollars a month. Government subsidies make some basic social services cheap. However, basic staples, clothing, and household items are mostly available only in dollar stores. For instance, last year during my trip, vegetables in the farmers markets were being sold for a dollar a pound, and a meal in some of the small *paladares* or family owned restaurants for two dollars or more. Inflation in Cuba is due to a combination of excess demand and insufficient competition.

The other dimension of these wage structures is that the best and the brightest defy labor legislation and whenever possible desert government jobs to work on their own. When they cannot leave, many become demoralized by their relative deprivation. This has resulted in a serious deterioration of public services and an increase in the commodification of social relations. What is more, many university graduates are leaving the universities to work in hotels and drive taxis for tourists in order to make dollars and provide for their families. After the government has made a substantial investment in education, Cuba is then losing on the next generation of professionals and wasting some of its human capital investment.

Increasingly, government officials state that incentives are applied "to each according to his efforts." This practice creates a lot of ethical and practical problems. Not only does it contradict the socialist nature of the regime, but more importantly it leaves a lot of room for abuse and patronage since it commands government officials to determine which and whose effort will be rewarded, when, and how. In addition, workers may put a lot of effort and dedication at work in their jobs in an industry that is not considered essential and so go unnoticed. Finally, this policy rewards the better endowed workers. This is normally not a problem in a situation that resembles a market meritocracy. But in Cuba, opportunities are highly politicized. In effect, this policy ends up rewarding those who supported the regime, gained access to more education and skills, and today can demonstrate their efforts more clearly than others.[10]

Labor Market

Tight labor markets are also affecting the structure of incentives and social justice in another ways. Salary structures are designated by professions, not by industries or collective bargaining, which are usually more competitive. Salaries are standardized nationwide by the state according to occupation. This was done as part of an attempt to assure egalitarianism during the 1970s. This experiment seems to have worked to a certain extent then when the economy was heavily subsidized. Today, the reality is different.

---

10. It is important to keep in mind that until recently educational and professional opportunities were exclusively open to those with unquestionable revolutionary credentials. For instance, the right to learn English or travel had to be earned with devotion to the revolution. Today, those who possess these endowments have a comparative advantage over the rest of the population.

With the government restructuring, earnings have become more significant and necessary than ever.

These rigid salary structures are practically impossible to overcome, regardless of individual experience, qualifications, or job performance in some cases. It stimulates low productivity and encourages illicit speculation. It also contributes to the desire to work in the informal sector. In fact, almost everyone I met during my trip was engaged in some form of unlawful activity justifying this practice as the only means to survive. But more importantly, these strictures violate the workers' basic rights to be rewarded for their labor and seem to contradict the official principle stated before of compensating each according to their efforts. Ironically, it was Marx who said that workers were only free when they were able to sell their labor freely in the market. He envisioned this as being one of the compliments of capitalism. In Cuba, we have a government of the people that denies the people's right to be free.

Networks and Hiring Practices

Lastly, but no less importantly, the fact that employment opportunities are not advertised anywhere encourages political patronage and arbitrariness in hiring practices. There is evidence that those with access to the most liberalized sectors of the economy, and therefore the most profitable jobs, are former government officials, their relatives or friends, and the supporters of the regime. This group has the contacts, the know-how, and experience to capitalize on emerging market opportunities. They are also given the benefit of the doubt about their revolutionary credentials and thus are less likely to be labeled or stigmatized as "capitalist" even if they behave like one. More importantly, many of these individuals still have friends in high government positions who can offer protection and information. They are also the most likely to be appointed to head the private or semiprivate enterprises in the island. The lack of institutionalized hiring practices not only encourages corruption, but also mediocrity and complacency. Individuals know "that it is not what you know, but who you know that matters." The extent of labor supply and widespread need increases the social pre-

mium, i.e., favor, obligation, etc., one pays for have access to good jobs.

Another recent trend in Cuba is to staff private companies with former military officers. A case in point is former General Julio Casas Regueiro, who at least until late 1995 was the head of the Gaviota Investment Group, a tourist conglomerate organized by Defense Minister Raúl Castro, with earnings in 1994 of $200 million or 15 percent of Cuba's foreign currency earnings, and a payroll of about 12,000 (*The Miami Herald*, January 23, 1995, p. 8A). During his military tenure, Mr. Casas Regueiro was, among other assignments, in charge of logistics for the military campaigns in Angola and Ethiopia. The argument can be made that many of the private companies set up in Cuba are designed to employ former military officers with the hope of diminishing any possible discontent and the possibility of a coup.

The problem with staffing private business with retired officers is that these ex- soldiers are socialized into not suppressing dissent. They tend to view those with little or no established track record of commitment to the revolution as enemies or simply not worthy of an opportunity to prosper. Furthermore, former military personnel view the armed forces institution as a fraternity and they are more inclined to assist those who were partly or closely associated with it. Finally, since there are no institutionalized employment channels personal networks and contact are the only way to grasp the best jobs available. Only a handful of people with strong ties to these former government officials might capitalize on labor market opportunities. Granted, not all job opportunities are controlled from above. Yet, based on my observations, workers, particularly the nonskilled, have had to rely exclusively on social ties for career advancement.

In sum, with regard to the political implications of the current changes underway in Cuba today, I would argue against those who assert that they are slowly eroding the authority of the state. Instead, I would argue that these reforms have increased substantially the power of the state, at least in the short term. With the current fiscal crisis, the regime has managed to get rid of some of its waste in the name of capitalism, which usually has a positive connotation. It is able to change patronage from ideology to market opportunities, thus giving the changes the appearance of reforms and legitimacy among sympathizers in Cuba and abroad. Since the unfolding, uneven market reforms have created much discontent, and hard-liners can claim some ideological gains which would make it easier for them to reverse these changes in the name of national welfare.[11] The government now has more information than ever about who is involved in which commercial trade, so if these trades become illegal again, presumably those who practiced them could be persecuted. More importantly, it is worth keeping in mind that the pace and extent of reforms continues to be dictated by the state. This is not a market-driven phenomena but one guided by political considerations, the most important of which is survival.

CONCLUSIONS

The reforms underway in Cuba today are not necessarily beneficial for the average citizen on the island and in fact may have enhanced the power of the state at the expense of human rights. Part of the problem is that the existing political impasse has made changes underway sectional rather than structural. It is clear the government of Fidel Castro has shown once more its determination to hold power rather than secure the comprehensive reforms the island needs to reverse its deteriorating living standard and infrastructure. Since the regime controls the extent of reforms, it is not clear that more "liberalization" would bring about the desired political changes everyone hopes. Rather, these initiatives will continue to strengthen the capacity of the regime to prolong its rule, since they are controlled from above.

BIBLIOGRAPHY

Amnesty International. *Cuba: Government Crackdown on Dissent* (April 1996).

Boletín de ANEIC (Marzo-Abril 1995).

Bourdieu, Pierre. *Outline of the Theory of Practice.* Cambridge: Cambridge University Press , 1990,

CIEM. *Economía Cubana: Boletín Informativo* 19 (Enero-Febrero, 1995).

Instituto Americano para el Desarrollo del Sindicalismo Libre, AFL-CIO. *Inversionistas Extranjeros: Lubricando la Maquinaria Gubernamental Cubana.* Washington, D.C. , Febrero 1995.

Ferriol, Angela. "El Empleo," *Economía Cubana: Boletín Informativo* 11 (Febrero 1995).

Lage, Carlos. "La Economía Cubana," *Economía Cubana: Boletín Informativo* 11 (Febrero 1995).

Pérez-López, Jorge. "Castro Tries Survival Strategy," *La Sociedad Económica,* Bulletin no. 47 (June 1995).

O'Connor, James. *The Fiscal Crisis of the State.* New York: St. Martin's Press, 1973.

O'Rourke, P.J. "Cubanomics," *Rolling Stone* (July 11-25, 1996).

Scarpaci, Joseph L. "Resolviendo! The Post Socialist Economy of Havana. Transitioning to Where?," unpublished paper, 1995.

Solchaga, Carlos. "Investing in Cuba." Washington, D.C.: Embassy of Spain, 1995.

Stern, Elizabeth Espin. *Free Market Cuba,* Vol. 3, No.2 (Spring 1995).

The World Bank. *Labor and Economic Reforms in Latin America and the Caribbean.* Washington, D.C., 1995

---

11. This is in fact occurring at present. A new wave of repression and demand for discipline is being undertaken by the old generation of orthodox Communist leaders who fear the tentative reforms promoted by a younger generation of scholars and government officials who did not participate in the insurgency against Batista.

COMMENTS ON

"Labor Effects of Adjustment Policies in Cuba" by Enrique S. Pumar

Ricardo L. Tejada

This paper raises several points of particular importance to the Cuban people today. First, it questions the Cuban government's rationale for the recent economic reforms and, in this context, argues that they were implemented in order to strengthen its own power. And second, the paper also opens the door to a debate which, although not explicitly addressed, seems to follow naturally: the question of the role of today's economic elite in a Cuba in transition.

Limited access to certain higher-paying occupations and sectors (with the ability to obtain hard currency), limited opportunities for profitable self-employment, and the growing problem with unemployment have all helped to create a dichotomy in the Cuban population. The paper establishes that, in Cuba, the place to be is in the lucrative "private" sector or in a job which allows access to dollars, but the government has limited the entrance to this part of the economy. Consequently, competition for these jobs is keen. Wages in other sectors, which pay in pesos, are often not sufficient to maintain a family

Dr. Pumar asserts that the Castro government has passed limited economic reforms solely as a measure to further tighten control over the population. Because competition for the new opportunities created as a result of Castro's reforms is intense, the government can select workers with a history of loyalty to the government to fill these sought-after positions. This is hardly disputable. However, this places new pressures on the government.

As the economic disparity increases between those who have access to lucrative jobs and those who do not, tensions will inevitably arise. In order to keep discord at bay, the government must respond to the portion of the population which does not enjoy the privilege of access to dollars or private sector jobs. It must do this through further oppression (thus increasing the dichotomy between the two groups) or further reforms. Only a large and sustained jump in economic growth could quell this situation—an unlikely scenario in the foreseeable future. Therefore, the current reforms are unstable. With this in mind, I must disagree with Dr. Pumar's premise that these reforms do not erode the power of the state. Power must indeed be eroded, as those denied access to this "new economy" become disaffected from the state. Certainly, this represents the vast majority of Cubans.

But looking forward, a further question arises which could be of particular importance to a Cuba in transition. This is the question of how this system of meritocracy will carry into a post-Castro economy. Will the scenario mirror that of Central and Eastern Europe where the most important players in the current economy are those who, under the previous regimes, enjoyed the highest of state privileges? These were the few with access to the highest levels of education, the most desirable skills, and perhaps most important, the personal connections necessary to succeed in a new market economy. Consequently, the former members of the ruling communist party once again enjoy positions of economic privilege based on their commitment to a previous regime. As objectionable as this situation might be to some, the economy can not afford to exclude those who hold the greatest human capital.

There exists a conflict here. An argument of politics versus efficiency. On the one hand, a true transition, one which would involve economic as well as political change, should reward the entire population. By no means should those who were denied access to coveted skills or the higher echelons of power find themselves in a position of economic disfavor relative to those who were not. However, a Cuba in transition will rely heavily on those skills that are held by those currently indulged by the revolutionary government. This is not a question which I would attempt to discuss in the limited scope of these comments but one which certainly deserves a closer look. I believe papers such as this one by Dr. Pumar provide an excellent forum for such questions.

UN "LOGRO" QUE TIENDE A DESMORONARSE

Marta Beatriz Roque Cabello

Estamos acostumbrados a que se resalten algunas actividades económicas y sociales del país como "logros" comparadas con el período anterior a 1959. Sin embargo, ya algunos de ellos comienzan a pesar, en el contexto de la falta de recursos para derrochar. En particular la seguridad social.

Mucho se ha reflexionado acerca de los beneficios que ha traído a los trabajadores cubanos el Sistema de Seguridad Social existente, pero los efectos negativos que se han desprendido de su adopción no se señalan.

Si el presupuesto estatal no tuviera que enfrentar los elevados gastos de seguridad social, el déficit presupuestario sería menor y también se reduciría la modorra que ha creado en los trabajadores la posibilidad de acogerse a certificados médicos o a jubilaciones prematuras con respecto a la edad, por problemas de incapacidad. El exceso de "bienestar" que preconiza el sistema trajo acompañado también un relajamiento en la disciplina laboral.

En la actualidad se ha llegado a la convicción de que es necesario rectificar la llamada benevolencia con que se ha enfocado la legislación vigente, pero se teme que las correcciones den al traste con una crisis. Es por ello que durante la discusión de la Ley Tributaria en la Asamblea Nacional del Poder Popular, quedó pendiente la aplicación de la contribución especial a la seguridad social por parte de los trabajadores.

No hay lugar a dudas que lo que se dio por un "logro" tiende a desmoronarse, el país no puede sostener un sistema propio de naciones altamente desarrolladas. Pero, antes de analizar las medidas que se pretenden tomar para subsanar las grietas que ha dejado el sistema, se podría hacer un pequeño recuento de cómo se ha legislado al respecto.

LA SEGURIDAD SOCIAL EN CUBA

Ya en 1913 se había elaborado la primera Ley de Seguridad Social en el país y en 1958 funcionaban 52 instituciones de Seguro Social, denominadas cajas fondo, cajas de retiro o seguro, y 50 cajas de retiro cuya funciones eran proteger a los trabajadores por pensiones de vejez, invalidez y muerte. También existían el régimen de accidentes del trabajo y el seguro de maternidad obrera. Aunque las instituciones protegían un poco más que el 46 por ciento de los trabajadores asalariados, el hecho de que no todos estuvieran cubiertos, no incidía para que todos se afanasen por trabajar.

La contribución que hacían los trabajadores a las cajas de retiro oscilaba entre el 3 y 6 por ciento del salario. Posterior a 1959 se han promulgado decenas de legislaciones vinculadas al Sistema de Seguridad Social, sin tener en consideración su mayor o menor importancia, algunas de ellas han sido demasiado "bondadosas," si se comparan con el costo social que implica manternerlas, como la Ley 1100 que garantizó un subsidio por 26 semanas al trabajador enfermo, prorrogable a otras 26 con el 40 por ciento del salario si estaba hospitalizado y el 50 por ciento si no lo estaba. La Ley 24 de 1979 extendió el derecho al cobro de subsidio por todo el tiempo que dure la enfermedad e incrementó en un 10 por ciento la tasa de los subsidios. Otras, han retirado parcialmente algunos de los beneficios que se suponía se recibieran del Sistema, como la Resolución 176 del Ministerio del Trabajo y el Ministerio de Salud Pública que ordenó que para los tres primeros días del certificado médico, la adminstración es quien justifica o no esos días. Este último aspecto, vinculado con el Sistema de Seguridad Social ha traído múltiples consecuencias adversas, entre ellas el relajamiento de la disciplina laboral, la pérdida de valores éticos por parte de los que emiten los certificados e indiscutiblemente el pago indebido de millones de días laborables, sin ningún respaldo productivo, como puede apreciarse en el Gráfico No. 1.

Ya los días promedio de ausencia por enfermedad en 1994 sobrepasaban los 17.22. Es algo contradictorio en un país en que oficialmente los indicadores de salud mejoran constantemente de año en año.

Si analizaramos la cantidad de jubilaciones y pensiones, nos encontraríamos ante una tendencia alta de crecimiento, la que comenzó al admitir la prueba testifical a los que acumulaban 25 años de trabajo y en los últimos 5 años se ha incrementado de forma insostenible, al extremo de que el Gobierno decidió revisar los expedientes de jubilación por incapacidad parcial o total de este período.

El número de beneficiarios asciende a 1,350,000 personas, con una tasa de crecimiento anual desde 1990 del 4.25 por ciento en físico y en valores monetarios del 6 por ciento. En 1980 la cifra absoluta era de 672,283, lo que implica que en 15 años se ha duplicado. Si se toma en cuenta el envejecimiento de la población cubana, se podría considerar normal, pero crecen en forma desproporcionadas las pensiones por invalidez, con cifras propias de países desarrollados, como se muestra en la Tabla No. 1.

La reducción que se nota en el último trimestre de 1995 es producida porque a nivel nacional se chequearon los expedientes y se viraron 807, con recomendaciones de buscarles solución sin jubilarlos. Las cifras relativas son elocuentes de lo que estaba pasando: si en 1990 el 25 por ciento de los jubilados fue por invalidez total, en los ocho primeros meses de 1995 ya ascendía al 38.5 por ciento.

Tabla 1. Casos de Invalidez Dentro de las Jubilaciones de 1994 y 1995

Trimestre	1994	1995	1995/1994 (%)
Primero	5416	7063	30.41
Segundo	6360	7919	24.52
Tercero	5136	9099	77.16
Cuarto	5427	4526	-16.6
Total	22339	28607	28.06

Con una esperanza de vida al nacer de 74.7 años, las mujeres se jubilan a la edad de 55 y los hombres con 60, lo que implica que el Estado debe proporcionarles ingresos mínimos por espacio de 20 y 15 años respectivamente como promedio, lo que resulta impropio de un país con tan bajo nivel de desarrollo económico. Sólo 60 de cada 100 trabajadores se retiran con la edad requerida, lo que aumenta la cantidad de años que hay que subsidiar al 40 por ciento de los jubilados.

Claro está, toda esta situación no se produce de forma espontánea, sino que a ella conducen factores de índole económico y social, sin excluirse los políticos. Hasta los propios organismos gubernamentales quieren resolver el problema de sus trabajadores "disponibles" y que están próximos a la edad del retiro, mediante la jubilación por invalidez. En algunas provincias se marca esta tendencia. Por ejemplo en Guantánamo en 1995 el 50 por ciento de los jubilados resultaron ser incapacitados totales para trabajar.

No cabe duda de que esta explosión está asociada al período especial—la pérdida del poder adquisitivo del salario y la posibilidad de obtener ingresos por otras vías ha influído en el hecho de que las personas se retiren antes de fecha. Posteriormente estos jubilados se incorporan nuevamente al trabajo de diferentes formas, una parte al sector estatal. En particular los jubilados de las Fuerzas Armadas y el Ministerio del Interior ocupan plazas de confianza,

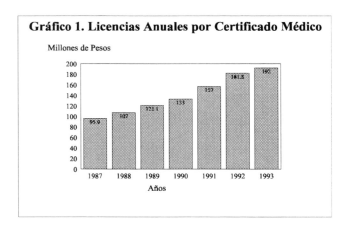

Gráfico 1. Licencias Anuales por Certificado Médico

Millones de Pesos

1987	1988	1989	1990	1991	1992	1993
95.9	107	121.1	133	157	181.8	192

Años

desde gerencias de tiendas y hoteles, hasta serenos. El sector cuentapropista también recoge una parte de estos, como puede apreciarse en la Tabla No. 2.

El hecho de que los jubilados opten por plazas estatales, con el déficit existente de ofertas de empleo de ese sector, hace que los jóvenes que arriban a la edad laboral, se encuentren en una situación desventajosa. Además de que el proceso de reducción de las plantillas infladas se detuvo, por su implicación política (dejar sin empleo a un millón de trabajadores, por concepto principalmente de ineficiencia de la fuerza laboral), anualmente se incorporan a la vida económicamente activa unas 140,00 personas, siendo el incremento potencial de la fuerza laboralanual de unas 100,000, porque de los que se incorporan hay que deducir las jubilaciones, los fallecimientos y otros factores (como los que emigran) por lo que todo atenta contra las posibilidades de nuevas fuentes de trabajo.

Tabla 2. Trabajadores por Cuenta Propia (Al cierre del primer trimestre de 1996)

	Número de Trabajadores	Por Ciento
Total	184,900	100.0
Con vínculo laboral	58,000	31.4
Desvinculados	50,300	27.2
Jubilados	47,300	25.6
Amas de casa	29,300	15.8

Nota: Al cierre de 1995, se reportaban 208,786 trabajadores por cuenta propia, de ellos el 47 por ciento desempleados y jubilados.

No hay que dejar de destacar, al tocar el tema, que poco se puede esperar de los jóvenes que tienen la oportunidad de incorporarse al trabajo, ya que desde el punto de vista productivo continuarán con el ejemplo que les dan sus antecesores, a los que el sistema ha convertido en su mayoría en malos trabajadores, trasladándoles la indolencia, el resquebrajamiento de la disciplina, la falta de exigencia personal y la desidia. Nadie trae al comienzo el rigor de los hábitos laborales y la cultura del trabajo, esto se va aprendiendo con la experiencia de un día tras de otro. Pero ¿cómo llegar a tener estos hábitos cuando el inicio es en un centro laboral donde reina el caos? Cuando se es joven se mira hacia el futuro trabajo, y las únicas expectativas que tiene la

vida de las generaciones venideras están ahí. Sin embargo entre las alternativas más comunes para estos jóvenes están estas dos: que no haya trabajo, o caer en el caos laboral.

En estos momentos se puede decir categoricamente que no hay relevo de la fuerza de trabajo y además, mientras se mantengan estos niveles salariales, no permitirían que se desarrolle.

Es como si existiera un acuerdo tácito entre el Estado y los trabajadores. El primero sabe que paga y la gente no trabaja; los segundos conocen que les pagan por debajo de sus necesidades y lo admiten. Las consecuencias de este convenio son la falta de bienes de consumo y servicios.

IMPACTO PRESUPUESTARIO

Al cierre de junio de 1995, la población laboral cubana llegaba a 4,330,000 personas, de las cuales 3,690,000 correspondían al sector estatal, y 640,000 al sector no estatal. Si tomamos en cuenta que el 43.35 por ciento de la población laboral es mujer y que son precisamente las mujeres que se jubilan con menor edad, así como que en el año 2000, uno de cada 7 cubanos tendrá 60 años o más, no cabe lugar a dudas que para esa fecha habrá una reducción de la Población Económicamente Activa, el Presupuesto Estatal se verá afectado por el número de jubilados y habrá adicionalmente una influencia en la demanda de servicios de salud y en el consumo de medicamentos.

Durante más de 30 años se ha mantenido una política artificial de empleo, superior al nivel óptimo. Oficialmente se calcula que el sobreempleo entre 1989 y 1992 se triplicó.

Lo hasta aquí explicado es un fenómeno incongruente con la esencia de los postulados sociales. La estructura de oportunidades para la sociedad estaba basada casi exclusivamente en el estudio y el trabajo.

De igual forma se hacen incoherentes los problemas financieros producidos por la crisis, que traen aparejado la necesidad de dinero fresco a través de préstamos internacionales y la necesidad de reducir el déficit del Presupuesto Nacional, sobre el cual influye de forma relevante el Sistema de Seguridad Social existente. En la Tabla No. 3 puede apreciarse el comportamiento de los gastos de seguridad social en el presupuesto del estado desde 1989.

Tabla 3.   La Seguridad Social y el Presupuesto del Estado (En millones de pesos)

Años	Gastos de Seguridad Social	Gastos de Seguridad Social como % de Gastos del Presupuesto del Estado
1989	1093.9	7.87
1990	1164.1	7.51
1991	1225.7	8.33
1992	1348.0	8.95
1993	1452.3	9.97
1994	1532.4	10.80
1995	1572.5	12.40

Tabla 4.   Comparación de los Ingresos Percápita en Cuba con Algunos Países de América Latina

País	Población	Ingreso percápita en dólares
Nicaragua	3,987,240	476
Costa Rica	3,264,776	2030
Honduras	5,170,108	800
El Salvador	5,636,524	1053
Panamá	2,579,047	2132
Guatemala	10,446,015	870
Cuba[a]	10,963,000	60

a.   Estimado por el ICEI a partir de informaciones oficiales y considerando la tasa de cambio de 21 pesos cubanos por un dólar de las Casas de Cambio.

En los Estados Unidos, donde existen diferentes programas de mantenimiento de los ingresos, en 1989 la Seguridad Social representó el 21 por ciento del gasto federal de ese año fiscal, con un monto de 234 mil millones de dólares. Si obviamos la cifra absoluta, el nivel poblacional, y la participación en el presupuesto, el 12.40 por ciento que invierte Cuba en la Seguridad Social, está muy por encima de sus posibilidades como país sin desarrollo económico.

No obstante el hecho de que no se hable de aumentar salarios, porque sería una forma de incrementar el circulante, vivir del salario es algo muy difícil y mientras este pago no tenga contrapartida material se eternizará la crisis. El ingreso percápita en el país es tan bajo que comparado con cualquier país de América Latina resulta irrisorio, según se puede apreciar en la Tabla No. 4. El 22.5 por ciento del total de los núcleos familiares es considerado de bajos ingresos (menos de 50 pesos percápita mensuales). Las provincias orientales concentran el 50 por ciento de los núcleos con bajos ingresos.

En la segunda mitad de los años 80, comienza a manifestarse el déficit presupuestario. Aunque no es el objetivo de este trabajo analizar este aspecto, si hay que dejar en claro que cuando cesa la ayuda del exbloque socialista, en particular de la Unión Soviética, es que sale a flote la preocupación gubernamental por este déficit. Sin embargo las repercusiones sociales no se hicieron esperar.

La clara imagen de bienestar de los trabajadores gracias a la bondad estatal, que ha querido proyectarse tanto externa como internamente, se ha oscurecido. Comienza a vislumbrarse el veradadero panorama que tiene frente la sociedad cubana, la que trata de salir del problema de diferentes formas, pero definitivamente va en busca de una transición, que llegará de una manera u otra, antes o después, en la misma medida en que sea más o menos tolerable la crisis.

Si se sumaran las circunstancias adversas que rodean cada uno de los llamados "logros" se podría constatar como tienden a minimizarse, pero en particular la Seguridad Social como sistema se hace insostenible y de ello están convencidos hasta los que lo mantienen.

FUENTES

Economía y Desarrollo, año 95, no. 2.

Samuelson, Paul A., y William D. Nordhaus. *Economía*.

THE OPTIMAL SIZE OF THE MILITARY IN A POST-CASTRO CUBA

Carlos Seiglie

In addressing the question of what is the optimal size of the defense sector in a post-Castro Cuba, we must first establish some criteria by which we can judge different alternatives. In this paper, the criteria that I use is one where the level of the military sector is determined by the preferences of the median voter. In other words, I assume that a representative democracy will exist in Cuba after Castro and that the decisive individual is the median voter. Allowing for different ways of collectively aggregating the preferences of different individuals, while yielding a different optimal level, will still possess all the characteristics of the approach used in this paper.

Individuals are assumed to make choices over consumption and national security. The latter is important because it can be seen as a way for individuals to *self-protect* against a future attack by an adversary who will confiscate some portion of their wealth if successful in its efforts. Defense serves to raise the cost of an attack to the perpetrator, i.e., it provides a means of deterrence to a country. Military spending is therefore a derived demand for an underlying commodity which is the increase in expected utility resulting from the higher probability of being able to consume one's wealth at a future period in time. The next section of the paper briefly outlines the theory and the final section discusses the optimal level of spending for Cuba under various different scenarios regarding the economic and political conditions which could prevail in Cuba.

THE DEMAND FOR NATIONAL SECURITY

This section generalizes the demand for national security in Seiglie (1988) in several directions. First, it introduces the possibility that expenditures by enemies decrease welfare just as those by allies increase welfare. Second, since the economy is open and in a steady state equilibrium, the budget constraint faced by individuals is altered. These extensions will be developed under the assumption that preferences take a particular functional form that generates linear military expenditure functions.

The amount of military capability produced or imported by a nation is not necessarily equal to the amount available for its consumption. Part of the difference is due to the public goods aspect of military alliances which has been discussed in the economic literature. The other part results from the fact that some proportion of an adversary's military capability spills over and decreases the effectiveness of the country's military defense, i.e., it reduces its national security. In the discussion that follows we denote the adversary of Cuba as country e (denoting enemy) and its potential ally as US. The proportion of country e's weapon stock that reduces Cuba's national security will be denoted by a_{ce}. Likewise, some proportion of Cuba's military capability reduces country e's national security; denote this as a_{ec}. These proportions differ for each country depending, for example, on the percentage of military spending directed towards offensive versus defensive purposes. If we represent the total amount of spillover from the adversarial country e towards Cuba by M_{ce} and the positive spillover from the ally, the US, by M_{cUS} then the total consumption of national security by Cuba is m_c, where

$$m_c = M_c - M_{ce} + M_{cUS} \qquad (1)$$

and M_c is the total amount produced by Cuba.

By our previous assumption,

$$M_{ce} = a_{ce}M_e + v_e \qquad (2)$$

$$M_{cUS} = b_{cUS} \ M_{US} \qquad (2')$$

where M_e is the total amount of military capability produced by country e and therefore, some fraction of that total, a_{ce}, reduces the effectiveness of Cuba's national security. The variable v_e is a measure of hostile actions by country e which signal intentions and is assumed independent of M_e. A similar interpretation holds for the positive spillover, M_{cUS} resulting from a military alliance, i.e., we assume some fraction b_{cUS} of the US military serves to protect Cuba.

Therefore, the total effective consumption of military capability for Cuba, m_c, is equal to:

$$m_c = M_c - a_{ce}M_e - v_e + b_{cUS} \ M_{US} \qquad (3)$$

Likewise, for country e which is assumed to be allied to country R,

$$m_e = M_e - a_{ec}M_c - v_c + b_{eA} \ M_R \qquad (4)$$

In the model, the coefficient a_{ij} is viewed as a measure of the degree of spillover embodied in the armament of the opponent. For example, if the weapons of the opponent were mainly offensive then a_{ij} would be high, but if the weapon systems of the opponent were mainly defensive then a_{ij} would be low. The other coefficient v_i can be viewed as a hostility signal. As such, it reflects the perception of threat or hostility directed towards country i from other nations. Analogously, b represents the spillins resulting from military alliances.

Let the representative citizen of country 1 have preferences represented by the following Stone-Geary utility function:

$$U(c_c \ , \ m_c) = (c_c - \overline{c}_c)^\alpha \ m_c^{1-\alpha} \qquad (5)$$

$$= (c_c - \overline{c}_c)^\alpha (M_c - a_{ce}M_e - v_e + b_{cUS} \ M_{US})^{1-\alpha}$$

where c represents consumption and $\overline{c}$ denotes a "minimum" subsistence level of consumption. We assume the Cuban economy is in a steady state with a capital/labor ratio, k^*, and an average propensity to save, s^*. For the overall economy with N individuals,

$$I = \sum_{i=1}^{N} E_i + \sum_{i=1}^{N} s_i \ I_i \qquad (6)$$

where I denotes national income; E_i the expenditure of the ith individual; I_i his income; and s_i his savings rate.

Cuba's defense expenditure is equal to $P_M \ M_c$ where P_M is the unit cost of maintaining a national defense of size M_c. The ith individual's tax share to finance these expenditures will be denoted by t_i, so that choosing consumption as the numeraire commodity, his budget constraint is:

$$c_c + \tau_c \ P_M \ M_c = (1-s_i) \ I_i = E_i \qquad (7)$$

Following Dudley and Montmarquette (1981), note that if the only tax rate, t, imposed by the government is proportional to income then

$$\tau_i = t I_i \ / \ \sum_{i=1}^{N} t I_i = I_i \ / \ (\sum (I_i \ / \ N) N)$$

$$= (1/ \ N) \ (I_i \ / \ Y) \qquad (8)$$

where Y is Cuba's per capita income.

Per capita income Y is a function of the degree of openness of the economy δ, i.e., $I(\delta)$ with $I'(\delta) > 0$. In other words, as the degree of openness of the economy increases, military spending increases.

Maximization of equation (5) subject to (7) yields the following first order conditions:

$$\alpha \ (c_c - \overline{c}_c)^{\alpha-1} \ m_c^{1-\alpha} - \mu = 0 \qquad (9)$$

$$(1-\alpha) \ (c_c - \overline{c}_c)^\alpha \ m_c^{-\alpha} - \mu\tau_c \ P_M = 0 \quad (9')$$

which when substituting

$m_c = M_c - a_{ce}M_e - v_e + b_{cUS} M_{cUS}$

along with our budget constraint yields the following demand (reaction) function:

$$M_c = (1-\alpha) \ [(1-s_i) \ I_i \ - \ \overline{c}_c] \ / \ (\tau_i \ P_M)$$
$$+ \ \alpha a_{ce} M_{ce} \ - \ \alpha b_{cus} M_{US} \ + \ \alpha v_e \qquad (10)$$

We can see from the above that the demand for defense is increasing in income and decreasing in the cost of maintaining the military, P_M.

Several other results emerge from equation (10). Firstly, M_c is increasing in the opponent's level of military weapons, M_e. Secondly, M_c is also increasing in the "degree of aggression," v_e, of the adversary, i.e., increasing in the level of conflict with adversaries. Thirdly, the weapon stock is decreasing in the level of weapons of the ally. This tendency to *free-ride* off the ally is increasing in the degree that the ally's weapons have the non-rivalness property of a public good and in the strength of the alliance. This degree of non-rivalness is implicitly incorporated in b_{cus}. This coefficient also captures the fact that an ally that is not very likely to intervene on behalf of Cuba will not greatly reduce the latter's level of armaments. M_c is also increasing in the threat of the adversary's weapons, a_{ce}. For example, the proximity of the two countries geographically is important if the countries do not possess long range missiles or bombers so that the closer they are the higher is a_{ce}, or if they are contiguous countries the mix of the weapon stock between offensive and defensive systems is important with an increase in offensive weapons implying a rise in a_{ce}. Finally, M_c is decreasing in the tax share, t_i.

The military expenditure function for Cuba, ME_c, which is equal to $P_M \ M_c$ is the following after substituting for τ and assuming that the representative individual's savings rate is equal to the steady state rate, s^* we get

$$ME_c = (1-\alpha)I \ - \ (1-\alpha)s^*I \ - \ [(1-\alpha)\overline{c}_c]\tau_i \qquad (11)$$
$$+\alpha a_{ce}ME_e - \alpha b_{cus}M_{US} \ + \ \alpha P_m v_e$$

$$=\beta_1 I \ + \ \beta_2 S \ + \ \beta_3 (1/\tau_i) \ + \ \beta_4 ME_c \ + \ \beta_5 ME_{US} \ + \ \beta_6 V_e$$

where I is real national income, S (equal to s^*I) is real national savings and β_1, β_4 and β_6 are greater than zero and β_2 β_3 and β_5 are less than zero.

Several propositions emerge from this expenditure function, namely that military expenditures should be increasing in: 1) income; 2) the opponent's expenditures; 3) the level of conflict or aggression directed towards it from other nations and decreasing in: 4) allies' expenditures; 5) the savings rate; 6) the tax share; 7) the minimum subsistence level; and 8) the strength of the alliance, b_{cus}.

Finally, the above assumes that countries trade at world market prices. Since the gains from trade are decreasing in distortions to world prices and since wars or international conflicts serve to raise the transaction costs involved in trade with the rest of the world, we expect that the greater that an economy is dependent on world trade and therefore, the greater is the sum of consumers' and producers' surplus derived from this trade, the greater will be its military expenditures in order to protect these gains. Therefore, military expenditures should be increasing in the extent that an economy is open to world trade.

ESTIMATES OF THE MILITARY EXPENDITURES FUNCTION

In this section, estimates are presented for the parameters of the expenditure function (equation 11) derived above. The variable O_i, denotes the degree of openness of the economy. We also introduce a constant to the equation, as well as an error term, e_i. The definitions of the variables are as follows. Our dependent variable, ME, denotes the real military expenditures of the country. As for our explanatory variables, I refers to the level of real GNP and S to the level of real national savings for country i. As for $(1/t_i)$, it is the inverse of the tax share of the representative individual in the country, which from equation (8) is equal to the inverse of the share of real income of the representative individual in GNP. As a proxy for this variable we have used a Gini coefficient of sectoral inequality published by the World Bank. A better proxy would have been a Gini coefficient based on individual income or households, but such a measure is unavailable for many of the countries used in our sample. We therefore expect that as inequality increases (the Gini coefficient rises, i.e., t_i falls and $(1/t_i)$ rises), the country's military expendi-

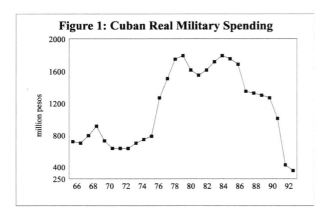

Figure 1: Cuban Real Military Spending

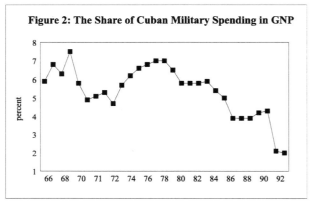

Figure 2: The Share of Cuban Military Spending in GNP

tures, ME_i, should rise. Therefore, we expect the sign of its coefficient to be positive.

As for the other variables, ME_j represents the military expenditures of the adversarial nation. We expect the coefficient, b_4 to be positive. Conversely, ME_k denotes the military expenditures of countries allied to country i. This captures the *spill-in* from the alliance's expenditure into the particular member country. Our model predicts the sign of this variable to be negative due to the free-riding problem inherent in public goods. As for our coefficient of aggression, v_j, which measures the aggression from the rest of the world towards country *i* we expect its sign to be positive, i.e., increases in foreign aggression should lead to increases in expenditures.

To arrive at a measure for this latter variable I have used the Conflict and Peace Data Bank (COPDAB)

developed by Azar (1980a, 1980b). The COPDAB consists of approximately 500,000 international events which occurred from 1948 to 1978. Each event entry in the data base lists the actor and target nation, the issue involved and the date of occurrence. The source of information is taken from close to 100 regional and international publications. The data base consists of a ranking of events according to a predetermined scale aimed at quantifying the intensity of the event ranging from the most cooperative given a value of 1, such as the voluntary unification of nation-states to the most conflictful which is given a value of 15, an extensive war act. In order to arrive at a level of aggression towards a country from the rest of the world (v_j) I have taken the average of the scaling of hostility from all countries in the data base towards that particular country during the year and conversely. So for example, if a country has had three international interactions in a particular year: 1) war was declared against it by a neighboring country (scale=15); 2) a country strongly attacked it verbally (scale=10); and 3) it formed a major strategic alliance with another country (scale=2), then the index of hostility for the year would be 9, (15+10+2)/3. This index was calculated for all countries in the sample listed in COPDAB for each year.

Correcting for the possibility of heteroscedasticity, the estimated military expenditure function is the following:[1]

$$ME_c = -25985 + .12\ I - .33\ S + 165\ (1/\tau_i) + .03\ ME_e - .02\ ME_{US} + 6352\ O + 2970\ V_e$$

Using these estimates for the variables we can analyze the level of defense expenditures in a post-Castro Cuba under various scenarios. Before we do so, Figures 1 and 2 shows the estimated size of the Cuban military for selected measures. It is obvious that there has been a sharp decline in the size of the military sector whether measured in real 1988 dollars or as a percentage of total output. Recent estimates place Cuban military spending in 1988 dollars at 354 million dollars and its share in total output declining to 2 percent.

---

1. All the variables are statistically significant and variables are in 1978 dollars.

The natural question to ask is if Cuba had different economic and political characteristics, what would be the optimal level of military spending? Given the space constraints, let me propose one of many plausible scenarios. Suppose that Cuba had a level of GNP (GDP) equivalent to that of Chile and a national savings rate of 20 percent (less than Chile's). Furthermore, assume that Cuba had as a natural adversary a country such as the Dominican Republic and that Cuba had the United States as an ally (as is the case for example, with Canada). Finally, assume that the Cuban economy is as open as that of the Dominican Republic or Jamaica. Under these conditions, Cuba would have to confront an international environment with a level of hostility towards it resulting in a COPDAB score of 9.2 to **justify having a military** for national security reasons. This score is defined as experiencing mild verbal hostility or discord with the rest of the world. More specifically, this corresponds to low-key objections to policy or behavior; expressing discontent through third parties; objections to explanation of policy and requests by other countries for a change in policy.

It is surprising that to justify current levels of Cuban military spending would require a value close to 10, which corresponds to a climate of strong verbal hostility towards it. Examples of this are strong condemnations by the international community of its actions or policies; threats of retaliation for acts it commits; denunciation of Cuba's leaders, system or ideology; strong propaganda attacks; postponement of head of state visits or withdrawal from meetings or summits; and blocking or vetoing actions in international bodies.

It may seem that this is the scenario that Cuba currently is facing in the world and this is what justifies its current levels (estimates). This is not in fact the case since the scores or values for the COPDAB is for an average of all countries' actions towards Cuba. Therefore, while the United States may have a hostile policy towards Cuba, the rest of the world has much better relations with it, and therefore, the value or score is lower. In conclusion, Cuba would have to be the subject of fairly widespread hostilities by members of the international community to justify a post-Castro Cuba having any significant military, if as I suggest, it proposes to ally itself with the United States (as is currently the case for NATO member countries or for that matter, Puerto Rico).

REFERENCES

Azar, E.E. "The Code Book of the Conflict and Peace Data (COPDAB): A Computer Assisted Approach to Monitoring and Analyzing International and Domestic Events," University of North Carolina, Chapel Hill (mimeo) (1980a).

Azar, E.E. "The Conflict and Peace Data Bank (COPDAB) Project," *Journal of Conflict Resolution* 24 (1980b) 142-152.

Benoit, Emile. "Growth and Defense in Developing Countries," *Economic Development and Cultural Change* 26 (January 1978) 271-280.

Bergstrom, T.C. and Goodman, R.P. "Private Demands for Public Goods," *American Economic Review* 63 (1973) 280-296.

Boulding, Kenneth E. *Conflict and Defense*. Boston: Harper and Row, 1961.

Brito, D.L. "A Dynamic Model of an Armament Race," *International Economic Review* 13 (1972) 359-375.

Brito, D.L. and M.D. Intriligator. "Conflict, War, and Redistribution," *The American Political Science Review* 79 (1985) 943-957.

Brito, D.L. and M.D. Intriligator. "Nuclear proliferation and the armaments race," *Journal of Peace Science* 2 (1977) 213-218.

Connolly, Michael. "Public Goods, Externalities and International Relations," *Journal of Political Economy* 78:2 (1970) 23-49.

Deger, S. "Economic Development and Defense Expenditure," *Economic Development and Cultural Change* 35 (October 1986) 179-195.

Deger, S. and S. Sen. "Military Expenditure, Spin-off and Economic Development," *Journal of Development Economics* 13 (August-October 1983) 67-83.

Dudley, L. and C. Montmarquette. "The Demand for Military Expenditures: An International Comparison," *Public Choice* 37 (1981) 5-31.

Findlay, Ronald. "Factor Proportions and Comparative Advantage in the Long Run," *Journal of Political Economy* (January 1970) 27-34.

Garfinkel, Michelle. "Arming as a Strategic Investment in a Cooperative Equilibrium," *American Economic Review* 80 (March 1990) 50-68.

Intriligator, Michael D. "Strategic Considerations in the Richardson Model of Arms Races," *Journal of Political Economy* 83 (1975) 339-353.

Isard, W. *Arms Races, Arms Control, and Conflict Analysis*. New York: Cambridge University Press, 1988.

Johnston, J. *Econometric Methods*. New York: McGraw-Hill Book Co., 1984.

Klein, Lawrence R. and M. Gronicki. "Defense Spending Among Warsaw Pact Countries: Implications for LINK Simulations of the Arms Race," mimeo, University of Pennsylvania (1988).

Komiya, R. "Non-Traded Goods and the Pure Theory of International Trade," *International Economic Review* (June 1967) 132-152.

Leontief, W., and F. Duchin. *Military Spending*. New York: Oxford University Press, 1983.

Murdoch, J.C. and T. Sandler. "Complementarity, Free Riding, and the Military Expenditure of NATO Allies," *Journal of Public Economics* 25 (1984) 83-101.

McGuire, Martin C. *Secrecy and the Arms Race*. Cambridge: Harvard University Press, 1965.

McGuire, Martin C. "A Quantitative Study of the Strategic Arms Race in the Missile Age," *Review of Economic and Statistics* 59 (1977) 328-339.

Olson, M. and Zeckhauser, R. "An Economic Theory of Alliances," *Review of Economics and Statistics* 48 (1966) 266-279.

Peltzman, Sam. "The Growth of Government," *Journal of Law and Economics* 23 (October 1980) 209-87.

Sandler, T. and J. Forbes. "Burden Sharing, Strategy, and the Design of NATO," *Economic Inquiry* 18 (1980) 425-444.

Sandler, Todd. "Impurity of Defense:An Application to the Economics of Alliances," *Kyklos* 30 (1977) 443-460.

Seiglie, Carlos. "International Conflict and Military Expenditures," *Journal of Conflict Resolution* 32 (1988) 141-161.

Seiglie, Carlos. "Determinants of Military Expenditures," in *Economics of Arms Reduction and the Peace Process*, edited by Walter Isard and C. Anderson. Amsterdam: North-Holland, 1992.

Seiglie, Carlos. "Causality in the Military Expenditures of Potential Adversaries," *Economics and Politics* (November 1996).

Schelling, Thomas C. *The Strategy of Conflict*. Cambridge: Harvard University Press, 1960.

World Bank. *World Tables*. Baltimore: Johns Hopkins University Press, 1976.

World Armaments and Disarmament--SIPRI Yearbook. London: Taylor and Francis Ltd., various years.

World Military Expenditures and Arms Transfers. Washington: United States Arms Control and Disarmament Agency, various years.

COMMENTS ON

"The Optimal Size of the Military in a Post-Castro Cuba" by Seiglie

Diego R. Roqué

It was professor Simon, the Nobel laureate, who once said that satisfizing is more often than not a far more attainable goal than optimizing. This was a recognition of how difficult it is to find optimal solutions of problems in the real world. This is what makes Professor Seiglie's effort even the more remarkable and worthy of consideration. It tackles the highest degree of difficulty possible. It is a very ambitious enterprise on a very complex arena.

The work of Seiglie, to begin with, contributes a mathematical model of how a society collectively defends its national interest. Herein lies a lot of its merit. All reasonable mathematical models are referential frameworks within which to organize thought. At the very least, they stimulate discussion of the subject matter in exposing their construct to criticism which is very easy to do. Let no one doubt that Professor Seiglie has made a significant contribution on this count alone and possibly much more.

When such models are sound, they have valuable explanatory power and general law and principle may be derived from them. Decision makers are wise to use such models. It is often practice or experimentation that lends models their validity and one may hope that Professor Seiglie's work will be some day subjected to such practice or experimentation. Continued development of this fundamental piece of work is a must to all those concerned with helping Cuba achieve a successful transition to democracy.

COMMENTARY

As a defense analyst, my experience has taught me that safeguarding the national interest or matters of national security are a very dynamic process subject to many random events in time almost demanding a stochastic approach to their analysis. Alliances, for example, are transient phenomena that vary with time and circumstances. If Professor Seiglie is not willing to call his model static, at the very least he is assuming some kind of stationarity or even yet a world in steady-state. This detracts somewhat from the amount of realism his work may offer.

Of fundamental importance in optimization work is establishing the criterion for what is considered best. In this context, the cornerstone of defense planning is a proper assessment and estimation of what constitutes the threat to the nation. This requires assembling the proper knowledge and expertise to keep the National Command Authorities, most of which represent the citizenry, properly informed. In national defense matters hardly ever is the citizen the decision maker. Properly informed representatives of the citizenry are the actual decision makers. This is because in a Republic, as opposed to a pure Democracy, the whole is much more than the sum of its parts or constituents. This is why I have to challenge Professor Seiglie's criteria for optimization as insufficient or incomplete. I quote: "In this paper, the criteria that I use is one where the level of the military sector is determined by the preferences of the median voter. In other words, I assume that a representative Democracy will exist in Cuba after Castro and that the decisive individual is the median voter."

A Republic, yes, but a pure Democracy, that is, a nation run on plebiscite, no. In matters of national security and of the supreme interest of the nation the responsibility entrusted to the representatives of the citizenry takes over and the individual voters seem to get lost. War, for example, is declared by the representatives and not the citizenry. The pressure to "dodge the draft," for example, sometimes surpasses the best interests of the collective. This is why the preferences of the median voter although having bearing and impact appear insufficient.

The author goes on to mention: "Military spending is therefore a derived demand for an underlying commodity which is the increase in expected utility resulting from the higher probability of being able to consume one's wealth at a future period in time." I seriously doubt whether voter output reflects any such well defined, conceptual or intuitive, utility function in matters of national defense.

Two other assumptions must not go unchallenged. One is that the economy of the Cuban nation will be in steady-state. We know it takes only trend to introduce non-linearity to a time series. True that sometimes one can extract trends and seasonality from a time series in order to isolate its stationary components but this is not the same as declaring the original time series stationary. This assumption definitely weakens the model. Another assumption is that "preferences take a particular functional form which generates military expenditure functions which are linear." No justification is given for this assumption nor is its sense of realism discussed.

To the author's credit, however, it must be stated that if one is willing to accept the imperfect premises of this model, if one wants to analyze the information they contain, then the author's construct can be viewed as one possessing a lot of internal consistency and well defined logical relations that do have bearing on national defense issues. The effort is a rational contribution shedding some light on matters that have previously been found very obscure and complex.

The optimization problem formulated by the author falls in the category of non-linear programming. He maximizes a non-linear utility objective function subject to one linear equality constraint. He fails to inform the reader that his non-linear program is convex (for a certain range of the parameter alpha) which is the key element in his claim of optimality. The Karuch-Kuhn-Tucker first order necessary conditions for optimality used to solve the optimization problem happen to be sufficient, as well, for global optimality, when the program is convex. Not using the term "necessary and sufficient first order conditions for global optimality" is a real disservice to the reader. The author also owes the reader an explanation as to why he does not incorporate into his formulation of the optimization problem non-negativity constraints of his two basic decision variables, namely consumption and the total amount of military capability produced by Cuba, and of the consequences of this.

As a result of the optimization, the author obtains two basic formulas, one for the total amount of military capability produced by Cuba (equation 10) and the other for the military expenditure function for Cuba (equation 11). The latter is derived from the former after some substitutions and one more assumption about the savings rate. The author successfully lends validity and credibility to the internal consistency of his model and the character of the basic relations used by demonstrating how the proper (read common sensical) monotonicity relationships exist between the dependent and independent variables of his equation 10. When it comes to equation 11, the same monotonicity relationships and many more now acquire the character of propositions. The model yields a lot of information about relationships among variables or quantities with real meaning that had previously remained unknown or unexplored. All the relationships, mathematically established, appear logical or supportable by common sense. Herein lies the fundamental merit of this work.

The author then uses equation 11 to embark on a quantification exercise. This requires estimating parameter and variable values for the right hand side of equation 11. This raises two questions: the first is how good and accurate are these estimates? The second is, even if the estimates are good, does the result have any value exogenous to the framework of the model? More specifically, may the result be accepted as universally valid in the real world?

In the first count, estimating the parameters, one must give the author the benefit of the doubt. His work appears professional indeed. The use of equation 11 is then a function of how valid and realistic are the different scenarios used to obtain or generate values of military expenditures for Cuba. But even if the scenarios are valid and realistic, the model may be at a very early stage of development to offer any more than broad guidelines. Certainly not deadly accurate realistic figures. Nevertheless, this elegant piece of work breaks new ground and permits the comparison of various alternative scenarios albeit within a limited framework. Only test, experimentation, and time can be the final arbiter of the adequacy of the model.

The author concludes: "Cuba would have to be the subject of fairly widespread hostilities by members of the international community to justify a post-Castro Cuba having any significant military, if as I suggest, it proposes to ally itself with the U.S. (as is currently the case for NATO member countries or for that matter Puerto Rico)." The author has established his case for this conclusion but the subject remains open to debate.

CONCLUSION

This work of Professor Carlos Seiglie will enrich the already extensive library of the Association for the Study of the Cuban Economy (ASCE) which will someday help restore sanity to the emergent institutions of the second Republic of Cuba. It rates very high in innovative thinking in an area of crucial importance to almost every nation. It would not surprise me at all if even the Pentagon shows an interest in this crucial development.

CUBAN MILITARY EXPENDITURES:
CONCEPTS, DATA AND BURDEN MEASURES

Jorge F. Pérez-López

The last two decades have seen the emergence of a rich literature on the military in socialist Cuba. The interest in studying the island's military institutions and functions was piqued in the 1970s by the overseas involvement of the Cuban military: overt intervention of Cuban forces in African wars; veiled involvement in Middle Eastern and Asian military campaigns; and threats of involvement in military conflicts in the Americas. Relatively well treated in the literature are Cuban military institutions (del Aguila 1989; Fernández 1989; Walker 1989 and 1995b), military mission and strategy (Buchanan 1995b; Goure 1989a; Walker 1995a, Zubatkin 1995), military relations with civil society (Buchanan 1995a; Domínguez 1974 and 1976; Suárez 1989), military relations with the Soviet Union (Goure 1989b; Goethals 1995), and military elites (Fermoselle 1987a and 1987b). Recent works have examined the adaptation of the military to the economic stringencies brought about by the economic crisis of the 1990s (e.g., Alonso 1995; Millett 1993; León 1995; Walker 1996). Less well studied are the implications of the Cuban military establishment and its activities for the civilian economy.[1]

What are the economic consequences—positive and negative—of various military activities? What are the trade-offs between military expenditures and other forms of public spending, such as nutrition, health, education, infrastructure, housing? Where is Cuba situated relative to this guns-versus-butter controversy?

To a large extent, the lack of attention to the economic implications of the Cuban military comes about because of the lack of adequate information. Reliable time series data on the structure and performance of the Cuban economy are difficult to come by and fraught with methodological questions.[2] Even scarcer are statistics on Cuban military expenditures, size of the armed forces, arms imports, and military foreign aid received or granted. Moreover, little is known about the precise definition of military expenditures used in Cuban statistics and how certain activities are treated.

This paper is a first attempt at examining the implications for the Cuban economy of the military, focusing on military expenditures. The first part of the paper looks at conceptual issues related to the definition of military expenditures. The second part reviews sources of military expenditures estimates. The third part focuses on official data and estimates of Cuban military expenditures, identifying some deficiencies in the data. The last part presents several measures of the military burden on the Cuban economy and compares them with similar measures for

---

1. Exceptions are Alonso (1995) and Roca (1980).

2. The classic evaluations of Cuban economic statistics are by Mesa-Lago (1969a and 1969b). See also Mesa-Lago and Pérez-López (1985).

other nations. The paper closes by raising some issues for further research.

THE CONCEPT OF MILITARY EXPENDITURES

The questions of how much of its resources a country devotes to military-related (or security-related) activities, and how the given country compares with others in this same regard, often do not result in unequivocal answers. There are several reasons for this. First, there are differences across countries—and even across organizations specializing on international security matters—with regard to the precise definition of military expenditures. Second, there is a tendency on the part of governments to restrict the amount of information they make public regarding military expenditures, arguing that potential enemies might profit from disclosure of sensitive information. And third, there are serious methodological problems in comparing military expenditures within the same country over time or across countries.

Definition of Military Expenditures

Conceptually, military expenditures (ME) can be broadly defined as all the material and human resources devoted by a state to its defense, and intended to: 1) guarantee its national independence, the integrity of its territory and, where appropriate, the respect of the international treaties binding the country to foreign states; and 2) maintain internal security and public order (Herrera 1994, p. 13). The first part of the definition concentrates on the defense of national territory and the ability to meet external challenges, while the second focuses on the maintenance of internal order. These motivations are virtually inseparable and their objective is the same: to ensure the proper functioning of a nation's society and economy, and basically to guarantee its survival, power and identity (Herrera 1994, p.13).

Military expenditures allow a state to purchase[3] a set of inputs from within the domestic economy and from foreign countries in order to produce an output called national defense. The most readily available data on ME for most countries is the budget of the Ministry of Defense or its equivalent within each country. While the Ministry of Defense budget may generally be a proxy for ME, there are practical problems in equating these two concepts. Some of the problems arise from differences across countries in accounting techniques and in the degree of state intervention in the economy. For example (Herrera 1994, p. 14):

- In some countries, the Ministry of Defense carries out functions related to infrastructure that are performed in others by the civilian sector. Examples are construction and maintenance of ports and airports, dredging of shipping channels, installation of telecommunications networks, land clearance, and surveillance of civilian productive equipment or lines of communication. Ministries of Defense in some nations can also be involved in providing certain services that are considered to be within the civilian sphere in others, e.g., air traffic control, customs services, meteorological information.

- On the other side of the ledger, some expenditures from the budgets of civilian ministries may be primarily for military purposes and therefore augment the budget of Ministries of Defense. Examples include research and development closely associated with weapons, construction of public infrastructures (roads and bridges to and from military bases, housing facilities for members of the military), research in areas such as nuclear power and airspace with military applications.

In part to address these national differences, the North Atlantic Treaty Organization (NATO), the International Monetary Fund (IMF), and the United Nations (UN) have developed standardized defini-

---

3. It is common for developing countries to receive foreign aid that allows them to augment their military expenditures beyond levels sustainable from domestic resources. In some instances, the military aid takes the form of loans or grants that allow the recipient country to increase their purchase of weapons systems and other inputs for the military. In others, it takes the form of the outright transfer or "gift" of military hardware, which therefore does not have to be purchased as such.

Definitions of Military Expenditures

North Atlantic Treaty Organization (NATO)

All current and capital expenditures on the armed forces, in the running of defense departments and other government agencies engaged in defense projects as well as space projects; the cost of paramilitary forces and police when judged to be trained and equipped for military operations; military R&D, tests and evaluation costs; and costs of retirement pensions of service personnel including pensions of civilian employees. Military aid is included in the expenditure of the donor countries. Excluded are items of civil defense, interest on war debts and veterans' payments.

International Monetary Fund (IMF)

All expenditure, whether by defense or other departments, for the maintenance of military forces, including the purchase of military supplies and equipment (including the stockpiling of finished items but not the industrial raw materials required for their production), military construction, recruiting, training, equipping, moving, feeding, clothing and housing members of the armed forces, and providing remuneration, medical care, and other services for them. Also included are capital expenditures for the provision of quarters to families of military personnel, outlays on military schools, and research and development serving clearly and foremost the purposes of defense. Military forces also include paramilitary organizations such as gendarmerie, constabulary, security forces, border and customs guards, and other trained, equipped and available for use as military personnel. Also falling under this category are expenditures for purposes of strengthening the public services to meet wartime emergencies, training civil defense personnel, and acquiring materials and equipment for these purposes. Included also are expenditures for foreign military aid and contributions to foreign to international military organizations and alliances. This category excludes expenditures for non-military purposes, though incurred by a ministry or department of defense, and any payments or services provided to war veterans and retired army personnel.

United Nations (UN)

The United Nations has drawn up an extremely precise and detailed accounting matrix with three categories of military expenditures: (A) operating costs; (B) procurement and construction; and (C) research and development.

A. Operating costs

(1) Personnel: a) conscripts; b) other military; c) civilian

(2) Operations and maintenance: a) current-use material; b) maintenance and repairs; c) purchased services; d) rent.

B. Procurement and construction

(1) Procurement: a) aircraft and engines; b) missiles, including conventional warheads; c) nuclear warheads and bombs; d) ships and boats; e) armored vehicles; f) artillery; g) other ordnance and ground force arms; h) ammunition; i) electronics and communications; j) non-armored vehicles.

(2) Construction: a) airbases; b) missile sites; c) naval bases; d) electronics and communications; e) personnel; f) medical; g) training; h) warehouses and depots; i) command, administration; j) fortifications; k) shelters.

C. Research and development

(1) Basic and applied

(2) Development, testing and evaluation.

tions of ME (see box). These definitions are used by the organizations to compile ME statistics that are widely used. There are several differences among the three definitions, among them with regard to: 1) the treatment of military aid; 2) financing of military pensions; 3) treatment of security forces not permanently engaged in national defense; and 4) research and development activities.

Secrecy of Military Expenditures

Perhaps a more significant problem than differences in the definition of ME is that "in the great majority of countries, if not all of them, information concerning questions of national defense are surrounded by an opaqueness symptomatic of the eminently political nature of this subject" (Herrera 1994, p. 23). The secrecy concerning statistical data on military expenditures is justified on the grounds that it reduces information available to other countries, who may be either potential or actual opponents. Another reason for the secrecy is, almost certainly, preventing the general public from knowing too much about their own military expenditures and potentially challenging the level of such expenditures through the political process (Ball 1988, p. 85).

The former Soviet Union and its military allies followed a pattern of dissemination of statistical data that has been described as "the fewer data published, the better" (Ball 1988, p. 84). Many developing countries have adopted this same approach. Even governments who make available substantial statistical information on ME are widely believed to understate their ME levels, although it is not possible to determine which countries understate their security expenditures, during which periods, and to what degree. Among the most frequently mentioned mechanisms used to obscure military expenditures are: double bookkeeping, the use of off-budget financing, highly aggregated budget categories, foreign assistance, and manipulation of foreign exchange and trade statistics. For example (Ball 1988, pp. 111-122; IISS 1994-95, pp. 279-281):

- It has been alleged that some countries keep two sets of ME accounts: one made public through the national budget and a second—more accurate—used only for internal government consumption. The degree of understatement of ME in the published accounts is not known with precision, but estimates range from 10 percent to "several times" the published figures.

- The essence of this mechanism is the creation within a country of funding sources independent of the national budget. A well-documented example is Indonesia, where off-budget military expenditures are financed by a special military fund fed by the earnings of Indonesia's many military-linked enterprises, engaged in mining (including oil production), plantations, banking, and trade; it has been estimated that in the 1970s, military enterprises generated 30-60 percent of the total ME of the country.

- Some countries publish only a single figure for their ME in their national budgets; this makes it relatively easy to manipulate the statistics to understate the level of resources devoted to the military. In some instances, the lack of detail about military expenditures is a function of the inability of the data collection systems to provide the necessary data. In others, however, it is a deliberate effort to obscure the true extent of ME. Examples of the latter cited in the literature include Saudi Arabia and Nigeria.

- Strictly speaking, military aid (whether grants or loans) given by a country to another should appear in the budget of the donor country as an expenditure; repayments of military loans should also appear as an expenditure in the budget of the recipient country as such transactions occur. There is ample evidence that many countries do not adhere to these rules.

- A portion of the foreign exchange earned by some countries through exports is often not entered into the national accounts and is instead set aside for special purposes, including the purchase of weapons. Some countries are also known to manipulate foreign trade accounts to disguise purchases of weapons, identifying them as purchases of "capital goods" for the civilian sector.

Comparability Problems

There are at least two critical methodological problems associated with the development of ME statistics that permit meaningful comparisons over time and across countries: 1) estimating military expenditures in real terms; and 2) converting measures of real expenditures in domestic currencies to a common currency base.

Deflation: In order to compare real ME over time, it is necessary to deflate current-value statistics to account for changes in prices, i.e., inflation. Ideally, different deflators would be used to adjust components of ME: personnel costs, construction, capital goods, imports of weapons systems, etc.

In practice, it is difficult to obtain even a single reliable measure of inflation for most economies, let alone the possibility of a family of deflators for different components of military expenditures. Thus, intertemporal comparisons of resources devoted to ME tend to be affected by the difficulties in properly adjusting for inflation.

Conversion factors: The military budget for each country is drawn up in that country's local currency. To make international comparisons of ME, it is essential to convert the expenditure streams expressed in national currency to a common currency or base monetary unit, usually the U.S. dollar. The choice of the appropriate exchange rate to convert each national currency to U.S. dollars is a methodological problem of considerable proportion.

One of the alternatives available is to effect the conversion from domestic currency to U.S. dollars using the official exchange rate between the national currency and the U.S. dollar. However, because official exchange rates tend not to correspond to the ratio between the average price levels of the two countries being compared, this method does not produce meaningful comparisons. Methodologically superior is the use of purchasing power parity (PPP) exchange rates to convert to a common basis. However, PPP exchange rates tend to available only for a limited set of countries and are often not up to date. As a result, analysts of ME generally have to rely on a combination of official and PPP exchange rates.

ESTIMATES OF MILITARY EXPENDITURES

The primary source of information on military expenditures is the national budget of each nation. Several national and international organizations compile and adjust central government expenditure (CGE) data to produce series that are comparable within

countries over time and also across countries. The best known of these specialized organizations are: 1) the U.S. Arms Control and Disarmament Agency; 2) the Stockholm International Peace Research Institute; and 3) the International Institute for Strategic Studies.

U.S. Arms Control and Disarmament Agency

Since the mid-1960s, the U.S. Arms Control and Disarmament Agency (USACDA) has been producing an annual compilation of data on military expenditures and arms transfers for a wide range of countries. The most recent issue, *World Military Expenditures and Arms Transfers 1993-1994* (USACDA 1995), contains ME, arms transfers, armed forces, and macroeconomic data for 166 countries over the 1983-93 decade.

- **ME** data in the USACDA publications for the members of the North Atlantic Treaty Organization (NATO) follow the NATO definition and therefore exclude expenditures on internal security. For other countries (except socialist countries), the data generally refer to expenditures of the Ministry of Defense; where the former data are known to include internal security expenditures, an adjustment has been made to exclude them. For socialist countries—notorious for the paucity of published data and the ambiguity of released information—the USACDA reports ME estimates by the Central Intelligence Agency and other sources.

- **Arms transfers** (arms exports and imports) statistics refer to the international transfer (under terms of grants, credits, barter, or cash) of military equipment, usually referred to as "conventional," including weapons of war, parts thereof, ammunition, support equipment, and other commodities designated for military use. Dual use equipment, which can have application in both military and civilian sectors, is included when its primary mission is identified as military. Statistics reflect the value of goods actually delivered during the reference year, in contrast both to payments and to the value of programs, agreements, contracts, or orders concluded during the period, which are expected to result in future deliveries. For the United States, arms transfers data originate from official statistics, while for other countries they are estimates by U.S. Government sources based on fragmentary information.

- **Armed forces** estimates refer to active-duty military personnel, including paramilitary forces if those forces resemble regular units in their organization, equipment, training, or mission; reserve forces are not generally included. Figures for the United States and other NATO countries originate from NATO sources, while all others are estimates by the U.S. Government.

- **Macroeconomic statistics** reported by the US-ACDA are the gross national product (GNP), CGE, and value of exports and imports. Where available, the statistics originate from national statistical sources; in other instances, they are estimates made by the U.S. Government and other sources. All value data in the report are expressed in U.S. dollars. Conversion of value data from domestic currencies to U.S. dollars is effected using market exchange rates of the most recent year for which data are available and adjusted for inflation using each country's implicit deflator.

Stockholm International Peace Research Institute

Beginning in 1968 and through 1992,[4] the Stockholm International Peace Research Institute (SIPRI) published estimates of ME and arms trade for a large number of countries in its annual yearbook, *World Armaments and Disarmament*. The SIPRI yearbooks included annual estimates of the value of ME in domestic currency at current prices and in U.S. dollars at constant prices; the conversion to U.S. dollars was effected using official exchange rates, with the consumer price index as deflator. The most recent SIPRI yearbook containing ME estimates—the yearbook

for 1992—contained statistics on 128 countries, of which 96 were developing countries.

SIPRI relied on NATO's definition of ME; SIPRI analysts adjusted national budget statistics to meet the NATO definition. Basically, the adjustments required taking into account the payment of pensions to retired members of the armed forces and the costs of maintaining paramilitary units and of military aid given to friendly foreign countries. The SIPRI yearbooks also contained data on the value of arms transfers; these data were reported in terms of constant dollars for each year.

International Institute for Strategic Studies

The London-based International Institute for Strategic Studies (IISS) is an independent research center concentrating on problems of security, armed conflict, and arms control throughout the world. The IISS publishes an annual report titled *The Military Balance* that contains information on the armed forces or arms stocks held by specific countries or regions, arms transfers, military assistance, and the official defense budget. The most recent issue of the report, *The Military Balance 1995-1996* (IISS 1995-96), included data on 160 countries.

The official defense budget for each country—the proxy for ME used by the IISS—is reported in the yearbooks at constant prices of a recent year in U.S. dollars; the conversion from national currencies to U.S. dollars is generally effected using the official exchange rate. A summary table consolidates data for individual countries on ME, per capita ME, the military burden (defense expenditures as a percentage of gross national product), and the size of the armed forces.

It should be noted that unlike the publications of the USACDA and SIPRI, which use the NATO definition of ME, IISS relies on the defense budget of each country and therefore the data reported lack compa-

---

4. Herrera (1994, p. 34) claims that SIPRI's decision not to publish military expenditures estimates in its 1993 yearbook resulted from the departure from that organization of key researchers who used to make these estimates and the lack of resources within SIPRI to continue to carry out this activity. SIPRI did not resume publication of the military expenditures data in the most recent issue of the yearbook—for 1994 (SIPRI 1994)—raising the possibility that the decision to discontinue publication of the military expenditures data in 1993 may be a permanent one.

rability within the same country over time (because of changes in budgeting systems) or across countries. Moreover, the IISS publications generally include ME estimates only for the two most recent years and a reference year in the recent past, all reported in U.S. dollars at constant prices; because the base year for developing the constant-price estimates varies from one issue of the IISS publication to another, it is not possible to put together time series on ME for any country or region from the IISS data.

CUBAN MILITARY EXPENDITURES

There are two sources of information on Cuban ME: 1) official statistics released by the Cuban government in the context of its annual central government budget exercise; and 2) estimates made by external organizations. This section of the paper describes these official data or estimates and raises some methodological questions and problems pertaining to them.

Official ME Data

Official information on ME in socialist Cuba is very sparse. For over a decade—from the mid-1960s to the late 1970s—there was a complete blackout on CGE statistics, including ME. Government expenditures data published since the late 1970s is highly aggregated. Moreover, little is known with respect to the definition of ME that is used by the Cuban government in its budget exercises and how certain components (e.g., arms purchases and military aid) are treated. All available official statistics on the Cuban budget are reported in pesos; presumably they are reported in current prices, although this is not explicitly stated.

Definition: Cuban budget statistics break down CGE into 8 large categories. One of those categories is "defense and internal order" (defensa y orden interior). The practice of reporting ME at highly aggregated levels—often a single budget line—was common for the Soviet Union and the socialist countries of Eastern Europe (Hutchings 1983; Crane 1987).

There is virtually no information on what is meant by "defense and internal order" in Cuban budget statistics. For example, Law No. 29, the budget law passed in 1980, does not throw any light on the components of this budget category ("Ley No. 29" 1980). The same is true for Resolution 156/181 of the State Committee on Finance (Comité Estatal de Finanzas), issued in October 1981, which set forth the system of expenditures in the central budget ("Resolución" 1981). The title of the category suggests that it includes expenditures on activities related to national defense, such as the uniformed services, as well as expenditures related to maintaining domestic order, such as activities of the national police and the Ministry of the Interior. Fidel Castro (1978, p. 3) has confirmed that "defense and internal order" includes all of the defense activities carried out by the Ministry of the Revolutionary Armed Forces and the Ministry of the Interior. It appears, then, that the definition of ME in Cuban budget statistics approximates the IMF definition, as both include expenditures related to maintaining internal order.[5]

ME data: In December 1977, Cuba's National Assembly of People's Power (Asamblea Nacional del Poder Popular, ANPP) approved a state budget for 1978.[6] This marked the first national budget approved by Cuban government since 1966. In that year, in the throes of an internal ideological debate over the socialist economic model that the country should pursue, the Cuban government abolished the Ministry of Finance (Ministerio de Hacienda)—the institution that traditionally prepared the nation's budget—and distributed its functions among other agencies. Responsibility for the preparation and implementation of the national budget was handed over to the Central Planning Board (Junta Central de Planificación, JUCEPLAN), but there is no evidence that a national budget was approved for subsequent years. It appears that the nation operated without a budget from 1966 through the late 1970s.

---

5. Recent ME expenditures data in a Cuban National Bank publication (BNC 1995) refer to expenditures for "defense and public order." It is not possible to ascertain whether this is the same category used in earlier periods titled "defense and internal order."

6. This section of the paper is based on Pérez-López (1992, pp. 5-13).

Table 1. Approved State Budgets, 1962-66 (in million pesos)

	1962		1963		1964		1965		1966	
	Value	%	Value	%	Value	%	Value	%	Value	%
Revenue	1854	100.0	2093	100.0	2399	100.0	2356	100.0	2745	100.0
Expenditures	1854	100.0	2093	100.0	2399	100.0	2356	100.0	2745	100.0
Financing of national economy	703	37.9	847	40.5	945	39.4	878	34.6	992	36.2
Housing and community services	NA	NA	114	5.4	130	5.4	136	5.4	133	4.8
Culture and social services	569	30.7	605	28.9	681	28.4	696	27.4	821	29.9
Central administration	195	10.5	150	7.2	155	6.5	137	5.4	136	5.0
Defense and internal order	247	13.3	214	10.2	221	9.2	213	8.4	213	7.8
Payment of public debt	116	6.3	134	6.4	157	6.5	163	6.4	174	6.3
Reserve	23	1.2	30	1.4	109	4.5	314	12.4	277	10.1

Source: Budget laws for each year from *Gaceta Oficial.*

With the adoption in the mid-1970s of the Economic Management and Planning System (Sistema de Dirección y Planificación de la Economía, SDPE), Cuba began to reintroduce economic controls, including national and local budgets. As noted above, the first budget approved by the ANPP was for 1978; the ANPP carried out this function regularly through 1990, when the economic crisis precipitated by the dissolution of the socialist community and the breakdown of economic relations with those countries brought about an austerity program known as the "special period in peacetime" (período especial en tiempo de paz).

For 1959, the first year of Cuba's revolutionary government, the national budget devoted 19.1 million pesos, or 14.5 percent of total CGE, to the Ministry of Defense ("Decreto" 1959). For 1960 and 1961, it appears that the Cuban government rolled over the 1959 budget, and a new set of budget priorities was not developed. For 1962, however, with the economy decidedly under governmental control and central planning already being introduced, the Council of Ministers began to issue annual laws proclaiming a national budget. The expenditures side of these annual budgets—for the years 1962-66—are reported in Table 1; among the allocations identified in the budget documents is "defense and internal order."

In 1962, budgeted Cuban CGEs were 1854 million pesos, 14 times the 132 million pesos budgeted for 1959; budgeted ME ("defense and internal order" expenditures) in 1962 amounted to 247 million pesos, a 13-fold increase from 1959, or 13.3 percent of CGE. ME declined in absolute terms and as a share of CGE in subsequent years, reaching a level of 213 million pesos and 7.8 percent of CGE in 1966.

As discussed above, after 1966 there was a hiatus of approximately a decade regarding a national budget. For the period 1978-90, ex ante budget expenditures, as approved by the ANPP, have been made public in official Cuban publications and are reproduced in Table 2. According to these data, ME were 784 million pesos (8.6 percent of CGE) in 1978; they peaked at 1471 million pesos (13.0 percent of CGE) in 1985, and reached 1380 million pesos (9.6 percent of CGE) in 1990. Ex ante budget expenditures for 1995 (not included in Table 2), have also been reported in an official Cuban publication (BNC 1995); according to this source, CGEs in that year were projected at 12683 million pesos, with 727 million pesos (5.7 percent of CGE) allocated to expenditures related to "defense and public order."

Prior to the publication of a report by the Cuban National Bank (Banco Nacional de Cuba, BNC) in 1995 (BNC 1995), the Cuban government had not published statistics on ex post, or realized, national budgets.[7] The mentioned BNC report contains statistics on the executed national budget for 1989-94, including for the category "defense and public order"; these data are reproduced in Table 3. While in earlier official publications, the ME category is referred to as "defense and internal order," the BNC

---

7. The exception was 1983. In 1984, the ANPP was presented a document with the realized budget for 1983 (ANPP n.d.).

Table 2.   Approved State Budgets, 1978-90 (in million dollars, at current prices)

	1978		1979		1980		1981		1982		1983		1984	
	Value	%	Value	%	Value	%	Value	%	Value	%	Value	%	Value	%
Revenues	9169	100.0	9413	100.0	9534	100.0	11201	100.0	9413	100.0	10496	100.0	11471	100.0
State sector	NA	NA	NA	NA	9417	98.8	11082	98.9	9290	98.7	10324	98.4	11275	98.3
Non-state sector	NA	NA	NA	NA	17	0.2	20	0.2	14	0.1	16	0.1	24	0.2
Population	NA	NA	NA	NA	100	1.0	99	0.9	109	1.2	156	1.5	172	1.5
Expenditures	9160	100.0	9409	100.0	9531	100.0	11197	100.0	9834	100.0	10300	100.0	11250	100.0
Productive sphere	4027	44.0	3883	41.3	3978	41.7	4672	41.7	3180	32.0	3558	34.5	3535	31.4
Housing and community services	327	3.6	398	4.2	364	3.8	412	3.7	483	4.9	508	4.9	731	6.5
Education and public health	1533	16.7	1684	17.9	1800	18.9	1848	16.5	2040	20.5	2158	21.0	2405	21.4
Culture and science	1150	12.6	1242	13.2	1315	13.8	1436	12.8	1546	15.6	1524	14.8	1767	15.7
Administration[a]	540	5.9	517	5.5	484	5.1	675	6.0	620	6.3	635	6.2	659	5.9
Defense and internal order	784	8.6	841	8.9	811	8.5	842	7.5	924	9.3	1116	10.8	1169	10.4
Other activities	399	4.4	451	4.8	443	4.7	767	6.9	544	5.5	450	4.4	527	4.7
Reserve	400	4.4	391	4.2	356	3.5	544	4.9	496	5.0	350	3.4	457	4.1
Surplus (Deficit)	9	—	5	—	4	—	4	—	(421)	—	197	—	222	—

	1985		1986		1987		1988		1989		1990	
	Value	%	Value	%	Value	%	Value	%	Value	%	Value	%
Revenues	11311	100.0	12018	100.0	11575	100.0	11721	100.0	11904	100.0	12463	100.0
State sector	11108	98.2	11761	97.9	11350	98.0	11506	98.1	11692	98.2	12188	97.8
Non-state sector	24	0.2	27	0.2	42	0.4	30	0.3	41	0.4	73	0.6
Population	179	1.6	230	1.9	183	1.6	185	1.6	170	1.4	203	1.6
Expenditures	11295	100.0	11997	100.0	11690	100.0	12312	100.0	13528	100.0	14484	100.0
Productive sphere	3329	29.5	3958	33.0	3740	32.0	4110	33.4	4975	36.8	5443	37.7
Housing and community services	724	6.4	788	6.6	879	7.5	913	7.4	860	6.3	870	6.0
Education and public health	2557	22.6	2626	21.9	2763	23.6	2940	23.9	2906	21.5	2953	20.4
Culture and science	1886	16.7	1965	16.4	1834	15.7	1947	15.8	2301	17.0	2506	17.3
Administration[a]	648	5.7	651	5.4	578	4.9	530	4.3	525	3.9	503	3.5
Defense and internal order	1471	13.0	1307	10.9	1303	11.1	1326	10.8	1377	10.2	1380	9.6
Other activities	446	4.0	310	2.6	166	1.4	182	1.5	305	2.2	245	1.7
Reserve	235	2.1	393	3.3	428	3.7	364	3.0	279[b]	2.1[b]	549	3.8
Surplus (Deficit)	16	—	21	—	(115)	—	(591)	—	(1624)	—	(1985)	—

Sources: Budget laws for each fiscal year, as published in *Gaceta Oficial* or *Granma* from Pérez-López (1992).

a.   Financing of operations of National Organs of People's Power, central state administration, courts, and prosecutorial system.

b.   Undistributed amount.

publication uses the title "defense and public order." It is not clear whether the different titles are the result of translation differences or substantive differences in definition.

Comparison of the ex ante and ex post ME figures for 1989 and 1990, the two years for which there is an overlap in data, raises a number of questions. In both instances, ex post or realized ME are significantly lower than the budgeted amounts; for 1989, the difference is about 9 percent (1377 million pesos v.

1259 million pesos), but for 1990 it is a whopping 38 percent (1380 million pesos v. 1002 million pesos). In contrast, realized CGEs in 1989 and 1990 were higher than budgeted CGEs, by 3 percent and 7 percent, respectively. The differences in ME in the two years suggest that they may in fact arise from different definitions of military expenditure.

According to the data in Table 3, realized ME ("defense and public order expenditures") declined steadily during the period 1989-94 both in absolute

Table 3. Realized State Budgets, 1989-94 (in million dollars, at current prices)

	1989		1990		1991		1992		1993		1994	
	Value	%	Value	%	Value	%	Value	%	Value	%	Value	%
Revenues	12501	100.0	13524	100.0	10949	100.0	10179	100.0	9520	100.0	12757	100.0
Expenditures	13904	100.0	15482	100.0	14714	100.0	15048	100.0	14567	100.0	14178	100.0
Education	1651	11.9	1616	10.4	1504	10.2	1489	9.9	1385	9.5	1334	9.4
Public health	905	6.5	925	6.0	925	6.3	977	6.5	1077	7.4	1061	7.5
Defense and public order	1259	9.1	1002	6.5	882	6.0	842	5.6	713	4.9	651	4.6
Social security	1094	7.9	1164	7.5	1226	8.3	1348	9.0	1452	10.0	1532	9.5
Administration	490	3.5	453	2.9	400	2.7	373	2.5	413	2.8	354	2.5
Housing and community services	40 6	2.9	353	2.3	281	1.9	322	2.2	260	1.8	316	2.2
Productive sphere	388	2.8	284	1.8	209	1.4	209	1.4	166	1.1	188	1.3
Other activities	1141	8.2	1198	7.7	996	6.8	993	6.6	968	6.6	1832	12.9
Variation in inventories	47	0.3	108	0.7	-55	—	-41	—	-73	—	4	—
Business activity	3465	24.9	3981	25.7	4722	32.1	5300	35.2	6168	42.3	4154	29.3
Investments	3060	22.0	4398	28.4	3625	24.6	3239	21.5	2038	14.0	2683	18.9
UBPC[a] aid	—	—	—	—	—	—	—	—	—	—	68	0.5
Reserve	—	—	—	—	—	—	—	—	—	—	—	—
Surplus (deficit)	(1403)	—	(1958)	—	(3765)	—	(4869)	—	(5050)	—	(1421)	—

Source: BNC (1995).

a.   Basic Units of Cooperative Production (Unidades Básicas de Producción Cooperativa).

terms and as a share of CGEs. ME fell by about one-half, from 1259 million pesos in 1989 (9.1 percent of CGE) to 651 million pesos (4.6 percent of CGE) in 1994.

Evaluation of official ME statistics: Numerous questions arise about official Cuban ME statistics. Some of the key questions refer to the coverage of the statistics, in particular whether ME statistics include costs such as: 1) training, procurement, and mobilization of reservists; 2) social security payments to former members of the defense establishment; and 3) imports of weapons and military equipment. More broadly, it is unclear how Cuban ME statistics treat dual purpose equipment and capital investments that serve military as well as civilian uses.

Commenting on the national budget for 1978, Fidel Castro (1978, p. 3) defended the accuracy of the statistics presented and raised the issue of the undervaluation of certain defense activities. He stated:

... something that aroused interest internationally was our expenses for defense and public order: 784 million pesos. ... [T]his is very interesting and attracted attention because our country has had to make such efforts and go through so much sacrifice in order to defend itself that many were taken by surprise. And if

is estimated that we have a formidable defense apparatus—which we must necessarily have!—this is a good standard to measure the kind of effort our country has made in regard to education and public health. These figures are exact; not a single cent has been changed. Everything is there: what corresponds to such and such sphere, to education, to public health, to defense, to public order. It's all there for everybody to see. Yes, almost eight percent is devoted to defense and public order, but we are not afraid to say it. The imperialists have forced us to develop powerful forces.

Needless to say, our efforts in defense are not measured in terms of pesos, in hundreds of millions. They are of a different nature that is very difficult to gauge, that is incommensurable, that is, the human effort! The tens of thousands of young people who devote part of their lives to military service; the tens of thousands of committed officers dedicated to the intense effort of the service; the noncommissioned specialists of our Armed Forces; our reservists; the hours, the time devoted to combat training. That's worth more than all those millions put together. And we do it with pleasure, because the imperialists forced all of us to become soldiers! ...

We don't have doubts of any kind. If for our homeland and our Revolution to survive it had been necessary to spend twice as much on defense as on other things, we would have spent twice as much on the defense of our country! We have no doubt about any of these matters.

Law No. 24 of 1979 is the main law regarding social security in Cuba, but it is not the only one. Personnel of the Ministry of the Revolutionary Armed Forces and of the Ministry of the Interior are covered by Laws No. 101 and 102. The terms and benefits received by eligible personnel pursuant to the latter laws exceed those available to the general population under Law No. 24 (Donate-Armada 1995). It is not clear whether benefits payed pursuant to Laws No. 101 and 102 are considered as ME or instead are considered in CGE statistics under social security expenditures.

The treatment in Cuban CGE statistics of military aid and arms imports is unknown; this is potentially a very important matter, as fragmentary information suggests that the flows into Cuba of foreign military aid and weapons were very significant. Mesa-Lago (1993, p. 149) cites a reference attributed to Minister of the Revolutionary Armed Forces Raúl Castro to the effect that Cuba received 10 billion rubles ($13.4 billion) in free military aid from the Soviet Union over the period 1960-86. Mesa-Lago (1993, p. 149) goes on to cite two Soviet sources, one who suggests that military aid was higher then the 10 billion rubles estimated by Raúl Castro and another who questioned whether all military shipments had been free, implying that some of the weapons shipments might have been financed by loans.

Former Soviet Ambassador and Foreign Ministry Official Yuri Pavlov (1994, p. 251), commenting on an article in the Soviet newspaper *Granma* on Cuban-Soviet relations, has said the following regarding Soviet weapons shipments to Cuba:

> *Pravda's* columnist omitted mentioning who was responsible for oversaturating Cuba with modern weapons. Soviet military representatives in Havana were doubtful at times of the wisdom of complying with all Cuban requests for more and more weapons. At one point, after the Cubans requested that more Soviet tanks be transported to Cuba to allow for the formation of additional armored battalions, a Soviet adviser told the Minister of the Revolutionary Armed Forces, "Raúl, you shouldn't ask for that much! The island won't keep afloat—it will sink into the sea under the load!" That does not exonerate, of course, Soviet leaders and military strategists of their responsibility for stimulating Castro's appetite for arms for offering them gratuitously, thus making it possible for the regime to build up a large, sophisticated military machine, whose continued maintenance was bound to constitute, particularly in the absence of free military supplies, an unbearable burden for Cuba.

Finally, there is no information on how Cuban CGE statistics treat dual purpose equipment and capital investments, such as trucks, ambulances, and road equipment that could be used for civilian or military purposes, and roads, bridges, airports or other forms of infrastructure that could serve both civilian needs and defense purposes. Similarly, there is no information on the valuation methods used for military construction and depreciation rates that used for military equipment and capital investments.

ME Estimates

Estimates of Cuban ME are available from three external organizations: 1) USACDA; 2) SIPRI; and 3) IISS. Because of the way the estimates are compiled and presented, it is not possible to develop continuous time series from the IISS estimates. The most recent ME estimates from all three sources are described below.

USACDA: The latest issue of the USACDA yearbook (USACDA 1995) contains estimates of Cuban ME made by that organization for the time period 1983-93. Two time series are presented (see Table 4): 1) annual estimates of Cuban ME in U.S. dollars at current prices; and (2) corresponding annual estimates of Cuban ME in U.S. dollars at constant prices of 1993. The cited USACDA publication is silent on the source of the basic Cuban ME information presented, the exchange rate that was used to make the conversion to U.S. dollars, or the deflator applied. Presumably, the estimates in the USACDA publication use the NATO definition of ME and therefore exclude expenditures related to maintenance of internal order.

Table 4. USACDA Estimates of Cuban ME and Military Burden (In million U.S. dollars, unless otherwise noted)

	ME		Armed Forces (000s)	GNP		Population (million)	ME/GNP (%)	ME/capita (U.S. Dollars)	Armed Forces/ 000 pop.
	Current	Constant		Current	Constant				
1993	426	426	175	21460	21460	11.0	2.0	39	16.0
1992	500	511	175	23850	24370	10.8	2.1	47	16.1
1991	1126	1218	297	26950	28300	10.7	4.3	113	27.6
1990	1400	1527	297	33690	36740	10.6	4.2	144	27.9
1989	1377	1567	297	35460	40350	10.5	3.9	149	28.3
1988	1350	1605	297	34720	41290	10.4	3.9	154	28.6
1987	1306	1613	297	33700	41620	10.3	3.9	157	28.9
1986	1307	1665	297	31420	40030	10.2	4.2	163	29.2
1985	1335	1747	297	29520	38630	10.1	4.5	173	29.4
1984	1386	1880	297	26990	36600	10.0	5.1	188	29.8
1983	1470	2082	250	25230	35740	9.9	5.8	211	25.3

Source: USACDA (1995, p. 60).

Table 5. USACDA Estimates of Cuban Arms Exports and Imports, 1983-1993 (In million U.S. dollars at current prices and at constant prices of 1993)

	Arms Imports (AM)		Arms Exports (AX)		Total Imports (M)		Total Exports (X)		AM/M (%)	AX/X (%)
	Current Prices	Constant Prices	Current Prices	Constant Prices	Current Prices	Constant Prices	Current Prices	Constant Prices		
1993	100	100	0	0	1700	1700	1500	1500	5.9	0
1992	100	103	0	0	2185	2240	2050	2102	4.6	0
1991	252	554	0	0	3690	3891	3585	3781	14.2	0
1990	1400	1534	0	0	6745	7393	4910	5381	20.8	0
1989	1200	1372	5	6	8124	9291	5392	6166	14.8	0.1
1988	1700	2032	230	275	7580	9060	5519	6596	22.4	4.2
1987	1800	2234	0	0	7584	9414	5401	6704	23.7	0
1986	1600	2049	0	0	9158	11730	6444	8252	17.5	0
1985	2400	3156	5	7	8677	11410	6503	8552	27.7	0.1
1984	1400	1908	20	27	8213	11190	6174	8415	17.0	0.3
1983	1300	1851	40	57	7235	10300	6416	9135	18.0	0.6

Source: USACDA (1995, p. 108).

The USACDA estimates suggest that Cuban ME at current dollars peaked at $1470 million in 1983, fell steadily through the second half of the 1980s, increased again at the end of the 1980s, and plummeted in the early 1990s; ME fell from $1400 million in 1990 to $426 million in 1993, or by nearly 70 percent. The latter decline is even sharper (72 percent) based on estimates in U.S. dollars at constant prices of 1993.

The mentioned USACDA publication points out that its ME estimates for Cuba omit expenditures for arms procurement. As a result, the USACDA probably significantly underestimates actual Cuban ME. Table 5 presents USACDA estimates of Cuban arms imports and exports during the period 1983-93, both in current U.S. dollars and in U.S. dollars at constant

prices of 1993. It is clear from these estimates that arms imports were very significant for Cuba during this period. During the second half of the 1980s, the value of arms imports was roughly one-fifth of the value of overall imports and in 1985 they were the equivalent of 28 percent. For each year in the second half of the 1980s and into the 1990s, USCDA estimates of the value of Cuban arms imports exceeded the level of overall ME estimated by that same organization!

SIPRI: Estimates of Cuban ME in domestic currency and in U.S. dollars at constant prices of 1988 made by SIPRI analysts are reproduced in Table 6. The time series refer to the period 1979-91; as indicated in the text, SIPRI ceased to publish estimates of ME for individual countries after 1991. As the US-

ACDA, SIPRI also used the NATO definition of ME, meaning that they did not cover expenditures related to the maintenance of internal order.

Table 6. SIPRI Estimates of Cuban ME and Military Burden

	ME (million pesos)	ME (million U.S. dollars; constant 1988 prices)	ME/NMP (%)
1991	1750	2255	NA
1990	1400	1804	NA
1989	1377	1775	10.0
1988	1350	1740	11.3
1987	1300	1676	10.7
1986	1307	1685	10.2
1985	1335	1721	9.6
1984	1386	1786	10.1
1983	1133	1460	8.8
1982	1109	1429	9.1
1981	1011	1303	8.8
1980	973	1254	9.9
1979	1009	NA	10.5

Source: SIPRI (1992, 1990).

Trends in SIPRI estimates of Cuban ME in Table 6 differ significantly from those obtained from official ME data or USACDA estimates. Thus, according to the SIPRI estimates, Cuban ME (in pesos or in U.S. dollars at constant prices of 1988) rose steadily throughout the 1980s and into the 1990s; the SIPRI estimates do not show the decline in ME in 1990 and 1991 that is observed from the official budget data or the USACDA estimates.

IISS: As mentioned above, the emphasis on the publications of the IISS is on the military balance for the most recent biennium. All ME estimates published by the IISS are reported in terms of U.S. dollars at constant prices of some reference year. Because the price basis for the estimates changes frequently, it is not possible to develop time series of any reasonable length.

Table 7 contains time series data—with some discontinuities—on estimates of Cuban ME (in U.S. dollars, at constant prices of 1985) for the period 1985-92. For the period under observation, ME peaked in 1988 and declined steadily thereafter.

Over the four-year period 1988-92, ME fell by 24 percent.

Table 7. IISS Estimates of Cuban ME, Armed Forces, and Military Burden

	ME (million U.S. dollars at 1985 prices)	Armed Forces (000s)	ME/GDP (%)	ME/capita (U.S. dollars)
1992	1272	175	5.0	117
1991	1491	175	5.0	140
1989	1535	181[a]	5.1	146
1988	1677	180	NA	162
1987	1344	NA	NA	131
1985	1597	162	9.6	158

Source: IISS (1994-95) and earlier issues.

a. 1990

THE MILITARY BURDEN ON THE CUBAN ECONOMY

ME statistics measure military effort by a country in absolute terms. In some instances, it is useful to examine relative indicators of military effort in order to examine military spending in the context of the overall resources of a nation or its public spending priorities and make comparisons with other countries. Several relative indicators of military effort—or military burden ratios—are commonly used by analysts:

- **Military expenditures to gross national product ratio (ME/GNP):** Perhaps the most widely used military burden measure, the ME/GNP ratio relates military spending to the size of the national economy. It scales the value of ME in a given year to the total value of goods and services produced by the economy over that same interval.

- **Military expenditures to central government expenditures ratio (ME/CGE):** The share of CGE devoted to ME is an indicator of the relative importance of the military within the spending priorities of the nation.

- **Military expenditures to population (ME per capita):** The ME per capita ratio relates the level of military expenditures to the size of the nation in terms of population. It complements the ME/

GNP ratio, providing information on the relationship between ME and the size of the nation in terms of population rather than wealth.

• **Armed forces to population (armed forces/ pop):** This ratio is an indicator of the degree of militarization of the population.

It should be noted that the calculation of military burden statistics—which typically compare ME or a related measure of military effort to other variables—introduces additional measurement problems. Typically, there are data availability and methodological problems associated with each of the non-military variables that are used to make the comparisons. This is particularly relevant for the ME/GNP ratio, as the measurement of the value of goods and services produced by an economy is problematic for many developing countries and for centrally planned economies.

Military Burden Ratios for Cuba

Tables 8 and 9 present several measures of the Cuban military burden based on official statistics. Table 8 uses ME statistics drawn from the ex ante official budgets for the period 1978-90 and the net material product (NMP)[8] as an indicator of the size of the national economy. Meanwhile, Table 9 relies on statistics drawn from the ex post official budgets for the period 1989-94 and the gross domestic product (GDP) as the measure for the size of the economy. Strictly speaking, the two military burden time series (for 1978-90 and 1989-94) are not comparable. Nevertheless, some general observations may be drawn from the individual and combined series.

The strongest, and most obvious, finding that flows from the data in Tables 8 and 9 is that socialist Cuba has devoted a substantial share of its national resources to the military:

• The ME/NMP ratio rose from around 8 percent in the late 1970s to double-digit shares by the end of the 1980s, peaking at 10.3 percent in 1985. The ME/GNP ratio shows a modest decline (about 1 percentage point) during the economic crisis of the 1990s.

• The ME/CGE ratios behave in a similar fashion to the ME/NMP or ME/GDP ratios: steady increase during the late 1970s and early 1980s, a peak in 1985—when 13 percent of CGEs were devoted to the military—and a decline in the 1990s. The steeper decline of the ME/CGE ratio compared to ME/GDP ratio during the 1990s is a function of the differences in the behavior of GDP and CGE during this period: while GDP shrunk by 32 percent between 1990 and 1994, budget expenditures remained at fairly high levels because of the need to provide subsidies to enterprises, payments to idled workers, etc., and only began to be controlled in 1993-94. Over the period 1990-94, CGEs fell only by about 8 percent.

• The ME/capita series also suggests that there was an increase in military effort through the 1970s and early 1980s; ME/capita peaked in 1985, remained at high levels in the second half of the 1980s, and fell significantly during the first half of the 1990s.

Selected military burden ratios for Cuba estimated by the USACDA, SIPRI and the IISS are reported in Tables 4, 6 and 7, respectively.

• Trends in ME/GNP and ME/capita ratios developed by the USACDA (Table 4) track closely those of official data (Tables 7 and 8). One significant difference, however, is that the ratios estimated by USACDA suggest that the peak in-

---

8. Following other socialist economies, Cuba used a methodology for its national economic accounts called the Material Product System (MPS). This system differs significantly from the System of National Accounts (SNA), the methodology used by most market economies. The main macroeconomic indicators under the MPS are the global social product (GSP) and the net material product (NMP); the corresponding indicators under the SNA are the gross national product (GNP) and the domestic product (GDP). One of the main differences between the two methods of national accounts is the treatment of "non material services" such as education, housing, public administration, public health, etc.; they are excluded from GSP and NMP but included in GNP and GDP. For further elaboration on the two accounting systems and their differences see Mesa-Lago and Pérez-López (1985). In the early 1990s, Cuba shifted away from the MPS and began to produce macroeconomic statistics based on the SNA.

Table 8. **Cuban Military Burden Measures, 1978-90, Based on Official Statistics (In million pesos)**

	NMP	CGE	Population (million)	ME	ME/NMP (%)	ME/CGE (%)	ME/capita (pesos)
1990	13592[a]	14484	10.603	1380	10.2	9.6	130
1989	13496	13528	10.577	1377	10.2	10.2	130
1988	13565	12312	10.468	1326	9.8	10.8	127
1987	13273	11690	10.356	1303	9.8	11.1	126
1986	13944	11997	10.246	1307	9.4	10.9	128
1985	14261	11295	10.152	1471	10.3	13.0	145
1984	13696	11250	10.043	1169	8.5	10.4	116
1983	12745	10300	9.946	1116	8.8	10.8	112
1982	12087	9384	9.848	924	7.6	9.3	94
1981	11504	11197	9.753	842	7.3	7.5	86
1980	9523	9531	9.694	811	8.5	8.5	84
1979	10051	9409	9.754	841	8.4	8.9	86
1978	9987	9160	9.686	784	7.9	8.6	81

NMP: Net material product (ingreso nacional creado), at constant prices of 1981.

CGE: Central government expenditures—ex ante budget expenditures from Table 2.

ME: Military expenditures—ex ante budget expenditures for defense and internal order from Table 2.

Source: AEC (1989) and Table 2.

a.   Estimated on the basis of the growth rate of GDP at constant prices for 1994.

Table 9. **Cuban Military Burden Measures, 1989-94, Based on Official Statistics (In million pesos)**

	GDP	CGE	Population (million)	ME	ME/GDP (%)	ME/CGE (%)	ME/capita (pesos)
1994	12868	14178	11.0	651	5.1	4.6	59
1993	12777	14567	10.9	713	5.6	4.9	65
1992	15010	15048	10.8	842	5.6	5.6	78
1991	16976	14714	10.7	882	5.2	6.0	82
1990	19008	15482	10.6	1002	5.3	6.5	95
1989	19586	13904	10.5	1259	6.4	9.1	120

GDP: Gross domestic product, at constant prices of 1981.

CGE: Central government expenditures—realized budget expenditures from Table 3.

Population: Estimated.

ME: Military expenditures—realized budget expenditures for defense and public order from Table 3.

Source: BNC (1995).

tensity in Cuban military effort occurred in 1983 rather than in 1985, as suggested by the official data. The armed forces/population ratio developed by USACDA follows the trend in other burden measures but suggests that this ratio peaked in 1984-86.

• SIPRI estimates of the ME/NMP ratio suggest substantial year-to-year fluctuations in military effort, with a clear trend line difficult to discern. As the series ends with 1989, it does not throw any light on the decline in military effort in the 1990s that is evident from other indicators.

• IISS estimates of ME/GDP ratios are very sparse, but nevertheless they suggest that the level of military effort declined from the mid-1980s to the early 1990s. Trends in the IISS ME/GDP ratios are similar to those of other military burden ratios.

Comparison with Military Burden Ratios for Other Countries

International comparisons of military burden require conversion of national military effort and macroeconomic statistics to common definitions and to a common currency. The painstaking work that is required to carry out such comparisons has been carried out by a number of organizations, such as the USACDA, SIPRI, and IISS.

For the very reasons that have been spelled out in the first two parts of this paper, there are significant differences in military burden ratios based on official statistics and on estimates made by external organizations. Moreover, there is no basis for singling out which of the measures are the most reliable. For 1989, for example, ME/GNP ratios range from 3.9 percent to 10.2 percent:

Official Cuban data: ME/NMP	10.2 percent
Official Cuban data: ME/GDP	6.4 percent
USACDA	3.9 percent
SIPRI	10.0 percent
IISS	5.9 percent

It stands to reason that extreme caution should be used in using any of the military burden ratios for serious policy analysis.

The most up-to-date and comprehensive set of military burden measures for Cuba is the one that has been developed by the USACDA. Thus, the comparison of Cuban military burden estimates with those of other countries in this section relies on the USACDA estimates.

Table 10 reproduces USACDA estimates of four military burden ratios for 1983, 1985, 1990, and 1993 for Cuba and several groups of countries: 1) the world; 2) the developing countries;[9] 3) Latin American countries; and 4) Central America and Caribbean countries. The last three groupings have been selected to compare patterns of Cuban military burden with those of like countries in terms of level of development, size, and geographic location.

It is evident from the data in Table 10 that military burden ratios of all countries declined substantially during the 1983-93 decade. Military spending began to decline in the mid-1980s and continued to do so through 1995. The decline, which extended to all

Table 10. Comparison of Measures of Military Burden

	1983	1985	1990	1993
ME/GNP				
World	5.7	5.4	4.4	3.3
Developing countries	6.1	5.4	4.4	3.1
Latin America	2.0	1.8	1.6	1.2
Central America and Caribbean	3.9	3.5	2.7	1.3
Cuba	5.8	4.5	4.2	2.0
ME/CGE				
World	19.0	18.6	16.6	11.5
Developing countries	20.1	18.2	18.2	12.6
Latin America	6.8	5.7	6.9	6.2
Central America and Caribbean	10.4	10.7	9.0	5.3
Cuba[a]	10.8	13.0	9.6/6.5	4.6
ME per capita				
World	255	255	222	157
Developing countries	70	66	60	49
Latin America	60	55	48	38
Central America and Caribbean	65	59	41	17
Cuba	211	173	144	39
Armed forces/000 population				
World	5.8	5.8	5.3	4.4
Developing countries	4.7	4.8	4.5	3.9
Latin America	4.6	4.6	3.6	3.1
Central America and Caribbean	8.9	10.5	8.7	5.9
Cuba	25.3	29.4	27.9	16.0

Source: USACDA (1995).

a. Based on Cuban statistics from Tables 7 and 8.

geographic regions of the world and to developed and developing countries alike, was in sharp contrast to the previous 25 years, when military expenditures rose substantially. The decline in military spending has been attributed to a combination of factors, including a slowdown in world economic activity, increased democratization, improvements in world security, and a fall in military aid ("Drop" 1996, p. 181). Several studies (e.g., Hewitt 1991a, 1991b, 1993) have documented the fall in military spending and offered reasons underlying this trend.

ME/GNP: According to estimates by the USACDA in Table 10, on average all countries of the world de-

9. The USACDA defines as *developed* countries all NATO members except Greece, Spain and Turkey; all former members of the Warsaw Pact except Bulgaria and the successor states of the Soviet Union (other than Russia); and Australia, Austria, Czechoslovakia, Finland, Ireland, Japan, New Zealand, South Africa, Sweden, and Switzerland. All other countries are considered as *developing* countries.

voted 5.7 percent of their GNP to military spending in 1983. Over the next decade, this share fell by over two full percentage points or by over 40 percent. Military spending by developing countries accounted for 6.1 percent of GNP in 1983—higher than the world average. The ME/GNP share for developing countries fell by three percentage points, or by 49 percent over the next decade, a sharper fall than for the world as a whole.

The ME/GNP ratios for countries of Latin America and Central America and the Caribbean were substantially lower than the corresponding rates for the world and for the developing countries. This reflects the much heavier intensity of military expenditures in developing countries and in Middle Eastern countries. Starting from lower levels, ME/GNP ratios for Latin America and for Central America and the Caribbean also dropped significantly over the period 1983-83, reflecting the overall reduction in military spending.

Cuba's ME/GNP ratio in 1983 was in line with the corresponding ratios for the world and for developing countries (which were influenced by military spending by NATO and the Warsaw Pact and by Middle Eastern countries). However, Cuba's ME/GNP ratio in 1983 was twice the corresponding level for Central America and the Caribbean (which itself is heavily influenced by Cuba's performance) and nearly three times that for Latin America. Cuba's ME/GNP ratio declined sharply over the period 1983-93; in 1993, this ratio was significantly lower than for the world and for the developing countries, but still nearly twice as high as the corresponding ratio for Latin America and for Central America and the Caribbean.

ME/CGE: In 1983, all countries of the world and the developing countries devoted about one-fifth of their public spending to the military. By comparison, the ME/CGE ratios for Latin America and Central America and the Caribbean were about one-third and one-half, respectively, of those for all countries and for developing countries. The USACDA does not produce estimates of the ME/CGE ratio for Cuba, but based on official data in Tables 8 and 9 it can be estimated that the island's ratio was higher—but

not significantly so—than for other Western Hemisphere countries. Over the 1983-93 decade, the ME/CGE ratio for all groupings reported in Table 10, as well as for Cuba, fell by about one half.

International comparisons of ME/CGE ratios are sensitive to the form of economic organization and the importance of the national budget as an allocator of resources within each economy . For all countries covered in the most recent USACDA yearbook, the ratio of CGE to GNP was around 30 percent (USACDA 1995, p. 27); this same average relationship for all countries of the world is mentioned in a study of public expenditures conducted by experts from the International Monetary Fund (Chu 1995, p. 8). The CGE/GNP ratio ranged from a low of 17 percent for East Asian countries—where the role of the public sector in the economy is quite limited—to 43 percent for Western European and 52 percent for Eastern European countries (USACDA 1995, p. 27). The larger the magnitude of CGE relative to GNP, the lower the ME/CGE ratio. The USACDA does not report CGE/GNP ratios for Cuba; based on the official data in Table 9, it can be estimated that the CGE/GDP ratio for Cuba in 1993 was 114 percent. Thus, it stands to reason that ME/CGE ratios for Cuba will be lower than for other countries where the role of the public in the economy is more limited.

ME/capita: As a consequence of the overall decline in military spending, ME/capita declined over the period 1983-93 for all country groupings in Table 10 as well as for Cuba. The drop for Cuba was particularly sharp: a five-fold decline from $211 in 1983 to $39 in 1993. For Latin America and Central America and the Caribbean, ME/capita fell less precipitously: to about one-half for Latin America as a whole and one quarter for Central America and the Caribbean. Despite the sharp decline, ME/capita in Cuba in 1993 was still substantially higher than in Latin America as a whole and twice as high as the corresponding level for Central America and the Caribbean.

Armed forces/000 population: The armed forces/population ratios fell during the 1983-93 period for all countries considered in Table 9, albeit at a more moderate pace than other military burden measures.

For the world as a whole, the reduction was about 25 percent, while it was 20 percent for developing countries, and about 33 percent for Latin American and Central America and Caribbean countries. For Cuba, it fell by about 37 percent. Nevertheless, in 1993, the index of armed forces per 1000 population in Cuba was 16.0, over 4 times higher than the index for the developing countries (3.9) and over 5 times higher than the corresponding index for Latin American countries.

CONCLUDING OBSERVATIONS

The examination of patterns of Cuban ME are hampered by the lack of adequate data. Official ME are scarce and those that are available are subject to numerous questions and uncertainties. The same is the case for estimates of ME made by external organizations.

The military burden measures presented in the paper—albeit very crude—suggest that revolutionary Cuba had a high degree of militarization and devoted a considerable share of its national resources to support its military establishment and activities. In the mid-1980s, Cuba devoted around 8 percent of its national income to ME; reductions in ME during the 1990s brought this share down significantly, but nevertheless Cuba devoted more than 5 percent of its national product to ME during the 1990s.

The preliminary analysis of Cuban ME carried out in this paper has raised numerous questions that deserve further attention and research. Hopefully, researchers will pursue some of these avenues, thereby increasing our common knowledge and understanding of Cuban ME and their economic implications. For example:

- What is the precise definition of military expenditures used in Cuban budget data? How are expenses on military pensions and costs associated with reservists handled?

- How are procurements of military equipment and capital construction valued and depreciated in budget statistics?

- How did Cuban international trade statistics treat imports and exports of arms and military equipment? Did Cuba follow the pattern of Eastern European nations of recording military equipment in machinery trade and of the Soviets of treating them in an unspecified commodity residual category (Crane 1987, p. 21).

- To what extent was foreign military assistance—mainly from the Soviet Union—already included in official data on ME, or did foreign assistance augment resources devoted to the military? Does it matter for these purposes whether the assistance took the form of grants (gifts) or loans?

BIBLIOGRAPHY

Alonso, José F. "Cuba's Armed Forces New Roles: Soldiers, Producers and Consumers," in *The Military and Transition in Cuba.* International Research 2000, mimeographed, March 17, 1995.

Asamblea Nacional del Poder Popular (ANPP). *Liquidación del Presupuesto del Estado 1983.* La Habana, n.d.

Ball, Nicole. *Security and Economy in the Third World.* Princeton: Princeton University Press, 1988.

Banco Nacional de Cuba (BNC). *Economic Report 1994.* La Habana, August 1995.

Buchanan, Paul G. "The FAR and Cuban Society," in *The Military and Transition in Cuba.* International Research 2000, mimeographed, March 17, 1995a.

Buchanan, Paul G. "The Mission and Objectives of the Cuban Revolutionary Armed Forces (FAR) in the Transitional Period," in *The Military and Transition in Cuba.* International Research 2000, mimeographed, March 17, 1995b.

Castro, Fidel. "Closing Speech at the Second Session of the National Assembly of People's Power, December 24, 1977." *Granma Weekly Review* (1 January 1978) 2-4.

Chu, Ke-young, et al. *Unproductive Public Expenditures: A Pragmatic Approach to Policy Analysis.* IMF Pamphlet No. 48. Washington: International Monetary Fund, 1995.

Crane, Keith. *Military Spending in Eastern Europe.* Santa Monica: RAND Corporation, 1987.

"Decreto No. 1709 del Ministerio de Hacienda." *Gaceta Oficial* (1 July 1959).

del Aguila, Juan. "The Changing Character of Cuba's Armed Forces," in Jaime Suchlicki, editor, *The Cuban Military Under Castro*, pp. 27-59. Coral Gables: Institute of Inter-American Studies, University of Miami, 1989.

Domínguez, Jorge I. "The Civic Soldier in Cuba," in Catherine M. Kelleher, editor, *Political- Military Systems: A Comparative Analysis.* Beverly Hills: Sage Publications, 1974.

Domínguez, Jorge I. "Racial and Ethnic Relations in the Cuban Armed Forces." *Armed Forces and Society* 2:2 (February 1976) 273-290.

Donate-Armada, Ricardo. "Preliminary Analysis of Retirement Programs for Personnel in the Ministry of the Armed Forces and the Ministry of Interior of the Republic of Cuba," in *Cuba in Transition—Volume 5.* Washington: Association for the Study of the Cuban Economy, 1995.

"Drop in World Military Spending Yields Large Dividend." *IMF Survey* (3 June 1996) 181-183.

Fermoselle, Rafael. *Cuban Leadership After Castro: Biographies of Cuba's Top Generals.* Coral Gables: Institute of Inter-American Studies, University of Miami, 1987a.

Fermoselle, Rafael. *The Evolution of the Cuban Military, 1492-1986.* Miami: Ediciones Universal, 1987b.

Fernández, Damián J. "Historical Background: Achievements, Failures and Prospects," in Jaime Suchlicki, editor, *The Cuban Military Under Castro*, pp. 1-26. Coral Gables: Institute of Inter-American Studies, University of Miami, 1989.

Goethals, Henry W. "Military Relationship Between Russia and Cuba," in *The Military and Transition in Cuba.* International Research 2000, mimeographed, March 17, 1995.

Goure, Leon. "Cuban Military Doctrine and Organization," in Jaime Suchlicki, editor, *The Cuban Military Under Castro*, pp. 61-97. Coral Gables: Institute of Inter-American Studies, University of Miami, 1989a.

Goure, Leon. "Soviet-Cuban Military Relations," in Jaime Suchlicki, editor, *The Cuban Military Under Castro*, pp. 165-197. Coral Gables: Institute of Inter-American Studies, University of Miami, 1989b.

Herrera, Rémy. *Statistics on Military Expenditure in Developing Countries: Concepts,* Methodological Problems and Sources. Paris: Organization for Economic Cooperation and Development, 1994.

Hewitt, Daniel P. *Military Expenditure: International Comparison of Trends.* IMF Working Paper WP/91/54. Washington: International Monetary Fund, 1991a.

Hewitt, Daniel P. "Military Expenditures in the Developing World." *Finance & Development* 28:3 (September 1991b) 22-25.

Hewitt, Daniel P. *Military Expenditures 1972-1990: The Reasons Behind the Post-1985 Fall in World Military Expenditures.* IMF Working Paper WP/93/18. Washington: International Monetary Fund, 1993.

Hutchings, Raymond. *The Soviet Budget.* Albany: State University of New York Press, 1983.

International Institute for Strategic Studies (IISS 1995-1996). *The World Military Balance 1995-1996.* London: Oxford University Press, 1995.

International Institute for Strategic Studies (IISS 1994-1995). *The World Military Balance 1994-1995.* London: Oxford University Press, 1994.

León, Humberto. "Impact of the Economic Crisis on the Cuban Revolutionary Armed Forces (FAR)," in *The Military and Transition in Cuba.* International Research 2000, mimeographed, March 17, 1995.

"Ley No. 29—Ley Orgánica del Sistema Presupuestario del Estado." *Gaceta Oficial* (12 December 1980).

Mesa-Lago, Carmelo. "Availability and Reliability of Statistics in Socialist Cuba." *Latin American Research Review* 4:1 (Winter 1969a) 59-91 and 4:2 (Summer 1969b) 47-81.

Mesa-Lago, Carmelo. "The Economic Effects on Cuba of the Downfall of Socialism in the USSR and Eastern Europe," in Carmelo Mesa-Lago, editor, *Cuba After the Cold War*, pp. 133-196. Pittsburgh: University of Pittsburgh Press, 1993.

Mesa-Lago, Carmelo, and Jorge Pérez-López. *A Study of Cuba's Material Product System, Its Conversion to the System of National Accounts, and Estimation of Gross Domestic Product per Capita and Growth Rates.* Washington: The World Bank, 1985.

The Military and Transition in Cuba. International Research 2000, mimeographed, March 17, 1995.

Millett, Richard L. *Cuba's Armed Forces: From Triumph to Survival.* Cuba Briefing Paper Series No. 4. Washington: Center for Latin American Studies, Georgetown University, 1993.

Neuman, Stephanie G. "Arms Transfers, Military Assistance, and Defense Industries: Socioeconomic Burden or Opportunity?" *The Annals of the American Academy of Political and Social Science* 535 (September 1994) 91-109.

Pavlov, Yuri. *The Soviet-Cuban Alliance 1959-1991.* New Brunswick: Transaction Publishers, 1994.

Pérez-López, Jorge F. *The Cuban State Budget: Concepts and Measurement.* Coral Gables: North-South Center, University of Miami, 1992.

Roca, Sergio. "Economic Aspects of Cuban Involvement in Africa." *Cuban Studies* 10:2 (July 1980) 55-80.

"Resolución No. 156/1981 del Comité Estatal de Finanzas—Norma Complementaria No. 2 de la Ley Orgánica del Sistema Presupuestario del Estado." *Gaceta Oficial* (1 October 1981).

Suárez, Andrés. "Civil-Military Relations in Cuba," in Jaime Suchlicki, editor, *The Cuban Military Under Castro, pp. 129-164.* Coral Gables: Institute of Inter-American Studies, University of Miami, 1989.

Suchlicki, Jaime, editor. *The Cuban Military Under Castro.* Coral Gables: Institute of InterAmerican Studies, University of Miami, 1989.

U.S. Arms Control and Disarmament Agency (USACDA). *World Military Expenditures and Arms Transfers 1993-1994.* Washington: USACDA, 1995.

Walker, Phyllis Greene. "The Cuban Military Service System: Organization, Obligations and Pressures," in Jaime Suchlicki, editor, *The Cuban Military Under Castro*, pp. 99-128. Coral Gables: Institute of Inter-American Studies, University of Miami, 1989.

Walker, Phyllis Greene. "The Missions and Doctrine of the Cuban Revolutionary Armed Forces," in *The Military and Transition in Cuba.* International Research 2000, mimeographed, March 17, 1995a.

Walker, Phyllis Greene. "The Personnel, Organization, and Capabilities of the Fuerzas Armadas Revolucionarias," in *The Military and Transition in Cuba.* International Research 2000, mimeographed, March 17, 1995b.

Walker, Phyllis Greene. "Cuba's Revolutionary Armed Forces: Adapting in the New Environment." *Cuban Studies*, volume 26, forthcoming, 1996.

Zubatkin, Mickail. "Revolutionary Armed Forces of Cuba: Role and Position, Today and Tomorrow" in *The Military and Transition in Cuba*. International Research 2000, mimeographed, March 17, 1995b.

CUBAN TELECOMMUNICATION INFRASTRUCTURE AND INVESTMENT

Larry Press

The economic embargo has been the centerpiece of U.S. policy and strategy toward Cuba, but information and communications issues and measures have not been ignored. For example, after the embargo began, AT&T was allowed to maintain pre-embargo links through their existing undersea cable to Cuba. The power of information is also recognized in the Radio Broadcasting to Cuba Act of 1983, which established Radio Martí; Public Law 101-246 of 1990, on TV Martí; the Cuban Democracy Act of 1992, which called for improving telecommunications connections and information exchanges in order to increase the potential for change in Cuba; and the Cuban Liberty and Democratic Solidarity Act of 1996, which amends the Cuban Democracy Act in restricting communication investment.

Communication technology and policy have increased in importance in recent years because of rapid technical progress and massive global investment in telecommunication infrastructure. Emerging computer networks are one, important manifestation of the growing importance of communication. Networks can improve the economic productivity, education, health, democracy and human rights, and quality of life of a developing nation such as Cuba [16].

With this background in mind, we conducted a study of Cuban networks and related issues and policy implications [17]. As background for that study, we investigated Cuban telecommunication infrastructure, which is described in this paper. We found that Cuba's international links and capacity are suffi-cient for today's demands, though more will be needed in the future, but that the internal Cuban infrastructure was poor and a bottleneck even today. The following sections discuss international and domestic telecommunication infrastructure and investment.

INTERNATIONAL TELEPHONE LINKS

Phone service between the U.S. and Cuba began in 1921 with AT&T's installing an undersea cable between Florida and Cuba. (The timeline in Figure 1 summarizes the history of U.S.-Cuba telephony.) After the embargo, AT&T was allowed to continue serving Cuba with the proviso that existing service continue, but new capacity not be added. AT&T deposited Cuban long-distance revenues in an escrow account. Calls from the U.S. were routed through an operator, and the FCC estimated that less than 1% of the 60 million annual call attempts were completed [6]. Cuban pressure and the rapid growth of Canadian companies providing call-back service in the U.S., led the State Department to issue guidelines calling for increased service in compliance with the 1992 Cuban Democracy Act [2], which allows an embargo exemption in support of "efficient and adequate telecommunication services between the United States and Cuba." Today we have direct dialing to Cuba and 953 authorized voice-grade (64 thousand bits per second, kbps) circuits. Of these 504 are in use. (See Table 1).

U.S. company WilTel has applied for permission to construct a 210 kilometer, 2.5 gigabit fiber optic cable that would have roughly 41 times today's combined authorized capacity. (John Williams, a founder

145

Figure 1. U.S.-Cuban Telecommunication Timeline

April 1921: Long distance service established through a submarine cable between Florida and Cuba.

July 1950: AT&T replaces original cable.

August 1957: Service enhanced by addition of over-the-horizon radio between Cuba and Florida.

October 1966: AT&T is exempted from the 1962 trade embargo for humanitarian reasons.

April 1987: Cable system fails, and service is diverted to radio relay towers.

April 1989: AT&T replaces failed cable system, but differences between Cuba and U.S. terms of agreement keep it inactive.

July 1992: The Cuban Democracy Act authorizes telecommunications facilities "in such quantities and of such quality as may be necessary to provide efficient and adequate telecommunications services between the United States and Cuba."

August 1992: Hurricane Andrew incapacitates radio system in Florida City, and calls are routed through Italy.

July 1993: Cuban Government cuts calls from the United States from approximately 20,000 minutes/day to 20,000 minutes/month.

July 22, 1993: U.S. State Department issues guidelines for long-distance companies doing business with Cuba.

July 27, 1993: FCC issues notice of acceptance of applications for Cuban service (Report No. I-6831).

March 1, 1994: WilTel agrees to construct than undersea fiber cable.

October 4, 1994: The FCC authorizes five carriers to provide switched voice and leased private-line services to Cuba: WilTel, MCI, LDDS, Sprint, and IDB. (WilTel, IDB, and LDDS subsequently merged to form WorlCom) and AT&T service is improved. (Report No. CC-588, Memorandum of Opinion, Order, Authorization and Certification DA 94-1098.)

December 9, 1994: The FCC authorizes the resale of switched services to Cuba (Report No. I-7079).

March 10, 1995: A State Department letter states that they have no objection to Spring offering direct packet data service via Canada or to GTE's Dominican Republic subsidiary CODETEL acting as a transit point for U.S.-Cuban telecommunications traffic.

June 19, 1995: An FCC letter authorizes AT&T Puerto Rico to temporarily operate 150 voice grade circuits pending approval of their permanent request.

---

of WilTel's parent company, was born in Cuba, and his family had business there until 1956.) While this is clearly excessive capacity today, video traffic and an evolved Internet in an environment of normal U.S.-Cuba relations could absorb that and more.

While motivated to some extent by current demand for calls (perhaps $250 million per year [8]) between U.S. family members and Cuba, WilTel is clearly looking forward to post-embargo expansion. Haines [8] writes:

WilTel Technology Ventures president, Jerry Seller, feels Cuba could play a key role in the development of communications in the Caribbean, emerging as a "very interesting hub to tie in the United States." Some U.S. analysts have gone further, suggesting that "Cuba could become a center for cable Communications between the U.S. and the Caribbean, later becoming the hub of a U.S./Caribbean/Central America/South America loop."

The WilTel application was made to the Commerce Department, which referred it to the State Depart-

Table 1.   Voice Channels from U.S. to Cuba (64 kbps)

Carrier	Link	Authorized by the FCC	In Use
AT&T	undersea cable	143	114
AT&T P.R.	Intelsat	150	150
MCI	Intelsat	150	120
Sprint	Intelsat	120	30
	Intersputnik		
Worldcom	Intelsat	390	90
	Columbia		
Totals		953	504

Note: The Worldcom figure is the sum of the authorizations of WilTel (120), LDDS (150), and IDB (120), which were merged. Further compression can increase these figures. WilTel (Worldcom) also has permission for occasional use of 2 satellite video links via Intelsat.

Source: Troy Tanner, Attorney-Advisor, FCC, Report No. CC-588, Memorandum Opinion, Order, Authorization & Certification DA 94-1098, and a letter from the State Department to AT&T dated June 19, 1995.

ment for an opinion. A positive opinion was given in November, 1994, and the application is back at the Commerce Department [10]]. WilTel says the cable can be in operation a year after they receive approval [8], but in the current political climate they do not expect rapid approval [3]. Sprint also confirmed that they plan to offer leased, private-line service. Though they would not comment on price at this time, this would support full Internet connectivity if it could be afforded [18].

There is also a $41 million joint venture between Cuba (51% ownership) and Italcable (49%) which provides long distance and international service through five portable earth stations in major tourist areas [8, 9]. I was unable to ascertain the capacity, but according to the Cuban Communications Ministry there are 1,109 total circuits. Italcable may account for the difference between this and the U.S. circuit count. Regardless, the majority of voice traffic is to the U.S.

While there is unused capacity for today's voice traffic, demand would increase dramatically if the trade embargo were revoked. Furthermore, today we have predominantly voice traffic, with little data transmis-

sion and fax services. A fiber cable would allow for video and other high-bandwidth data types and services. Still, for now, the internal Cuban infrastructure is a greater constraint on Cuban telecommunications than international connectivity.

INTERNAL TELECOMMUNICATION INFRASTRUCTURE

Cuban telecommunication infrastructure lags behind much of the world and the Caribbean region. Table 2 compares the number of main lines[1] in Cuba with larger Caribbean nations and with nations in various income groups and geographic regions. Cuba has fewer main telephone lines as a proportion of population and GDP than any Caribbean nation but Haiti, and is closer to the low-income nations than the lower-middle group in which it falls.

Armando Coro, a telecommunications expert and University of Havana professor states that "The U. S. embargo has had a devastating effect on Cuba's telecommunications" [21]. The interruption of supplies of spare parts from Eastern Europe after the Soviet dissolution and a lack of hard currency has exacerbated the problems. Table 3 shows that Cuba has added some main lines since 1992, but that growth is much slower than in other developing nations or the world.

Enrique López, a principal of the AKL Group, a telecommunications consulting firm with wide experience in Cuba, reported that central office equipment dates back as far as the 1930s, and calls are very difficult to make. The poor infrastructure causes echo and disconnects and hinders both voice and fax calls [11]. Haines [8] estimates that 40% of the Cuban telephone systems was installed in the 1930s and 1940s. Professor Coro confirms this, and states that Cuban equipment comes from Alcatel and Thomson-CSF (France), Western Electric and GTE (U.S.), Northern Telecom and Mitel (Canada), and L. M. Ericsson (Scandinavia), East Germany, and Hungary [19, 21]. This mix, the embargo, and a lack of hard currency make interoperability and maintenance difficult.

---

1. *Main lines* are telephone lines connecting a customer's equipment (e. g., a phone or fax machine) to the public, switched (dial-up) telephone network.

Table 2. Caribbean and World Main Lines

Country	Population (millions)	1993 GDP (billion dollars)	Mains (thousands)	Mains/ million pop.	Mains/ million GDP
Cuba	11.0	12.9	350	31.8	27.2
Bahamas	0.3	3.1	76	282.2	24.6
Dominican Republic	7.7	7.3	474	63.3	65.0
Jamaica	2.4	3.8	251	103.1	65.9
Puerto Rico	3.7	35.8	1315	360.2	36.7
Haiti	7.0	2.6	45.0	6.4	17.3
Low income nations	3147.2	1276.0	46522	14.8	36.5
Lower middle	1110.6	1616.6	93190	83.9	57.6
Upper middle	508.4	2242.8	71893	141.4	32.1
High income	838.9	18850.2	435522	519.2	23.1
Africa	700.6	422.2	11497	16.4	27.2
Americas	795.0	8422.2	213495	279.1	25.3
Oceania	28.0	341.5	10811	386.5	31.7
World	5605.0	23985.6	647127	115.5	27.0

Source: Based on data in *World Telecommunication Development Report,* International Telecommunications Union (March 1994). The Cuban figures were supplied by the Cuban Ministry of Communications after publication, and vary slightly from the published version.

Table 3. Caribbean and World Main Lines: Change 1992-1994 (In percent)

Country	Population (millions)	1991 GDP (billion dollars)	Mains (thousands)	Mains/ million pop.	Mains/ million GDP
Cuba	1.89	-14.27	4.03	2.10	21.34
Bahamas	-10.0	-6.06	-4.15	6.5	2.03
Dominican Republic	0.00	0.00	0.00	0.00	0.00
Jamaica	-2.80	-2.56	49.02	53.31	52.94
Puerto Rico	1.39	59.11	29.52	27.75	-18.60
Haiti	3.53	0.00	0.00	-3.41	0.00
Low income nations	-2.18	28.22	80.36	84.39	40.67
Lower middle	40.62	39.04	67.27	18.95	20.31
Upper middle	-20.36	-0.24	-16.51	4.83	-16.31
High income	1.45	8.52	7.19	5.66	-1.22
Africa	2.38	1.81	14.10	11.44	12.07
Americas	2.91	13.65	10.36	7.23	-2.90
Oceania	2.45	-1.56	7.81	5.23	9.52
World	2.42	10.14	12.75	10.09	9.52

Source: *World Telecommunication Development Report,* International Telecommunications Union (March 1994). The Cuban figures were supplied by the Cuban Ministry of Communications after publication, and vary slightly from the published version.

There is a digital central office in Havana, identifiable by the "33" phone number prefix. These 33 numbers are available for dollars, and are used by phone company officials, foreign business people, diplomats, and so forth.[2] Cubans can theoretically have phones installed for an installation charge of 6.25 pesos, but in practice, they are not affordable by most. Those with 33 numbers can directly dial international calls, but others must request a call from an operator who places the call and calls them back when the connection is established. CIBGnet, and presumably other computer networks, pay for their domestic lines in pesos, but CIBGnet Technical Director Carlos Armas fears that may change.

Some developing nations have been installing cellular systems as a substitute for decrepit landline systems. Cubacel is a joint venture partner with Iusacell ($8 million investment [5, 8]), owner of the Mexico City cellular franchise. (Iusacell is a publicly-traded subsidiary of Industrias Unidas, S. A.) Calls are routed via satellite through Italy. Demand is low, and as of

---

2. The increase in main lines between 1992 and 1994 may be attributable in large part to this office.

148

Table 4. Cuban Telecommunications Indicators

	1992	1993	1994
Population (thousands)	10786	10856	10989
Havana population (thousands)	2142	2158	2175
Homes (thousands)	3031	3120	3147
Gross domestic product (million pesos)	15010	12777	12868
Main telephone lines	336945	349000	349471
Main telephone lines in Havana	153287	155100	156937
Main telephone lines in Havana (%)	45	44	45
Installed capacity (lines)	447340	455708	459168
Capacity used (%)	75	77	76
Lines to automated Central Office (CO) (%)	99	99	99
Lines to digital CO (%)	1	1	1
Residential lines (%)	63.0	63.5	64.8
Public telephones	10003	7508	5814
International circuits	262	442	1019
Telex subscribers	4728	4523	4337
Fax machines	392	na	na
Cellular subscribers	234	600	1152
Radio paging subscribers	632	734	859
Private leased lines	1006	na	na
X.25, 28 subscribers	na	na	266
Faults/year/100 lines	14.9	25.1	29.2
International calls (million minutes)	7.5	7.5	11.2
Residential installation (U.S. dollars)	$100	$100	$100
Monthly residential charge (U.S. dollars)	$6.25	$6.25	$6.25
Monthly commercial charge (U.S. dollars)	$9.25	$9.25	$9.25
Charge per 3 minutes	none	none	none
Cellular installation (U.S. dollars)	$120	$120	$120
Monthly cellular charge (U.S. dollars)	$40	$40	$40
Cellular charge/3 minutes (U.S. dollars)	$0.40	$0.40	$0.40
Full time employees	16900	17363	15696
Total revenue (million U.S. dollars)	221.5	241.4	283.8
Annual investment (million U.S. dollars)	26.7	na	na
TV sets (thousands)	1918	2061	na
Satellite antennae	na	na	260

Note: Figures reported in U.S. dollars assume an exchange rate of 1 U.S. dollar per peso, but this is unrealistic. Cuban residential service is paid in pesos, but lines to the digital office (33 prefix) and cellular fees are paid in dollars.

Source: Ministry of Communications, Havana, Cuba, provided by the International Telecommunications Union (September 1995).

1994 there were only 1,152 cellular subscribers in Cuba (Table 4). Cellular charges are also in dollars. Table 5 shows overall Cuban telecommunication in a global context.

The major hope for improving the Cuban telephone infrastructure rides on a joint venture between the Monterey, Mexico holding company Grupo Domos Internacional (Domos) and the Empresa de Teleco-municaciones de Cuba, S. A. (ETECSA). In June, 1993, Cuba decided to privatize telecommunication, and invited proposals for joint venture partners. Iusa-cell was selected first, but withdrew to concentrate resources for competition in Mexico when the

Telmex monopoly ends in 1997. (Dolan [5] speculates that there may also have been fear of interference by the Cuban bureaucracy.)

In June, 1994 Domos, through their subsidiary CITEL (Corporación Interamericana de Telecomu-nicaciones), agreed to purchase a 49% interest in the Cuban phone system for a reported $1.5 billion [1]. ETECSA was separated from the Ministry of Telecommunications, and established as a private joint venture. The Ministry regulates the phone system and sets rates, so one can assume there are close ties between it and ETECSA.

Table 5. Cuban Telecommunications in a Global Context

Indicator	Cuba	Low Income	Lower Middle Income	Upper Middle Income	High Income	World Average
Basic Indicators						
Population (million, 1994)	11	3506	956	496	839	5606
Population density (per km2)	96	86	23	22	25	41
GDP (billion U.S.$, 1993)	13	1400	1535	2210	18850	23994
GDP per capita (US$)	1331	433	1619	4555	22617	4360
Main telephone lines						
Lines (1984)	257	8947	43485	31619	304793	388844
Lines (1993)	349	47205	92590	70084	424141	634019
Compounded annual growth rate, CAGR (% change, 1984-94)	3.5	18.1	7.9	8.3	3.4	5.0
Lines/100 inhabitants (1984)	2.6	0.3	5.3	7.6	39.6	8.2
Lines/100 inhabitants (1993)	3.2	1.4	9.6	14.1	50.8	11.4
CAGR (% change, 1984-94)	2.5	15.9	6.2	6.4	2.5	3.3
Local telephone network						
Capacity used (%, 1992)	75.1	65.2	84.9	84.8	89.6	85.5
Automatic (%, 1992)	99.0	97.5	97.6	99.8	100.0	99.5
Digital (%, 1992)	1.0	75.0	29.7	55.3	67.4	61.6
Residential (%, 1992)	63.0	55.6	73.9	74.3	73.3	72.7
Faults/100 lines/year (1992)	14.9	170.6	50.0	33.3	10.1	23.8
Tele-accessibility						
Residential lines (thousands, 1992)	217	13315	62154	48320	276868	400657
Households (thousands, 1992)	3031	382798	174162	97332	277539	931831
Lines/100 households (thousands, 1992)	7.2	2.9	28.5	41.8	9829	37.5
Payphones (thousands, 1992)	10	317	676	1109	4479	6581
Payphones/1000 population (1994)	0.9	0.1	0.7	2.3	504	1.2
Urban concentration						
Population in capital (%, 1994)	19.8	4.7	11.6	16.8	7.8	8.2
Lines in capital (thousands, 1994)	157	4517	21673	18336	30150	74677
Lines in capital (%, 1992)	45.0	29.7	25.8	31.2	8.9	15.0
Capital teledensity (1994)	7.2	4.8	20.2	23.3	56.1	22.4
Rest of nation teledensity (1994)	2.2	0.6	7.6	10.4	48.4	11.2
National teledensity (1994)	3.2	0.8	9.0	12.5	49.0	12.1
Text communications						
Telex subscribers (thousands, 1988)	4.3	109.7	167.1	317.1	959.7	1553.5
Telex subscribers (thousands, 1992)	4.7	129.4	185.5	246.4	457.2	1018.6
Telex CAGR (% change, 1988-94)	2.3	4.2	2.7	-4.9	-16.9	-10.0
Fax machines (thousands, 1992)	0.4	284.5	512.5	1641	23439	25877
Data communications						
Leased circuits (thousands, 1992)	1.0	39.9	80.4	591.5	19540	20252
Mobile subscribers						
Cellular phones (thousands, 1992)	0.2	1756.2	1913.3	3339	42243	49252
Cellular as % of all phones (1994)	0.1	4.3	2.1	4.7	13.3	9.5
Radio paging (thousands, 1990)	0.6	481.0	39.9	516.1	18771	19808
Radio paging (thousands, 1992)	0.6	1742.5	1832.1	2750	44239	50564
Radio paging CAGR (% change, 1990-94)	6.5	38.0	160.3	51.9	23.9	26.4
International traffic						
Million minutes (1992)	5.3	1880	3558	4032	38402	47872
Minutes per capita (1994)	0.5	0.6	4.2	8.5	46.0	9.1
Minites per line (1994)s	32.1	54.1	44.5	61.6	90.8	79.5
International circuits (thousands, 1992)	0.3	30.5	103.7	75.5	413.2	623.1
Telecommunications staff						
Staff (thousands, 1992)	16.9	1293	1327	511	2080	5212
Lines/employee (1992)	19.9	28.0	66.0	135.0	203.0	118.0

Table 5. Cuban Telecommunications in a Global Context *(continued)*

Indicator	Cuba	Low Income	Lower Middle Income	Upper Middle Income	High Income	World Average
Telecommunications revenue						
Total revenue (million U.S.$, 1994)	284	14091	18895	42262	400388	475635
Revenue/capita (U.S. $, 1994)	25.8	4.3	20.7	87.0	479.6	86.7
Revenue/line (U.S.$, 1994)	812.1	304.0	233.0	620.0	946.0	764.0
Revenue/employee (thousand U.S.$, 1994)	18.1	11.4	14.7	81.8	195.6	100.9
Telecommunications investment						
Investment (million U.S.$, 1994)	27	11138	6621	17473	93449	128681
Investment/capita (U.S.$, 1994)	3.5	3.6	7.3	36.0	112.7	24.2
Lines added (thousands, 1993-94)	0.5	14407	6772	4525	12170	37874
Investment as a % of revenue (1994)	0.1	0.8	0.4	0.4	0.3	0.3
Television						
Total sets (thousands, 1993)	2	371	175	116	500	1161
Sets/100 inhabitants (1994)	18.9	11.4	18.3	23.9	59.9	21.0
Sets CAGR (% change, 1984-94)	1.1	21.8	2.9	5.7	2.6	6.2

Source: Non-Cuban data from International Telecommunications Union, *World Telecommunication Development Report* (October 1995). Cuban data from Ministry of Communications, September 1995.

Billed as the first large scale privatization in Cuba since the revolution, the agreement was announced during a one-day trip to Cuba by then Mexican President Salinas, who also took the opportunity to speak against the U.S. embargo. (Subsequent to his presidency, Salinas spent two months in Cuba.) In April, 1995, Domos announced "completion" of the purchase, and the sale of 25% of their interest to STET International Netherlands, N. V., a wholly-owned subsidiary of the Italian State Telecommunication Company for $291.2 million. ETECSA is jointly managed with 4 Cuban Vice Presidents, 3 Mexican, and one Italian. It will be interesting to see how the management of the operation and its relationship to the state evolves. Dolan [5] states that Domos is seeking further equity investment to reduce their share of ETECSA to 25%.

According to Domos spokesman Héctor Cuéllar [4], ETECSA has a concession for 25 years (the first 12 on an exclusive basis) with two possible 12-year extensions to provide basic national, domestic long distance, and international telecommunication services, data transmission, telex, public telephone, trunked radio communication, subscription TV, paging, and other value-added services (all but cellular telepho-

ny). The agreement "valued" ETECSA at $1.442 billion, but promised investment "on the order of" $1.5 billion, including cancellation of Cuban debt to Mexico of $300 million.[3] Domos says they will invest an additional $700 million in the next 7 years for expansion and modernization of telecommunications, like the digitization of the network, refurbishing 200,000 existing lines, and expanding the network to a total of a million lines. The goal is to have 11 lines per 100 people (20 in Havana) in 7 years. Dolan [5] estimates that ETECSA already handles 20,000 international calls averaging 12 minutes daily.

The Domos plans sound optimistic, but I was unable to determine anything specific about their long and short term plans or actual improvements currently under way. I had many questions on the technology, money flow, and actual financial terms and commitments. When I asked, Cuéllar referred me to a contact at ETECSA, and I also contacted the Cuban Interest Section in Washington. Both invited me to submit follow-up questions (see Figure 2) via fax, but neither has answered despite several follow-up calls. One cannot infer from this that there are no concrete plans, but it is not encouraging. Moreover, *The Mexico Report* [20] recently characterized Domos as being

---

3. Domos refers to the debt swap as $300 million, Haines [8] as $200 million, and Dolan [5] as a $200 million payment for debt with a face value of $300 million.

Figure 2. Questions Regarding Grupo Domos' Investment Plan

1. Will competition be allowed after their 12-year exclusive arrangement expires?

2. You state you will invest $700 million over the next 7 years, but did not provide details on how it would be used, for example:

    •   What percentage will be in Havana as opposed to other cities?

    •   Which cities will be connected with fiber?

    •   What percentage of Havana will be connected with fiber and digital switches?

    •   Has anything been done so far?

    •   What is the timetable for the expenditure over the next 7 years?

3. Has there been any joint planning with CENIAI or other Cuban Internet organizations?

4. Has there been planning with key industries like tourism or biotechnology?

5. Are there plans for services such as ISDN, frame relay, or ATM?

6. Is there an overall communication infrastructure plan?

Note: These questions were posed to representatives of ETECSA in Havana and the Cuban Interest Section in Washington, who were asked that their answers be faxed. Answers were not received.

"in default on a $350 million payment due Cuba for the purchase of that country's phone company."

I made informal contact with an ETECSA employee who does not wish to be identified. He said there were plans for some renovation with digital switches in Havana, and that $3 million had been allocated for a 64kbps X.25 network.[4] The choice of X.25 instead of frame relay was the result of a lack of technical expertise. He also stated that generally nothing had changed within the company. There is still a lack of funds for investment in modern technical infrastructure, and no competitive approach. Top management is not market oriented. They are conservative, and trying to maintain the current voice infrastructure, rather than starting over from scratch in the data communication business with a market orientation. He also mentioned reports of a plan for a national satellite network in support of tourism, though he had no details. This would be designed for telephony, not data.

At a Havana networking conference in May, 1996, it was announced that the X.25 network would have a 2 million bits per second (mbps) data rate in Havana (connecting each Ministry), and that Domos would be building fast microwave links to four provinces. This is a bit more than my anonymous reporter indicated, but substantially the same.

Pérez-López [13] argues that while investments are important to Cuba, they may be of less than face value for a number of reasons. Several of these—multi-year disbursement, contingency of the investment upon future events, use of existing assets (in Mexico and Cuba) rather than fresh investment, payment for management of existing facilities rather than new construction, debt for equity swapping ($200-$300 million in this case), supplier credits rather than equity investments, and business delays—might apply in the case of this joint venture.

An additional cloud hangs over the Domos investment. ETECSA has inherited assets of the nationalized Cuban Telephone Company, an ITT subsidiary, and ITT has an outstanding claim for $131 million against the Cuban Government [13]. Domos received a warning from the U. S. shortly after the

---

4. X.25 is a 20-year old data transmission protocol which is well established, but generally less efficient for computer networks than the newer frame relay protocol (though X.25 is a more rational choice in a nation with poor infrastructure than one with modern infrastructure because it contains an error correction mechanism.)

passing of the Cuban Liberty and Democratic Solidarity Act, and this may give them second thoughts and further hamper their effort to raise capital or find other equity investors.

To summarize, the internal Cuban telephone infrastructure is obsolete and deteriorating. While investment has been promised, the details—questions such as those raised in Figure 2—are not specified, and Domos appears to be having difficulty making good on their promises. For some time, voice and data communication within Cuba will continue to be poor, and there may be opportunity for further investment.

CONCLUSION

We have seen that Cuba's international telecommunication infrastructure is in better condition and better able to meet current and future demand than their internal infrastructure. The U. S. has been a major investor in international connectivity, and plans more as the political situation allows.

Demand for telecommunication is rising in spite of the economic effects of changes in relations with Eastern Europe and the former Soviet Union and the embargo. Key industries which generate hard currency, for example tourism and biotechnology, require communication, and their requirements are being slowly funded. Four Cuban networks have international Internet connectivity. They grew substantially during 1992-95, are significant by Caribbean standards [14, 15], and are working to connect their networks internally creating a Cuban "intranet," which will eventually be permanently connected to the Internet (current links are dial-up only). A committee "regulating the policy on global information networks"[5] has been formed, and an Internet plan formulated [12].

We can expect gradual investment in Cuban telecommunication. In spite of the political risks, Castro sees that modern communication and computer networks are necessary for the economy. (This "dictator's dilemma" is being faced in many nations.)[6]

U. S. companies have invested in international telecommunication links. It was arguable that U.S. investment in internal telecommunication infrastructure was allowed under the terms of the Cuban Democracy Act, since that is where the major communication bottleneck is, and communication was to be encouraged. (Encouraging political communication without strengthening the economy and internal security is the "democrat's dilemma.") However, the Cuban Liberty and Democratic Solidarity Act seems to have closed that option. It allows the "delivery of telecommunication signals to Cuba," but amends the Cuban Democracy Act with a prohibition of investment in "the domestic telecommunications network within Cuba."[7]

If the investment by Domos materializes, ETECSA will make significant equipment purchases. They may also find new equity partners who will supply equipment and service. In addition to basic communication equipment, networking equipment like routers will be needed, and could possibly be supplied by U.S. firms. At the very least, we should allow direct investment in the equipment needed to support the services we offer. For example, Alan Garatt, an MCI spokesman, reported that problems with Cuban infrastructure caused difficulty and a four month delay in establishing their current service [7].

5. This was taken from *Granma* according to a Reuters release on June 20, 1996.

6. The policy implications of improved networks and telecommunications are complex and mixed. See [16], for a discussion of the likely impact of improved telecommunication and computer networks on free and fair elections, civil liberties and human rights, movement toward a free market economy, Cuban living standards, Cuba-U.S. trade, finding new forms of management and state/enterprise relationships, protection of the environment and conservation of natural resources, and access to Cuban scientific information.

7. This sounds like it refers to the telephone network, and routers and other computer networking equipment could conceivably be treated differently—the line between computing and communication equipment barely exists—however, this is an unlikely interpretation.

REFERENCES

1. Bardacke, Ted, "Mexicans to Buy 49% of Cuban Phone System," *Washington Post* (June 14, 1994).

2. Beird, Richard C., letter from Beird, Senior Deputy U. S. Coordinator, Bureau of International Communications and Information Policy, U. S. Department of State to FCC Chairman Reed Hundt, October 3, 1994.

3. Broyles, Gil, interview, July, 1996.

4. Cuéllar, Héctor, telephone and fax interview.

5. Dolan, Kerry A., "Their Man in Havana," *Forbes* (September 11, 1995), pp 60-68.

6. FCC, Common Carrier Action, Report No. CC-588, October 5, 1994.

7. Garatt, Alan, telephone interview, August, 1995.

8. Haines, Lila, "Cuba's Telecommunications Market," *Columbia Journal of World Business*, 30:1 (Spring, 1995), pp 50-57.

9. International Technology Associates, "Market Trends," *Latin American Telecom Report*, vol. 3, no. 1 (January 1, 1994).

10. Lockman, Laura, State Department Desk Officer, telephone interview, August, 1995.

11. López, Enrique, telephone interview, August, 1995.

12. Martínez, Jesús, "Profile of the Cuban Scientific Network Project," email document received, February, 1995.

13. Pérez-López, Jorge F., "A Critical Look at Cuba's Foreign Investment Program," Meeting of the Latin American Studies Association, Washington, D. C., September 28-30, 1995.

14. Press, L. and Snyder, J., "A Look at Cuban Networks," *Matrix News* 2(6), Matrix Information and Directory Services, Austin (June 1992).

15. Press, L., and Armas, C., "Cuban Network Update," *OnTheInternet* (January/February 1996). Pp. 46-49.

16. Press, L., "The Role of Computer Networks in Development," *Communications of the ACM*, Vol. 39, No. 2 (February 1996), pp 23-30.

17. Press, L., *Cuban Telecommunications, Computer Networking, and U. S. Policy Implications*," DRR-1330-OSD. Santa Monica, CA: RAND Corporation, February 1996.

18. Savageau, John, R., email interview, October 1995.

19. Scaefelen, Steve, "A Different Kind of Revolution," *In Perspective* (Summer 1994).

20. *The Mexico Report*, Vol. 5, No. 10 (June 3, 1996), http://l-r-i.com/mexrpt.html, info@l-r-i.com, (202) 363-8168.

21. Wallace, David, "Rebuilding Cuba's Network," *Telephone Communication*, Vol 98, No 20 (October 15, 1994), p. 28.

FOREIGN INVESTORS' PROPERTY RIGHTS AND LEGAL GUARANTIES AGAINST NON-COMMERCIAL RISKS IN CUBA[1]

Sergio A. Leiseca

There is a framework under Cuban law which establishes (i) property rights for foreign investors, and (ii) legal guaranties protecting foreign investors against non-commercial risks. For property rights, it derives from the Constitution of the Republic of Cuba and the Law on Foreign Investment. For legal guaranties protecting against non-commercial risks, the framework results from international bilateral treaties for the reciprocal promotion and protection of investments, as well as from the Constitution of the Republic and the Law on Foreign Investment.

My first purpose is to review that legal framework. It is not to advocate for amendment or replacement of the legal framework. I am implicitly assuming that (a) the framework will remain in existence following the date when it becomes lawful under U.S. law to trade and invest in Cuba, subject only to the dynamics of the political process which will eventually take place in Cuba, and (b) U.S. persons and companies will wish to trade with and invest in Cuba even while

Cuba's domestic political process unfolds. Accordingly, my second purpose is to begin to educate U.S. persons and companies on the general status of Cuban law concerning foreign investors property rights, and legal guaranties against non-commercial risks.

FOREIGN INVESTORS' PROPERTY RIGHTS

The Constitution of the Republic of Cuba

In accordance with the national Constitution,[2] the property rights of foreign investors will depend upon the type or category of the respective assets. Assets are generally divided into (i) assets forming part of the "socialist state patrimony," (ii) small agricultural holdings, and (iii) assets derived from personal work.

Foreign investors cannot acquire or hold rights to small agricultural holdings, pursuant to Article 19 of the national Constitution.[3] These assets may be owned only by "small agricultural producers," and may be transferred only to agricultural cooperatives and other "small agricultural producers," subject in

---

1. These comments were prepared for delivery in Miami, Florida at the Conference on The Future For Investment and Economic Development in Cuba, held on February 29 and March 1, 1996 at the Radisson Hotel Conference Center.

2. *Official Gazette of the Republic of Cuba,* Extraordinary Edition, No. 7 (August 1, 1992).

3. The following is an English translation of the text of the provision: "The State recognizes the ownership of small agricultural producers to the lands which legally belong to them, and to the other immovable and movable goods which may be necessary for them to carry on the exploitation to which they are engaged, in accordance with that established in law. The small agricultural producers, upon prior authorization of the competent state organism and the compliance with the remaining legal requirements, may incorporate their lands only to cooperatives for agricultural production. They may also sell them, exchange them or otherwise transfer them to the State, and to cooperatives of agricultural production or to small agricultural producers in those cases and in accordance with the forms and conditions established in law, without prejudice to the preferential right of the State to acquire them by means of payment of their just price. Leasing, sub-division, mortgage loans and any other act implying a lien or assignment of the rights derived from the ownership of small agricultural producers to their lands are prohibited. The State supports the individual production of the small agricultural producers who contribute to the national economy."

each case to the State's preferential right of acquisition for a "just price."

Foreign investors may be able to acquire and hold rights to assets derived from personal work. They are defined by Article 21 of the national Constitution[4] as the assets acquired by individuals through personal work, including personal residences. Article 21 of the national Constitution does not prohibit owners of assets derived from personal work from transferring the assets, but legislation specifically governing the particular assets would have to be reviewed during the course of due diligence to determine whether it prohibits or restricts transfers to foreign investors.

Foreign investors can acquire and hold rights pursuant to Article 15 of the national Constitution[5] to assets forming part of the "socialist state patrimony," but in each case upon prior and specific approval of the Council of Ministers of the Republic.

The concept of "socialist state patrimony" is broadly defined by Article 15 of the national Constitution to include "all lands not owned by small agricultural producers or cooperatives formed by small agricultural producers, the subsoil, mines, living and nonliving natural resources located within the economic maritime zone of the Republic, forests, waters, roads, sugar mills, factories, fundamental means of trans-

portation, and all enterprises, banks and installations which have been nationalized and expropriated from the imperialists, large landowners and bourgeois, as well as the factories, enterprises and economic installations and scientific, social, cultural and sports centers constructed, developed or acquired by the State, and those which it may construct, develop or acquire in the future."

Accordingly, foreign investors may acquire property rights perhaps with respect to assets derived from the personal work of the transferor, and undoubtedly and most importantly, to assets included within the "socialist state patrimony," which are the significant economic assets in Cuba. The property rights may include even ownership rights. The single exception is limited to means of public communication, for example, media as well as radio and television stations, which in accordance with Article 53 of the national Constitution[6] may not be privately owned.

Foreign investors may do so indirectly through "mixed enterprises, companies and economic associations" organized in accordance with the laws of Cuba.

The Cuban State recognizes ownership rights with respect to those entities, pursuant to Article 23 of the

---

4. The following is an English translation of the text of the provision: "Private ownership to income and savings derived from personal work, to the housing possessed with just title of ownership, and to the other goods and objects used for the satisfaction of the material and cultural needs of the individual are guaranteed. Likewise, ownership to the means and instruments of personal or family work, which may not be used to obtain income derived from the exploitation of the work of third parties, is guaranteed. The law will establish the amount up to which conditions of personal property may be attachable."

5. The following is an English translation of the text of the provision: "a) all lands not owned by small agricultural producers or cooperatives formed by small agricultural producers, the subsoil, mines, living and nonliving natural resources located within the economic maritime zone of the Republic, forests, waters, roads; b) sugar mills, factories, fundamental means of transportation, and all enterprises, banks and installations which have been nationalized and expropriated from the imperialists, large landowners and bourgeois, as well as the factories, enterprises and economic installations and scientific, social, cultural and sports centers constructed, developed or acquired by the State, and those which it may construct, develop or acquire in the future. The property of these goods may not be transferred to natural or legal persons, other than in exceptional cases in which the partial or total transfer of any economic objectives will be dedicated to the development purpose of the country, and do not affect the political, social and economic foundations of the State, upon prior approval of the Council of Ministries or its Executive Committee. The transfer of other rights with respect to these goods to State enterprises or other authorized entities, for the fulfillment of their purposes, will be made in accordance with the provisions of law."

6. The following is an English translation of the text of the provision: "The liberty of speech and press of citizens in accordance with the purposes of the socialist society is recognized. The condition material to their exercise exist by the fact that the press, radio, television, films and other means of public broadcasting are state or social property, and in no case may be the subject of private ownership, which guarantees their use for the exclusive service of the working people and the interest of society. The law will regulate the exercise of these liberties."

national Constitution.[7] It reads as follows in relevant part: "The State recognizes the ownership of the mixed enterprises, companies and economic associations which may be organized under law." Moreover, it mandates that "use, enjoyment, and disposition of assets belonging to [their] patrimonies will be governed by the provisions established by law and in treaties, as well as by the particular articles and bylaws by which they are governed".

The Law on Foreign Investment

The foreign investors' property rights are substantially similar regardless of the business entities through which they engage in business. Generally, the Law on Foreign Investment[8] contemplates three forms of business entities, namely, (i) "mixed enterprises" or joint ventures, (ii) "contracts of international economic association" or unincorporated consortiums or partnerships, and (iii) "enterprises entirely of foreign capital," or companies wholly-owned by one or more foreign investors.

Foreign investors have indirect property rights with respect to the assets of the respective business entities, which in turn will have rights of ownership or use, management and disposition of their assets pursuant to Article 23 of the national Constitution as noted above, and their constituent documents. These assets will certainly include assets originally forming part of the "socialist state patrimony," but transferred by the Cuban State with the approval of the Council of Ministers of the Republic.

One point bears emphasis. The Law on Foreign Investment does not prohibit Cuban partners from transferring ownership of assets to joint ventures and unincorporated consortiums or partnerships. It therefore allows for the possibility of direct ownership of assets by the joint ventures and unincorporated consortiums or partnerships, and indirect ownership thereof by their foreign investors.

Similarly noteworthy is that foreign investors might acquire ownership to real estate, even if indirectly. Pursuant to Article 16 of the Law on Foreign Investment,[9] real estate may be used by foreign investors only to construct tourist facilities, and housing and offices for foreign investors. The acquisition will be subject to ad hoc or specific conditions, in accordance to Article 18 of the Law on Foreign Investment,[10] to be established in the particular authorization.

Foreign investors in joint ventures and wholly-owned foreign companies have constitutionally recognized ownership rights with respect to their shares of capital stock. On the other hand, foreign investors participating in unincorporated consortiums or partnerships maintain direct ownership rights with respect to their capital contributions, pursuant to Article 14 (1)(d) of the Law on Foreign Investment.[11]

---

7. The following is an English translation of the text of the provision: "The State recognizes the ownership of the mixed enterprises, companies and economic associations which may be organized under law. The use, enjoyment, and disposition of assets belonging to [their] patrimonies will be governed by the provisions established by law and in treaties, as well as by the particular articles and bylaws by which they are governed."

8. Law No. 77, published in *Official Gazette*, Extraordinary edition (September 6, 1995).

9. The following is an English translation of the text of the provision: "1.Under the authorization of this Act, investments can be made in real estate and acquire ownership and other property rights over that real estate. 2. The investments in real estate discussed in the previous paragraph can be utilized for: a) Housing and other structures destined for private residence or tourism activities of persons who are not permanent residents in Cuba; b) Housing or offices of foreign companies; c) Real estate development for use in tourism."

10. The following is an English translation of the text of the provision: "The conditions and terms under which the purchase and transfer of real estate discussed in Article 16 of this Act are determined in the authorization and must be in accord with current legislation."

11. The following is an English translation of the text of the provision: "1. d) Each contracting party makes separate contributions, which constitute a cumulative amount which they own at all times, and even though they do not constitute capital stock, it is in their interest to establish a common fund, as long as the portion of ownership belonging to each of the parties is well defined."

Foreign investors are entitled in accordance with Article 6 of the Law on Foreign Investment[12] to purchase the shares of capital stock or equivalent equity interests of the other foreign investors in their joint ventures and unincorporated consortiums or partnerships in the event the latter wish to sell their shares of capital stock or equivalent equity interests. The foreign investors may freely establish transfer prices.

Foreign investors have the right as well under Article 6 of the Law on Foreign Investment to sell their shares of capital stock in their joint ventures and wholly-owned foreign companies, and their equivalent equity interests in their unincorporated consortiums or partnerships, either to the Cuban State or to third parties. Except in cases of wholly-owned foreign companies, all transfers are subject to the previously noted right of first refusal. Each transfer requires approval of the Ministry or agency of the Cuban government which approved the respective foreign investment. Transfer prices may be freely established by the parties, or at their elections, by internationally recognized appraisers licensed by the Ministry of Finances and Prices or the Ministry for Foreign Investment and Economic Collaboration to operate in Cuba. They are payable in freely convertible currency unless otherwise agreed by the parties.

Upon liquidation of their joint ventures, unincorporated consortiums or partnerships and wholly-owned foreign companies, foreign investors are entitled, pursuant to Article 4(2) of the Law on Foreign Investment,[13] to payment of their prorata shares of the liquidation proceeds. The allocations may be freely established by the parties, or at their election, by internationally recognized appraisers licensed by the Ministry of Finances and Prices or the Ministry for Foreign Investment and Economic Collaboration to operate in Cuba. They are payable in freely convertible currency unless otherwise agreed by the parties.

Property Claims of U.S. Citizens and Companies

We cannot conclude our review of foreign investors' property rights without discussing at least briefly the effects of the unsettled claims of U.S. citizens and companies, and Cuban exiles generally, on those property rights.

First, the claims of U.S. citizens and companies, which derive from two sources: the International Claims Settlement Act of 1949, and more recently, the Cuban Liberty and Democratic Solidarity (Libertad) Act of 1996.

Claims derived from the International Claims Settlement Act of 1949:[14] These are the unsettled claims of nationals of the United States and companies more than 50% beneficially owned by nationals of the United States against the Government of Cuba for losses generally resulting from expropriations occurring between January 1, 1959 and October 16, 1964.

They are protected under international law, which requires governments to pay "just compensation" to aliens upon expropriation of their properties.[15]

The claims have been certified by the Foreign Claims Settlement Commission to the Secretary of State for use in the future negotiations of a claims settlement agreement with the Government of Cuba. They total

---

12. The following is an English translation of the text of the provision: "1. At any moment, subject to the consent of all parties, the foreign investor in an international economic association can sell or transfer its total or partial share of the company to the State or a third party, subject to government authorization, receiving the corresponding price in freely convertible currency, except in the case of an express agreement to the contrary. 2. The foreign investor in a company with totally foreign capital can at any moment sell or transfer, in any form, to the State or a third party and subject to authorization by the Government, its total or partial share of the company, receiving the corresponding price in freely convertible currency, except in the case of an express agreement to the contrary."

13. The following is an English translation of the text of the provision: "2. If the period is not extended, at the time of its expiration, the joint venture, international economic-association contract or company with totally foreign capital shall be liquidated, as stipulated in the constituent documents and existing legislation, and the portion due to the foreign investor shall be paid in freely convertible currency, except in the case of an express agreement to the contrary."

14. See, e.g., Foreign Claims Settlement Commission of the United States, *1989 Annual Report.*

15. Restatement (Third) of the Foreign Relations Law of the United States § 712 (1987).

US$1,851,057,358 in principal only. Pursuant to U.S. law, the decisions of the Foreign Claims Settlement Commission are final and conclusive on all questions of fact and law, and are not subject to review by any other agency of the United States, or by any U.S. court.

The settlement agreement between Cuba and the United States will be binding on the certified claimants. It will take the form of payment of a lump sum by Cuba to the United States, which will then be distributed prorata by the U.S. Treasury among the certified claimants. Accordingly, settlement and payment of these claims will not involve restitution of assets to any of the certified claimants, and will not affect the property rights of foreign investors.

Incidentally, it is reasonable to expect the United States to settle these claims for considerably less than face value. For example, the United States settled claims totaling US$ 70,466,019 in principal against the former USSR for US$ 8,658,722, or 12.29 percent and claims totaling US$ 196,681,841 in principal against China for US$ 80,500,000, or 40.93 percent. However, the United States settled claims totaling US$99,471,984 in principal against Vietnam for US$203,800,000, or 204.88 percent.

Claims derived from the Cuban Liberty and Democratic Solidarity (Libertad) Act of 1996: Generally, any U.S. party, including but not limited to claimants certified by the U.S. Foreign Claims Settlement Commission, may file a claim in U.S. federal district court against the non-U.S. party deemed to be "trafficking" in the "confiscated" "property" of the U.S. national after November 1, 1996. The entitlement originally on November 1 as well now accrues on April 1, 1997. The concept of "property" is broadly defined to include any tangible as well as intangible asset having a value of at least $50,000, and excluding only residential properties. Liability will be the greater of (i) the value of the property as evidenced by the U.S. national's claim, if any, certified by the

U.S. Foreign Claims Settlement Commission, plus interest, or (ii) the amount established by the U.S. national, plus interest, or (iii) the fair market value of the property, calculated as being the then current value of the property, or the value of the property when confiscated, plus interest, whichever is greater. It may be tripled in the event the defendant receives notice of the claim of ownership from the U.S. national.

These claims are not protected under international law, if the claimant was not a U.S. national at the time of the taking of the property.

Settlement and payment of these claims might, but need not, involve restitution of assets to the claimants. Defendant foreign investors may not own or otherwise have legal capacity to transfer the respective assets, or be willing to do so. However, defendant foreign investors will at least be indirectly, and perhaps materially, affected by the settlement and payment of these claims. That possibility will clearly affect the certainty of foreign investments in Cuba, and indirectly, the property rights of foreign investors.

Second, the claims of Cuban exiles generally, and their descendants.[16] They are not protected under international law. Whether claims are deemed to exist, and if so, the rules which will govern their settlement will be entirely a question of Cuban law and policy.

The following points bear emphasis: (i) It is less than clear whether the Cuban government violated Cuban law when it expropriated the property of its citizens after January 1, 1959. The claimants argue that the expropriations violated the rules established by the Constitution of 1940, but the argument is not conclusive because of the irregular constitutional status of Cuba at the time. The Government of General Fulgencio Batista, which preceded the current Government of Cuba, suspended the national Constitution in 1952, several years before the expropriations.[17] (ii) It is unreasonable in my view to expect

---

16. Juan C. Consuegra-Barquín, "Cuba's Residential Property Ownership Dilemma: A Human Rights Issue under International Law," *Rutgers Law Review,* Vol. 46, No. 2 (Winter 1994).

17. Constitutional Act of 1952.

the Government of Cuba to repudiate its expropriations of the properties of its citizens. (iii) As a matter of policy, the Government of Cuba might ultimately decide to repudiate expropriations at least of commercial assets to encourage local investments by the Cuban exile community. If so, the resulting privatizations may involve restitution of assets, which in turn may affect the pace and certainty of foreign investment in Cuba, as well as the property rights of foreign investors.

LEGAL GUARANTIES PROTECTING FOREIGN INVESTORS AGAINST NON-COMMERCIAL RISKS

The Constitution of the Republic of Cuba

The national Constitution does not generally prohibit expropriations, or mandate payment of "just, adequate and effective compensation" to foreign investors in the event they occur. Instead, Article 25 of the national Constitution authorizes expropriation in exchange for "the proper indemnification." It provides as follows:

> "The expropriation of assets is authorized for reasons of public utility or social interest and with the proper indemnification.
>
> The law will establish the procedure for the expropriation and the bases for determining its utility and necessity, as well as the form of indemnification, taking into account the economic and social interests of the expropriated party."

The Law on Foreign Investment

The Law on Foreign Investment strengthens considerably the constitutional protections against expropriations by establishing standards which are consis-

tent with generally recognized principles of international law.

Pursuant to Article 3 of the Law on Foreign Investment,[18] no foreign investment, including reinvested earnings, may be expropriated other than for reasons of public utility or social interest, declared by the Government, in accordance with applicable provisions of the national Constitution, then current law, and most importantly, international treaties for the reciprocal promotion and protection of investments.

Moreover, Article 3 of the Law on Foreign Investment mandates payment equal to the "commercial value" thereof in exchange for the expropriated foreign investment, in freely convertible currency. In the event of disagreement with respect to its amount, the "commercial value" of the foreign investment would be established by internationally recognized appraisers licensed by the Ministry of Finances and Prices or the Ministry for Foreign Investment and Economic Collaboration to operate in Cuba.

In addition to protection against expropriations, foreign investors are guaranteed remittance and repatriation rights. This probably does not mean that foreign investors will be guaranteed availability of freely convertible currency; instead, it likely means that foreign investors having access to freely convertible currency may acquire the currency to carry out the remittances and repatriations.

Specifically, foreign investors are entitled to remit earnings derived from their foreign investments, in freely convertible currency, pursuant to Article 8.1 (a) of the Law on Foreign Investment.[19] They have the right under Article 8.1 (b) of the Foreign Invest-

---

18. The following is an English translation of the text of the provision: "The foreign investors within Cuban national territory enjoy full protection and security and their assets cannot be expropriated, except for reasons of the public good or in the interest of society, as declared by the Government, in accordance with the Constitution of the Republic, current legislation, and international agreements covering the mutual promotion and protection of investments undertaken in Cuba. In the case of expropriation, indemnification is made in freely convertible currency and is equal to the commercial value established by mutual agreement. If an agreement is not reached, the price is set by an organization with international recognized prestige in the assessment of business assets, authorized by the Ministry of Finance and Prices and contracted for that purpose with the assent of all parties, or of the foreign investor and the Ministry of Foreign Investment and Economic Cooperation, if the affected party is a company with totally foreign capital."

19. The following is an English translation of the text of the provision: "The State guarantees the foreign investor the free transference abroad, in freely convertible currency, free from taxes or any fee related to such transference, of: 1. a) Net profits or dividends obtained as a result of the investment."

ment Law[20] to remit, in freely convertible currency, the proceeds derived from the sale of their shares of capital stock in their joint ventures and wholly-owned foreign companies, and their equivalent equity interests in their unincorporated consortiums or partnerships, to the Cuban State or to third parties.

Finally, upon liquidation of their joint ventures, unincorporated consortiums or partnerships and wholly-owned foreign companies, foreign investors are entitled in accordance as well with Article 8.1 (b) of the Foreign Investment Law to repatriate their prorata shares of the liquidation proceeds, in freely convertible currency.

International Treaties for the Reciprocal Promotion and Protection of Investments

Cuba's international treaties for the reciprocal promotion and protection of investments are the third and last element of the framework protecting foreign investors against non-commercial risks.

The international treaties for the reciprocal promotion and protection of investments between Cuba, on the one hand, and Spain,[21] the United Kingdom of Great Britain and Northern Ireland,[22] on the other, are illustrative. They are substantially similar, and may provide the general blueprint of an eventual investment treaty between Cuba and the U.S.

The treaties cover "foreign investments" made by nationals and companies of Spain or the U.K. in Cuba, and viceversa. The concept of what constitutes a "foreign investment" is broadly defined to mean all assets, without distinctions, including intellectual property rights, know-how and business concessions.

In the case of Cuba, all protected foreign investments are entitled to the following treaty guaranties:

1. *Protection:* This generally means freedom from unreasonable or discriminatory measures in Cuba which would impair management, maintenance, use, development, enjoyment, sale or liquidation of the foreign investment.

2. *National treatment and most-favored-nation benefits:* This generally means fair and equitable treatment in Cuba, no less favorable than the treatment from time to time given by Cuba to foreign investments of third country nationals and companies.

3. *Expropriation:* This means that Cuba cannot expropriate a foreign investment except for non-discriminatory reasons of public utility, and against prompt, adequate and effective compensation in freely convertible currency. The amount of compensation must equal the fair market value of the foreign investment before the expropriation became publicly known. This guaranty is therefore substantially similar to the one established by Article 3 of the Law on Foreign Investment, which as noted also prohibits any expropriation other than for reasons of public utility, and mandates payment in freely convertible currency of compensation equal to the "commercial value" of the foreign investment.

4. *Convertibility:* This means that a protected foreign investor is entitled to transfer from Cuba, in freely convertible currency, all earnings and proceeds derived from the respective foreign investment. It assumes local availability of freely convertible currency, as does the similar guaranty contained in Article 8 of the Law on Foreign Investment.

---

20. The following is an English translation of the text of the provision: "The State guarantees the foreign investor the free transference abroad, in freely convertible currency, free from taxes or any fee related to such transference, of: 1. b) The moneys due him or her in the cases discussed in Articles 3, 4 and 6 of this Act."

21. "Acuerdo 110/000138 Entre el Reino de España y la República de Cuba para la Promoción y Protección Recíproca de Inversiones," La Habana, May 27, 1994, published in *Boletín Oficial de las Cortes Generales* (December 23, 1994).

22. "Agreement between the Government of the United Kingdom of Great Britain and Northern Ireland and the Government of the Republic of Cuba for the Promotion and Protection of Investments," London, January 30, 1995, published in Treaty Series No. 50 (London : HMSO, 1995).

5. *Compensation for losses:* This generally means compensation upon loss to or of the foreign investment in Cuba due to war or other armed conflict, a state of national emergency, revolt, insurrection or riot. The compensation must be equal to compensation paid to Cuban nationals and third country nationals under similar circumstances.

6. *Dispute resolution:* This means that the protected foreign investor, at its election, may require Cuba to arbitrate any dispute concerning any treaty obligation. The protected foreign investor may choose the forum generally from the International Court of Arbitration of the International Chamber of Commerce, on the one hand, or on the other, an ad hoc panel to be established under the Arbitration Rules of the United Nations Commission on International Trade Law. The resulting award will be final and non-appealable. Incidentally, Cuba has ratified the United Nations Convention on the Recognition and Enforcement of Foreign Arbitral Awards, or New York Convention. Spain and the U.K. have too, as has the U.S. Accordingly, Cuba's submission to international arbitration to resolve investment disputes is a significant benefit to foreign investors entitled to invoke these international treaties for the reciprocal promotion and protection of investments.

CONCLUSIONS

We can draw at least four conclusions from this review of Cuba's framework establishing (i) property rights for foreign investors, and (ii) legal guaranties protecting foreign investors against non-commercial risks.

First, foreign investors have direct ownership rights with respect to their shares of capital stock and equivalent equity interests in their joint ventures, unincorporated consortiums or partnerships and wholly-owned foreign companies, and indirect rights of ownership or use, management and disposition with respect to assets of the latter. These assets will certainly include assets previously in the "socialist state patrimony," because they represent the most significant economic assets in Cuba, and may now even include real estate.

Second, the guaranty against expropriation of foreign investments is consistent with generally accepted principles of international law.

Third, the guaranty of free convertibility effectively removes exchange controls as a non-commercial risk for foreign investors while freely convertible currency is available.

Fourth, foreign investors of countries having international treaties with Cuba for the reciprocal promotion and protection of investments enjoy the significant treaty benefit of being able to submit investment disputes to binding arbitration pursuant to international rules of arbitration.

AGRIBUSINESS INVESTMENT IN
CUBA'S POST EMBARGO PERIOD

James E. Ross

Research being conducted at the University of Florida, secondary data and information, and three visits to Cuba—1993, 1994 and 1996—are the basis for my comments on foreign agribusiness investment in Cuba.

Studies by the University's International Agricultural Trade and Development Center (IATDC) are supported by a grant from the John D. and Catherine T. MacArthur Foundation. The grant has made it possible to carry out the work in cooperation with the Center for Research on the International Economy (CIEI) at the University of Havana.

With that background, I would like to comment on: 1) the traditional areas of U.S. agribusiness investment in Cuba; 2) the current foreign agribusiness investment situation; and 3) potential areas of opportunity for U.S. agribusiness in a post-embargo period.

TRADITIONAL AREAS OF AGRIBUSINESS INVESTMENT

Prior to the 1959 revolution, the United States was the largest foreign investor in Cuba in terms of both number and size of investments. Other foreign investors, largely in non-agricultural enterprises, were from Canada, Mexico, Latin America and Europe.

U.S. investments in Cuba before the 1959 revolution were diversified and present in most economic areas of the country. In the agricultural sector, many of the largest U.S. corporations held investments in the sugar sector, cattle ranches, and tobacco plantations. Several small entrepreneurs were investing in production of rice, oilseeds, tomatoes, swine, poultry, and beef and dairy cattle.

Following the revolution in 1959, all foreign corporations were taken over by the revolutionary government. This included agricultural, as well as non-agricultural, corporations.

It was not until the early 1980s, more than 20 years after the overthrow of Batista, that the Cuban government took "steps to foster and encourage economic associations with foreign capital." The first step was approval of Law-Decree No. 50, "On Economic Association Between Cuban and Foreign Entities," in February 1982.

Six years later the first joint enterprise was established. A "foreign economic association" was made with Spanish investors to build and operate a hotel in the tourist center of Varadero. By the early 1990s there was increased interest in foreign investment, with a gradual extension to non-tourist investments—including agribusiness.

In July 1992, the National Assembly convened for three days to amend the 1976 constitution. Changes, in addition to abolishing references to the former Soviet bloc, included permitting joint foreign investment. On September 5, 1995, Cuba passed a new law aimed at attracting foreign capital—Law No. 77 on Foreign Investment.

Foreign investment plays a key role in Cuba's economic reforms. By turning over a limited amount of economic activity to private individuals and foreign investors, and by loosening government control over the economy, Cuba hopes to achieve increased productivity in all sectors of the economy.

CURRENT FOREIGN AGRIBUSINESS INVESTMENT

More than $5 billion in foreign investments in all sectors of Cuba's economy have been announced; however, less than $750 million have been committed, according to data reported by *El Nuevo Herald* on May 12, 1996. Over 90% of the anticipated capital is from Mexico, Canada, Australia, Spain, South Africa, Holland, Brazil, and Chile—in that order. Mexico, alone, accounts for two-fifths of the investments announced and one-third of the capital actually committed.

There are, according to Cuban officials, "international economic associations" constituted in 34 different branches and sectors of the country's economy, with capital from 55 countries. More than 200 "international economic associations" have been established in Cuba since 1988—over 90% of them since 1992. Tourism, mining, telecommunications, and basic industry are the major areas of investment.

Of the government's recorded 212 foreign "economic associations," only about 10% involve agribusiness. According to data compiled by the Cuban consulting firm Consultores Asociados of Havana, 10 agricultural economic associations with foreign capital have been registered with the Cuban Government since 1991. Registered investments in businesses related to agriculture, e.g., food processing, accounts for the estimated additional 5%.

While foreign investment in agribusinesses is relatively small, information does indicate that there is increasing interest in Cuba among international agribusiness investors.

Companies from Israel, Greece and Chile have made substantial investments in production, processing and marketing of citrus. Firms from Spain, France and the United Kingdom have significant investments in tobacco production and marketing. Investors from Honduras, Canada, Italy, and France, also, have notable investments in African palm, beer, rum, mineral water, sugarcane, vegetables and food pro-

cessing. Russia and Holland also have made some investments in Cuba's agribusiness.

Citrus

One of the largest agribusiness projects is an international economic association involving an Israeli Corporation and the Cuban National Citrus Corporation (Corporación Nacional de Cítricos). The Israeli investment is made through the **BM Corporation**, which is registered in Panama. It is an international economic association contract, not a joint venture. The objective of the project is to increase productivity and improve the quality of *citrus* being produced on 38,750 hectares in Jagüey Grande—considered the largest contiguous citrus grove in the world. The project was initiated in the 1960s, ended when Cuba broke diplomatic relations with Israel, and was renewed in 1990. The Israeli investment, reportedly, is $22 million. Fruit is marketed under the brand name "Cubanita."

A second economic association of the National Citrus Corporation is with Chilean companies **POLE** and **INGELCO**. Citrus, mainly grapefruit, is being produced on 11,000 hectares on the Isla de la Juventud. In addition, there is an economic association to produce and market 30 million liters of citrus juice annually under the brand name "Tropical Island." Recent information, however, indicates that the association with **POLE** has been terminated.

A third citrus project, which is a joint venture, has been established by the National Citrus Corporation with **Lola Fruit S.A.** The company was created in May 1993 by Lomar Shipping Ltd. (U.K.) and the Lavina Shipping Corporation (Greece). Lola Fruit leases 31,000 hectares of oranges, grapefruit and limes in Ciego de Avila from the Cuban National Citrus Corporation. A juice factory, producing frozen concentrate and oil extract, controls an additional 14,000 hectares in the central area of Cuba. Again, recent information indicates that the association with **Lola Fruit** has been terminated.

Tobacco

Other economic associations involve the production, manufacture and marketing of tobacco. Pre-financing agreements were signed in 1994 with two state tobacco monopolies, **Tabacalera** of Spain and **Seita** of France. The two agreements bind a large part of Cuba's tobacco exports.

Tabacalera, reportedly, agreed to pre-finance one-half of the Cuban tobacco harvest. One source reported Tabacalera agreed to provide $25 million per year to finance inputs and market tobacco from 21,875 hectares in Pinar del Río. Another source said the agreement was worth $30 million and included the supply of 25,000 tons of fertilizer, fuel and lubricants and parts for 350 tractors. **Seita** of France is reported to be providing a $3.5 to $4 million line of credit to finance inputs and market tobacco in France. Holland's **Lipoelif** is reported to also have been a provider of credit for harvest of Cuba's tobacco crop during the 1995-96 season.

The cost for the tobacco harvest ending in May, 1996 was estimated at $50 million. Production in 1995-96 was reported at 31,818 metric tons. This level of production is expected to enable Cuba's export-oriented cigar industry to produce 70 million cigars in 1996, 10 million more than in 1995. World demand for Habanos is estimated to be 120 million units.

A third economic association involving tobacco is a joint venture between the Cuban Tobacco Union and **Souza Crus**, a Brazilian subsidiary of the British-American Tobacco Company. The joint venture factory in Havana, BrasCuba, has six production lines producing 15,000 cigarettes per minute. Plans are to expand production to five billion units per year. Cigarettes will be exported under the Brazilian brand, "Continental." The Cuban brand, "Popular," will be produced for the domestic market. An initial investment of $10 million is expected to be recovered in three years.

Sugar

The most significant new agribusiness area in Cuba to become open to foreign investment is the sugar industry. Efforts to encourage foreign investment in the sugar sector appears to be focused on financing the production and marketing of sugar—not on the acquisition of assets such as sugar mills and refineries. Eight "territorial financing programs" have been es-

tablished with international sugar producers and financial institutions, according to secondary sources.

For the 1995/96 sugarcane crop an estimated $200 million was secured from European sources for the pre-financing of essential inputs such as petroleum and fertilizers. Terms of financing, reportedly, reflected the risk involved. It was estimated production of sugar would need to increase one million tons to cover the pre-financing cost. With sugar production for 1995/96 at 4.4 million metric tons, that increase would have been achieved.

For the 1996/97 sugarcane crop, the Ministry of Sugar is reportedly seeking $60 million in additional financing. Investors would, in addition to interest payments, receive 25% of the profits from increased production over the average of the previous two harvests. They also would be given the first option to sell inputs to the industry at competitive prices.

Sugar production for the 1996/97 season is forecast by the U.S. Department of Agriculture at 4.2 million metric tons. A delay in completing sugarcane plantings and the extended 1995/96 harvest are the main reasons for the lower forecast. If sugar production is lower in the 1996/97 season, it may reduce the availability of foreign financing for future sugarcane crops.

Other Areas

As a result of efforts to reduce agricultural imports and to supply the tourist hotels, Cuba has opened investments in agriculture for non-export crops such as rice and beans, as well as pork and dairy products. By mid-1995 it was reported that over 200 foreign firms had discussed these new investment opportunities with Cuban officials. Negotiations to form economic associations in production of animal feed, rice and dairy products were said to be well advanced.

A British company was reported in 1995 to have signed an agreement to fund rice production in the provinces of Pinar del Río and Sancti Spíritus. Rice production in 1995 was only 80,000 metric tons, approximately one-half of pre-revolution production levels and less than one-third of record harvests in the late 1980s. Foreign credits, according to Miguel Rodríguez, Rice Union Director in the Ministry of Agriculture, will raise 1996 rice production to 180,000 metric tons. Rodríguez said Cuba could meet domestic demand projected at 450,000 metric tons by the year 2000. (An estimated additional 100,000 metric tons of rice was sold through the new agricultural markets in 1995.)

Sherritt International, a Canadian company that mines nickel-cobalt in a joint venture at Moa (near the eastern tip of Cuba), has established a 200-acre experimental farm. The objective of the farm is to demonstrate how strawberries and green peppers can be grown for the export market and for sale to the tourist industry in Cuba. The agricultural company formed by Sherritt International is known as Sherritt Green.

Production of cotton and tomatoes is being supported by Spain, primarily the Spanish Agency for International Cooperation. The project, "Project for Development of Rural Integration," is being carried out in Pinar del Río. Among the resources, reported to be valued at some $3,976,000, will be high quality seeds, tractors, harvesting machinery, and systems for leveling land with laser beams. The project also includes a cotton gin and a tomato processing plant.

Another international economic association includes production of African palm on 20,000 hectares. **FACUSS' Foods** of Honduras, reportedly, is providing $100 million over seven years to finance inputs and manufacture soap using the palm oil.

In addition to the international economic associations involving agricultural production, there are a number of other economic associations involving processing of agricultural products. The products include processed foods, bottled water, rum and beer. Some of the mixed companies include:

- Meztler of Canada, established in 1994. The company produces instant drinks, pasta, hot chocolate, crackers, soda biscuits, etc. It manufactures in Havana.

- Confitel S.A., a joint venture with Russia. The firm produces cookies and candies.

- CONAICA, a Cuban-Spanish operation, produces caramelos of all types.

- Diego Montero is a mineral water joint venture with Spain.

- Emprea Confitera Gamby is a Cuban-Italian operation started in 1995. It produces a line of pastas for the dollar trade at tourist hotels.

POTENTIAL AREAS OF AGRIBUSINESS OPPORTUNITY

In Cuba's post-embargo period, agribusiness opportunities will depend largely on three principal factors. They are: 1) the degree of Cuba's openness to agribusiness trade and investment; 2) effective domestic demand, and 3) competition in international markets.

Openness to Trade and Investment

The first factor is perhaps the most important and least predictable of the three. Cuba's decision to open its borders to foreign investment under Law No. 77 was borne of economic necessity. It was not an enthusiastic political decision.

In the post-embargo period, policies reflecting the degree of openness to trade and investment in Cuba may be affected equally by politics and economics. It is conceivable that the government in control will not be reluctant to encourage foreign trade and investment. In fact, Cuba may earnestly invite foreign agribusiness investment in an effort to reconstruct a poorly managed sector of the economy.

Effective Domestic Demand

The second factor is effective domestic demand. It seems clearly predictable that, in a post-embargo situation, there will be pent-up demand in Cuba for the products of agribusiness.

The failure of agriculture in Cuba since 1959 is well known. Production of many food items has fallen from the 1959 production level, e.g., milk, pork, beef, poultry meat and eggs, corn, beans, rice and sugar. At the same time, Cuba's population has grown from 6.7 million in 1959 to over 11 million. Thus, there is an increase in the need for food of more than 60% merely to maintain the same food consumption level sustained 37 years ago.

For some agricultural products, output has fallen by a larger percentage than the population has increased. Corn production, for example, has fallen from the pre-revolution period by more than 60%. Thus, production of corn has not only not keep pace with population growth, it has fallen dramatically. Along with less corn for animal feed, there has been decreased production of animal proteins—beef and veal, pork, and poultry meat. These are food products that are consumed in larger quantities as incomes rise.

Also, as a result of lower agricultural production, especially sugarcane, there has been less foreign exchange earned from agricultural exports to import food products. Based on data for 1951-55, Cuba was the number one country in the world for sugar production, accounting for 15% of the world's supply. In 1993-94 Cuba ranked eighth among all countries and accounted for less than 4%.

With lower per capita production levels and less foreign exchange to import food, there is bound to be a pent-up demand in Cuba for higher quality foods and food products. The real question is not whether there will be an increase in demand for food, but will there be an increase in effective demand? Will the Cuban consumers have money to buy the products generated by foreign agribusiness investment?

Again, it seems plausible that following lifting of the embargo there will be a substantial capital inflow combined with the introduction of new technologies. Capital and technology will increase productivity. The result will be increased employment opportunities, higher wages and a significant and steady rise in personal real income. Thus, Cuban consumers will have more money to buy agricultural products, including more processed and higher value foods.

Competition

The third factor is competition. This includes competition in Cuba among agribusiness traders and investors from other countries, and in the markets abroad where Cuban products might be sold.

Agribusiness companies already established in Cuba will have an advantage over companies new to the market. It is also likely that they will increase their investments in the post-embargo period to take advantage of the expanding market. The mixed-capital companies that have had substantial experience in the Cuban market will be strong competition for new agribusiness investors.

Companies new to the market, but with proven records of efficiency and substantial capital backing, however, will have an opportunity to become competitive. The companies that can produce for both the Cuban domestic market and the export market will be especially competitive.

As I mentioned at the beginning, historically the United States has been the major investor in Cuban agriculture. U.S. corporations held major investments in Cuba's sugar, cattle and tobacco industries. While all three industries will offer significant opportunities for investment in the post-embargo period, I believe that U.S. agribusiness investments in Cuba's post-embargo period will be more diversified than in the past.

Cuba's citrus industry has become a major area of foreign investment. U.S. investors, particularly Florida firms, may be interested in exploring investment opportunities in production, marketing and processing of oranges and grapefruit. Cuban citrus is on the world market about one month before that of Florida.

In addition to the current export crops of sugar, tobacco and citrus, U.S. exporters and investors may find trade or investment opportunities in the following products:

- **Bulk agricultural:** wheat, coarse grains, rice, soybeans, pulses and cotton.

- **Intermediate agricultural:** wheat flour, vegetable oils, live animals, semen, embryos, complete feeds and supplements (protein meals, vitamins, minerals and trace minerals), and seeds.

- **Consumer-oriented agricultural:** fresh, chilled, frozen and processed meats, dairy products, poultry products, tropical fruits, potatoes, wine, beer, snack foods and other consumer-ready food products.

- **Manufactured agricultural**: fertilizers, pesticides, tractors and other agricultural machinery and equipment.

Foreign investment in these areas of opportunity, following lifting of the embargo, will be essential for rapid growth of Cuba's agriculture. Capital and technology transferred by the investments will have a major impact on agricultural productivity, which will be a key factor in Cuba achieving increased economic growth.

BIBLIOGRAPHY

Alvarez, José. *Cuba's Sugar Industry in the 1990s: Potential Exports to the U.S. and World Markets*, IW92-2, Food and Resource Economics Dept., University of Florida, Gainesville, February 1992.

American Institute for Free Labor Development, AFL-CIO. *Foreign Investors: Oiling the Cuban Government Machine. A Special Report.* Washington, D.C. February 13, 1995.

Business Tips on Cuba. February 1995.

Caribbean Basin Commercial Profile. A joint publication of Caribbean Publishing Co. Ltd. and Caribbean Latin American Action. Grand Cayman, Cayman Islands, D.W.I., 1996.

Caribbean UPDATE. June 1995; July and August 1996.

Cuba Foreign Trade. Cuban Chamber of Commerce. No. 1, 1996.

The Cuba Report 4:9 (March 1996), p. 3, and 4:8 (February 1996), p. 11.

"Cuba's Foreign Investment Law No. 77." Chapter II.

Economics Press Service, *Información Quincenal Sobre Cuba* 9:4 (29 de Febrero 1996).

The Economist Intelligence Unit. *Country Report—Cuba.* 4th Quarter 1994.

Free-Market Cuba Business Journal 3:2 (Spring 1995).

Granma International. May 1, 1996. p. 13.

"An Index of Foreign Investment in Cuba." *Bulletin* no. 43, La Sociedad Económica, September 1994.

Messina, William A., Jr. "An Overview of Cuba's Agricultural Sector Prior to the Special Period." Background Paper, January 1996.

El Nuevo Herald. May 12, 1996.

Rúa, Manuel. "Cuba's Program to Attract Foreign Investment." Cuba Transition Workshop. Shaw, Pittman, Potts & Trowbridge and Oceana Publications, Inc. Washington, D.C., January 26, 1996.

"A Survey of Cuba," *The Economist* (April 6, 1996).

Tetzeli, Frederick E. "Foreign Investment in the Cuba of Yesterday." Cuba Transition Workshop, Shaw, Pittman, Potts & Trowbridge and Oceana Publications, Inc. Washington, D.C., January 26, 1996.

U.S. Department of State Dispatch 4:8 (February 22, 1993), p. 105.

Weiss, Kenneth D. "Outlook for Agribusiness in the Western Hemisphere." IAMA Symposium. Caracas, Venezuela. May 18, 1995.

CUBA Y EL ESTADO DE DERECHO: PASADO, PRESENTE Y FUTURO[1]

Alberto Luzárraga

La definición del Estado de Derecho ha sido objeto de muchas formulaciones. En su acepción más simple se ha definido como: "saber a que atenerse." Así se hace resaltar el factor de estabilidad necesario a toda relación jurídica que afecte el conjunto social pero es necesario ir más allá. La estabilidad tiene que estar basada en la legitimidad del sistema que dicta, aplica e interpreta la ley y de la justicia con que actúe.

La justicia fué definida por los romanos como "la voluntad *continuada* de dar a cada cual lo que le corresponde." Explicar el requisito de continuidad es fácil, la justicia esporádica no es justicia; pero no lo es tanto el explicar en que consiste dar a cada cual lo que le corresponde y aquí entramos en el tema de los derechos naturales que son la base de los derechos individuales.

Hay ciertos derechos naturales anejos a la persona humana que exigen protección inmediata y son relativamente fáciles de enunciar. Casi todas las constituciones los declaran y establecen esferas de libertad individual que el ciudadano precisa para desenvolverse en sociedad.

Hay tres esferas de protección: la supervivencia individual, la supervivencia de la especie y el desarrollo del hombre como ser social. Sin pretender crear una lista enumeremos algunos derechos usualmente protegidos en cada esfera de libertad. Se protege la esfera de la supervivencia del individuo amparando por ejemplo la propiedad; la esfera de la supervivencia de la especie amparando la familia y la procreación; y la esfera del desarrollo del individuo como ser social, amparando derechos tales como la libertad de expresión, la libertad de cátedra y las relaciones entre gobernantes y gobernados.

Ejemplos de lo último son la inviolabilidad de la correspondencia y del domicilio y el derecho de "habeas corpus" que no son sino límites impuestos al poder expansivo del Estado, que en un constante flujo y reflujo histórico se expande y sufre limitaciones a medida que las sociedades cobran conciencia de que las autoridades existen para servir a los gobernados y no para abusar de ellos. Los siglos XVIII y XIX fueron prolíficos en este proceso que culminó con la definición del estado de derecho basado en el respeto a una carta fundamental y a los derechos básicos allí establecidos.

Sin embargo pronto se tomó conciencia de que las enunciaciones puramente declarativas de derechos no eran más que palabrería rimbombante si no existía un recurso para hacer que se cumpliera lo garantizado por las constituciones. Fué así que surgieron los tribunales constitucionales, dotados de la facultad de declarar y hacer valer los derechos ciudadanos frente a la arbitrariedad o el exceso de la administración.

---

1. Este trabajo se basa en el contenido de dos mesas redondas verificadas el 9 y el 10 de Agosto de 1996 durante la reunión anual del ASCE en Miami. Participantes: José D. Acosta, Alberto Díaz Masvidal; Jorge Hevia; Alberto Luzárraga; Pedro Pablo Llaguno; Manuel Mariñas; Fernando A. Roa; y Silvio Sanabria

Pero esto requiere que exista un Estado de Derecho acatado por los que gobiernan lo que en resumen nos trae a completar la definición: existe Estado de Derecho cuando el gobierno actúa a través de la ley (y de ley dictada previo examen y libre controversia por un parlamento libremente elegido) sometiéndose al examen y/o revocación judicial de sus actos cuando sean contrarios a derecho.

De más está decir que el poder de *examen y revocación* requiere sumo cuidado en la organización, selección y régimen de inspección y gobierno del poder judicial que precisa estar por encima de toda duda. Por ello se concede a los jueces ciertos beneficios como la inamovilidad, en muchos países se les exige acceder a sus cargos previo examen y se regulan los ascensos mediante concurso oposición y/o confirmación por el cuerpo legislativo.

Apliquemos el caso a nuestra historia. La historia de Cuba siempre ha estado transida de constitucionalismo y deseo de limitar el poder central. Recordemos que por excesivo celo constitucionalista se produjo la deposición de Céspedes tachado injustamente de "dictador." Los patriotas del 68 estaban tan decididos a no tener una república que imitase a los desmanes que se veían por entonces en Sur América que sacrificaron a Céspedes en aras de ese prurito. La entrevista de Martí con Gómez en New York donde le espetó: "General, un país no se gobierna como un campamento" es otro ejemplo y también lo es la entrevista de Martí con Gómez y Maceo en La Mejorana donde Maceo se queja de las exigencias legales del "Doctor Martí."

Como patriotas al fin, depusieron sus diferencias y la República en armas así como la de la paz nació con una Constitución que establecía un poder civil al que debía estar supeditado el ejército. Si continuamos examinando nuestra historia veremos una lucha constante por limitar el poder central. Las revoluciones, alzamientos, etc., han sido tan sólo la reacción del pueblo de Cuba contra un poder arbitrario, centralizante y absorbente.

¿Cómo pues con esta historia hemos podido apartarnos tanto del camino que llevaba nuestra sociedad? La respuesta tiene tres vértices. Uno es la tergiversación absoluta de la historia jurídica e institucional de Cuba por el gobierno actual. Otro fué la falta de desarrollo adecuado de nuestras instituciones que estaban "cuajando" por así decirlo hasta el golpe de 1952. Y finalmente el peor y más grave es el sistema actual que pretende ser legal y que ni siquiera alcanza un grado mínimo de pudor jurídico, tanto en la forma como en el fondo, produciendo un vacío en la formación ciudadana que habrá que llenar en su momento a través de una intensa labor educativa.

Veamos los dos primeros puntos. La historia jurídica de Cuba no tiene nada que envidiar a la de ningún país. Es más dado su tamaño nuestra nación ha producido talentos jurídicos en exceso de lo que pudiera esperarse. El Poder Judicial fué organizado desde temprano por su Ley Orgánica promulgada el 27 de enero de 1909. Sus redactores entre otros incluyeron patriotas de la talla de Juan Gualberto Gómez.

La ley y sus modificaciones posteriores establecieron en Cuba el sistema de ingreso a la judicatura mediante examen, calificándose a los examinados, que a su vez ocupaban las plazas vacantes de acuerdo con el puesto que hubieren alcanzado en la calificación. Los ascensos se regulaban y existía el concurso oposición que garantizaba el ascenso por méritos entre los que se incluía el desempeño en el cargo, la producción de obras jurídicas y un examen teórico-práctico ante la Sala de Gobierno del Tribunal Supremo.

El sistema de méritos, independencia e inamovilidad fué mantenido y reiterado por la Constitución del 40. La judicatura en Cuba era básicamente honesta y respetada. Los tribunales funcionaban. El recurso de "habeas corpus" era común. Muchos de los dirigentes actuales se acogieron a sus preceptos empezando por Fidel Castro.

La Constitución del 40 recogió en sus preceptos el recurso de inconstitucionalidad y organizó el Tribunal de Garantías como límite al poder. Y aún así el gobierno actual habla de la República "mediatizada," República que el 31 de Mayo de 1949 desarrolló a través de la Ley No. 7 la legislación orgánica del recurso de inconstitucionalidad previsto en los artículos 172, 182, 183 y 194 de la Constitución del 40 y reguló asimismo el recurso de abuso de poder.

Si algo pudiera criticarse a la mencionada ley era su excesiva apertura. El recurso de inconstitucionalidad podía plantearse como recurso independiente o alegarse dentro de actuaciones judiciales tanto por la persona afectada como por 25 ciudadanos que impugnasen la constitucionalidad de una ley o reglamento; lo cual convertía a toda la ciudadanía en defensora de la legalidad.

Planteado el recurso de inconstitucionalidad dentro de actuaciones judiciales los jueces estaban obligados a suspender los procesos y remitirlos al Tribunal de Garantías y además la ley los facultaba a acudir de "motu propio" en consulta ante el Tribunal de Garantías cuando surgiesen dudas sobre si la ley aplicable era o no constitucional.

El recurso de abuso de poder protegía a las organizaciones político administrativas de nivel intermedio, o sea la provincia y el municipio, de usurpaciones de funciones por el poder central facultándolas para solicitar la suspensión y/o anulación de órdenes o actos administrativos contrarios a derecho y violadores de la autonomía municipal o provincial establecida por la Constitución y las leyes, algunas de las cuales (como la Ley Orgánica de los Municipios) databan de principios de siglo.

El progreso institucional era evidente pero se precisaba más tiempo de funcionamiento para que llegase en toda su profundidad al conocimiento del pueblo. Intuitivamente llegó lo suficientemente lejos para propiciar la rebelión contra Batista pero no había suficiente apego a las instituciones para defenderlas del ataque despiadado y mendaz de que fueron objeto a partir de 1959.

Hay una realidad histórica que es preciso entender: el sistema anterior con todos los defectos humanos o estructurales que puedan señalársele daba facilidades para la protección del ciudadano y tenía tras de sí una vieja prosapia jurídica que hacía que los gobiernos se sintieran obligados a plasmar en leyes o a respetar al menos en parte (como hizo Batista) los lineamientos básicos del sistema.

No es cierto pues que no existiese nada valioso como afirma el gobierno actual; lo cierto es que dicha afirmación es necesaria para obnubilar al pueblo y justificar el adefesio jurídico que hoy en día pasa por Constitución de la República. Examinemos el caso y por el momento, olvidemos que hoy en Cuba no existe un proceso electoral serio y que sólo el partido único (comunista) tiene acceso a los medios de comunicación y controla los organismos de intimidación. Concentrémonos solamente en lo escrito por el mismo régimen que revela mejor que nada la patología jurídica del sistema.

La Constitución del 76 y su modificación subsiguiente están hechas a la medida de un hombre y su camarilla. La Asamblea Popular que supuestamente es el poder supremo del Estado debe aprobar las leyes. Pero sesiona por un corto período y en el interín el Consejo de Estado legisla. Cuando sesiona y a veces se trata de sólo 3 o 4 días (pues obviamente es muy eficiente) la Asamblea no sólo vota nuevas leyes sino que ratifica las modificaciones a las leyes "votadas" por ella que fueron a su vez modificadas por el Consejo de Estado durante el período de vacaciones de la Asamblea. La redacción constitucional no permitía dicho procedimiento pero pronto se modificó a resultas de un dictamen del ex-presidente Dorticós que justificó la necesidad de un cambio. La Asamblea con su complacencia habitual facultó al Consejo de Estado para actuar de esa forma y así se anuló totalmente la única facultad teórica de dicho parlamento gomígrafo.

El Consejo de Estado, verdadero órgano legislativo, se compone de 31 miembros supuestamente también miembros de la Asamblea del Poder Popular. La Asamblea los "elige" así como al Presidente del Consejo de Estado que es a la vez el Jefe del Estado y del Gobierno y como tal preside el Consejo de Ministros. Entre las facultades omnímodas del Presidente se encuentra la de asumir la dirección de cualquier Ministerio sin necesidad de dar razón para ello.

Olvidemos también que la Asamblea disciplinadamente elige siempre a quienes le indiquen los dos hermanos Castro y pensemos solamente en el sistema. Poder Ejecutivo y Legislativo concentrados en un sólo organismo, mezcla de funciones y ausencia de incompatibilidades para cargos diferentes. Cuba es tal vez el único país del mundo donde se puede ser juez y diputado simultáneamente y donde se puede concentrar en una persona la investidura de diputado local, provincial y nacional.

¿Inamovilidad judicial? Los jueces son nombrados por las Asambleas nacionales locales o provinciales y pueden ser removidos por ellas cuando les parezca. Y para colmo se establece el sistema de integrar jueces legos (no letrados) junto a los letrados; jueces que son designados como puede preverse de entre los adeptos del partido que son de confianza absoluta. Así se remacha el sistema, no suceda que algún juez letrado y estudioso se contagie con lo que lee y decida administrar justicia.

Esta olla podrida de funciones incompatibles concentradas en pocas personas refleja la *esencia* del sistema. El poder se ejerce para perpetuarse y el diseño es consistente con el objetivo. Otras Constituciones socialistas han sido más pudorosas (por lo menos en el papel) en cuanto a delimitar funciones. En Cuba se ha carecido hasta del más elemental sentido de dignidad jurídica y nacional, concentrando el poder cuando así lo exigió Fidel Castro pues suya fué la "sugerencia" de que los jueces y diputados pudieran ostentar ambos cargos a lo cual se plegó la Asamblea con su acostumbrada maleabilidad. Pudiéramos extendernos considerablemente y señalar muchos otros aspectos pero la muestra es suficiente. El contraste con nuestro pasado es avergonzante.

La "constitución"castrista (no merece mayúscula) es pródiga en enumerar derechos individuales pero constantemente los refiere a la ley que debe regular su ejercicio. Este régimen ha dictado más leyes que todos los otros gobiernos de nuestra historia corroborando la máxima latina de "plurimae lege corruptisima republica" pues pretende regularlo todo ya que la libertad individual es la única amenaza a su permanencia.

Veamos una muestra de su pregonada justicia. El artículo 73 del Código Penal vigente establece el estado de peligrosidad por *conducta antisocial* y bajo una definición tan amplia ordena la remisión del así considerado a un hospital psiquiátrico, un colectivo de trabajo u otro establecimiento por períodos que van de uno a cuatro años. Es la forma de crear el control absoluto aún antes de que se produzca una conducta adversa al régimen.

Como de costumbre el régimen no inventó nada constructivo sino que corrompió los preceptos del Código de Defensa Social de 1937 y se apropió del concepto y la definición de peligrosidad (muy precisa en ese Código) para cambiarla y darle un contenido genérico que permita al Estado controlar cualquier tipo de conducta que juzgue contraria a sus intereses.

El artículo 103 del Código Penal castiga con prisión de uno a ocho años el "delito" de propaganda enemiga definido como "incitación contra el orden social....o el *Estado socialista* mediante propaganda oral escrita o en cualquiera otra forma" y asimismo establece que incurre en ese "delito" aquél que "difunda noticias falsas o predicciones maliciosas tendientes a causar alarma o *descontento* en la población." La sanción llega a quince años si se trata de un medio de difusión masiva. ¡Cuidado con escribir artículos en revistas o hablar en público fuera de lugar! La prensa y la televisión son del Estado y es un dueño celoso.

La Constitución del 40 por el contrario garantizaba en su artículo 33 la libre emisión del pensamiento "de palabra, por escrito o por cualquier otro medio gráfico u oral de expresión, utilizando ... todos los procedimientos de difusión disponibles."

El artículo 206 del Código Penal crea un increíble y novedoso "delito" denominado "abuso de la libertad de cultos" que se integra por "oponer la creencia religiosa a los objetivos de la educación." Sanción: de tres meses a un año. ¡Cuidado con intentar educar moralmente a los hijos! También sus almas son propiedad del Estado.

El artículo 35 de la Constitución del 40 decía: "es libre la profesión de todas las religiones ....y el ejercicio de todos los cultos."

El artículo 208 del Código Penal castiga las asociaciones ilícitas con sanción de tres meses a un año. Son ilícitas todas las que no estén previamente autorizadas por el gobierno. Las reuniones también son propiedad del Estado.

El artículo 36 de la Constitución del 40 decía: "los habitantes de la República tienen el derecho de reunirse pacíficamente y sin armas y el desfilar y asociarse para todos los fines lícitos de la vida."

El artículo 216 del Código Penal castiga al que intente salir del territorio nacional sin cumplir "las formalidades legales" con prisión de uno a tres años. Si hay fuerza en las cosas o intimidación en las personas la pena es de tres a ocho años. Las personas físicas también son propiedad del Estado y los esclavos no deben ausentarse sin el visto bueno del patrón.

El artículo 30 de la Constitución del 40 decía: "toda persona podrá entrar y permanecer en el territorio nacional salir de él, trasladarse de un lugar a otro y mudar de residencia sin necesidad de carta de seguridad, pasaporte u otro requisito semejante."

La Ley de Procedimiento Penal es otra indicación objetiva de como se piensa. En vez del juez instructor que establecía la antigua Ley de Enjuiciamiento Criminal, tenemos ahora un instructor que no es otro que un funcionario de la seguridad del Estado. En nuestro sistema tradicional una vez procesado el acusado tenía derecho a participar en las actuaciones y a proponer pruebas antes de que se abriera el juicio oral. Hoy en día está indefenso hasta que se presenta a juicio. Naturalmente, esto se ha cambiado puesto que ser procesado en la Cuba de hoy por un "delito" del cariz de los expuestos equivale a ser condenado y no se desean molestias ni abogados que compliquen el proceso de "prueba." La palabra del amo es definitiva.

Por el contrario la Constitución del 40 concedía a los jueces facultades amplísimas para proteger al detenido, tanto así que en su artículo 29 estipulaba: "es absolutamente obligatoria la presentación ante el tribunal que haya expedido el 'habeas corpus' de toda persona detenida o presa, cualquiera que sea la autoridad o funcionario persona o entidad que la retenga, *sin que pueda alegarse obediencia debida*...los jueces o magistrados que se negaren a admitir la solicitud de mandamiento de 'habeas corpus' *serán separados de sus cargos* por la Sala de Gobierno del Tribunal Supremo."

El contraste entre una simple muestra de algunos los derechos establecidos en la Constitución del 40 (corroborados por la Declaración Universal de los Dere-

chos Humanos) y la legislación vigente en Cuba nos hace ver que la "constitución castrista" con gran desparpajo dice garantizar todo lo que después el gobierno se ocupa de prohibir en la legislación complementaria.

¡Pobres patriotas que gestaron la independencia! El preámbulo de la constitución del 76 se refiere a ellos como inspiración y se pretende que este triste documento sea la continuidad de su esfuerzo.

Frente a esta ceguera y falta de civismo es necesario que el Estado de Derecho en la Cuba futura tenga una base jurídica del más alto nivel moral y técnico. El texto falaz que hoy rige en Cuba, pues rige solamente a efectos propagandísticos, tendrá que ser sustituído por una Constitución como la que disfrutábamos que establezca una judicatura independiente y un Tribunal Constitucional que haga valer los preceptos constitucionales. Las Leyes complementarias violadoras de las constituciones se controlan por este medio. Es obvio que en Cuba el gobierno hace lo que quiere porque no hay independencia judicial ni respeto por la judicatura que hoy en día está al servicio de la camarilla imperante y no es sino un instrumento más del poder absoluto.

El gran desafío de la Cuba libre será llevar a la mente del ciudadano común la simple idea de que puede y debe ser protegido en el ejercicio de sus derechos y para ello hay que crear un control de la legalidad pues de lo contrario no hay Estado de Derecho. Ese control se llama Tribunal Constitucional y tiene que organizarse en Cuba con gran independencia y el más alto prestigio para que sus decisiones sean respetadas por el Poder Ejecutivo y por la ciudadanía. Un Tribunal Constitucional respetado y competente no sólo controla a un Poder Ejecutivo desbordado sino que también controla al Congreso en caso de que la mayoría imperante decida pasar leyes inconstitucionales para congraciarse con sus electores. Y aún más actúa como control de la judicatura si ésta no cumple con su obligación de aplicar la Constitución y amparar al ciudadano. Es la verdadera garantía del Estado de Derecho y la Constitucionalidad y constituye la pieza más importante del sistema en todo cuanto se refiera a su estabilidad pues proporciona una alternativa a los disconformes que no es la violencia o la revolución.

Afortunadamente contamos con antecedentes muy valiosos que han permanecido en la conciencia nacional tanto en el exilio como en Cuba. También es cierto que nuestra tradición jurídica contó con el aporte del movimiento legislativo de fin del siglo XIX que influyó definitivamente en la legislación española modernizándola y creando buenos Códigos como el Civil de 1888 y otros que fueron implantados y regían en Cuba hasta el año 1959. Esta legislación para fortuna nuestra ha seguido desarrollándose en España de acuerdo con las necesidades de los tiempos y así por una coincidencia histórica contamos hasta con una fuente de jurisprudencia dentro de las líneas de nuestra tradición e idioma que será muy útil para el desarrollo de la legislación futura incluyendo la nueva ley del Tribunal Constitucional de ese país y su excelente jurisprudencia.

Nuestra tarea más importante, aquélla que asegurará el futuro de las generaciones venideras será crear instituciones basadas en la justicia, respetarlas, protegerlas y acostumbrar al ciudadano a acogerse a ellas. La fuerza y la revolución de por sí no son fuentes de derecho. Decir lo contrario como afirman los creyentes de que la ley positiva equivale al derecho es hacer caso omiso al hecho de que existen derechos naturales inviolables que trascienden las situaciones de fuerza y que acaban por imponerse porque como decíamos son anejos a la persona humana. El transcurso del tiempo sí crea situaciones de hecho que será necesario reconocer y tratar con justicia pues en definitiva el derecho lidia con la vida y la realidad. Pero una cosa es adaptarse a una situación de hecho con medidas transitorias que faciliten el tránsito hacia una sociedad más justa y otra es no poner fin al desastre institucional que ha gestado el presente régimen.

Este cambio requerirá un esfuerzo ingente y la buena voluntad de todos los cubanos que deben entender que su deber patriótico es crear un Estado de Derecho y entender en que consiste. El Estado de Derecho no es cosa de abogados (aunque su aportación es importante), es cosa de ciudadanos que deben estar bien familiarizados con los recursos que se ponen a su alcance para poder desenvolverse civilizada y productivamente. No se trata como piensan algunos tan sólo de que me respeten *mi derecho* sino de que se respete *el de todos* y se pueda convivir en una sociedad justa, lo cual implica *deberes y respeto* mutuos pues nuestro derecho termina precisamente donde comienza el de los demás.

Sólo así lograremos una Cuba "con todos y para el bien de todos."

CUBA'S NEW AGRICULTURAL COOPERATIVES AND MARKETS: ANTECEDENTS, ORGANIZATION, EARLY PERFORMANCE AND PROSPECTS

José Alvarez and William A. Messina, Jr.

Land tenancy in Cuban agriculture has experienced three pronounced changes since the beginning of the revolution in January 1959. The first agrarian reform law was enacted in May of that year. It proscribed the latifundia (described as estates larger than 405 hectares), and initially distributed some land and encouraged the development of cooperatives on large estates. Most of these cooperatives, however, had been converted into state farms by 1962.

The second agrarian reform law, enacted in October 1963, expropriated the land of most farmers with more than 67 hectares. The state then became the owner and manager of the vast majority of Cuba's agricultural lands. This situation lasted exactly thirty years, until the creation of the Basic Units of Cooperative Production (UBPCs) in October of 1993, which is considered by many as a third agrarian reform.

The objectives of this paper are: (a) to summarize the causes and effects of the current Cuban economic and agricultural crises; (b) to study in some detail the organization and operation of both UBPCs and new agricultural markets; and (c) to discuss the implications of these changes for Cuba's future agricultural productivity.

ANTECEDENTS[1]
The General Economy
In mid-September of 1990, Cuban officials announced that the country was entering a "Special Period in Time of Peace" as a result of the demise of socialism in Eastern European countries and the changes taking place in the Soviet Union. The subsequent collapse of the Soviet Union and of the Council for Mutual Economic Assistance (CMEA) eliminated the framework within which the majority of Cuba's commerce and economic activity were taking place.

At the end of the 1980s, Cuba was conducting around 80 percent of its external commercial relations with the member countries of the CMEA. This group of countries was purchasing the majority of Cuba's total exports (63 percent of sugar, 73 percent of nickel, 95 percent of citrus), and was the origin of around 86 percent of Cuba's total imports including 63 percent of food, 86 percent of raw materials, 98 percent of fuels and lubricants, 80 percent of machinery and equipment, and 57 percent of chemical products (Alvarez González and Fernández Mayo, 1992, pp. 4-5). Furthermore, the trade relations between Cuba and the CMEA took place under favorable terms of trade for the Cuban economy. For example, Alvarez González and Fernández Mayo

---

1. González Jordán (1995, pp. 84-88) contains a brief but interesting account of agricultural developments going back to the early days of the revolution.

175

(1992, p. 4) estimate that, during the period 1980 to 1990, Cuban import revenues were about 50 percent higher than they would have been if their exports had been sold at world market prices.

In 1989 Cuban imports exceeded 8 billion pesos, but by 1992 they had decreased to 2 billion pesos for a decline in value of more than 70 percent in only three years (Alvarez González and Fernández Mayo, 1992, pp. 4, 8). As a result, the living standard of the general populace in Cuba deteriorated during the Special Period. Food availability in the official distribution system (rationing system) continually worsened, oil shortages for power generation grew so critical that rolling power black outs became a regular part of life throughout the country, and gasoline and repair parts for automobiles and buses became so scarce that a large proportion of the population was relegated to using bicycles as their primary means of transportation. However, perhaps the most significant event of the Special Period was the development of food scarcity into a crisis.

The Food Crisis

Food scarcity in revolutionary Cuba is not a new phenomenon. It dates back to 1962 when it was the motivation for the introduction of the rationing book. Wide variations in food availability (in terms of both quantity and variety) have been experienced since that time. The present crisis is the result, in order of importance, of the inefficiencies inherent to central planning, the demise of the Council of Mutual Economic Assistance (CMEA), and the U.S. economic embargo.

The failure of central planning to solve the food scarcity problem is well documented in the literature. For example, Alvarez and Puerta (1994) have shown that, as the state intervention decreased among Cuba's agricultural production units, the quantity and quality of output of most commodities under study generally increased despite more limited access to factors of production and other resources. In addition,

Peña Castellanos and Alvarez (1996) have shown that the intensive use of land and inputs, and high levels of investment, along with the specific forms of organization and management that characterized Cuba's sugarcane extensive growth model during the 1980s, could not overcome the challenges posed by the need for close coordination between sugarcane crop production and corresponding industrial processing activities. Furthermore, Alvarez and Puerta (1994, p. 1666) demonstrated that nonstate farms performed better than state farms in each of the last 21 harvest seasons for which official data are available. To make things worse, state agricultural enterprises were subsidized to cover all of their losses even when the losses were the result of poor management (González Jordán, 1995, p. 92).[2]

Research has not only shown differences in productivity but also disparities in income levels among workers in farms with different agricultural production. Field research conducted in three different Cuban municipalities show that peasant households (in regions characterized by sugarcane, mixed cropping, and livestock production) generate the highest income levels in the agricultural sector. Moreover, private sector incomes were considerably higher than those of households of state farm wage workers (Deere et al., 1995). According to these authors, the relatively high incomes earned by members of Agricultural Production Cooperatives are indicative of the higher profitability and, hence, productivity of Cuba's production cooperatives as compared to the state farms (p. 231).

Nova González (1994) confirms that, in the last fifteen years, and particularly since 1986, Cuba's agricultural and livestock activities in general experienced production declines, loss of efficiency, and/or stagnation in key production areas. This happened despite the strong investment process that took place in agriculture (around 30 percent of total investments in the country during the decade of the 1980s), the high availability of tractors, high use of

---

2. This practice, however, is being discontinued at present. Despite that fact, data from the Cuban Ministry of Finance show that subsidies to state enterprises comprised 42.3, 29.8 and 26 percent of the country's total budget in 1993, 1994 and 1995, respectively (CIEM, 1996, p. 25).

nutrients per hectare, as well as continuing increases in productive expenses and in the labor force. Furthermore, while 39 percent of state agricultural enterprises showed positive financial results in 1986, only 27 percent did so in 1990.

The Food Plan (*Plan Alimentario*, PA) was the most recent attempt at solving Cuba's food problem through central planning.[3] Although this plan dates back to the mid-1980s following the closing of the free farmers' markets, it increased in importance after the establishment of the Special Period in September of 1990. The general objective of the PA was to make Cuba self-sufficient in most agricultural commodities. After initial mixed results, and facing increasingly labor and input shortages, the PA was abandoned in 1993.

With the severe economic crisis, and the resultant food crisis, the Cuban government was facing after the demise of the former Soviet bloc, the above evidence prompted the Cuban leadership to break up the large state farms into smaller units that could perform as well as the private and cooperative sectors (Acuerdo, 1993; Varela Pérez, 1993). The Basic Units of Cooperative Production, or *Unidades Básicas de Producción Cooperativa* (UBPC) were born in September of 1993. This radical change is especially significant from a philosophical point of view when one considers that Fidel Castro had consistently referred to the state farms as the "superior form of agricultural production."[4]

THE BASIC UNITS OF COOPERATIVE PRODUCTION (UBPC)

Establishment and Organization

On 20 September 1993, the Council of State enacted Law-Decree No. 142 establishing the Basic Units of Cooperative Production on state lands (*Gaceta*, 1993, p. 15). Article 1 states that the activity of the UBPCs will be based on the following principles:

a. the linking of the man to the land;

b. the self-sufficiency of the workers' collective and their families, with a cooperative effort, and the improvement of their living conditions;

c. the workers' earnings will be rigorously related to the production achieved; and

d. to develop the autonomy of management and to administer their resources with the objective of achieving self-sufficiency in the productive process.

Article 2 establishes that the UBPCs will:

a. have the usufruct of the land for an indefinite period of time;

b. be the owners of production;

c. sell their production to the state through the enterprise or in the manner that the state decides;

d. pay insurance premiums;

e. manage bank accounts;

f. purchase the fundamental means of production on credit;

g. collectively elect its leadership who will render periodic accounts to its members; and

h. fulfill the corresponding fiscal responsibilities as their contribution to the general expenditures of the Nation.

---

3. For detailed descriptions of the PA, consult Deere (1993) and Roca (1994).

4. This effort is being complemented with a significant land distribution program to families who are willing to move to the countryside. According to Orlando Lugo, president of ANAP, until early 1995, about 6,000 families had received around 12,000 ha of land in usufruct for tobacco production in the province of Pinar del Río; more than 430 urban families, especially in the province of Santiago de Cuba, had moved to the mountains after receiving land for coffee production, while 2,600 individuals were in the process of obtaining such approval; and 369 livestock workers and their families had received 19,870 ha and livestock for dairy production in the province of Ciego de Avila (Alfonso, 1995a).

Table 1. Average Farm Size for State Enterprises in 1990 and UBPCs in 1994, by Main Activity (in hectares)

Main Activity	State Enterprise	UBPC	Average decline in size (%)[a]
Sugarcane	13110	1190	91
Mixed crops	4276	456	89
Citrus and other fruits	10822[b]	100	99
Rice	32760	5132	84
Tobacco	2778	241	91
Livestock	24865	1595	94

Source: Compiled by González Jordán (1995, p. 90) from several Cuban sources.

a. Calculated by the authors.

b. Does not include the Jagüey Grande enterprise with 48,200 hectares.

Through August 2, 1994 the total number of sugarcane and non-sugarcane UBPCs established amounted to 2,643, with a total area of 221,300 *caballerías* (cabs.), or 7.4 million acres, and more than 257,000 members. This represented approximately 50 percent of the total area in state hands, with 93.5 percent of state cane area going to cane UBPCs and 29 percent of state non-cane area allocated to non-cane UBPCs. Average UBPC size is 84 cab. (2,800 acres), with 97 members per UBPC, or 1.2 workers per cab. (33.3 acres) of total area (Comité Estatal de Estadísticas, 1994, p. 2).[5]

One of the indications of the magnitude of the change is the difference in average farm size between state enterprises in 1990 and UBPCs in 1994 (Table 1).

Although the Table reflects the average UBPC to be less than 10 percent of the size of the average state farm, González Jordán (1995, p. 91) believes that the average UBPC size is still too large and may be the

reason for their low productive and economic efficiency.

During several field visits conducted by the authors during 1994, 1995 and 1996, cooperative leaders and members provided useful information concerning their experiences with the UBPCs' establishment and organization.[6] Former state farm workers were given the option of becoming members of the new UBPC and the coop members elected their leaders (referred to as a "Direction Board") from among their membership. Cooperative members also have the right to vote on the addition of new members and the termination of members who may not be adequately conducting their duties at the UBPC.

UBPCs were given the right to farm their land in perpetuity, although title to the land remains with the state. While in some cases, each UBPC was assigned a proportionate share of machinery and equipment from the former state farm (without any input from coop members); in other cases the members selected the amount and type of machinery and equipment they wanted to purchase from the state enterprise. However, each coop has complete control over which and how many of the pieces of equipment they maintain and use. Provisions were made with the Cuban National Bank for the UBPCs to obtain low interest loans to purchase the machinery and equipment from the state.

UBPCs still have production quotas which they must sell to *acopio* (the state collection agency). In the interest of maintaining a balance of production between crops throughout the country, the state enterprise which supervises the UBPCs offers them relatively little autonomy in what to produce as their primary crops at the present time. For example, UBPCs which were formed from a state farm producing mostly bananas and plantains must continue to pro-

5. In addition, in 1992 there were 383 sugarcane CPAs and 185 CPAs of miscellaneous crops, with a total area of 14,500 and 36,000 acres, respectively (Polo Científico, n.d., pp. 9, 10).

6. One important point to recognize is the similarities between, but also discrepancies among, sugarcane UBPCs and non-sugarcane UBPCs. Perhaps the most important difference is that sugarcane UBPCs maintain their dependence on the Ministry of Sugar's former Agro-Industrial Complexes, or CAI (vertically integrated organizations), while non-sugarcane UBPCs' relationship is with state enterprises under the Ministry of Agriculture.

duce similar volumes of bananas and plantains. There is speculation (and hope) that more autonomy may be permitted in the future.[7]

This autonomy is expected to develop as part of the process of negotiating production quotas which occurs annually between the UBPC Direction Boards and the state. Annual "production potentials" (i.e., goals) for the principal commodities produced by the UBPC are initially based upon a proportionate share of the previous state farm's quota. However, UBPC Board members hope that, over time, they may be able to convince the state negotiators to allow them to increase the production of crops which they are more efficient at producing and decrease those which they are less.

The Incentive System[8]

With the opening of the agricultural markets (discussed later in the paper), policy changes were also implemented for the UBPCs which provided important production incentives. Once the production goals are agreed upon between the state enterprise and the UBPC Direction Board, the UBPC quota for sale to *acopio* is established at 80 percent of the overall production goals. This quota is broken up into monthly commitments levels. The UBPC is free to sell the remaining 20 percent of the production goal and 20 percent of any excess above the production goal to the agricultural markets.

UBPCs have some degree of autonomy within this system. For example, they are free to sell surplus production in any agricultural market they choose; it obviously costs less to transport their crops to local markets, but prices in these markets are typically lower than the prices in the markets in the city of Havana. Conversely, the government charges a lower tax rate on crops sold in agricultural markets in the cities than they do at rural markets to encourage shipment of food into the cities. UBPC leaders understand these tradeoffs and carefully assess the relative costs

and benefits when deciding where to market their surplus. Indeed, two neighboring UBPCs visited made different decisions with regard to where to market their crops because they produced different commodities. For one of them, the additional cost of transporting their crops to markets in the city of Havana was more than offset by the lower taxes and high prices which they received while the other UBPC elected to sell in the local markets because their crops did not command a sufficient premium in the city market. The UBPC Simón Rodríguez sells its surplus of mixed crops in the city, while the neighboring UBPC Fidel Borrego elected to sell its bananas and plantains locally.

Furthermore, UBPCs do not actually need to produce any volumes beyond that which they are obligated to sell to *acopio*. For example, some UBPCs that were visited had found that, since bananas and plantains remained relatively plentiful in Cuba at that time, the price which they received for these products in the agricultural markets did not even cover their production costs. These UBPCs therefore had chosen to only produce their quota requirements of bananas and plantain for *acopio* and reallocate the inputs (labor as well as limited amounts of fertilizer and pesticides) to production of crops which will return a profit.

Actually, the UBPC members do not use the term profit, preferring instead to use the term "surplus." These surpluses are extremely important because, in addition to being the source of funds that the UBPC uses to pay off its equipment loans, they also are the source of incentive compensation to the individual workers.

Despite their different areas of specialization, all UBPC members are considered to be the same level and generally receive the same base wage for their work. Individual UBPCs have a great deal of flexibility in how they structure the incentive system for dis-

---

7. In fact, this is one of the issues of the current internal debate concerning UBPCs. More information about it may be found in later sections of this paper.

8. In discussing current Russian reforms, Bromley (1993, p. 6) states that the key economic issue is not that of nominal "ownership" but the institutional arrangements that define the incentives under which production is to be undertaken.

tributing their surplus. For example, one UBPC visited divided their members into three-person work brigades. Each brigade was assigned a specific small plot of land and their compensation from the UBPC surplus was tied to the level of production which they were able to generate on their plot. This arrangement requires an elaborate system of record keeping and control and not all UBPCs choose to use such a complex system. Indeed, the structure of the system varied depending upon both the type of crops produced and the mix of crops within the UBPC. UBPCs which produced a large variety of crops recognized the difficulties in measuring productivity of the individual members or groups of members when they were producing different crops and their systems therefore tended to share the surplus fairly equal among members. Conversely, UBPCs which produced chiefly a single crop tended to have more elaborate methods of measuring productivity to provide incentives to the individual members or groups of members. One UBPC was actually attempting to adjust its compensation plan for work brigades whose plots were on the windward side of banana fields because of losses which their plots sustained from heavy winds and storms.

A common practice among UBPCs is to distribute 50 percent of their surplus to the workers. The other half is used to pay off equipment loans and for other production-related expenses such as purchasing inputs. The balance of these monies remains in a common fund for construction of facilities for the coop members such as housing, recreational facilities, expanded health care, technical training, and others.[9]

Differences Between UBPCs and CPAs

The similarities between the Agricultural Production Cooperatives (CPAs) and the UBPCs are obvious. In fact, the latter were developed following the economic framework and the means of collective and individual remunerations of the former.

The only major exception is land ownership in legal terms. CPA members are the owners of their land while the UBPC leases state lands for an indefinite period of time. An additional difference exists on members' affiliation to a mass organization. CPA members belong to the National Association of Small Farmers (ANAP). UBPC members, on the other hand, remain enrolled in the Agricultural, Livestock, and Forestry Workers' Union. Under this arrangement, CPAs have a greater degree of autonomy than UBPCs.

Although we believe the autonomy issue to be a temporary difference, it surfaced dramatically during a visit to one sugarcane CPA and a neighboring sugarcane UBPC a few weeks after the conclusion of the 1993-94 sugarcane harvest. The CPA had standing cane belonging to different stages of the production cycle. The UBPC did not. The CPA officials had refused to harvest any of this cane in order not to disrupt the normal production cycle despite pressure from the CAI. The contiguous UBPC, however, had to yield to the CAI's "persuasion" to fulfill a national production goal. This difference is explained by the fact that, from the outset in the mid-1970s, the CPA members have been the owners of their land and equipment and had been granted a degree of autonomy they were not willing to relinquish.

Early Performance

The performance of the UBPCs is very difficult to evaluate for two obvious reasons. First, it is a very short period of time to allow the UBPCs to grow and mature; and, second, this drastic transition has taken place within an economy going through its worst economic crisis in many decades. What follows is a summary of statistics provided by Cuban officials and a description of the results of two major efforts aimed at finding the causes for the first-year apparent disappointing performance.

Although established in late 1993, UBPCs' preliminary performance results were being released in early 1995. According to Alfredo Jordán, Minister of Agriculture, Cuban agricultural production in 1994 (1,050,000 short tons), declined by 200,000 short tons when compared with the previous year, and by 600,000 short tons when compared with 1992. The

---

9. This is identical to what Agricultural Production Cooperatives (CPAs) do (Junta Directiva, 1994, p. 7).

figures include total production (grains, fruits, tubers, roots, and vegetables) except sugarcane (Alfonso, 1995b). Later, the National Council of the Agricultural, Livestock, and Forestry Workers' Union met to analyze the losses and low productivity inherited by the UBPCs from the former state farms. Salvador Valdés, general secretary, enumerated a long list of material difficulties the UBPCs are facing (Alfonso, 1995d), most of which are discussed later in this section.

The sugarcane UBPCs did not fare any better. In mid-March of 1995, Raúl Trujillo, first deputy Minister of MINAZ stated that, during the 1993-94 harvest, only 127 (9 percent) of the 1,426 UBPCs in operation increased production and generated profits; another 712 (50 percent) have many problems that could be solved within a one-year period, while the remaining 587 (41 percent) show a series of problems without immediate solution (Alfonso, 1995c).

The release of these statistics generated opposite reactions among scholars who study the Cuban situation. Carmelo Mesa-Lago, a professor of Economics at the University of Pittsburgh, stated: "The co-ops are not working. They don't have the proper incentives. The majority of the cooperative members say, 'Why should I be productive for the state, if the state is going to pay me much less?'" Julio Carranza, an economist with Havana's Center for the Study of the Americas, however, believes that the "UBPCs constitute the transformation of the economy. Results are not high enough, but that does not mean they are a mistake. It's just that they haven't matured" (Alvarez, 1995, p. 4A). Two studies conducted in Cuba may shed some light on the issue.

One of these studies was conducted by the Center of Demographic Studies at the University of Havana, and the National School of Union Leaders "Lázaro Peña" (Molina Soto and García Santiago, 1995). Research objectives included determining what needs to be done in the UBPCs to reach the following goals: (a) obtain the necessary labor force; (b) link remuner-

ation to all members to their productive results; (c) obtain the necessary working tools; (d) satisfy the food needs of the workers and their families; and (e) advance in the building of housing for their members.

A questionnaire was developed to obtain information on actions taken and date of expected fulfillment of the previous goals. A sample of 774 UBPCs was drawn from Cuba's 14 provinces and the Special Municipality of the Isle of Youth in May 1995, resulting in 630 actual UBPCs visited. The interviews were conducted in pairs by 1,100 students of the provincial schools of union leaders during one week. Most of the UBPCs visited included sugarcane, miscellaneous crops, and cattle.

A summary of the research findings are reported in relation to the goals:

a. *obtain the necessary labor force:*[10] The total number of workers required is 79,790, for a shortage of 18,844 workers, or 23.6 percent of the necessary labor force (p. 4). Of special importance is the fact that 74.1 percent of the worker shortage was in sugarcane, followed by miscellaneous crops with 10.2 percent (p. 5). The majority of UBPCs will fulfill this goal in 1996, while the rest will do so in 1997 (p. 6);

b. *link all members to their productive results:* 40.8 percent of the UBPCs are already working in that direction, while 27.9 percent are not doing anything in that regard. In addition, 19.4 percent are linking members to their areas, and the remaining 11.9 percent are doing so to their productive results (p. 8). Sugarcane UBPCs are doing better than the rest in the fulfillment of this goal (p. 7) although no specific dates were given for achieving this goal;

c. *obtain the necessary working tools:*[11] It was estimated that 26,114 animals were necessary and that there was a shortage of 10,664, or 40.8 percent. Highest needs are present in sugarcane

---

10. The study does not specify what criteria were followed to determine the number of workers needed by UBPC.

11. Also in this area, the study does not define the criteria followed to determine the number of necessary tools, especially animals.

(63.7 percent), livestock (19.2 percent), and miscellaneous crops (11.5 percent) (p. 9). Achievement of this goal is expected between the years 1996 and 1998 (p. 11);

d. *satisfy the food needs of the workers and their families*: 63.7 percent of the UBPCs are already working in self-provisioning plots, while the remaining 36.3 percent are not. Figures by type (crop) of UBPC are very similar to the national averages. Expected dates of fulfillment for the majority of the UBPCs is 1996, and 1997 for the rest (p. 12); and

e. *advance in the building of housing for their members*: Of the 20,250 dwellings needed, there is a deficit of 10,273 units, or 50.7 percent. Livestock UBPCs show the lowest shortage (30.2 percent), while citrus UBPCs have the highest (78.9 percent) (pp. 15, 16). Housing needs are expected to be fulfilled between 1998-2010 because of the current lack of construction materials (p. 17).

The second study was directed by Polo Científico de Humanidades (1995) at the University of Havana (UH), although actual participation included seven research centers at the UH and three at other institutions.[12] This project consisted of several multidisciplinary efforts with the common goal of researching problems in the UBPCs in the provinces of La Habana, Cienfuegos, Ciego de Avila and Granma through the use of questionnaires and surveys.

Although results are still considered preliminary, the following seven themes (Coordinación, 1995, pp. 5-9), can be considered relevant due to the consistency of the replies to the questionnaires:

a. *the UBPCs' autonomy*: It is a key structural element to improved efficiency of the UBPCs. As

stated above, sugarcane UBPCs' linkages with the CAI and MINAZ are very strong since the CAI receives the production and offers technical services such as machinery repairs, land preparation, and oil supplies. Non-sugarcane UBPCs depend of the Ministry of Agriculture's enterprises. These historical ties of subordination represent one of the most important obstacles to overcome. There exist numerous examples of the CAIs and enterprises continuing to function with their old styles of control, which they exerted on the state farms, leading to the obstruction of the UBPCs' development. Some examples include (1) close operational control such as the sale of oil being tied to detailed reporting on how it was used; and (2) imposing strategies that do not correspond to the realities faced by the UBPCs such as prohibiting the burning of sugarcane fields not suitable for hand harvesting, and an obligatory planting schedule;

b. *leadership and technological organization, especially in the area of economics*: It became evident that there are difficulties for exercising these roles because of lack of knowledge, which have an effect on the system of participative democracy that must characterize the UBPCs. For example, there exists ignorance in the complexities of the accounting system, calculation of production costs and the relationship between advanced payments and profits. This is related to the low qualifications of the personnel involved;

c. *use of agricultural biotechnology*: The use of science and technology becomes critical during the Special Period, which provides a favorable framework for emphasis on the use of substitutes of fertilizers and chemical pesticides, leading to the shift from conventional to an economically

---

12. This impressive and objective summary of research on the UBPCs contains an introduction by Coordinación (pp. 1-9), and articles on labor force issues by Capó Pérez and Colectivo (pp. 39-41); on accounting by Castillo Díaz (pp. 37-38); on general issues in miscellaneous crops by Díaz et al. (pp. 31-36), Lorenzo Delgado et al. (pp. 44-45), and Romero Valcárcel et al. (pp. 42-43); on computing for sugar CAIs by González Surribas and Jhones Menéndez (pp. 26-30); on sugarcane by Jústiz García and Díaz Pérez (pp. 10-16), Limia David and Salazar (pp. 17-19), and Pampin Balado et al. (pp. 20-25); on dairy by Martínez Figueredo et al. (pp. 47-50); on marketing by Miranda Forés et al. (p. 51); on livestock by Molina Soto (p. 46); and, finally, on the agricultural markets by Rodríguez Castellón (pp. 52-54).

efficient sustainable agriculture. However, a change in attitudes is a must. The use of substitutes is considered by many as a transitory ill of the Special Period because the aspiration to return to traditional production practices remains alive;

d. *stabilization of the labor force*. There are problems in this area, which differ between sugarcane (most critical) and non-sugarcane UBPCs. The problems are related to the lack of housing and self-sufficiency. The members' exodus results in a non-stable labor force since they have to be replaced by mobilized workers. The study recommend the recruitment among the members' family, avoiding mistakes such as the formation of mixed brigades where women are expected to perform like men;

e. *lack of a broad-based appreciation for the concepts of property and ownership*. There is a challenge to convert the workers into self-managed owners. This is the result of all the factors discussed from (a) through (d), in addition to the strong traditional forces within a paternalistic state;

f. *living conditions*. Where housing shortages exist, it is necessary to be flexible regarding conditions which would facilitate multiple families living in a single domicile. In addition, there is a strong demand for recreational activities, job transfers, and bicycles; and

g. *immediate effect of the establishment of the agricultural markets*. Although not fully discernible yet, there appears to be a positive impact on production increases in UBPCs of miscellaneous crops. This issue should be investigated in sugarcane UBPCs.

THE AGRICULTURAL MARKETS
Establishment and Organization

Initially, the UBPCs operated under the same system as the CPAs, where they sold their quota volumes to the state at the fixed official price and they received a premium for production in excess of their quota. During the late 1980s this system provided incentives for the CPAs to produce in excess of their quota levels and sell the extra production to the state. However, food shortages which developed in the early 1990s caused a dramatic increase in prices on the black market, thus the incentive to sell excess production to the state declined significantly (Deere, 1995, p. 15).

The lack of ability to import foodstuffs, coupled with declining agricultural production and the incentive to redirect excess production (and, in some cases, even quota production) to the black market created severe food shortages in the ration stores in Cuba. These shortages are, in part, considered responsible for the civil unrest which developed in Cuba in mid-1994 and culminated in the rafters or refugee crisis that summer. This, in turn, helped to bring about the second major policy change for the agricultural sector: the opening of the agricultural markets (*mercados agropecuarios*, MA). The decision was somewhat surprising based on an earlier experiment with free farmers markets (*mercados libres campesinos*, MLC) which the Cuban government had attempted during the 1980s and closed six years later for a variety of reasons.[13]

On September 19, 1994, the Council of Ministers enacted Decree No. 191 establishing the agricultural markets (Pagés, 1994, p. 3).[14] The main objective of these markets is to increase the production levels of food intended for the population's consumption. The MA are organized by the Bureau of Commerce

---

13. For more information on the MLC, see Alonso (1992), Alvarez and Puerta (1994, pp. 1670-1672), Benjamin et al. (1986, pp. 57-77), Deere and Meurs (1992, pp. 829-836), Figueroa and García (1984), Mesa-Lago (1988, pp. 69-72), Pérez-López (1995, pp. 83-90) and Rosenberg (1992). In addition, Espinosa (1995) discusses the agricultural markets from political and ideological perspectives.

14. In fact, the disclosure had been made by Raúl Castro in an interview conducted on September 11 and published on September 19 (Báez, 1994) —the same day that Decree No. 191 was enacted by the Council of Ministers and two days before it appeared in the official press. Rumors on the establishment of these markets, however, had been circulating throughout the island since the second half of August (Torres and Pérez, 1994, p. 32).

of the Administrative Councils of Popular Power, who determine the number and location of these markets in each municipality.

Only the surplus beyond the production agreement between the farmers and the state agency will be saleable at the MA. Thus, the more production, the higher the quantities that will be available to be sold at prices agreed upon freely between buyers and sellers. Sellers have to pay a tax for the space and other services provided. The Administrative Councils supervise and control the functioning of the MA, according to current regulations. Producers who fail to fulfill their obligations with the state but sell in the MA will have to pay a penalty equal to the product of multiplying the unfulfilled volume times the highest price at the MA at the time of the violation. The Ministries of Agriculture and Internal Trade will be responsible for regulating the organization and functioning of these markets. In addition, the Ministries of the Revolutionary Armed Forces, Interior, and other state central organizations, will establish their own regulations to participate in the MA.

On September 30, 1994, the Ministries of Agriculture and Internal Trade signed a Joint Resolution regulating the participation in, and products to be sold at, the MA (Pagés, 1994, p. 3). The following entities and individuals, or their appointed representatives, will be able to participate in the agricultural markets: (a) state farms and enterprises; (b) non-cane basic units of cooperative production (UBPC); (c) agricultural production cooperatives (CPA); (d) farms under the Working Youth Army (*Ejército Juvenil del Trabajo*, EJT); (e) cooperatives of credit and services (CCS) representing their members; (f) small farmers; (g) budgeted enterprises and units that produce in their areas for self-consumption; (h) producers in areas allocated for family self-consumption; and (i) producers in yards and small parcels.

The following products are excluded from the MAs: bovine, buffalo and equine beef; fresh milk; coffee, tobacco and cocoa, as well as their derivatives; and rice from the agro-industrial complexes (which will be entirely contracted with the state). The sale of some of these products, however, may be authorized in certain periods and territories.

The characteristics of the MAs during the first 15 days of operation was studied by Lee (1994) and summarized by Torres and Pérez (1994, pp. 35-39). The description focussed on three major topics:

- *participation by sectors.* On opening day, 1,491 sellers showed up in the 121 MAs of the country to face hundreds of consumers, some of whom had been waiting since the previous night. During the first days there was a strong presence of the state sector with a relatively low showing of the independent farmers, but the opposite was true by day 15;

- *volumes, variety, display, and quality of products.* In terms of volumes, seasonality dictated the strong presence of *viandas* (68.5 percent of the total), while vegetables represented only 5.5 percent (Table 2). However, although pork accounted for only 2.9 percent of the volume, it represented 30.3 percent of total sales value. In addition to seasonality, the scarcity of beans and vegetables is explained by the early absence of independent farmers since they produce about 72 percent of the beans and 45 percent of vegetables. In general, the level of management was poor and was reflected in the disorganized and uncleaned manner in which the products were displayed. The presence of health inspectors, however, guarantees the sale of livestock products in good conditions;[15]

- *demand, price movements, conditioning and organization.* The presence of consumers, especially in the city of Havana, was very high in the first days and continued at high levels thereafter. For example, the total national value of sales was of 14.5 million pesos in the first two days, and of 61.9 millions during the first 15 days. During the first days of operation, prices in the MAs were high in relation with the purchasing power

---

15. Our observations indicate that this problem is the result of the lack of marketing savvy on the part of sellers.

Table 2. **Sales During the First 15 Days of Cuba's Agricultural Markets (October 1 to October 15, 1994), by Commodity and Volume**

Commodity	Volume (cwt)	Percent
Viandas[a]	112765	68.5
Plantains	42000	25.5
Cassava	32000	19.4
Sweet Potato	27000	16.4
Pumpkin	9200	5.6
Other	2565	1.6
Vegetables	9105	5.5
Peppers	2200	1.3
Garlic	2030	1.2
Other	4875	3.0
Citrus and fruits	24572	14.9
Citrus	12368	7.5
Avocado	5270	3.2
Papaya	2600	1.6
Other	4334	2.6
Rice	4618	2.8
Beans	1154	0.7
Pork	4782	2.9
Ovine Beef	1080	0.6
Other	6836	4.1
Total	164912	100.0

Source: Adapted from Torres and Pérez (1994, p. 37) as it appears in Lee (1994).

a. In addition to those listed, the term *viandas* also includes taro and potato.

of average Cubans.[16] Sellers price their products according to market conditions at the beginning of the day. Prices are adjusted throughout the day depending on a variety of factors. However, a negative influence is the fact that taxes are imposed based on the price of the products at the beginning of the day. The average tax is of 8 percent of the gross value, but it is 5 percent in the city of Havana and 15 percent in other areas of the country. The MA occupy the facilities where previous markets and the MLCs were located. Availability of facilities and equipment is low and varies from place to place. Warehouses are scarce. Times of operation are not fixed.

Differences Between the MA and the MLC

There are three major differences between the free farmers' markets (MLCs) of the 1980s and the new agricultural markets (MAs):

- First, in addition to independent farmers and their representatives, participation in the MAs includes CPAs, non-cane UBPCs, state enterprises and organizations (such as farms under the Working Youth Army, EJT), and all other individuals and collectives who work on self-sufficiency plots. The first three, however, must show proof of having met their delivery quotas to the state.

- Second, MAs are subject to a taxing system that has been designed to generate revenues for the state during the current economic crisis. It ranges from 5 percent of the value of projected gross sales in the city of Havana (to channel the greatest volume to the capital, where food shortages are potentially the most politically volatile) to 15 percent in the small, rural markets of the interior (Deere, 1995, p. 16).

- And third, as opposed to the MLCs where this phenomenon was insignificant, sales of processed foods are an important part of the new MAs (Torres and Pérez, 1994, p. 36).

Early Performance

Although the previous section also contains some description of the early performance of the agricultural markets, there are additional important issues for discussion. Torres and Pérez (1994, pp. 39-41) report a series of statements from both buyers and sellers about the benefits and early performance of the MA. In general, they deal with the advantages of the access to the markets by the working population, the availability of fresh products as opposed to the ones purchased in the state stores, and the expectations about future declines in prices.

The first specific positive impact of the MA has been the lowering of prices that had prevailed in the black

16. For example, while the average monthly salary of a Cuban worker amounts to 180 pesos, the price of one pound of pork was 45 pesos and a pound of turkey cost 30. Likewise, one orange or one banana cost one peso.

Table 3. Selected Average Prices of All Participants in the Agricultural Markets in the City of Havana and in the Country, by Month, October 1994 Through March 1995 (Cuban pesos/pound)

Item	BO CH	1994						1995			
		October		November		December		January-February		March	
		WC	CH	WC	CH	WC	CH	WC	CH	WH	CH
Rice	45	10.3	10.7	9.4	9.7	8.6	9.1	7.5	8.5	7.66	8.52
Beans	30	16.4	25.4	17.0	24.1	14.9	19.5	11.6	12.6	11.37	12.19
Pork	75	37.4	41.2	38.9	41.9	38.5	42.1	35.7	38.8	35.88	38.87
Sweet Potatoes	6	1.3	1.8	1.2	1.5	1.1	1.4	1.4	1.9	1.52	2.01
Cassava	6	1.5	3.0	1.5	2.7	1.5	2.6	1.6	2.6	1.59	2.50
Taro	15	7.3	8.3	7.0	7.8	6.5	7.2	5.4	7.0	5.64	7.11
Garlic	30	20.0	23.6	20.8	20.6	19.9	19.9	23.4	22.7	21.26	19.52

Notes: BO—Before the opening of the agricultural markets; CH—City of Havana; WC—Whole country.

Source: Compiled by Nova González (1995a, p. 66) from "Ventas en el Mercado Agropecuario," Oficina Nacional de Estadísticas, 1994 and 1995.

Table 4. Selected Prices in Three Agricultural Markets in Havana, 1994-1996 (in Cuban pesos/pound)

Item	Black Market June 1994	Agricultural Markets		
		January 1995	June 1995	January 1996
Rice	50	7	9.5	4
Black beans	30	13	9	9
Pork steak	75	45	35	28
Jam	150	70	60	45
Cassava	15	2.5	2.5	1
Sweet potatoes	15	2.5	3	1.5
Pumpkin	40	5	3	2

Source: Summarized from Deere (1996).

market (Scarpaci, 1995, p. 14). For example, the presence of the state enterprises was responsible for bringing the price of pork down from its June 1994 black-market level of 75 pesos to 45 pesos per pound. Also, rice prices in the black market were around 50 pesos per pound in June 1994 but decreased to between seven and 10 pesos per pound in January 1995 in the MAs. Similarly, the price of cassava went down from 15 pesos a pound to between two to three pesos during the same time period (Deere, 1995, p. 16). More detailed (sometimes contradictory) information appears on Tables 3 and 4. However, prices still remain high relative to the purchasing power of the average consumer.[17] On the other hand, quantities sold have remained relatively stable (Table 5), while independent farmers seem to control the highest percentages of most of the commodities sold in the markets (Table 6).

Perhaps the most important contribution of the agricultural markets to the economy in general has been the depreciation of the U.S. dollar in relation to the Cuban peso. Deere (1995) states that the dollar reached a peak of 120 pesos in the black market in July 1994. By the following June, the dollar was valued at between 30 to 35 pesos (p. 17). During the authors' last visit in the spring of 1996, the exchange rate of the dollar had declined to between 21 and 23 Cuban pesos.

IMPLICATIONS FOR FUTURE AGRICULTURAL PRODUCTIVITY

Who would have thought that we, so doctrinaire, who fought foreign investment, would one day view foreign investment as an urgent need?

— Fidel Castro, 26 July 1993

This quote is a powerful confirmation of the magnitude of the transformation which is currently under way within Cuba.[18] The two most important changes in the agricultural sector have been partially de-

17. This gap has prompted requests for governmental intervention. (See, for example, Economics Press Service, 1996.)

18. We have excluded any discussion of foreign investment in the agricultural sector (Pagés, 1995), despite its importance (Nova González, 1994, p. 4), because it is largely occurring in only a few isolated commodity sub-sectors almost exclusively for export, and therefore it has relatively little influence on domestic food supply.

Table 5. **Sales in the Agricultural Markets, by Month, October 1994 through March 1995 (1000 cwt)**

Product	1994				1995				% Change IQ 1995/ IVQ 1996
	October	November	December	IV Quarter	January	February	March	I Quarter	
Agricultural	294.2	262.7	399.0	955.9	321.7	311.4	316.6	949.7	-6.2
Meat	13.5	14.2	17.9	45.6	12.9	13.7	15.7	42.3	-3.3
Total	307.7	276.9	416.9	1001.5	334.6	325.1	332.3	992.0	-9.5

Source: Complied by Nova González (1995d, p. 71) from "Ventas en el Mercado Agropecuario," Oficina Nacional de Estadísticas, January-April 1995.

Table 6. **Percentage Participation of Independent Farmers in the Agricultural Markets, by Selected Commodities, October 1994 through March 1995 (percent)**

	1994			1995	
	October	November	December	January - February	March
Taro	82.6	89.7	92.3	92.4	92.0
Cassava	41.3	49.5	56.7	69.7	71.3
Tomato	54.3	72.0	73.7	74.1	74.5
Onion	87.4	93.3	93.3	90.6	88.0
Garlic	86.5	86.1	87.8	94.8	91.5
Pepper	43.6	56.9	65.4	74.3	66.1
Rice	69.9	77.0	79.8	85.1	85.0
Bean	57.7	69.9	77.0	90.3	91.4
Pork	71.6	80.5	78.6	82.4	85.2
Corn ear	63.7	62.6	64.6	47.4	60.3
Banana	12.7	18.3	21.3	30.2	31.0

Source: Compiled by Nova González (1995d, p. 66) from "Ventas en el Mercado Agropecuario," Oficina Nacional de Estadísticas, October-December 1994 and January-March 1995.

scribed in this paper. The establishment and organization of the UBPCs and MAs have important implications for future agricultural productivity. Since the two organizations are complementary, the issues are discussed together.

UBPCs and MAs

Let us start with a series of statements and direct quotes appearing in the Cuban publication Economics Press Service (1995, pp. 6, 7):

- The production takeoff of agricultural food did not materialize as expected six months after the opening of the agricultural markets in the island [Official sources].

- The production increase due to the stimulus of participating in this market has not been achieved yet. Although the overstocking of the stands may point to the contrary, all seems to indicate that what is being sold "already existed" but, simply, was not delivered to the state collection agency. A good portion of these products were being sold in the black market and at prices

even higher than those being exhibited now in the agricultural markets where the law of supply and demand governs [*Granma*].

- From October through March [of 1995], these markets only sold 19 percent of the total tons of agricultural products distributed to the population, although their variety is wider than the one collected and sold by the state in the places of rationed sales [Official sources].

- As a farmer, one has to fulfill a quota of sales to the state but the payment is sometimes laughable. You sell and, when you go to the nearest's town market, you find your orange three or four times more expensive [An independent producer].

- The fact that prices in agricultural markets do not go down is another more than sufficient proof that agricultural production has not experienced the expected takeoff. "When it happens, deliveries to the state collection agency as well as supplies will increase, and prices will tend to decrease," specialists stated [*Granma*].

• The Cuban countryside has been stagnant during a long period of time and one can not revive it overnight. One has to plant and wait for the results [An anonymous economist].

In fact, while the economy as a whole experienced a modest growth of 0.7 percent in 1994 with respect to 1993 (Oficina, 1995, p. 3), activity in the agricultural sector decreased by 4.9 percent (p. 4). Modest growth was present in rice, corn, fruits, milk, eggs, and poultry and pork, while *viandas* and vegetables decreased by 16.6 percent (p. 5).

The previous quotes and statements serve as good background for the discussion. The main issue revolves around the reasons for the stagnant agricultural production. It is true that dramatic production increases, within the current economic crisis, can not be realized in a short period of time. But it is also true that there are mechanisms that hinder such increases. For example, as the independent producer expressed above, *acopio* prices are very low when compared with prices at the MA. In addition, as discussed earlier, there is little incentive to produce beyond the established production goal since 80 percent of any surplus will also have to be sold to the state agency at very low prices.

An important point is that most agricultural markets have a relative abundance of multiple agricultural commodities. When one observes this fact, the question arises about the remaining 80 percent that was supposed to be delivered to *acopio* since most of these products are not available in the ration stores.

After examining the differences in gross and net revenues (Table 7) and average costs of production (Table 8) between the state and non-state sectors, one wonders about the reasons for the existence of some state farms. There is speculation that some state farms are being held by the government as potential joint venture operations. Or, it simply may be that, since the majority of state farms have already been converted to UBPCs, the incentive to complete the process has decreased. Nevertheless, the fact that the majority of state farms have been broken up into UBPCs is a clear indication of the commitment on the part of the Cuban government to this fundamental policy change.

Table 7. Average National Gross and Net Revenues in the State and Non-State Agricultural Sectors, by Crop, 1993 through December 1995 (in thousand pesos/*caballería*)

Item	State		EJT[a]		UBPC[b]		CPA[c]	
	GR	NR	GR	NR	GR	NR	GR	NR
Sweet potato	90.1	29.3	95.1	33.7	83.5	24.2	105.0	41.5
Taro	491.7	365.4	515.3	387.1	361.6	254.6	326.9	268.6
Cassava	94.7	12.2	172.4	74.1	91.0	8.7	126.4	72.2
Banana	704.2	384.5	836.2	599.6	863.7	527.5	1234.6	793.3
Plantain	498.4	248.7	489.9	242.9	439.2	190.5	294.8	152.9
Tomato	411.8	277.2	523.0	376.1	328.0	203.1	499.9	378.1
Onion	1548.0	1274.6	1282.4	1033.5	804.6	612.6	1175.1	1001.0
Garlic	474.8	328.4	907.3	717.7	697.3	508.8	1108.9	930.4
Pepper	206.4	85.2	761.4	576.5	444.9	295.7	400.1	306.3
Pumpkin	39.8	12.9	38.5	11.7	32.5	6.5	49.8	26.9
Rice	554.8	468.8	562.5	475.5	620.8	527.4	484.0	407.3
Bean	77.1	52.9	75.9	51.8	49.2	28.8	158.1	131.1
Corn ear	36.3	12.1	60.3	32.9	27.7	4.6	22.9	6.1

Note: GR—Gross Revenue; NR—Net Revenue; 1 *caballería* equals 33.3 acres.

Source: Compiled by Nova González (1995d, p. 68) from several official Cuban sources.

a. *Ejército Juvenil del Trabajo* (Working Youth Army).

b. *Unidades Básicas de Producción Cooperativa* (Basic Units of Cooperative Production).

c. *Cooperativas de Producción Agropecuaria* (Agricultural Production Cooperatives).

Table 8. Average Costs of Production in the State and Non-State Agricultural Sectors, by Commodity (pesos/cwt)[a]

Item	State	CPA	Independent (Private)
Sweet potato	28.43	4.36	2.99
Taro	86.68	13.89	10.05
Cassava	72.04	5.64	2.64
Banana	11.55	2.43	2.43
Plantain	10.46	13.50	7.50
Tomato	27.87	5.05	3.29
Onion	67.64	16.43	9.39
Garlic	272.93	70.97	40.28
Pepper	82.94	11.69	7.78
Pumpkin	33.03	3.94	2.82
Rice	8.13	8.04	5.62
Bean	203.21	43.38	43.38
Corn ear	39.73	5.04	5.04

Source: Compiled by Nova González (1995d, p. 69) from Cuban official sources.

a. Date or time period not specified.

State Collection Agency (*Acopio*)

The role of the state collection agency (*Acopio*) is extremely important in any discussion of the implications of the two new agricultural entities. *Acopio* has been the official link between producers and consumers since the early years of the revolution. Through the years, it has become a highly centralized entity intended to collect and distribute all farm production. Production, however, could never be recorded in its totality since it excluded on-farm consumption, barter, and sales in the black market. During the time period when the MLCs were in existence (1980-1986), surplus production was legally sold directly to consumers. When these markets were closed, the state assumed total control of procurement and distribution.

With that goal in mind, *Acopio* was completely reorganized at that time both in terms of collection and distribution by: (a) placing the system under the Ministry of Agriculture rather than the municipal Councils of People's Power where it had been until then; (b) establishing the Enterprise of Selected Fruits (*Empresa de Frutas Selectas*), also under the Ministry of Agriculture, to purchase the surplus fruits and vegetables from private farmers and Agricultural Production Cooperatives and sell them directly to the population and to the tourist sector; (c) increasing the prices paid to producers, especially those paid by the newly created Enterprise of Selected Fruits, to avoid drastic decreases in farmers' incomes after the closing of the free farmers' markets (Torres and Pérez, 1994, p. 30); and (d) investing in additional refrigerated trucks and warehouse facilities (Deere and Meurs, 1992).

Restructuring of *Acopio* at the national and local levels continued during the early 1990s with the establishment of a new procurement process and an increase in the number of *Acopio* procurement personnel (*visitadores de Acopio*).[19] Multiple collection points were created in the countryside for peasants to deliver their products on a given day of the week. According to an official interviewed, the probability of the Acopio official, the cashier who pays for the crop, and an *Acopio* truck all converging at the same point at the same time, is most unlikely. Despite success in production plans and deliveries in different areas and products, further debate concerning the new structure includes, among others: (a) the possibility of ANAP officials and extension agents performing the role of area chiefs as well as increasing number of state officials; and (b) as discussed earlier, the continuing state intervention on farmers' cooperatives.

Facing the economic realities of the Special Period within a process of economic reforms in the agricultural sector, one has to wonder about the feasibility of maintaining a system originally designed to operate within a highly centralized and subsidized agricultural sector. The debate has already started in Cuba. Carriazo (1994) states that the UBPCs are tied to a system of *acopio*, inefficient by itself and now suffering greater limitations such as in transportation

---

19. What follows in this paragraph is a summary of field research conducted by Deere et al. (1994, pp. 224-228) in three municipalities located in the three natural geographical regions of Cuba: Güines, in the western province of La Habana; Santo Domingo, in the central province of Villa Clara; and Majibacoa, in the eastern province of Las Tunas.

and containers (p. 23). And he adds that *"Acopio's* pricing system reveals its rigidity by not reflecting with the required celerity the changes in supply, demand, quality, cost and other factors" (p. 24). He ends by questioning whether the UBPCs should be required to render all of their production to a system of *acopio* traditionally inefficient and lacking transportation resources (p. 24). González Jordán (1995, p. 91) criticizes *Acopio's* current pricing system for not "stimulating" either production or sales to the state. The reason is low prices that do not correspond with the economy's general price level. Orlando Lugo, president of the National Association of Small Farmers (ANAP) has stated that the mechanisms developed through *Acopio* are now obsolete, and the norms used by *Acopio* to purchase from the farmers do not respond to the present realities (García Luis, 1994, p. 5).

Some of the early difficulties due to the lack of transportation have been mitigated. Soon after the creation of the agricultural markets, Resolution 178/94 of the Ministry of Transportation authorized state enterprises and private parties involved in public service activities, who posses the corresponding operative license, to engage in the transportation of products to the markets.

This, however, is a timid step. More radical reforms are needed. For example, Torres and Pérez (1994), in addition to several recommendations to improve the markets, one could also think in the explosion in the number of commercialization chains, marketing cooperatives and others that would serve as the intermediaries between producers and consumers, taking charge of the purchase, transport, cleaning, promotion and sales. Such chains would not only operate in the agricultural markets, but in supermarket chains and other small businesses (p. 42).

The above recommendation does not seem to enjoy official support at present. At the end of May 1996, the weekly *Trabajadores* (official organ of the Confederation of Cuban Workers, CTC) sent a strong message to the "new rich", alluding specifically to the middlemen in agricultural markets (Noticias, 1996, p. 1B). A few days before, however, Vice-President Raúl Castro, in an unusual open letter to the Minis-

ter of Agriculture published in the official daily *Granma*, strongly criticized the state *Acopio* system. He stated that one-fourth of agricultural commodities intended for distribution under the state system for Havana residents in April were rotten and had to be discarded (Raúl, 1996, p. 9A). Such problems, however, have been constantly present. Pérez Marín and Muñoz Baños (1991, p. 4), for example, estimated losses of 225 kg/ha (13 kg/capita) in tubers, roots, vegetables and grains left unharvested in the fields.

CONCLUSION: "IT DEPENDS ON THE MARKET"

The statement "it depends on the market" was the reply received by the authors on numerous occasions from UBPC Direction Board members in response to questions related to how they decide what commodities to send to the market, which market (city or local) to send their crops to or when to send them. This demonstrates that, despite having lived for over 30 years under a planned economic system, there is an understanding of the operation of markets.

The degree of control and autonomy which UBPC members have in the operation of their coop is certainly limited as compared to what farmers in market economies have. However, even this limited ability to influence production and marketing decisions is a substantial improvement over their days as workers on large state farms. As a result, UBPC members are beginning to feel a new sense of stewardship toward the land and other productive assets. At the same time, they recognize the UBPC as a mechanism to potentially improve their personal well being. These are important incentives, but, they will not continue to motivate without further reinforcement.

The decision to dismantle the state farms into UBPCs and to establish the agricultural markets would appear to have created a window of opportunity for the Cuban government to improve domestic agricultural production and food availabilities. As discussed earlier in this paper, obstacles still exist which hinder the efficient operation of these new institutions in Cuba. Even if these obstacles are removed, chronic shortages of fertilizers, pesticides and fuel oil will restrict the ability of the agricultural sector to respond in dramatic fashion. However, if the obstacles are not removed, the failure to increase agricultural output and food accessibility could potentially lead to another food crisis and further civil unrest.

REFERENCES

"Acuerdo del Buró Político: Para Llevar a Cabo Importantes Innovaciones en la Agricultura Estatal," *Granma* (September 15, 1993), p. 1.

Alfonso, Pablo. "Cobra Auge Entrega de Tierras a Trabajadores Agrícolas," *El Nuevo Herald* (February 21, 1995a), p. 1B.

Alfonso, Pablo. "Producción Agrícola Continúa su Descenso," *El Nuevo Herald* (January 10, 1995b), p. 3A.

Alfonso, Pablo. "Sin Avance las Cooperativas Cañeras," *El Nuevo Herald* (March 10, 1995c), p. 1B.

Alfonso, Pablo. "Son Improductivas las Cooperativas Agrícolas," *El Nuevo Herald* (January 13, 1995d), p. 3A.

Alonso, José. "The Free Farmers' Markets: A Rejected Approach but a Possible Solution," *Cuba in Transition—Volume 2*. Washington: Association for the Study of the Cuban Economy, 1992, pp. 166-184.

Alvarez González, Elena and María Antonia Fernández Mayo. "Dependencia Externa de la Economía Cubana," Documento INIE. Ciudad de la Habana: Instituto de Investigaciones Económicas, 1992.

Alvarez, José and Ricardo A. Puerta. "State Intervention in Cuban Agriculture: Impact on Organization and Performance," *World Development* 22:11 (1994), pp. 1663-1675.

Alvarez, Lizette. "Using Capitalism to Save Socialism," *The Miami Herald* (March 28, 1995), pp. 1A, 4A.

Báez, Luis. "Entrevista a Raúl Castro: Si Hay Comida Para el Pueblo no Importan los Riesgos," *Trabajadores* (September 19, 1994).

Benjamin, Medea, Joseph Collins and Michael Scott. *No Free Lunch: Food and Revolution in Cuba Today*. New York: Grove Press, Inc., 1986.

Bromley, Daniel W. "Revitalizing the Russian Food System Markets in Theory and Practice," *Choices* (Fall Quarter 1993), pp. 4-8.

Capó Pérez, José R. and Colectivo de Autores. "Estudio Sobre las Expectativas de la Fuerza de Trabajo en las Nuevas Formas Organizativas de la Producción Agropecuaria en la ECV Melena del Sur," in Polo Científico de Humanidades (Ed.), *Colectivos Laborales de Nuevo Tipo: Resumen de Investigaciones Sobre las UBPC*. La Habana: Programa Flacso, Universidad de la Habana, January 1995, pp. 39-41.

Carriazo, George. "Cambios Estructurales en la Agricultura Cubana: La Cooperativización," *Economía Cubana - Boletín Informativo*, No. 18, Centro de Investigaciones de la Economía Mundial (November 1994), pp. 14-29.

Castillo Díaz, Miguel. "Trabajo de Organización Contable: UBPC 'Marcos Martí,' Municipio Quivicán," in Polo Científico de Humanidades (Ed.), *Colectivos Laborales de Nuevo Tipo: Resumen de Investigaciones Sobre las UBPC*. La Habana: Programa Flacso, Universidad de la Habana, January 1995, pp. 37-38.

Comité Estatal de Estadísticas. "Unidades Básicas de Producción Cooperativa -UBPC- Características de las UBPC y Algunos de los Cambios Provocados en el Sector Agropecuario con su Introducción," Dirección Agropecuaria y Silvicultura, La Habana, August 1994.

Coordinación. "Introducción," in Polo Científico de Humanidades (Ed.), *Colectivos Laborales de Nuevo Tipo: Resumen de Investigaciones Sobre las UBPC*. La Habana: Programa Flacso, Universidad de la Habana, January 1995, pp. 1-9.

"Cuba: Hechos y Cifras," *Economía Cubana - Boletín Informativo*, No. 25, Centro de Investigaciones de la Economía Mundial (January-February-March 1996), pp. 20-31.

Deere, Carmen Diana. "Cuba's National Food Program and Its Prospects for Food Security," *Agriculture and Human Values* 10:3 (Summer 1993), pp. 35-51.

Deere, Carmen Diana. "Implicaciones Agrícolas del Comercio Cubano," *Economía Cubana - Boletín Informativo*, No. 18, Centro de Investigaciones de la Economía Mundial (November 1994), pp. 3-14.

Deere, Carmen Diana. "Reforming Cuban Agriculture: The Challenges of the 1990s," unpublished manuscript (March 1996).

Deere, Carmen Diana. "The New Agrarian Reforms," *NACLA Report on the Americas* 29:2 (September/October 1995), pp. 13-17.

Deere, Carmen Diana and Mieke Meurs. "Markets, Markets Everywhere? Understanding the Cuban Anomaly," *World Development* 20:6 (1992), pp. 825-839.

Deere, Carmen Diana, Ernel Gonzales, Niurka Pérez and Gustavo Rodríguez. "Household Incomes in Cuban Agriculture: A Comparison of State, Cooperative, and Peasant Sectors," *Development and Change* 26:2 (April 1995), pp. 209-234.

Deere, Carmen Diana, Niurka Pérez and Ernel Gonzales. "The View From Below: Cuban Agriculture in the 'Special Period in Peacetime,'" *Journal of Peasant Studies* 21:2 (January 1994), pp. 194-234.

Díaz, Beatriz et al. "Cooperativización Agrícola: Retos y Alternativas. Estudio de Caso en la UBPC de Cultivos Varios 'Marcos Martí', Quivicán," in Polo Científico de Humanidades (Ed.), *Colectivos Laborales de Nuevo Tipo - Resumen de Investigaciones Sobre las UBPC*. La Habana: Programa Flacso, Universidad de la Habana, January 1995, pp. 31-36.

Economics Press Service. "Agricultura: Mercado Agropecuario no Disparó la Producción de Alimentos," *Información Quincenal Sobre Cuba*, Año 8, No. 7 (April 15, 1995), pp. 6-7.

Economics Press Service. "Mercado Agropecuario: Precios Estremecen los Bolsillos Cubanos," *Información Quincenal Sobre Cuba*, Año 9, No. 4 (February 29, 1996), pp. 13-14.

Espinosa, Juan Carlos. "Markets Redux: The Politics of Farmers' Markets in Cuba," in *Cuba in Transition—Volume 5*. Washington: Association for the Study of the Cuban Economy, 1995.

Figueroa, Víctor and Luis A. García. "Apuntes Sobre la Comercialización Agrícola no Estatal," *Economía y Desarrollo* 83 (1984), pp. 34-61.

Gaceta Oficial de la República de Cuba (September 21, 1993), p. 15.

García Luis, Julio. "Lo Principal es Cómo Elevar la Producción y el Acopio, que es lo que Salva al País," *Trabajadores* (July 11, 1994), p. 5.

González Jordán, Benjamín. "La Agricultura Cubana: Un Balance Crítico," *Economía y Desarrollo* 118:2 (December 1995), pp. 81-97.

González Surribas, Aracely and Eliézer Jhones Menéndez. "Sistema Computacional A3CAI: Actividad Agropecuaria de Autoconsumo en los CAI Azucareros," in Polo Científico de Humanidades (Ed.), *Colectivos Laborales de Nuevo Tipo - Resumen de Investigaciones Sobre las UBPC*. La Habana: Programa Flacso, Universidad de la Habana, January 1995, pp. 26-30.

Junta Directiva. "Informe Anual de la CPA," Cooperativa de Producción Agropecuaria "Amistad Cuba Laos," Bauta, Provincia de La Habana, July 1994, Mimeographed.

Jústiz García, Elizabeth and Hilda Díaz Pérez. "Resumen de los Principales Resultados de la Investigación Socio-económica Dirigida a las Unidades Básicas de Producción Cooperativa Cañeras del País Durante 1994," in Polo Científico de Humanidades (Ed.), *Colectivos Laborales de Nuevo Tipo - Resumen de Investigaciones Sobre las UBPC*. La Habana: Programa Flacso, Universidad de la Habana, January 1995, pp. 10-16.

Lee, Susana. "Amplio Examen de las Experiencias del Mercado Agropecuario. Reunión de Presidentes de las Asambleas Provinciales," *Granma* (October 20, 1994), p. 4.

Limia David, Miguel and Graciela Salazar. "Las UBPCs Cañeras como Forma Embrionaria de Nuevo Tipo de Colectivo Laboral en Cuba," in Polo Científico de Humanidades (Ed.), *Colectivos Laborales de Nuevo Tipo - Resumen de Investigaciones Sobre las UBPC*. La Habana: Programa Flacso, Universidad de la Habana, January 1995, pp. 17-19.

Lorenzo Delgado, Raudel, Juan Molina Soto, Blanca Morejón Seijas and Gloria Valle Rodríguez. "Estudios Sociodemolaborales: Un Enfoque para la Investigación," in Polo Científico de Humanidades (Ed.), *Colectivos Laborales de Nuevo Tipo - Resumen de Investigaciones Sobre las UBPC*. La Habana: Programa Flacso, Universidad de la Habana, January 1995, pp. 44-45.

Martínez Figueredo, Antonio, Gregorio Núñez Lage and Argelio Castro Villa. "La Finca Lechera 'Siberia' Hacia la Producción Sostenible," in Polo Científico de Humanidades (Ed.), *Colectivos Laborales de Nuevo Tipo - Resumen de Investigaciones Sobre las UBPC*. La Habana: Programa Flacso, Universidad de la Habana, January 1995, pp. 47-50.

Mesa-Lago, Carmelo. "The Cuban Economy in the 1980s: The Return of Ideology," in Sergio D. Roca (Ed.), *Socialist Cuba - Past Interpretation and Future Challenges*. Boulder: Westview Press, 1988.

Miranda Forés, Rubén et al. "Caracterización de la Producción y Comercialización en el Mercado Interno de los Productos Agrícolas," in Polo Científico de Humanidades (Ed.), *Colectivos Laborales de Nuevo Tipo - Resumen de Investigaciones Sobre las UBPC*. La Habana: Programa Flacso, Universidad de la Habana, January 1995, p. 51.

Molina Soto, Juan. "Estudios Sociodemolaborales: En la Rama Pecuaria (Resultado de Caso)," in Polo Científico de Humanidades (Ed.), *Colectivos Laborales de Nuevo Tipo - Resumen de Investigaciones Sobre las UBPC*. La Habana: Programa Flacso, Universidad de la Habana, January 1995, p. 46.

Molina Soto, Juan and Ermela García Santiago. *Informe Sobre el Perfeccionamiento de UBPC Seleccionadas*. La Habana: Centro de Estudios Demográficos de la Universidad de la Habana and Escuela Nacional de Cuadros Sindicales Lázaro Peña, July 1995.

"Noticias de Cuba," *El Nuevo Herald* (May 28, 1996), p. 18.

Nova González, Armando. "El Mercado Agropecuario Cubano," *Economía y Desarrollo* 118:2 (December 1995a), pp. 65-79.

Nova González, Armando. "La Reactivación Económica del Sector Agropecuario Cubano," *Economía y Desarrollo* 117:1 (September 1995b), pp. 85-90.

Nova González, Armando. "La Reorganización de la Agricultura en Cuba - Factor Clave de la Estabilización Económica," Instituto Nacional de Investigaciones Económicas (INIE), La Habana, May 1994, mimeographed.

Nova González, Armando, et al. "Mercado Agropecuario: ¿Apertura o Limitación?," *Cuba: Investigación Económica* No. 4, Instituto Nacional de Investigaciones Económicas (December 1995c), pp. 21-54.

Nova González, Armando. "Mercado Agropecuario: Factores que Limitan la Oferta," *Cuba: Investigación Económica* No. 3, Instituto Nacional de Investigaciones Económicas (October 1995d), pp. 63-72.

Nova González, Armando. "Mercado Agropecuario: 'Futuro Escenario'," *Información Quincenal Sobre Cuba*, Año 9, No. 4, Economics Press Service (February 29, 1996), pp. 21-22.

Oficina Nacional de Estadísticas. "La Economía Cubana en 1994," La Habana, June 1995.

Pagés, Raisa. "Inversiones en la Agricultura No Cañera: No Presentamos un Negocio Color de Rosa," *Granma Internacional* (May 10, 1995), p. 11.

Pagés, Raisa. "Mercado Agropecuario: Decreto y Resolución," *Granma* (September 21, 1994), pp. 1, 3.

Pampin Balado, Blanca R. et al. "La Organización y Estimulación del Trabajo en la Producción Cañera. UBPC 'Jose Vázquez Martínez' y CPA 'Amistad Cubano Nicarangüense,'" in Polo Científico de Humanidades (Ed.), *Colectivos Laborales de Nuevo Tipo - Resumen de Investigaciones Sobre las UBPC*. La Habana: Programa Flacso, Universidad de la Habana, January 1995, pp. 20-25.

Peña Castellanos, Lázaro and José Alvarez. "The Transformation of the State Extensive Growth Model in Cuba's Sugarcane Agriculture," *Agriculture and Human Values* 13:1 (Winter 1996), pp. 59-68.

Pérez-López, Jorge F. *Cuba's Second Economy: From Behind the Scenes to Center Stage*. New Brunswick: Transaction Publishers, 1995.

Pérez Marín, E. and E. Muñoz Baños. *Agricultura y Alimentación en Cuba*. La Habana: Editorial de Ciencias Sociales, 1991.

Polo Científico de Humanidades. "Grupo: Estudios Socio-económicos de Producción Cooperativa y Campesina." La Habana: Instituto Superior de Ciencias Agropecuarias de La Habana (ISCAH), n.d.

Polo Científico de Humanidades. *Colectivos Laborales de Nuevo Tipo - Resumen de Investigaciones Sobre las UBPC*. La Habana: Programa Flacso, Universidad de la Habana, January 1995.

"Raúl Castro Critica a Ministro por Derroche en Dura Carta Abierta," *El Nuevo Herald* (May 27, 1996), p. 9A.

Roca, Sergio G., "Reflections on Economic Policy: Cuba's Food Program," in Jorge F. Pérez-López (Ed.), *Cuba at a Crossroads: Politics and Economics After the Fourth Party Congress*. Gainesville: University Press of Florida, 1994, pp. 94-117.

Rodríguez Castellón, Santiago. "Algunas Consideraciones Sobre el Mercado Agropecuario," in Polo Científico de Humanidades (Ed.), *Colectivos Laborales de Nuevo Tipo - Resumen de Investigaciones Sobre las UBPC*. La Habana: Programa Flacso, Universidad de la Habana, January 1995, pp. 52-54.

Romero Valcárcel, Lázaro, Prisco Barroso Fernández and Ramón Díaz Menéndez. "Vías para el Perfeccionamiento de la Actividad Socioeconómica de la UBPC '9 de Abril,'" in Polo Científico de Humanidades (Ed.), *Colectivos Laborales de Nuevo Tipo - Resumen de Investigaciones Sobre las UBPC*. La Habana: Programa Flacso, Universidad de la Habana, January 1995, pp. 42-43.

Rosenberg, Jonathan. "Cuba's Free-Market Experiment: Los Mercados Libres Campesinos, 1980-1986," *Latin American Research Review* 27:3 (1992), pp. 51-89.

Scarpaci, Joseph L. "On the New Economic Geography of Havana's Food and Paladar Markets,"

Cuba in Transition—Volume 5. Washington: Association for the Study of the Cuban Economy, 1995.

Torres, Cary and Niurka Pérez. "Mercado Agropecuario Cubano: Proceso de Constitución," *Economía Cubana - Boletín Informativo*, No. 18, Centro de Investigaciones de la Economía Mundial (November 1994), pp. 29-42.

Varela Pérez, Juan. "Nuevos Conceptos en la Agricultura: Mayor Autonomía en la Producción Cañera," *Granma* (September 19, 1993), p. 3.

BACK TO THE FUTURE: THE SOCIOPOLITICAL DYNAMICS OF MIRAMAR'S REAL-ESTATE MARKET

Joseph L. Scarpaci

A key factor in understanding the transition of the real-estate markets in cities of Eastern Europe and the former Soviet Union hinges on the transition from state to private ownership. Buildings, commercial centers, homes, and even vacant lots suddenly become prime targets for real-estate speculation and foreign investment. During the Cold War, small amounts of private property or, at least private employment, existed in Eastern Europe and the former Soviet Union (Szelenyi 1983). There was also a pool of entrepreneurs who have become increasingly important as a bridge between the impending global market on the outside, and newly emerging democracies and markets from within.

In Cuba, however, the loosening of state controls over a centrally-planned economy unfolds cautiously, and with joint-venture operations. Unlike its former socialist trading partners, Cuba held practically an insignificant amount of private entrepreneurs until recently (Pérez-López 1995). The demise of the socialist trading bloc (Council for Mutual Economic Assistance, CMEA) has brought a growing number of foreign investors to Cuba, all of whom require locations for the new operations. The district of Miramar in Havana affords amenities and some infrastructure that accommodates these new headquarters. By locating in Miramar, new questions and concerns arise about the use of public and semi-private spaces in contemporary Cuba.

This paper examines the changing use of these spaces. It begins with a brief review of the residential changes that Miramar has experienced in the past 50

years or so. I then summarize a land-use study I conducted in June 1996 on the location of foreign and joint-venture firms that have offices or retail outlets in roughly a 60-block area of oceanfront property in Miramar. This inventory of foreign investment includes the following streets: it is bounded east-west by 2nd and 60th streets, respectively; they run north-south and are perpendicular to the Florida Straits. It is outlined north-south by the ocean and extends to Fifth Avenue *Quinta Avenida* (running east-west, parallel to the Florida Straits) (Figure 1). The approach in this land-use survey is largely empirical, providing a 'snapshot' only of those firms vying for the choicest locations and, supposedly, paying greater rent to the Cuban government. Accordingly, these land uses are surrogate measures of potentially profitable investment areas, or at least those areas deemed appropriate for investment by the Castro government.

Figure 1: Study Area

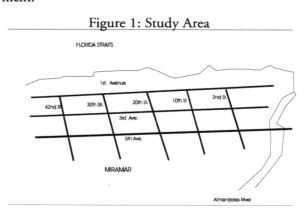

MIRAMAR: PERIODS OF GLORY, PERIODS OF PERIL

A defining feature of Havana's urban geography is the wandering trek of its center-city and economic and political functions. In the parlance of urban geographers, these functional nodes or downtowns reflect the economic, political, residential, and symbolic elements of a given city. Since its founding in 1519 until the mid-19th century, Havana was a walled city. Three main town squares anchored the oval-shaped core of Old Havana: Plaza de la Catedral, Plaza de Armas, and Plaza Vieja. By the early 19th century, the old walls had clearly failed to contain urban growth. Neighborhoods to the south (Cerro, Jesús María) and west (Centro Habana, Vedado) opened up to house new businesses and upper-income homes. By the turn of this century, Centro Habana functioned as the commercial locus of the city's economy.

During U.S. occupation from 1898-1902, the Army Corps of Engineers modernized Havana's infrastructure. The Americans improved roads, telegraph and telephone lines, port facilities, and sewers. A major contribution to the city's transportation network included the extension and widening of the Malecón—Havana's seaside promenade—westward, from its beginning at the Prado. The construction of the Hotel Nacional at what is now La Rampa district of Vedado, anchored what was then the end of the Malecón, about 3 kilometers from Habana Vieja. During the latter 19th and early 20th century, Vedado grew as a center of middle- and upper-income residences.

Miramar remained fairly isolated from Havana's push westward. Separated from Vedado by the Almendares River, the area was accessible only south of the waterfront, over higher land. In the mid-1920s, engineers bridged the Almendares. This facilitated the opening up of Miramar as an attractive, bedroom community. Designed in the spirit of the City Beautiful movement in the United States (characterized by landscaped boulevards and town squares), automobile access capitalized on this level, oceanfront suburb of Havana. By the late 1940s and early 1950s, the Malecón had been extended some 8 kilometers,

reaching the Almendares River. At that time, a French-Cuban venture completed a tunnel under Havana Bay as well as under the Almendares River. In 1957, a tunnel joined Línea Street in Vedado and *Quinta Avenida* in Miramar. Commuting time for Havana's merchants who worked in one of the downtown areas (Vedado, Centro Habana, or Habana Vieja) had been greatly enhanced by the tunnel. One could now travel in about 20 minutes from the center of Miramar, along the Malecón, to Parque Central at the end of the Prado.

The Revolution of 1959 ended that pattern of suburban commuting but it did not immediately change the 'look' of Miramar. By the late 1950s, Miramar had come to hold a huge stock of solid homes, most of which were modest in design and scope, although many were palatial. Some of the Caribbean's finest Art Nouveau, Art Deco, and Modern designs can be found in Miramar. A large out-migration of Cubans in the early years of the Revolution left many vacancies. In the early 1960s, the revolutionary government used these empty houses as student boarding houses, as well as lodging for foreign technicians and advisors and *dirigentes* from the revolutionary leadership. Throughout the 1970s and 1980s, the number of protocol houses (*casas de protocolo*), government ministries, foreign embassies, and houses for Cuban Communist Party officials increased in Miramar.

With the onset of the Special Period in the early 1990s, foreign investors were aggressively courted. Their charge was to help arrest the downward spiral in which Cuba found itself after trade and aid from the former Soviet Union ended (Carranza, Gutiérrez and Monreal 1995). Miramar, as it had done in the past, positioned itself to accommodate this new demand for prime real estate.

LAND USES IN THE CREME DE LA CREME: JOCKEYING FOR OCEANFRONT POSITION IN MIRAMAR

I conducted a land-use survey of commercial establishments as noted by the presence of a sign on the property. I conducted the survey over a two week period in June 1996. The reconnaissance covered approximately 60 city-blocks. When I had a question about the nature of the commercial enterprise, I inquired directly at the office or with neighbors or workers.

I recorded about 120 non-residential establishments, of which 92 had a clear commercial focus. Slightly more than half (57 percent) of the seemingly commercial establishments were Cuban entities (Figure 2). Most of these Cuban firms work in the area of tourism or in other services (advertising, telecommunications, office furniture, interior design, laundry and dry-cleaning). A second concentration of Cuban-owned firms was hard-currency charging retailers: film developing, jewelers, restaurants, and beauty salons. The majority of those Cuban firms worked in the service sector: import-export, tourism, and restaurants.

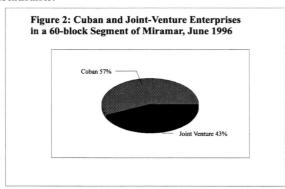

Figure 2: Cuban and Joint-Venture Enterprises in a 60-block Segment of Miramar, June 1996

Figure 3 displays the commercial land-use breakdown of the 60-block area of Miramar under study. The data refer to both Cuban and foreign (joint-venture) commercial establishments. Leading land uses in descending order are import-export firms, tourism and other services, retail, restaurants, and banks.

Forty-three percent of the commercial firms were foreign (joint-ventures). I determined by the signs posted that there were investors from Spain, Mexico, Canada, Bermuda, Italy, Panama, Japan, and China. Almost all of the joint-venture firms concentrated on imports-exports. There was also a strong presence of foreign embassies (n=15), but I did not include them in this survey of commercial enterprises. If included, however, they would shift the land uses of commercial buildings in Miramar to about half Cuban and half joint-venture businesses.

Along with the great majority (>90 percent) of buildings in Miramar that remain residential, there are a

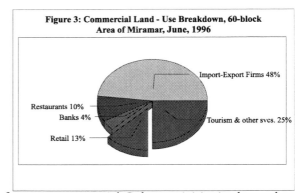

Figure 3: Commercial Land - Use Breakdown, 60-block Area of Miramar, June, 1996

few non-commercial Cuban activities in the study area. One clinic, two schools, several churches, government offices, two museums, and an indeterminate amount of mom-and-pop restaurants (*paladares*) operate in the area (Scarpaci 1995).

LEGAL CONTEXT OF FOREIGN PROPERTY OWNERSHIP

Land-use planning and regulation in 20th century Havana has been shaped largely by master plans (Table 1). Most of these plans represented broadly sketched and normative features of the city; they presented idealistic views of how residential, commercial, industrial, and other spaces should be allocated throughout Havana. However, they lacked a comprehensive approach to deal with urban problems. Instead, "the role of zoning concepts in these 'plans' was very strong" (Núñez 1996, 6).

Table 1. 20th Century Master Plans in Havana

Year	Plan
1870	Francisco Albear Plan
1922	Enrique Montoulieu Plan
1925	Pedro Martínez Inclán Plan
1926	J. Nicolás Forestier Plan
1951	Eduardo Cañas Abril Plan
1958	Wiener, Sert, Schultz, Romañach Plan
1964	First Schema for Master Plan by Mario González and Luis Espinoza
1971	Baquero, Ascue, Garatti Plan
1984 & 1990	Technical and Economic Basis for the Master Plan

Source: Núñez, 1996; Segre, Coyula and Scarpaci, forthcoming.

After 1959, the Revolutionary leadership nationalized about 90 percent of land in Cuba, while in Havana, about 70 percent came under state control. Along with the elimination of what was perceived to be widespread corruption and speculation, so too disappeared any semblance of a real-estate market (Hamberg 1994). Conceptual concerns of equity and social justice outweighed matters of efficiency. The government set rent at 5-10 percent of gross incomes. Commercial space was leased at ridiculously low prices. The strategy also sought to improve the home-work ratio (i.e., clustering homes close to the workplace).

With the onset of the Special Period and the need to accommodate foreign investment, Havana's land market began changing. In the early 1990s, only a few activities financed by foreign capital were permitted (tourism, textiles, trading operations). In September 1995, the Cuban Parliament passed the Foreign Investment Law which broadened the scope of investment. In essence, land will still remain property of the state, but terms of lease will reflect the necessary periods of time for the foreign investor to recoup an investment and earn a profit. Put another way, real-estate laws in Havana address tenancy, not property rights.

The impact of this law in Havana—especially in Miramar and other 'choice' locations—is both profound and confusing. On the one hand, the government began reneging on its post-1959 commitment to satisfy housing demands. Instead, it began searching for hard currency. How can the government, for instance, justify investing heavily in repairing buildings designated for joint-venture operations when, right across the street, there is an overcrowded home in dire need of repair? Although public discourse on this is constrained, officials justify these actions because of the (i) the economic quagmire of the dissolution of CAME; (ii) the 35 year old U.S. blockade against Cuba; or, more recently, (iii) the looming impact of the Helms-Burton Act on Cuba's economic future. My conversations with dozens of Miramar residents showed that there is public concern about

this new preference for business enterprises at the expense of residential construction needs.

On the other hand, confusion surrounds real-estate investment. There is little institutional capacity to handle this new investment. Government agencies have little experience with this economic activity. Because foreign investment must be approved at the highest levels of government, it is paramount that local, mid-level and national government agencies work closely together (Núñez 1995). Staff do not have clear signals about how to handle requests for property renovation or securing material inputs (paint, plaster, electrical wiring, glass) for remodelling. In brief, there is little 'transparency' about the norms and regulations surrounding real-estate developments (Núñez 1996, 14). When clarity or approval for a real-estate deal is reached, it usually violates the prevailing master plan.

Despite the widespread attention given to Cuba's shift to market criteria, real-estate development in Havana is slow, cumbersome and expensive. Ricardo Núñez (Núñez, 1996, 17), an economist who works with a semi-autonomous Cuban urban design and planning institute in Havana, describes the situation this way:

> The over-centralization in the decision-making process, the strong sectoral approach in the economic behavior, the narrow concepts to measure the development agencies' performance, the lack of integrity in the implementation process and the over-estimation of the scale[,] are the causes of high cost urban development [in Havana].

The Grupo para el Desarrollo Integral de la Capital held a symposium to address this changing real-estate market in May 1996. The conference was held in Miramar and was titled, *Havana on the Eve of the New Millennium: Challenges and Opportunities.*[1] It included some 30 Cuban and foreign experts and po-

---

1. The full name in Spanish was *La Habana ante el Nuevo Milenio: Retos y Oportunidades. Taller de Ideas sobre Desarrollo Inmobiliario y el Suelo Cubano.* The sponsors (Grupo para el Desarrollo Integral de la Capital) house a large three-dimensional scale model (1:1,000) of Havana. They serve as an advisory board to metropolitan, provincial, county (*municipio*) and local planning agencies. Their operative document, *Estrategia*, sets out a series of goals and objectives for controlling the city's growth and addressing its problems. Unfortunately, they are not always consulted. For instance, the 21-floor Spanish hotel, Meliá Cohiba, was erected one block off the Malecón in Vedado—adjacent to turn-of-the-century structures and the modernist landmark, Hotel Riviera, without any consultation. This underscores the problems of coordination identified by Núñez.

tential investors. The sponsor's goal was to "ensure that any land investments are made in an orderly fashion and that they will develop areas in need of an injection of foreign capital but will not change the flavor of the lovely city" (RHC 1996). The challenges, to which we turn in the next section, are not small.

MIRAMAR'S NEW LOOK

The amenities of Miramar continue despite changes in land use over the past 37 years. It is still one the thickest, tree-covered sections of the city. Third Avenue, running parallel to the ocean and set back just one block, is a principal bicycle thoroughfare. It eases the flow of some of the city's 1 million bicycles (about one for every two habaneros) (Scarpaci and Hall, 1995). Prestigious Quinta Avenida still retains its neatly landscaped pedestrian mall in the middle, and is flanked on both sides by two-lane, unidirectional roads. Because of the risks of car bombs and attempts against Fidel Castro's life, automobiles cannot be parked on Fifth Avenue, nor can buses or private trucks pass through it. Quinta Avenida is now sprouting more commercial establishment headquarters for joint-venture operations, as well as its longstanding endowment of embassies and diplomatic residences.

Several phases characterize street life in the 1990s. At the beginning of the Special Period (1990-1993), few cars passed through the streets because of strict gas rationing. Blackouts prevailed and travel on the roads at night was often unsafe. The liberalization and decriminalization of the dollar in 1993 brought a greater number of small entrepreneurs to the neighborhood. Home restaurants (*paladares*), bicycle repair shops and parking lots, refreshment and snack stands, and other activities began changing the look of driveways, porches, back garages, and property fronts. Since 1994, a flurry of remodeling has taken hold. Financed mainly by Cuban and joint-venture firms, these activities refurbish the large homes that once held students who came from the provinces to study in the capital, or many migrants from the eastern provinces. Construction efforts remodel these homes to furnish businesses with office space, sales rooms, dining areas, and apartments for foreigners.

Unlike any time in the history of the Revolution, Miramar displays a collection of 'haves' and 'have nots' that are distinguished by their access to dollars, an unprecedented situation in Socialist Cuba.

DISCUSSION: BACK TO THE FUTURE? RESIDENTIAL SEGREGATION IN HAVANA

The out-migration of a large bourgeoisie left a huge housing stock in Miramar and adjacent districts for the revolutionary government to use. Government leaders took pride in promoting the new social integration taking place in this corner of the city. Soldiers, literacy campaign volunteers, students, and government officials were often rewarded with homes or apartments in this coveted section of Havana. If any section of the city represented a radical transformation, it was Miramar. Class, race, and occupational skills mattered little when it came to assigning housing.

Since the foreign investment 'boom' of the 1990s, Miramar is again becoming a highly segregated social space. Not only is there a growing number of foreigners there, but the area is heavily patrolled by Tourist Police and regular police. When power blackouts strike, the roars of gasoline engines that serve as power backups identify which buildings are foreign owned. The contrast between the illuminated and freshly painted foreign structures next to the darkened homes of Miramar residents—patiently waiting on their porches or front steps for power to return—is a strong reminder of the new segregation taking hold. The contrast of Miramar with the broader structural changes sweeping Cuba is perhaps best illustrated by the motto of a foreign tourist company posted on *Quinta Avenida*: "The Ultra, Inclusive, Exclusive Resort." To be sure, Miramar is paradoxically both inclusive and exclusive.

SUMMARY AND CONCLUSIONS

In just a few years, the rental market development and property renovations of Havana have taken place at unprecedented levels. This new investment is not directed towards the traditional socialist thrust of providing new housing. Instead, it is designed to attract and retain overseas investors. While the State still maintains ownership of these new rental properties, foreign investment is leaving its stamp on the cityscape.

The residential amenities of Miramar hold great appeal for these new economic actors. In the process of providing the necessary office space and homes, however, a new rift has appeared in the social fabric of the city. Miramar is quickly becoming a highly segregated place with distinct zones of exclusivity. While the district has been home to many embassies during the course of the Revolution (and therefore has always been a special place for foreigners), the presence of multinational and Cuban companies is creating a new look.

This paper reported on the commercial land uses of more than 100 buildings in a 60-block area next to the ocean. Although 57 percent of these commercial complexes are Cuban, the breakdown is about half foreign and half Cuba once foreign embassies and their residences are included. About half of the foreign establishments (47 percent) serve as headquarters for import-export firms. As Cuba tries to reassert insert itself into a global economy, this land-use survey should serve as a benchmark for subsequent changes in Helms-Burton legislation, the ongoing U.S. trade embargo, and the real success Cuba will have in attracting foreign investment. Future research should address the growth and expansion of this new commercial real estate. It will also be helpful to know how residents of Miramar feel about the subtle and overt changes in their buildings and streets.

BIBLIOGRAPHY

Carranza, J., Gutiérrez, L., and Monreal, P. 1995. *Cuba: La Restructuración de la Economía. Una Propuesta para el Debate.* La Habana: Editorial de Ciencias Sociales.

Hamberg, J. 1994. *The Dynamics of Cuban Housing Policy.* Unpublished Ph.D. dissertation, Columbia University, New York.

Núñez, R. 1995. *The Influences of Government Relations and Institutional Environment on Urban Issues in Cuba.* La Habana: Grupo para el Desarrollo Integral de la Capital.

_____. 1996. *Land Planning and Development in Havana City: Two Study Cases. The New Investment Context Regarding Land.* La Habana: Grupo para el Desarrollo Integral de la Capital.

Pérez-López, J. 1995. *Cuba's Second Economy.* New Brunswick, NJ: Transaction Books.

RHC. 1996. Workshop on real estate and urbanism underway in Havana. From Radio Havana (via the Internet) (June), 2 pp.

Scarpaci, J. 1995. "Havana's Emerging Food and Agricultural Markets." In *Cuba In Transition—Volume 5.* Washington, DC: Association for the Study of the Cuban Economy.

Scarpaci, J., and Hall, A. 1995. "Cycling through Havana." *Transport Development.* No. 5 (Fall), pp. 2-4. (New York: Institute for Transportation and Development Policy).

Segre, R., Coyula, M., and Scarpaci, J. forthcoming. *Havana: Two Faces of the Antillean Metropolis.* New York and London: John Wiley & Sons.

Szelenyi, I. 1983. *Urban Inequalities under State Socialism.* London: Oxford.

THROUGH THE CRACKS OF SOCIALISM:
THE EMERGING PRIVATE SECTOR IN CUBA

Ana Julia Jatar-Hausmann

The free market reforms that Cuba undertook in the wake of the collapse of the Soviet Union have propelled the country into uncharted waters as it improvises to find solutions to its economic crisis. The harsh realities of a world without the massive Soviet aid on which Cuba had become so dependent forced the government to tolerate considerable reductions in the state's control of the economy.

However, the market reforms of the 1990s are not the first free market experiments that Cuba has conducted to try to alleviate the problems that its highly centralized socialist economic model generates. The island has flirted with capitalist concessions since the revolution and has seemed to alternately embrace and reject limited economic openings throughout the socialist period. The desire to spur employment and provide for Cuban consumers has run into conflict with Fidel Castro's devotion to socialist ideals and his need to prevent an entrepreneurial class from challenging his political hegemony. A perennial, politically charged balancing act between the drive for efficiency and adherence to socialist principles has been the result.

This paper describes the reforms, it attempts to understand their logic, and evaluates their impact. The main conclusion is, that in contrast with the liberalizations of 1985, the current reforms are here to stay.

PRIOR REFORMS: PLAYING WITH CAPITALISM FOR A WHILE

An examination of earlier Cuban reforms reveals that they foreshadow the 1990s reforms. Free peasant markets, the legalization of certain kinds of private enterprise, and the liberalization of real estate sales are examples of recent Cuban reforms that had been instituted in years past, then backed away from, for various ideological and practical reasons. These antecedents can be seen as part of a cycle in which reforms are tolerated until, perhaps inevitably, they produce results that are anathema to socialist ideals. When income inequality, corruption, and profiteering reared their heads in Cuba in the mid-1980s, the Rectification Process was initiated and capitalist openings, such as the peasant markets, were closed down. Cuba has certainly witnessed greater changes in recent years than those which brought about the Rectification Process, and those changes have challenged some of the basic tenets of Cuban socialism. Furthermore, Castro is firmly in control and remains a committed socialist. Will the pendulum swing back toward a more thoroughgoing socialism? How do the current reforms compare with earlier ones?

Prior Reforms in the Agricultural Sector

Since the 1959 revolution in Cuba, the agricultural sector has been at the forefront of most economic activity not entirely dictated by the socialist model. Indeed, private farms have existed throughout the history of modern Cuba. The 1959 Agrarian Reform Law created private farms; many of the farmers who received land were sharecroppers and tenant farmers before the revolution. These farms number about 102,000 and range in size from 20 to 60 hectares. Until 1980, the private farmers sold their products to the government, which controlled the distribution, wholesale and retail of the goods. In 1986, approximately seven percent of arable land in Cuba was in private hands, 13 percent was owned by cooperatives and 80 percent was owned by the government. The private farms have had consistently higher productivity rates than the government-run farms, despite the fact that they generally have less access to fertilizers and machinery.

By 1980, Cuba's centralized system had produced bottlenecks and inefficiencies that hurt the agricultural sector's ability to meet production goals. Some of the shortcomings of the planning system, the Sistema de Dirección y Planificación de la Economía (SDPE), were obvious to Cuban officials. Modeled after Soviet planning systems and intended to improve efficiency through the introduction of an economic accounting system and certain profitability incentives, the SDPE was hampered in this effort by centrally fixed, static prices, which did not allow optimal resource allocation or production choices. Input shortages had become rampant and were aggravated by enterprises' hoarding in response to uncertain supply.

Cuban agriculture had suffered under the rigidities of the SDPE, and authorities turned to further decentralization to redress the problems. To alleviate food shortages, the government legalized free farmers markets, or *mercados libres campesinos* (MLCs), through Decree 66 approved by the Council of Ministers in the spring of 1980. By the mid-1980s, 250 such MLCs had been established. Private farmers were permitted to sell their products at the MLCs at free prices, provided they first met quotas for sales to the government. The MLCs undercut the black market and alleviated some shortages. Cubans flocked to the markets and enjoyed the greater variety that they offered, though complaints of high prices were common. Meats such as chicken, rabbit and lamb (beef was still controlled by a state monopoly) and vegetables and fruit became more readily available to Cuban consumers almost overnight.

The government had hoped to improve the productivity of state-run farms and thereby be able to sell at lower prices than the private farmers if their prices climbed too high. The private Cuban farmers, how-

ever, proved to be adept at working this small capitalist opening to their advantage; they closely monitored what the state stores were offering and then brought to the free markets goods they knew were not available from the government. The ensuing sellers' market drove prices up and led to allegations of widespread corruption. In 1982 government investigators cracked down on the markets, arresting 165 people for "irregularities," including involvement of middlemen in the markets and the sale of products stolen from the government. The Cuban Domestic Commerce Minister at the time, Manuel Vila Sosa, claimed that 60 percent of the goods sold at the MLCs had been stolen from the government. After the crackdown, government controls were imposed on the peasant markets, including a 20 percent sales tax and a progressive income tax ranging from five to 20 percent. Despite the stricter controls, the markets continued to thrive.

Prior Self-Employment Reforms

Free market reforms affected other sectors of the economy as well in this period. In 1978, limited self-employment was first allowed by the state. Certain professionals such as carpenters, plumbers, electricians and artisans were allowed to work privately, provided they had fulfilled their time commitment to the state first. Those who were able to buy a state license could essentially go into business for themselves. They charged whatever rate they could get, and payment was often made in kind with goods such as chickens or vegetables. They were not allowed to hire any staff, but they could form business alliances with colleagues.

The 1978 legalization of self-employment was considered an attempt to control what had been occurring for quite some time. Artisans and handymen had seemingly always worked outside of the state apparatus, risking detention by the authorities as they attempted to improve their standard of living. Even after the 1978 reforms such work was a potentially dangerous proposition. The state strictly controlled the number of licenses issued for private work, and crackdowns such as the trial of a score of artisans in a public square in Santiago de Cuba in June of 1985 for selling jewelry without a license, were common.

The government instituted other changes that brought a degree of flexibility to the economic system. In 1979, "resource fairs" were embraced as a way to deal with the growing stocks of unused inputs within enterprises. The state allowed enterprises to trade directly with each other as a way to overcome inefficiencies and errors committed by the State Committee on Technical-Material Supplies, the central organization for resource allocation. In 1980, 40 million pesos of inputs were traded at the fairs.

Incentives on Wages

Some initiatives date back to the earliest days of Cuba's socialist history. Even in the 1960s under Minister of Industry Ernesto "Che" Guevara, a committed Marxist, workers were paid 0.5 percent of their wage for every 1 percent of overproduction achieved. Castro himself held forth on the need to achieve a balance between material and moral incentives in the workplace when he declared: "Material incentives must be used together with moral incentives, without abusing one or the other, because the latter would lead us to idealism while the former would develop individual selfishness."

The record of wage incentives in Cuba reflects the general pattern that capitalist reforms have followed in the country: they were adopted, then disavowed when it was determined that they were undermining socialist ideals, then adopted again when economic realities demanded it. In 1967, authorities believed that a communist consciousness had been gained which obviated the need for wage incentives, and incentives were abandoned. The resulting fall in productivity and standards of living produced another reversal; in 1973, wage incentives were reinstated.

The position of wage incentives in the functioning of the Cuban economy was codified with the General Wage Reform of 1980. The Reform raised the average wage by 4.5 percent and firmly established the connection between wages earned and the quantity and quality of work done by individuals. Prices of certain products which had been frozen since 1962, despite rising input costs, were raised. The results of

the Reform were drastic; labor productivity leaped 10 percent in 1981. In a speech in July, 1981, Castro claimed that the Reform had increased industrial production by 14 percent, that food production had risen 10 percent, construction was up 19 percent, and investment had increased 16 percent.[1]

Prior Investment Reform

Another significant development in Cuba that anticipated the market reforms of the 1990s was the passage of decree-law 50 in 1982. This law permits foreigners to own up to 49 percent of local businesses, to control labor, pricing and production policies, and to repatriate profits. The law was structured to compel international investors to bear more risk than would be the case if finance capital were invested. Negotiations for some investment projects with Canadian and West European companies were initiated after decree-law 50 came into effect, but pressure from the Reagan administration on potential investors limited the benefits of the law. Decree-law 50 was the base upon which the current foreign investment environment was created; in 1992 it was expanded and became a cornerstone of Cuban economic policy.

Other noteworthy liberalizations were effected during this period as well. In 1984, Cubans who rented apartments from the government—the majority were city-dwellers—were allowed to own them; rent payments were converted into mortgage payments. Furthermore, individuals could sell housing to private citizens for the first time, and the construction of private homes was legalized. Construction materials became easier to obtain, and a housing and construction boom ensued.

The Reversal of Reforms and the Return to Socialist Ideology

By 1986, these reforms had generated considerable tensions in Cuban politics and society. The MLCs and the liberalized construction materials market, for example, diverted valuable resources from state to private uses. The specter of the much-hated "middleman" had arisen in the MLCs, persons who would

---

1. *The Washington Post* (October 5, 1981).

exploit the free farmers' lack of transport by buying produce cheaply in the countryside, then bring the goods to the cities to sell at a hefty profit. Income differentials were becoming more obvious to Cuban citizens, as truck drivers typically made many times more than what physicians were earning. Housing law reforms unleashed a speculative boom in real estate, and prices shot up. Government officials were concerned about the negative effects the reforms might have on the people's socialist fervor as well as the undue influence that might be gained by the beneficiaries of reform. At the same time, however, the government fully realized the positive economic impact of liberalization. Indeed, the need for further decentralization had been described in various government documents and speeches in the months preceding the 1986 Third Congress of the Cuban Communist Party, particularly at the 1985 Fourth Plenary session.

The Third Party Congress was the scene of vigorous discussions over the direction that the economy should take. The role of material incentives in a socialist system was once again the subject of fierce debate in Cuba. Economic realities precipitated a turn toward a more orthodox brand of socialism. In 1986, a 2 percent growth rate, low sugar prices, and several years of drought combined to deplete Cuba's hard currency earnings by almost 50 percent, or $600 million. Cuba's failure to secure a new $300 million loan at the Paris Club meetings that summer exacerbated the crisis and produced a serious shortage of imported inputs, which in turn greatly reduced outputs in the economy. Material incentives were weakened by a lack of goods to spend money on. The lack of foreign exchange stalled the impetus for further changes as the government tried to marshal all the resources it could, to complete several long term investment projects. The result was a period of renewed socialism and a rejection of many of the capitalistic openings of the late 1970s and early 1980s known as the Rectification Process.

There was clearly a political and ideological element in the government's turnabout as well. Corruption had infected all levels of the bureaucracy to some extent. A political purge which saw some of the veterans of the revolution ousted was initiated simultaneous with Rectification. Volunteerism was revived with the resurrection of the "micro-brigades" of unemployed and temporarily laid off workers, originally a Guevara innovation. Castro, who visited North Korea in 1986 and was impressed by that country's hard line Communism, adopted a more virulent anti-capitalist tone, reminiscent of the early days of the revolutionary period.

Decrying what he called the "thousands of wheeler-dealers who cheat, sell and steal," Castro summarily closed the MCLs on May 15, 1986. At a meeting of 4,000 representatives of Cuba's farm cooperatives two days before the announcement of the shutdown, Castro anticipated this most significant step in the rectification: "Our fight against these neo-capitalists that have arisen will not be limited to the elimination of the free farmers' markets: we are going to fight against these tendencies and manifestations on all fronts and in all places," he stated at the time. "In the search for economic efficiency, we have created a culture for a heap of evils and deformation and what is worse, corruption....it is a moral question, one of principle and dignity not to enter into that commercialism and that speculation," he told the coop farmers. The six year experiment in free enterprise had grown to be a serious irritant for the regime, which was willing to sacrifice the $83 million worth of produce that the MLCs sold to the public annually. Furthermore, the sudden removal of private forms of transportation worsened food scarcity and led to food wastage of up to 35 percent of certain crops.[2]

Other free market openings were abandoned as well. The 1984 housing law was amended to give more control to the state and halt the speculation and corruption that had arisen. The regime decreed that all housing sales must be approved by a state agency that would regulate prices. The government began again

2. Reuters (June 6, 1986).

to exercise its legal right to buy all housing for sale on the market.

Also in 1986, Castro labeled the thousands of self-employed Cubans "corrupt parasites" on the public sector and curbed their activities with tighter regulations. In an effort to gain greater control over resources, the government imposed a system in which taxi drivers, artisans, and street vendors and private service workers such as plumbers and electricians had to obtain all materials via a state-issued certificate. The number of private wage workers and workers for their own account fell from 52,100 in 1985 to 43,200 in 1987. In monetary terms, private non-farm incomes fell from 102.5 million pesos to 67.8 million pesos in the same period. During the Rectification Period, wage incentives for the population as a whole were also scaled back.

The Return to Market Oriented Reforms

We have seen many of the free market reforms of the 1978-1985 period adopted once again in the 1990s. MLCs have been reinstated, private enterprises and occupations have been legalized to an unprecedented extent, foreign investment is being actively courted. Accompanying these changes are the conditions that prompted the abandonment of free market reforms in 1986. Inequalities are even more drastic today because Cubans are allowed to hold dollars and a dual economy has resulted. Those Cubans with jobs in the tourism sector or with well-off relatives in the United States typically live far better than physicians, scientists and others who have been most loyal to the regime, a situation that spawns deep resentments. A new generation of Cubans that missed the heady early days of the revolution and is witnessing increasing inequality, has begun to press for change, as have other sectors of an emerging civil society. According to the formula that has established itself, the time is ripe for a backlash against these market oriented tendencies.

Our main thesis in this paper is that some key differences between the Cuba of 1986 and that of 1996 preclude any such reversal today. In the 1980s, economic openings were attempts to ameliorate the systemic scarcity, inefficient investments, and widespread waste that typically plague centrally planned economies. Cuban officials experimented with the reforms, but even the MLCs never had a major impact on the workings of the economy. Cuba was experiencing the end of a period of relative prosperity in 1986 and was still securely dependent on heavily subsidized trade with the Soviet Union.

In the 1990s, however, the collapse of Soviet Union has altered the playing field dramatically. Free market reform, once a tentative experiment, is now Cuba's lifeline. Cuba is attempting to fill the gaping hole left by the removal of Soviet patronage with foreign investment and tourism, and reforms are necessary to develop these sectors and assure an influx of foreign exchange. Further, material incentives are more effective as previously unavailable goods can now be purchased at dollar stores. Without a generous and forgiving sponsor, Cuba has no choice but to become more efficient and insert itself into the international system in order to survive. This requires economic reforms, from which there is no turning back.

THE 1989 CRISIS AND THE INITIAL ADJUSTMENT

Driven more by external reality than any internal conviction, Cuban policy makers have been introducing market reforms since 1989 in order to adjust to major changes in external trade relations. One of the most controversial results of these changes has been the emergence of the small Cuban entrepreneur, the capitalist expression of a socialist defeat. Already fighting for survival after three years of continuous growth and expansion, this small private sector is currently targeted by the tax authorities and followed with suspicion by the communist party leaders. Nevertheless, in spite of some conflicting signals received from the government—reflecting the contradictions of the current system—we will argue that the Cuban entrepreneur, this time around, is here to stay.

Since the economic transformation began seven years ago, the Cuban government has been opening different sectors of the economy, previously under its control, for private investment. The development of a strong private sector—foreign and local—is vital to achieving sustained growth in Cuba. Nevertheless, for a society that praises equality and takes pride in its socialist achievements, this is a formidable challenge indeed. As Carlos Lage, a principal architect of the reforms, stated in 1993,

> We are not an economy in transition, nor are our people or our party in transition towards capitalism. We will make the changes that are necessary but we will never make a single concession.

Since the downfall of communism in the former Soviet Union in 1989 and until 1993, the Cuban economy went through a major contraction. The cut off of the Soviet aid and the collapse of the commercial arrangements within the socialist bloc—which had accounted for 80 percent Cuba's trade—had a devastating impact in the economy of the island. The Soviet Bloc provided Cuba with 95 percent of its needs on fuels and lubricants, 80 percent of the machinery and equipment and 63 percent of the foodstuffs. Cuba on the other hand, placed in those markets—usually through barter agreements—63 percent of its sugar, 73 percent of the nickel produced and 95 percent of the citrus fruits.[3]

As a consequence, exports plunged from $5.4 billion in 1989 to $1.7 billion in 1993 due mainly to the collapse in sugar production, which fell from 8 million tons in 1989 to 4 million tons in 1993 and 3.3 million tons in 1995.[4] GDP fell over 40 percent during the same period. Imports were brought down from $8.1 billion in 1989 to $2.2 billion and the trade deficit was kept low, in line with the meager external financing.

Though they decided to make the necessary changes to face the crisis, Cuban policy makers expressed that they will maintain the socialist orientation of the system.

In summary, the reforms would permit the transition from a classical model of socialism to another kind of socialism ... which would require to give to the market an active role, neither exclusive nor dominant in the allocation of resources and in the economy as a whole.[5]

> We will have to improve and perfect socialism, make it efficient but not to destroy it. The illusion that capitalism is going to solve our problems is an absurd and crazy chimera for which the masses will pay dearly. This is another reason why, not only because socialism is more just, more honorable, and more human in every sense, but because is the only system that would provide us with the resources to keep our social conquests.[6]

Cuba is a socialist regime. This is an important premise to understand the particular speed and sequencing of the reforms that the government undertakes and which are usually introduced with great caution. Policy makers are particularly careful not to alter the already fragile social equilibrium between those working in the emerging private sector and the those trapped in the lethargic peso economy. Viewed from outside changes seem structurally *insufficient*, but for Cubans, on the contrary, the transformations are perceived as *dramatic*. They proudly announce their reluctance to "follow other models." They see reforms in the former Soviet Union as a tragic disappointment while Latin-American reforms are dismissed with the following view:

> The neo-liberal model adopted in Latin America characterized by price liberalization, the reduction of

---

3. Banco Nacional de Cuba, *Economic Report 1994*, p. 2.

4. This shock was partly the result of the elimination of price subsidies on sugar and nickel by the former Soviet Union. Total Soviet subsidies to Cuba averaged US$2100 million per year during the 1960-1990 period. Also the collapse of sugar production was caused by the lack of access to imported inputs and the break-up of large, capital-intensive state farms into smaller labor-intensive cooperatives.

5. Julio Carranza, Luis Gutiérrez, and Pedro Monreal, *Cuba: La Restructuración de la Economía* (La Habana: Editorial de Ciencias Sociales, 1995), p. 10.

6. Fidel Castro, speech at the National Assembly (December 28, 1993).

Table 1.   Fiscal and Monetary Data (in millions of pesos)

	1989	1990	1991	1992	1993	1994	1995
Fiscal Income	12486	14601	9175	11362	9556	11913	11482
Fiscal Expenditure	13886	16706	12332	16162	14567	13528	12682
Fiscal Deficit	-1400	-2105	-3157	-4800	-5051	-1617	-1200
Fiscal Deficit as a % of GDP	7.2	10.5	26.8	34.8	40.0	12.0	9.3

Sources: CEPAL, *Cuba: Evolución Económica durante 1994*; U.S. Trade and Economic Council; Ariel Terrero, "Tendencias de un ajuste," *Bohemia* (October 26, 1994); Banco Nacional de Cuba, *Economic Report 1994*; Cuban state budget for 1996.

real wages and welfare programs was never consulted with the people and increased dramatically the already terrifying levels of inequality in those countries.[7]

Insufficient or dramatic, the government usually ends up enacting too-little-too-late changes, generating further imbalances which in turn lead to more reforms. In the face of the massive contraction of export revenues, the Cuban government relied on a set of measures designed to mitigate the social impact of the adjustment. These measures have generated important economic disequilibria, which at the same time are promoting further reforms.

The adjustment through foreign exchange rationing instead of devaluation is generating important inefficiencies. In market economies, an adjustment to an external shock of this magnitude would have required a massive devaluation to reduce the demand for imports and increase the profitability of export and import-competing sectors, so as to efficiently return to external balance. Such real devaluations would require a lower real wage, an unpopular decision opposed by the National Assembly and the government. This was made clear by the Finance Minister in a public speech:

> Taking into account the positive experiences from other countries like China and Vietnam, we avoided a sudden currency devaluation. This would have added terrible (social) consequences to the already difficult economic crisis faced by the country.[8]

Thus, as a centrally planned economy, Cuba reacted to the sudden shortage of foreign exchange not by devaluing, but by *rationing* foreign exchange and *administratively distributing* dollars to different sectors.

In spite of the objectives of the Cuban government, the use of this arbitrary process as a substitute for devaluation has generated serious inefficiencies and Cuba is paying their cost. On the one hand, since products are neither more expensive nor more profitable—as would have happened with devaluation—shortages develop as output contracts and demand grows at the set low prices. In other words, the system does not generate the price incentives to produce or save dollars. Imports are extremely cheap at the distorted official exchange rate of 1 peso per 1 US dollar.

Also, the serious efforts oriented to attract foreign private capital in the tourist sector increased the circulation of dollars in the economy and the proliferation of the black market for goods. Further, the original intention of opening tourism alone to foreign investment was soon defeated by reality. When important export sectors like nickel, tobacco, citrus and biotechnology were lagging behind due to technological obsolescence and lack of hard currency to buy inputs, the government opened up these sectors to foreign investment as well. Only sugar, the traditional source for foreign exchange in Cuba, remained closed to direct foreign investment. Nevertheless, since it continued to perform poorly—in the 1994-1995 harvest, sugar production plunged to 3.3 million tons, the worst performance in the country's modern history—Cubans had to leave behind mis-

---

7. Osvaldo Martínez, Representative from Sagua de Tánamo to the National Assembly, National Assembly Debates, *Granma* (December 29, 1993).

8. José Luis Rodríguez, Minister of Finance, at the World Economic Forum in Davos, Switzerland (February 1996).

conceived notions of nationalism and accept private investment in sugar.[9]

Given the government reluctance to devalue, Cubans were left with more purchasing power—measured at the official prices—than the actual supply of goods which they had available. This led to greater rationing and higher black market prices for goods. Also insufficient adjustment led to a fiscal deficit that reached 40 percent of GDP in 1993.

The government could not stop spending, while exports, the economy, and fiscal revenues were collapsing. Given the absence of external financing and of internal capital markets, the government had very little choice but to cover the deficit by printing money. As a consequence, the economy was flooded with liquidity. The number of pesos in circulation increased from 5 billion in 1990 to 11.4 billion in 1994.

In a market economy, excess liquidity creates inflation. In a centrally planned economy the effects are different. Since official prices do not change and people have more money to spend than products to buy, huge shortages and black markets develop. By the end of 1993 the official exchange rate was 1 peso per U.S. dollar, while it reached 150 pesos per dollar in the black market.

In 1993, the government finally realized that the solution to the crisis was not to be found in cosmetic changes made at the periphery of the system. In contrast, it would require profound revisions of the socialist order and also of its incentive structure. Since then, a sequence of reforms has characterized the period from 1993 to date. Among others, the legalization of hard currency, the creation of agricultural cooperatives, the introduction of monetary incentives to increase labor productivity, the opening of free markets for farmers and artisans, the legalization of the creation of foreign firms with 100 percent foreign capital, the authorization of free zones; and the liber-

alization of 157 economic activities to be performed by self-employed workers, are some of the expression of the revision that the government of Cuba has made at all levels.

THE TURNAROUND AND THE 1993-1996 REFORMS

The Cuban economy is recovering. After suffering a 40 percent decline in GDP over four years (1989-1993), it touched bottom in 1993 and has been recuperating ever since. After timid growth of 0.7 percent in 1994 and 2.5 percent in 1995, the prospects for this year are more ambitious after the announced 9.7 percent growth for the first semester of 1996.

According to the 1994 ECLAC report, 18 industrial sectors grew during the 1993-94 period. For the first time, tourism displaced sugar as the principal source of foreign exchange, providing US $800 million in 1994, which represented 35 percent of Cuba's total hard currency revenue. Evidently the economy has adjusted to a lower level of activity. GDP stopped contracting in 1994 thanks to the expansion in new activities such as tourism, mining, oil, and non-sugar manufacturing. Foreign investment in these new activities has also been growing. For 1996, due to important growth in all sectors of the economy—including traditional ones such as sugar and nickel, which were until now holding back the GDP

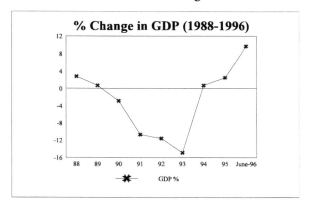

9. In order to make these changes and private investment legally possible, Cuba's National Assembly passed in 1992 a number of amendments to the 1976 Constitution providing the legal basis for transferring state property to joint ventures with foreign partners. They also abolished the State monopoly on foreign trade and relaxed the concept of central planning by changing the concept of *one plan* (plan único) to that which "guarantees the programmed development of the country."

rebound—predictions are for an estimated 7 percent increase in GDP for the year.

The sugar harvest of 1996 is only one of the many good examples of hard currency salary incentives increasing labor productivity.[10] Around 400,000 workers in the sugar industry alone receive dollar incentives for meeting or exceeding their work quotas. According to official estimates, around one million workers, 25 percent of the labor force, is now receiving some form of payment in dollars.

Table 2. Percentage Growth Rate in Selected Sectors

Sectors	1993	1994	1995	1996[a]
Traditional				
Sugar	-40.1	-4.8	n.a.	33.6
Nickel	-32.9	-9.6	n.a.	31.0
Non-traditional				
Tourism	25.3	15.2	n.a.	n.a.
Non-sugar manufactures		9.2	n.a.	10.0
Construction		8.1	n.a.	30.0
Oil	22.2	18.2	n.a.	46.0
Mining[b]		10.2	n.a.	n.a.

Source: CEPAL, *Cuba: Evolución Económica durante 1994*; Informe Económico, Primer Semestre 1996, Ministerio de Economía y Finanzas.

a. For the first semester 1996

b. Copper, gas and zeolite.

Another good sign in the economy has been the recovery of the peso. After reaching 150 pesos per dollar in 1993, it began to fall until December 1995, when it stabilized at 22 per dollar. In spite of that important recovery, the situation is still far from stable. The huge distortions generated by the differences between the official and the unofficial rates are responsible for significant inefficiencies in the allocation of resources. For example, since income in dollars represents 22 times more purchasing power than income in pesos, there has been a mass exodus of university

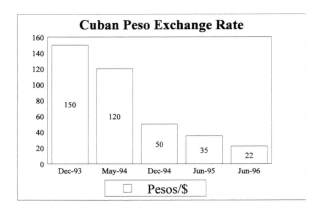

Cuban Peso Exchange Rate

professionals to less skilled activities that provide dollar remuneration.

In evaluating the adjustment and partial recovery of the Cuban economy after 1994, some important issues must be kept in mind in order to assess the real dimensions of the efforts ahead. The economy has experienced a dramatic contraction in a very short period of time, and growth rates, though high in some sectors, will not necessarily produce a rapid recovery. For example:

- In order to recover the standard of living of the average Cuban in 1988, the economy will have to grow for eight years in a row at a rate of seven percent.

- To substitute the foreign exchange earnings from sugar and nickel that Cuba had in the 1980s, tourism would have to grow from one million to about three million tourists per year. Over one billion dollars more in foreign investment would be needed to boost tourism to those levels.

Hence, while the economy has stopped contracting, it has done so at a very decreased level of income which will take a long time to reverse.

Nevertheless, the economy has reacted with a dynamism that shows no signs of fatigue yet. New reforms have been announced in an attempt to solve the increasing contradictions between the new, market-ori-

---

10. To buy fertilizers and spare parts, the government borrowed about US$200 million at interest rates between 15 and 18 percent. At current international sugar prices, the harvest had to be at least 4 million tons to break even. The official figure for sugar production of 4.5 million tons (33 percent higher than last year) guarantees important growth rates for this year.

ented sectors of the economy and the controlled, centrally planned, socialist economy. In other words, the system has developed a dynamic of its own, which has been forcing the government to make more changes than originally planned. We believe that those changes will bring more economic freedom and with it, undesirable inequality. In this context, the Cuban government will be increasingly exposed to political challenge arising from social tensions. The following are some examples of how this scenario is developing.

Legalization of Hard Currency: The Solution for the Expanding Black Market

As consequences of the reforms to attract tourism and foreign investment, the dollar economy began to expand and black market activities boomed. Since illegal transactions in dollars became common practice among Cubans, the government had no choice but to legalize dollar holdings. On July 26th, 1993, Fidel Castro made the following historic statement: "today life, reality ... forces us to do what we would have never done otherwise. ...we must make concessions." Among others, he made the following announcements: 1) Cubans would be permitted to have foreign currency and to spend it in special stores; 2) the government would introduce a national currency which would be convertible (this commitment was made effective in December 1994); 3) bank accounts in dollars would become legal; and 4) Cubans could pay for the services of other Cubans in dollars. The objectives of these measures were to eliminate the hard currency black market and to stimulate dollar remittances from families abroad.[11] Different sources estimate dollar remittances from Cubans in exile to be in the vicinity of US$500 million annually, despite the controls imposed by the U.S. government.

The reforms have resulted in important inequalities between those who have access to dollars and those who only have pesos. There are two Cubas, drifting apart; they live different lives and hope for different things. Nevertheless, the good news is that the number of Cubans participating in the dollar economy has been constantly growing since the legalization of hard currency. Subsequent reforms designed to expand the dollar economy, such as authorizing farmers and self-employed to charge in dollars or pesos, are the principal causes of the increase. According to a government survey, the amount of foreign currency in the hands of the population is increasing substantially.

Foreign Investment: A New Source of Dollars and Technology After the Breakup of the Soviet Union

Before 1989, it was the Soviet Union who provided Cuba with the hard currency and the technology it needed to support the economy. Now the Cuban government relies on foreign investment for such purposes. However, Cubans fear becoming once again overly dependent on any one country or sector.

> We went to bed one night and when we woke up, the Soviet Union was not there anymore and we had to begin all over again. The same thing had occurred years before with the United States. This is not going to happen again to us.[12]

If the Cuban government has shown firm commitment to anything since the beginning of the economic crisis, it has been to attracting investors from as many countries as possible to bring their dollars to Cuba. Different sources suggest that foreign investment agreements for around 2 billion U.S. dollars—up to the year 2005—have been signed between the Cuban government and investors from over 15 countries, including Australia, Canada, France, Germany, Great Britain, Israel, Italy, Mexico, Spain and others.

Originally, the government intended to attract foreign investment only in tourism; this was seen as the safest way to keep the capitalist exercise limited to a peripheral activity. Reality though, forced Cuba to open other sectors to private capital in the search for new technologies and hard currency. The most widely opened sectors behind tourism are: agriculture (mainly tobacco and citrus), mining (nickel, lead,

---

11. In August 1994, the U.S. Government prohibited dollar remittances to Cuba in response to increases in illegal immigration.

12. Conversation with the Minister of Basic Industry, 1995.

gold and chrome), oil and coal, telecommunications and textiles.

Cuba has signed investment protection agreements with most investor countries guaranteeing equal treatment, abstention from nationalization, and the right to repatriate profits and capital. With the objective of attracting more private capital, the new foreign investment law, enacted in September 1995, allows 100 percent private ownership. It also permits investment in real estate and the creation of free trade and export manufacturing zones.

Discussions in the National Assembly over the Foreign Investment Law were heated. The two most controversial features of the bill were: a) allowing Cuban exiles to invest in Cuba with the same rights as other foreign investors; and b) allowing foreign companies to hire employees directly. Only the former was approved.

The system may change in the future in response to the growing criticism from abroad. Except in special free trade zones, foreign companies can only hire Cuban workers through a government agency, ACOREC, which assigns workers according to the individual qualifications and also keeps the dollar salary, paying the employees in pesos. Since the official exchange rate is still one peso per U.S. dollar, workers consider this policy sheer robbery. They would not mind paying the 20 percent tax that the government has instituted if they could exchange their dollars at the unofficial exchange rate. Because they cannot, workers consider the income tax an insult to injury, especially after the government opened exchange houses where they were allowed to buy back their dollars, but at the unofficial (much higher) exchange rate.

The impact of the Helms-Burton Act has yet to be seen. Cuban officials are expecting a slowdown in foreign investment, especially for the second semester of 1996.

Solving the Fiscal Problem: More Taxes and Less Subsidies

The recent fiscal reform has also been highly controversial. Reductions in the fiscal deficit required the introduction of some very unpopular measures. The fiscal gap was reduced from 40 percent of GDP in 1993 to 12 percent in 1994 and 9 percent in 1995. In order to obtain these results, the government had to widen its sources of income and at the same time reduce expenditures, especially subsidies and salaries.

- On the *income* side, taxes were increased by 24 percent. A new income tax was imposed on the self-employed, farmers and cooperative members. There was an substantial increase in prices of some goods and services such as tobacco, liquor, electricity,[13] transportation, gas and mail services, among others.

- On the *expenditures* side, there was a reduction of nine percent, achieved by a major cut in the size of the central government: 15 ministries were eliminated and many subsidies in education and health were reduced. A social security contribution of up to 12 percent of wages was introduced in early 1995 to pay for the country's financially onerous pensions.

These policies were the subject of contentious debate at the National Assembly. Tax reforms were particularly hard to accept. Almost 30 years after Cuba abolished personal income taxes as irrelevant to a communist society, confusion reigns over what its re-adoption really means:

> we had the money to do what we did, we even had the money to subsidize those who got used to subsidies, but under the current situation, we cannot escape the need to impose taxes, a policy which is also oriented to clean up our internal finances.[14]

It took more than two years for the members of the National Assembly to agree on the need to reinstate taxes. The debate, long known to capitalist societies,

---

13. Ninety percent of Cuban households have electricity. The price increase has only affected 50 percent of the households for consumption in excess of 100 kwh per month.

14. Ricardo Alarcón, President of the National Assembly.

is still in its infancy in Cuba. The reforms adopted to date are not enough, and there is an agreement among some high Cuban government officials that a more comprehensive tax reform is needed in the future. It is obvious that the political viability of this policy will depend on the development of a profitable private sector. The size to which this private sector should be allowed to grow is also a source of debate.

The Small Scale Cuban Entrepreneur: Political Challenge and Economic Hope

Since 1990, the Cuban government has constantly emphasized the significance of foreign investment in stimulating the economy and in accessing dearly-needed hard currency. Big corporations, mainly joint ventures between foreign investors—including Cubans in exile—and the government, are doing business on the island. But local Cubans are not allowed to do so because their businesses are limited by law to the very small scale.

The Self-Employed—Conflicting Objectives from the Government Perspective:

Part of the success in the arena of fiscal policy has been the reduction of the deficit by decreasing expenditures, cutting costs, and decentralizing and reducing the size of the central government. By allowing self-employment, the government has provided job opportunities to those laid off from public enterprises. According to some estimates, close to one million people out of the total work force of four million must be laid off in order for state enterprises to become efficient. Ricardo Alarcón, president of the National Assembly, said that expanding self-employment was the "logical solution to unemployment." The second objective, less politically correct and also less publicized, is to incorporate more Cubans into the dollar economy. Increasing tensions between the dollar and the peso economy have led to social discontent and frustration. While doctors, members of the armed forces, and educators wonder why they are earning 20 times less than the self-employed, the government tries to find ways to close the uncomfortable gap. The policy thus far has been to expand the number of services and activities authorized to be offered by the self-employed. Finally, the legalization of self-employment

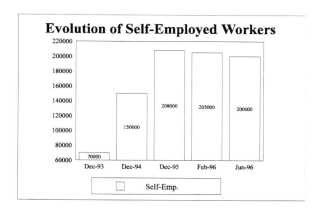

also has the objective of increasing fiscal income by widening the tax base.

In other words, the change in government policy towards the self-employed in Cuba is driven by three elements: a) the increase in the number of workers who are and will be unemployed; b) the need to bridge the growing inequalities between the peso and the dollar economy by providing dollars to those who can earn them; and c) the need to increase fiscal revenues. This last objective is being achieved by not only expanding the number of self-employed but also by introducing a highly controversial tax reform. Unfortunately, increasing tax rates limit the government's ability to address the first two factors, and the number of self-employed workers is shrinking for the first time.

The Expansion and Contraction of Self-Employment:

According to different sources, there were between 110,000 and 160,000 self-employed workers in Cuba by December 1994. Pedro Ross, President of the Confederation of Cuban Workers, said that out of the 2.2 million persons employed by public enterprises, 500,000 could be "pushed out of their jobs and encouraged to become self-employed." Further, around 80,000 Cubans who join the labor force every year will consider self-employment as an option. By the end of 1995, the number of Cubans with self-employment permits reached approximately 208,000 workers, over 5 percent of the island's labor force of four million. Also, according to some official estimates, another 200,000 persons are working in similar activities but without licenses.

In June 1996, the Government authorized 40 new occupations for self-employment but increased the monthly flat fee that it charges for carrying out each occupation. The schedule of fees, which when established in 1993 ranged from zero (exempted or free) to a maximum of eighty pesos per month, changed to a new range of from ten to four hundred pesos per month. The most successful activities have been taxed with the highest fees. Also, university graduates—previously banned from participating in any activity as self-employed—have been recently allowed to do so. Unfortunately, they are restricted to the 157 legalized activities and may not be self-employed in their field. This new decision is an attempt to alleviate the increasing discontent of some of the traditional elite who feel unjustly left out.

After an impressive initial boom, the number of self-employed workers has stagnated and even decreased as a consequence of the introduction of new taxes. Official figures show that the number of self-employed workers fell from 208,000 in December 1995 to 200, 000 in June 1996. In fact, these small entrepreneurs have been suffocated by mountains of regulations which define in incredible detail exactly what they can and cannot do. In December 1994, artisan markets were created in order to allow the sale of a variety of "light manufactures" and artisan goods. Cubans can charge in pesos or dollars for these goods and services. Some professions such as health and educational services have been excluded because they are intensive in a form of human capital—nurses, doctors and professors—that has been traditionally provided by the State. The government's justification for excluding these fields is that these professionals have a duty to pay back to society what the system has invested in their education.

The introduction of a tax reform is perceived by this small, emerging private sector as another manifestation of the government obsession with control. "Now all the self-employed workers will have to pay taxes. We are not working for the rich," said Castro to the National Assembly in December 1995. But in spite of Castro's words, the decrease in the number of self-employed has alarmed Cuban officials. Afraid of having gone to far with the controls, they are easing them in practice and have not been enforcing them as rigidly as before.

The debate—loosening political control in exchange for what?: In spite of the ongoing ideological debate over the ideal size of the private sector and the increasing suspicion of some communist leaders, the regulatory body has been relaxed.[15] More people are allowed to enter the system and the authorized activities have been expanded.

Table 3. Selected Authorized Activities for Self-employment: Monthly Flat Fee in Cuban Pesos

Activity	1993	1996
Artisan	45	200
Taxi driver	40	100
Home restaurant	not authorized	400
Food and beverage stand	not authorized	200
Shoe producer/seller	45	200
Art restorer	not authorized	100
Baby sitting	0	10
Tax collector	non existent	40
Plumber	40	80
Electrician	45	45

The New Constituency in Favor of the Reforms: A View from the Streets: Though not yet the majority, there is an increasing number of Cubans engaged in economic activities that did not even exist three years ago. According to government officials, there are approximately 500,000 Cubans working in activities related to self-employment activity. Another half million are receiving dollar incentives from the big government enterprises and thousands are earning dollars in activities related with the tourism industry. They all represent a growing constituency for the reforms. Furthermore, the huge spread between the official and unofficial exchange rate is pushing the government to incorporate more Cubans into the dollar economy.

---

15. Law-decree 141 of September 8, 1993 and the Regulations for the Exercise of Self-Employment of 18 April 1996.

THE NATIONAL ASSEMBLY, DECEMBER 28, 1993 DEBATE OVER THE LEGALIZATION OF SELF-EMPLOYED WORKERS

Arguments against:

Profiteering:

- "People will be selling at high prices what has been produced by others."

- "People will be selling products and services with subsidized inputs (gasoline or flour) or with stolen supplies from state enterprises."

"Small businesses will not take us anywhere. It would have been better to create cooperatives." Fidel disagreed, reminding the Assembly of the negative experiences of some cooperatives in the Soviet Union: "We cannot turn everything into cooperatives," he said.

"It may become such an attractive job alternative that it may compete and create labor shortages for the State enterprises."

"It can generate deformations in the system. Minuscule businesses are not the answer, this not socialism and is not big capitalism either."

"Many people outside Cuba would want us to have their democracy and their capitalism. The problem is that they want us to copy the way poor countries have them."

Arguments in Favor:

- It is a complement to the State.

- It is a good job alternative for the unemployed.

- It will satisfy the needs and will supply the goods and services that are not provided by the State.

- The government gains control by legalizing and regulating widespread illegal activities. For example, "there are hundreds of illegal food vendors in spite of the prohibitions."

- The State can collect taxes: "Now we have the worst situation: there are illegal activities everywhere and the State is not benefiting from them."

- "It is a popular decree; people like it. It would be very sad if the members of the National Assembly who are supposed to represent the people decide against something that the people want."

The structure of the Cuban economy has undergone a transformation which guarantees a period of growth. Nevertheless, the dual nature—a dollar and a peso economy—of this structure is generating social tensions and growing inequalities.

For an egalitarian society pounded flat by socialism for over 35 years, accepting the inequalities that come with capitalism is difficult. Small scale entrepreneurs are engaged in a wide range of authorized activities. Trapped between socialism and capitalism, this new breed is doing wonders to make a profit in spite of the restrictions and distortions imposed by the socialist logic. These structural limitations—in frank contradiction with the entrepreneurial spirit—are nearly ubiquitous in the regulations for the private sector. Among other restrictions to eventual growth the following are the most critical:

a. The total lack of access to bank credit;

b. The illegality of hiring other workers;

c. The lack of a legal way to buy the required supplies;

d. The prohibition of the use of intermediaries;

e. Very high income tax rates.

All of these bottlenecks will have to be resolved in the near future. Further reforms must tackle the current restrictions, since they are badly needed for the private sector to grow. And this time around, the good health of the government depends on the survival of the entrepreneur.

VIGNETTES FROM HAVANA: THE INCREASING SOCIAL TENSION

For Clara, opening a small restaurant in her tiny house facing the Havana "Malecón" or seaside boulevard, is a source of hope and dollars. She now makes in a month with this *paladar* almost ninety times what she used to earn as an accountant in a government agency. Clara observes, "The worst is over. We were hungry and desperate, things are much better now, people are happier, don't you see?" She points at a couple of Cubans talking and laughing while eating rice, beans, pork and drinking a local beer. "Finally we have the chance to have a night out." Sitting at other tables, Italian, Spanish and German tourists seem to enjoy the local cuisine.

Clara buys most of the food she needs for her US$1.25 menu at the farmers' markets, also legalized less than a year ago. There, prices are not controlled by the government. Like many other Cubans, Clara enjoys the novelty of buying shoes at the free artisans' market, and dresses, detergent, and olive oil in dollar specialty stores.

José Luis is 18 years old. He makes wood statues out of pieces of mahogany he usually finds in collapsed buildings. He sells them to tourists at the artisans' market near the Cathedral, but he does not want to study art. He wants to be "important," he wants to be a doctor. His excellent grades in high school have almost guaranteed him access to medical school next year: "I still have to do very well on the admission tests. You know, to be a doctor, you need to be the best." José Luis makes around US$200 a month selling statues, much more than the salary of a medical doctor.

Antonio, 34, is a medical doctor. He is a revolutionary. He fought in Angola. He is frustrated and depressed. "The situation gets worse every day. How can the owner of a *paladar* or a waiter make more money than a neurosurgeon," he asks me while shamefully accepting a present for his eight year old girl. "All these years have been a waste," he continues, "teenage prostitution, beggars on the streets ... we did not have that before, this is not socialism, it is not worth the sacrifice anymore."

CONCLUSIONS

In spite of previous setbacks in Cuba's reform attempts, this time around the Cuban private sector is here to stay. Without the generosity of the Soviet Union, there is no choice left for Cuba but to become more efficient and to insert itself into the international system.

In contrast with earlier attempts at reform—which were reversed with ideological rhetoric and Soviet help—the reforms of the 1990s are sustained by a growing constituency, both foreign and local, with market oriented objectives. This constituency, in contrast with the former experiences, continues to push the reforms forward toward greater liberalization. The government, on the other hand, cannot survive without the dollars and the taxes provided by this emerging private sector.

The Cuban government is committed to Marxism and also to preserving the egalitarian society which was forged by almost four decades of socialism. In such efforts, important reforms such as foreign exchange unification, have been delayed in order to mitigate their negative social impact. Paradoxically, in spite of all these efforts, Cuba's social tensions have increased and political discontent exacerbated. The coexistence of two exchange rates has caused enormous distortions, making those earning dollars significantly richer than those trapped in the stagnant peso economy.

The self-employed, the owners of the *paladares*, the farmers, and the artisans are leaping at the opportunities with the hope of a better life. Others, like doctors, educators, scientists, and artists, who have sacrificed years climbing up the traditional socialist ladder, feel unjustly left behind.

OPPORTUNITIES AND RESTRICTIONS FOR THE SMALL ENTREPRENEUR: A CONVERSATION AT A FARMER'S MARKET

Supply and demand are the first words you hear upon entering a Havana free market. There is no electricity, poor ventilation, no fans and no refrigeration. But under the hot sun at 35 degrees, Cubans buy and sell pork, ham sausages, goats, live hens, vegetables and fruits. "The price of pork is now 28 pesos but, you know, it all depends on the supply and demand."

Jorge was a medical student and he is now a *representante*; he got a license to sell at the market. He is eager to explain that he does not buy the meat from the farmers, he sells it *for* them and they share the profits. Pedro is the farmer. He has always worked at the farm. He is 55 years old and is afraid and ashamed to speak. He raises pork. He has always worked the land—he was 10 years old when his father got the piece of land he still works on. He does not sell to the consumer; his responsibility is to slaughter the animals and to transport them from the farm to the market by truck. "I pay the owner of the truck; he also has a license; he also has to pay taxes." The owner of the truck is also self-employed and his job is to transport pork and other products to the market. He got the truck by trading his old car to a friend working in a cooperative.

The farmer refuses to say how much money he is making. Profit is not a popular word in Cuba these days. The *cuenta propias* or *no asalariados* are being harshly criticized by those who earn salaries in pesos as selfish and unscrupulous. The farmer insists that he does not do the selling. It is Jorge, a thin but muscular 20 year old with inquisitive eyes who does the selling "and the cutting, so what?" He learned to cut meat from an uncle, and he carries a bag with his utensils: three big knives, a huge sharpener, and a glove made out of a kind of steel thread for his left hand, so he does not get hurt. He does the cutting with great skill. Jorge was a medical student until he decided to quit and become a

farmer's agent (*representante*). He cuts meat and deals with the clients, and he is responsible for the pricing and sale of the meat. He pays the taxes and the rent; he is also "in charge of the numbers" and uses a calculator all the time. "I quit medical school because the state does not have a job to offer me that would be sufficient to have a decent life." He is sick and tired of paying taxes to the government. "I might have to go out of business soon because taxes are too high, they do not know what they are doing." Jorge has to pay five percent of his daily sales in taxes, plus 200 pesos a month, 125 pesos per day for the rent of the stand, and an annual tax, which they do not know yet how much it will be. But Jorge's greed has its limits: when an elderly woman asks for the price of the pork chops and complains, he gives her a pound for free: "don't worry *compañera*, I know the way you feel. My mother is also retired and cannot afford these prices."

Jorge is the *representante*, a new word allowed by the government to avoid the use of the word intermediary, or middle man, which carries a stigma from former attempts at liberalization. The *representante* sells and pays the farmer his share, 20 pesos per pound, of what they sold during the day. What is not sold and uncut, the farmer takes away. The unsold cut meat is the risk run by the *representante*. Jorge works 12 hours a day, 7 days a week, and says he would like to make more money and get married someday. He lives with his mother who is not working anymore; she is retired and gets 120 pesos a month (US $4) for her pension. Life is tough, very tough, but Jorge sings a well known Mexican song: "con dinero y sin dinero hago siempre lo que quiero" (with money or with out it, I do what I please). I push him by continuing the song "y mi palabra es la ley" (and my word is the law). He laughs and says "that part I leave to Fidel."

In order to ease this increasing tension, the government has been steadily expanding the areas where private activities are allowed: the more Cubans that have access to dollars, the better. This government objective though, is being limited by significant bottlenecks that restrict the growth of the private economy. New reforms can be expected in these areas in the future. The most sorely needed changes are the following: the unification of the exchange rate, the liberalization of the supply market for the self-employed, the creation of small and medium size enterprises, bank reform (to permit the financing of small businesses and access to credit), and a labor reform legalizing the hiring of non-family employees.

Thanks to the reforms introduced to date, the Cuban economy has touched bottom. It is now growing and will continue to grow. After coping with the crisis, Cubans face the daunting task of managing growth. In the midst of great economic distortions, the principal challenge ahead is to resolve the increasing social tensions that accompany them.

The achievements of the old system are eroding, while the benefits of the reforms are timidly emerging through the cracks of socialism. This fragile equilibrium is driving more reform and liberalization. How fast Cuba will proceed and what shape its emerging economic system will take is still a puzzle for all.

CINCO AREAS DE ACCION ESTRATEGICAS PARA LOGRAR EL MILAGRO ECONOMICO CUBANO: UNA RAPIDA RECUPERACION CON UN ALTO Y SUSTENTABLE CRECIMIENTO CON EQUIDAD E INCLUSION SOCIAL[1]

Rolando H. Castañeda y George Plinio Montalván[2]

"En última instancia, lo que cuentan son las personas. A la postre, el proceso de transición de un país se juzgará desde la perspectiva de si su población vive mejor que antes...Esto es particularmente cierto en los países en transición, donde es posible que los responsables de las políticas no puedan mantener las trascendentales reformas en pro del crecimiento si grandes segmentos de la población consideran que la transición los ha marginado".

— Banco Mundial (1996, p. 80)

"The evolution of ideas:
First stage: 'How absurd; can any sensible person believe such things?.' **Second Stage:** 'These ideas are dangerous; they must be suppressed.' 'Of course, everyone knows that; whoever doubts it?'"

— Alvin Hansen, citado por Wolf (1993, p. 49)

Según la CEPAL Cuba tuvo el peor comportamiento económico de la región en el quinquenio 1991-1995, con una reducción media anual del producto interno bruto (PIB) real del 7.0 por ciento. Ello se debió a la reducción del comercio exterior y la ayuda del antiguo bloque socialista, a la ineficiencia del sistema económico existente, a las deficientes e insuficientes políticas económicas para hacerle frente a la crisis económica y al endurecimiento del embargo económico, primero por la Ley Torricelli de 1992 y después por las expectativas de la aprobación de la Ley Helms-Burton de 1996. Cuba tiene que replantear y rediseñar fundamentalmente su política económica y sus instituciones para mejorar sus resultados económicos.

Luego del inmovilismo del período 1989-julio de 1993, Cuba comenzó un cauteloso proceso de reformas económicas a partir de agosto de 1993, orientado a superar los problemas anteriores a la crisis, pero agudizados por ella, tales como el alto nivel de la deuda externa, y por otros que han sido resultado de las políticas económicas adoptadas durante de la década de los noventa, tales como el déficit fiscal, el excedente monetario y la dolarización. El gobierno está realizando un esfuerzo por mantener los niveles de empleo y los servicios

---

1. Entendemos por equidad brindar condiciones de vida mínimas aceptables a toda la población en términos de ingreso y servicios sociales básicos. Equidad no es mantener la distribución del ingreso igualitaria sino brindar igualdad de oportunidades a toda la población. Inclusión es que la población participe adecuadamente en los beneficios de la recuperación y el crecimiento económico mediante oportunidades adecuadas de empleo, así como eliminar la dualidad existente creada por la segmentación y la dolarización. En este sentido, equidad e inclusión están en conflicto con la existencia de pobreza extrema, pero no con el enriquecimiento de personas, ni aún con mayores desigualdades en la distribución del ingreso existente, especialmente en las primeras etapas de la transición.

2. Las opiniones aquí expresadas son de exclusiva responsabilidad de los autores y de ninguna manera reflejan sus vínculos institucionales.

sociales de salud, educación y seguridad social, los cuales son elevados para el nivel de desarrollo del país.

La experiencia de los antiguos países socialistas europeos muestra que el proceso de transición hacia una economía de mercado puede ser muy costoso en términos de inflación, reducción de la producción, aumento del desempleo, reducción de los servicios sociales y aumento de la pobreza extrema. Tal vez esto explique el resurgimiento de los comunistas en casi todos estos países, excepto en la República Checa. En contraste, los países socialistas asiáticos han logrado incorporar elementos importantes de una economía de mercado con altas tasas de crecimiento económico, tasas de inflación y desempleo moderadas y reducción de la pobreza extrema, pero su sistema político sigue siendo totalitario. No existe un estado de derecho, ni un sistema judicial independiente e imparcial, y se rechazan las libertades y derechos individuales, y el pluralismo político.

Como consideramos que parte de los resultados de la transición europea se debieron a políticas erróneas y no a la transición en sí, que han generado una resistencia a la forma de hacer el cambio, este ensayo propone una estrategia innovativa con cambios fundamentales en las políticas e instituciones económicas para estabilizar la economía sin recesión y recuperar rápidamente el crecimiento con énfasis en la equidad, centrada en el tratamiento de cinco áreas estratégicas. Así se podrán evitar los errores de política económica de varios de los antiguos países socialistas europeos. Consideramos que dados los bajos niveles de ingreso existentes y la vulnerabilidad de la economía cubana, un proceso de ajuste similar al de los países de Europa Oriental o la antigua Unión Soviética, tendría efectos negativos que podrían desatar una oposición o boicot a las reformas y terminar en una severa crisis social y política cuya

secuela podría durar muchos años, o convertirse en un verdadero juego de suma-cero. En cualquier caso, en el contexto de la globalización de la economía mundial, de la intensa competencia internacional y del dinámico cambio tecnológico, Cuba necesita una recuperación basada en altas tasas de crecimiento sustentable manteniendo equidad social.

La propuesta está orientada específicamente a eliminar los siguientes errores de la transición de muchos de los países de Europa Oriental y la antigua Unión Soviética: (1) Realizar una liberalización prematura de precios y al comercio internacional y una flotación cambiaria antes de lograr una estabilización efectiva, descartando cierta secuencia requerida y la necesidad de ciertas instituciones, lo que determinó una inercia inflacionaria y que fuera necesario aplicar posteriormente un proceso de choque monetario que conllevó una significativa recesión. (2) No distinguir que las políticas monetarias, cambiarias y fiscales tienen objetivos distintos y se deben aplicar en forma diferente en las etapas de estabilización y de recuperación del crecimiento. (3) No diseñar ni aplicar una estrategia orientada a lograr una pronta recuperación de la economía cuando el proceso de crecimiento pudo hacer una importante diferencia en la aceptación y el apoyo de la comunidad al proceso de reformas y para evitar la dependencia de abultadas redes sociales para compensar el alto desempleo con sus distorsiones.[3] (4) Disminuir los servicios sociales y los niveles de empleo y aumentar la pobreza extrema que crearon oposición de un grupo importante de ciudadanos, frenando el proceso de reformas. (5) Poner énfasis en la restitución, la cual detuvo innecesariamente la privatización, el uso de los activos disponibles y el proceso de inversión.

El ensayo propone una solución para mejorar la calidad de vida del cubano e insertar al país en la comunidad internacional basada en el crecimiento

---

3. El Informe del Banco Mundial de 1996 sobre las economías en transición señala: "Según investigaciones recientes realizadas en distintos países, parece que el nivel de confianza de los ciudadanos en que el gobierno pondrá en práctica las políticas anunciadas o cumplirá sus obligaciones tiene una relación positiva con el crecimiento económico a largo plazo. En estudios independientes sobre las empresas privadas realizados en 1995 se observa que el nivel de credibilidad conseguido por el gobierno de la República Checa es elevado, mientras que en Rusia es mucho más bajo" (Banco Mundial, 1996, p. 113).

sustentable con equidad y descarta las posiciones de: (1) mantener el *status-quo* del socialismo real, que ya es pretérito y que ha atrapado a Cuba en el atraso económico y social en un mundo muy dinámico y competitivo; (2) volver a la situación de los años 1950, ya que las realidades de Cuba y del mundo han cambiado significativamente; así como (3) implantar una solución social de corte neoliberal, porque nunca ha estado en las aspiraciones del pueblo cubano como lo muestran la tradición política y cultural previa, así como los principios fundamentales y la orientación de la Constitución Política de 1940 que estableció derechos sociales no contemplados en la Constitución de los Estados Unidos (Sánchez-Roig, 1996).

El ensayo está organizado de la siguiente forma. La primera sección describe la situación general y en las áreas relevantes de Cuba en la actualidad (las condiciones iniciales que es necesario enfrentar), así como las ventajas y posibles aportes de la comunidad cubana en el exterior. La segunda sección resume las experiencias y lecciones de la transición hacia una economía de mercado de los países europeos y asiáticos en 1989-1995. La tercera sección presenta una estrategia macroeconómica para lograr una rápida y efectiva recuperación económica de Cuba con equidad e inclusión social dentro de un espíritu de reconciliación nacional, así como cinco áreas de acción de políticas y de desarrollo institucional que habría que aplicar coherente y decididamente. La cuarta sección analiza el probable efecto de las cinco áreas de acción estratégicas. La quinta sección analiza la consistencia de las áreas de acción y el posible efecto agregado sobre los objetivos deseados. La sección final presenta el resumen de las principales conclusiones del ensayo.

LAS CONDICIONES INICIALES DE CUBA: LA SITUACION GENERAL Y EN LAS AREAS RELEVANTES EN LA ACTUALIDAD. VENTAJAS Y POSIBLES APORTES DE LA COMUNIDAD EN EL EXTERIOR

Según el Informe del Banco Nacional de Cuba (IBNC) de 1994, la producción nacional a precios de 1981 se contrajo de CU$19,585.5 millones (CU$=pesos cubanos) en 1989 a CU$12.868.3 millones en 1994, o sea una disminución del 34.3 por ciento (ver Cuadro 1). La producción se contrajo en 2.9 por ciento en 1990, 10.7 por ciento en 1991, 11.6 por ciento en 1992 y 14.9 por ciento en 1993, experimentando una recuperación del 0.7 por ciento en 1994 y del 2.5 por ciento en 1995.[4]

Cuba tiene un significativo excedente monetario. La circulación monetaria, definida como el efectivo en circulación y los depósitos en las cuentas de ahorro, aumentó de CU$4,152.5 millones en 1989 a CU$9,939.7 millones en 1994, es decir, una expansión del 139.4 por ciento. La relación entre dichos activos monetarios y la producción real pasó del 21.2 por ciento en 1989 al 77.2 por ciento en 1994. Dado que los precios oficiales o controlados se han mantenido prácticamente fijos, ello explica la fuerte presión inflacionaria "reprimida" a los precios oficiales vigentes. El IBNC de 1994 no presentó cifras sobre la inflación en los años recientes, ni sobre el circulante y los depósitos en cuentas de ahorro denominados en "pesos convertibles" que comenzaron en diciembre de 1994.

El déficit fiscal aumentó del 7 por ciento del PIB en 1989 al 40 por ciento del PIB en 1993, pero se redujo al 9.3 por ciento en 1995. Por otra parte, Cuba se declaró en moratoria de su deuda externa en 1986. Según el BNC la deuda externa, excluyendo la

---

4. La zafra azucarera de 1996 establece dudas sobre un crecimiento del PIB real del 9.6 por ciento en el primer semestre de 1996, tal como fue anunciado por el Vicepresidente Carlos Lage el 23 de julio de 1996 (Lage, 1996, p. 1). El gobierno incurrió en un financiamiento de US$300 millones para comprar insumos importados y expandir la producción azucarera sobre los niveles de 1995 (3,300,000 toneladas méetricas), pero el aumento de producción logrado (menos de 1,200,000 toneladas métricas) apenas alcanzó para pagar el principal y los intereses del financiamiento (US$350 millones). Consecuentemente, el crecimiento del PIB real con base en la expansión del azúcar parece exagerado, porque el PIB generado por el azúcar es la diferencia entre las exportaciones e importaciones de dicho sector, o sea sólo US$50 millones y el PNB es cercano a cero debido al pago de elevadas tasas de interés. El informe del BNC reconoce que las tasas de interés que Cuba paga ocasionalmente duplican las que prevalecen en los mercados internacionales y que los préstamos que recibe son poco flexibles (BNC, 1994, pp. 21 y 25).

Cuadro 1. Cuba: Indicadores Económicos Seleccionados, 1986-1995

VARIABLES E INDICES	1986-89	1990-94	1989	1990	1991	1992	1993	1994	1995P
Producto Interno Bruto (PIB)									
(CU$ miles de millones a precios de 1981)	19.4	15.4	19.6	19.0	17.0	15.0	12.7	12.9	13.1
% Cambio Anual del PIB real	0.2	-8.1	0.7	-2.9	-10.7	-11.6	-14.9	0.7	2.0
PIB per capita (CU$ a precios de 1981)	1,890	1,420	1,861	1,787	1,580	1,385	1,172	1,174	1,190
% Cambio Anual del PIB per capita real	-0.8	-8.8	1.1	-4.0	-11.6	-12.3	-15.5	0.3	1.4
Exportaciones, FOB (CU$ miles de millones)	5.4	2.5	5.4	5.4	3.0	1.8	1.1	1.3	1.5
Importaciones, CIF (CU$ miles de millones)	7.7	3.6	8.1	7.4	4.2	2.3	2.0	2.0	2.1
Producción de Azúcar									
(millones de toneladas métricas)	7.6	6.2	7.6	8.0	7.6	7.0	4.2	4.0	3.3
Ingresos Brutos por Turismo (CU$ millones)	136	553	168	243	387	567	720	850	986
Moneda en Circulación (CU$ miles de millones)	3.6	7.3	4.2	5.0	6.7	8.4	11.0	9.9	9.2
Moneda en Circulación como porcentaje del PIB	19	56	21	26	39	56	85	77	70
Déficit Fiscal (CU$ miles de millones)	0.8	3.4	1.4	2.0	3.8	4.9	5.1	1.4	1.0
Déficit Fiscal como porcentaje del PIB	4	23	7	11	22	33	40 ·	11	8
Deuda Externa en moneda convertible									
(CU$ miles de millones)	5.9	8.0	6.2	6.8	7.4	8.1	8.8	9.1	9.2

P=Preliminar

Fuentes: Para 1986 a 1989: CEPAL, *Economic Survey of Latin America and the Caribbean*, 1989 o estimado por los autores con base en los datos de la CEPAL; para 1989-1994: Banco Nacional de Cuba, *Economic Report, 1994*

contraída con el antiguo bloque socialista, ascendía a US$9,082.8 millones en 1994. Esto compara con las exportaciones de bienes y servicios de US$2,258.5 millones en ese año e implica relaciones de la deuda al PIB y de servicio de la deuda muy por encima del promedio latinoamericano (Martínez-Piedra y Pérez, 1996, pp. 22-24).

El gobierno realizó un amplio proceso de confiscaciones de todas las grandes y medianas empresas en 1960 y posteriormente confiscó casi todas las pequeñas empresas, mediante la llamada "Gran Ofensiva Revolucionaria" de 1968. Sólo existen pequeños propietarios individuales u organizados en cooperativas que ocupan el 14.9 por ciento de la tierras agrícolas (3.4 por ciento y 11.5 por ciento, respectivamente) y en el área de servicios y artesanías (trabajo por cuenta propia). A junio de 1996 había 208,000 personas autorizadas como cuentapropistas en 160 ocupaciones, aunque se estima que hay 190,000 adicionales trabajando clandestinamente (Alfonso, 1996).

Cuba tiene una amplia comunidad residente en el exterior (unos 1,200,000 habitantes) que podría contribuir decisivamente a la recuperación y crecimiento económico sustentable y al desarrollo de una economía de mercado, con demostrada experiencia y capacidad empresarial, tecnológica, profesional y gerencial, recursos financieros y con experiencia en la penetración de mercados internacionales. Esta comunidad, alentada y motivada por políticas apropiadas, podría hacer un aporte significativo, obteniendo un considerable provecho de ello, a la vez que mejoraría las condiciones de vida del pueblo cubano.

EXPERIENCIAS Y LECCIONES DE LA TRANSICION DE LOS PAISES EUROPEOS Y ASIATICOS HACIA UNA ECONOMIA DE MERCADO EN 1989-1995

En su transición hacia una economía de mercado, los antiguos países socialistas de Europa han experimentado en general un proceso recesivo, el cual ha sido mayor y más persistente de lo esperado. Las recesiones fueron amplias y profundas, con una reducción acumulativa del producto real del 33.6 por ciento (Fischer, et. al, 1996b, p. 229), con tasas de inflación de tres dígitos, niveles de desempleo de dos dígitos, una reducción en los servicios sociales prestados y un aumento de la pobreza extrema[5] (ver Gráficas 1, 2 y 3).

---

5. "No cabe duda de que la pobreza aumentó en las etapas iniciales de la transición—en muchos países considerablemente" (Banco Mundial 1996, p. 85).

La exclusión de amplios sectores de la población y el trastorno en el tejido social tal vez explique el resurgimiento de los comunistas en casi todos estos países, excepto en la República Checa. Dos artículos recientes de Fischer, et. al. (1996a y 1996b) resumen las características más importantes de esta transición y concluyen que el crecimiento retornó a los países aproximadamente dos años después que se controló el proceso inflacionario. Aunque la mayoría de los economistas está de acuerdo con el proceso de ajuste que se ha aplicado en esas economías, hay diversas opiniones críticas en cuanto a varios elementos de la política empleada que incluyen desde de la política cambiaria (Sachs, 1996), la política de estabilización innecesariamente recesiva (Berthelot, 1996, p.5), lo drástico de la apertura comercial realizada y la política industrial que ello implica (Amsdem, 1994), el pasivo papel del estado en orientar el proceso de transición (Kochanowics y Taylor, 1994), y los problemas de ajuste a nivel de las empresas estatales que requieren tiempo por problemas de información asimétrica y contratación (Blanchard y Kramer, 1996).[6]

En cambio, los países socialistas asiáticos comenzaron un proceso limitado y gradual de utilización de los mecanismos de mercado y de la propiedad privada (economías que combinaron primero la planificación y el mercado, y que después se definieron como socialismo de mercado) que les ha permitido obtener altas tasas de crecimiento con niveles moderados de inflación y desempleo (el índice de miseria de Okun), mantener los servicios sociales a la población y reducir la pobreza extrema durante el proceso de transición (ver Gráfica 4).[7]

Tanto en los países europeos como en los asiáticos, el crecimiento se ha basado principalmente en el nuevo y dinámico sector privado de las pequeñas y

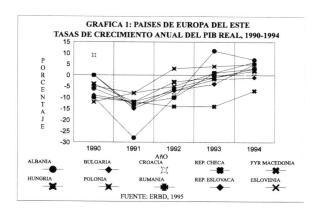

medianas empresas, a veces con apoyo de la inversión extranjera en la forma de empresas mixtas en los países asiáticos. Sin embargo, la producción del sector estatal se ha contraído sustancialmente en los países europeos, mientras que se ha mantenido o se ha expandido más modestamente que la del sector privado en los países asiáticos.

UNA PROPUESTA DE ACCION PARA LOGRAR UNA RAPIDA Y EFECTIVA RECUPERACION Y CONSOLIDACION ECONOMICA DE CUBA CON EQUIDAD E INCLUSION SOCIAL DENTRO DE UN ESPIRITU DE AMPLIA PARTICIPACION CIUDADANA Y RECONCILIACION NACIONAL

Cuba ha sufrido un fuerte proceso de ajuste causado por el corte de la ayuda y el comercio con el desaparecido bloqueo soviético y la deficiente política de ajuste, lo que ha significado una reducción del producto real de más de 30 por ciento. Por ello es difícil considerar que Cuba pueda seguir un proceso de transición a una economía de mercado similar al de los antiguos países socialistas europeos sin severas repercusiones políticas y sociales.

---

6. "In the absence of either plan or market institutions for dealing with specificity, the introduction of private opportunities can lead to the collapse of output under market imperfections, such as asymmetric or incomplete contracts" (Blanchard y Kramer, 1996, p. 1). "The available evidence suggests that disorganization has played a limited role in the major Central European countries, some role in Russia and the Baltics, and a major role in the other republics" (Blanchard y Kramer, 1996, p. 19).

7. "Ambos tenían un elevado número de pobres cuando emprendieron la reforma, pero en el curso de ese proceso lograron significativas reducciones del nivel de pobreza. En los dos países esa mejoría fue consecuencia del rápido crecimiento y de la modificación de la política en favor de la agricultura" (Banco Mundial, 1996, p. 85).

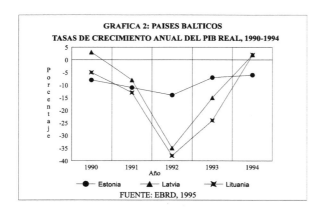

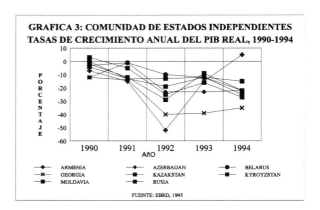

Los objetivos de Cuba al diseñar una estrategia de ajuste deben ser: (1) estabilizar la economía rápidamente sin recesión, condición previa a lograr la efectiva recuperación y consolidación de la economía, y (2) altas y sustentables tasas de crecimiento. Estas fases de la transición deben realizarse en forma tal que sean lo más equitativas posible, apoyen efectivamente una amplia reconciliación nacional y tengan una amplia participación de la población para que los ciudadanos sientan que ellos pueden influir efectivamente las decisiones del gobierno y que las autoridades públicas son realmente responsables ante ellos. Los objetivos de equidad e inclusión social son esenciales en las propuestas de solución a problemas económicos que se basan en principios de solidaridad humana (ver por ejemplo, Martínez-Piedra y Pérez, 1996). El gobierno deberá reenfocarse fundamentalmente, adoptando una filosofía de servir al pueblo y no de ser su dictador, así como de ser lo más eficiente y efectivo en brindar los servicios públicos requeridos.

El logro de los tres objetivos (estabilización, recuperación y equidad) deberá tener efectos que se refuercen mutua y sinérgicamente, ya que, aunque sus interrelaciones son variadas y complejas, generalmente son positivas. Así, por ejemplo, será posible consolidar la estabilización en la medida que la oferta agregada comience a crecer sostenidamente y se desarrolle un sistema financiero con instrumentos de ahorro a largo plazo. Obviamente existen ciertas incompatibilidades estáticas entre lograr un mayor crecimiento y una mayor equidad; sin embargo, desde un punto de vista dinámico, las sociedades que han alcanzado mayores niveles de equidad (los países asiáticos en 1960-1995 y Chile a partir de 1984) han tenido un mayor crecimiento a mediano y largo plazo.

El logro de la estabilización se basa en la eliminación de las causas principales de las presiones inflacionarias reprimidas: el déficit fiscal, el excedente monetario y la dolarización. A su vez, el logro de la recuperación y consolidación del crecimiento sustentable se basa en la progresiva liberalización y desregulación de los mercados y la institucionalización de una economía de mercado (reformas estructurales).[8] Asimismo, la privatización de la infraestructura y el reenfoque del gobierno deberán contribuir a una mayor eficiencia y a un mayor crecimiento sustentable. El logro de la equidad social se basa en mantener, y aún mejorar, la calidad de los servicios sociales básicos y brindar suficientes oportunidades de empleo a todos los ciudadanos. Una posible alternativa al proactivismo en el empleo sería crear una red de seguridad social que tendría que financiarse a través de niveles de impuestos elevados o de endeudamiento externo, lo

---

8. La recuperación de la economía consiste en utilizar adecuadamente la capacidad productiva existente lo cual no conlleva mayores inversiones sino utilizar la mano de obra calificada y profesional mediante la liberalización del trabajo por cuenta propia, la agricultura, y la micro, pequeña y mediana empresa. Altas y sostenidas tasas de crecimiento conllevan un aumento de la inversión física.

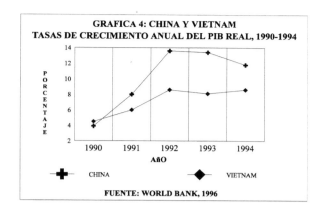

GRAFICA 4: CHINA Y VIETNAM
TASAS DE CRECIMIENTO ANUAL DEL PIB REAL, 1990-1994

FUENTE: WORLD BANK, 1996

que tendría efectos negativos sobre la asignación de los recursos y la eficiencia de la economía. El aumento relativo del gasto social en los países europeos en transición parece haber sido compensatorio y tener esos efectos (Banco Mundial, 1996, pp. 139, 140).

Cinco áreas de acción tienen una importancia crucial y deberán utilizarse en forma consistente para hacer viable y compatible el logro efectivo y eficaz de los objetivos indicados anteriormente y orientar el sistema económico en la dirección deseada: (1) las políticas monetarias y cambiarias utilizadas para eliminar el excedente monetario y la dolarización, así como para lograr la ampliación y profundización financiera, las cuales a su vez deberán tener significativos impactos en el logro y la consolidación del proceso de estabilización; (2) el financiamiento externo y la renegociación de la deuda externa, por su impacto en la inversión y en el crecimiento de la economía; (3) la compensación en vez de la restitución (devolución) de las propiedades confiscadas, por su posible impacto en los procesos de inversión nacional y extranjera y con ello en el crecimiento de la economía; (4) el mantenimiento de los servicios sociales básicos a la población; y (5) el mantenimiento de los niveles de empleo, estos dos últimos por su impacto en la equidad social.

ANALISIS Y DETERMINACION DE LOS POSIBLES EFECTOS DE LAS CINCO AREAS DE ACCION ESTRATEGICAS Y COMO UTILIZARLAS CONSISTENTEMENTE PARA

TENER EL IMPACTO DESEADO EN LOS OBJETIVOS PROPUESTOS

Paquete de medidas monetarias y cambiarias para lograr la desdolarización, la monetización y la profundización financiera sin recesión ni choque monetario

Cuba tiene un significativo excedente monetario en relación con su nivel de actividad económica y de precios, lo que se debe en parte a la represión y al escaso desarrollo institucional financiero, y es agravado por la dolarización y la segmentación financiera. El país debe eliminar la dolarización y el excedente monetario, acumulados por varios años de déficits fiscales y de políticas monetarias y cambiarias deficientes, mediante un paquete coherente de medidas de reforma monetaria, devaluación y régimen cambiario fijo con respecto al dólar (al menos temporalmente), del establecimiento de un banco central independiente y un sistema de regulación y supervisión financieras prudentes que logren la estabilización y eviten el choque monetario y la consecuente recesión que han sufrido los antiguos países socialistas europeos. Posteriormente, deberá comenzar un proceso gradual de liberalización, desregulación e institucionalización para lograr la ampliación, profundización y diversificación financieras, que son tan importantes para el crecimiento económico y la privatización de la economía.

El paquete de medidas monetarias y cambiarias propuesto presenta ventajas importantes sobre la liberalización de precios, la flotación cambiaria y el choque monetario que crearía fuertes inercias, conductas especulativas e histéresis inflacionarias y recesivas (recesión con inflación) que inhibirían el desarrollo de la institucionalización y profundización financieras debido a la inestabilidad y las incertidumbres que desatan. El paquete propuesto fomentaría una mejor gerencia y disciplina financiera de las empresas, alentaría el ahorro y la inversión al brindar información pertinente a los agentes económicos, y evitaría casos generalizados de

Efecto Principal de las Areas Estratégicas Consideradas sobre los Objetivos y Relación Sinérgica entre los Objetivos y las Areas

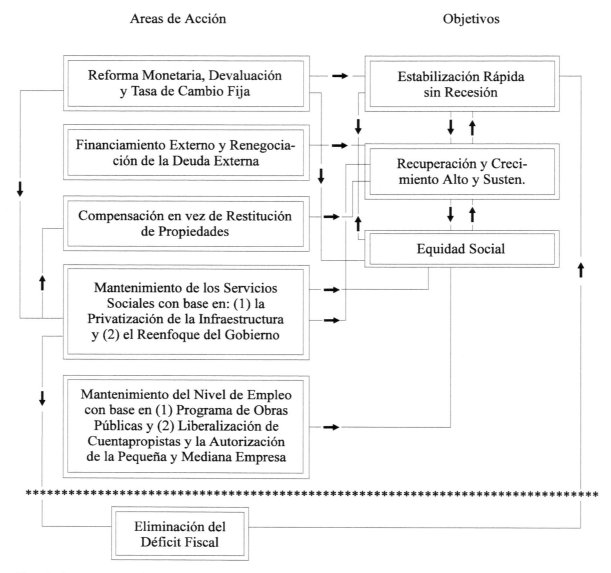

Areas de Acción   Objetivos

Nota: Un diagrama más completo se presenta en el anexo I.

corrupción y fraude financieros que crean histéresis[9] e inhiben el desarrollo de este importante sector y postergan el proceso de privatización.[10] El diseño y aplicación de un paquete similar fue utilizado por Yugoslavia para estabilizar con éxito y rápidamente en 1994 en condiciones de bloqueo externo y de guerra (Avramovic, 1996).

La literatura reciente señala y muestra empíricamente que las estabilizaciones no tienen que ser

9. "...escándalos financieros socavan las normas de comportamiento tanto público como privado" (Banco Mundial, 1996, p. 115).

10. Una elaboración más detallada de este tema se presenta en Castañeda y Montalván (1996).

Cuadro 2. Probable Efecto de las Areas de Acción Individuales sobre los Tres Objetivos Propuestos

Áreas de Acción Estratégicas	Objetivos Propuestos		
	Estabilización	Crecimiento	Equidad
I. Reforma Monetaria	+	?	?
Devaluación	+	+	+
Tasa de Cambio Fija (Temporalmente)	+	+	?
Ampliación, Profundización e Institucionalización Financieras	+	+	?
II. Financiamiento Externo y Renegociación de la Deuda Externa	+	+	?
III. Compensación en Vez de Restitución de las Propiedades	+	+	+
IV. Mantenimiento de los Servicios Sociales y Mejoramiento de su Calidad	?	+	+
Programa de Privatizaciones, Concesiones y Contratos de Administración de Infraestructura	+	+	+
Reenfoque del Gobierno	+	+	?
V. Programa de Obras Públicas Municipales	?	+	+
Programa de Vivienda Social	?	+	+
Liberalización del Trabajo por Cuenta Propia y la Autorización de la Pequeña y Mediana Empresa	+	+	+

contraccionarias (Easterly, 1996). Asimismo, que la ampliación, diversificación y profundización financieras es un factor *determinante* y no *resultante* del crecimiento económico y del aumento de la productividad (King y Levine, 1993; Greenwood y Smith, 1993) debido a las contribuciones que hacen a la innovación y la reducción del riesgo para los empresarios y a la selección de ellos. King y Levine (1993, p. 537) destacan que los países que han hecho reformas económicas en el marco de un sector financiero reformado han logrado mayores éxitos con el conjunto de reformas que los países que no lo tenían. La experiencia chilena de 1984-1996 muestra que la liberalización y desregulación financieras a partir de un marco de regulaciones y supervisión prudentes son muy importantes en la transición hacia una economía de mercado no sólo para facilitar el ahorro interno requerido, sino también para mejorar la asignación de inversiones, apoyar el proceso de privatización y proveer el señoreaje que el gobierno necesita en las primeras etapas del proceso de transición.

La movilización de un monto adecuado de financiamiento externo y la renegociación de la deuda son más importantes que obtener términos concesionales para el financiamiento

Dado sus bajos niveles de ahorro interno y de desarrollo, Cuba necesita montos significativos de recursos externos netos (financiamiento externo) y en los términos más favorables posibles (menor costo de los recursos) para asegurar la recuperación y consolidación económica en el futuro próximo y altas y sustentables tasas de crecimiento posteriormente. El bajo nivel de ahorro interno del país es determinado por el bajo nivel de ingreso, la represión financiera existente y la carencia de instituciones financieras básicas e instrumentos de ahorro a largo plazo adecuados que fomenten y asignen el ahorro y faciliten la inversión, tales como: fondos privados de pensión, compañías de seguros, bonos, acciones, fondos mutuos, etc. Sin embargo, dadas las necesidades de inversión existentes en el país, lo más importante es conseguir un monto adecuado de recursos externos complementarios en vez de darle prioridad a la concesionalidad de los recursos, la cual está tendiendo a desaparecer.

A pesar de lo indicado anteriormente, todavía hay disponibles fuentes concesionales de recursos externos (por ejemplo, recursos "blandos" de la Unión Europea, así como de FOMIN, CTFONDOS y fuentes japonesas en el BID y en el Banco Mundial) que se pueden y deben movilizar para asistir a un país de bajo nivel de ingreso por habitante, como lo es Cuba actualmente.

Una forma efectiva de recibir financiamiento concesional neto del exterior y movilizar recursos adicionales en el futuro es mediante la renegociación de la deuda externa, tanto en lo referente a su monto como en cuanto a sus condiciones (tasa de interés, plazo de amortización y período de gracia), dada la capacidad real de pagos del país y las reformas que se adoptarían para hacerle frente a las obligaciones. Este enfoque es consistente con los planes "Baker" y "Brady," se podría basar en los llamados términos de Nápoles, permitirá movilizar recursos mayores y disminuiría la salida de recursos externos netos en el futuro.

Empleo de la compensación en vez de la restitución de propiedades como norma para desagraviar a los confiscados [11]

Cuba enfrenta no sólo el reto de restablecer una economía de mercado dinámica y competitiva, sino también de establecer y desarrollar un régimen de propiedad privada que sea aceptable y apoyado por la población para que funcione eficientemente, pueda ser vigilado efectivamente, y sustente una clase media de amplia base con intereses que propicien y consoliden una rápida y robusta expansión del sector privado y de la economía de mercado. Esto crearía cohesión social y facilitaría la reconciliación nacional.[12]

Cuba deberá evitar la experiencia de los países bálticos y de Europa Oriental donde la restitución se ha convertido en *un difícil obstáculo y una larga demora* a la clarificación y seguridad de los derechos de propiedad, al funcionamiento adecuado del sistema de justicia porque lo ha congestionado con litigios, y al desarrollo de conductas apropiadas y procesos fundamentales de utilización de activos, reconstrucción y privatización.[13] Aún en esos países la restitución se ha limitado a los reclamos presentados por ciudadanos individuales dentro de un plazo determinado para viviendas, bienes raíces y tierras agrícolas, las que a su vez se han limitado en extensión y deberán ser aprovechadas directamente por los propietarios. Como las otras empresas generalmente se consolidaron y expandieron y es prácticamente imposible determinar qué pertenece actualmente a quién, sus propietarios han sido compensados (Brada, 1996, pp. 68-70).

Por ello, el país deberá, en primera instancia, mantener la política de negociar acuerdos bilaterales con otros países, especialmente EUA, para compensar globalmente a grupos grandes de empresas e individuos cuyos activos fueron confiscados.[14] En los demás casos, se deberá buscar formas de compensar directamente a los agraviados, por ejemplo, otorgándoles derechos o acciones sobre las empresas y los bienes privatizados—que podrían incluir bases militares decomisadas y corporatizadas—o sobre el fondo compensatorio a ser establecido con la privatización de la infraestructura y las empresas de servicios públicos que se propone en la sección siguiente, asegurándoles mayores ingresos futuros al igual que al resto de la población. Esto adelantaría el proceso de privatización al separarlo claramente del proceso de compensación.

Mantenimiento de los servicios sociales básicos (educación, salud y seguridad social)

El gobierno, para responder mejor a las necesidades de bienestar del pueblo, debería concentrar prioritariamente los gastos públicos en áreas sociales

---

11. Para una recomendación diferente ver Gutiérrez (1996). Nuestra recomendación es similar a la que la Fundación Nacional Cubano Americana hizo originalmente sobre el tema de privatización y compensación *versus* restitución: "to avoid social upheaval and resentment by Cubans in the island against exiles, prevent inequities stemming from the return of some materially altered confiscated properties and discriminate against non-property owner victims of the communist dictatorship" (descrito por Gutiérrez, 1996, p. 25, en base a J. Tamayo, "Divining Cuba's Future," *Miami Herald*, September 29, 1991, pp. 1C, 6C).

12. El Informe del Banco Mundial de 1996 sobre la transición hacia una economía de mercado señala que "los análisis comparativos entre países demuestran que las sociedades con grandes desigualdades en la distribución de los ingresos o de los activos suelen ser, política y socialmente, menos estables y tener tasas más bajas de inversión y crecimiento" (Banco Mundial, 1996, p. 15).

13. A veces se da el caso que hay bienes raíces inutilizados por litigios, mientras las nuevas empresas tienen que operar en kioscos o en vehículos estacionados en las calles. "...muchos edificios y lotes de tierras se han devuelto a quienes habían sido sus propietarios antes del régimen comunista, aun cuando a veces ni quieren ni pueden hacerse cargo de ellos" (Banco Mundial, 1996, p. 59).

14. Véase, por ejemplo, el acápite "The Standard 'Lump Sum' Settlement Approach," en Travieso-Díaz (1996, pp. 673-676).

básicas—tales como: proveer salud, educación[15] y capacitación suficientes y de mejor calidad a la población (capital humano fundamental)—así como en garantizar un ingreso mínimo decoroso a *todos* los ciudadanos por razones de dignidad humana mediante empleo en obras públicas municipales de interés social, como Chile lo hizo en la segunda mitad de la década de los ochenta. Dichas obras podrían estar orientadas a mejorar los sistemas sanitarios y la situación del déficit y hacinamiento habitacionales, mientras la recuperación de la economía es capaz de reabsorber a los desempleados y se alienta la iniciativa y el espíritu empresarial del cubano.

Los gastos sociales se podrían racionalizar (aumentar su eficiencia interna) y hacer más efectivos (aumentar su eficiencia externa). Por ejemplo, se podrá eliminar gastos excesivos e ineficientes, entre ellos la jubilación anticipada que trae un relajamiento en la disciplina laboral, e introducir y ampliar la aplicación de técnicas presupuestarias para medir eficiencia, efectividad y costos en los servicios prestados; concentrar los gastos en los sectores más pobres de la sociedad; permitir la práctica privada, incluyendo a las instituciones voluntarias, para traer la presión de la competencia del sector privado a estas importantes áreas; cobrar parcialmente por algunos servicios prestados; darle más autoridad a los empleados de línea en las decisiones; y descentralizar el diseño, administración y ejecución de los servicios a nivel de los municipios de tal forma que los proveedores sean más responsables ante los ciudadanos por los resultados y la calidad de los servicios prestados. Como hemos indicado en otro ensayo, deberán establecerse fondos privados de pensión y concentrar los servicios públicos de seguridad social en los sectores más pobres de la sociedad (Castañeda y Montalván, 1993).

El gobierno cubano deberá establecer y desarrollar marcos y organismos regulatorios y de supervisión estables y creibles, con incentivos y mecanismos arbitrales, que atraigan competitivamente la inversión para promover altos estándares de servicios y desarrollen la eficiencia para privatizar u ofrecer en regímenes de concesiones, leasings o contratos de administración privada para construir, rehabilitar, equipar, reparar, mantener y operar la infraestructura económica básica.[16] También deberán establecer bonos de protección y sanciones adecuados que protejan el interés público, establecer los criterios para fijar las tarifas generales y establecer los subsidios, si corresponden, para los usuarios de bajos ingresos.

El país requiere con urgencia modernizar y actualizar su nivel tecnológico aplicando las mejores prácticas y técnicas internacionales, mejorar la calidad de vida y de servicios a la población, lograr un alto y sustentable crecimiento económico, y despolitizar las actividades económicas rápidamente. Con este enfoque para la infraestructura, el gobierno de Cuba podría reducir sus esfuerzos administrativos parcialmente, los gastos públicos corrientes y de capital en estos rubros y concentrarlos en áreas sociales prioritarias, tal como lo viene haciendo Chile, así como generar fondos para la compensación a los confiscados (ver sección anterior). Los gastos públicos de inversión, reparación y mantenimiento de la infraestructura han caído significativamente en los antiguos países socialistas europeos (Banco Mundial, 1996, pp. 140-141). Una infraestructura adecuada deberá alentar inversiones en los sectores productivos y facilitar la orientación de la economía hacia el exterior.

El enfoque de privatizaciones, concesiones, leasings y contratos de administración de las empresas de servicios públicos y de la infraestructura económica dará flexibilidad y eficiencia a la economía. Pasará el

---

15. Habrá que realizar ajustes en algunos componentes de la educación (adquisición de conocimientos, destrezas, actitudes y valores culturales) para adaptarlos a una sociedad más libre, y dar mayor iniciativa y responsabilidad individuales.

16. Ferrocarriles; servicios de buses urbanos e interurbanos; carreteras; puentes; túneles; puertos; aeropuertos; terminales; generación, trasmisión y distribución de energía eléctrica y gas; teléfonos y otras telecomunicaciones; acueductos; alcantarillados; canales; recogida, tratamiento y disposición de desechos.

reto de la modernización al sector privado; permitirá atraer y movilizar el amplio capital financiero, el talento empresarial y gerencial, y la experiencia profesional de los cubanos en el exterior; con lo cual también se alentará la entrada de recursos privados de otras fuentes. Esto es especialmente importante en las primeras etapas de la transición cuando los mercados financieros y de capital estarán en proceso de desarrollo y consolidación.

Para el enfoque del sector público propuesto (mejores servicios sociales, una gestión pública más eficiente y honesta, así como la privatización de la infraestructura económica), Cuba necesita reenfocar el gobierno y sus prácticas administrativas para servir mejor las necesidades de sus ciudadanos basado en tres principios básicos: (1) que los servicios públicos a brindar deben ser esenciales; (2) deben ser rápidos y no burocráticos; y (3) debe dársele suficiente autoridad al funcionario de línea que atiende directamente al ciudadano para que pueda servirlo mejor y sea innovativo en sus funciones.

Mantenimiento del nivel de empleo

El gobierno cubano deberá realizar un esfuerzo por mantener el nivel de empleo existente para brindar ingresos a la población y evitar su rechazo a la transición, ya que todo el proceso de reformas y de privatización podría detenerse o aún revertirse. Sin embargo, deberá mantener el empleo, no a nivel de las empresas individuales en los sectores productivos (agricultura, manufactura, servicios comerciales como el turismo) para que estas actividades puedan reajustarse rápida y efectivamente y desarrollar una robusta competitividad externa, sino mediante una amplia liberalización y desregulación del trabajo por cuenta propia—eliminando licencias burocráticas, controles detallados y a veces contradictorios e impuestos prácticamente confiscatorios que son más intensos que los que popularizó Hernando de Soto y que se acentuaron en mayo de 1996 con la Resolución Conjunta de los Ministerios de Trabajo y Seguridad Social, y de Economía y Precios—y potenciando la postergada micro, pequeña y mediana empresa. Los nuevos trabajadores por cuenta propia y la nueva pequeña y mediana empresa deberían ser

alentados con una exención tributaria sobre la renta por dos años, siguiendo el ejemplo de Rumania.

Cuba también deberá desarrollar un programa de obras de interés social intensivo en mano de obra, complementario al programa de concesiones privadas que se propuso en la sección anterior, el cual conllevaría una expansión extraordinaria de la construcción y permitiría absorber en parte la mano de obra excedente de las empresas de los sectores productivos. Las obras de interés social consistirían en pequeñas obras públicas o mixtas (de cooperación entre los sectores público y privado), tales como obras municipales sanitarias y de desarrollo urbano, y lotes con servicios, que ofrezcan fuentes temporales de empleo a la vez que le permitan al país aliviar la solución básica de vivienda en esta área tan deficitaria. El mejoramiento de la situación habitacional es imprescindible para aumentar la movilidad de la fuerza de trabajo.

CONSISTENCIA DE LAS AREAS DE ACCION CONSIDERADAS Y POSIBLE EFECTO GLOBAL SOBRE LOS OBJECTIVOS DESEADOS

No todas las áreas de acción consideradas tienen el efecto adecuado sobre cada uno de los tres objetivos deseados, tal como lo muestra el Cuadro 2 anterior. Sin embargo, tienen, en general, un efecto muy positivo sobre la recuperación y consolidación del crecimiento de la economía. Tienen un efecto mayormente positivo sobre la estabilización, excepto por los gastos de obras públicas municipales, vivienda social y servicios sociales; de ahí, la importancia de los programas de reenfoque del gobierno y de las privatizaciones, concesiones, contratos de administración de las empresas de servicios públicos y de la infraestructura económica para liberar recursos públicos que permitan concentrar y hacer más efectivo el gasto público (corriente y de capital) en los sectores sociales y evitar posibles presiones inflacionarias. En cuanto a los efectos sobre la equidad, las áreas de acción propuestas descansan y dependen mucho de las actividades que crean directamente empleo o que mantienen los servicios sociales, ya que el efecto de las otras áreas de acción es incierto en el mejor de los casos.

En consecuencia, las cinco áreas de acción consideradas en su conjunto tendrán el efecto adecuado sobre los objetivos propuestos y si éstos se logran se reforzarán mutuamente y tendrán efectos sinérgicos significativos.

RESUMEN Y CONCLUSIONES

Cuba enfrenta el difícil desafío de hacer la transición hacia una economía de mercado para mejorar la calidad de vida de sus ciudadanos y reinsertarse en la comunidad internacional, partiendo de una severa y prolongada recesión, un excedente monetario, la dolarización de la economía, un déficit fiscal, la moratoria de la deuda externa, una tasa de cambio distorsionada y fragmentada, y un compromiso del gobierno de mantener los niveles de empleo y los servicios sociales.

Por ello, deberá aplicar una estrategia innovativa orientada a lograr efectivamente la estabilización sin recesión y recuperar el crecimiento económico con equidad social, utilizando, cinco áreas de acción que hacen compatibles y viables los objetivos: (1) un paquete coherente de medidas cambiarias y monetarias (consistente en la reforma monetaria, la devaluación del peso, un régimen cambiario fijo con respecto al dólar y el establecimiento de un régimen regulatorio y de supervisión financiera prudentes); (2) la movilización de recursos externos netos mediante el financiamiento externo y la renegociación de la deuda externa; (3) el uso de la compensación en vez de la restitución de propiedades como régimen para desagraviar a los confiscados; (4) el mantenimiento de los servicios sociales mediante el reenfoque del gobierno para hacerlo más eficiente y un programa de concesiones, privatizaciones y contratos de administración de servicios para la infraestructura económica y las empresas de servicios públicos; y (5) el mantenimiento del nivel de empleo mediante la liberalización y desregulación del trabajo por cuenta propia, la pequeña y mediana empresa, así como un programa de lotes con servicios y de obras municipales de saneamiento y desarrollo urbano.

Este paquete coherente de cinco áreas de acción aplicado decididamente tendrá un efecto positivo en estabilizar sin recesión y lograr la recuperación económica con equidad rápidamente.

Anexo I: Efecto Principal del Paquete Propuesto de Medidas sobre los Objetivos y Relación Sinérgica entre los Objetivos

Medidas   Objetivos

Medidas Macroeconómicas de Estabilización

Eliminación del Déficit Fiscal
Reforma Monetaria y Ajuste Tasas de Interés
Devaluación, Unificac y Tasa Cambiaria Fija

→ Estabilización Rápida sin Recesión

Libertades y Derechos Indiv.

Medidas Macroeconómicas de Crecimiento

Sistema Tributario con Incentivos Apropiados
Ampliación y Profundiz. del Sistema Financ.
Régimen Cambiario de Competitividad Externa

Reconciliación Nacional

Medidas Microeconómicas de Crecimiento

Desregulación y Liberalización de Mercados
Privatización de Empresas Productivas
Institucion. de Economía Social de Mercado
Reestructuración Productiva y Compensación
Retorno y Reintegración de Emigrados

→ Recuperación y Crecimiento Alto Sustentable

Medidas de Movilización de Recursos Externos

Alentar Transferencias Unilaterales
Movilizar Financiamiento Externo Oficial
Renegociación de Deuda Externa Oficial
Alentar la Inversión Privada Extranjera
Estrategia de Promoción de Exportaciones

→ Reinserción Internacional

Medidas de Equidad Social y Empleo

Moderniz. del Estado y Manten. Gasto Social
Privatización Infraestructura Económica
Programa de Obras Públicas Municipales

→ Equidad e Inclusión Social

BIBLIOGRAFÍA

P. Alfonso. "Apuntes sobre la situación económica de Cuba," in this volume.

A. H. Amsden, J. Kochanowics and L. Taylor. *The Market Meets Its Match.* Cambridge, Mass., Harvard University Press, 1994.

D. Avramovic. "Lessons from the Transition: The Case of Yugoslavia 1994-96." Ensayo presentado en el "Development Thinking and Practice Conference", auspiciada por el BID, setiembre de 1996.

Banco Mundial. *Informe sobre el desarrollo mundial 1996: De la planificación centralizada a la economía de mercado.* Washington, DC: Banco Mundial, 1996.

Banco Nacional de Cuba. *Economic Report, 1994.* La Habana: Banco Nacional de Cuba 1995.

Y. Berthelot. "Lessons from Countries in Transition." Ensayo presentado en el "Development Thinking and Practice Conference," auspiciada por el BID, setiembre de 1996.

J. C. Brada. "Privatization Is Transition-Or Is It?" *The Journal of Economic Perspectives* (Spring 1996), pp. 67-86.

R. H. Castañeda and G. Plinio Montalván. "Transition in Cuba: A Comprehensive Stabilization Proposal and Some Key Issues." *Cuba in Transition—Volume 3.* Washington: ASCE, 1993, pp. 11-72.

R. H. Castañeda y G. Plinio Montalván. "Cuba: Estabilización sin Recesión ni Choque Monetario," in this volume.

W. Easterly. "When is Stabilization Expansionary?" *Economic Policy*, No. 22 (1996), pp. 65-107.

Economic Commission for Europe, United Nations. *Economic Survey of Europe in 1994-1995.* Paris: UNECE, 1996.

S. Fischer, R. Sahay and C. Végh. "Economies in Transition: The Beginnings of Growth." *The American Economic Review* (May 1996a), pp. 229-233.

S. Fischer, R. Sahay and C. Végh. "Stabilization and Growth in Transition Economies: The Early Experience." *The Journal of Economic Perspectives* (Spring 1996b), pp. 44-66.

J. Greenwood and B. D. Smith. "Financial Markets in Development, and the Development of Financial Markets." *Journal of Economic Dynamics and Control* (1993).

N. Gutiérrez. "Righting Old Wrongs: A Survey of Restitution Schemes for Possible Application to a Democratic Cuba," in this volume.

R. King and R. Levine. "Finance, Entrepreneurship, and Growth: Theory and Evidence." *Journal of Monetary Economics*, 32 (December 1993), pp. 513-542.

C. Lage. "*Cuba: Informe Económico, 1er semestre 1996*". La Habana: Ministerio de Economía y Planificación, mimeo (23 de julio de 1996).

A. Martínez-Piedra y L. Pérez. "External Debt Problems and the Principle of Solidarity: The Cuban Case," in this volume.

J. Sachs. "Economic Transition and the Exchange-Rate Regime." *The American Economic Review* (May 1996), pp. 147-152.

R. Sánchez-Roig. "Cuban Constitutionalism and Rights: An Overview of the Constitutions of 1901 and 1940," in this volume.

M. F. Travieso-Díaz. "Alternative Remedies in a Negotiated Settlement of the U.S. Nationals' Expropriation Claims Against Cuba." *University of Pennsylvania Journal of International Economic Law*, Vol. 17, Number 2 (Summer 1996), pp. 659-690.

H. Wolf. "The Lucky Miracle: Germany 1945-1951." In R. Dornbusch, W. Nolling, and Richard Layard. *Postwar Economic Reconstruction and Lessons for the East Today.* Cambridge, MA: The MIT Press, 1993.

MARXISM AND THE MARKET: VIETNAM AND CUBA IN TRANSITION

Julie Marie Bunck

The collapse of the Soviet bloc severely jolted the remaining communist world. Two long-time Soviet allies, Vietnam and Cuba, suddenly found their chief benefactor, from which substantial assistance had consistently flowed, to have vanished. Consequently, their leaderships had to attend immediately to sorting though alternative policies that might bring about rapid economic growth while averting the disintegration of the socialist state and the unraveling of communist-party dominance.

This paper compares the economic transitions of Vietnam and Cuba and argues that Vietnam has moved into the post-Cold War world era more adroitly and painlessly than has Cuba and that Vietnam's economy has integrated into regional and global markets less disruptively than has the Cuban economy. Seven political factors may help to explain the differences in approach between the Vietnamese and Cuban transitions and the relative success of Hanoi: the degree of Cold War economic dependence, the reaction to the collapse of the Soviet empire, the extent of policymaking consistency, the characteristics of the leaderships, the nature of traditional culture, the nature and substance of regional relationships, and the degree of commitment to long-term economic reform.

THE DEGREE OF COLD WAR ECONOMIC DEPENDENCE

Initially, the Marxist regimes in Cuba and Vietnam each achieved important successes; however, each confronted grave crises by the end of the first decade in power. One decade after its revolutionary triumph, Cuba's national effort to harvest ten million tons of sugar ended in an unprecedented economic crisis marked by widespread mismanagement, acute food shortages, a flourishing black market, rapidly falling agricultural and non-agricultural production levels, and increasing vagrancy and worker absenteeism. Likewise, by 1985, a decade after reunification, the Vietnamese government confronted raging inflation, low productivity, economic mismanagement, famine in some provinces, rising numbers of fleeing refugees, the drying up of Chinese and Western aid after Hanoi's exceptionally expensive invasion and occupation of Kampuchea, and the toll of resisting China's retaliatory invasion.[1]

Cuba and Vietnam responded to these similar problems by seeking different objectives, emphasizing dissimilar priorities, and adopting divergent policies. The Cuban regime launched its second decade of rule by fortifying economic and political ties to Moscow. The Cuban leadership adopted Soviet planning and management mechanisms, strengthened the communist party, adopted a Soviet-style constitution, and focused attention on bolstering the island's

---

1. George Irvin, "Vietnam: Assessing the Achievements of *Doi Moi*," *Journal of Development Studies* 5, 31 (June 1995), p. 729.

economic base. In return for Castro's compliance, Moscow provided unprecedented levels of economic and military assistance. According to recent estimates, Soviet subsidies to Cuba soared to perhaps $8 billion a year, roughly $800 per capita, equal to nearly 40 percent of Cuba's gross national product.[2] Such a level of support allowed Castro to claim correctly that Cuban citizens enjoyed a higher quality of life than citizens in many other comparable developing countries. Cuba, in fact, enjoyed an illusion of prosperity, based in the final analysis on extraordinary external dependence.[3]

Vietnam never came to rely on Soviet economic aid to the extent that Cuba did. Indeed, throughout the Cold War Vietnam never received more than $1 billion ($14 per capita) annually in military and non-military aid from the Soviet Union.[4]

THE REACTION TO THE COLLAPSE OF THE SOVIET EMPIRE

By 1986, although the Soviet bloc was supplying approximately 84 percent of Cuba's imports, the sweetheart relationship between Havana and Moscow began to falter. The Soviet leadership began to distance itself from its Cuban counterparts, subtly at first, but more pointedly over time. The Soviet media came to criticize openly Cuban production levels and even to lambast Castro for failing to meet his sugar commitments. Moreover, the Kremlin moved to improve relations with the United States. Despite these early warning signs, the Castro regime, mindful of its vulnerability and dependence, quietly endured the withdrawal of aid and the stinging comments of those Soviet critics who publicly questioned the prudence of Moscow's aid to Cuba.[5]

By the late 1980s the Castro regime desperately needed a potent dose of creative thinking to find some enterprising solution that might counter, mitigate, or postpone the impending economic blow. Instead, the leadership retreated from the intellectual challenge before it. The government rejected any move toward a Cuban *perestroika* and reasserted the time-worn ideals of the 1960s: moral incentives, ideological purity, and centralized decision-making. Meanwhile, the Cuban leaders continued to plead for economic refuge in the familiar nest of a critically ailing Marxist-Leninist superpower.

The death rattle of the Soviet bloc in 1989 plainly exposed the extent of Cuba's reliance on Moscow and its satellites. Profound divisions marked the December 1990 Soviet-Cuban trade agreement and soon thereafter Moscow substantially scaled back its Cuban commitments.[6] Even as the Soviet Union dis-

---

2. David Rieff, "Cuba Refrozen," *Foreign Affairs* (July/August 1996), p. 63. Some economists estimate the number to be closer to $4 billion a year, about $400 per capita, equal to nearly twenty percent of Cuba's gross national product. See Andrew Zimbalist, "Treading Water: Cuba's Economic and Political Crisis," in *Cuba and the Future*, ed. Donald E. Schulz (Westport: Greenwood Press, 1994), pp. 7-8; Carmelo Mesa-Lago, "The Economic Effects on Cuba of the Downfall of Socialism in the USSR and Eastern Europe," and "Cuba's Economic Policies and Strategies for Confronting the Crisis," in Mesa-Lago, *Cuba After the Cold War*, pp. 133-257. Brundenius and Zimbalist argued in 1989 that the magnitude of Soviet aid to Cuba had been overstated as a result of faulty methodology. Jorge Pérez-López, however, has rejected their methodology, based on Cuban official prices, as conceptually inappropriate for constructing indices that reflect economic growth. See Andrew Zimbalist and Claes Brundenius, *The Cuban Economy: Measurement and Analysis of Socialist Performance* (Baltimore: The Johns Hopkins Press 1989); *Cuba's Political Economy: Controversies in Cubanology*, ed. Andrew Zimbalist (Boulder: Westview, 1988).

3. Cole Blasier, "The End of the Soviet-Cuban Partnership," in *Cuba After the Cold War*, ed. Carmelo Mesa-Lago (Pittsburgh: University of Pittsburgh Press, 1993), p. 73.

4. Frederick Z. Brown, "Vietnam Since the War: 1975-1995," *Wilson Quarterly* 19, no. 1 (Winter 1995), p. 79; author's confidential interview with official from the Foreign Ministry, Hanoi, Vietnam, November 8, 1995.

5. Susan Kaufman Purcell, "Cuba's Cloudy Future," *Foreign Affairs* 69 (Summer 1990), p. 113; Robert Legvold, "The Revolution in Soviet Foreign Policy," *Foreign Affairs* 68, 1 (1988/89), p. 86; K. W. Ellisen, "Succeeding Castro," *The Atlantic Monthly* (June 1990), p. 38. See also Jorge I. Domínguez, *To Make a World Safe for Revolution: Cuba's Foreign Policy* (Cambridge: Harvard University Press, 1989), p. 110; *Cuba at a Crossroads: Politics and Economics after the Fourth Party Congress*, ed. Jorge Pérez-López (Gainesville: University Press of Florida, 1994).

6. Blasier, pp. 88-89.

integrated in 1991, the Cuban regime could muster no striking counter-move. Rather, it continued to muddle along with economic policies that must have seemed anachronistic even to those of a Marxist persuasion. Hampered by ineffective policies, between 1989 and 1994 Cuban exports dropped by 80 percent and Cuba's gross domestic product (GDP) was halved.[7]

Not until late 1993 did the Castro regime seriously attempt to resolve its painful predicament. Once the economy reached a state of irrefutable dilapidation, the regime adopted notable reforms. It legalized circulation of the dollar, authorized limited self-employment, established open produce markets, allowed privately owned restaurants, and transformed state farms into cooperatives. In 1995 Cuba reformed foreign investment laws and imposed taxes.[8] These changes mitigated the crisis and helped to attract considerable foreign investment. By the end of 1995 estimates of foreign investments in Cuba since 1992 range from $800 million to $1.5 billion.[9]

The Vietnamese regime confronted the economic crisis triggered by changes in the Eastern bloc much earlier and more decisively than did the Cuban state. As early as the mid-1980s Vietnamese leaders, especially Politburo member Nguyen Van Linh, recognized the gravity of their country's food shortages. Vietnamese leaders thus consciously and deliberately focused on raising domestic production while decreasing external economic dependence. To increase the food supply, the Vietnamese regime introduced modest market-oriented agricultural reforms. For instance, the government allowed families in cooperatives to sell on the open market any excess produced above a state quota. Such limited incentives, offered to virtually all farmers, increased production significantly.[10]

In December 1986, after hardliner Le Duan's death, the distribution of power within the party shifted to the reformist wing and the party chose Linh as its new leader. Inspired by Mikhail Gorbachev, Linh quickly introduced *Doi Moi*, a far-reaching *perestroika*-like policy of economic renovation.[11] *Doi Moi* continued to emphasize diminishing the annual $1 billion in Soviet economic aid by carrying out reforms singlemindedly aimed at driving production levels higher.[12] The government legalized and encouraged private entrepreneurship in a range of enterprises. It dismantled agricultural collectives and returned land to families to farm. It opened the country to foreign trade and investment. Moreover, the regime unified and sharply devalued the currency, raised interest rates to levels above the inflation rate, and cut fiscal deficits drastically, chiefly by slashing budgetary subsidies to state-owned enterprises. The government also imposed financial discipline on state firms. It trimmed the number of state enterprises by 5000,[13] laid off 900,000 workers without guarantees of other public-sector employment, and exposed some state firms to competition from the growing private sector. Today, most state enter-

---

7. *Miami Herald* (October 21, 1994), p. 1C.

8. See Jorge Pérez-López, *Cuba's Second Economy: From Behind the Scenes to Center Stage* (New Brunswick: Transaction Publishers, 1995); and Julio Carranza, Luis Gutiérrez, and Pedro Monreal, *Cuba la reestructuración de la economía* (La Habana: Editorial de Ciencias Sociales, 1995). See also *Washington Post* (September 6, 1995), pp. A1, A25; *Washington Post* (September 9, 1995), pp. C2, C3; *Washington Post* (September 12, 1995), p. A14; *Washington Post* (April 13, 1996), p. A25.

9. *Miami Herald* (October 21, 1994), p. 1C; see also Manuel Lasaga, "A New Look at Cuban Statistics," *CubaNews* (February 1995), p. 2; Carmelo Mesa-Lago, "How Good are Those 1995 Predictions?" *CubaNews* (May 1995), p. 2.

10. Brown, p. 79.

11. Brantly Womack, "Political Reform and Political Change in Communist Countries: Implications for Vietnam," in *Reinventing Vietnamese Socialism: Doi Moi in Comparative Perspective*, eds. William S. Turley and Mark Selden (Boulder: Westview Press, 1993), p. 282. See also George Irvin, p. 729.

12. Brown, p. 79; author's confidential interview with official from the Foreign Ministry, Hanoi, Vietnam, November 8, 1995.

13. Approximately 3000 of these firms merged with other larger firms. The remaining 2000 closed.

prises are decentralized and increasingly subject to market forces.[14]

In response to these dramatic reforms, the output of state enterprises climbed steadily, and tax yields jumped from 6 to 11 percent of GDP in just 3 years. Party leaders also agreed to offer lucrative incentives for improved performance and to reduce their daily administration of the economy by abandoning price controls. Although fuel, electricity, public transport, and food staples were not subject to the initial reforms, market forces drove down prices of many commodities, industrial goods, and services. In agriculture the regime eliminated all quotas and endorsed free trade at market prices. These policies further boosted food production and created a surplus that might be exported in exchange for hard currencies. In fact, by 1989 Vietnam had become and remains the world's third largest exporter of rice.[15]

Despite the sweeping lay-offs, many workers and managers survived the reforms without exceptional hardships. The agricultural sector and the new non-state industrial and service sectors, which together account for about 60 percent of GDP and 85 percent of employment, grew rapidly. These sectors effectively absorbed workers laid off in the public sector. This fundamental reorientation of the Vietnamese economy raised national production levels significantly.

Doi Moi thus embraced decisive free-market reforms. In 1989, while Moscow repeatedly scaled back deliveries to Vietnam of fuel, fertilizer, steel, chemicals, and cotton, the Vietnamese harvested a record-breaking rice crop. By 1991 the communist regimes of Eastern Europe and the Soviet Union had collapsed and all assistance had ceased. Naturally, the resulting sharp decline in foreign trade weakened Vietnam's

economic performance. A brief recession occurred. Nevertheless, the government maintained the momentum of reform and by 1993 had restored macroeconomic stability.[16] In fact, aided by strategic thinking, the *Doi Moi* economic philosophy, and a timely oil boon, Vietnam adjusted to transformed international circumstances without any substantial drop in output. Since 1992 inflation has remained below 10 percent and growth has held steady and impressive at around 9 percent. Vietnam now ranks as the fastest-growing economy among developing Asian countries.

In September and October 1993, Vietnam cleared its $142 million debt with the International Monetary Fund (IMF). A month later, the World Bank and the Asian Development Bank pledged loans worth $800 million for infrastructure development, while the IMF provided a $223 million credit. In November 1993, the Paris Donors' Conference offered another $1.86 billion in pledges, of which the Japanese pledged more than half. At present, Vietnam owes its major outstanding debt—$11 billion in 1989—to Russia. At the current ruble exchange rate, however, the debt is of negligible concern.[17]

THE EXTENT OF POLICYMAKING CONSISTENCY

The World Bank's 1996 *World Development Report* states: "in every case [of transition] what matters is the breadth of policy reforms attempted and the consistency with which they are maintained."[18] The report continues: "Get policies right; stick with them. ...Countries will only fully exploit [their] potential by being consistent over time."[19] In fact, the Vietnamese leadership has governed with remarkable consistency from reunification in 1975 to the transition of the 1990s. The leadership, comprised of five individuals,

14. Irvin, p. 727.

15. Douglas Pike, "Uncertainty Closes In," *Asian Survey* 24, no. 1 (January 1994), p. 65; also see Peter Janssen, "So Much for Theory: Now for Practice," *Asian Business* (April 1994), p. 43; George Irvin, p. 730.

16. See Vo Nhan Tri, "The Renovation Agenda: Groping in the Dark," in *Vietnam Today: Assessing the New Trends*, ed. Thai Quang Trung (New York: Taylor & Frances, Inc., 1990).

17. Irvin, p. 734.

18. *World Development Report 1996: From Plan to Market* (Washington, D.C.: World Bank), p. 17.

19. *World Development Report 1996*, p. 27.

customarily reaches decisions after a drawn-out round of discussions and negotiations in which input from many party members is sought. Even changing policy ever so slightly requires approval from various power centers and is frequently accomplished after a tedious process. While not without serious drawbacks, this form of governance lends itself well to consistency. Since the mid-1980s the regime has steadfastly maintained its long-term plan of economic reform. Even the recent Eighth Party Congress, which flourished with conservative rhetoric and rumors of dramatic changes, deviated only slightly from well-established strategies.

The Cuban regime has historically taken a different tack altogether in its approach to policymaking, one that is perhaps most notable for its inconsistency. While Castro's long-term goal of survival has remained constant, he has adopted a zig-zag approach to policymaking. For example, over the years the regime has moved from encouraging material incentives to promoting moral incentives to re-establishing material incentives. Castro has experimented with private enterprise, abolished it, and then re-introduced it. The leadership has regularly initiated grandiose construction projects, only to abandon them unfinished.

Although this extraordinary flexibility has proven valuable at times, the fact that the regime has vacillated rather than to articulate and focus singlemindedly on a long term strategy has seriously handicapped efforts at economic reform. Cuba's failure to articulate and focus singlemindedly on a long-term strategy for economic recovery has led to repeated failures.

THE CHARACTERISTICS OF LEADERSHIP

It is increasingly clear that in attempting to cope with cataclysmic political changes, Cuba's inability to maintain a steady course reflects the personality and whims of Fidel Castro. While he orchestrated the revolution's early successes, Castro's inclination to control all aspects of Cuban governance has repeated-ly silenced pragmatic views and stifled consistent political reform. The problem of centralized, unchallengeable, and erratic decisionmaking has dominated Cuban politics and economics, just when international developments require more prudent and consistent policymaking. Cuba seems to have become a dysfunctional member of the post-Cold War international community: its economy is unable to grow and mature so long as Castro retains unchallenged control.

One key distinction between the Vietnamese and Cuban experiences is the continued presence of a domineering persona in the Cuban leadership, but not in Vietnam's. Charismatic leader Ho Chi Minh, founder of socialist Vietnam, died in 1969, well before the reunification. Thus, in determining how to navigate through the uncharted waters of transition, the post-1975 government has not had to contend with a single manipulative or domineering founding father. Rather, Ho Chi Minh left to the party unifying memories and a legacy of writings. The revolutionary leadership built upon his myth but never had to contend with a personality cult or a leader intent on retaining personal power. Perhaps as a result, the Vietnamese government in the 1980s responded to their crisis readily and adopted a realistic, less ideological approach with relative ease.

THE NATURE OF TRADITIONAL CULTURE

The goal of creating a revolutionary culture clearly derives from Marxist ideology. Karl Marx argued that the pernicious influence of capitalism, intrinsically destructive to human beings, alienates citizens, foments greed, and spawns materialism.[20]

According to Marx, the revolutionary overthrow of capitalism and the ensuing transformation of institutions would liberate mankind. However, for the Marxist master plan to succeed, a socialist regime would have to reeducate its citizens so that they would know how to think and act in their new society.

---

20.   Erich Fromm, *Marx's Concept of Man* (New York: Frederick Ungar, 1961), pp. 20-21, 25, 63, 151; Joseph Cropsey, "Karl Marx," in *History of Political Philosophy*, eds. Leo Strauss and Joseph Cropsey (Chicago: University of Chicago Press, 1987), pp. 809, 824-825; John McMurtry, *The Structure of Marx's World-View* (Princeton: Princeton University Press, 1978), p. 20.

As two of the more doctrinaire Marxist-Leninist regimes, both Cuba[21] and Vietnam initially viewed transforming culture with the utmost seriousness and each expended tremendous energy in carrying it out. Cuban and Vietnamese leaders believed that the creation of a utopia depended upon their efforts to mold a socialist citizenry. Viewing their prerevolutionary cultures as products of Western capitalism and imperialism, the leaders sought to transform or replace anti-revolutionary attitudes with a more appropriate set of beliefs and values. In their efforts to transform culture, the Cuban and Vietnamese leaders employed an array of strategies, from nonmaterial rewards to reeducation to incarceration.

What would constitute the characteristics of the model socialist citizen? In general terms these governments urged citizens to cultivate obedience and an eagerness to toil, deference and loyalty to authority, self-denial, selflessness, and an orientation toward the state.[22] The "new man" would combine all of these qualities into mental, physical, and ideological strength. This effort to overhaul society's traditional culture proved to be a formidable task for both regimes. For the Castro leadership, however, it proved to be especially challenging. The revolutionary culture that Castro envisioned starkly differed from Cuban reality. The regime urged Cuban citizens—traditionally individualistic, competitive, and entrepreneurial, oriented toward self and family, suspicious of authority, and disdainful of manual labor—to change fundamentally their attitudes and behavior to meet revolutionary standards and goals. The leadership encouraged citizens to shun individualism and entrepreneurship and adopt a communitarian mentality, to reject competition for cooperation, to repudiate family loyalties in favor of a more nation-oriented perspective. Moreover, the leadership

attempted to imbue citizens with a wholly transformed labor ethic devoid of the influence of Spanish colonialism, Cuban slavery, and Western capitalist domination.[23] Ernesto "Che" Guevara urged citizens to think of manual labor as "man's greatest dignity."[24]

Despite its efforts, the Cuban government largely failed to sway its citizens. For 35 years the Cuban regime consistently battled quiet forms of dissidence, unruly and "undisciplined" citizens, and annoying and pervasive problems such as vagrancy, absenteeism, plummeting production, and destruction of state property. Cuba's "revolutionary culture" of the 1990s barely resembled the ideal culture that the government had long sought to create.[25] These cultural obstacles continually dogged the revolutionary government and cost the leadership a stunning amount of resources and anguish.

Vietnam's Marxist leadership also recognized the importance of a hardworking, highly productive work force. The Le Duan government incessantly implored citizens to labor selflessly to consolidate the "reunification." Vietnam's communist leadership, however, enjoyed a substantial advantage over the Castro regime. Traditional Vietnamese culture—dominated by ancient Confucian values, but also containing elements of Buddhism, Taoism, and other influences—viewed manual labor as honorable, valuable, and a fundamental civic obligation in order to promote the common good. As an official in the Foreign Ministry recently explained, "we have collectively viewed toil as a required service to the country. This has always been seen as a profoundly important duty—long, long before the liberation."[26]

21. See Julie Marie Bunck, *Fidel Castro and the Quest for a Revolutionary Culture in Cuba* (University Park: Pennsylvania State University Press, 1994).

22. The ambivalence with which Marxists approach the concept of the state in theory and practice is curious. For a discussion of this matter see Michael Ross Fowler and Julie Marie Bunck, *Law, Power, and the Sovereign State: The Evolution and Application of the Concept of Sovereignty* (University Park: Pennsylvania State University Press, 1995), pp. 128-130.

23. For a discussion of these three historical legacies, see Bunck, pp. 127-128.

24. Quoted in Bunck, p. 125.

25. Bunck, pp. 182-184

26. Author's confidential interview with government official, Hanoi, Vietnam, March 15, 1995.

Moreover, for centuries Vietnamese society has emphasized social harmony (what the Vietnamese call *yin*), communal cooperation and an orientation toward the group rather than the individual, and unabashed loyalty and deference toward authority. Traditional Vietnamese society has also stressed the importance of social duty, loyalty (*trung*), discipline, and perseverance (*nghia*).[27]

In Vietnam, traditional culture provided a solid foundation upon which the revolutionary regime could promote a wide array of Marxist-Leninist attitudes and values. A strong element of continuity existed between the traditional culture and that which the regime aimed to create. To ask Vietnamese citizens to adopt the ideal Marxist characteristics seemed neither radical nor absurd.

Consequently, post-1975 Vietnamese society has been less conflictive and competitive, more deferential and disciplined, and more broadly supportive and cooperative than has Cuba's revolutionary society.

THE NATURE AND SUBSTANCE OF REGIONAL RELATIONSHIPS

Once members in good standing of the global family of socialist states, by the early 1990s Cuba and Vietnam found themselves orphaned. Vietnam, however, quickly fell in with relatively congenial neighbors and avoided regional isolation. In July 1993 the U.S. removed the restraints that had long interfered with potential IMF and World Bank assistance to Vietnam. The following February the U.S. lifted the trade embargo. Just a few years after the fall of the Soviet Union the practical and psychological barriers between the Vietnamese economy and the international market were tumbling down.

By spring 1994 key officials from Taiwan, Thailand, Australia, and the Philippines had visited Vietnam, as had also Singapore's senior minister, Lee Kwan Yew. During this same period Hanoi's communist party chief, Do Muoi, had traveled to Malaysia, Singapore,

and Thailand, and Vietnam took an increasingly active role in the United Nations and other international fora. In July 1995 the United States normalized diplomatic relations with Vietnam and opened an embassy in Hanoi.[28] Finally, in September 1995, Vietnam joined the Association of Southeast Asian Nations (ASEAN), an increasingly influential regional organization. At present, the Vietnamese government is aggressively lobbying for membership in the Asia Pacific Economic Cooperation (APEC) forum.

Vietnam has thus successfully compensated for the deterioration of its global socialist family by aggressively pursuing regional ties and vastly increasing diplomatic and economic contact with the West. The new regional support system, in turn, encouraged the regime to establish a different focus, seek new objectives, and expand its markets and trade partners. The rapidly developing Little Tigers of Asia, especially Singapore, Taiwan, and Korea, took tangible initiatives to support their words of counsel. Their companies began to invest heavily, and their public and private sectors promoted the development of the Vietnamese infrastructure.

Cuba, on the other hand, has remained more economically isolated since the Soviet downfall. Cuba has joined CARICOM, the English-speaking Caribbean common market, but has found it of negligible usefulness. While certain neighboring countries have increased trade with Cuba, most possess limited resources and a few of the larger, such as Mexico and Venezuela, are struggling with their own grave economic difficulties. Castro has been encouraged by some Canadian and European investments, yet Cuba's large neighbors seem unable or unwilling to provide much support. Although efforts to integrate economies in Central America have repeatedly occurred, none has yet achieved the noteworthy successes of ASEAN. And, given the hostile relations between the United States and Cuba, Cuban membership in the North American Free Trade Agreement is certainly not forthcoming. Thus, in

27. Neil L. Jamieson, *Understanding Vietnam* (Berkeley: University of California Press, 1993), pp. 15-24.
28. See *New York Times* (July 11, 1995), p. 1A; *Washington Post* (July 12, 1995), p. 1A.

contrast to Vietnam, no unified neighboring family of states has reached out to offer Cuba a new identity and purpose in the post-Cold War era.

Given Castro's inability to generate stronger regional ties, he has shifted his attention to the global stage. Last year Castro traveled as widely as ever before. He visited China, Japan, and Vietnam, the Caribbean and Latin America, and Europe and the United Nations. Other high-level Cuban officials, including Foreign Minister Roberto Robaina and Francisco Soberón, president of the Central Bank, have logged significant air time. This diplomatic offensive aims to ward off isolation by finding new friends abroad and cultivating a few old ties.[29] Despite these efforts, to date, the Castro regime has failed to replace the Soviet bloc with new trading partners. In fact, Cuba has few exports that other countries covet and little hard currency with which to buy the items it needs or wants. Thus, although Japan and a few European and African countries have slightly increased trade with the Castro regime, overall Cuba has not been able to find new partners or generate new regional or global markets to compensate for the loss of Soviet aid. Consequently, the island has witnessed a 73 percent drop in overall trade during the 1990s—a development in stark contrast to that in Vietnam.[30]

THE DEGREE OF COMMITMENT TO LONG-TERM ECONOMIC REFORM

Vietnam's commitment to promote economic change and development runs deep. Several pieces of evidence build a case that Vietnam will continue and possibly further accelerate its efforts toward market transformation. First, ASEAN and APEC provide powerful incentives to the Vietnamese leadership to continue the reform process. Nurturing the support of ASEAN has, after all, long been a centerpiece of Vietnam's strategy for weaning itself of dependence

on the Soviet Union and balancing the power of China, which despite its ideology is viewed as Vietnam's chief national security threat. ASEAN members have clearly stated that they intend to hold Vietnam to its commitments to reduce tariffs by the year 2006 and to carry through with its economic opening. Given the controversy surrounding Vietnam's membership in the organization, the member states will likely require full compliance. If Vietnam is going to "mobilize the foreign and domestic capital it needs in order to meet its ASEAN commitments, it will have to reform much more," explained a foreign economist.[31]

Likewise, Vietnam has applied for membership in the APEC forum. The APEC agenda chiefly promotes liberalizing trade and investment. APEC members have not yet decided whether to approve Vietnam's membership. Unquestionably, Vietnam's performance over the next year will significantly influence the decision. It seems clear that Vietnam will be expected to press on with considerably more trade liberalization if it is to gain membership in APEC.[32]

Since Vietnam desperately wants to be a respected member of both organizations, ASEAN and APEC requirements create weighty disincentives to the Vietnamese regime to retreat from, or even slow, the reform process. Rather, the momentum to continue to open up will be difficult to resist. And, current members will press Hanoi to make sacrifices that the regime has thus far been able to avoid.

Whether the government will move toward a greater opening in order to gain and preserve these regional memberships likely depends on the extent to which economic reforms are seen as weakening party control. However, some evidence suggests that, when pressed, the Vietnamese leadership will make the necessary changes.

29. *Financial Times* (January 4, 1996).

30. See Mark Falcoff, "Cuba's International Relations," in *Cuba in Crisis* (Washington: Cuban American National Foundation, 1993), pp. 49-55. See also Ariel Terrero, "Tendencias de un ajuste," *Bohemia* (October 28, 1994).

31. "There is genuine concern within ASEAN," an official in the ASEAN secretariat stated in June 1996. "Our interactions with the Vietnamese tell us that the policies of freer market access will remain in force. It is implementation of policies which will be critical and which concerns us most." *AsiaWeek* (June 28, 1996), p. 29. See also *Far Eastern Economic Review* (July 11, 1996), p. 16

32. *Foreign Broadcast Information Service* (FBIS) (June 28, 1996).

Perhaps more important, developing and earning the respect and friendship of neighbors is of profound important among Asian states. The identity of Asian regimes is perhaps more group-oriented than that of the regimes of other regions. Leaders of Asian states tend to measure their own performance against that of their neighbors. A regional leader tends to view his or her country's domestic economic growth as bolstering the regional community as a whole and as a sign of the individual leader's intelligence, prudence, and wisdom. High performers earn regional respect; low performers are scorned. The Vietnamese government, reflective of traditional Asian culture, apparently believes that some measure of self respect depends upon respect by the surrounding community. The Vietnamese have signaled that nurturing a positive identity within the group is a notable national interest. To keep from being dismissed from the group, which might signify failure of their long standing strategy and cause them to lose face in the region and at home, Vietnam's leaders may be prepared to undertake considerable additional economic reforms.

Cuba's revolutionary leadership has not pursued any comparable overarching goals within the region. Castro has been intent on garnering international publicity and ensuring regime survival, but his heart has never been in development. The regime has done and continues to do what it must to survive. Even while the Cubans enjoyed from $6 billion to $8 billion annually from Moscow, the leadership squandered the aid and failed to invest it wisely. As one observer recently wrote, "One has only to imagine what the Singaporean leader Lee Kuan Yew or the military bosses of South Korea, Taiwan or Thailand would have done with 25 years of subsidies on the order of those the Soviet Union funneled to Castro to appreciate how badly the regime has bungled the economy."[33]

Perhaps on account of the lack of official commitment, the economic record of revolutionary Cuba appears ever more dismal. Since the early 1990s, the Cuban regime has met with very little success beyond survival. Although dollar remittances from overseas Cubans and foreign investment have brought some relief over the past three years, both have subsided since February when Cuban MiGs shot down two unarmed private American Cessnas over international waters.

Meanwhile, the Castro regime has failed to present any real and enduring solutions for the island's economic problems. Even relatively progressive moves, like opening farmers markets and attracting foreign investment, have been hedged about with debilitating restrictions. Foreign investors must operate through the state. Farmers must still sell approximately 80 percent of their crop at government rates well below market prices. Indeed, the regime seems to have relied upon a series of failed initiatives: tourism, mining, and a focus on the sugar industry. As one observer recently wrote, "if these can be said to offer hope, it is only in the sense that they have offered hope to Jamaica or the Dominican Republic, still chronically impoverished after decades of trying these remedies."[34]

Recently the Cubans have boasted that the economy has weathered the storm and that increased tourism coupled with a booming sugar harvest and higher petroleum and nickel production will markedly raise living standards this year.[35] Yet this optimistic rhetoric is eerily reminiscent of the mistakes and misjudgments of previous economic policies. In the catastrophic sugar campaign of 1970 the leadership mobilized the entire country and targeted all resources on this one symbolic goal. While the Cubans reached their 10-million-ton goal, they did so at the expense of virtually all other sectors. The effort left the economy in shambles.

---

33. Rieff, p. 69.
34. Rieff, p. 67.
35. Rieff, p. 70.

This year the Cubans have borrowed $300 million in short-term loans to buy equipment and fuel to run the tractors and sugar refineries. To obtain these loans, the government is paying interest rates estimated at between 14 and 20 percent. Even if the government reaches the 4.5 million-ton goal, the interest payments alone are likely to negate the benefit from increased sugar sales. Moreover, this year's harvest lasted months beyond the average, which suggests to some that the harvest has cut dangerously into next year's crop.[36] And, while the regime has targeted sugar, tourism, and nickel production, other ignored sectors may well be deteriorating rapidly.

In Cuba, while progressives have met with some success in advancing a reform agenda, the Castro leadership has refused to remain consistent. The regime initiates reforms, the economic crisis eases up a bit, and the regime retreats. Achievements, such as Castro's public-relations success in New York or growing foreign-investor interest, are viewed as signs that fur-

ther reforms are not required. A foreign diplomat recently commented that the Castro government is "once again acting in a triumphalist manner."[37] A *New York Times* article stated that Cuban leaders "seem to be drawing the wrong lesson from what has happened. Instead of looking on the promising results they have obtained thus far as a signal to press on even further, they appear to be telling themselves that they have now done all they need to get by."[38] Once again, in marked contrast to the goals of Vietnamese leaders, simply surviving appears to be the chief objective of the Cuban regime.

In conclusion, while Cuba and Vietnam have faced comparable post-Cold War challenges, Vietnam has fared considerably better than has Cuba. The seven factors assessed above not only help us to explain Vietnam's relative success thus far, but suggest the measures Cuba must take in order to achieve comparable development.

---

36. Rieff, pp. 69-70.

37. Edward Gonzalez, *Cuba: Clearing Perilous Waters?* (Santa Monica: RAND, 1996), p. 83.

38. Gonzalez, p. 84; taken from *New York Times* (November 19, 1995), p. 3.

COMPARISON OF INTERNATIONAL MONETARY FUND AND WORLD BANK CONDITIONALITIES AND CUBA'S ECONOMIC REFORMS OF THE 1990S

Ramón C. Barquín III

The economic reforms that have been implemented in Cuba in recent years bear similarities to the structural adjustment programs of the International Monetary Fund (IMF) and the World Bank (WB). Pressured by the economic crisis of the early 1990s, the Cuban government has moved toward deregulation of foreign investment and partial privatization of state enterprises through joint ventures in some sectors of the economy. This paper compares the measures taken by the Cuban government and the traditional IMF and WB conditionalities and attempts to forecast the possible performance of the new—if it can be considered new—Cuban economic system.

IMF AND WB CONDITIONALITIES

Structural adjustment loans made by the IMF and the WB to member countries are predicated on the adoption by the recipient country of certain policies, generally known as conditionality. Generally, IMF and WB officials advise governments to cut budget deficits by reducing government expenditure and to implement orthodox structural adjustment programs to stabilize the economy and control inflation (Cardoso and Helwege 1995, p. 173). According to the orthodox view, economic stabilization and control of inflation is achieved by reducing government subsidies, bureaucracy, and by privatizing state enterprises.

In addition, following the orthodox view, officials from the IMF and WB recommend an increase in interest rates, a liberalization of imports and currency exchange controls, an elimination of price regulation, and a devaluation of the national currency in order to stabilize the economy. Furthermore, these officials suggest a restructuring of the tax system in order to increase taxes, and as a result, increase government income. As will be discussed below, many of these same policies have been recently implemented in Cuba, with others soon to follow.

In line with structural adjustment programs similar to the ones recommended by the IMF and WB to third world countries like Chile, Bolivia, Brazil, Peru and Ghana, the Castro regime has decreased government subsidies, stimulated exports, indirectly pushed import substitution, increased taxes on cigarettes and rum, increased admission fees to sports and cultural events and established currency exchange houses (for the first time in thirty six years), presumably in an attempt to control inflation and advance economic growth by curtailing the money supply and increasing the government's revenue.

The bulk of these changes, however, seem to be directed towards the goal of gaining admission into the IMF and WB. Admission into these international monetary institutions would provide the Cuban government with economic financing and aid, thus, extending the life of the Castro regime.

Furthermore, the dilemma is that Cuban laws are only on paper, since in actuality almost everything depends on the will of Fidel Castro. There is little due process in Cuba; it is not a country of laws.

Therefore, the structural adjustment programs that are trying to be implemented in Cuba are an illusion, since the obsession of Fidel Castro against profit, capitalism and the "Yanquis," would never allow a full free market economy. However, it is possible that the half-hearted economic reforms implemented by the government might nevertheless unleash a real economic liberalization process that escapes the control of the government.

All in all, however, the Cuban government is also developing its own structural adjustment program and economic model by combining it with orthodox and neoconservative approaches to stabilization. Still, this "cubano" structural adjustment program appears to be an attempt by the Castro government to portray the island as an open economy and prolong its control over the people.

EARLY REFORMS

Foreign Investment

The first measure implemented was in 1991 after the Fourth Cuban Communist Party Congress. At that time, the Cuban government amended the Law-Decree 50 of 1982 (the Foreign Investment Law) in order to attract foreign investment (Barquín 1995a, p. 11). The Cuban government needed to attract foreign investment, since the island's economic activity decreased by more than 50 percent after the elimination of Soviet subsidies connected to the disappearance of the Council of Mutual Economic Assistance and the Soviet Union.

In September 1995, the investment law was amended again, allowing 100 percent foreign ownership of enterprises and further liberalizing the export economy in an attempt to stimulate investment and enhance the faith of foreigners in the economic reform process. Supposedly the new investment law reduced the bureaucratic "red tape" in the approval and licensing process of foreign investment and allowed foreigners for the first time in the Island's communist government to engage in real estate transactions. However, the deregulation and stimulus of foreign investment has been small, since government licensing and approval of foreign investment and joint ventures is highly regulated. Furthermore, decision-making and oversight is exercised by the Executive

Committee of the Council of Ministries, or by the Council itself. Thus, a decrease in the decision-making bureaucracy has not been significant.

Nevertheless, foreign investment has increased rapidly. Between 1989 and 1996 it has more than doubled. The Cuban government reports that foreign investment has surpassed $2.1 billion. However, according to Gareth Jenkins, president of the consulting company, Cuba Business Ltd., and publisher of *Cuba Business*, less than 25 percent of the reported foreign investment has been delivered. Yet, economic activity between Cuba and members of the international community is continuously increasing.

The exemption of foreign and joint venture enterprises from tariffs, duties, and prior government approval on imports and exports, the flexible policy on taxes—except for social security—and the authorization to do business in hard currency, are supposed to be incentives for foreigners to invest in Cuba. Therefore, at the present large corporations are heavily investing and establishing joint ventures in the island. These foreign investors include (US-Cuba Trade and Economic Council 1995c):

- Canadian Sherritt and MacDonald Mines corporations (Investment: Mining and Tourism);

- Japan's Mitsubishi and Suzuki Motor Corp. (Investment: Automotive, Tourism) and Komatsu (Investment: Industry-Heavy Machinery);

- Germany's Mercedes Benz (Investment: Industry-Heavy Machinery);

- United Kingdom's Castrol (Investment: Oil) and Unilever (Investment: Soap, Detergent);

- South Africa's Anglo-American Corporation and AMSA (Investment: Mining);

- Venezuela's Cervecera Nacional (Investment: Beer) and Gibraltar Trading Corporation (Investment: Steel);

- Mexico's Pemex (Investment: Oil) and Grupo Domos (Investment: Communications);

- Brazil's Petrobras S.A. (Investment: Oil);

- France's Total Corporation (Investment: Oil);

- Israel's World Textile Corp. S.A. (Investment: Textile and GBM (Investment: Citrus);

- Italy's Benetton (Investment: Textile), Spain's Grupo Hotelero Sol and Guitart Hotels S.A. (Investment: Tourism); and

- Australia's Western Mining Corp. (Investment: Mining).

Furthermore, an increasing number of foreign businesses, including large corporations in the United States, are anxious to invest in Cuba once the U.S. embargo is lifted.

Recently, the Helms-Burton Act was signed by the president of the United States. Consequently, a temporary decrease in the flow of foreign investment into the island as a result of the strengthening of the U.S. embargo will occur. Canadian, Spanish, Mexican, Israeli, Chilean, Italian and French companies will think twice before investing in Cuba, when they take into consideration the stress that would be imposed on their economic and political relationship with the United States.

Furthermore, even after the law is challenged in the International Court of Justice, North American Free Trade Agreement, and the World Trade Organization, it will take months and perhaps years until the cases are settled in the United States legal and political institutions. Therefore, some foreign investors in Cuba will exit the island to prevent an economic or legal confrontation with the United States. Others, however, will counter-attack the Helms-Burton law with similar policies towards the United States.

Meanwhile, the similarities between the IMF and WB economic policies for economic development and the Cuban economic reforms increase. Traditional IMF recommendations consist of political and economic reforms geared towards a reduction in the size of the government and a stabilization of the balance of payments through the promotion of exports and foreign investment (Cardoso and Helwege 1995, p. 176). Today, according to Cuban government sources (US-Cuba Trade Council 1995b, p. 4), more than 600 foreign businesses are represented in Cuba, approximately 4,000 non-United States companies

are involved in economic transactions with the island (US-Cuba Trade Council 1995b, p. 1), and over 230 have established joint-ventures (Pérez-López 1995b). Foreign investment in Cuba as of May 1995 was reported at $2.1 billion, joint-ventures being the most common form of investment (Pérez-López 1995b, p. 5). According to the US Cuba Trade and Economic Council (1995b), "the Republic of Cuba maintains commercial dealings with over 4,000 foreign businesses in more than 80 countries," and "total announced intended foreign investment exceeds $4 billion by more than 100 businesses from 30 countries." Even though the above figures are debatable, it has been a good first step towards a real economic liberalization. Still, these figures are insignificant if we compare them with foreign investment in Colombia, Venezuela, Chile, Argentina, Panama, Costa Rica and even the Dominican Republic.

Stimulus of Private Enterprise

The stimulus to productivity and private enterprises has been pursued by the deregulation of foreign investment activity and the passage of law decrees aimed at increasing food availability and self sufficiency through sustainable development.

In September 1992, Law-Decree 141 decriminalized some forms of self-employment and small, family operated private enterprises, in an attempt to reduce the unemployment produced by the decrease of activity in the state-controlled sectors of the economy and increase the availability of goods and services that the government is not able to provide efficiently. In addition, the government could generate revenue by taxing the self-employed and reduce its expenditure by decreasing subsidies to agriculture, sports events, and unemployment compensation.

But, self-employment is still tightly controlled by the state bureaucracy; which prevents students, professionals, and individuals classified as "essential" from being self-employed. This excessive regulation has induced an increase in the second economy and loss of government income through taxation. Today Cuba has more than 200,000 licensed self-employed, in comparison to 28,600 in 1989 (Rodríguez 1995), and between 1.5 to 2 million unofficial self-employed in the second economy (Mesa-Lago 1995, p. 34).

Privatization

Some early forms of privatization have occurred either through foreign enterprises, joint ventures or cooperatives. After the initial round of reforms in 1992, the government transformed most of the managed and state owned agriculture sector into cooperatives (Unidades Básicas de Producción Cooperativa). The ownership is passed to the farmers, who are allowed to keep or sell excess production beyond state production quotas. Not only is this supposed to increase food supply, but should help reduce the budget by eliminating government subsidies to the agricultural sector. Furthermore, it stimulates domestic production to improve import substitution, while creating the necessary conditions to potentially increase the exports of some products. This exchange of "ownership" could be considered a form of Orthodox style privatization.

Stabilization

To date, the elimination of price controls has been minute. Most of the economic activity is controlled by the state. Perhaps, the only area where prices are decided by the interaction of supply and demand is in the special sites of farmers and artisans markets, where some products (after production quotas have been met) are allowed to be sold at unregulated prices. However, the government still maintains a strong oversight on the operation of these markets, since price caps have been established in an attempt to prevent excessive accumulation of capital and emergence of "capitalistas."

Neoconservative policies recommend market liberalization, fixed exchange rates, free entry and exit of capital into the economy, prices reflecting costs, freely determined interest rates, and an elimination of control over the allocation of credit (Cardoso and Helwege 1995, p. 180). These policies became popular during the 1970s in the authoritarian regimes of Argentina, Chile, and Uruguay. These countries lowered wages, eliminated export taxes, decreased trade barriers, decreased government subsidies, engaged in wide-scale privatization, and restricted labor unions.

Today, similar measures are being applied in Cuba. For example, unionization of labor and collective bargaining—since the late 1960s—is severely limited in Cuba as it was in Chile, Argentina and Uruguay. Pursuant to the September 1995 Foreign Investment Law, Cuban employees in the hard currency sector (tourism, joint ventures) are employed through a Cuban agency that receives the pay in hard currency and in turn pays them lower wages in national currency (Gaceta Oficial 1995). In addition, a decrease in government subsidies to its bureaucracy has been attempted; sixteen ministries were eliminated and restructured into six new ministries; reducing the number of employees from 12,879 to 8,228 (Quijano 1995).

The Cuban government, as in Argentina, Chile, and Uruguay twenty years earlier, has decreased subsidies in attempts to decrease the government budget and increase its income. For example, according to a report in *Cuba News* in September 1995 from the Vice Minister of Agriculture, Eduardo Chao, subsidies to agriculture decreased from 370 million pesos in 1994 to 57 million in the first six months of 1995 ("Agriculture" 1995). Furthermore, he said that "the ultimate goal is to eliminate agricultural subsidies altogether" ("Agriculture" 1995). The difference between Cuba and the above mentioned Latin American countries is that the decrease in subsidies was partially achieved through privatization, something that has not occurred in Cuba.

Traditional subsidies of tobacco, rum, beer, gasoline, and communications were reduced by increasing their prices (Quijano 1995). Fees charged for utilities and transportation have also increased since October, 1994 (Quijano 1995). Through these actions the government has managed to decrease the budget deficit. However, we should not base this result on a comparison between the 1993 and 1996 budget deficits, since 1993 was not a normal year for the Cuban economy.

There has been a reallocation of government resources from idle and inefficient enterprises to tourism, mining, and oil exploration. Since the tourism and mining industries have increased dramatically their share of the gross domestic product in recent years, and their ability to generate hard currency and high and quick rate of return on investment makes them desirable, the government has decreased subsidies in manufacture and agriculture transferring resources to the dollar economy infrastructure. Consequently, the government is improving its allocation of resources, pressured by market mechanisms.

Similar to the three South American countries mentioned above, privatization was pursued in Cuba to a lesser degree. Presently, many formerly state owned enterprises in Cuba have been transformed either into joint ventures or cooperatives, which are still controlled by the government. However, under the September 1995 Foreign Investment Law, quasi-governmental, foreign and joint-venture enterprises have freedom to export and import; which to some academics is a an example of the economic liberalization process that is emerging in the island. Therefore, foreign trade has been significantly deregulated with the decrease in export and import tariffs, and the creation of industrial parks and free trade zones (FTZ) as of mid-1996.

SECOND ROUND OF REFORMS
Exchange Rate

While orthodox policies rest on the belief that less government involvement in the economy is better, heterodox policies take the view that government intervention is necessary to control inflation and "to settle the struggle between workers and firms over relative shares of national income" (Cardoso and Helwege 1995, p. 188). Heterodox and neoconservative policies attempt to stabilize and restructure the economy not only through market liberalization, but by fixing the exchange rate. On August 13, 1993, the Cuban government legalized the use and possession of hard currency and allowed Cubans to open savings and bank accounts at market interest rates between 1 to 4 percent ("Budget Deficit" 1995). The exchange rate was fixed at one peso equal to one dollar. The government also slightly liberalized interest rates and monetary transactions from its control. These measures led to a "dollarization" of the Cuban economy, and inflation rose instead of being controlled through the capture of excess national currency in circulation. According to Hiram Marquetti Nodarse,

from the Center for the Study of the Cuban Economy in Cuba, "the dollar market represents more than $400 million per annum."

Consequently, the Cuban government enacted a second round of economic reforms aimed at reducing inflation and stimulating economic growth. Farmers markets were created, where products could be sold after meeting the state production quota and prices are regulated by supply and demand. Also, *paladares* (small, family owned restaurants) were legalized again under strict government licensing and taxation (Pérez-López 1995a). Through the creation of farmer and artisan markets, the legalization of *paladares* and an increase in the allowed number of small enterprises and self-employed, the government seeks to reduce the scarcity of food and to capture the hard currency in circulation. Since the government taxes and charges licensing fees to the self-employed (including operators of *paladares*), individual farmers, artisans, and small entrepreneurs, excess national currency in circulation has been reduced ("Excess Liquidity" 1995). Thus, inflation has decreased and the peso has been strengthened, with a current value in the black market of 25 to 30 pesos to the dollar. Still, some academics in the field believe that a behind the scenes influx of dollars prompted by the government enabled these changes to take place. In addition, there are many complaints about how excess taxation is hurting *paladares*, farmers and artisans.

According to Cardoso and Helwege (1995, p. 189), during the mid-1980s programs like the Cruzado Plan (1986) in Brazil, the Austral (1985) in Argentina, and the Inti Plan (1985) in Peru, established "new currency emissions as a symbol of policy change and to fight the expectation of inflation." Today Cuba has done something comparable by creating the "convertible peso" and establishing currency exchange houses as part of a larger financial and banking reform at the end of October, under the name of Casas de Cambio S.A. ("Exchange Houses" 1995). The official exchange rate was established at 25 to 30 pesos to the dollar. In the black market the peso has maintained value of 25 pesos to the dollar since September 1995, "following the sudden strengthening of the peso prompted by the unexplained availability of dollars in the black market" ("Exchange Houses" 1995). However, according to Francisco Soberón, president of the National Bank of Cuba, "the official rate of one peso to the dollar will continue to exist for international trade, government to government operations and other bookkeeping purposes" ("Exchange Houses" 1995). The Cuban government seems not too supportive about the idea of devaluating the national currency ("Budget Deficit" 1995).

Taxation

The Cuban government has increased taxes and in June 1995, established an agency to collect tax revenue similar to the Internal Revenue Service, the Oficina Nacional de Administración Tributaria (National Office for Tax Administration). These reforms have been in line with traditional IMF and WB adjustment programs in Third World countries.

In August 1995, a new income tax law was approved, imposing income taxes on all hard currency earners (10 - 50 percent) beginning on January 1, 1996. In addition, the Ministry of Finance and Prices has said that the establishment of a "progressive peso income tax on the self-employed would be announced before the end of 1996" (US-Cuba Trade Council 1995a, p. 3). Cubans already pay admissions fees to sport events, cultural activities, transportation, and recreational activities, activities which used to be free to consumers as they were subsidized by the state. Additionally, corporate taxes were implemented throughout 1995: 14 percent tax on employers for social security, 25 percent tax on gross payroll, 35 percent on foreign companies (Quijano 1995). Furthermore, there is a present debate on the creation of a sales tax (Quijano 1995).

The increase in taxes and the creation of a national tax agency not only will increase government income by collecting hard currency, reduce the excess of pesos in circulation, and help decrease the government deficit, but the tax should also aid in controlling inflation in order to stimulate economic growth. On the other hand, if the increase in taxes is directed towards the self-employed, as it seems to be, then the emerging and struggling "working" and entrepreneurial sectors of the population could be severely harmed.

Import Substitution

Other structural adjustment policies implemented by the Cuban government to cope with the economic depression of the 1990s are either original or have been used before with some success. Import substitution, a by-product of the lack of imports and necessary input during the present economic crisis, promoted the use of alternate fuel resources, the use of oxen to replace tractors in agriculture, and the use of bio-agriculture. Import substitution rapidly increased in every day activities from cooking to personal hygiene. For example, many Cubans citizens began to marinate and cook grapefruit peel as a substitute to beefsteak, and to raise pigs, chicken, cattle, goats, rabbits and other animals for consumption.

While this may be good for the environment, the import substitution "a la cubana," however, is perhaps the saddest outcome of the Castro regime. An island that pre-1958 enjoyed one of the highest standards of living in the developing world is now suffering badly for lack of food production. The island's per capita daily food consumption before the Revolution surpassed 2,680 calories per person, third place in Latin America and only preceded by Argentina and Uruguay (Molina 1995, p. 259).

Although positive in terms of reducing imports, stimulating self sufficiency instead of state and foreign dependency, and even improving the environment in some areas, this awkward import substitution as positive as some academics have, it has created serious problems like the misuse of natural resources. With the reduction of fuel imports by 60 percent (Rivero 1994), Cubans increasingly turned to wood as cooking fuel. As a result, many trees have been cut and deforestation has significantly increased. Deforestation not only destroys the ecological environment and increases global warming, but it prevents the trees from holding part of the rain which now falls completely into the ground inducing floods and decreasing soil fertility.

This "cubano" style import substitution, has stimulated the use of alternate fuel resources produced with cattle and agriculture manure (bio gas), alcohol produced from sugar cane, and solar and hydroelectric energy production (Barquín 1995a). Still, how positive is this outcome for an island that pre-1958 enjoyed abundance of imported oil to produce energy?

CONCLUSION

Even though the economic picture that the Cuban government conveys may be brighter than reality, Cuba may have started a process of economic reform and recuperation.

- According to Vice President Carlos Lage, the economy grew by 0.7 percent in 1994 and over 2.5 percent in 1995. Further, according to National Bank of Cuba's President Francisco Soberón, the economic growth for 1996 should surpass 7 percent (US-Cuba Trade Council 1995a, p. 3).

- International reserves have increased by more than 50 percent since 1992; and the fiscal deficit has been reduced from 5 billion pesos in 1993 to 1.4 billion in 1994—a reduction of more than 60 percent, to 5 percent of the Gross Domestic Product (GDP), compared to 33 percent a year earlier ("Economic Indicators" 1995).

- According to Foreign Trade Minister Ricardo Cabrisas, exports increased by 18 percent in 1994 ("International Trade" 1995).

- Industrial production has slightly increased and import substitution has been successful in some areas. Tariffs have been reduced in trading activities conducted by quasi-government agencies, joint-ventures and private foreign enterprises.

- Production in the agriculture, mining, tobacco, and sugar industries has increased; and tourism has experienced significant growth in the last five years ("Economic Indicators" 1995).

Perhaps the most important trend is the aggressive encouragement of trade in the export economy and entry of capital through foreign investment. However, the changes in the rigid control on interest rates and capital markets has been minimal, domestic investment is restricted, and further liberalization of trade is needed. Hence, more economic reforms are needed; but they need to be implemented gradually in order to prevent the collapse of the government during the restructuring process.

According to Cardoso and Helwege (1995, p. 177), the implementation of economic stabilization programs can be more successful in authoritarian regimes, because of their tight control on domestic policies. Based on their recommendations for structural reform and stabilization (Cardoso and Helwege 1995, p. 200), the Cuban government should move towards a "gradual stabilization, more realistic exchange rates, and promote export production and import substitution (in industry and agriculture)." These are the policies that the Cuban government has pursued in recent years.

The Cuban government has been implementing orthodox structural adjustment programs *a lá* IMF and WB which attempt to improve the economic indicators and reestablish the balance of payments to service the foreign debt. By servicing the foreign debt the Cuban government would attempt to gain some credibility with the IMF, WB, the Inter-American Development Bank, the Club of Paris and the London Club, institutions that could assist Cuba in its reform process. Furthermore, smaller banks and individual creditors would increase their activities in the island once the IMF and WB were involved in Cuba, increasing the availability of financial resources to the Cuban economy. Admission into the IMF and WB may be the objective of the soft line on economic reform and hard line on politics that the Cuban government has adopted.

BIBLIOGRAPHY

"Agriculture Subsidy Declines." *Cuba News* (September 1995), p. 4.

Barquín, Ramón C., III. "La capitalización de Cuba," paper presented for LAS-100 Seminar on Cuba, Brandeis University, Spring 1995a

Barquín, Ramón C., III. "Cuba Today: The Economic Development of Cuba ... But Preserving the Environment," research paper presented at an independent study course under the Latin American Studies Department, Brandeis University, Fall 1995b.

"Budget Deficit Cut More than 70%," *Financial Times* (September 26, 1995).

"Calculan en $6 mil millones el comercio con EE.UU.," *Diario las Américas* (September 13, 1995), p. 1-A.

Cardoso, Eliana, and Helwege, Ann. *Latin America's Economy: Diversity, Trends, and Conflicts.* Cambridge: The MIT Press, 1995.

"Cuba I, II, III, IV," *Financial Times* (September 26, 1995).

Cuba Info, Vol. 7, No. 15 (November 30, 1995).

De Córdoba, José. "Cuba's Business Law Puts Off Foreigners," *The Wall Street Journal* (October 10, 1995), p. A16.

"Economic Indicators." *Cuba News* (February 1995), p. 2.

"Excess Liquidity Reduced." *Cuba News* (November 1995), p. 3.

"Exchange Houses Open in Havana and Varadero." *Cuba News* (November 1995), p. 3.

Gaceta Oficial de la Republica de Cuba (September 6, 1995).

Halebsky, Sandor, and Harris, Richard L. *Capital, Power, and Inequality in Latin America.* Boulder: Westview Press, 1995.

Inter-American Dialogue. *The Environment in US-Cuban Relations: Opportunities for Cooperation.* Washington, DC: Inter-American Dialogue, April 1995.

"International Trade: 1994 Exports Grew." *Cuba News* (October 1995), p. 4.

Mesa-Lago, Carmelo. *Are Economic Reforms Propelling Cuba to the Market?* Coral Gables: North-South Center, University of Miami, 1995a.

Mesa-Lago, Carmelo. "Mountain of Foreign Debt Keeps Lenders Away," *Cuba News* (September 1995b), p. 2.

Molina, Antonio J. *Curiosidades Históricas.* Hato Rey, Puerto Rico: Ramallo Bros. Printing, Inc., 1995.

Pérez-López, Jorge F. "Coveting Beijing, But Imitating Moscow: Cuba's Economic Reforms In A Comparative Perspective." In *Cuba in Transition—Volume 5.* Washington: Association for the Study of the Cuban Economy, 1995.

Pérez-López, Jorge F. "A Critical Look At Cuba's Foreign Investment Program." Paper presented at the 1995 Meeting in Latin American Studies Association, Washington, September 28-30, 1995.

Quijano, Carlos. "Vietnam v. Cuba: Institutional and Legal Reforms; Structural and Macro-economic Policies," August 3, 1995.

Rivero, Nicolás. "Later Phases of the Transition: Reactivation of Production and Distribution," paper presented at the conference Strategies for the First Year of Cuba's Transition, January 27, 1994.

Rodríguez, Magdaly. "Subsistencia a base de ingenio y malicia," *El Nuevo Día* (November 22, 1995).

"Sign of the Times:Tax Office Opens." *Cuba News* (August 1995), p. 3.

Travieso-Díaz, Matías F. "Cuba's Sham Investment Law," *The Journal of Commerce* (October 25, 1995).

US.-Cuba Trade and Economic Council, Inc. "Economic Eye On Cuba." New York, November 20-26, 1995a.

US.-Cuba Trade and Economic Council, Inc. "Realities of 'Market Cuba.'" New York, 1995b.

US.-Cuba Trade and Economic Council, Inc. "Non-United States Companies and the Republic of Cuba." New York, 1995c.

THE 1995-1996 SUGAR ZAFRA:
RESULTS AND IMPLICATIONS—THE MACHINERY SECTOR

Alfredo Blanco, Jr.

Sugar production in Cuba during the 20th century has never been curtailed by the installed industrial capacity. It is easy to increase the cane grinding rate on a short notice in such a manner as to process any expansion of the cane supply within the normal harvesting season. The communist government was fortunate the mills it seized had an industrial capacity to crush all the cane it has made available up to the present date. In contrast, augmenting cane quantity takes years from planting to harvesting, with weather vagaries ever present.

In certain years, for example in 1930-40 and 1953-60, international marketing agreements set export quotas for Cuban sugar. After 1960, the Communist regime pulled out from, or discarded, quota pacts and Cuba has been producing sugar freely, limited only by the available cane.

We estimate that in Cuba—before Castro—the cost of growing and delivering cane to the mill amounted to 58% of the total sugar production cost, whereas the processing of cane into sugar by the mill represented 27%, for a ratio of 2.14 (58/27).[1] Thus cane cost within the total production cost carries a heavier weight than the industrial cost.

Furthermore, the mill processing cost among countries shows a small deviation from the international average cost, a consequence of the machinery being very much alike in all countries. On the other hand, the cane cost is subject to wide swings throughout

the various nations, the upshot of the diverse characteristics of soils, climate and labor.

It can be concluded that:

- The cost of the raw material—cane—is the most important component of the cost of production of sugar in Cuba. Also, it determines the competitiveness in the international export market due to its variation among countries

- Sugar output in Cuba is limited by the cane supply under current conditions inasmuch as the crushing capacity of the mills greatly exceeds the available cane.

We raise these points because customarily most of the attention of seminars is devoted to the factory equipment, perhaps because it is easier to deal with machinery than with agriculture with its myriad facets and uncertainties.

MANAGEMENT'S GOALS IN THE SUGAR INDUSTRY OF CUBA

The prime objective of Cuba's communist government is to stay in power, regardless of consequences. Accordingly, every aspect of the governmental structure and its derivatives, like the sugar industry, has been designed to keep absolute control of all activities in the hands of Communist Party members.

The top executive in every mill is the Communist Party Secretary of the Mill Nucleus. All projects and

---

1. Alfredo Blanco, Jr., "Financial Projection of the 1994 Sugar Crop of Cuba," unpublished manuscript, 1993.

decisions must be cleared with him. He has authority to overrule technicians in every matter including technical advice. His superior is the Communist Party Secretary of the Region.

Technical positions (Chief Engineer, Fabrication Chief, Laboratory Chief) are filled with technically unqualified personnel, often without degrees or training, based on political merits or connections, rather than competence. For example:

- In 1993, Juan Herrera, an engineer and a competent sugar technologist, was replaced as Minister of the Sugar Industry by Nelson Torres, a civil engineer, chief of the Communist Party of the Province of Cienfuegos, with no sugar experience.

- In 1985, in the Province of Matanzas, not a single one of its 21 mills had an experienced, qualified Chief Engineer. All individuals filling this position had been recently drawn from lathe operators, mechanics, welders, etc.

- No renowned Cuban sugar technologist has been produced by the communist regime. Ironically, a surplus of engineers is available, but they do not actively participate in mill operations, as we will explain below.

The pernicious effects of the communist system on the functioning of the sugar industry and its workers in Cuba will be pointed out in the course of this report.

PERFORMANCE OF THE INDUSTRIAL SECTOR OF THE SUGAR INDUSTRY
Sources of Information
Our data on the industrial sector comes mostly from Cuban technicians who have worked in high positions in the industry, some of them of recent arrival in Miami. Their information is much better, in greater detail, than the news reaching us through the media. Their names have been omitted in this report in order to avoid reprisals to their relatives in Cuba.

The latest statistics published by the Cuban Government on the sugar industry pertained to the 1988-89 crop. Even these were incomplete and of questionable reliability in some cases. Everything in Cuba is subject to unpredictable, whimsical changes that take time to reach us. Thus, some of our data might not be current.

Systems and Patterns in the Industrial Sector
With the onset of communist control in 1961, many new systems and patterns emerged in the industrial sector that seriously impaired its efficiency. Later on, the economic crisis unleashed by the demise in 1990-92 of Communism in Europe and the suspension in 1992 of the subsidy by the Soviet Union to Cuban sugar, forced mills to operate with a reduced budget which translated into smaller cane deliveries. The effect on the performance of the factory may be termed deleterious.

An outline of problems and practices found in the industrial sector in the 1995/96 crop follows.

Cane Crushing: A striking characteristic is the intermittent crushing of all mills, which plays havoc with the entire process of juice extraction and the heat balance of the factory. Insufficient cane delivery is the main cause of interruptions, followed by machinery breakdowns and rains.

Deficient cane deliveries stem from the lack of coordination of cane harvesting and/or transportation from canefield to mill. The cane shortfall may result from insufficient cane ready for harvesting, or cane harvesting machine breakdowns, or a labor shortage. Transportation equipment, nowadays mainly trucks, with their steep depreciation, are prone to be taken out of service on account of breakdowns and lack of spare parts.

Statistics of the vital parameters for assessing the performance of cane grinding (e.g., percent sucrose extraction, cane sucrose, percent sucrose, percent sucrose and moisture of bagasse) have not been published. Needless to say, a mill with frequent stoppages is bound to show a low extraction and outside fuel (Bunker C) will have to be burned for processing the sugar containing products (cane juice, syrup, molasses, massecuites) filling the boiling house (clarifiers, evaporators, syrup and molasses tanks, vacuum pans, crystallizers). Once crushing stops, any stored surplus bagasse will be promptly used up and outside energy will have to be called upon for the quick processing of the sugar containing products in order to avoid their loss through fermentation. The capacity of the transformer substations connecting the public power grid to mills have been increased manifold. Through this channel, outside electric power supplements the energy demand in shutdowns for driving injection and vacuum pumps for condensers, and centrifuges. No precise figures on the energy cost during stoppages are available, but undoubtedly the cost is a high one.

A weird mitigation of the energy shortage occurred at the Vertientes Sugar Mill in 1995. Wagons with stale cane, unsuitable for sugar production, were set aside at a railroad spur. When a large number of wagons had accumulated and the mill shut down in one of its frequent stoppages, the stale cane was discharged in the cane conveyor and crushed as regular cane, the only difference being that the fermented juice thus extracted was discarded down the drain while the mill got the benefit of storing its bagasse for future energy requirements.

Ordinarily the crushing machinery determines the factory capacity. It represents the most expensive industrial department to which the remaining departments (boiling house, boilers, e tc.) must adjust. We estimate the current installed crushing capacity of Cuban mills at 732,410 metric tons of cane per day (MTCD)[2] as compared to 555,821 MTCD in 1952, an increment of 176,589 MTCD or 31.77%. Assuming a sugar 96° polarization yield of 10.59%, the country could make in a normal crop of 132 days (115 days effective, 17 days lost time or 12.88%) some 8,919,655 MT of sugar, 96° polarization. Assuming that the duration of the 1995/96 grinding season spanned 156.5 days, with 35% (54.8 days) lost time while sugar output was reportedly 4.5 million MT, installed capacity was used as follows:

Sugar production	4,455,000 MT
Crop days (assumed)	156.5 days
Lost time (156.5 days X 35%)	54.8 days
Effective days (156.5 - 54.8)	101.71 days

Sugar 96°/Cane yield	10.59%
Estimated sugar production 96° at rated capacity (732,410 MTCD X 101.71 X .1059)	7,888,853 MT
% capacity utilized (1995/96) (4,445,000 / 7,888,853)	56.47%
% idle capacity (100.00 - 56.47)	43.53%

The question arises, how is this 43.53% unused capacity allocated? This matter first came up in the 1992/93 crop, when sugar output plunged to 4,245,716 MT from 7,218,804 MT in the previous year. First, in late April 1993, the government declared that for the 1992/93 campaign, 5 out of the 20 mills in Northern Villaclara Province (25%) had not operated.[3] Extrapolating 25% to the total number of mills in the country (157) yields an estimate of 39 idle mills. This method checked for Matanzas Province; for the rest of the country we could not get the data.

This policy of shutting down mills completely was modified in all subsequent crops by:

- Rotating mill closures: For example, the Cuba Sugar Mill (5,750 MTCD) ground in 1993, and shut down in 1994, while its neighbor Dolores Sugar Mill (2,000 MTCD) shut down in 1993 and ground in 1994.

- Shutting down some mills for extended periods of time: Some mills, after being shut down for 3 years—for example, Mercedes Sugar Mill (4,600 MTCD), Limones Sugar Mill (2,600 MTCD)—were reconditioned with some outside equipment, ground for a few days and were shut down again.

- Multi-tandem mills (2 or 3 tandems) grinding mostly with one tandem. For example, the España Sugar Mill (7,000 MTCD), a two-tandem mill, operating with one tandem since 1991.

- Shortening (or token) grinding of many mills. Many mills operating a few days (5 days, 15 days, etc.).

---

2. Alfredo Blanco, Jr., "Projected Production Capacity of the Cuban Sugar Industry, Year 1993," unpublished manuscript.

3. Pablo Alfonso, "Rains Interrupt Harvest in Las Villas," *El Nuevo Herald* (April 21, 1993).

The conclusion, shared by people from sugar mill localities, is that the regime is frantically trying to keep all mills mobilized for the purpose of its image, offering hope for the future. The government does not want ghost towns.

In view of the acute economic crisis and the surplus capacity available, dismantling and/or cannibalization of existing mills provides a temptation for a quick, albeit irreversible remedy. As far as we know, the government has not, to this date, resorted to said systems in a large scale.

The sugar factories seized by the communist takeover in Cuba comprised the best machinery inventory in the world's sugar industry at the time, notwithstanding statements to the contrary by some experts lacking operational knowledge.[4] No other country could compete with Cuba, in crushing capacity, efficiency and product quality.

After an initial campaign against the sugar industry (1959-60), the regime realized its worth and entered into marketing agreements with the Soviet Union at high prices. Reversing its stand, the government embarked on a modernization and expansion program of the sugar industry. In the Crushing Department, the program translated into:

- Cane preparation prior to grinding: All mills equipped with 2 sets of cane knives.

- Individual power drives (steam turbine or electric motor) in large mills. Replaced steam engines from large mills substituted steam engines in small mills. New steel gears, finished teeth. Power drives (turbines) and gears—mostly Skoda (Czechoslovakia), good quality. Power drives (electric motors)—from Russia. Not sure about the quality.

- Donnelly chute and fourth roller for forced bagasse feeding in a few mills.

- Boilers: All fire tubes replaced by water tubes. A boiler tube plant, straight tubes, 150 p.s.i., built at Sagua la Grande.

- Cane and bagasse conveyors equipped with new, good quality chains.

- Capacity increment over 1952: 32%.

Boiling House (Fabrication Department): Our preceding assertion of the top ranking of the Cuban sugar industry when the Communists confiscated it in 1958 is valid also for the boiling house. The following changes have occurred to the Fabrication Department since 1959:

- Juice heaters, clarifiers, evaporators, vacuum pans, mud filters: Modernization of existing equipment, installation of new equipment for increasing capacity by at least 35% over year 1952 by the addition of new units. Juice heaters, clarifiers, evaporators, vacuum pans, mud filters manufactured locally from imported materials; mud filters manufactured at a foundry in Sagua la Grande.

- Centrifuges (for separation of sugar and molasses) "A" and "B" sugar (batch centrifuges): All belt driven centrifuges replaced by automatic, electrically driven batch centrifuges. Manufacturer: ASEA (Sweden), Silver Brand, excellent quality, comparable to U.S. centrifuges.

- Centrifuges for "C" sugar (low grade sugar): Continuous centrifuges, electrically driven, have displaced the batch centrifuge for "C" sugar. Its power consumption is much lower, needs no labor, cheaper; a continuous centrifuge will perform the task of several batch centrifuges. Installation of continuous centrifuges for "C" sugar in all mills, fully automatic. Manufacturer: foundry at Unión de Reyes from imported materials. Electric motors imported from Poland.

- Entire centrifuge station ("A", "B", "C" sugars) supervised solely by one or two workers per shift, no other workers.

---

4. Alfredo Blanco, Jr., "Economics of the Cuban Sugar Industry and Data on Its Industrial and Agricultural Sectors (for NAFTA Negotiators)," unpublished manuscript, 1993.

- Capacity increment over 1952: 35%.

All mills converted to bulk raw sugar shipments, at mill (handling and warehousing), transportation from mill to port, and vessel loading. Railroad wagons and truck vans for bulk sugar locally built. Sizeable savings in packing (formerly jute bags) and labor at mill and port loading. About 40% of total factory workers eliminated (bag numbering, packers, sewers, cart workers), stevedoring (stacking at warehouse, railroad wagon or truck loading), centrifuge operators. It should be noted, however, that the bloated personnel in other departments more than offset the labor savings of bulk sugar.

No laboratory reports are available regarding the quality of sugar for individual mills or for the entire industry. Said data has been declared confidential by the regime and its disclosure would bring a severe penalty. Thus, we have to glean available production statistics and accounts by technicians from inside Cuba for an assessment of the work of the Boiling House, however unreliable these reports might be.

The missing indicators of Boiling House efficiency include analysis of cane juice entering Boiling House, analysis of sugar produced, analysis of final molasses, and analysis of mud filter cake. Available statistics are cane ground (until 1989), sugar produced (up to 1996), yield of sugar 96° polarization (until 1989), and final molasses produced (up to 1996).

According to *Anuario Estadñstico de Cuba* (Statistical Yearbook of Cuba), 1988, printed by the Cuban Government, for the 1985/86 crop, the yield of sugar 96° polarization, was 10.59%. Meanwhile, in 1952, the corresponding yield was 12.46% and the 1952-58 average was 12.79%.

Evidently the sugar yield % cane in the communist period has fallen by around 17.20% compared to the 1952-58 period, at a time when said yield has been rising in most nations as an outgrowth of sweeter cane varieties being developed and improvement in the mill machinery. At first glance, the overall performance of a Cuban mill with 10.59% sugar yield is a dismal one. The fault, however, rests to a large extent on the low quality of the cane delivered to the mill, received several days after harvesting, with a high trash percentage, plus the numerous interruptions of grinding. Lacking the juice analysis we are unable to determine the Boiling House Efficiency.

Before Castro, Cuban sugar set the norm for sugar quality. Nowadays, Cuban raw sugar is an inferior quality product unwanted/depreciated in sugar refining countries. In Venezuela, for example, in 1989 some refiners refused to refine imported Cuban raws due to their bad quality. A complaint by the Venezuelan Government (the raws importer) to Cuba was settled by Cuba accepting to supply some 2,000 MT raws free as compensation. The reason for the low quality of the raws was presumably poor quality cane juice and, very likely, the low technical level of the Cuban mill personnel as explained above.

INNOVATIONS STILL MISSING

The Communist period deserves credit for the investment in the modernization, improvement and capacity expansion of mill factories until 1991. Beneficial as these changes have been, they have lagged behind the introduction of the latest technological advances. For instance:

- Installation of Donnelly chutes and fourth roller for forced bagasse feeding was started in 1994 and probably has been halted by now.

- Continuous vacuum pans for "C" sugars.

- Continuous vacuum pans for "B" sugars.

- Automation of mill operations.

- Cogeneration of electric power for sale to public utilities, as in Florida, Guatemala, etc. Boilers at 600 p.s.i. are needed to do this, instead of regular 150 p.s.i. boilers.

- Eight new mills built with medium size tandem rollers (7 foot-wide rollers rather than 9 foot-wide).

WORKERS' CONDITIONS

Wages in the Sugar Industry

Shortly after consolidating its control of the labor unions (1961), the Cuban communist government enacted a decree freezing wages in all industries, up to the present. The only exception in the sugar industry was the minimum agricultural wage of 3.15

pesos daily, which was raised to 4.00 pesos. A ceiling of 10 pesos daily (300 pesos per month) was set. Historical (old) wages were respected. but promotions must abide by new nomenclature with lower wages.

In pre-Castro time, the salaries of sugar workers were regulated by an escalator clause linked to the price of sugar in international markets. In 1958, the world market sugar price was $0.0496/lb F.O.B. Cuban port; currently it is $0.1260/lb FOB. The differential between wages at the international sugar price (Contract No. 11, New York Sugar Exchange) and the frozen wages at $0.0496/lb has proven to be a bountiful source of revenues for the regime, at the expense of workers' economy.

According to our calculations, in the 20-year interval 1972-91, with average international sugar price at $0.2423/lb FOB, and using a exchange rate of 1 peso=$1, the wage differential amounted to $31.0 billion, which was retained by the government.[5] For the five-year period 1992-96, the average international sugar price was $0.1083/lb FOB; using an exchange rate of 85.38 pesos=$1, the wage differential has amounted to $2.7 billion,[6] which has also been pocketed by the government. Such deprivation of sugar workers of their hard-won remuneration has made them despondent to work. At the present exchange rate of 25.00 pesos=$1, the minimum salary of 4.00 pesos daily is equivalent to $0.16, and the monthly minimum salary of 120 pesos to $4.80; the maximum daily salary of 10 pesos is equivalent to $0.40, and the maximum monthly salary of 300 pesos is equivalent to $12.00.

Table 1 compares the real minimum wage, in U.S. dollars, of Cuban agricultural and industrial sugar workers in 1958 and 1996. Cuban agricultural wages in 1958 were twenty times higher than in 1996; minimum daily wages for mill workers were 31 times higher in 1958 than in 1996. Table 2 compares min-

imum daily wages in 1996 with the hypothetical wage (in U.S. dollars) that Cuban sugar workers would have earned based on the wage they earned in 1958 and the international market price escalator. The hypothetical wage was 52 times higher than the actual wage for agricultural workers, and 84 times higher for industrial workers. These two tables show clearly the blatant exploitation inflicted on sugar workers by the regime.

Table 1. Minimum Daily Wages in the Sugar Industry (In U.S. dollars)

| | Real Minimum Daily Wage | | Difference | |
	1958	1996	Amount	Percent
Agriculture	3.15	0.16	-2.99	-94.92
Mill	4.91	0.16	-4.75	-96.74

Note: The official minimum daily wage during 1961-96 is 4.00 pesos/day; the exchange rate for 1996 is 25 pesos=$1.

Workers' Morale

Cuban workers receive the following food per person/month per their ration books:

Rice	5 lbs
Beans	0.25 lbs
Cooking oil/fat	0.25 lbs
Sugar (raws)	4 lbs

Many months no cooking oil/fat is available. No meat is available through the ration book, although some off-quality meat mixed with soybean, inedible to many, is distributed irregularly. Rationed goods last a person 12-13 days. After that every individual is on his/her own.

The prices of rationed goods are subsidized. Prices in the black market are dollarized and too high for workers earning Cuban pesos.

Workers loaf at the work place, due to lack of incentive, dissatisfied with a miserable salary. There is an absence of discipline, high absenteeism, and manage-

---

5. Alfredo Blanco, Jr., "Computation of Sugar Salaries Unpaid by the Communist Government (Years 1972- 91)," unpublished manuscript, 1991, p. 21. See also National Federation of Sugar Workers of Cuba (in Exile), "Castro Has Stolen From Sugar Workers More than 25 Thousand Million Dollars During 20 Years," *Diario las Américas* (August 25, 1991).

6. Alfredo Blanco, Jr., "Cuba's Communist Regime Continues Stealing the Salary Differential from Cuban Sugar Workers (1992-96)," unpublished manuscript, 1996.

Table 2. **Actual and Hypothetical 1996 Minimum Daily Wages of Cuban Sugar Workers (In U.S. dollars)**

| | 1996 Minimum Daily Wage | | Difference | |
	Actual	Hypothetical	Amount	Percent
Agriculture	0.16	8.30	-8.14	-98.07
Mill	0.16	13.51	-13.35	-98.82

Note: Hypothetical minimum wage based on 1958 wage and current international sugar price (average price, Contract No. 11, New York Sugar Exchange) of $0.1260/lb FOB for January-May 1996.

ment has lost authority. Management is aware of the harmful situation, but reluctant to enforce order out of fear of upheaval.

Personnel: Many new, unnecessary jobs have been created in the sugar industry of a bureaucratic nature. In the Tinguaro Sugar Mill (5,700 MTCD), for example, there are 5 additional engineers and 1 boiler technician who do not participate in the mill's operations. There are currently 3 shifts in the machine shop (compared to a single shift before) with 8 mechanics each (compared to one mechanic per shift before).

In 1981, the government enacted a decree establishing at the mill factory, during the crushing season, 4 shifts instead of the existing 3.[7] Its implementation was delayed until the early 1990's. This measure increases the factory payroll by 33%.

CONCLUSIONS CONCERNING THE MACHINERY OF MILLS

Cuba can still muster the basic industrial capacity for processing 7.0-8.0 million MT sugar/year. The government has kept the existing 157 mills in operational condition despite the surplus capacity for the current 4.5 million MT sugar/year production.

The lack of proper maintenance since 1992 has caused a marked deterioration of the machinery, although the damage could yet be redressed if abundant funds become available. Cannibalization has started in some mills but still is not widespread.

Management is in the hands of Party politicians, not technicians. Performance is at a low level. Work ethic, morale and organizational efficiency are in absolute disarray.

The low sugar yield ratio of 10.59% is shameful. The blame falls mainly on the poor quality of the raw material (cane) and frequent stoppages due to deficient cane deliveries. On the other hand, the incompetence of management and personnel in key positions aggravates problems.

Overall, the sugar factory performance under Communism gets very low marks as contrasted with the top ranking of prerevolutionary Cuba.

IMPLICATIONS OF THE CURRENT CROP

The industrial sector was capable of processing the available cane supply to produce 4.5 million MT of sugar and could conceivably do it for a much larger crop if the machinery receives proper maintenance. Currently Cuba's production is limited by the available cane and it seems it will remain so in the near future.

The overall performance of the whole Cuban sugar industry is a dismal one in agriculture and in industry. It is likely to continue in wretched conditions— even with sufficient funds—while its management and organizational structure pursue Communist political objectives as their primary function.

The infusion of funds through the foreign financing of inputs in the current crop appears to have had a beneficial effect on cane output. It remains to be seen whether the improvement can be sustained.

Large scale shortchanging of workers' salaries and repression continue, along with workers' resentment and despondency, while harsh Communist measures are in effect.

7. Jorge F. Pérez-López, *The Economics of Cuban Sugar* (Pittsburgh: University of Pittsburgh Press, 1991), p. 75.

CUBA: AN UNRELIABLE PRODUCER OF SUGAR

Juan Tomás Sánchez

The Cuban government has recently reported that the 1996 *zafra* produced 4.45 million tons of sugar—a 35% increase over the 3.3 million tons of sugar produced in 1995, following a decline of 18% from the 4 million it had claimed in 1994. In effect, Cuba's sugar output has fallen off the bottom of the historical statistical charts.

Who could have anticipated *zafras* of 4.5 million tons or less following previous reports of very high agricultural yields, major increases in financing to purchase fertilizers and equipment and improve cultivation and cutting, no climatological disasters or plagues? These latter factors had no adverse impact on the 95/96 output.

I think that 95/96 harvest reports can be good for Castro or bad for Castro, whatever the writer wants to say—but the issue is so grave that it deserves careful review to identify the problems and implications. The primary problems contributing to the failure of Cuba's last *zafra* are:

First, the total absence at the individual level of any economic incentive to grow or harvest sugar cane for one's self or for the state.

And second, this is compounded by the fact that the communist state has been the worst farmer on the face of the earth. Cuba's most obvious economic failures and potential solutions lie in farming.

In the Prologue by Dr. Pelayo García to the 1925 edition of Alvaro Reynoso's 1869 *Ensayo Sobre el Cultivo de la Caña de Azucar*,[1] he says that success in modern agriculture depends more on the size of the farmer than on the size of the farm. The contribution of the Cuban art of farming to modern agriculture was summarized in an influential Venezuelan newspaper about Florida's sugar industry, stating that the Cuban art of farming and making sugar had combined with American technology to give Florida the state-of-the-art in cultivation, harvesting and grinding of sugar cane.

The reason for the absence of economic incentives during the 95/96 crop in Cuba following more than 30 years of communist dictatorship with average sugar prices of over 20 US cents per pound is:

- The drop in agricultural wages to 4 Cuban pesos per day, or 16 US cents per day.[2]

In sharp contrast, the results after the first 60 years of this century (1900-1959), with average sugar prices of 2 US cents per pound, was:

- Minimum field labor wages equivalent to the FOB sugar price of 50 pounds of sugar, at no less

---

1. Alvaro Reynoso is a Cuban sugarcane scientist who wrote the *Manual for Cultivation of Sugarcane* in 1865. The manual was translated and used by the Dutch growers in Java to change their routine cultivation practices making them the best producers. The Java method, known as the "Reynoso System," was copied all over the world. British equipment manufactures advertised their equipment as suitable "For the Reynoso System."

2. National Public Radio reported recently from Washington, D.C., that sportswear manufacturers like Nike are moving their operations to Vietnam where wages are US 88 cents per day.

than 5 US cents per pound, plus other benefits equaling to $3.16 US dollars per day.

Other contributing factors to the last *zafra*'s failures, and a threat to all future crops while the communist government remains in power, are: 1) the dollarization of the Cuban economy in 1991; and 2) the total absence of value of a sugar stalk as a commodity in the black or unregulated market. In the farm management function, in the UBPCs[3]—a new name for the same state farms—the state continues as a boss: opportunistic and disoriented.

The 95/96 *zafra* is proof that Cuba is not a reliable supplier of sugar to its markets, and that it will remain so as long as the present form of government in Cuba continues.

---

3. Cuba's new form of agricultural organization, called the Basic Unit of Cooperative Production, or the State Cooperative.

DECENTRALIZATION, LOCAL GOVERNMENT AND CITIZEN PARTICIPATION IN CUBA

Nelson Amaro

The collapse of socialist regimes after 1989 reflects more bankruptcy than political change. The "old revolutionaries" and/or "counter-revolutionaries"—depending on the perspective—have been left unemployed. Before, a subversive agenda existed for "would be" destroyers or builders of "Ancient Regimes," "Betrayed Revolutions," and "Restorations." Their prescriptions were very similar to the way Fidel Castro seized power in Cuba. These prescriptions were summarized, with historic descriptions, in Curzio Malaparte's (1932) classic book on "coup d'etat techniques," a very popular book in Cuba prior to Batista's departure.[1]

The demise of socialism does not come about in this way. At some point in time, the parties in power realize that the system does not function as it was anticipated and begin to remedy this situation through policies to manage the regime effectively. Policy prescriptions run in the direction of establishing "market" mechanisms. These reforms tend to be temporary orthodox economic measures. For example,

Lenin's "New Economic Policy (NEP)" relatively soon after socialism began in the Soviet Union.

Former socialist countries followed this same pattern in 1989. The degree to which they allowed autonomy at the enterprise level varied, permitting some decisions to be based partly on costs, prices and earnings. Recent research suggests that these reforms come in cycles. They intend to solve critical short-term economic problems, but in the long run they do not address the root of the problem. These deeper obstacles were related to the basic premises of the socialist system itself.[2] They attempted to correct the "Stalinist" version of socialism derived from the experiences of the former Soviet Union since 1917, later extended to Eastern European countries after the Second World War.

The realistic alternative is to change the system. The economic breakdown associated with "bankruptcy" has opened the way for political transformations of the system.[3] Cuba, however, is an exception to this

---

1. The coup d'etat required general crises in a country coupled with "revolutionaries" who had the political will to control through action the regime's central systems of command posts, communications and infrastructure.

2. See Kaminski (1994). Poland passed through these stages in 1956-58, 1964-65, 1969-70, 1971-73, 1981-83 and 1988-89. "However, once each of the crisis was eased, Polish radical components of the reform were typically dropped. Thus, politics played a major role" (p. 154).

3. The best description of this process is given in Solnick (1996). What is important is the expectations of lower agents in the bureaucracy that perceive breakdowns in "property rights" and hierarchy structures to their advantage. The generalization used by this author is similar to the inverse of a "panic" or "depositors' run" affecting a specific bank. When panic reaches its peak, all principals (clients) run to save what belongs to them of what is left. The inverse relationship refers to the fact that in the case of systemic bankruptcy, panic stems from top authorities when is confirmed by them that lower agents in the chain of command are challenging their control and they do not want to appeal to force or punishment for compliance. At that point in time, all actors make decisions to capture power and resources (institutions, enterprises and fiscal benefits) for their own use. The system—namely the authority, power and political structures—then break down. This is different from a "coup d'etat" or a revolutionary take over.

last generalization. Some have argued that the Cuban regime, resilient to the changes needed, may become a "socialist museum."[4] This thought is widespread among many Cuban intellectuals who are attempting to search for answers to the situation within the island.

This conceptual paper will discuss the present situation in Cuba and different alternatives that may help to extend economic changes to the political sphere. It will describe the objectives and transitions in the Soviet Union and Eastern Europe in an effort to derive lessons that might be helpful in analyzing the Cuban situation. Furthermore, it will examine the extent to which "capitalist" thinking has been introduced into the Cuban political, legal and social structures regarding decentralization, local government and citizen participation. Finally, it will suggest major ways in which the Cuban experience differs from that of other countries, particularly those in Latin America. In addition, this paper will suggest measures that are needed to bring Cuban decentralization, local government and participation efforts in line with other countries, particularly Latin American and the Caribbean nations, that are in the mainstream of modernization of the state and strengthening of municipal governments.

LESSONS FROM THE SOVIET UNION AND FORMER SOCIALIST COUNTRIES

One paramount lesson from the experience of the Soviet Union and the former socialist is that the process of "transition to market systems" is an integrated effort involving multidisciplinary variables rather than an economically unidimensional process. Economic growth policies such as investment and structural adjustment mechanisms do not necessarily work when there is no market in place. Emphasis should be placed in developing the needed arrangements and institutions that eventually would evolve into rational behavior that will give rise to market signals and intended effects. Economic policies should be pursued in a context of "capacity building" of institutionalized patterns of behavior.[5]

Decentralization, local government and participation changes draw their strength from simultaneous contextual changes. From the economic side, macroeconomic reforms such as structural adjustment and stabilization policies are only one dimension. In addition, there is a need to expand foreign trade and investment geared toward the participation of the economy in the "globalization process"; expand the private sector, encompassing the self-employed as well as small and medium businesses and transnational corporations; strengthen financial institutions and labor markets; and develop more efficient marketing and distribution systems of goods and services, public as well as private.

From the social and political perspective, other measures that need to take place at the same time as economic changes, are needed. For example, political authorities should:

- enhance and make transparent property rights, protected by an independent judiciary operating under the rule of law;

- disentangle the links between the Executive and the Legislative power, ensuring minority and alternate systems of representation trough fair and certifiable elections;

- redirect the educational system towards "globalization" and competitiveness;

- strengthen civil society, encouraging a variety of social organizations such as community associations, pressure and lobby groups, non-governmental and private voluntary entities;

- deregulate all spheres that have dampened human initiative;

- eliminate all monopolies or privileges around state power through privatization and the cre-

---

4. For example, see a recent work by a Cuban living inside the island that still has hopes of survival, Juan Antonio Blanco (circa 1996). Blanco says: "Cuba is today, certainly, a museum and a promise" (p. 2).

5. This approach is advanced in Rondinelli (1994).

ation of a reliable and independent civil service; and

- create a social safety net for the transition as a whole.[6]

Only when implementation of these measures is well advanced and documented with results, is it possible to see significant developments in democratization, decentralization, local government and social participation. Opening at the central level is needed to enact reforms. Zealous civil servants have to relinquish their positions; new competencies and financial functions at all levels have to emerge; and links with intermediary levels have to be built. To isolate only one of these elements and fail to take action with respect to the others would be a futile attempt at reforming the system.

A recent United Nations conference dealing with transition of former socialist countries ("Decentralization" 1995) identified major trends regarding decentralization and local government. On the basis of studies regarding Bulgaria, the Czech Republic, Hungary, Poland and the Slovak Republic, the following conclusions for all countries in transition were reached:

> "the reform...weakened the powers of central government and, in most cases, eliminated or weakened the intermediary levels at the regional and district levels ... reform has set up or reinforced the powers and autonomy of local government authorities at the lowest level as the most authentic expressions of local self-government ... and has favored the grass-roots level ... reflecting a desire to bring the government closer to the governed ("Decentralization" 1995, p. 9).

These findings portray a massive transfer of state property ownership to municipalities and passage of extensive legislation giving to the local level competencies and independent financial means under the principle of "self-government." This drive was effect-

ed in Hungary by proclaiming "all power to corporate democracy, more restriction to public administration, the weakest possible center and the strongest possible local autonomy" (Balázs and Bertók 1995, p. 60). The Hungarian experience is not far from decentralization efforts in Latin America and elsewhere (see, e.g., Amaro 1990, 1994 and 1996). Nevertheless, apart from political statements and isolated studies, scholars either in Cuba or in the United States have not said much in this area for the transition of Cuban socialism.[7]

DECENTRALIZATION CHANGES IN CUBA

There is no doubt that Cuba has already entered into an economic cycle with state modernization reforms which point toward the market system. This is a trend similar to that of other former socialist countries before 1989. Measures implemented by the Cuban government, however, are limited to specific areas and show contradictory trends and attitudes on the part of those that proclaim them. The legalization of the use and holding of foreign exchange (August 1993) has checked speculation in the black market but has stimulated a division between the "haves" and the "have-nots" regarding dollars. The revolutionary leadership is looking at this development with concern. The creation of the Basic Units of Cooperative Production (September 1993) and the authorization of self-employment also have been approved in the midst of concerns about increasing income distribution inequalities.

In addition, the military budget and personnel have been reduced (March 1994) and a Tax Law (August 1994) coupled with a law seeking to curb fiscal evasion (July 1994) have been approved. Unemployment and the informal sector of the economy have shown considerable growth and are expected to increase even more in the future. Subsidies have been cut and prices increased to try to reach macroeconomic balance. Paying lip service to "the excesses of

---

6. This last measure has been elaborated in Alonso, Donate-Armada and Lago (1994).

7. We should acknowledge an article by Cuban analysts (Dilla, González, and Vicentelli 1995) which is part of a wider study that has not been published. Nevertheless, once in a while a sense of triumphalism emerges in this piece of work inadvertently: "Posiblemente no existe en nuestro continente un sistema de gobiernos locales tan vigoroso y participativo..." referring to the Cuban system. A pioneering work in this area is by Ritter (1985).

capitalism," a law against "illicit enrichment" was also approved (May 1994). Taxes are being used to curtail earnings. Fees payable to the state by self-employed workers have been raised to moderate authorized self-employment.

A modest reorganization of state agencies has been launched. The Central Planning Board (JUCE-PLAN) has been merged with other organisms such as the one that used to coordinate external assistance from socialist countries (State Committee for Economic Cooperation, CECE). All experts on the subject agree that these measures have had an impact on the availability and reliability of statistics, which are notably contradictory and absent. This lack of information must be deliberate. It reinforces the "secrecy" that surrounds these regimes and underlines the accountability limits of the recent opening.

The Cuban National Bank has been strengthened and decentralized through the consolidation of banking functions under its jurisdiction and expansion of subsidiaries. Activities of the Cuban National Bank in the areas of foreign commerce and tourism have been encouraged. Susan Brandwayn (1993, p. 367) says:

> "...among the most radical changes in Cuba's public management system is the decentralization of foreign trade... Until recently, import and export procedures were almost completely standardized: what worked for one enterprise would be applied to all others. Now any enterprise producing exportable goods may export and import directly..."

A Ministry of Tourism has been created. Joint ventures with transnational corporations are common. Incentives for managers and intensive training are being applied with better results than expected. No doubt some progress has been made. A new managerial style has been instituted and foreign investors from several countries are investing in Cuba (Pérez-López 1995). But will that be enough to overcome the secular stagnation of socialist regimes?

After all, "the International Country Risk Guide for 1991 showed that investors ranked Cuba 116th out of 129 countries in which to invest" (Brandwayn 1993, p. 374). For 1995, *Euromoney* magazine ranked Cuba "behind Somalia, just ahead of Haiti" among 181 countries (Werlau 1996, p. 15). María C. Werlau estimates, according to the highest official figures, that "in five years Cuba has satisfied 12 percent of the estimated loss of one year of subsidies and assistance from the former Soviet Union, if we rounded to US$6 billion annually" (Werlau 1996, p. 46). The Helms-Burton Law has increased risks for prospective investors in Cuba to even higher levels.

In addition, no "capacity building" is observed beyond the specific sectors designated for change, such as limited structural adjustment and macroeconomic stabilization; expansion of foreign trade and investment with some "globalization" attempts; and reorganization of the labor market (more as an outlet to unemployment through self-employment than an encouragement of the private sector in a large scale restructuring of the labor force). Other reform measures are completely absent, particularly trends toward the strengthening of civil society and reduction of the state influence in everyday life of ordinary citizens.

Even from an economic perspective, changes have been introduced with extreme caution, as the law on "illicit enrichment" documents. The most emphatic statement was made by Carlos Lage, a Vice-President of the Council of State, who to a great extent is operationally responsible for the changes: "...haremos reformas pero sólo para salvar el socialismo."[8]

The basic power structure as defined in the 1976 and 1992 Constitutions remains in place, but specific government dependencies are responsible for economic priorities which are suffering drastic changes. A new cycle of temporary "capitalism" has been introduced. Decentralization has occurred when economic requirements have determined the need to make this concession. The model is economic reform without political change.

---

8. Pumar (1996, p. 2), quoting from *El País* (19 June 1994), p. 32.

China, the most authoritarian state in South East Asia during certain periods, and Chile under Pinochet, seem to be the models for accomplishing these objectives.[9] They offer examples of societies that were open to economic changes but, at least for some time or permanently, refused to open their political systems to opposition forces. Cuba is following this development model at present.

LOCAL GOVERNMENT IN CUBA

Concerns about regional imbalances may be traced back to the beginning of the revolution. The first decade witnessed successful attempts to diminish migration from rural areas to the Capital City.[10] The Institute of Physical Planning (Instituto de Planificación Física, IPF), attached during its first stage to the Ministry of Construction, was founded in 1963 and concentrated on the location of new investments (Boisier 1987, pp. 23-24).

These policies were relaxed during the second decade and beyond. In addition, the territorial dimension was better integrated into national plans in the mid-seventies but suffered when these instruments were rejected as unsuitable to address Cuban realities during the "Process of Rectification of Errors and Negative Tendencies" in 1986. This attitude deepened when the "Special Period" was declared after 1989. From this point forward, former Cuban allies increasingly left Cuba at its own.

Table 1 depicts Cuba's territorial and population distribution by provinces and municipalities in 1992. Ciudad de la Habana and Santiago de Cuba provinces have the largest population in absolute numbers, following patterns that were present before the Revolution took place. Nevertheless it is remarkable that the province of Holguín is very close in population to Santiago de Cuba.

The number of municipal jurisdictions usually follows unpredictable patterns in many countries.

There is a tendency to grant municipality status to territories when constituencies press congressmen to comply with their wishes. The new Cuban distribution of provinces seems to have considered homogeneity criteria to define their limits. The number of municipalities per province vary between 8 and 19, with the exception of Isla de la Juventud.

The percentage distributions by province of municipalities and population tend to be fairly close, except in those provinces where the population is heavily concentrated—Ciudad de la Habana and Santiago de Cuba. For the other provinces, there is a certain balance between the two indicators, except in Ciudad de la Habana, where the relationship is inverse. The latter is the only territory, together with Isla de la Juventud, that deviate from the pattern.

The crucial test of homogeneity is the number of people per municipality (municipalization degree), which is given in the last column of Table 1. The province of La Habana appears as the province with lowest level of population per municipality, 34,810 inhabitants, well below the average of 64,318 inhabitants per municipality. Nevertheless both figures are manageable. Only municipalities in the provinces of Ciudad de la Habana, Santiago de Cuba, Holguín and Isla de la Juventud exceed the national average. The rest vary between 34,810 in the province of La Habana and 63,449 in Las Tunas. These figures are not very far from each other. This analysis provides a preliminary basis to consider if present provincial jurisdictions have been constructed considering rational criteria. On the basis of homogeneity criteria, which is only one dimension, the territorial division seems reasonable.

The new 1992 Constitution appears to provide for decentralization and local government in Cuba, but in fact there has been little change since the former 1976 Constitution. As all socialist countries, Cuba

---

9. Carlos Lage said at the end of 1992 that the "experience" of China should be "studied, analyzed and kept...present" by the Cuban leadership (free translation by the author). By 1991 exports from Cuba to China had slowed somewhat but the latter country had become Cuba's second most important market after the Russian Federation; imports have increased placing China only after Russia and Spain. See Domínguez (1995, p. 38).

10. The outcome of these measures is well documented for the first decade in Amaro and Mesa-Lago (1970).

has institutionalized the "Principle of Double Subordination." Marta Harnecker (1979, p. 20) says:

"The main criteria prescribe that all enterprises and budgeted units that work for the community, namely for the locality, ought to be transferred to the locality. Those that work for the municipality should depend on the Municipal Assembly; those that work for the province should be transferred under the authority of the Provincial Assembly and those that work for the whole country remain on the hands of central organizations."

The consequences of this principle are readily seen at the local level, where administrative organs of "Poder Popular" (People's Power) are responsible for a myriad small businesses: pharmacies, candy shops, bakeries, dry cleaning shops, restaurants, cafeterias, movie theaters, etc., are under the Principle of Double Subordination. This is a heritage of measures taken during the "Revolutionary Offensive" at the end of the sixties; radical changes at that time resulted in government control of 100 percent of industrial and commercial activities.

The Principle of Double Subordination is applied to these operations units through administrative directorates. Consequently, these directorates depend on state provincial and central organizations such as ministries, committees, assemblies and institutes. These entities are in charge of elaborating policies to make operations uniform at the local and provincial level. Tourism, for example, is managed at the central level because it is a national priority. The same happens with sugar production.

The concept being applied in Cuba, as in all socialist countries, is deconcentration. Subsidiaries are created, but decisions ultimately remain within the boundaries of central government authorities. The approach is eminently administrative. A sense of "rights and duties" involved in self-government and autonomy is absent. At any moment, central government authorities can revoke any decision taken at lower levels. The French model (well regarded in Latin America) which has improved its decentralization

components recently, offers a good example of the above regarding the relationship between the central government (the prefect) and local authorities (Marcou 1995, p. 125):

"...the new general rule is that local government public power decisions are subject only to legality supervision... If the prefect considers the decision unlawful, he refers it to the administrative court... the prefect will notify to the local authority the unlawfulness to be removed, and will appeal to the court only in case of conflict with the local authority... Financial tutelage was also abolished and replaced by supervision both by prefects and new and independent regional chambers of accounts."

Local self-government is ruled out in Cuba. The 1992 Constitution is clear about the endorsement of centralism when it states that Cuba has a socialist economy (Article 14) with a comprehensive central plan.[11] It also states that "decisions taken by higher state organs are mandatory on lower ones"(Article 68(d)) and "lower state organs are responsible to higher ones and have to report to them about their management" (Article 68 (e)). An Executive Council composed of the President of the State Council (Fidel Castro himself) and Ministers appointed by him, may decide matters which are the competence of the Ministers' Cabinet (Article 97). The Cabinet may revoke decisions of subordinated administrative organs accountable to Municipal Assembly (Article 98).

The Cuban municipal system resembles the "weak mayor-strong council" model, which means that after elections are held for delegates to the Municipal Assembly, the President of the Municipal Assembly is also the President of the municipality or the Mayor. The Municipal Assembly is equivalent to a large Municipal Council and has faculties to revoke the mandates of the Executive Council managed by the Mayor. This last organ is in charge of managing the production and delivery of basic social services (health, education, social security) or economic operations such as the ones mentioned under the Principle of Double Subordination.

---

11. All quotations are taken from Constitución (1992). Free translation by the author.

Table 1. Cuba: Territorial Organization and Municipal Indicators

Provinces	Population 1992	Number of municipalities	Municipalities: percentage distribution	Population: percentage distribution	Municipalization degree: Population/ per municipality
Camagüey	761,855	13	7.69	7.01	58,604
Ciego de Avila	382,766	10	5.92	3.52	38,277
Cienfuegos	376,333	8	4.73	3.46	47,042
Ciudad de la Habana	2,160,901	15	8.88	19.88	144,060
Granma	810,939	13	7.69	7.46	62,380
Guantánamo	507,414	10	5.92	4.67	50,741
Holguín	1,010,658	14	8.28	9.30	72,190
La Habana	661,395	19	11.24	6.08	34,810
Las Tunas	507,595	8	4.73	4.67	63,449
Matanzas	627,114	14	8.28	5.77	44,794
Pinar del Río	709,867	14	8.28	6.53	50,705
Sancti Spíritus	441,025	8	4.73	4.06	55,128
Santiago de Cuba	1,015,106	9	5.33	9.34	112,790
Villa Clara	820,801	13	7.69	7.55	63,139
Isla de la Juventud	75,982	1	0.59	0.70	75,982
TOTAL	10,869,751	169	100.0	100.0	64,318

Source: Programa de Naciones Unidas para el Desarrollo (1996) on the basis of information given by CEPAL-GTZ, *La Descentralización Financiera: la Experiencia Cubana*, Política Fiscal Ser. 62, (Santiago de Chile: CEPAL-GTZ, n.d); and INSIE-CEE, *Anuario Demográfico de Cuba* (La Habana, 1993).

The problems facing these municipal authorities vary by size, migration and urban/rural components (Dilla et al. 1995, pp. 65-73):

- A municipality like Havana-Center presents lower levels of efficiency in services because of the variety and difficulty of problems encountered.

- Another municipality, Bayamo, is much more integrated but unemployment is rampant and female representation in political affairs and labor force is notably absent.

- Santa Cruz is a small municipality suffering from sudden migrations but not pressures on basic services. Integration problems revolve around difficulties with neighbors from other areas that are rejected by old settlers.

- Chambas is a rural municipality where the population is dedicated to agricultural activities. Chambas has not changed much in two decades and does not seem that its future would be different from what it is now. The provincial government is taking away many of the functions formerly performed by the municipality of Chambas.

What comes out of the analysis of sub-territorial units is the complete dependence of the units on the central government. For instance, independent statistics of municipal budgets have never been published. There are indications that some taxes presently gathered at the local level are allocated to municipalities directly without having to channel these funds to the central level. Nevertheless, the fact that statistics on these revenues have never circulated in thirty-six years of revolutionary government is the best indicator of the importance given in the past and present to local governments. Changes brought about by the Rectification Process and the Special Period do not involve any modification of this structure except the elimination of regions as intermediary administrative units, new electoral laws, and the emphasis given to People's Councils (Consejos Populares, bodies where local authorities and neighbors sit together). The following description of the situation in Poland before 1989 may fit the current Cuban situation (Stepien et al. 1995, p. 80):

"Local government loses the reason for its existence, and local authority is attached to structures of a so-called uniform system of state authority... The non-partisan public service apparatus is replaced with the so-called "nomenklatura" system. In essence, this is a catalog of senior officers in administration, army, policy, and—what is very important—in the judiciary staffed by people approved by the party... They lose the right to own property and to execute budgets independent from those of the state. They do not have separate self-governmental staff at their disposition, and their councils are not freely elected."

The structure and situation of Cuban municipalities as well as their efficiency depend on factors that are beyond their control. On the other hand, decentralization is not a panacea. It is a means for certain goals related to the development model that has been adopted at the central level. This is the way basic needs are satisfied at the local level. On the other hand, many other factors intervene in the chain of command between municipal authorities and the highest authorities which are also beyond what a local government can do. These forces from above tend to take away the few competencies that municipalities exercise. This is particularly relevant in a socialist country where centralism is the adopted system of government.

CITIZEN PARTICIPATION

Recently, there have been changes regarding citizen participation: the Electoral Law (1992), the "Consejos Populares," and the extension of the so-called "Rendimiento de Cuentas" (accountability), which is a mechanism that forces elected representatives to report to their constituency. The Electoral Law intends to open political spaces to people from the grassroots. This is a very important point to clarify because it can put in doubt statements made above regarding the similarity between the Cuban and the Polish municipal systems. After the enactment of this law, there will be two kinds of direct and secret elections in Cuba: to elect deputies to the National Assembly of the "Poder Popular" (each for 5 years) and to elect delegates to Municipal Assemblies (each for 2 years and a half). Before the electoral reform, the provincial and national representatives were elected indirectly by the Municipal Assembly once that body was elected.

The principle of both the nomination and the election of representatives by the people is the main argument to defend the new electoral system. This argument runs against the control of who should be elected by the structures of the party. "The multi-party system is a concession—says Fidel Castro when discussing this law—which can never be accepted."[12] The system attempts to reconcile the existence of one party system with democracy. No doubt that this unique party, as in the Polish case, is the Cuban Communist Party. Any citizen has the choice to vote for one candidate, two candidates, all candidates or none from the Cuban Communist Party. The crucial test is that any candidate should have 50 percent of the electorate plus one vote to be considered elected. Otherwise a second round may take place to make this possible.

For making this principle effective, a Candidacy Commission has been created. It is presided by the *Confederación de Trabajadores de Cuba* (Confederation of Cuban Workers, CTC) and composed by mass organizations such as *Federación de Mujeres Cubanas* (Federation of Cuban Women, FMC) and *Comités de Defensa de la Revolución* (Committees for the Defense of the Revolution, CDR) and others. In the past, this Commission was headed by the Communist Party. An effort has been made to prevent the influence from the only political party existing in the country in distorting the elections, according to Cuban authorities.

The Organs of People's Power consist of five-tier set of assemblies. From lower to higher levels they consist of: neighborhood, electoral districts (*circunscripción*), municipal, provincial and national levels (Ritter 1985, p. 273). The Candidacy Commission takes the nomination of candidates to the neighborhood jurisdiction. Neighbors approve these candidates by a show of hands. Candidates for the neighborhood are nominated as possible delegates for the electoral districts (*circunscripción*). Usually only one person is nominated and appointed, although other potential candidates may be taken to this assembly at the neighborhood level, anticipating the possibility of rejections.

Experience shows that actual rejection is rare. Ritter (1985, p. 280) states that during the end of the seventies—before the more recent changes took

---

12. See, e.g, Castro (1992, p. 4) and (1993, pp. 2-7).

place—"...it is highly unlikely that a candidate with a questionable background, of a noncompliant disposition, or openly hostile, would let his or her name stand as a nominee, thereby risking public embarrassment."[13] Circumstances have not changed since these statements were made. The process of nomination of candidates now is more structured than in the past. Mass organizations and the Party at the local level are often composed by the same people. Candidates at the municipal level are elected by direct and secret vote of all of the circumscriptions.[14] Thus, the elected circumscription delegates constitute the Municipal Assemblies. These elections take place every two years and a half with the difference that every other election, they also serve as elections for provincial and national office.

Electoral commissions have the task of distributing photos and biographies of all candidates at the local level. Electoral campaigns by individual candidates are forbidden. The attitude of the revolutionary elite regarding political campaigns has always been negative. For the revolutionary elite, political campaigns are synonymous with "politicking." The vices of democracy—particularly those that prevailed before the Revolution—are often brought up in public by the old leaders. According to the revolutionary elite, these shortcomings should be avoided, just as it is important to avoid the proliferation of parties that will divide the Cuban nation.

Another measure that tends to enhance representation from below is a rule that stipulates that 50 percent or less of all elected deputies for the provincial and national level, must be drawn from the Municipal Assembly. This rule tends to balance representation, giving grassroots leaders who are young and unknown a better change of being elected to higher-level bodies.

Recently, Raúl Castro (1996), when reporting to the Central Committee of the Cuban Communist Party, summarized the results of these changes. Elections held in February 24, 1993, had a 99.57 percent turnout of eligible voters. For the elections held in January, 1995, turnout was 97.1 percent. The decrease in support was expressed publicly from one point in time to another. While people casting blank or not valid ballots in 1993 was 7.0 percent, this percentage reached 11.3 percent in 1995.

Some scholars believe these figures reflect a political reality where participants show trust in the system.[15] An alternative explanation, which portrays a better understanding of the situation, is given by Marifeli Pérez-Stable (1995, p. 163):

"I ask myself: this citizenry, those university graduates, technicians, qualified workers, who the majority of them became adults after 1959, do they have their own ideas different from the leadership on the particular situation that Cuba faces as well as on the Cuban Nation? I assume so and even in some cases I know in fact that this is the way they think, but we do not know that for sure because the political system does not offer guarantees for debating differences of opinion and, especially in different projects and visions."

No alternatives have been presented to the Cuban people in a way that a decision can be made without pressures and manipulations. External pressures as well as internal social control has prevented authentic expression. The very high voter turnout rates may be explained, in addition to trust on the system, by inertia in the way attitudes are expressed, family or friendship ties, fear, mobilization capacity of the Communist Party and mass organizations, ignorance, survival, double standards of morality, political ambitions, attitudes toward stepping up in the social ladder, "politicking" for a single party, conservative behavior to keep a job in government

---

13. In view of this statement, it is difficult to understand the conclusion reached by Ritter (1985, p. 281) that "local level OPP (Organs of People's Power) assemblies do permit local initiative and participation" in leadership selection.

14. For an illustration see the information in Castro (1992).

15. For example, Rodríguez Beruff (1995) says that "the high level of participation (98 percent) and the relatively reduced number of blank and invalid ballots, according to official figures, make unreliable the scenario of catastrophic bankruptcy of the political order that some analysts and political sectors predicted in recent times."

payrolls, or any combination of all these factors. Participation rates in elections approaching 100 percent of the population who cast their vote, were not rare among the socialist countries—the former Soviet Union and Eastern European countries—just a few years ago. Thus, these figures and their publicity as a success, may be deceptive.

Electoral procedures violate the right to secrecy at the neighborhood level. In addition, pressures arising from zealous militants may create an atmosphere of fear and distrust which are difficult to overcome. Some neighborhoods may show a greater consensus. On the other hand there are 50 percent of candidates at the provincial and national level that are considered national personalities or figures, and their popularity only tested within that context. In these cases, the population has no other alternative. There is no way to determine by certified, independent observers that the consensus is valid and reliable as the leadership claims either at the local, provincial or national level.

Before the 1993 elections, the only organ of People's Power that could send forward nominees to the Provincial and National Assemblies, was the Municipal Assembly. Typically, the Municipal Assembly would do this after its delegates were elected. A report by a Cuba analyst (Dilla 1995, p. 77) referring to all elections through the beginning of the 1990s stated that on average, 70 percent of the elected representatives or delegates belong to the Communist Party or the "Unión de Jovenes Comunistas" (Young Communists League, UJC), despite the fact that this group represents only 17 percent of the population.

Another report (Ritter 1985, p. 281) states that "in 1979, 6 percent of Provincial delegates and 3.3 percent of National delegates were unaffiliated (to the Communist Party); 99.2 percent and 100 percent of Provincial Executive Committee and National Council of State members, respectively, were Party members." Despite the new arrangements to give greater importance to mass organizations, the earlier tendency approximates what also has happened in the 1993 elections. In Poland (Stepien et al. 1995, p. 80), the system has been described as "a tri-level structure (provincial, county, gmina), where the

councils are established on the same undemocratic basis...and executive bodies are subordinated to the central, as well as local, structures of the Communist Party."

The other institution which is emphasized in terms of promoting more participation, is the "Consejos Populares" (People's Councils). Although this organization was contemplated in the 1992 Constitution (Article 104) and was experimented before in the Matanzas province in 1974, according to Cuban sources (Asamblea Nacional 1995), conditions are now better for its implementation. These conditions include the elimination of intermediary levels (the regions) and the increase in the number of provinces from 6 to 14. In addition, new responsibilities were placed on the local level during the "Special Period," such as the collection of taxes and the approval and control of self-employment and economic plans, which require greater collaboration between community organizations and municipal authorities.

At present, there are 1,551 "Consejos Populares" in the whole country. The 14,000 Delegates of the Consejos Populares and of the Municipal Assemblies (Councilmen) select a President for this organization among themselves for each "city town, neighborhood, settlement or rural zones" (Article 104 of the 1992 Constitution). They work with mass organizations (CDRs, women organizations, small farmers, workers and representatives of social services and production centers in each jurisdiction). These organizations collaborate with local governments working for greater efficiency in production and services activities and to strengthen popular participation and the quality of life of ordinary citizens. They also exercise fiscal supervision over all entities rooted at the municipal level regardless of their subordination status.

An important accountability institution is the "rendimiento de cuentas," where each elected delegate reports his or her work performance to the electorate twice a year. The delegate reports information and establishes a dialogue with the population. As a result, solutions are found to problems and agreements are reached with the participation of neighbors. According to official figures 31.2, 24.4 and 22.0 percent of the electorate participated in these events in

Guantánamo, Las Tunas and Santiago de Cuba between November and December 1995, respectively (Asamblea Popular 1995, p. 4). This institution, however, has been put into effect only since the end of the 1970s. In any event it will reinforce reforms being enacted at the local level as a result of direct elections of provincial national assemblies.

Recruitment at the grassroots level at a time of crisis seems to be a genuine concern. According to Pareto's Law on the "Circulation of Elites," revolts and revolutions emerge when channels to political power are curtailed and a capable leadership emerges from below. These leaders do not have other alternatives to exercise their skills and are able to challenge top authorities. In this sense, the measures to increase participation are an attempt to prevent this danger and ensure the continuity of the revolution.[16]

Another trend may be detected by analyzing the interplay between the Communist Party and mass organizations *vis-a-vis* the charismatic leadership of Fidel Castro. One constant characteristic throughout time is Castro's resilience to be intermediated by institutionalized organizations. During calm times, e.g., the 1970s, he has relied on institutional mechanisms. When difficult times come, then he turns to mass organizations to survive. The swings from left to right and back which have characterized the Cuban Revolution and its leadership exemplify this process. During crises, somehow, some form of "direct democracy" is seen as a viable solution without much intermediation. The Rectification Process and the Special Period are no exceptions.

Changes made at the local level reflect more a unique characteristic of the Cuban Revolution and less of a concession to align Cuba with similar accountability and democratic concerns at the international level. Nevertheless, this concession gives territorial responsibilities to the Central Organization of Trade Unions, an organization that has been far away from local structures and has not played a significant role in any stage of Cuba's political development.[17] This inclusion may be an internal compromise between the Communist Party and the charismatic leadership of Fidel Castro. In any event, the top hierarchy of mass organizations are interchangeable with the top hierarchy of the Communist Party. Often Party leaders shift positions in mass organizations and viceversa.

In addition, phenomena such as "sociolismo" (a popular expression mocking the word "socialism" and meaning dubious partnerships) and survival through illegal exchanges in kind, where goods belonging to the state are appropriated if not openly stolen, are so subtle that it is difficult to draw the line between corruption and proper behavior on the part of civil servants. These concerns were raised during the Sixth Congress of the Communist Party in May 1992. Accusations of "improper behavior," such as participating in the black market, trafficking in foreign exchange and prostitution, were quoted as "contaminating" members of the Union of Young Communists and the Communist Party (Domínguez 1995, p. 30). To apply the law strictly would amount to putting on trial a significant portion of the population, including government authorities. Therefore the "accountability" exercise seems rather ritual when one examines the underlying phenomena where a significant percentage of the Cuban population are involved in illegal activities and many authorities either profit from these illegal exchanges or tolerate them.

---

16. Since the Rectification Process at the beginning of the 1990s, there has been a concern with this problem. For example, at present 14 of the 25 members of the Political Bureau of the Communist Party are new, and only 6 members remain of those elected at the First Congress in 1965. Concerns revolve around the perception of the revolutionary leadership that new generations are out of touch with the realities and sufferings experienced by their generation before the Revolution. They believe that new generations take for granted the benefits they enjoy. See del Aguila (1996, p. 397). The meteoric career of Roberto Robaina, current Minister of Foreign Relations, responds to these concerns.

17. Dilla (1995, p. 118) confirms this statement.

NON-GOVERNMENTAL ORGANIZATIONS (NGOS) ALLOWED BY THE REGIME

According to Raúl Castro (1993, p. 5), the revolution defines civil society as mass organizations such as the CDRs and the FMC. In a report presented before the Central Committee of the Cuban Communist Party, Raúl Castro classified NGOs according to whether they contribute or not to the so-called "Track Two." In this last category fall all social organizations, universities or international donors that, according to the revolutionary elite, harbor intentions to subvert the revolution while hiding behind research activities or wish to strengthen civil society in Cuba. "Track One" corresponds to organizations that are openly opposed to the revolution.

Under these circumstances, the statements made by Raúl Castro (1996) to revolutionary intellectuals is not surprising. He calls to their attention to the danger of making individual foreign policy decisions when dealing with international donors and NGOs. He warns that this path may lead them to play into the hands of the enemies of the revolution. Raúl Castro (1996, p. 34) said:

"...those who want to use the NGOs as a disguise for their subversive and counter-revolutionary organizations, which were created, are subordinate to or are promoted by the imperialists to destroy the revolution and Cuba's independence, haven't the slightest possibility of success in our country."

Changes promoted by the regime tend to strengthen national organizations more so than local jurisdictions. In addition, all state dependencies related to mass organizations have been left unchanged, especially those belonging to the Ministry of Interior and the Ministry of the Armed Forces. This lack of action puts in doubt the autonomy of mass organizations, whose hierarchies are interchangeable with state authorities. Leaders of the Cuban Communist Party at the national level are appointed as heads of many of these mass organizations. Raúl Castro's wife Vilma

Espín, for example, was for a long time the Head of the FMC.

Maida Donate-Armada (1996), who left Cuba only 3 years ago, has said that the CDRs

"are the organization that permitted the government to exercise social control in neighborhoods, supplanting other neighborhood associations and preventing the establishment of other forms of neighborhood-based associations independent of the state. As a mass organization, [the CDR] brought about the permanent presence of the social control system carried out by the state within family units."[18]

This organization deserves study in depth. In other countries there has been attempts to set them up, but in nowhere else has this organization played the paramount role that it played—and still plays—in Cuba. Such an attempt was made in Nicaragua, but the Nicaraguan families in the urban and rural neighborhoods rejected the Sandinistas' policies. Specifically they resented, and expressed that attitude at the ballot box, the compulsory military service of their children to fight an uncertain war. Electoral results were unfavorable and the Sandinistas had to relinquish power.

In this sense, CDRs have been a unique contribution of the Cuban Revolution to the heritage of modern day dictatorships. The CDRs and FMC were created in the sixties, when internal strife was at its maximum and the radicalization of the revolution was taking place. These organizations developed their projection without the existence of a Communist Party.

To a great extent, the passionate militancy that accompanied the creation and growth of CDRs and FMC at the neighborhood level was an urban phenomenon. Its basis was the Urban Reform, that together with the radicalization process encouraged the departure of hundred of thousands of Cuban citizens to the United States and other countries. Most of those who departed came from to the Cuban high

---

18. The author has compared the views of Donate-Armada (1996) with information received from independent sources interviewed by the author in early 1987 and later. The two sets of views do not differ very much. In addition, the author has consulted United States Information Agency (1988, pp. 107-109). The paragraphs that follow are based on these sources.

and middle social classes, and left behind their homes and properties. Their distribution of those properties among those who were using them or those who were loyal to the Revolution, may be called the Cuban "Piñata." This process is equivalent to what occurred in Nicaragua at the end of the seventies. Behind extreme revolutionary attitudes and militancy rejecting any negotiated solution with exile community may be the fear by the rank and file that these properties could be reclaimed by their original owners, as was the case in Nicaragua.

The same may be said of the "Revolutionary Offensive," which expropriated thousands of small businesses at the end of the sixties. The Cuban Communist Party reached higher status in the seventies when the institutionalization process was accepted and diplomatic relationships with the Soviet Union peaked. The Rectification Process prompted a revival of mass organizations beginning in 1986. Therefore, the new roles assigned to mass organizations during the current "Special Period" have antecedents.

On the basis of changes made in 1987, which allowed certain information to be made public, the author took the pains of tracing the links between organizations at the block level and the state security and military apparatus. Recent verification of this information confirms that basically this is the structure that prevails nowadays. The structure is shown in Figure 1.

The CDR VOP (Vigilancia y Orden Público—Vigilance and Public Order) Front works directly with the uniformed police. At the end of the 1980s, CDRs were reorganized, with each sector now consisting of several city blocks with one person assigned control. Each morning, the sector controller meets with the CDR officials (the president, vice-president, or other official), particularly those in charge of VOP, at each block and obtain the daily log of activities in that particular block.

The CDR officials have the duty to know the activities of each person in their respective blocks. There is an individual file kept on each block resident, some of which reveal the internal dynamics of households. For this reason Maida Donate-Armada (1996) says

that "perhaps the greatest contribution (of the CDRs) to the history of world espionage may be to have raised to the level of counterintelligence the daily gossip (*chismes*) and disagreements (*bretes*) that go on at the neighborhood level. Citizens must be careful of their actions and of what they say, as they are being constantly monitored by the block CDR.

The structure consists of a president, vice-president, a treasurer, an organizer, an official responsible for the work force, and another for ideological control. CDRs al include an important component, referred to as the CDR Vigilance and Public Order Front (Vigilancia y Orden Público). After the September 1986 CDR Congress, a special component (front) was introduced to assist those young people who neither work nor study. This division of the CDR is referred to as the Prevention and Education Front. This front notifies the police department of all pertinent information regarding young people who are neither in school nor working.

CDR characteristics probably vary according to population size, prevalence of common crime or acts against the state, extremism of the CDR authorities, educational level, etc. An important variable is the lack of commitment of the rank and file at the local level.

Militancy in CDRs is interchangeable with other organizations such as the FMC, the Communist Party, or the League of Young Communists. Any militant of the Party or of the Youth must show that he or she is a member of the CDRs and/or FMC. These last two organizations, together with the Party and the Youth are the most active at the local level. The statutes of the Cuban Communist Party of Cuba, Chapter VIII, Article 73, states:

"The Party guides and directs the work of the mass and social organizations, based on the principle of full and conscious acceptance of its leadership role and of the influence its members and aspirants have in the mass organizations, while recognizing the organic independence of those organizations."[19]

Within each block, there is one other agent who deals indirectly with the CDRs: this person reports directly to an officer of the security apparatus of the Ministry of Interior. Very rarely are the secret duties of this person known to other block citizens or CDR officials. In order for a CDR official to be informed of the duties of this person, there must be a working relationship on a particular case.

The organization of the CDRs by sectors and blocks follows the national-regional-province-municipality-zone-sector-block pyramid structure. The sector controller holds a full-time job. They patrol on foot since they do not have other means of transportation. Their work hours might vary from 9:00 a.m. to as late as 11:00 p.m. Most of them do not even live in the sectors they patrol. The president of the CDR provides all pertinent information to the sector controller. Frequently, however, the sector controller does not trust the CDR president and usually verifies this information with VOP Front Officials.

Figure 1. Cuba: Links between the CDR's Vigilance System and Government Bodies

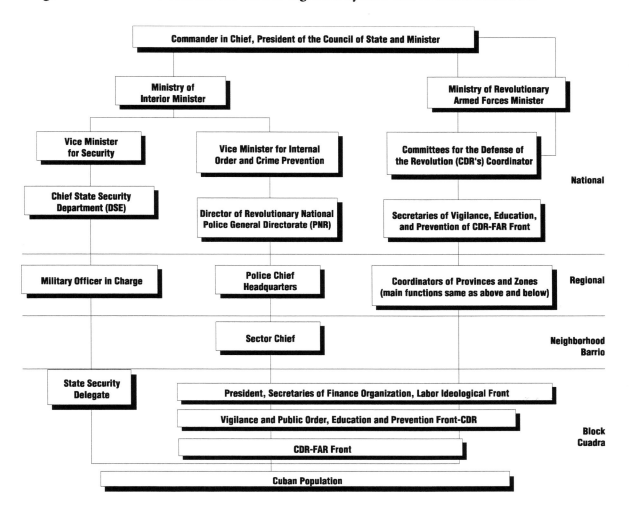

---

19. As quoted in Ritter (1985, p. 277).

If enough evidence of wrongdoing is found regarding a particular citizen, the sector controller meets with that individual. Three warnings are given to each citizen, with the first two given in written form. After one warning, the citizen's file is classified as category A; after two warnings, as B. The third warning results in the arrest of the citizen and classification of his or her file as category C.

There are national, provincial, municipal, and zone meetings for all CDR presidents, who then pass on the information to their block officials and citizens. The VOP Front consists of people who have shown extreme loyalty to the revolution, and who are willing to go to great means to discover wrongdoing. The background of the Front officials varies from retirees to people who have served in international missions. The ideological control person usually has a college degree.

As is depicted in Figure 1, the Ministry of Interior and the CDRs have parallel structures. Security bodies (intelligence and counterintelligence) and police back-stop this mass organization. Designation of officials for different posts within CDRs, especially for being in charge of "vigilance," are subject to consultation with the MININT officer in charge.

This network in turn is linked to the chiefs of "defense zones" and territorial militia, which are the lower layer of the so-called "Republic of Cuba's Unique System of Exploration" and the mobilization chain for any war action. "Defense zones" are in charge of evacuating the civil population and destroying cities and towns if the socialist system is in danger. These activities are connected to the Ministry of Armed Forces.

There are "Voluntary Brigades of Activists" that are mobilized according to instructions of the state security apparatus. The Brigades are sometimes called into action by the police. They are the direct antecedent of the so-called "Brigadas de Respuesta Rápida" (Quick Response Brigades) that hold "repudiation meetings" in front of the homes of undesirable neighbors, sometimes when it is known that they plan to leave the island. The Brigades are a sort of para-military organization backed by the Cuban authorities established for the purpose of harassing and fighting—physically sometimes, with sticks, bricks, and hammers—dissident neighbors and families.

The notion of civil society is alien to the policies that the Cuban leadership is pursuing at present. The theories of "transmission belts" and an "enlightened vanguard" suit more closely regime's goals and modus operandi. The essence of civil society lies in the possibility that social groups could be autonomous, particularly from military and government tutelage and control. This is impossible in today's Cuban society. The leadership has a horizontal circulation system that allows the same faces and names to transfer from government to mass organizations to military positions. This revolving system has been operating for 36 years.

The Party, the State and mass organizations are intertwined. To claim that Cuban mass organizations represent civil society is to deny that the latter has any right to exist as an independent force. This is the kind of participation Nazi and fascist regimes encourage, together with the "personality cult" of the leader. The revolutionary leadership and the leader himself have designed a totalitarian society; changes to the control mechanisms and reforms are attempts to strengthen this grip.

BRINGING CUBAN DECENTRALIZATION AND LOCAL GOVERNMENT EFFORTS IN LINE WITH OTHER COUNTRIES

Concerns with decentralization and local government are common worldwide. These concerns have emerged in the former socialist countries as well as in Latin America. Comparing the agenda in these countries with what is occurring in Cuba, suggests that Cuba differs from the other countries with regard to the following:

(a) The decentralization and local government drive in Latin America and the Caribbean and elsewhere is aimed at improving democracy, based on multiparty elections. A multiparty system is out of the question for the revolutionary elite in Cuba.

(b) There is an effort elsewhere to reduce the influence of the state by changing its orientation to make it focus on essential functions (internal order, international relations, defense and provision of needed infrastructure) and an efficient delivery of services based on citizens preferences. Cuba's 1992 socialist Constitution runs counter to these objectives.

(c) There is a consensus that the delivery of services may be carried out by the state, by the for-profit private sector, or by NGOs. The latter two may intervene directly, do so through franchises or contracts, receive subsidies or special bonuses, or use any combination of all these options. The creation of a market where different service providers can compete is not the purpose of changes that have been taking place in Cuba. NGOs are regarded as entities dedicated to espionage and subversive activities. Despite statements to the contrary, the Communist party pervades all mass organizations.

(d) The trend elsewhere is for countries organized with federal governments (Argentina, Brazil, México and Venezuela) to implement fully the federal system as opposed to ancient traditions of centralism. For countries with unitary systems of governments—the rest of Latin America—the tendency is to federalize. Cuba remains a unitary system of government.

(e) Cuba has rejected the concept of regions while countries more advanced in the decentralization process have created sub-divisions that absorb some of the functions of the central government and receive "situados" (funds) or revenues from specific taxes that can be used directly and autonomously by territorial sub-units. Without financial independence of subterritorial units, it is a chimera to talk about autonomy or "independence."

(f) Local government autonomy, a long term claim expressed by people in municipal jurisdictions, is granted in Latin America with very few controls. In the case of Brazil, for example, this autonomy extends to fiscal management. All Latin American constitutions—except for Cuba—currently grant autonomy to municipalities. Further, most former socialist countries have rejected the principle of double subordination, which Cuba maintains.

(g) The most important "bridge" is between municipal authorities and local organizations, tied to problems of their jurisdictions, rather than national organizations. Local organizations such as Local Administrative Boards (Juntas Administradoras Locales) in Colombia and Juntas de Vecinos (Neighbors' Boards) and Consejos Económicos y Sociales Comunales (Community Economic and Social Councils) in Chile are already under way in these countries and have millions of affiliates.[20]

(h) Changes to state organization made by the Cuban leadership recently have been primarily motivated by economic concerns. They have followed a pattern of decentralization where enterprises and state dependencies have been given new responsibilities formerly executed at the central level, but still decisionmaking comes from above. What is being searched in former socialist countries and most countries of Latin America is not decentralization, but the devolution of authority, which includes policies to strengthen autonomous organizations and self-government of subterritorial units.

(i) Employment in Cuban state payrolls has been reduced but the scope of reduction appears limited. This situation contrasts with significant efforts made in Latin America regarding decentralization and strengthening of local government. For instance, Colombia has been engaged in state modernization since 1974. A new (1991) Constitution has been approved which makes significant reforms at the central and sub-national level. The central government has reduced its size significantly in Chile and Colombia through reorganizations taking into account sub-territorial layers. Large numbers of former central gov-

---

20. "Juntas Administradoras Locales" exist in Colombia since 1986. By 1994, it is reported that 30 cities had their neighbors organized. It is estimated that these cities cover 40 per cent of Colombia's population. In the case of Chile, pursuant to Law 18.893 on Territorial and Functional Territorial Community Organizations, affiliations grew significantly during the period between 1973 and 1988, when there were serious restrictions on these organizations imposed by the military regime. By 1991, three years after the law was enacted, affiliations reached close to 3 million members, a figure that exceeded levels attained before 1973. For the Colombian case see Santana (1994); for the Chilean case, see República de Chile (1993).

ernment workers have been transferred to local governments.

CONCLUSIONS

The experience of the Soviet Union and former socialist countries indicates that the approach to systemic transitions should be multi-dimensional approach. Structural adjustments and macroeconomic stabilization policies are not enough. They must be accompanied by capacity building of institutional patterns of behavior around the rule of law, private enterprise, globalization, competitiveness, state modernization, municipal strengthening and human resources training, among others, in order to stimulate market forces and rational behavior.

Decentralization steps and changes in local government and citizen participation in Cuba seem to be limited to specific sectors such as foreign trade and tourism. They resemble the usual "capitalist" cycles undertaken by former socialist countries in the past. They aim to isolate the political sphere and, therefore, its power structure, from economic openings. Cuba is not following the model of countries undergoing democratic transitions and is instead pursuing that of countries with authoritarian rule seeking economic openings to the rest of the world. It may be useful to examine the extent to which other regimes—for example, Spain during the last years of Franco; China with its four modernization principles; Chile under the military regime after the plebiscite; Taiwan under the influence of Chinese emigrants at the beginning but suffering political changes after the death of Chiang; Singapore with its present regime; Indonesia under Sukarno and Suharto; Korea since the sixties until recent democratic changes at the end of the eighties introduced effective multi-party systems, balance of power and anti-corruption practices—have managed to accept greater political opening than Cuba.

There is no doubt that former socialist countries closer to the category of developing countries seem to be more resilient to change. There are distinctions between the less developed socialist countries—such as China, Viet Nam, Romania, Bulgaria, Albania, Cuba, the Democratic's Republic of Korea and Laos— where there is still a commitment to socialist ideology and the expectation of a greater role for the state, and post-socialist states such as Poland, Hungary, and the former Czechoslovakia and German Democratic Republic (GDR), which are undergoing drastic political and economic changes toward market behavior and closer relations with Europe and the United States.[21] The former Yugoslavia is a middle-of-the-road example where non-socialist parties took control of the Federal Republics of Slovenia and Croatia, while the remaining areas are more attached to former socialist structures. It should be recognized that these are dynamic situations, and changes may be in store that will make some of these judgements seem premature.

Within the sample of authoritarian countries, Chile was able to make the transition toward democracy even though military influence still prevails in certain areas. Taiwan and Korea also offer similar transitions after authoritarian periods. Taiwan as well as Chile had regimes with a strong degree of personalism. Spain offers a good comparison as Franco shared many characteristics with Fidel Castro: Galician origin, anti-Americanism, military background, language and cultural heritage, although they had very different ideological approaches. However, there is nothing in Cuba like the Spanish monarchy that could play the role of an intermediary institution. The revolution did not leave any competing organization intact. Perhaps, the Catholic and some Protestant churches, together with powerful foreign countries, could play this role. Recently the hierarchy of the Catholic church has called for change and reconciliation through a national dialogue between the regime and its opponents in Cuba and in the exile community (Aguila 1996).

A similar contrast may be made with Augusto Pinochet in Chile, with the difference that Pinochet has preferred to guide his succession while he is still alive and protected by the military. In this sense, Pi-

---

21. I owe this distinction to Sobhan (1994, p. 38).

nochet seems to be at some point between Franco and De Gaulle regarding the concern for the legitimacy of his regime and succession. If Castro does not take steps in the direction of legitimacy of successors, polarization will prevail. So far, Castro has been careless, slow and stubborn regarding alternatives to the present system. The odds at present are against the survival of the Cuban revolutionary heritage in historic terms, that is, beyond the life span of any individual.

The top leaders have their mind on pursuing economic reform measures but not their hearts. Their attitudes are contradictory. Human initiative is curtailed if growth entails palpable inequalities, such as those related to dollarization of the economy. State technocrats give autonomy to managers of enterprises but within certain limits. These constraints may lead to artificial results. The zealousness of maintaining everything under state control leads to bargaining negotiations between technocrats and managers because market mechanisms simply are not there. This has been the case in former socialist countries.

Changes made at the local level follow a logic that has characterized the Cuban Revolution since its beginning. It reflects a genuine concern regarding the greater participation of young people and a lower level of concern regarding local leadership at all levels of the power structure. The new electoral legislation eases the difficulties of young people in reaching higher positions within governmental structures.

Issues tackled by other countries in regarding decentralization and local government seem very far from concerns being addressed by Cuba's government. Democracy as it is known in most parts of the world is not a goal of the Cuban regime; autonomy of subterritorial units is not a concern; fiscal decentralization is not relevant; NGOs are attacked and legitimacy of their activities is questioned; market-building steps are absent; privatization is out of the agenda except in for some narrow areas; and state organization remains much as it is defined in the 1976 Constitution.

This approach, to a large extent, also reflects the circumstances of the special period. Again, the sense of being under attack and the drama for the Cuban population, still being asked to make more sacrifices without hope that the future will bring greater rewards may be influencing these outcomes. Openness may be synonymous with betrayal. The revolutionary leadership feels that is entitled to select their opposition among Cuban political forces within and outside the island: their own scholars, their capitalists, and now even their own NGOs. The discourse behind recent changes regarding decentralization, local government and participation also reflects this cautious approach. The trend is toward greater degree of social control instead of less government intervention in the private life of ordinary citizens.

The Cuban revolutionary leadership has been in power for 36 years. To a great extent the basis for the legitimacy of its social order is still charismatic, resting on the personality of Fidel Castro. This is not strong ground for stability in the future. The charismatic leader has to continue working miracles to keep beliefs alive. Gone are the heroic times when the revolution broke with the Cuban establishment promising the millennium to a radicalized population. Gone are the long speeches and the revolutionary appeals—the "two or three Vietnams" in Latin America and international revolutionary duties in Angola and the Third World, the nationalizations, the "revolutionary offensive," the pursuit of a "New Man," the 10 million-ton sugar harvest, and the "birth of a communist society in one generation." The top leadership has asked heroic achievements from succeeding generations of Cubans and continues appealing for more achievements and sacrifices during the "Rectification Process" and "Special Period."

Now it is the turn of ordinary citizens. They have been subject to mobilizations and military enlistments; voluntary labor; salary cuts; food rations; "vigilante" activities; and family divisions. Not even sport activities have been free from these manipulations. To follow a path of self-fulfillment in baseball, such as joining a professional U.S. major league team, a rather innocuous action in any country in normal times, becomes a "betrayal" and evidence of "counter-revolutionary" behavior. Pressures has being created from internal as well as external sources. Foreign 'invasions," "embargoes," isolation policies, and mere indifference has helped sustain an otherwise critical situation for years without any sight of light at the end of the tunnel. The search for a political structure adjusted to human needs calls for a halt to any kind of pressures. The only sensible measure to put an end to these sufferings, pressures and manipulations is to let the Cuban people express their will. If the people is the sovereign, as Sarmiento once said, let's educate the sovereign.

The Cuban people are entitled to be fully informed so that they can make the best decisions. Information should flow freely to make this possible. Then, a national election, certified by international observers, should take place. It is the only basis to bring about legitimate decentralization, local government and participation at present. However, the attitude of the Cuban revolutionary leadership toward the Nicaraguan elections preclude a positive reaction to this suggestion. The Cuban reality today is very far from these goals.

REFERENCES

Aguila, Juan M. del. "Development, Revolution, and Decay in Cuba," in *Latin American Politics and Development*, Howard J. Wiarda and Harvey F. Kline (eds.). Boulder: Westview Press, 1996.

Alonso, José F., Donate-Armada, Ricardo, and Lago, Armando. "A First Approximation to the Design of a Safety Net for Democratic Cuba," in *Cuba in Transition—Volume 4*. Washington: ASCE, 1994, pp. 88-154.

Amaro, Nelson. "La Descentralización en los Países Unitarios de América Latina y el Caribe en la Actualidad: Cuatro Dilemas Gerenciales," paper presented at the "Conferencia Regional sobre Cooperación Política en Materia de Descentralización en América Latina," Caracas, Venezuela, 1-2 de agosto de 1996 (sponsored by the United Nations Development Program, Proyecto RLA/ 92-030 sobre "Gobernabilidad y Desarrollo Humano.")

Amaro, Nelson. *Descentralización, Gobierno Local y Participación-América Latina/Honduras*. Honduras: Guaymuras, 1994.

Amaro, Nelson. *Descentralización y Participación Popular en Guatemala*. Guatemala: Serviprensa/ INCEP, 1990.

Amaro, Nelson, and Mesa-Lago, Carmelo. "Inequality and Classes," in *Revolutionary Change in Cu-*

ba, Carmelo Mesa Lago (ed). Pittsburgh: University of Pittsburgh Press, 1970.

Asamblea Nacional del Poder Popular. "Algunas Consideraciones sobre la Descentralización hacia los Organos Locales de Gobierno de Cuba," paper presented at the "Conferencia Regional sobre Cooperación Política en Materia de Descentralización en América Latina," Caracas, Venezuela, 1-2 de agosto de 1996 (sponsored by the United Nations Development Program, Proyecto RLA/ 92-030 sobre "Gobernabilidad y Desarrollo Humano.")

Balázs, Istvan and Bertók, Janos. "Modernization of the Hungarian Public Administration," in *Decentralization and Administrative Modernization in Central and East European Countries*, Report of a Workshop held in Maastricht, The Netherlands, 30 November-30 December 1993, Governance and Public Administration Branch, United Nations. New York: United Nations, 1995.

Blanco, Juan Antonio. *Cuba: ¿"Museo Socialista" o Laboratorio Social? (Carta a un amigo europeo)*. Manuscript (circa 1996).

Boisier, Sergio. *Ensayos sobre Descentralización y Desarrollo Regional*. Santiago de Chile: Cuadernos de ILPES, 32, 1987.

Brandwayn, Susan. "Cuba's Economic and Management Policy Response to the Changing Global Environment," *Public Administration and Development* 13 (1993), pp. 361-75.

Castro, Fidel. "Esta ley perfeccionará nuestro sistema y todo el poder popular," *Gramma* (30 October 1992).

Castro, Fidel. "Estas elecciones han enseñado más a nuestro pueblo que millones de conferencias sobre democracia," *Granma* (23 February 1993), pp. 2-7.

Castro, Raúl. "Informe del Buró Político," *Granma* (27 March 1996).

Castro, Raúl. "Maintaining Revolutionary Purity," in *Cuba: Political Pilgrims and Cultural Wars.* Washington: The Free Cuba Center of Freedom House, 1996.

Constitución de la República de Cuba. La Habana: Editora Política, 1992.

Decentralization and Administrative Modernization in Central and East European Countries, Report of a Workshop held in Maastricht, The Netherlands, 30 November-30 December 1993, Governance and Public Administration Branch, United Nations. New York: United Nations, 1995.

Dilla, Haroldo, González, Gerardo and Vicentelli, Ana Teresa. "Participación y Desarrollo en los Municipios Cubanos," in *Cuba en Crisis: Perspectivas Económicas y Políticas,* Jorge Rodríguez Beruff (ed.). San Juan, Puerto Rico: Editorial de la Universidad de Puerto Rico, 1995.

Dilla, Haroldo. "Socialismo, Empresas y Participación Obrera," in *Cuba en Crisis: Perspectivas Económicas y Políticas,* Jorge Rodríguez Beruff (ed.). San Juan, Puerto Rico: Editorial de la Universidad de Puerto Rico, 1995.

Domínguez, Jorge. "Cuba un Nuevo Camino," in *Cuba en Crisis: Perspectivas Económicas y Políticas,* Jorge Rodríguez Beruff (ed.). San Juan, Puerto Rico: Editorial de la Universidad de Puerto Rico, 1995. 23-44.

Donate-Armada, Maida. "Sociedad Civil, Control Social y Estructura del Poder en Cuba," in this volume.

Harnecker, Marta. *Cuba: Dictadura o Democracia.* 8a. ed. corregida y aumentada. México: Siglo XXI Editores, 1979.

Halebsky, Sandor and Kirk, John M. (eds.) *Cuba: Twenty-Five Years of Revolution, 1958-1984.* New York: Praeger, 1985.

Kaminski, Bartlomiej. "The Failure of the Transition from Direct to Indirect Controls in Poland in the 1980s," in *The Role of the Public Sector in Promoting the Economic Development of Developing Countries,* Proceedings of a United Nations Interregional Seminar held in Nairobi, Kenya. New York: United Nations, 1994, pp. 148-171.

Malaparte, Curzio. *Coup d'etat, the Technique of Revoution.* New York: E.P.Dutton, 1932.

Marcou, Gerard. "Decentralization in France: Constitutional and Legal Aspects," in *Decentralization and Administrative Modernization in Central and East European Countries,* Report of a Workshop held in Maastricht, The Netherlands, 30 November-30 December 1993, Governance and Public Administration Branch, United Nations. New York: United Nations, 1995.

Pérez-López, Jorge. *Odd Couples: Joint Ventures between Foreign Capitalists and Cuban Socialists.* North-South Agenda Papers 16. Coral Gables, North-South Center, University of Miami, November 1995.

Pérez-Stable, Marifeli. "La Cuba que Aún Puede Ser," in *Cuba en Crisis: Perspectivas Económicas y Políticas,* Jorge Rodríguez Beruff (ed.) San Juan, Puerto Rico: Editorial de la Universidad de Puerto Rico, 1995.

Programa de Naciones Unidas para el Desarrollo. "Informe del Proyecto sobre `Gobernabilidad y Desarrollo Humano,'" paper presented at the "Conferencia Regional sobre Cooperación Política en Materia de Descentralización en América Latina," Caracas, Venezuela, 1-2 de agosto de 1996 (sponsored by the United Nations Development Program, Proyecto RLA/92-030 sobre "Gobernabilidad y Desarrollo Humano.")

Pumar, Enrique S. "Labor Effects of Adjustment Policies in Cuba," in this volume.

Reilly, Charles (ed.) *Políticas Urbanas: Las ONG y los Gobiernos Municipales en la Democratización Latinoamericana.* Arlington, Va.: Fundación Interamericana, 1994.

República de Chile, Ministerio del Interior, Subsecretaría de Desarrollo Regional y Administrativo. *Manual de Gestión Municipal.* Santiago de Chile: Talleres de LOM, 1993.

Ritter, Archibald. "The Organs of People's Power and the Communistg Party: The Patterns of Cuban Democracy," in, *Cuba: Twenty-Five Years of Revolution, 1959-1984,* Sandor Halebsky and John M. Kirk (eds.). New York: Praeger, 1985.

Rodríguez Beruff, Jorge (ed.) *Cuba en Crisis: Perspectivas Económicas y Políticas.* San Juan, Puerto Rico: Editorial de la Universidad de Puerto Rico, 1995.

Rondinelli, Dennis A. "Capacity-Building in Emerging Market Economies: The Second Wave of Reform," *Business & The Contemporary World* 3 (1994), pp. 153-167.

Santana, Pedro Rodríguez. "Gobiernos Locales, Descentralización y Democracia en Colombia," in *Políticas Urbanas: Las ONG y los Gobiernos Municipales en la Democratización Latinoamericana,* Charles Reilly (ed.). Arlington, Va.: Fundación Interamericana, 1994, pp. 191-210.

Sobhan, Rehman. "The Public Sector: Review of Role, Trends, Constraints, Conclusions," in United Nations, Department for Development Support and Management Services, *The Role of the Public Sector in Promoting the Economic Development of Developing Countries,* Proceedings of a United Nations Interregional Seminar held in Nairobi, Kenya. New York:United Nations, 1994.

Solnick, Steven L. "The Breakdown of Hierarchies in the Soviet Union and China: A Neoinstitutional Perspective," *World Politics* 48 (January 1996), pp. 209-238.

Stepien, Jerzy, Gintowt-Jankowicz, María, Rabska, Teresa and Ruszkowski, Jacek. "Local Government in Poland and Problems of Decentralization," in *Decentralization and Administrative Modernization in Central and East European Countries,* Report of a Workshop held in Maastricht, The Netherlands, 30 November-30 December 1993, Governance and Public Administration Branch, United Nations. New York: United Nations, 1995.

United Nations. *The Role of the Public Sector in Promoting the Economic Development of Developing Countries,* Proceedings of a United Nations Interregional Seminar held in Nairobi, Kenya. New York: United Nations, 1994.

United States Information Service, Voice of America, Offfice of Research & Policy, Radio Martí Program. *Cuba Annual Report, 1987.* New Brunswick: Transaction Publishers, 1988.

Werlau, María C. "Foreign Investment in Cuba: the Limits of 'Commercial Engagement' as a Policy Prescription," in this volume.

Wiarda, Howard J., Kline, Harvey F.(eds.) *Latin American Politics and Development.* Boulder: Westview Press, 1996.

SOCIEDAD CIVIL, CONTROL SOCIAL Y ESTRUCTURA DEL PODER EN CUBA

Maida Donate-Armada

En el estado moderno, la condición gregaria del ser humano impone un conjunto de normas y participación, directa o indirecta, que se expresan en las organizaciones, asociaciones y agrupaciones, oficialmente reconocidas, oficiosas y autónomas. En este trabajo se le llama *sociedad civil* (SC) a esas normativas y modalidades de participación.

Toda sociedad necesita de control social por razones de orden y armonía. Los principios y objetivos del sistema socio político son consecuentes con la manera en que el grupo en el poder ejerce el control social, y establece la relación voluntaria o impuesta entre los representantes del estado y los diferentes grupos y subgrupos que componen la SC.

En las sociedades abiertas y democráticas, la relación se logra por negociación y balance entre los grupos en el poder y sus opositores. Las partes interesadas debaten y negocian hasta llegar a un acuerdo o pacto en favor de intereses particulares y de cambios que promueven el desarrollo de la nación. En las totalitarias se impone el criterio del grupo en el poder y las decisiones se toman en función de mantener la permanencia y estabilidad política.

Las tres grandes esferas del pacto social son: la económica, la política y la social. El contenido del pacto depende del tipo de sociedad y de la importancia estratégica coyuntural que tenga una esfera específica, para mantener el status quo del poder. Lograr un pacto social con un equilibrio proporcional entre las esferas económica, política y social, sigue siendo la máxima aspiración de los movimientos y cambios de la sociedad contemporánea.

Para controlar la ejecución del pacto social, el grupo en el poder necesita de una estructura institucionalizada o en vías de institucionalización. Esa estructura distingue las sociedades entre sí y se modifica y adapta según las exigencias del desarrollo socioeconómico.

La estructura de control del pacto exige consenso y un determinado grado de represión para mantener el orden y la armonía. Cada grupo en el poder diseña su propia estructura y da mayor o menor importancia al aspecto represivo, en dependencia de su proyecto socio político. En el totalitarismo el Estado asume el monopolio de la violencia como vía de supervivencia y reafirmación.

La actual crisis de la sociedad cubana no comenzó con la caída del campo socialista. El socialismo real en Cuba se ha caracterizado por una ambivalencia política permanente, basada en el control militar de la sociedad civil según convenga a la élite de poder, lidereada por Fidel Castro. Los militares salen de los cuarteles para "cumplir y hacer cumplir las orientaciones," cuando se necesita que la decisión "de arriba no se puede cuestionar." Por ejemplo, la zafra de los 10 millones (1970), la Constitución de la Asamblea Nacional de los Poderes Populares (1976), la creación de las empresas mixtas (1986), la neutralización y desestructuración de la influencia política y económica del MININT (1989). Regresan a sus cuarteles en los períodos en que se gestan nuevas decisiones de control. La "normalidad" produce el espejismo de ciertas libertades: económicas (tímidas modalidades de economía de mercado) e intelectuales (intercambios culturales y académicos con el extranjero). Ese tira y encoge de la militarización de la sociedad cubana es parte de la estrategia que mantiene el poder actual.

Este trabajo presenta las estructuras y mecanismos de poder para ejercer el control social en Cuba, a través de las organizaciones de masas. La lógica de la exposición se basa en experiencias profesionales y personales, enfocadas y organizadas como observación participante, en un intento por entender la sociedad cubana en la etapa de la revolución.

ANTECEDENTES

A partir de enero de 1959, las rencillas por el poder entre las organizaciones que lucharon contra Batista, no se hicieron esperar. Independiente de sus orígenes políticos, no pocos vistieron el uniforme verde olivo y reclamaron un lugar en la nueva organización militar que se gestó. A medida que se consolidó el socialismo en Cuba, el Ministerio de las Fuerzas Armadas (MINFAR) nacido del fidelismo más profundo—el Ejército Rebelde—evolucionó hacia la sovietización, la formación y asesoría de la oficialidad pronto pasó a ser soviética. El Ministerio del Interior (MININT), apoyado por la relación del Partido Socialista Popular (PSP) con el Soviet Supremo de la URSS, nació asistido por la KGB, y evolucionó hacia el fidelismo.[1]

El análisis de los orígenes y evolución de estos dos ministerios, de los antagonismos entre ambos, y de la procedencia política de los oficiales de sus respectivos estados mayores, provee el entendimiento del desarrollo de las principales tendencias políticas dentro del gobierno cubano. El balance de las tendencias entre los militares es importante para garantizar la lealtad de la oficialidad al "Comandante en Jefe" y mantener bajo control a los cuerpos armados, en el sentido más amplio del término.

La identificación y apoyo a la política de la revolución se ha logrado a través de la participación de la población civil en las estructuras militares, modificadas y adaptadas, según las circunstancias y necesidades de control social de cada situación histórica específica.

En 1959, los que no habían participado directamente en la lucha contra Batista, debieron demostrar su apoyo a la Revolución inscribiéndose en las Brigadas Estudiantiles Universitarias "José Antonio Echevarría" (BUJAE), si era estudiante universitario, y en las Milicias Nacionales Revolucionarias (MNR),[2] todo hombre o mujer mayor de 14 años de edad, que estuviera dispuesto a defender con las armas en la mano, "la independencia de Cuba" contra los "enemigos," internos y externos. Ambas instituciones dependían del Ejército Rebelde.

Con las BUJAE y las MNR se inició la organización, neutralización y control de la población civil, bajo disciplina militar. Había interés especial en los estudiantes universitarios: sector con prestigio político histórico y alta capacidad de reflexión, que esperaba del nuevo orden la restauración y respeto de la autonomía universitaria, y las garantías necesarias para la libre participación en la política nacional.

La delicada situación que se vivió en octubre de 1962, cuando la Crisis de los Misiles, fue otro momento de movilización militar total de la población civil. La propaganda oficial centró la atención en el diferendo Cuba-Estados Unidos y obvió el alcance internacional de la crisis.

Entre 1963 y 1965 las actividades militares masivas de la población civil se redujeron a las guardias que se realizaban en los centros de trabajo, y a las movilizaciones de determinados grupos (jóvenes en su mayoría) para la "Lucha contra Bandidos," en particular, la "Limpia del Escambray."

---

1. La estructura y el modelo de acción del G-2 cubano integraron la experiencia de la conspiración urbana y la táctica de la guerra de guerrillas, con los métodos y técnicas del espionaje profesional.

2. En abril de 1961, cuando el desembarco de Bahía de Cochinos/invasión de Playa Girón, muchas personas se inscribieron en las MNR como una manera de expresar sus sentimientos nacionalistas frente a lo que se ha definido como ataque a la soberanía nacional e injerencia de los Estados Unidos en los asuntos internos de Cuba.

Se observa en el grupo de poder cierta regularidad de procedimiento en la lucha contra la oposición activa: se combinan acciones demagógicas populistas con formas de represión extremas. Por ejemplo, reforma agraria, rebaja de alquileres, campaña de alfabetización, reconocimiento del salario histórico y "pleno" empleo, con fusilamientos, sentencias de largos años en prisiones de extrema crueldad. Escala salarial según calificación del trabajador, ampliación del acceso a la educación, campañas masivas de vacunación a la población infantil con lucha contra los alzados (fusilamientos in sito, traslado forzoso de las familias del Escambray hacia la zona occidental del país).

En 1966 aparece en el discurso del "Máximo Líder" la definición del concepto de construcción paralela del socialismo y el comunismo, el país comienza a preparar la zafra de los diez millones (1970), y se reanima la preparación combativa de los milicianos, especialmente en las universidades. En La Habana se revitaliza el Batallón de la Milicia Universitaria y se crea la cátedra militar.

En esa ocasión, la vuelta al militarismo popular está mezclada con acciones de política interna y externa. La consolidación del estado totalitario en Cuba (marzo de 1968) coincide con el auge de la influencia cubana en las guerrillas de América Latina, el movimiento de los No Alineados, la Conferencia Tricontinental, la fundación de la OSPAAAL, la OLAS, la OCLAE.

Después de la extinción de la guerrilla boliviana, la muerte del Che Guevara (octubre de 1968) y el fracaso de la zafra de los 10 millones (1970), se procedió a la institucionalización de la revolución. Se organizó el I Congreso del Partido (diciembre de 1975), en el que se adoptaron nuevas estructuras de gobierno y se acordó el primer plan quinquenal de desarrollo socio económico (1976-1980). En esa etapa la movilización militar de la población civil disminuyó en intensidad y devino en rutina.

En los años ochenta, en el momento de la mejoría económica, el auge del mercado libre campesino, la cierta liberalización del mercado estatal, la apertura de los viajes familiares a los Estados Unidos, se produjo una nueva reactivación y exigencia de militarización de la población civil. La inscripción en una organización de corte militar como las Milicias de Tropas Territoriales (MTT), variante de las primeras milicias (MNR), fue la nueva prueba de fidelidad a la revolución exigida al pueblo, en primer lugar, a la militancia del Partido y la juventud comunista, con el mismo pretexto y palabras de siempre: "nunca antes la defensa de la patria socialista y la seguridad nacional han estado en peligro de ataque más inminente por el imperialismo yanqui que ahora"(sic).

La población civil se comenzó a movilizar bajo el lema de *Listo para la defensa* y en los organismos de la administración central del estado e insituciones de ámbito nacional, se creó el *Departamento Uno*. ¿Qué importancia podía tener esta nueva orientación de control militar? ¿Acaso no era el mismo perro con diferente collar? Obviamente, no.

El MININT, además de las tradicionales funciones de su competencia, en 1986 había logrado un aparato de control de la sociedad casi absoluto. A nivel de comunidad, apoyado en los Comité de Defensa de la Revolución (CDR). En los centros de trabajo y estudio, comprometió a la militancia del Partido y de la juventud, como cuestión de principio.

La estrategia de control social del gobierno cubano concibe cada centro de trabajo y estudio como un objetivo de atención para la seguridad del estado. Toda la estructura del Estado está reproducida en la contrainteligencia cubana del MININT. Para cada ministerio, dependencia, organización de masas, etc., hay un oficial que contacta, sistemática y establemente, con el jefe del organismo, el secretario del núcleo del Partido y el responsable del secreto estatal. El control también abarca a ciertos trabajadores del centro, a quienes se les recluta uno a uno y en forma directa. Nadie debe saber quiénes son los informantes del MININT en el centro de trabajo o estudio, ni siquiera el jefe administrativo ni los dirigentes políticos, porque ellos también son vigilados. Algunos tratan de adivinar quiénes son por la manera en que se expresan. Los íntimos se lo comunican entre sí, sin que el oficial del MININT lo sepa.

A lo anterior se suma la "Red de recogida de opinión del pueblo"—paralela a la del Equipo del mismo nombre del Comité Central del Partido—que diariamente procesa y sirve de termómetro del estado de ánimo de la población. Ese equipo de investigación social, política y económica, incluye a profesionales civiles, especialistas en las diversas esferas del conocimiento científico y técnico, para analizar la información. Son reclutados en las universidades, institutos de investigación, organismos, etc.

La información de la opinión pública nacional que diariamente recibe el Ministro del Interior en funciones, es la más confiable. Hasta las causas No. 1 (Ochoa-La Guardia) y No. 2 (Abrahantes) se tramitaba esa información sin censura interna. Los informantes decían lo que oían y daban sus opiniones. Gran parte de los informes eran sobre las insuficiencias y deficiencias de las administraciones de los centros de trabajo y estudio. A nivel de la contrainteligencia se iba nutriendo un expediente que se mantenía oculto hasta el momento que fuera "políticamente necesario," por ejemplo, decidir cambios institucionales, una nueva estructura, la sustitución del jefe del organismo, etc.

El Ministro del Interior en funciones recibe la información internacional propia de su cargo y—en el caso cubano—en coordinación con el Departamento de América del Comité Central controla el alcance de la influencia de Cuba y las relaciones con los países del continente, especialmente, con Estados Unidos. Cuando se puso en marcha el "proceso de rectificación de errores y tendencias negativas" (1986), la perestroika y la glanost comenzaron a ser objeto de conversación entre la población—militantes y militares incluídos. Se resquebrajaron el control y los mecanismos de movilización interna.

Después de 1986 la tramitación de la información que recibía y generaba el MININT, quedó a discreción del Ministro del Interior—José Abrahantes—quien cada día ampliaba más su radio de acción y control, y aumentaba los recursos que manejaba en moneda dura a través de las "corporaciones."[3]

En 1988 se activó el plan *Listo para la Defensa*, bajo la dirección del MINFAR. Fue el antídoto de Castro para limitar y protegerse del poder que estaba cobrando el MININT, a partir de la estrategia que él mismo había trazado. Estar "listo para la defensa" es una condición que se otorga por etapas a los centros de trabajo y territorios político administrativos (provincias, municipios, regiones y zonas), que cumplan determinados requisitos: todos los trabajadores (y estudiantes según el centro) deben estar inscritos en una organización o institución militar definida, y tener constancia de ello en el carnet de identidad. Como parte del plan de defensa, se imparten sistemáticamente clases, charlas, conferencias sobre preparación combativa al colectivo de trabajadores. Se controla la asistencia. En las clases se da especial atención a la explicación y asimilación del Sistema Unico de Exploración de la República de Cuba (SU-ERC)[4], con el objetivo de convertir a la población en centinela y concientizarla de que su vida cotidiana es objeto de obervación militar permanente.

El MINFAR controla la actividad estatal civil a través del *Departamento Uno*, cuyo jefe recibe órdenes del Estado Mayor. El *Departamento Uno* centraliza la documentación clasificada y accede a los archivos de personal y cuadros de los centros de trabajo y estudio. Para determinar si un centro está o no listo para la defensa, el jefe del *Departamento Uno* y el jefe del organismo—o el funcionario designado por éste—asisten a reuniones convocadas por el Estado Mayor del MINFAR, en las que se explica uno a uno los pasos a seguir.[5] Deben presentar los documentos específicos pertinentes y preparar una exhaustiva expli-

---

3. Las coorporaciones controladas por MC, fueron una variante económica que dió a Fidel Castro mayor libertad para manejar fondos monetarios en moneda dura al margen del presupuesto nacional.

4. El nombre actual es Sistema Unico de Vigilancia y Protección de la República de Cuba (SUVPRC). La vigilancia defnine como "actividad enemiga" a la oposición política interna, la matanza clandestina de ganado vacuno y equino, y el "desvío" de productos agrícolas para la venta a ciudadanos particulares.

5. Por ejemplo, cómo actuar en caso de un GAMS (Golpe Aereo Masivo Sorpresivo), después que pase el bombardeo, hacia dónde dirigirse para emprender la evacuación de las ciudades, mantener en silencio todos los planes que se hacen para que el "enemigo" no los escuche, la elaboración de los planes para "tiempo de guerra."

cación, por escrito y verbal, de la actividad de su organismo, para que los oficiales del MINFAR se puedan "compenetrar" mejor con las instituciones civiles que asesoran militarmente.

Cuando ocurrieron los sucesos del verano de 1989, los dos ministerios militares tenían sus propias vías de control sistemático de la actividad estatal civil. El MININT, además, tenía acceso a fuentes económicas y políticas internacionales. Después de la causa seguida contra Arnaldo Ochoa y Antonio de La Guardia, el MINFAR concentró el control social y dirigió la intervención y desestructuración del MININT, obviamente bajo la tutela del "Comandante en Jefe." La militarización del control social y la exigencia a la población de participar en organizaciones y actividades militares, tiene inhibida y solapada la participación de la SC.

PRINCIPALES ORGANIZACIONES DE MASAS Y JUVENILES

Hay organizaciones que existen en otros países como formas de asociación de grupos de poblaciones similares, por ejemplo, las mujeres, los vecinos, los jóvenes y los trabajadores. En Cuba esas formas de agrupación están bajo la dirección del Estado y son vías de reafirmación para militarizar la población civil.

Federación de Mujeres Cubana (FMC)

La FMC fue creada el 23 de agosto de 1960. Tiene acaparada, en exclusiva, toda la diversidad y posible participación femenina en la gestión social. Las mujeres cubanas no pueden optar por ninguna otra manera de agrupación que no sea a través de la FMC.

La FMC permitió a la política estatal entrar en la familia a través de su elemento catalizador más dinámico: la mujer, en especial, las amas de casa. Se aprovechó de la influencia emocional, útil y decisiva de la mujer, para comunicar y consolidar a nivel familiar. La propaganda escogió—y mantiene—la miliciana y combatiente, la mujer militarizada, como la imagen de la federada destacada.

El acceso e incorporación a ocupaciones no tradicionales en la mujer se ha identificado con la incorporación femenina a la artillería antiaérea y otras especialidades militares. A Celia Sánchez, "la guerrillera por excelencia," se la fotografió de uniforme con una flor, y Alicia Alonso, la "etérea Giselle," se vistió de verde olivo para bailar "Avanzada"—coreografía inspirada paradójicamente en la fotografía de los "marines" en la batalla de Iwo-Jima. Ninguna mujer cubana: "federada, miliciana, cederista destacada," puede preocuparse por las condiciones de vida. Ninguna debe preguntar por qué se gasta en acciones militares lo que debía gastarse en comida.

Internamente, esta organización permite al gobierno centralizar la información, manipular la divulgación nacional y mediatizar la comunicación de las cubanas con inquietudes sobre el tema de los derechos económicos, políticos y sociales de la mujer. Externamente, posibilita establecer contactos con los movimientos femeninos a escala mundial, y presentar como fénomeno aislado y único, "logro del socialismo," las transformaciones estructurales de la participación femenina ocurridas en Cuba, durante la etapa de la revolución.

Si se comparan las agendas de los congresos de las feministas cubanas de la década de los años veinte con las agendas de los congresos de la FMC, encontramos que en los últimos prima la intrascendencia política y social de los asuntos discutidos, para la mujer cubana.

En Cuba no hay organización en la que la élite dirigente, con su presidenta a la cabeza, Vilma Espín de Castro (esposa del Ministro de las Fuerzas Armadas y cuñada del Comandante en Jefe), esté más distante de la realidad, ni represente menos a sus afiliadas que la FMC. Desde el IV Congreso del Partido (1991) hubo consenso entre las propias federadas, en particular las trabajadoras y parte de las militantes del Partido y la juventud, que esta organización debía desaparecer en su estructura actual porque no representa a las mujeres cubanas, no cumple funciones de utilidad y recarga el presupuesto de tiempo, de por sí escaso, de la población femenina.

Aunque existen mujeres que han logrado sobresalir por méritos propios y continúan rechazando y reafirmando que no se sienten representadas por la organización femenina oficial, la FMC se mantiene como única posibilidad de organización femenina en Cuba.

En sus inicios la FMC tenía entre sus funciones tareas propias relacionadas con la incorporación de la mujer al trabajo, la escuela de los hijos y acciones de salud pública en la comunidad que sus afiliadas realizaban en el lugar de residencia. En la práctica, la FMC no ha jugado un papel trascendente en la incorporación de la mujer cubana al trabajo. La modernización del derecho laboral femenino lo heredó la revolución de las luchas de los movimientos feministas anteriores a 1959. Posterior a esa fecha, los logros restantes han sido variaciones sobre el mismo tema.

En la relación familia-escuela, el papel de la FMC como organización femenina es puramente formal. No tiene incidencia sobre la política educacional del país. Al grupo de madres que están más relacionadas con la escuela de sus hijos se las "estimula" reconociéndolas como parte del movimiento de "*madres combatientes por la educación.*" La agenda que resulta de esta inducción pavloviana está muy ajena a las cuestiones personales que las madres "combatientes" enfrentan para educar a sus hijos y garantizarles el sustento. A partir del II Congreso del Partido (1981), la FMC perdió gran parte de su misión. A solicitud de las afiliadas, que debían realizar las mismas actividades con el CDR, se decidió que, a nivel de vecindario, ambas organizaciones compartieran los círculos de estudio, el trabajo voluntario a nivel de vecindad, el apoyo a las acciones de salud pública y, sobre todo, las relacionadas con la distribución de los alimentos. Esta decisión redujo la cantidad de actividades extralaborales, a la vez, evidenció la falta de trascendencia social y redundó en la pérdida del carácter femenino de la organización. En la actualidad, a nivel de base, sólo se realiza independiente la cotización. El pago es trimestral, $0.25 por mes, más igual cantidad para ayudar al finaciamiento de las MTT.

Al presente, la FMC cumple una función preventiva, evitando que la mujer se organice en organizaciones distintas a la Federación. También cumple funciones simbólicas. La mayoría de las federadas cotiza, equiparando esto con "la masiva participación femenina en la Revolución" y cada 23 de agosto, cumpliendo la orientación de los "niveles superiores" preparan algún platillo para celebrar el aniversario de su fundación a nivel de barriada.

A nivel de base el ambiente es otro. Las dirigentes de base se quejan de la poca ayuda que les dan las otras afiliadas. El trabajo recae en las amas de casa y las mujeres de baja calificación profesional. De hecho, se ha reabierto la servidumbre como función femenina, ahora en misión civil estatal, socialmente masificada, sin pago y "voluntaria." En las reuniones no se discuten en ninguna instancia de la organización los problemas específicos de la mujer cubana como grupo social.

La participación de la mujer es esencial para el desarrollo de la SC. En Cuba, la supeditación de la FMC al Estado no permite que se cumplan a cabalidad las funciones que corresponden en las sociedades modernas occidentales a las organizaciones femeninas. Entre las mujeres cubanas la necesidad de organizarse para atender sus propias agendas se mantiene latente. En un futuro cambio, la actual estructura monopólica, bajo influencia estatal, de la FMC desaparecerá, dando paso al surgimiento de diversas formas de asociación y agrupación que permitan a las cubanas participar como grupo, de manera más efectiva en la concertación del pacto social.

Comités de Defensa de la Revolución (CDR)

Los CDR, creados el 28 de septiembre de 1960, son la organización que permitió el ejercicio del control social en las zonas de residencia, sustituyendo a las asociaciones de vecinos y cerrando cualquier otra modalidad de asociarse sobre bases vecinales independientes del estado. Como organización de masas, completó la presencia permanente del sistema de control que ejerce el régimen en el seno de la familia.

Los CDR han desarrollado su labor en tres áreas principales. La "primera misión" es defender la revolución, que incluye la vigilancia revolucionaria para inmovilizar al "enemigo" e impedirle cualquier movimiento en el territorio nacional y controlar sus posibles contactos con el extranjero. Las otras dos funciones son: la vigilancia y el control de la población civil en la zona de residencia. Los militares, los dirigentes y los militantes del Partido, hasta cierto nivel, no son objeto de atención sistemática, y tienen que recibir autorización para vigilarlos. Después de sus primeros años se le agregaron funciones auxiliares, de tipo paraprofesional, en apoyo a los sectores de salud y educación.

Desde que fueron creados, para ser miembro de la FMC hay que serlo del CDR. El miembro del CDR tiene un puesto asignado en la defensa, es decir, está bajo control militar. Todo militante de la juventud y del Partido, tiene que ser a su vez miembro del CDR, y las mujeres de la FMC.

Los CDR fueron el punto de apoyo para iniciar en los años 60 el racionamiento de la distribución de alimentos. A través de ellos se hizo el "censo de la manteca." Estos "líderes de los CDR" después continuaron en la vigilancia y control de los miembros del núcleo familiar y en la entrega de las "libretas" de productos alimenticios e industriales. Con la aparición paralela del mercado negro, los diagnosticadores e inspectores se convirtieron paulatinamente en los "traficantes" más populares, ejerciendo estas "nuevas reponsabilidades" con los Jefe de Sector de la Policía y vecinos miembros del Partido, de la Seguridad del Estado o militares, lo que les ha garantizado cierta impunidad mediante el contubernio de la "confiabilidad política."

La amplia cobertura de la organización se aprovechó para ejecutar los programas de prevención de salud—campañas de vacunación y realización de pruebas para la detección de enfermedades evitables por diagnóstico precoz. La manera de realizar las tareas en cada área, ha variado en el tiempo según las circunstancias.

Inicialmente, la vigilancia ponía énfasis en las personas que expresaban desacuerdo con las medidas del gobierno revolucionario y, en particular, con los que pedían la salida definitiva del país. Se instruyó a los CDR que debían estar alertas de las posibles actividades contrarrevolucionarias de los que emigraban, y que éstos no repartieran, cambiaran o vendieran, entre sus conocidos y familiares, la vivienda, automóvil, equipos domésticos, muebles, ropas y demás pertenencias. En los inventarios que se hacían a los emigrantes, debían estar presentes dos cederistas—el presidente o el organizador y el responsable de vigilancia—acompañando a los oficiales de inmigración. Era una manera solapada de alimentar "el reclamo de distribución social más justa." Mientras se hacía gran alharaca aparentando que se protegía "el patrimonio nacional," de hecho se repartían los bienes de los que salían del país. Primero, en premio a los revolucionarios más conocidos, y eventualmente, aunque ya sin verse, llegaban por compra—a precio de descuento—o como regalo a "sus superiores." El sistema se destapó treinta años después, cuando comenzó el cambio de oro, plata y objetos de arte, para "generar divisas para la Revolución." En ese momento, muchas personas se dieron cuenta que de pronto, "austeros" dirigentes y funcionarios, que hasta ese momento se vanagloriaban de su humilde origen social, y de deberle a la revolución y a Fidel todo lo que poseían, iban y cambiaban objetos de alto valor que jamás habían adquirido por su trabajo o por medios legales. Hubo quien reconoció en manos de conocidos dirigentes y funcionarios pertenencias de antiguos vecinos y familiares que se habían marchado del país supuestamente inventariadas en los 60.

Los puestos claves en cada CDR son: el presidente, el vicepresidente—antes el organizador—y el responsable de vigilancia. Los dos primeros se eligen entre los miembros del CDR por votación directa a mano alzada. Para elegir al tercero, hay que consultar antes de la asamblea con el responsable de vigilancia de la zona—divisón territorial que abarca varios CDR—que a su vez, tiene que consultar con el oficial del MININT que lo "atiende," a ver si el propuesto "es confiable." Este oficial verifica contra los archivos de la Dirección Nacional de Investigaciones (DNI), los antecedentes penales del propuesto, y si ha sido "objeto de atención" por Seguridad del Estado. Con el visto bueno de las "instancias correspondientes," se presenta la proposición en la asamblea de los cederistas y éstos votan, aceptándola o no. En el momento de la votación, es muy difícil que alguien se oponga, porque se teme que ello se interprete como "discrepancia con el MININT," en última instancia, el criticón puede señalarse como contrarrevolucionario por hacer preguntas impertinentes, "destacarse" como contestatario y tener que enfrentar represalias.

El responsable de vigilancia es quien organiza, lleva el control de la guardia nocturna de los cederistas y guarda el libro del registro de direcciones de los ciudadanos residentes en el área del CDR. En el registro debe escribir los datos generales de cada persona—nombres y apellidos, sexo, edad, fecha de nacimiento, número de identidad permanente, ocupación, si trabaja, estudia, está jubilado, etcétera, militancia política y "lugar asignado" en la defensa.

Aunque el responsable de vigilancia es la cara visible de contacto con el MININT, en cada CDR hay una red de activistas—que puede incluir o no a los dirigentes del CDR—con la función de ser escuchas e informantes[6] de todo lo que acontece en el barrio. Estos informantes son independientes del CDR. No tienen que ser militantes del Partido o de la juventud, siempre son vecinos que conocen a las personas que viven en el barrio, pueden identificar a los líderes de información y a los extraños en la comunidad. El MININT los contacta directa y aisladamente. No se identifican como sus colaboradores ante ninguna institución ni organismo. Muchas veces prestan sus viviendas como "casas de contacto" para las entrevistas operativas de los oficiales del MININT con los "agentes." Algunos, a nivel municipal, están organizados territorialmente en grupos denominados "Brigada de Activistas Voluntarios" del MININT. Son movilizados según los intereses de Seguridad y, a veces, de la Policía.

Popularmente se conoce el mecanismo, pero no siempre a las personas específicas que lo mantienen activo, de hecho, puede ser cualquiera. Ahí radica la efectividad del método: actúa anónimamente como controlador social y autoregulador impersonal de la conducta, porque estas personas no sólo vigilan, sino también provocan para "probar" al provocado.

Estos grupos existen desde siempre y son el antecedente verdadero y directo de las Brigadas de Respuesta Rápida.[7] El régimen pretende presentar las acciones de estos grupos verdaderamente

paramilitares, como un fenómeno de masas espontáneo.

Esta forma de organización de la vigilancia permite que el sistema propio de información de la contrainteligencia, se mantenga siempre activado desde la misma base, aún cuando a veces sea necesario modificarlo, según las circunstancias. A nivel de CDR, los activistas actúan como conspiradores e informan todo lo que acontece en su radio de acción. Para ellos, cualquier persona sin excepción, es un "enemigo" solapado o en potencia. Quizás el mayor aporte de los cubanos a la historia del espionaje mundial, sea haber institucionalizado a la categoría de contrainteligencia la afición por el *chisme* y el *brete* cotidianos a nivel de barrio. Ese ha sido, sin duda, el aporte de la Cuba revolucionaria al método policiaco universal: una Stazi tropicalizada y ampliada, envidia probable de los ex compañeros de la RDA.

En la discusión del Llamamiento al IV Congreso del Partido, se cuestionó la existencia del aparato estructural de los CDR por inmiscuirse "demasiado" en lo privado. Se interpretó que su función de vigilancia— al ser contínua, sistemática y secreta—traspasaba los límites políticos tolerables y se inmiscuía demasiado en la vida personal de los ciudadanos. Ante este exceso, el cubano medio quedaba indefenso, sin posibilidad de apelación ni protección judicial, a los comentarios que dieran sobre ellos, las "personas de confianza" del CDR.

La impopularidad de los CDR aumentó en 1987 con la despenalización de delincuentes convictos y la aceptación oficial de la delación como una actividad rehabilitadora del delincuente. Siguiendo "orientaciones superiores" el régimen promovió la incorporación a los CDR de delincuentes conocidos en los barrios, que habían delinquido contra el orden social—robo, homicidio, asesinato. Legalmente se les indultaban condenas de las que habían cumplido menos de la mitad, aduciendo que eran ciudadanos

---

6. Son la base del Sistema Unico de Vigilancia y Protección citado.

7. Al principio se les llamó de Acción Rápida, pero se les ha querido dar el matiz de que son la "respuesta" popular "inmediata" a las acciones que se consideren desestabilizadoras del régimen.

"descarriados," "reminiscencias del capitalismo" y ya no atentaban contra el orden político establecido.

Bajo la consigna de "Guerra de todo el pueblo" (1988), las zonas de los CDR y los bloques de la FMC, quedaron subordinados a las órdenes de los jefes de las "Zonas de Defensa," que son el eslabón inferior del "Sistema Unico de Vigilancia y Protección de la República de Cuba" (SUVPRC), y de la "Cadena de Movilización de la Reserva," en caso de una acción de guerra. Cada Zona está encargada de garantizar la evacuación de la población civil, y de la destrucción de pueblos y ciudades, en caso que peligre mantener el orden socialista.

Hoy día, un cederista promedio, cotiza trimestralmente, una cuota de $0.25 por mes, más igual cantidad para el financimamiento de las MTT. Asiste a las reuniones que se citan, si no tiene otro remedio, y a las que tratan temas relacionados con asuntos del vecindario (distribución de materiales de construcción para reparar las viviendas, limpieza de calles y aceras). Los militantes del Partido, los jubilados y los militares, son los que están haciendo la guardia nocturna y no siempre. Además, realizan algún que otro trabajo voluntario de higienización de las calles y aceras conjuntamente con las amas de casa.

La rudeza de la vida cotidiana ha modificado, en parte, las relaciones entre los vecinos y el CDR, sustituyendo la intransigencia por cierta tolerancia mutua. Pero, la estructura, tal y como se concibió inicialmente, no se ha abolido, se matiene y se utiliza como control represivo, cada vez que es necesario y con amparo oficial, dizque para la estabilidad política del régimen.

En la evolución y desarrollo de la SC, la invasión de la privacidad y las tareas de vigilancia permanente entre vecinos y el control del racionamiento de alimentos y productos industriales, no tienen cabida. Una asociación saludable de vecinos es incongruente con esas aberrantes funciones y tareas. La asociación saludable de vecinos deberá tomar un cauce diferente y recobrar la esencia de las organizaciones de base vecinal: servir de expresión y apoyo al desarrollo de la comunidad.

Unión de Jóvenes Comunistas (UJC)

En octubre de 1960, en la clausura del I Congreso de Estudiantes Latinoamericanos, Fidel anunció que los jóvenes cubanos, bajo el lema "Estudio, Trabajo y Fusil," se integrarían en una organización única: la Asociación de Jóvenes Rebeldes (AJR). Con su sucursal infantil, los niños se agruparían en la Unión de Pioneros Rebeldes (UPR).

El presidente Joel Iglesias, el soldado más joven de la columna comandada por el Che—se había alzado en armas a los catorce años de edad—en la Sierra Maestra, después de sobrevivir de milagro a varias heridas de bala, le habían otorgado el grado de Comandante. Joel era de origen campesino muy humilde. Estaba en proceso de alfabetización con lenta asimilación aunque ya tenía dieciocho años. Mutilaciones en las cuerdas vocales, en la cadera y en las extremidades inferiores, que le dificultaban el habla y su capacidad de movimiento, Fidel lo escogió como símbolo histórico, indiscutible ejemplo y de emulación para la juventud cubana revolucionaria de todos los tiempos.

El nuevo símbolo necesitaba, sin embargo, de un "apoyo" para cumplir con su delicada misión estratégica como dirigente de la nueva organización juvenil cuyo radio de acción estaba, fundamentalmente, entre los estudiantes de la enseñanza media.[8] El mentor ideológico escogido fue Aníbal Escalante. En sus labores más visibles impartía conferencias, presidía reuniones de trabajo, daba orientaciones metodológicas, hasta el momento en que fue separado de su puesto de dirección política, después de ser identificado públicamente por Fidel, como el instiga-

---

8. Muy pronto se eclipsó la aureola mítica alrededor de los primeros jóvnes rebeldes—los Cinco Picos—por las limitaciones de las capacidades intelectuales y los orígenes delincuenciales de una buena parte de ellos. Procedían de centros correccionales y de ambientes sociales problemáticos, muchos tenían trastornos de personalidad y presentaban psicopatologías sociales. Los universitarios fueron menos susceptibles porque no se sentían representados intelectualmente por la AJR. La Federación de Estudiantes Universitarios (FEU) siguió siendo hasta 1966, el símbolo de la organización de los estudiantes universitarios.

dor de conductas sectarias, particularmente entre los jóvenes, dirigidas a debilitar la unión de los revolucionarios. Todo esto nutrió los archivos penales del conocido "proceso de la microfacción," iniciado en 1962 y concluído en 1968.

En abril de 1962 hubo nuevos cambios en la AJR y UPR. En el I Congreso de la Juventud, se proclamó el nuevo carácter, estructura, y nombre de la organización: Unión de Jóvenes Comunistas (UJC), y su ad hoc infantil, la Unión de Pioneros de Cuba (UPC).

Como grupo social, los jóvenes y los adolescentes, han sido y son, objeto de atención y manipulación especial de Fidel Castro y su régimen marxista-leninista-stalinista-fidelista, como lo identifica Monseñor Carlos Manuel de Céspedes. En el desarrollo del socialismo en Cuba, se observa como regularidad histórica, que los procesos de cambios estructurales han estado precedidos por cambios en las estrategias y líneas de acción política en la organización juvenil. Entre sus funciones están la integración a la Revolución—léase a la domesticación—de las nuevas camadas de jóvenes o de capas generacionales, detectar el grado de desvío en las ya incorporadas y evidenciar las agendas que deba entretener la dirigencia para que los históricos sigan mandando con el Máximo Líder de eje y en la cima.

Es importante entender la dinámica de estos procesos y la división de tareas que asumen sus actores principales. Se inician con una etapa de debate sobre "los cambios necesarios," según los expresan las distintas tendencias toleradas dentro de los límites del dogma marxista-leninista. Cuando una de ellas empieza a predominar, con sus posibles líderes ya identificados, de manera automática, Fidel asume el papel de árbitro. Corta por lo sano y se define en la tendencia contraria, posición que siemrpe coincide con la optimización del poder para los históricos.

Hasta el momento del arbitraje, el juego lo hace el Máximo Líder en aparente contraposición con su hermano Raúl, quien asume el papel de defensor u opositor, dependiendo del momento concreto. Todo el proceso no es más que una división de tareas entre los dos hermanos de la "primera familia del país" para resolver los potenciales conflictos políticos que enfrenta la dirigencia, donde Fidel siempre es el que manda y Raúl el que ejecuta. Los tres casos más conocidos hasta ahora sucedieron en la Universidad de La Habana, en la segunda década de los sesenta: con los estudiantes de las Facultades de Arquitectura, Psicología y Humanidades, con el departamento de Filosofía y con la revista *Pensamiento Crítico*.

A la fecha, se pueden identificar tres grandes grupos generacionales que han militado en la organización juvenil comunista cubana. Cada uno tuvo sus propios requisitos de ingreso y maneras de evolucionar a fin de "crear al hombre nuevo." En los primeros años hubo que captar a los jóvenes que tenían un desarrollo intelectual acorde con el biológico: eran los que estaban preparados educacionalmente para convertirse en los cuadros profesionales de la revolución, tanto en la actividad civil como militar. Los miembros del "glorioso" ejército rebelde (en su mayoría auténticos guajiros del campo), no tenían la instrucción ni la capacidad intelectual necesaria para asumir el papel esperado de ellos. Pero, a esos "privilegiados" jóvenes, había que recordarles sistemáticamente, parodiando al poeta: *sobre los huesos de qué muerto, estaban vivos...* y con ese recordatorio bien asimilado, podían seguir estudiando. En esos tiempos Cuba había dejado de ser *una república de generales y doctores, para ser de comandantes y licenciados.* Esta creencia nunca ha sido abandonada por el credo revolucionario cubano: el talento civil sólo tiene valor si va unido al militar.

Este "inseparable matrimonio" empezó desde muy temprano. En el curso 1960-1961, en los Institutos de Segunda Enseñanza se hicieron captaciones para pasar cursos de artillería antiaérea, y otras especialidades militares para las que se requería "determinado nivel de escolaridad." A ciertos bachilleres graduados se les propuso estudiar la carrera universitaria en los países socialistas de Europa con becas gestionadas a través del PSP.

En la misma época, durante los primeros cinco años de la revolución, un sector significativo de la juventud emigró a Estados Unidos, desencantados con la Revolución o como meros acompañantes de sus padres emigrados. Aunque el resultado a largo plazo iba a ser diferente, en la opinión pública se asumió la salida del país por cualesquiera de estas vías como una manera de evadir el rigor que empezaba a sentirse en la sociedad cubana. La solución del poder fue exigir como requisito de selección, a los que solicitaban beca para irse a estudiar en Europa del Este, esperar la respuesta de aceptación sembrando eucaliptos en la península de Guanahacabibes, como parte del plan de repoblación forestal de la zona occidental.

Desde entonces, ser seleccionado para ir a estudiar a los países socialistas, se convirtió en una opción de estudio diferente y en un mérito, hasta que empezó el proceso de la perestroika y la glasnost. El desmoronamiento del campo socialista cortó de golpe el flujo de estudiantes universitarios cubanos becados a Europa Oriental.

Para contrarrestar la inevitable influencia en el desarrollo de la personalidad que suponía estar lejos—mínimo cinco años—del control directo de la política ideológica del Partido, se instrumentó un doble discurso: se dió por cierta la predisposición al cuestionamiento político y a estilos de vida "extranjerizantes" en los estudiantes y graduados "fuera" de Cuba. A la vez, que se exigían pruebas de las condiciones políticas individuales y familiares, para ser seleccionado a estudiar en el extranjero. Se creó un aparato burocrático-administrativo para la atención de los becados en el exterior con subordinación al departamento de relaciones exteriores del Ministerio de Educación Superior (MES) y al MININT, *por lo estratégico que resultaba para la seguridad nacional la formación de los jóvenes especialistas cubanos.*

Una parte de los estudiantes de la enseñanza media superior que se quedó en Cuba, subió a las montañas orientales como maestros voluntarios. Más tarde fueron los primeros alumnos de la escuela de administradores de empresas, organizada por el Che cuando era Ministro de Industrias.

En abril de 1961 se interrumpió el curso escolar, y se convocó, en especial a los estudiantes de la enseñanza media, a incorporarse a la Campaña de Alfabetización, principalmente en las zonas rurales. Al regresar un año después, encontraron estructurados los nuevos planes de estudios, basados en un gigantesco plan de becas, todas de internado. Resaltan los cambios de forma y contenido que se hicieron al sistema de formación del magisterio: las Escuelas Normales para Maestros fueron sustituídas por las tristemente célebres, Escuelas Pedagógicas "Antón Makarenko," dirigidas por la difunta Elena Gil, que por vivir fuera de su época—pero hacia atrás—y obsesionada por probar que la moral socialista era lo máximo, sus dotes pedagógicas las hubieran envidiado en pleno medioevo. En aquellas escuelas se aprendía que el mejor sistema de educación es el que se basa en el quebranto de la voluntad del educando, porque del sacrificio como estilo de vida, sale el verdadero disfrute de la condición humana y la reafirmación del ser social.

A partir de entonces, se iniciaron las temporadas de trabajo voluntario en el campo. Las primeras movilizaciones de estudiantes fueron a la recogida de café en las montañas. La participación sistemática en jornadas de trabajo voluntario en labores agrícolas que se exige a muchos cubanos—en especial a los jóvenes, de manera notable a los capitalinos—son el complemento de la filosofía de la expiación permanente por el hecho *de consumir sin gastar esfuerzo físico, lo que otros producen.* Estas movilizaciones ayudan a mantener en movimiento constante a la población juvenil y en los miembros de la familia crean el sentimiento de desestabilización y desarraigo.

Como la mayoría de los muchachos realiza esta actividad por compulsión social, la rebeldía típica de la adolescencia y la juventud se distorsiona provocando conductas que pueden resultar inexplicables para alguien que observa de lejos esa realidad. En Cuba, los jóvenes, mujeres y hombres, no tienen alternativas oficiales de agrupación por intereses comunes que sean ajenos a la política. En consecuencia, el exceso de politización y la limitación del espacio existencial provoca un contrario. En la actualidad los jóvenes rechazan cualquier posible análisis político, dando imagen de indolencia o materialismo radical como filosofía de vida. Algo relativamente nuevo y contrario a las tradiciones de rebeldía de la juventud cubana durante la República, y en especial, de los jóvenes universitarios.

El primer grupo generacional de jóvenes comunistas está en torno a los cincuenta años de edad. Se caracteriza por haber roto las costumbres y tradiciones en las relaciones de la familia cubana. Una buena parte de ellos salió del hogar al inicio de la adolescencia y de la temprana juventud. Su ímpetu rebelde, típico de esa etapa de la vida, fue utilizado como catalizador del nuevo régimen, por lo cual se les autorizó un cierto umbral de participación en la discusión política, siempre en los límites del reconocimiento individual y colectivo, de lealtad a la autoridad "indiscutible" de Fidel.

Su formación profesional fue orientada estatalmente hacia carreras técnicas y de ciencias. Las humanidades fueron consideradas no útiles o inútiles, socialmente cuestionadoras y no susceptibles de tomarse en cuenta. El haber cursado la carrera universitaria en Cuba o en universidades de países socialistas europeos, marcó una diferencia importante en los referentes exitenciales de este grupo generacional. Desde entonces, a los que han estudiado fuera de la Isla, se les adjudica—explícita o implícitamente—mayor propensión a la desviación ideológica.

Algunos siendo casi niños, participaron en la movilización de Bahía de Cochinos, otros en la Lucha del Escambray. Durante la Crisis de Octubre estuvieron movilizados en los centros de estudio y trabajo. Conforman el grueso de los milicianos fundadores.

Ese es el grupo generacional al que se le exigió para ser militantes de la juventud comunista, haber participado en la mayoría de las actividades anteriormente referidas, y la renuncia a toda relación con familiares, amigos y personas que no aceptaran, sin condición, la ideología de la Revolución. Ante la obra revolucionaria, se les exacerbó e impuso una constante declaración de vocación para el sacrificio y sentimientos de culpa y humildad.

A esta generación se la conoce como la "generación de la escoba," porque Fidel la cogió para barrer todo lo que le estorbaba. Como no subieron a la Sierra Maestra ni fueron pioneros, tienen la "deuda eterna," porque nada de lo que han adquirido lo deben "a su propio esfuerzo," sino al "sacrificio desinteresado" de los que hicieron la Revolución, es decir, los que for-

maron el Ejército Rebelde en las montañas orientales no "pudieron estudiar" y siguen "sacrificados" en el MINFAR y las principales posiciones de gobierno hace más de treinta años.

Esta es la generación que actualmente consume más psicofármacos, está presentando lo que se ha dado en llamar "síndrome de neurosis situacional." Tiene padecimientos de hipertensión arterial, mortalidad temprana por infarto del miocardio y accidentes cerebrovasculares. Son los que dispararon en la década de los setenta la tasa de suicidio.

Los que están en el Partido son los más críticos y reflexivos de la situación actual, se sienten comprometidos con lo que existe y tratan de plantear soluciones. No han perdido, totalmente, el hábito de la discusión, que tuvieron oportunidad de ejercer en alguna medida y con dudoso éxito, alguna que otra vez.

El grupo siguiente, los menores de cuarenta y cinco y más de veinticinco años, es la "generación de la orientación," son los que, si Fidel sigue en el poder, serán los "jóvenes ancianos" (con Robaina al frente de la procesión). A éstos no se les ha dejado crecer, aunque constituyen el potencial intelectual, profesional y técnico, más importante conque cuenta la nación cubana en la actualidad. Los que ingresaron en los Jóvenes Comunistas, lo hicieron casi por costumbre o norma social: habían sido pioneros, se portaban bien en clases, estudiaban, iban a las escuelas al campo y, a los catorce años, se habían inscrito en los CDR, y las muchachas en la FMC. Sus compañeros los proponían en asamblea de ejemplares, y si querían, se analizaba la proposición de ingreso a la juventud, lo que significaba tener mejores oportunidades de estudio y desarrollo personal.

Educados bajo el concepto del "hombre nuevo," fueron los primeros que en su infancia gritaron: Pioneros, ¡por el comunismo! ¡seremos como el Che!, y ostentaban como máximo galardón de conducta la más absoluta obediencia al orden establecido.

Hijos de la generación anterior, heredaron el prestigio político de sus padres, intelectuales o militares. Con ellos se agudizó el nepotismo, particularmente en el MININT y en el MINFAR. Son el grueso de los "hijos de papá" y la cantera priorizada, para ser miembros de las Tropas Especiales o acceder a las posibilidades de desarrollo intelectual, en el país y en el extranjero.

Estudiaron becados, en las escuelas en el campo, la enseñanza media y preuniversitaria. En su educación se hizo énfasis en el estudio de las matemáticas, física, química y biología: la literatura, el español y la historia, se les enseñó sin estimular el pensamiento reflexivo. En esa etapa como segundo idioma, comenzó a generalizarse el ruso.

Entre ellos están los "ceperitos," los "de la Lenin," los "camilitos" y los "de los preuniversitarios vocacionales" de las capitales de provincia. Son los del 100 por ciento de promoción escolar. Para ellos obtener una calificación de 96 puntos de promedio, sobre el máximo de 100, durante los tres años de estudios preuniversitarios, equivalía a una catástrofe emocional, y sentirse candidato a ser un fracasado social: todos estaban destinados a estudiar carreras universitarias para trabajar... ¿dónde?...

Inauguraron la cátedra militar en los preuniversitarios. Los hombres que continuaron estudios universitarios y no habían pasado el servicio militar general, al terminar la carrera debían trabajar en el MINFAR durante seis meses. Por ser graduados de nivel superior, se les otorgó el grado de teniente en la reserva militar. Este grupo no participó en las estructuras militares civiles de los primeros tiempos, y fue el mayor protagonista, más por voluntarismo que por exigencia, de las guerras de Angola y Etiopía.

Al cumplir treinta años, se les analizó para ingresar al Partido y—para asombro de la jerarquía—comenzaron a acogerse al principio de voluntariedad, decían no sentirse que cumplían con los requisitos para ser militante del Partido, a pesar de haber estado en la juventud comunista desde los catorce años de edad.

Entre los que han pasado a militar en el Partido, se pueden identificar tres grupos fundamentales:

- Primero, los que están en el entorno de los cuarenta, que tratan de hallar la lógica y explicar lo que está sucediendo en el país y están senti-

mentalmente ligados a la generación anterior, más por razones familiares que personales;

- Segundo, los que tienen treinta y algo y llegan con actitud crítica-interrogante, esperando respuesta "racional" para los desatinos políticos, no se sienten comprometidos con lo que sucede, y les cuesta trabajo tomar decisiones propias, porque necesitan, con antelación, el visto bueno de la decisión por alguna "autoridad de los niveles superiores";

- Y tercero, los que—con independencia de la edad—intentan copiar los patrones de conducta política de los líderes históricos y arremeten, contra toda lógica, siempre que tengan certeza o intuyan, estar haciendo lo deseado por sus superiores. Aspiran al poder para hacer lo que ellos desean, el problema está en que son muy inestables en sus deseos.

Los menores de veinticinco, la "generación del Malecón," son los "impronosticables" e "incontrolables" para el gobierno. Han aprendido a desdoblar su personalidad, de tantas maneras como sea necesario. A decir lo que las "instancias superiores" quieren escuchar, y hacen lo que a ellos les viene en ganas. Son los campeones de la doble moral. Ni se sienten comprometidos a sacrificarse ni a obedecer. Son contestarios por omisión y sus planteamientos están despolitizados en el sentido estricto del término.

Se intenta involucrarlos en la disciplina militar—incluídas las mujeres—a través del servicio militar general, haciendo captaciones para ingresar en las fuerzas regulares, en particular, las de tropas especiales y la policía. Muchos de los que entran a estos cuerpos lo hacen deliberadamente para insertarse en la corrupción como medio de vida.

No les interesa ser militantes de la juventud. Los que son militantes, están entregando, en número "preocupante," el carné o lo pierden adrede junto con el expediente político, aprovechando la un cambio de centro de estudio o trabajo.

La calidad de la educación de este grupo ha descendido acelerada y ostensiblemente. Entre otras razones, por la falta de libros y materiales de información actualizada, unida a la orientación dogmática y esquemática de la enseñanza en Cuba, que al tratar de evitar el pensamiento reflexivo en los estudiantes, jóvenes y adolescentes, inhibe la creatividad y engendra la actitud pasiva y displicente que observan los foráneos y de la que se quejan los intelectuales cubanos.

A este grupo generacional el nombre le viene porque en el verano de 1992, ante la llegada de las vacaciones, y la imposibilidad de ofrecer a la población en general—a la juventud en particular—lugares de recreación donde pasar el tiempo libre, surgió la idea del Malecón habanero, como alternativa para descongestionar las playas del este y el transporte de la capital. Los dirigentes juveniles, alicates y martillos en mano, a la voz de su jefe, Roberto Robaina—ahora canciller—quitaron los carteles de *Prohibido bañarse*, que se habían puesto años antes sobre el muro del conocido paseo—por orientación del Ministerio de Salud Pública, en coordinación con la Academia de Ciencias, debido al alto nivel de contaminación del litoral—cuando el ex secretario del Partido en Ciudad de La Habana, Julio Camacho Aguilera, había anunciado el Proyecto Malecón y comentado que esa zona quizás pudiera ser buena para los baños de mar.

La alta dirección de los jóvenes comunistas se mofó de las conclusiones de los científicos que atentaban contra soluciones prácticas, en favor de la estabilidad política del socialismo cubano, y no veían las ventajas de esparcimiento y recreación que brindaba el muro del Malecón.

El resultado no se hizo esperar: los médicos comenzaron a reportar un incremento de infecciones de la piel, de las vías respiratorias, vaginales y de otros tipos, en personas que estaban haciendo suya la consigna de bañarse ese verano en el Malecón. El escándalo se produjo tras las bambalinas del secreto político: *para no ayudar al "enemigo."* Fidel no quiso criticar a Robaina, porque su equivocación había sido por tratar de ayudar al Partido y al gobierno a dar solución al problema de las vacaciones de los jóvenes ese verano.

Se suponía que ese grupo fuera la primera hornada del "hombre nuevo," sin embargo, no hay referencias en la historia de Cuba, de grupo generacional juvenil más despolitizado. Para esta última camada de jóvenes, sean o no de la UJC la consigna inicial de la organización se ha convertido en sal y agua. El estudio ha perdido incentivo—por adoctrinador, poco interesante y desfasado—no estimula la creatividad, obstaculiza el pensamiento reflexivo y está absolutamente falto de información actualizada. Consideran que existen serias limitaciones para acceder a las pocas oportunidades de estudio que existen, agravadas por las brumosas perspectivas de lograr un trabajo de utilidad social, acorde con la califiación profesional y que responda a la motivación individual.

El trabajo no se visualiza por los jóvenes—tampoco por la población más adulta—como la vía más eficaz, inmediata o futura, de satisfacción de las necesidades, en un país que se vanagloria de ser una sociedad de trabajadores. El fusil se traduce en la preparación para el final absoluto, la muerte como única solución o como un medio de vida con garantías de privilegios, aunque sea por corrupción, en especial si se logra ascender, por mérito o matrimonio, a las familias de las "altas esferas."

La UJC no tiene el peso que tenía hace unos años atrás. En los centros de estudio, donde antes se seleccionaba, se ha comenzado a tratar de captar a los jóvenes. La mayoría de los que cumplen con los requisitos para ingresar a la organización, se acoge al principio de voluntariedad (forma política de rechazar el pertenecer al Partido). En los centros de trabajo, el comité de base se ha convertido en un problema para el núcleo del Partido, por el cuestionamiento permanente de las orientaciones y la falta de "disciplina" militante que el Partido espera.

Los "novedosos métodos políticos" que está utilizando la juventud comunista para movilizar a sus militantes y los jóvenes en general, es la oferta de: camisetas, discos, cassettes de audio, pasadores de moda, y similares... ¿Novedad revolucionaria?

¿Es la juventud cubana actual menos sólida moralmente que las anteriores? Definitivamente, no. Sucede que cada generación sólo puede generar un estilo de represión.[9] Si una generación mantiene el control social por tiempo, las nuevas generaciones aprenden y crean sus propios mecanismos de defensa, que se convierten en respuestas novedosas, innovadoras frente al poder represivo—instituído y estancado—en circunstancias psicológicas y sociales diferentes. Llegado ese hito, el poder establecido comienza a perder la eficacia de su hegemónico control, símbolo triunfante de sus tiempos gloriosos.

Los jóvenes cubanos se desarrollan en el debate de la doble moral que les impone el discurso político del gobierno cubano, con Fidel a la cabeza. Los hacen cohabitar con la tolerancia, cada día menos encubierta, de manifestaciones extremas de degradación moral como la prostitución—femenina y masculina, heterosexual y homosexual—y otras conductas asociadas al sexo y la pornografía. Ninguna de estas "desviaciones" atentan contra el poder político establecido y, por el contrario, ayudan a la "recuperación económica" del país: traen dólares.

En Cuba se puede ejercer la prostitución, incluso ser delincuente, pero no discrepar. Si uno se convierte en disidente a la luz pública, se le tratará de acusar de cualquier cosa degradante y nunca se le reconocerá como disidente, menos de opositor. La oposición sólo existe fuera del país y nunca dentro del régimen.

La sobrecarga ideológica que durante los años de revolución se ha dado a la juventud sin que ésta pueda ver resultados individuales y familiares en la vida cotidiana, relacionados al esfuerzo propio y de sus padres, ha agotado el discurso político tradicional. Ha vuelto insonora la oratoria grandilocuente, la misma que plantea soluciones irracionales en plazos humanamente inalcanzables. Las monsergas paralizantes ya no surten efecto.

La acción grupal se expresa de manera muy evidente en la etapa de la juventud. La rigidez de las estructuras de la organización juvenil, la UJC,[10] no ha eliminado el deseo de asociación y agrupación por intereses y motivaciones comunes. Así han surgido grupos espontáneos—entre jóvenes artistas e intelectuales—que mantienen en jaque a la dirección política del Partido. Los intentos que se han hecho por suprimirlos han devenido en efecto de Hidra de mil cabezas, cuando le cortan una, resurgen con efecto multiplicador. La juventud cubana ha estado experimentando diversas formas de agrupación que contienen en su esencia los elementos más informales y de más potencia de la SC.

Central de Trabajadores de Cuba (CTC)

Mucho antes del triunfo de la revolución, los trabajadores cubanos se habían organizado en sindicatos y organizados en la Central de Trabajadores de Cuba (CTC). Las luchas sindicales y obreras siempre estuvieron presentes en el quehacer político, económico y social de la sociedad cubana. Fueron protagonistas principales de pactos sociales trascendentes en la historia de la nación: la Constitución de 1940, el diferencial azucarero, los derechos de los portuarios.

La evolución que ha sufrido la CTC en el período socialista reafirma la esencia antidemocrática, totalitaria y antitrabajadora del proceso revolucionario. Entre debates y "bates," se llegó al XII congreso de la CTC en 1966, y con él se dió el tiro de gracia a los sindicatos. Miguel Martín, hasta entonces secretario de la UJC, pasó a ser el secretario general de la organización de los trabajadores, con la misión explícita, de parte de Fidel, de desarticular la organización sindical. En su lugar se propuso desarrollar el "movimiento de avanzada," que en la práctica quería decir lo contrario. A partir de entonces, las palabras claves del

---

9. Existen estudios realizados en sociedades con altos niveles de represión—El Salvador durante la guerra, España cuando el franquismo, la Alemania nazi—en los que se observa que una vez en el poder, el grupo "triunfador" asume su aparato represivo como la base del éxito, y comienza un proceso de repetición de los métodos y las acciones. Repetición que permite a los opositores focalizar las fisuras del sistema y facilita las modalidades de adaptación, evasión y lucha.

10. En este trabajo no se analizan la Federación de Estudiantes Universitarios (FEU), la Federación de Estudiantes de la Enseñanza Media (FEEM), la Asociación Hermanos Saíz—parte de la Unión de Escritores y Artistas de Cuba (UNEAC)—porque todas de una u otra forma están bajo la orientación de la Unión de Jóvenes Comunistas (UJC). Reflexión aparte merece la Unión de Pioneros de Cuba (UPC) para entender el proceso de ideologización de la niñez cubana.

discurso a los trabajadores serían: erradicar la vagancia, reconocer el sacrificio del que trabaja, estimular ante el colectivo y la sociedad la humildad y modestia de los que crean la riqueza del país, etc.

Resulta significativo que el desmantelamiento total de la CTC ocurrió paralelo a la desestructuración del Ministerio del Trabajo (MINTRAB). Es decir, para consolidar el control sobre los trabajadores se actuó paralelamente en la esfera sindical y la estatal administrativa.

En el informe central al I Congreso del Partido (1975), en el acápite "Los errores cometidos," se reconoció la desarticulación del movimiento sindical y la desestructuración del MINTRAB, pero se advirtió que la reorganización y reorientación del aparato sindical y administrativo se haría bajo estricto control, según los intereses del Estado y el Partido, es decir, desde y por el grupo en el poder.

En la actualidad, la organización sindical es una pura formalidad. Los trabajadores cubanos no tienen participación en la gestión social de dirección. Sus relativos derechos se miden en función del grado de pertenencia a las organizaciones dirigidas por el Estado. Las movilizaciones militares en las que el trabajador haya participado a los largo de su vida le dan los créditos para ser reconocido en su trabajo específico y poder optar por una vivienda o un equipo electrodoméstico. Formalmente no existe reemplazo, ni competencia, en relación a organizaciones sindicales disidentes, hoy estimadas en más de 90 grupos sin reconocimiento legal. Probablemente, la continuidad de la actual organización sindical como parte del desarrollo de la SC en Cuba, sea la más precaria y difícil de lograr.

A MODO DE CONCLUSION

Cabría preguntar: si las mujeres, los vecinos, los jóvenes y los trabajadores no tienen alternativas de asociación independiente reconocidas por el Estado... ¿cómo enfocar entonces, la cuestión de la SC en Cuba?

La nación cubana tiene 12 millones de habitantes, de los cuales, un millón y algo vive en el extanjero y once en el territorio nacional. Una revolución es un hecho social que conmueve todas las estructuras de la sociedad donde se produce y deja consecuencias para el grupo humano que es su actor principal. La cubana no es la primera, ni la única, ni la última revolución del mundo. Lo distinto es que nosotros los cubanos, somos sus actores principales y estamos en la escena todo el tiempo, para afirmar o negar la estadía.

Fidel Castro centra el gobierno que subió al poder a consecuencia de la revolución hace poco más de treinta y siete años. A esta fecha se puede hablar de algunas regularidades de su método de dirección:

- Estructurar la discusión de las tendencias contrarias y adversas, entrando siempre él como árbitro.

- Este árbitro decide imponiendo o cambiando las reglas necesarias, siempre que el cambio engrandezca o no afecta su posición de máximo poder.

- Ensaya con los jóvenes, y los utiliza, para realizar las estrategias y tácticas de los cambios en la política interna.

- Responde dinámicamente a los momentos de conflicto internos con nuevas estructuras militares que abarcan, cada vez, más sectores de la población civil.

- Promueve discusiones y asambleas catársicas que tienden a diluir la responsabilidad del grupo en el poder.

- Mantiene estructuras paralelas de gobierno a las oficialmente instituídas (Grupo Central, Equipo de Coordinación y Apoyo) para que el resto del poder—a partir de la cúspide—sea siempre un objetivo cambiante.

- Exacerba a grupos sociales marginales— incluídos los delincuentes—exaltando la "responsabilidad" de la sociedad civil por sus conductas socialmente incordes.

- Mantiene activo juego político doble, en el que el único beneficio seguro sea siempre la estabilidad y permanencia en el poder, a cualquier precio, de Fidel Castro.

Tales métodos de dirección han creado una cuerte de caos en la sociedad cubana, que se nos presenta virtualmente atrapada y sin salida. Quizás en la discusión sobre las alternativas de cambio sería conveniente focalizar la factibilidad social, política y económica de:

- La reclamación de las propiedades confiscadas por la revolución.

- Mantener la garantía de accesibilidad a la educación y a la salud de la población.

- Dar soluciones que mitiguen el desempleo creciente en la sociedad cubana. El país no puede salir de la crisis actual con más del 25 por ciento de desempleo.

- El nuevo proyecto no puede partir de ayudas económicas concesionarias.

- La restauración—sin distinción—de los derechos civiles y políticos de todos los cubanos.

- Amnistía de los presos de conciencia.

THE FUTURE FACES OF THE CUBAN ECONOMY: A BAYESIAN FORECAST

Barton J. Bernales

On March 12, 1996, President Clinton signed into law the Helms-Burton Act. Title III of the Helms-Burton law provides for sanctions against third-country companies, with assets in the United States, if they do business with properties in Cuba which are subject to claims before U.S. courts.[1] In response, during a weekend meeting held March 23-24, 1996, President Fidel Castro told the ruling Communist Party's central committee that:

> "Never has revolutionary ideology been as necessary as now...Socialism has no alternative in this country, the revolution has no alternative."[2]

Unlike the leaders of the former Soviet Union and Eastern Europe, Fidel Castro remains vehemently opposed to making a complete transition to a market economy. Thus far the Castro regime has chosen to implement both economic and political reforms incrementally, largely in response to worsening conditions. Many Cuban analysts believe these efforts are inadequate because they prolong popular suffering and serve only to temporarily delay economic collapse. There is a strong consensus that unless the Castro regime proceeds along the most direct path to a market economy, the Cuban economy is doomed to meander aimlessly. Even though the abandonment of socialist economic ideals seems inevitable, there exists a critical period of transition for Cuba. It is during this period that Castro's decisions and their impact upon selected target variables can be assessed and the associated probabilities of economic direction charted.

The future direction of the Cuban economy and the extent of its recovery may be ascertained by employing fundamental decision theory combined with Bayesian analytical methods. The purpose of this paper is to examine the potential for using a Bayesian approach to forecast the direction of the Cuban economy in the short (1-2 years) to medium (3-5 years) term. Much of the recent literature dedicated to Cuba's "life after the Soviet Union" addresses strategies of economic reform and reconstruction or presents political and economic scenarios possible in the near term, whereupon possible future scenarios implicitly imply the direction of the Cuban economy. This study will explicitly determine the probabilities of Cuba sustaining a centrally planned economy or transitioning to a mixed or predominantly market economy based upon the conditional dependence of specific variables: foreign exchange earnings, import substitution, political control, economic reforms, integration into the international finance community, and the policies of international or regional actors. Armed with such probabilistic outcomes, a forecast of Cuba's economic direction can be proposed given an observed sequence of relevant events.

---

1. Jorge A. Banales, "U.S. Briefs NAFTA Partners on Cuba," UPI (Washington, D.C.): April 26, 1996.
2. Frances Kerry, "Cuba must confront U.S. pressure with ideology-Castro," Reuter (Havana): March 26, 1996.

ORGANIZATION AND APPROACH

According to Adolf Lowe (1965), the aim of a socialist economy in transition is a terminal state (of nature) with an efficient use of resources and a higher rate of growth, and not necessarily the marketization and privatization of the economy. The terminal state is defined in terms of specified macroeconomic goals and institutional changes instrumental to their achievement. What remains to be determined is whether the envisioned institutional structure creates the necessary motivations to move the economy to the desired terminal state. Presented in the second section is a brief description of the decision environment within which Cuba's economic decisions are most likely to be influenced. In the third section, the specifications of the Bayesian forecasts are defined in terms of the mutually exclusive and exhaustive states of nature and the analytical translation of select target variables into relevant events. The probabilistic calculation of Cuba's economic direction is formalized by the forecast mechanics presented in fourth section. Finally, conclusions drawn from the forecasts and their implications regarding economic direction and recovery are presented. Contained within Appendix A is a numerical example using hierarchical inference to calculate the assigned probabilities of relevant events.

An econometric approach, although feasible, may prove too complex and cumbersome in assessing a generalized sense of economic heading; considering the difficulty of establishing, mathematically, production functions without reliable data and the crisis mode in which the Cuban economy is currently operating. A time-series model, which extrapolates past economic trends into the future, usually occurs in cases where a large number of data points are available. A single-equation regression model attempts to explain the variable under study by a single, often time-dependent, function (linear or non-linear) of explanatory variables. Similarly, a multi-equation simulation model seeks to relate the explanatory variables, through a set of equations, not only to the variable under study, but to each other as well. All of these approaches requires a thorough understanding of the economic interrelationships and processes being studied, and consequently, the construction of

such models may prove extremely difficult (Pindyck and Rubinfield 1976: xiv-xv). The dynamics of the Cuban economic crisis force a collateral reevaluation of the processes at work and thereby compound the necessary mathematical formulations. Pursuant to the obstacles expressed thus far, a Bayesian forecast appears to be an applicable, appealing alternative; even though no similar application of the methodology was discovered upon reviewing the literature.

Bayes' theorem provides a formal procedure for revising the probability assessments of hypotheses concerning a situation such that evidence upon which the revisions are based is (1) more systematically considered than it would be intuitively and (2) is given more weight than if it were intuitively aggregated and judged. Thus more information can be extracted from the available data because the technique allows each piece of evidence, whether central or marginal, to add its weight to the final assessment in a systematic way (Hunter, 1984). Bayesian analysis calls for all probability assessments to be subjective and therefore risks reflection of undue bias or genuine disagreement among analysts. Bayesian techniques seek to overcome these shortfalls by assigning a formal role to subjective (non-data) information, allowing the forecaster to evaluate the impact of such information on the conclusions via a sensitivity analysis.

Theorizing that the Cuban economy can be qualified as either a centrally planned economy, a mixed economy or a predominantly market economy, specifies a set of mutually exclusive and collectively exhaustive possible outcomes that constitute the hypotheses under analysis. Following the tenets of decision theory and Bayesian analysis the following approach results: (1) each of the possible outcomes is subjectively assigned a probability of occurrence; (2) considered next are events and/or evidence that would support the aforementioned outcomes; (3) the indicators related to these events and/or evidence are identified; (4) quantitative linkages (conditional probabilities) are established between adjacent levels based upon existing knowledge or information and hierarchical inference, as dictated by the fundamental principles of decision theory; (5) lastly, as new events occur or evidence is received, the use of Bayes' theorem leads to the revision of the original probabilities assigned.

As a result of the Bayesian forecast, a graphical representation of the initial and revised probabilities of the hypotheses will be used to illustrate the overall trends of the Cuban economy as relevant events occur. In addition, a sensitivity analysis of the forecast will be performed by substituting high or low values into various probability assessments and re-calculating the hypotheses' outcome probabilities, thereby providing a range and an idea of the relative sensitivities involved. The originally assigned probabilities can also be adjusted in response to changing political or economic events and the forecast revised to reflect other probabilistic scenarios.

THE DECISION ENVIRONMENT

Examined in this section are the dominant political and economic environments that affect Cuba's attempt at acheiving the terminal state desired by Fidel Castro.

The Political Environment

The political environment under which turmoil and change exist in Cuba is defined by the leadership of Fidel Castro and his commitment to Cuban socialism despite civil discontent over decreasing levels of domestic consumption and social benefits. Influential to the short-to-medium term economic decisions undertaken by the Castro regime will be the perceived intensity, extent and duration of popular opposition, and the regime's ability to suppress or appease. If the Castro regime is to remain in control, it must find ways to re-legitimize itself through economic recovery and political revitalization (Gonzalez and Ronfeldt 1994).

The Economic Environment

The decisions made by the Castro regime in response to the current crisis have thus far focused on three economic areas: the major production sectors of the economy, foreign direct investment and the increasing significance of the black market. Key to any re-equilibration, or recovery strategies within the intermediate term are the major sectors of the Cuban economy that are capable of earning hard currency or providing import substitutes. Similarly, the success-

ful attraction of foreign direct investment could considerably factor into the output production matrix of the Cuban economy, particularly if it materializes as capital. The black market in Cuba yields both aggravation and reprieve to economic planners. The history of monetary dualism in Cuba as discussed by Sanguinetty (1994) seems to reveal a reoccurring theme, "...the development of the dollar-peso dualism followed...the need to finance government expeditures." While the black market accelerates the dollarization of the Cuban economy and is contradictory to socialist political and economic aims, it also serves to alleviate some economic and social pressures. In addition, the black market sets the (un)official Cuban peso/dollar exchange rate.

SPECIFICATION OF THE FORECASTS

States of Nature

The hypotheses put forth in a Bayesian analysis are mutually exclusive and exhaustive and serve to specify the possible "states of nature," or outcomes, with respect to a particular issue. For the purposes of this paper the systemic forces at work in the decision environment are such that the possible states of nature characterizing the Cuban economy are: a centrally planned economy (CPE), a mixed economy (MIX) or a predominantly market economy (MKT). Each of the possible outcomes is assigned a prior probability representing the assessor's degree of belief concerning the truth of the various hypotheses. Based on the recent works of Mesa-Lago and Fabian (1993), Ritter (1993), and Gonzalez and Ronfeldt (1994) the following prior probabilities are assigned to the economic direction of the Cuban economy in the short-to-medium term:

Probability	Justification
P(CPE) = .20	the former dependence upon Soviet subsidy and the CEMA trade bloc has left Cuba without economic support in time of crisis
P(MIX) = .65	the bifurcation of the Cuban economy and the concern for preserving social gains
P(MKT) = .15	the steadfast reluctance of Fidel Castro to accept market reforms and capitalism

Target Variables

Target variables, within a Bayesian context, represent those factors, pieces of evidence or activities readily translated into events from which revised conditional probabilities of the possible hypotheses are assessed. According to fundamental probability theory, two events are independent if the probability assigned to one event is unaffected by the knowledge that the other event has occurred. The conditionally independent form of Bayes' Theorem can only be used if it can be justified mathematically, often an arduous theorectical exercise. In the case of economic or political applications, prior events may in fact be essential to formulating a valid probability assessment and therefore, using conditional dependence represents a more accurate and realistic approach (Hunter 1984: 144-150). There are several target variables, dependent on other activities, that are relevant to the possible hypotheses regarding the Cuban economy. Although several more could be postulated, six target variables assumed to be conditionally dependent have been chosen:

1. Foreign Exchange Earnings,
2. Import Substitution,
3. Political Control,
4. Economic Reforms,
5. Financial Integration into Global Financial Community, and
6. External Policies of International and Regional Actors.

The analytical translation of these variables into relevant events (E1-E6) is discussed below.

Event 1—Foreign Exchange Earnings Exceed $4 Billion

Cuban foreign exchange earnings are a direct calculation of the revenues generated by both the commodity and service sectors added to foreign direct investments. The earning potential of major Cuban exports such as sugar and nickel will depend not only on production output but also on world market prices, unless more favorable bilateral agreements materialize. Increased foreign direct investment in the form of joint ventures may partially compensate for the low world prices of Cuban commodities particularly if selected industries become more efficient and benefit from long-term capital.

Event 2—Import Substitution Meets 50 Percent of Consumption

The most significant import substitution efforts undertaken by the Castro regime address energy and foodstuff self-sufficiency. The lack of energy inputs severely curtails the production output of Cuba's most important industries. In addition, regularly scheduled electricity blackouts throughout the country serve as a daily reminder of the unabated crisis conditions. A significant discovery and refinement of Cuban oil reserves or the completion and successful operation of the Juraguá nuclear plant could lessen energy rationing restrictions. The satisfaction of consumer demand for foodstuffs represents a prominent catalyst of civil unrest. Should Cuba earn sufficient foreign exchange to purchase 30 to 40 percent of its foodstuffs abroad, and should import substitution meet 50 percent of domestic consumption, the remaining 20 to 10 percent could be absorbed by private production or the black market.

Event 3—Political Control is Maintained by Castro

Maintaining political control within Cuba involves the Castro regime being able to respond quickly and decisively to civil or military challenges. Central to this issue is the ability of the Castro regime to sustain its claim of legitimacy in the face of alternate claims from outside the regime. Black market activity may also provide information indicative of the potential for civil discontent or disobedience. Should staple consumer goods become increasingly scarce, even on the black market, the unofficial exchange rate (peso/dollar) will rise, reflecting inflationary pressures. Inflation of black market prices left unchecked could ultimately result in desperate popular actions. According to Edlestein (1995), a socioeconomic structure must be created in which the social relations of production draw individual and sectoral short-term interests closer to the needs of long-term socialist development.

Event 4—Economic Reforms Result in Less Centralization

The relevant economic policies include those affecting institutional structures, as well as internally and externally oriented policies (Alonso and Rathbone 1993: 19). The internal and external economic policies that result in less centralization include: liberalizing prices, privatizing state industry, instituting tax reform, adopting a realistic exchange rate, restructuring incentive policies, reducing state subsidies, and encouraging private enterprise. The tradeoff is a loss of state control over the allocation of resources and economic activity, from which income distribution inequalities result. Economic centralization, as stated by Edlestein, lacks the flexibility to adapt to changing conditions and technologies, and is inadequate to provide for continued growth under conditions of reincorporation into the global economy.

Event 5—Integration into the Global Financial Community

A major obstacle thwarting the integration of Cuba into the global financial community is its inability to service a $11 billion debt owed to Western lenders.[3] The effect of Cuba paying its foreign debt is to reduce the foreign exchange available for imports and investments. For Cuba to cover interest and principal on its debt an increased trade surplus or a renegotiated repayment schedule is necessary. Cuba is not a member of the International Monetary Fund nor the World Bank and therefore is unable to secure desperately needed financial credits. Prospective lender-nations remain skeptical of Cuba's economic and political future and are reluctant to extend credit other than in the form of investments in joint ventures, or "debt swap" deals as accomplished by Mexico. The "governance" criteria of Western aid donors, as identified by Betancourt (1994), include the legitimacy of government; accountability of political and official elements of the government; competence of governments to formulate policies and deliver services; and respect for human rights and rule of law. Should significant oil reserves be discovered in Cuba, access to financial credits could be considerably facilitated.

Event 6—Foreign Trade/Aid Policies Benefit Cuba

The external foreign policies of international and regional actors such as the U.S., EU, OAS, and CARICOM could quite literally throw Cuba a lifeline. Such action could entail development aid similar to that pledged to the economic reconstruction of Haiti following the return of exiled president Jean-Bertrand Aristide in mid-October 1994. The most debated foreign policy issue remains the lifting of the U.S. trade embargo, which undoubtedly would increase foreign investment but not necessarily eliminate tension between the two countries, considering the $1.8 billion in expropriated properties claimed by American businesses and the $7 billion claimed by Cuban exiles. According to Sanguinetty (1994), given the size of Cuban markets, the state of current technologies, and the economies of scale, Cuba's growth prospects are dependent on its ability to export. The efficacy of the Helms-Burton Act is yet to be determined in its totality. Debate regarding any legally binding interpretation under the General Agreement on Tariffs and Trade (GATT), by such agencies as the World Trade Organization (WTO), and the economic policy reaction or retaliation by Cuba's major trade partners remain unresolved.

SCENARIO FORECASTS

The scenario forecasts assume the continuation of Fidel Castro in a position of unchallenged political and economic leadership into at least the medium term (5-8 years). Under the first five scenarios, U.S. policy toward normalizing relations with Cuba and lifting the embargo remains unchanged, as does Cuba's indefinite moratorium on the servicing of its foreign debt. Under these conditions, Event 5 and Event 6 can be excluded from Scenarios I-V. A word of caution is necessary with respect to the specific time order of relevant events. If no specific time order can be specified for the events under consideration, different orders will represent different composite events and one should expect to calculate different final products for the different probability judgments assigned (Hunter 1984: 168). Event 1 through Event 6 have

---

3. John Rice, "Cuba to Open New Banks, Talking with Foreign Creditors," AP (Mexico City): October 25, 1995.

Table 1A. Assigned Probabilities for Scenario I

j	P(H$_j$)	P(E1⎮H$_j$)	P(E2⎮E1 & H$_j$)	P(E3⎮E2 & E1 & H$_j$)	P(E4⎮E3 & E2 & E1 & H$_j$)	Rev. Prob. of Hj
1	.20	.05	.35	.70	.10	.002
2	.65	.45	.55	.80	.65	.598
3	.15	.65	.75	.90	.85	.400

Table 1B. Revised Probabilities for Scenario I

Event	P(CPE)	P(MIX)	P(MKT)
None	.200	.650	.150
E1	.025	.731	.244
E2	.015	.677	.308
E3	.012	.653	.334
E4	.002	.598	.400

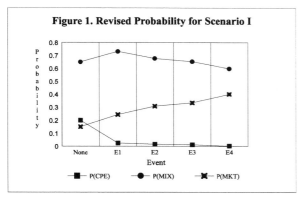

Figure 1. Revised Probability for Scenario I

sequence of events is ordered E1-E2-E3-E4. Table 1A lists the prior probability of each hypothesis, the conditional probabilities associated with the sequence of events, and the revised probabilities calculated after the sequence has occurred.

The generalized trends of the Cuban economy subsequent to the given sequence of relevant events for Scenario I are depicted in Figure 1.

As each relevant event occurs the probability of each hypothesis (CPE, MIX, MKT) is recalculated (revised) using Bayes' theorem. These results are listed in Table 1B, and correspond to data points which determine the revised probability graph in Figure 1.

Under the conditions of Scenario I the assigned probability of each hypothesis was affected by the associated sequence of events as follows: P(CPE) decreased by 99.1%; P(MIX) decreased by 8%; and P(MKT) increased by 167%.

been placed in a logical order of succession without regard for the discrete time intervals between successive events. Event 1 through Event 4 are interchangeable; however, Event 5 and Event 6 most likely would succeed Event 1 through Event 4 regardless of their order. All assigned probabilities are subjective, and are intended to appeal to the prescience of the reader.

Due to the initial definition of Event 4, the conditional probability, P(E4⎮H$_1$), is assigned a low value and factors to significantly decrease P(CPE) regardless of the sequence of relevant events. For this study Event 4 is considered an applicable variable to the direction of the Cuban economy, and therefore has been included in each scenario.

Scenario I—Events Occur 1-2-3-4

Scenario I reflects the limitations of a Cuban CPE with respect to earning foreign exchange receipts in excess of $4 billion; considerably more favorable conditions exist under a mixed or market economy. The

Scenario II—Events Occur 4-3-2-1

Scenario II considers the same pretense as in Scenario I, but instead assumes the events occur in reverse order. Similar to the previous case, Table 2A lists the prior probability of each hypothesis, the conditional probabilities associated with the sequence of events, and the revised probabilities calculated after the sequence has occurred.

The generalized trends of the Cuban economy subsequent to the given sequence of relevant events for Scenario II are shown in Figure 2.

As before, the revised probabilities associated with the occurrence of each relevant event have been calculated and appear in Table 2B.

Under the hypothetical conditions of Scenario II: P(CPE) decreased by 97%; P(MIX) decreased by 4.6%; and P(MKT) increased by 149%.

Table 2A. Assigned Probabilities for Scenario II

j	P(H_j)	P(E4|H_j)	P(E3|E4&H_j)	P(E2|E3&E4&H_j)	P(E1|E2&E3&E4&H_j)	Rev. Prob. of H_j
1	.20	.10	.40	.25	.25	.006
2	.65	.65	.65	.45	.40	.620
3	.15	.85	.85	.55	.50	.374

Table 3A. Assigned Probabilities for Scenario III

j	P(H_j)	P(E3|H_j)	P(E4|E3&H_j)	P(E1|E4&E3&H_j)	P(E2|E1&E4&E3&H_j)	Rev. Prob. of H_j
1	.20	.40	.20	.25	.25	.018
2	.65	.60	.40	.45	.40	.522
3	.15	.80	.75	.55	.50	.460

Table 2B. Revised Probabilities for Scenario II

Event	P(CPE)	P(MIX)	P(MKT)
None	.200	.650	.150
E4	.035	.741	.224
E3	.020	.702	.277
E2	.011	.667	.322
E1	.006	.620	.374

Table 3B. Revised Probabilities for Scenario III

Event	P(CPE)	P(MIX)	P(MKT)
None	.200	.650	.150
E3	.136	.661	.203
E4	.061	.595	.344
E1	.032	.568	.400
E2	.018	.522	.460

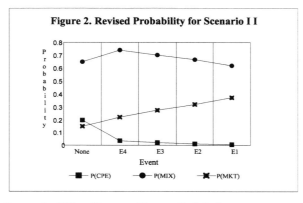

Figure 2. Revised Probability for Scenario I I

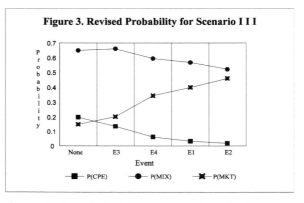

Figure 3. Revised Probability for Scenario I I I

Scenario III—Events Occur 3-4-2-1

Scenario III considers the conditions under which both political control and decentralization are less likely to occur coincident with a CPE. Under this scenario the Cuban government would fail to provide the most basic foodstuffs or no longer guarantee the social gains of the revolution. As a result, civil opposition would increase its demands for more market reforms and less centralization. The sequence of relevant events is ordered E3-E4-E2-E1.

The generalized trends of the Cuban economy subsequent to the given sequence of relevant events for Scenario III are depicted in Figure 3.

The revised probabilities associated with the occurrence of each relevant event appear in Table 3B.

Under the hypothetical conditions of Scenario III: P(CPE) decreased by 91%; P(MIX) decreased by 19.7%; and P(MKT) increased by 207%.

Scenario IV—Events Occur 2-3-4-1

Scenario IV reflects the condition under which import substitution efforts to meet 50 percent of consumption needs are not likely to succeed in the near term regardless of the economic system in place. Table 4A lists the prior probability of each hypothesis, the conditional probabilities associated with the sequence of events, and the revised probabilities calculated after the sequence has occurred.

Table 4A. Assigned Probabilities for Scenario IV

j	P(H$_j$)	P(E2|H$_j$)	P(E3|E2&H$_j$)	P(E4|E3&E2&H$_j$)	P(E1|E4&E3&E2&H$_j$)	Rev. Prob. of H$_j$
1	.20	.10	.65	.20	.25	.002
2	.65	.20	.75	.40	.45	.543
3	.15	.30	.85	.70	.55	.455

Table 5A. Assigned Probabilities for Scenario V

j	P(H$_j$)	P(E1|H$_j$)	P(E2|E1&H$_j$)	P(E3|E2&E1&H$_j$)	P(E4|E3&E2&E1&H$_j$)	Rev. Prob. of H$_j$
1	.333	.05	.35	.70	.10	.002
2	.333	.45	.55	.80	.65	.256
3	.333	.65	.75	.90	.85	.742

Table 4B. Revised Probabilities for Scenario IV

Event	P(CPE)	P(MIX)	P(MKT)
None	.200	.650	.150
E2	.011	.734	.254
E3	.009	.711	.279
E4	.004	.590	.405
E1	.002	.543	.455

Table 5B. Revised Probabilities for Scenario V

Event	P(CPE)	P(MIX)	P(MKT)
None	.200	.650	.150
E1	.043	.391	.565
E2	.023	.329	.648
E3	.019	.305	.676
E4	.002	.256	.742

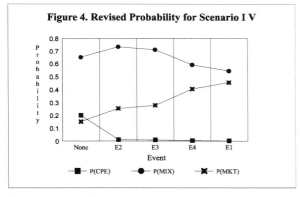

Figure 4. Revised Probability for Scenario I V

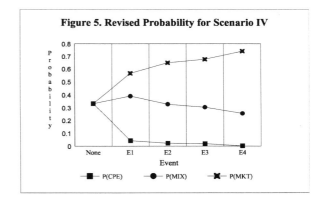

Figure 5. Revised Probability for Scenario IV

The generalized trends of the Cuban economy subsequent to the given sequence of relevant events for Scenario IV are depicted in Figure 4.

The revised probabilities associated with the occurrence of each relevant event appear in Table 4B.

Under the hypothetical conditions of Scenario IV: P(CPE) decreased by 99%; P(MIX) decreased by 16.5%; and P(MKT) increased by 203%.

Scenario V—Equiprobable Hypotheses

Scenario V assumes that each of the three hypotheses has an equal probability of occurring, i.e., P(CPE) = P(MIX) = P(MKT) = 0.333. Such an equiprobable occurrence is most unlikely in the case of Cuba, however, it will be examined to illustrate an initial lack of information or intuition. The condition represents

an assessor's judgment that the situation is independent of the probabilistic outcome of each economic system prior to the sequence of relevant events. The remaining assigned probabilities are identical to Scenario I as is the sequence of relevant events, which is ordered E1-E2-E3-E4. Listed in Table 5A are the prior, conditional, and revised probabilities.

The generalized trends of the Cuban economy subsequent to the relevant events for Scenario V appear in Figure 5.

The revised probabilities associated with the occurrence of each relevant event appear in Table 5B.

Table 6A.   Assigned Probabilities for Scenario VI

j	P(H$_j$)	P(E1|H$_j$)	P(E2|E1&(H$_j$)	P(E3|E2...(H$_j$)	P(E4|E3...(H$_j$)	P(E5|E4...(H$_j$)	P(E6|E5...(H$_j$)
1	.20	.05	.35	.70	.10	.20	.25
2	.65	.45	.55	.80	.65	.30	.35
3	.15	.75	.75	.90	.85	.40	.45

Table 6B.   Revised Probabilities for Scenario VI

Event	P(CPE)	P(MIX)	P(MKT)
None	.200	.650	.150
E1	.025	.731	.244
E2	.015	.677	.308
E3	.012	.653	.334
E4	.002	.598	.400
E5	.001	.528	.471
E6	.001	.465	.534

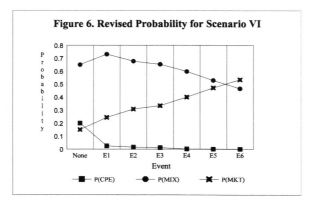

Figure 6. Revised Probability for Scenario VI

Under the hypothetical conditions of Scenario V: P(CPE) decreased by 99.4%; P(MIX) decreased by 23.1%; and P(MKT) increased by 122.8%.

Scenario VI—A Road to Recovery

Scenario VI is identical to Scenario I, with the additions of Event 5 and Event 6. This scenario incorporates the conditions that allow for Cuba's foreign debt to come under control and the external trade policies of other nations and organizations to significantly benefit Cuba; neither is expected in the near term. Such a situation could arise as the Cuban economy displayed signs of sustainable growth. Global perceptions of political and economic risk would be replaced by estimates of expected recovery. The sequence of relevant events is, ordered E1-E2-E3-E4-E5-E6. Table 6A lists the prior probability of each hypothesis, and the associated conditional probabilities.

The generalized trends of the Cuban economy subsequent to the relevant events for Scenario VI appear in Figure 6.

The revised probabilities associated with the occurrence of each relevant event appear in Table 6B.

Under the hypothetical conditions of Scenario VI: P(CPE) decreased by 99.6%; P(MIX) decreased by 28.4%; and P(MKT) increased by 255.7%.

Scenario VII—An Economic Lifeline

Scenario VII considers the same pretense as Scenario VI, but instead assumes the events occur in reverse order. This scenario represents a concerted effort by the international financial community and other nations and organizations to actively perpetuate the economic recovery of Cuba. In essence, an economic lifeline would be thrown to the Castro regime. The likelihood of such a coordinated effort prior to any major economic reforms within Cuba is low. Table 7A lists the prior probability of each hypothesis, and the associated conditional probabilities.

The generalized trends of the Cuban economy subsequent to the relevant events for Scenario VII appear in Figure 7.

The revised probabilities associated with the occurrence of each relevant event appear in Table 7B.

Under the hypothetical conditions of Scenario VI: P(CPE) decreased by 94.5%; P(MIX) decreased by 13.8%; and P(MKT) increased by 186%. Before interpreting the scenario forecasts and formulating any conclusions, the probability assessments require a sensitivity analysis.

Sensitivity Analysis .

Sensitivity analysis is used to investigate the extent to which the revised probability of a hypothesis is influenced by any particular conditional probability. The sensitivity of a forecast to any assigned probability can be determined by varying the probability of in-

308

Table 7A. Assigned Probabilities for Scenario VII

j	P(Hⱼ)	P(E6|Hⱼ)	P(E5|E6&(Hⱼ)	P(E4|E5...(Hⱼ)	P(E3|E4...(Hⱼ)	P(E2|E3...(Hⱼ)	P(E1|E2...(Hⱼ)
1	.20	.10	.25	.15	.70	.65	.60
2	.65	.20	.35	.55	.80	.75	.70
3	.15	.30	.45	.65	.90	.85	.80

Table 8A. Probabilities for Sensitivity Analysis P(E1|H₁)

j	P(Hⱼ)	P(E1|Hⱼ)	P(E2|E1&Hⱼ)	P(E3|E2&E1&Hⱼ)	P(E4|E3&E2&E1&Hⱼ)	Rev. Prob. of Hⱼ
1	.20	.85	.35	.70	.10	.029
2	.65	.45	.55	.80	.65	.582
3	.15	.65	.75	.90	.85	.389

Table 7B. Revised Probabilities for Scenario VII

Event	P(CPE)	P(MIX)	P(MKT)
None	.200	.650	.150
E6	.103	.667	.231
E5	.071	.643	.286
E4	.019	.643	.338
E3	.016	.618	.366
E2	.013	.590	.396
E1	.011	.560	.429

Table 8B. Revised Probabilities for P(E1|H₁) = .85

Event	P(CPE)	P(MIX)	P(MKT)
None	.200	.650	.150
E1	.304	.522	.174
E2	.203	.548	.249
E3	.176	.545	.279
E4	.029	.581	.389

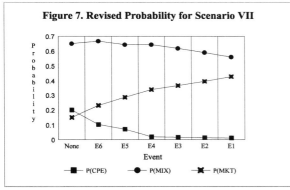

Figure 7. Revised Probability for Scenario VII

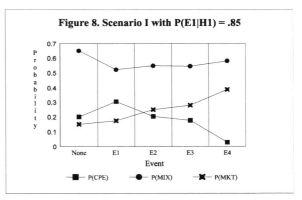

Figure 8. Scenario I with P(E1|H1) = .85

terest, recalculating the revised probabilities, comparing these values to the original set of probabilities, and evaluating any significant differences that result. Considerable variance between the two sets of revised probabilities would require additional justification, analysis or information to ascertain the optimum value for the conditional probability in question. (Barclay, Brown, Kelly, Peterson, Phillips and Selvidge 1977: 99-102)

The Foreign Exchange Earnings Under a CPE

In each of the scenarios the foreign exchange earning potential of a centrally planned economy was assessed to be significantly lower than that of a mixed or predominantly market economy. To demonstrate the sensitivity of a forecast to the earning potential of

a CPE, a value higher than conditionally warranted is used to calculate a new set of revised probabilities. Consider Scenario I with the condition that the occurrence of Cuban foreign exchange earnings exceeding $4 billion is, by contrast, most probable under a CPE. How is the forecast of Scenario I affected if all other conditional probabilities are unchanged? Listed in Table 8A are the assigned prior, and conditional probabilities, with the value for P(E1|H₁) appearing in **bold italics**.

The revised probabilities associated with the occurrence of each relevant event have been recalculated and appear in Table 8B.

Table 9A. Probabilities for Sensitivity Analysis of P(E3|H₁) and P(E1|H₁)

j	P(Hⱼ)	P(E1|Hⱼ)	P(E2|E1&Hⱼ)	P(E3|E2&E1&Hⱼ)	P(E4|E3&E2&E1&Hⱼ)	Rev. Prob. of Hⱼ
1	.20	**.80**	.35	.70	.10	.029
2	.65	.45	.55	.80	.65	.582
3	.15	**.40**	.75	.90	.85	.389

The sensitivity of the Scenario I forecast to the conditional probability, P(E1|H₁) = .85, is evident upon examining the revised probabilities of a CPE in Table 8B up to the occurrence of Event 3 and comparing them with corresponding values for P(CPE) listed in Table 1A. With the condition that P(E1|H₁) = .85, P(CPE) decreases by only 12% after Event 3 has occurred, compared to a decrease of 93.8% calculated for Scenario I. The revised generalized trends of the Cuban economy subsequent to the given sequence of relevant events for Scenario I with P(E1|H₁) = .85 are depicted in Figure 8.

The current economic situation in Cuba precludes the justification for assigning the occurrence of a Cuban CPE earning foreign exchange in excess of $4 billion a high probability. Despite the sensitivity at high values of P(E1|H₁), an assigned probability ranging from .05-.65 will not significantly influence a scenario forecast.

Political Control and a CPE

The sensitivity of a forecast to the conditional probability of political control, P(E3|H₁), is analyzed similar to the case of P(E1|H₁). The ability of the Cuban government to maintain political control under a centrally planned economy is now assessed to be higher than under a mixed or predominantly market economy. This condition alone is sufficient to influence P(MKT), but when combined with an increased conditional probability for P(E1|H₁) it significantly affects P(CPE) as well. Scenario III is chosen for this example, and a new set of revised probabilities calculated. Table 9A lists the associated probabilities, with the amended values for P(E3|H₁), P(E3|H₃) and P(E1|E4&E3&H₁) appearing in *bold italics*.

The revised probabilities have been recalculated and appear below in Table 9B.

Table 9B. Revised Probabilities for P(E3|H₁) = .80, P(E3|H₃) = .40 and P(E1|E4&E3&H₁) = .85

Event	P(CPE)	P(MIX)	P(MKT)
None	.200	.650	.150
E3	.262	.639	.098
E4	.137	.669	.193
E1	.223	.574	.203
E2	.144	.594	.262

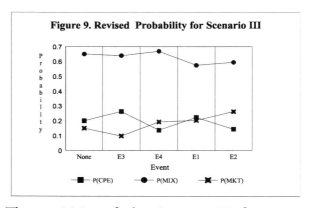

Figure 9. Revised Probability for Scenario III

The sensitivity of the Scenario III forecast to P(E3|H₁) and P(E3|H₃), given a high value for P(E1|H₁), is determined by contrasting the values for P(MKT) and P(CPE) listed in Table 3A with the new set of revised probabilities. Under the above conditions, P(MKT) increases by 74.7%, and P(CPE) decreases by only 28% after the relevant events occur, this compared to a P(MKT) increase of 207% and a P(CPE) decrease of 91% calculated for Scenario III. The revised generalized trends of the Cuban economy subsequent to the relevant events for Scenario III with P(E3|H₁) = .80, P(E3|H₃) = .40 and P(E1|E4&E3&H₁) = .85 are depicted in Figure 9.

The Cuban state security apparatus poses a portentous force to any civil opposition. However, as the economic crisis worsens increased repression of civil unrest will undoubtedly reach a threshold beyond

Table 10A Assigned Probabilities with P(E1|H₃) = .10

j	P(H$_j$)	P(E1|H$_j$)	P(E2|E1&H$_j$)	P(E3|E2&E1&H$_j$)	P(E4|E3&E2&E1&H$_j$)	Rev. Prob. of H$_j$
1	.20	.05	.35	.70	.10	.029
2	.65	.45	.55	.80	.65	.582
3	.15	*.10*	.75	.90	.85	.389

Table 10B. Revised Probabilities for P(E1|H₃) = .10

Event	P(CPE)	P(MIX)	P(MKT)
None	.200	.650	.150
E1	.031	.921	.047
E2	.020	.916	.064
E3	.017	.911	.072
E4	.003	.904	.093

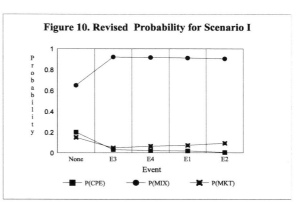

Figure 10. Revised Probability for Scenario I

which its effectiveness will be minimal. Arguably in the case of Cuba, definite political control is seen to be jeopardized by the adoption of free market mechanisms, as lesser economic controls could intensify a concurrent appetite of organized opposition for more political freedoms. Ascribing high values to P(E3|H₁) in the near term cannot be readily justified, and the sensitivity of a scenario forecast assigned such a conditional probability exceeding 0.60 will prove significant.

The Foreign Exchange Earnings Under a Market Economy

Each of the scenarios previously examined assesses the foreign exchange earning potential of a predominantly market economy (MKT) to be significantly higher than either a mixed economy or CPE. Consider Scenario I with the condition that Cuban foreign exchange earnings exceeding $4 billion is considerably less probable under a MKT. In this case, the forecast sensitivity to P(E1|H₃), is determined by using a lower conditional probability. Listed in Table 10A are the assigned prior, conditional and revised probabilities, with the value for P(E1|H₃) in **bold italics**.

The revised probabilities have been recalculated and appear below in Table 10B.

The sensitivity of the Scenario I forecast to a low value of P(E1|H₃), is analyzed upon comparing the values for P(MKT) and P(CPE) listed in Table 1B with the new set of revised probabilities in Table 10B.

P(MKT) decreases by 38%, and P(MIX) increases by 39.1% after the sequence of relevant events has occurred, this is contrasted with a P(MKT) increase of 167% and a P(MIX) decrease of 8% previously calculated for Scenario I. The generalized trends of the Cuban economy subsequent to the given sequence of events for Scenario I with P(E1|H₃) = .10 are depicted in Figure 10.

Assigning P(E1|H₃) a low value relative to P(E1|H₁) and P(E1|H₂) does not accurately reflect the foreign exchange earning potential of a predominantly market economy. Associating a relatively higher conditional probability to P(E1|H₃) is justified, given the historic inefficiencies of Cuba's CPE and the limited number of autonomous export earning enterprises expected to operate in a mixed Cuban economy. To overcome forecast sensitivity at low values of P(E1|H₃), its assigned conditional probability should be greater than 0.55 or the difference between P(E1|H₃) and both P(E1|H₂) and P(E1|H₁) at least 0.20.

Pessimistic and Optimistic Probability Judgments

Sensitivity analysis may also confirm if a scenario forecast is influenced by overly optimistic or pessimistic probability judgments of a particular event. Consider Scenario I with the condition that Cuban foreign exchange earnings exceeding $4 billion are

Table 11A. Assigned Probabilities for Pessimistic Assessment of E1

j	$P(H_j)$	$P(E1|H_j)$	$P(E2|E1\&H_j)$	$P(E3|E2\&E1\&H_j)$	$P(E4|E3\&E2\&E1\&H_j)$	Rev. Prob. of H_j
1	.20	*.05*	.35	.70	.10	.008
2	.65	*.10*	.55	.80	.65	.575
3	.15	*.15*	.75	.90	.85	.417

Table 11B. Revised Probabilities for Pessimistic Assessment of E1

Event	P(CPE)	P(MIX)	P(MKT)
None	.200	.650	.150
E1	.102	.667	.231
E2	.062	.637	.301
E3	.053	.618	.328
E4	.008	.575	.417

Figure 11. Revised Probability (Pessimistic Case)

considerably less probable under each of the hypotheses: CPE, MIX, and MKT. In this example lower assigned values of P(E1|Hj), j = 1,2,3; define a pessimistic assessment of Event 1. Table 11A lists the assigned prior, conditional and revised probabilities, with the affected values for P(E1|Hj) shown in **bold italics**.

The revised probabilities have been recalculated and appear below in Table 11B

For the sake of argument the original conditional probabilities listed in Table 1A are considered an optimistic assessment of Event 1. Under the optimistic condition, P(CPE) decreased 99%, P(MIX) decreased 8% and P(MKT) increased by 167%. The revised forecast, incorporating the pessimistic probabilities, resulted in P(CPE) decreasing 96%, P(MIX) decreasing 11.5% and P(MKT) increasing by 178%. The economic trends of Scenario I with a pessimistic assessment of Event 1 appear in Figure 11.

As this example illustrates, sensitivity analysis can be extended to establish the sensitivity of a forecast to the "pessimistic/optimistic" assessment of a particular event. All assigned conditional probabilities specific to the event must be re-evaluated before proceeding with any analysis of the revised probabilities. For Scenario I, a pessimistic assessment of E1 results in a revised probability over four times higher than calculated in the optimistic case for P(CPE) after each event occurs. The revised probabilities calculated after the occurrence of the final event, however,

do not appear significantly influenced by the quantification of a pessimistic assessment.

FORECAST RESULTS AND CONCLUSIONS
Forecast Results
The forecast results of Scenario I reveal a sharp increase (62.7%) in P(MKT) coinciding with a sharper decline (87.5%) in P(CPE) after Cuban foreign exchange earnings exceed $4 billion. As subsequent events occur both P(MKT) and P(CPE) continue to increase and decrease respectively, but at a much less pronounced rate. The differences between the systemic attributes of a CPE and MKT directly affect their capacity to achieve the necessary conditions for Event 1. It is this disparity that accounts for the dramatic divergence between P(MKT) and P(CPE) in Scenario I. The probability associated with a mixed economy, P(MIX), exhibits a steady decline of only 3%-8% after a modest initial increase of 12.4%. Overall, the probabilistic estimate of Cuba's economic direction under the conditions for Scenario I suggests a steady convergence towards a 60%-40% split between P(MIX) and P(MKT) after the sequence of relevant events occurs.

The forecast results of Scenario II essentially parallel those of Scenario I, with P(MKT) demonstrating a slightly lower rate of increase. The most recent political and economic events in Cuba more closely resemble the sequence assumed under Scenario II, however, the revised probabilities calculated for both forecasts are approximately the same.

The forecast results of Scenario III reveal a large displacement for both P(MKT) and P(CPE) after the occurrence of Event 4. The revised probability for a MKT increases by 69.4% while the revised probability of a CPE decreases by 55.1%. The probability associated with a MIX exhibits a steady decline of 4%-10% after an initial increase of only 1.7%. The facility of implementing economic reforms resulting in less centralization under a MKT versus a CPE explains the divergence. Such reforms represent a compromise by the Castro regime to counter increased civil unrest and preserve political control. Of the seven scenarios analyzed, the forecast results of Scenario III offer the closest approximation to a 50%-50% assessment of P(MKT) versus P(MIX).

The forecast results of Scenario IV are similar to those of Scenario III, displaying the most significant probability shift after the occurrence of Event 4. In this case, however, marked convergence is evident between P(MKT) and P(MIX). The revised probability for a MKT increases by 45.2% while the revised probability of a MIX decreases by 17.0%, closing the previous gap between the two by 57.2%. The revised probability associated with a CPE exhibits an initial decrease of 94.5%, reflecting its inability to meet import substitution levels descriptive of Event 2. The forecast results of Scenario IV approximate those of Scenario III since the scarcity of basic commodities necessary for daily survival in Cuba could spark the civil disobedience and unrest examined under Scenario III.

The forecast results of Scenario V consider equal probability of the three hypotheses: CPE. MIX, MKT. The revised probabilities immediately diverge from one another with P(MIX) experiencing the least change after the sequence of events has occurred, ultimately resulting in an approximate 74%-26% split between P(MKT) and P(MIX). The dominance of P(MKT) after the sequence of events has occurred is not unexpected since the conditions most favorable to each event is optimum under a predominantly market economy.

The forecast results of Scenario VI postulate Cuba's economic direction in the medium term. The revised probabilities portray an extension of the converging economic trends examined under Scenario I. Importantly, the revised probabilities of P(MKT) and P(MIX) cross and separate after Event 5, but before the occurrence of Event 6. It is at this point that P(MKT) overtakes P(MIX) suggesting the likelihood of Cuba integrating into the global economy as a predominantly market economy given Events 1 through 6 have transpired.

Similar to the analogy drawn between Scenarios I and II, the forecast results of Scenario VII parallel those of Scenario VI. The revised probabilities of Scenario VII depict steady convergence between P(MKT) and P(MIX). The probability of a mixed economy, however, remains approximately 13 percentage points higher than the probability of a predominantly market economy after the sequence of events has occurred. Upon initial observation, the forecast results of Scenarios VI and VII lend some support to principals advocating the continued imposition of the U.S. trade embargo against Cuba as a means to bring about a free market economy there. The inferences will not be pursued and are beyond the scope of this study.

Cuba's Economic Direction

The conditions guiding Cuba's economic direction are dominated by the Cuban socialist experience, the supremacy of Fidel Castro, and the stark isolation which confronts the Cuban economy. The course taken by the Cuban economy in the near term is conditionally dependent upon reform measures directed at preserving the two former conditions and resolving the third. It is this conditional dependence that lends itself to a Bayesian formulation of possible scenarios and a forecast indicative of economic direction. The examination of each scenario forecast reveals probabilistic outcomes subsequent to a specific sequence of events deemed relevant to Cuba's economic future. The juxtaposition of the event order represents varying combinations of both economic and political priorities critically challenging the Castro regime. Whether taken individually or compositely the scenario forecasts suggest either a mixed economy or a predominantly market economy as the most probable path given the economic challenges ahead. The perpetuation or resurrection of a centrally planned economy by the Castro regime does not seem practical or probable if economic rationality prevails.

Cuba's Economic Recovery

As postulated, the scenario forecasts presented in Section V do not explicitly determine the probability of Cuba's economic recovery in absolute terms. Inferred from the Bayesian data analysis is the probabilistic response of three hypothetical outcomes to a set of conditions that may occur along a path to economic recovery. The construction of a Bayesian forecast requires the subjective definition of relevant conditional probabilities, which determine the revised probability of an outcome given that an event or sequence of events has already happened. As defined, Events 1 through 6 establish a conceivable set of occurrences marking a path for Cuba's economic recovery. The prescribed sequence of events generating each scenario is a simple permutation of the event set, whose intent is not to exclusively characterize all possible paths, but to allow for analytical balance. The scenario forecasts calculate the revised probabilities of each possible outcome (CPE, MIX, MKT), and therefore can be interpreted as an updated estimate of outcome consequential to Cuba's incremental progress towards favorable economic conditions and recovery.

The economic recovery of Cuba is contingent upon more than the occurrence of Events 1 through 6 in any particular order. Other target variables such as measured economic growth rates, and monetary and fiscal policy reforms are also principal factors to consider. A lack of information, however, will complicate the translation of these variables into relevant events and make the subjective probability assignments increasingly more difficult. For example, there may be a time lag between economic successes and the actual measured economic growth where essential data has yet to be compiled. Cuba's economic recovery presents a slightly different problem from estimating the future direction of the Cuban economy. Resolution of either conundrum reveals their conditional dependence and requires caution to preclude

or identify events prejudicial to a particular outcome or economic strategy. Events 1 through 6 are justifiable since a different sequence of events less skewed towards market reforms, does not accurately portray the events, initiatives and debates currently taking place in Cuba. Deduced from the scenario forecasts, Cuba may indeed muddle through with a mixed economy, but to advance the conditions most favorable for economic recovery will warrant a predominantly market economy.

Applicability of Bayesian Forecasting

Bayesian forecasting proves to be an acceptable method by which to explicitly determine the probabilistic outcomes of the Cuban economy given the occurrence of a single event or a sequence of relevant events. The strength of the analysis lies in the flexibility afforded to the forecaster to readjust assigned probabilities as the political and economic currents shift in Cuba. To incorporate the postulations of a different sequence of relevant events or additional events, congruent with the dynamics of the Cuban crisis, the forecaster need only formalize the associated conditional probabilities. The forecast results, derived from the deductive vice inductive judgments of the information or evidence available at the time, in essence assign a degree of precision to the uncertainty of Cuba's economic future. A sensitivity analysis finalizes the Bayesian forecast of the Cuban economy identifying subjective conditional probabilities that will considerably affect the scenario forecasts should their values vary significantly. The sensitivity analysis also provides the means by which to compare Cuba's pessimistic, optimistic, and realistic case scenarios.

A Bayesian forecast of the Cuban economy is not without its shortcomings. Essential to the analysis is a clear definition of the relevant events whose translations, from key target variables, risk idiosyncratic or situational bias. Such prejudice may be unavoidable if complete information is unavailable or existing information suspect. In addition, to expand the possible Cuban economic hypotheses beyond 3-5 mutually exclusive hybrid classifications would require extensive probability computations, most likely aided by a computer algorithm.

APPENDIX A. AN EXAMPLE OF HIERARCHICAL INFERENCE

The following is an example of how hierarchical inference is used to calculate the assigned probability of a relevant event.

Problem: How to incorporate the available data on Cuban nickel production and world market prices into the calculation of the assigned probability of Cuban foreign exchange earnings exceeding $4 billion (Event 1) for a predominantly market economy (MKT), under the conditions of Scenario VII.

Solution: The sequence of events for Scenario VII occur in the following order: E6-E5-E4-E3-E2-E1, and when combined with the hypothesis of a market economy represent the most favorable conditions for Cuban nickel production. The data presented in Table 1 is extracted from the CIA Trade Statistics for Cuba 1993.

From these data it is assumed that export earnings from sugar, tourism, nickel, tobacco, and citrus account for 91 percent of the total. Event 1 stipulates that foreign exchange earnings exceed $4 billion, which implies that: ($4 bn) x (.91) = $3.64 bn must be earned by Cuba's major export oriented sectors listed in Table 1.

Event 1 is conditionally dependent on sub-events derived from the 1990-91 average values with slight, justifiable modifications:

1. sub-event e1: Sugar export earnings > $2.885 bn (less than average due to the recent decline in sugar harvests)
2. sub-event e2: Tourism earnings > $ 0.250 bn (more than average due to the recent increases in the sector)
3. sub-event e3: Nickel export earnings > $0.285 bn (less than average due to lost CEMA markets)
4. sub-event e4: Tobacco export earnings > $0.095 bn
5. sub-event e5: Citrus export earnings > $0.125 bn

For the purposes of simplicity sub-event e3 is itself assumed to be conditionally dependent upon two events, *e1* and *e2*:

1. *e1*: Cuban nickel production > 45 thousand metric tons (this value represents a maximum estimate)
2. *e2*: the world price for nickel > $6400/metric ton

A tabular array of assigned probabilities is constructed, which includes the revised probabilities calculated using Bayes' theorem. The results are shown in Table 2, with the negation of sub-event e3 (nickel export earnings are less than $0.285 bn) denoted by ê3.

From the data presented in Table 2 it is clear that the probability of Cuban nickel earnings exceeding $0.285 bn has increased to 64% (from 30%) given that output production is in excess of 45 thousand metric tons and the world price for nickel is greater than $6400 per metric ton. This revised probability

Table 1. Major Export Earnings 1990-1991

Row		1990	1991	Average (90-91)
1	Total Exports (in $bn)	4.910	3.550	4.230
2	Sugar	3.690	2.670	3.180
3	Tourism	0.125	0.144	0.135
4	Nickel	0.362	0.272	0.317
5	Tobacco	0.095	0.100	0.975
6	Citrus	0.150	0.100	0.125
	Total of Rows 2-6	4.422	3.286	3.855
	% of Row 1	0.90	0.92	0.91

Table 2. Probabilities for Sub-Event e3

	Prob.	P(Ie1)	P(Ie2&e1)	Rev. Prob. of Hj
e3	.30	.55	.45	.64
ê3	.70	.20	.30	.36

now becomes an assigned probability which is combined with those associated with the other sub-events, and Bayes' theorem is again applied to determine the revised probability of Event 1. The results appear in Table 3, with the negation of Event 1 denoted by Ê1.

The probability for E1 given that all the sub-events, e1...e5, have occurred has been revised to .80 as shown above. As the final step in the hierarchical inference process, this value is incorporated into the assigned probabilities of Scenario VII. It appears as $P(E1|E2\&...\&E6\&H_3)$ in the seventh column, third row of Table 7A.

Table B3. Probabilities for Event 1

	Prob.	P(Ie1)	P(Ie2&e1)	P(Ie3&e2&e1)	P(Ie4&...&e1)	P(Ie5&...&e1)	Rev. Prob. oHj
E1	.15	.79	.68	.64	.57	.55	.80
Ê1	.85	.15	.50	.40	.45	.35	.20

REFERENCES

Alonso, José F. and John Paul Rathbone. 1993. Panel Discussion: "Current Political and Economic Trends in Cuba." In *Cuba in Transition—Volume 3*. Washington: Association for the Study of the Cuban Economy.

Barclay, Scott, Rex V. Brown, Clinton W. Kelly III, Cameron R. Peterson, Lawrence D. Phillips, and Judith Selvidge. 1977. *Handbook for Decision Analysis*. McLean, VA: Decisions and Designs, Inc.

Betancourt, Ernesto F. 1994. "Governance and Post-Castro Cuba". In *Cuba in Transition—Volume 4*. Washington: Association for the Study of the Cuban Economy, p.313- 329.

Edlestein, Joel C. 1995. The Future of Democracy in Cuba. *Latin American Perspectives* 87, vol. 22, no. 4, 7-26.

Gonzalez, Edward and David Ronfeldt. 1994. *Storm Warnings for Cuba*. Santa Monica, CA: RAND.

Hunter, Douglas E. 1984. *Political/Military Applications of Bayesian Analysis*. Boulder: Westview Press.

Lowe, Adolf. 1965. *On Economic Knowledge Toward a Science of Political Economics*. New York: Harper and Row.

Mesa-Lago, Carmelo. 1993. "Cuba's Economic Policies and Strategies for Confronting the Crisis." In *Cuba After the Cold War*, ed. Carmelo Mesa-Lago, 197-251. Pittsburgh: University of Pittsburgh Press.

Pindyck, Robert S., and Daniel L. Rubinfield. 1976. *Econometric Models and Economic Forecasts*. New York: McGraw-Hill.

Ritter, Archibald R. M. 1993. "Exploring Cuba's Alternate Economic Futures." In *Cuban Studies* 23, ed. Jorge F. Pérez-López, 3-32. Pittsburgh: University of Pittsburgh Press.

Sanguinetty, Jorge A. 1994. "Monetary Dualism as an Instrument Towards a Market Economy: The Cuban Case". In *Cuba in Transition — Volume 4*. Washington: Association for the Study of the Cuban Economy.

COMMENTS ON

"The Future Phases of the Cuban Economy" by Bernales

Jorge Luis Romeu

This paper by Barton J. Bernales constitutes a positive contribution to ASCE's work for it develops a Bayesian model to analyze and forecast the Cuban process. As we have said before in these meetings, it is necessary to foster the presentation of quantitative papers, like the present one by Bernales, that analyze Cuban issues. For it is through the extensive and adequate use of quantitative models that we gain: (i) a better understanding of and (ii) a more detached and, hence, productive discussion about, the Cuban problem. And this reflects very positively on ASCE and on its work.

In general, if one is able to establish a quantitative model, with its variables and relationships, one necessarily exercises one's taxonomy and synthesis capabilities. And this allows us to obtain a better understanding of a problem components and a larger picture of the issues involved and their interrelationships. As it often occurs in simulation modeling, for example, a large part of the problem is solved during the model building stage. For, with a better understanding of the underlying problem structures and factors we are able to see things we were missing before, to approach them better informed and to find more efficient solutions.

By using quantitative models we also are able to engage in a less partisan and more detached analysis and discussion of the issues. Anyone can disagree on the values of the model factors, on the factors themselves, or even on the model structure. For example, one can argue that it should be a multiplicative and not an additive model, etc. But these are useful discussions where everyone can contribute something. In a qualitative paper, on the other hand, the weight of the arguments are often based on the personal opinions of the author, making it more difficult to debate without falling into partisan attacks and controversies.

Therefore, just on the count of having provided an example of Bayesian statistical techniques applied to the analysis and forecast of the Cuban economy, Bernales' paper is a valid contribution to our meeting. We can verify how it joins other such papers (a short list of selected quantitative papers presented to ASCE is given at the end of this paper). And we see how they are becoming more frequent in our meetings, a very positive trend.

Now, directly analyzing Bernales' paper we verify how its main purpose is well defined from its introduction: "to examine the potential for using Bayesian approach to forecast the direction of the Cuban economy (...)". Bernales shows us how there is a good potential for bayesian techniques here too. In what follows, we will comment on several elements in Mr. Bernales' paper that can be improved upon, making his paper more complete and solid.

Bernales has compared his Bayesian approach with the econometric one, with regression and with simulation. He has pointed out the respective strengths and weaknesses and has concluded that the Bayesian approach has several solid advantages he would like to explore. Bernales defines several events, outcomes or states of the Cuban economy. And, following the Bayesian approach, he provides them with prior probabilities. The three events constituting the partition of the universe are: a centrally planned economy, a mixed economy and a market economy. And here we would like to make a brief side comment.

One additional advantage of quantitative modeling is that it triggers the development of other such models. Bernales' paper is an example of this. By studying his approach for this discussion, we have thought of using a Markov Chain model to describe the Cuban economy as a stochastic process that moves through time, among the above three states. We propose using these three states and time periods of, say, a trimester or a semester. The transition probabilities could depend on: (i) the state in which the process (Cuban economy) currently is and (ii) a series of internal and geopolitical factors that depend on the process contextual situation. We suggested such a Markov model and there are already two ASCE members interested in developing it for next year's annual meeting.

Continuing with Bernales' paper, we now want to comment on his specific assignment of the (subjective prior) probabilities corresponding to his above mentioned three events. Instead of using his own probabilities, we suggest that Bernales conduct a survey of knowledgeable economists and obtain a "distribution" of them. He could then use the mean, median, max, min, weighted average or other combination of each of these probabilities to look into different scenarios. Such Delphi techniques are very useful when data points are few and event evaluation is uncertain, as occurs in the present case.

We also want to comment on Bernales' particular definition of "market economy" and of the other two states or events. We believe that these three events are ill-defined, from a quantitative point of view. We suggest Bernales say, for example, that a market economy is one where 80 percent or more of the GDP comes from private producers, a mixed economy is one where between 30 to 80 percent come from private entrepreneurs and a centrally planned economy one where less than 30 percent of the GDP originate from the private sector. Such numerical val-

ues may be obtained from the literature or by consensus via a Delphi survey.

Bernales then defines six very interesting "target variables": Foreign Exchange Earnings, Import Substitution, Political Control, Economic Reforms, Financial Integration and External Policies. His objective is to define new events from these six variables. We find this a promising approach.

The first two of these variables, Foreign Exchange and Import Substitution, and their corresponding events, are well defined. For example, the event "Foreign Exchange is Greater Than Four Billion Dollars" is a well defined event, whose probability is somehow obtainable. However, we find that the four remaining variables and their respective events are ill defined.

For example, there is no precise quantification of the variable "Political Control." It could be defined on the basis of the number of political prisoners or on the number of independent and operating radio stations and newspapers, or NGO's or other organizations of the "civil society." Because the variable is not well defined, it is not possible to establish a well defined event, either. An event such as, say, high political control, could be defined as one where there were no independent radio and TV stations or newspapers operating in the country. And an event such as low political control would be defined as one where no constraints existed for the operation of such organizations. Under the present limitations of the variable, such events are not yet refined.

The same comment applies to the remaining three "target variables": Economic Reforms, Integration into Global Financial Community and Foreign Trade/Aid.

- Variable Economic Reforms may be quantified in terms of privatization efforts. For example, as a given percentage of the GDP produced with recently privatized (and previously state-operated) economic units. Then, the event in question is whether this percentage is above or below a specified value.

- Variable Integration to Global Economy may be measured in terms of either the percentage of the foreign debt being serviced or the number of international organizations (e.g. World Bank, IMF, etc) willing/able to provide Cuba with economic assistance. Then, the event of interest may be defined as Cuba achieving an economic assistance beyond a prespecified value.

- Variable Foreign Trade can be similarly treated and measured in terms of dollars of exports to European, North American, G-7 Group countries, or any grouping of countries. And the event of interest may then be defined, for example, as Cuba achieving a pre-established amount of export dollars, expanding trade to at least so many countries, etc.

Our final technical comment pertains to the "scenarios" defined by Bernales, which in turn define the events of interest for which he obtains a posterior distribution. Bernales establishes several orders under which the six "target variables" could occur, as different scenarios. We propose that, instead of such orders, different events of interest be established (say that privatization occurs at a very low level, at medium level or at high speed). And that their relationship to the partition events (state, mixed and open economy) be studied.

Summarizing, we believe that Bernales' paper constitutes a valuable contribution by providing a first example of the use of Bayesian statistics in the analysis of the Cuban economy. As with any first approximation to a problem, this first example is still open for refinement and additional work. We have discussed several suggestions for such improvements and for the revision and/or additional work. And we look forward to other such high quality, quantitative papers in future ASCE meetings.

Addendum: Selected Quantitative Papers at Earlier ASCE Meetings

1. "Commodity-Linked Transactions and Recapitalization Needs for Privatizing the Economy in a Democratic Cuba: The Case of Sugar." F. Alvarez and J. Alvarez (1991).

2. "The Industry Composition of Production and the Distribution of Income by Race and Ethnicity in Miami." R. D. Cruz (1991).

3. "Non Walrasian Properties of the Cuban Economy: Rationing, Labor Supply and Output." Jorge Sanguinetty (1992).

4. "Endogenous Political Structures." L. Locay and C. Seiglie (1992).

5. "Una Política o un Sistema Monetario Optimo." J. L. Moreno-Villalaz (1992).

6. "A First Approximation of the Foreign Assistance Requirements of a Democratic Cuba." J. F. Alonso and A. Lago (1993).

7. "Notas Sobre los Principios Arcos Para la Inversión Extranjera en Cuba." R. Asón (1994).

8. "More on the Statistical Comparison of Cuban Socioeconomic Development." J. L. Romeu (1995).

9. "A First Approximation Model of Money, Prices and Exchange Rates in Revolutionary Cuba." J. F. Alonso and A. Lago (1995).

10. "The Optimal Size of the Military in a Post-Castro Cuba." C. Seiglie (1996).

THE EFFECT OF SOCIALISM ON THE ENTREPRENEURIAL ABILITIES OF CUBAN-AMERICANS

Luis Locay and Jorge Sanguinetty

The transformation of centrally planned economies into market economies has met with varying degrees of success. In several countries the process of economic reform has not gone very far or it has stalled, and in some instances it is even in danger of being reversed.[1] High on many observers's lists of possible important causes for the difficulties encountered in turning centrally planned economies into market economies is the general lack of understanding of how market economies work. According to this argument, years of unchallenged Marxist indoctrination about the evils of capitalism, together with no experience of living under capitalism, have left the populace of many transition economies with widespread prejudices and misconceptions of all aspects of a market economy. Commenting on the situation in Russia, Alexander Solzhenitsyn (1991) states:

> After seventy years of propaganda our brains have been instilled with the notion that one must fear private property and avoid hired labour as though they were the work of the devil: that represents a major victory of ideology over our human essence.

The citizens of these previously socialist societies often do not understand the importance of even the basic institutions of market economies, such as private property and contract law, or how market friendly reforms can benefit them. Their prejudices against the "market" and their ignorance of how it functions makes them more susceptible to manipulation by political demagogues.[2] This is the basic thesis in Sanguinetty (1995), who argues that decades of socialism in Cuba have hardened anti-market attitudes and led to great ignorance as to how markets function. The author views such biases and attitudes as a significant obstacle to successful market reform in current transition economies and in a future Cuba. Successful economic reform in Cuba, he further argues, should be accompanied by a campaign of public economic education.

Confirmation that anti-market views are common in socialist or transition societies comes from a survey conducted in New York City and Moscow in 1990. The survey was conducted by an American economist (Robert J. Shiller), a Soviet economist (Maxim Boycko) and a Soviet sociologist (Vladimir Korobov). Most of their questions were aimed at determining attitudes, but a few attempted to gauge understanding of how markets work. The authors found concerns, especially with fair prices and income inequality, that "might help prevent change to a market economy."

---

1. Even in Russia itself, the main challenger to Yeltsin in the mid-June elections, Gennady A. Zyuganov, proposed an economic program which would bring back many features of the Soviet-era economy, including protectionist trade policies, price and wage regulation and control of production. See Shogren (1996).

2. By the "market" we refer to an economic systems where for the most part individuals own the means of production and goods and services are voluntarily traded.

The most surprising finding by Shiller et al (1991), however, is that the views expressed by Muscovites were no less market friendly than those of New Yorkers. The authors conclude that the concerns that many observers had expressed that the pace of economic reform was significantly constrained by anti-market sentiments, is probably exaggerated.[3]

Even if anti-market attitudes in transition economies are not an important obstacle to successful economic reform, poor market skills may be. It seems plausible that life under communism can create a mind set that is not alert to profit opportunities. After all, entrepreneurship is likely to be, at least to some extent, an acquired skilled. The impressions of most observers is that the levels of market skills in transition economies, especially entrepreneurial skills, are low. In their concluding section, Shiller et al give an example of a soap shortage in the Soviet Union in 1990 that went unexploited by would-be entrepreneurs. They believed the soap example was typical of the sort of problem economic reform was encountering in the then Soviet Union. Such failure to exploit an apparently clear profit opportunity may have been due to a regulatory climate not conducive to enterprise, or it may have been due atrophied entrepreneurial abilities, the most important type of market skill.[4]

Low levels of market skills will result in a slower and more difficult transition to a market economy, increasing the chances the full transition will never take place. The key question is how long does it take for a people to rebuild to normal levels market skills that

have atrophied over decades of very limited use? If the recuperation is quick there is no need for concern. If the recuperation of market skills is a slow process, then it should be seriously considered in any transition strategy for previously socialist societies.[5]

Our ultimate aim is to gauge the impact that decades of socialism in Cuba may have had on the entrepreneurial skills of its population. This paper is a first step in achieving that aim. The work presented here is very preliminary and it is primarily descriptive and exploratory in nature. We approach the problem indirectly by looking at the self-employment rate of Cuban immigrants to the United States. We view self-employment as being related to entrepreneurial skill, and we will look to see if the likelihood that a Cuban immigrant is self-employed is negatively related to the amount of time the immigrant spent in Cuba after 1959. The main advantage to studying this group is that it allows us to abstract from the effect of a regulatory environment hostile to enterprise—a problem that would be encountered by any study looking at entrepreneurship in a socialist or a transition economy. The main drawback is that the process of emigration is likely to select people in a way that is not independent of their entrepreneurial skills.

In the next section we describe the data and discuss briefly some of the relationships it suggests. Then we perform some descriptive estimation. We conclude with a brief summary and some thoughts on future work.

---

3. We are skeptical of the basic finding of Shiller et al (1991) that attitudes toward the market are very similar in socialist and market economies. We cannot consider here all our reasons for our reservations. We only mention that we do not believe that New York and Moscow are representative of the respective populations. Moscow was a center of political and economic reform in 1990, and we would be surprised if attitudes there were not more favorable to markets than was typical of the rest of the Soviet Union. New York may well be the "business and financial 'capital' of the United States," as the survey authors refer to it, but that does not mean that a large portion of its residents are business persons or professionals in financial firms. We suspect that other characteristics of New City, such as its large welfare population, its high proportion of minorities, and its liberal voting record, makes it likely that its residents have attitudes toward the market more hostile than the rest of the United States.

4. Shiller et al consider only the former explanation. The question then arises why such a regulatory system was then in place? The conclusion they draw from their survey is that the explanation *was not* that in the Soviet Union the population was more anti-market than in market economies.

5. If recovery of market skills is slow, incorporating economic and business education into the reform plan may be of considerable value.

Table 1. Basic Data on Self-Employement by Cuban-Americans

	Fraction Self-employed	
	Total	Excluding Medical and Law
Born in U.S.	0.113	0.101
Age of immigration less than 10	0.131	0.118
20+ years of age in 1959:		
Year of immigration 1960-65	0.246	0.230
Year of immigration 1965-75	0.195	0.184
Year of immigration 1975+	0.140	0.135
10-20 years of age in 1959:		
Year of immigration 1960-65	0.250	0.237
Year of immigration 1965-75	0.222	0.216
Year of immigration 1975+	0.181	0.177
10 or less years of age in 1959:		
Age of immigration 10-15	0.131	0.120
Age of immigration 15-20	0.149	0.147
Age of immigration 20-25	0.153	0.152
Age of immigration 25-30	0.180	0.179
Age of immigration 30+	0.172	0.172

DESCRIPTION OF THE DATA

Our data are taken from the Public Use Microdata Samples of the 1980 and 1990 U.S. Census of Population and Housing. In keeping with the preliminary nature of this work, we restricted our sample to men residing in the state of Florida. To be included in our sample a man had to be of Cuban origin, and be between the ages of 16 and 65. He had to be employed, not in the military, and could not be a student. We also excluded any man reporting non-zero farming income or farming as his occupation.

Neither the 1980 or the 1990 census records what country an immigrant came from. We assume throughout that every foreign born man in our sample came to the United States directly from Cuba. This is, of course, not true, but we believe the biases it introduces in the case of Cuban immigrants to the U.S. is small. Another difficulty is that both censuses report year of immigration as falling in a range. We used the midpoint of each range as the year of immigration in computing time in the United States and time in Cuba in our statistical work.[6] In future work we will avoid such an imputation.[7]

Table 1 presents some basic data on self-employment for various groups of Cuban-Americans. Column 2 provides total self-employment rates, which includes both incorporated and non-incorporated businesses. Column 3 excludes medical professionals and lawyers, two occupations with high rates of self-employment. We have divided the sample into mutually exclusive, but not exhaustive, groups, representing different levels of exposure to life under socialism. In going from top to bottom the groups roughly increase in exposure to life in post-1959 Cuba.

Let us first consider the group of immigrants whose members were more than 20 years old in 1959. Among them we see the pattern we would expect to find if living under socialism reduced one's entrepreneurial skills. Earlier immigrants have substantially higher rates of self-employment than later immigrants. A similar pattern can be seen among immigrants who were between 10 and 20 years of age in 1959. Other explanations, of course, are possible. The various immigrant cohorts, for example, differ in the amount of time they have been in the United States. If the likelihood of becoming self-employed

---

6. Such imputed values will sometimes result in a negative age of immigration. In those cases we assumed the individual migrated in his first year of life.

7. In future estimation we will include each possible year of immigration in our likelihood functions, with each possibility weighted by the fraction of Cuban immigrants for the relevant period entering the United States that year.

Table 2. Potential U.S. Work Experience of Self-Employed

	Fraction Self-Employed/Potential U.S. Work Experience					
	0-5	5-10	10-15	15-20	20-25	25+
Born in U.S.	0.022	0.104	0.102	0.241	0.153	0.180
Age of immigration less than 10	0.043	0.104	0.166	0.253	0.184	0.200
20+ years of age in 1959:						
Year of immigration 1960-65	NA	NA	NA	0.231	NA	0.227
Year of immigration 1965-75	NA	0.137	0.165	0.207	0.237	NA
Year of immigration 1975+	0.104	0.129	0.138	0.000	0.143	0.185
10-20 years of age in 1959:						
Year of immigration 1960-65	NA	0.182	0.103	0.243	0.229	0.290
Year of immigration 1965-75	NA	0.185	0.185	0.229	0.266	NA
Year of immigration 1975+	0.103	0.207	0.157	0.353	0.100	0.167
10 or less years of age in 1959:						
Age of immigration 10-15	0.040	0.093	0.136	0.181	0.209	NA
Age of immigration 15-20	0.036	0.167	0.111	0.207	0.400	NA
Age of immigration 20-25	0.027	0.176	0.310	0.182	NA	NA
Age of immigration 25-30	0.082	0.203	0.273	NA	NA	NA
Age of immigration 30+	0.107	0.225	NA	NA	NA	NA

rises with years in the U.S., later immigrants will be less likely to be self-employed because they have been here a shorter amount of time, and not necessarily because they have lower entrepreneurial skills

Time in the United States is an observable characteristic, and we are able to control for it. This is done in Table 2, where each group is further divided according to potential U.S. work experience. Potential U.S. work experience is defined as age minus the largest of the following: age of immigration, years of education plus six, or 16. As expected, self-employment rates tend to rise with potential U.S. work experience, especially in the earlier years.[8] Table 2 also suggests that age may have an independent effect. In the first column, corresponding to 0-5 years of potential work experience, the highest self-employment rates are among groups that would tend to have higher average ages.

Returning to Table 1 and looking across all groups we see a pattern which is not supportive of the hypothesis that life under socialism reduces the likelihood of being self-employed. All immigrant groups have higher rates of self-employment than Cuban-Americans born in the United States. Among immigrants, those with the least exposure to socialism, i.e.,

those who migrated under the age of ten, have the lowest self-employment rates. Of course, the groups in Table 1 differ more than in just exposure to socialism. The various groups differ in terms of several observable variables such as education, English proficiency, and age, that may contribute to the group patterns observed in Table 1. Table 3 shows group means for potential U.S. work experience, age, education and English proficiency, variables that likely to be associated with self-employment. As can be seen, those born in the United States tend to have low potential work experience and tend to be younger, both of which would lead that group to have lower self-employment rates. They also tend to have higher education and speak English well, characteristics we will see below are negatively related to self-employment. Two other groups which also had low self-employment rates in Table 1—those who immigrated under the age of 10 and those who were less than 10 in 1959 and immigrated between the ages 10 and 15—have similar average values to those of the U.S. born. In the next section we will see to what extent these variables account for the observed differences in self-employment rates.

---

8. The pattern is not perfect across cells, but that is probably due some of the cells having few entries.

Table 3.   Characteristics of Self-Employed

	Sample Averages			
	Potential U.S. Work Experience	Age	Education	Speaks English Well
Born in U.S.	9.5	26.4	12.8	1.00
Age of immigration less than 10	9.01	28.0	12.9	0.98
20+ years of age in 1959:				
Year of immigration 1960-65	21.5	54.7	11.8	0.65
Year of immigration 1965-75	15.2	53.9	9.4	0.35
Year of immigration 1975+	11.7	56.1	9.2	0.35
10-20 years of age in 1959:				
Year of immigration 1960-65	21.1	41.8	13.0	0.92
Year of immigration 1965-75	15.4	43.4	10.8	0.56
Year of immigration 1975+	9.5	44.5	10.6	0.40
10 or less years of age in 1959:				
Age of immigration 10-15	11.0	29.8	12.6	0.97
Age of immigration 15-20	9.8	28.4	11.1	0.75
Age of immigration 20-25	8.2	30.9	11.1	0.50
Age of immigration 25-30	7.9	35.5	11.0	0.45
Age of immigration 30+	6.0	39.0	11.1	0.34

Besides differences in observable characteristics, men in our sample also differ in unobservable characteristics that affect of self-employment rates. If those unobservable characteristics are correlated with observable ones, they will bias our estimates of the effect of the latter on self-employment. We suspect that the process of emigration from Cuba selects people who tend to have high entrepreneurial skills. This can happen for at least two reasons. First of all, entrepreneurs and would-be entrepreneurs would have been among those who had the most to lose from confiscation of assets and from loss of livelihood, especially in the early stages of the revolution.[9] If entrepreneurial skills are transferable, or if early immigrants managed to take out some of their assets, they would have a higher likelihood of being self-employed in the United States. It also seems possible, even probable, that entrepreneurial skills are positively correlated with characteristics, such as willingness to take risks, that are associated with immigrants.

The hypothesis that emigration from Cuba has tended to select out persons with higher than average entrepreneurial skills is consistent with the difference observed in Table 1 between immigrants and the U.S. born, and it also accounts for some of the patterns among the immigrant groups. Consider first those who were more than 10 years old in 1959. Their self-employment rates are lower the later is the period of their immigration, which is consistent with the most entrepreneurial leaving first. For those who were less than 10 years of age in 1959 we find that self-employment rates rise with age of immigration. This paradoxical pattern is also consistent with the process of emigration selecting those with better entrepreneurial skills. The younger immigrants left Cuba because their parents did. Whatever the selection process, it was operating on their parents, and not on them. In any case, the selection by unobservable characteristics that the process of immigration introduces into the data is a problem which must be kept in mind. It is also one which may not be surmountable.

SOME DESCRIPTION OF ESTIMATES

We refer to the estimation we report on in this section as being "descriptive" because we do not wish at this point to make claims to having identified chains of causation. In Table 4 we present parameter estimates for some logit probability models. The logit

---

9. A similar point with respect to earnings is made by Borjas (1994).

Table 4. Parameter Estimates for Logit Probability Models

Variable	Logit Estimation Estimates			
	I	II	III	IV
Constant	-5.90**	-5.43**	-5.31**	-5.54
PUSWE - Potential U.S. Work Experience	0.74**	0.96**	1.03**	1.08**
PUSWE^2	-0.20**	-0.19**	-0.19**	-0.15**
AGE - Age at Time of Census	1.66**	1.42**	1.32**	1.35**
AGE^2	-0.19**	-0.17**	-0.15**	-0.15**
PUSWE X AGE	0.06	0.02	0.02	-0.03
English Proficiency:				
Well		0.11*	0.10	0.09
Not Well		0.32**	0.30**	0.29**
Not at All		0.25**	0.24*	0.22*
Years of Education		-0.10	-0.10	-0.12
MARIEL: Immigrated During 1980-81 at an Age of 16+			0.21**	0.19*
Mean Log-Likelihood	-0.437	-0.436	-0.436	-0.435
Number of Cases	11958	11958	11958	11958

** Significant at the 1% level.
* Significant at the 5% level.

was used for its simplicity of estimation, though it may not be the best functional form for the problem at hand. Column I gives the estimates for the set of basic variables: potential U.S. work experience, age, their squares, and an interaction term. As expected the probability of self-employment rises with potential U.S. work experience and with age, but at a decreasing rate.[10] Except for the interaction term, al the other coefficients of the basic variables are significant at the 1% level. These general features remain the same when other variables are included in columns II-IV.

Column II expands the set of variables to include English proficiency and education. Those who speak only English or speak it very well make up the excluded English proficiency category. Interestingly, the lower English proficiency categories are associated with higher rates of self-employment. The estimated coefficients do not change much when other variables are included, though the significance levels fall. Education is also negatively related to self-employment, though its coefficient is not significant at conventional levels (it would be significant at 10%). Tabulations not shown here suggest that the relationship between education and self-employment may be more complicated, and may be different for the various groups.

In column III we add a variable labeled MARIEL. This is a dummy variable that takes on the value one if a man immigrated to the United States in the interval 1980-81 and was at least 16 years old at the time. The overwhelming number of Cuban immigrants in those years, of course, were those of the Mariel boat lift of 1980. It involved the immigration, primarily to South

Florida, of a large number of individuals over a very short period of time. Even though there is some evidence that the Mariel influx did not lower wages in South Florida, there is the possibility that labor market pressures may have induced an unusually high number to enter self-employment. This our justification for including the variable MARIEL. Its coefficient is indeed positive and significant in the two logits in which it was included.

Finally, column IV adds to the variables in column III a set of dummy variables representing the groups in Tables 1-3. The estimated coefficients for the

---

10. The units of potential U.S. work experience and age are tens of years.

Table 5. Estimated Coefficients for Logit Probability Models

	Coefficients for Group Dummies	
	I	II
Born in U.S. - Excluded Group	NA	NA
Age of immigration less than 10	0.22	0.22
20+ years of age in 1959:		
Year of immigration 1960-65	0.22	0.15
Year of immigration 1965-75	0.13	-0.00
Year of immigration 1975+	0.04	-0.16
10-20 years of age in 1959:		
Year of immigration 1960-65	0.19	0.14
Year of immigration 1965-75	0.23	0.10
Year of immigration 1975+	0.26	0.03
10 or less years of age in 1959:		
Age of immigration 10-15	0.04	0.02
Age of immigration 15-20	0.43*	0.26
Age of immigration 20-25	0.45*	0.18
Age of immigration 25-30	0.49*	0.21
Age of immigration 30+	0.49*	0.24

* Significant at 5% level

group dummies appear in Table 5. Besides the group dummies, the logit for column I of that table includes the basic variables (as in column I of Table 5). Column II includes English proficiency, education, and MARIEL, in addition to the basic variables. In both columns of Table 5 the estimated coefficients measure effects relative to the excluded group, the one composed of those born in the United States. To obtain the relative effect between any two groups, one has to take the difference of the coefficients of the respective groups. To get a feel for what the magnitudes of these coefficients means, consider the following numerical example. If the probability of a U.S. born Cuban-American is 0.10, then an identical man from another group with coefficient 0.20 would have a predicted probability of self-employment of about 0.119. If the group coefficient had been 0.50, the predicted probability for the immigrant would be about 0.154.

Most coefficients in both columns are positive, implying higher self-employment rates, but only four in column I are significant at conventional levels. The coefficients in column II are lower than their corresponding value in column I, and none are significantly different from zero. The differences across the two columns appears primarily to be the result of the

inclusion of the variable MARIEL in column II (see column IV of Table 4).

SUMMARY AND CONCLUSIONS

The raw data presented in table 1 did not offer strong support for the notion that the entrepreneurial skills of Cuban-Americans as measured by self-employment rates was adversely affected by exposure to socialism in Cuba. Even after controlling for some variables that we would expect to be important, immigrants still tend to have higher self-employment rates. Most problematic are the groups whose members were less than 10 years old in 1959. Not only do they tend to have the highest self-employment rates after other variables are controlled for (Table 5), but within those groups there seems to be no tendency for self-employment to decline with length of time in Cuba. The most that can be said in support of the original hypothesis is that when the Mariel influx is controlled for, (1) the group effects are statistically insignificant, and (2) for those over 10 years of age in 1959, the relative sizes of the group effects falls with length of time in Cuba.

Our preliminary findings are consistent with emigration from Cuba selecting out those with greater entrepreneurial skill. The biases such selection implies could, in principle, distort our estimates considerably. In some cases it may mask the effect we were looking for. In others it may create a pattern that can be mistaken for time in socialist Cuba leading to a decline in self-employment in the United States. We do not know whether we will eventually be able to correct for this sample selection bias. The problem is difficult because we have data only on those who migrated to the United States. In any case, the necessary next step is to develop an explicit model of the decision to become self-employed in the United States and to emigrate from Cuba. Such a model will have to show how entrepreneurial ability develops over the life cycle, and how it interacts with labor market con-

ditions in the United States and Cuba, as well as with the emigration process. A more complicated choice process, perhaps involving income determination, may be considered.

One final note on the two hypotheses of entrepreneurial skills deteriorating under socialism, and the most entrepreneurial emigrating from socialist Cuba. Both result in a reduction the in entrepreneurial skills of the population remaining on the Island. For some purposes it may not be crucial to distinguish between the two causes, but simply to measure the combined effect.

REFERENCES

Borjas, George J., "The Economics of Immigration," *The Journal of Economic Literature* (December 1994) 1667-1717.

Sanguinetty, Jorge, "Economic Education for a Market Economy: The Cuban Case," in *Cuba in Transition—Volume 5*. Washington: Association for the Study of the Cuban Economy, 1995.

Shiller, Robert J., Boycko, Maxim, and Korobov, Vladimir, "Popular Attitudes Toward Free Mar-

kets: The Soviet Union and the United States Compared," *The American Economic Review* (June 1991) 385-400.

Shogren, Elizabeth, "Yeltsin's Opponent Proposes Return to Soviet-Style Economy," *The Miami Herald* (May 29, 1996).

Solzhenitsyn, Alexander, *Rebuilding Russia*. London: Harvill, 1991.

COMMENTS ON

"The Effect of Socialism on the Entrepreneurial Abilities of Cuban Americans" by Luis Locay and Jorge Sanguinetty

Silvia Pedraza

This paper has been a very interesting one for me to assess because it has brought together two of my intellectual interests and effectively married them. At present, I have two research projects on-going: one on the causes and consequences of self-employment in ethnic enterprises among various immigrant groups in the city of Chicago (Cubans, Mexicans, Puerto Ricans, Koreans, Chinese, and Filipinos); and the other on the causes and consequences of the various waves of the Cuban exodus, in its relationship to the changing stages of the Cuban revolution. Usually, I keep the two completely separate and compartmentalized—in different parts of my head and my heart. Reading this paper by Luis Locay and Jorge Sanguinetty has forced me to bring them together, and to think about the relationship between the two.

First, I want to underscore that the intellectual effort this paper makes—the question it asks and tries to answer—is extremely interesting and worthwhile. Even more, to have undertaken to answer it via manipulating the data from the U. S. Census is downright valiant. As someone that has at times also milked the Census data to study immigrants, I can guarantee you that they have also milked that cow for all it is worth. Moreover, the paper also attempts to take into account the difference in "political generations" (a term that comes from the work of Karl Mannheim) that developed over the course of the Cuban revolution and exodus—an issue that is very

dear and near to my heart and mind. Thus, the paper seems to me to be ambitious (in the best sense of that word) as it asks an interesting question, and is also on the right tack to answering it. However, before it really succeeds, the authors need to select their sample and code their variables in a manner more appropriate to the question asked. I will return to this point later. Before I do so, I need to develop another point further.

In my view, taking the issue of different "political generations"—different generations of lived social and political experience that are thereby marked by a different consciousness—seriously into account, as this paper attempts to do, is extremely important for understanding *any* aspect of the Cuban experience, both for Cubans in Cuba as well as among the immigrants in exile. A friend once told me that the use of the word "revolution" to describe the vast upheaval and social transformation that we are all familiar with came from the French (the first such vast social transformation) and their use of the word révolution—because of its literal meaning of taking a complete turn. In Cuba, those complete turns—social, political, and economic—were extremely swift and profound, making the lived experience and, therefore, the understanding of that felt experience, markedly different for people who were not, in fact, very far apart in years. Let me give some stark examples from the hypothetical but typical lives of two young men in Cuba and in exile, examples that will hopefully

328

show the difference that only 10 years (half a generation!) can make.

If a young man came to *el exilio* in 1960, at the age of 20, it is very likely that he would go on a year later to join the *Brigada 2506,* together with all his friends, and would arrive in Cuba to fight in the shores of *Bahía de Cochinos* in 1961. However, if in that same year of 1960, a young boy arrived in el exilio at the age of 10, it is very likely that 19 years later he would go on, together with many of his friends, to join the *Brigada Antonio Maceo* and to write for the journal *Areíto,* arriving in Cuba to do voluntary work in the fields in 1979.

If the young man remained in Cuba, and was 20 years old in 1960, it is very likely that he participated in the literacy campaigns of the early years. Moreover, until the age of 28, in 1968, he may well have worked in the small business his father and uncle owned, working side by side with them in their restaurant, until the "revolutionary offensive" of 1968 confiscated those small enterprises typical of *la petite-bourgeoisie.* But before they confiscated his father's restaurant, he was able to work there and gain the knowledge and hands-on experience involved in trading—an apprenticeship in buying and selling that is often the route to business ownership later. However, if the young boy who remained in Cuba was 10 years old in 1960, 10 years later at the age of 20 he may well have participated in *la zafra de los diez millones* of 1970. But he will never have been able to gain from an apprenticeship in his family's business, because those small businesses simply disappeared before he reached adulthood, leaving him without the opportunity to learn the ropes of trading.

Taking this, quickly, all the way to 1994: the young man who was 20 in 1960 would then be 54. If he remained in Cuba all the time, he is still young enough to help and teach his children, nieces and nephews, who now want to enter the new labor market of *trabajo por cuenta propia*—self-employment during the *período especial.* The uncle (now 54) is now helping his niece (30) open up and run a rather nice *paladar* in Centro Habana, drawing on the knowledge and skill he gained as a young man working in his father's

restaurant. If, however, that same man (54 in 1994) had left Cuba in the Summer of 1994, in a *balsa,* when he arrived in Miami (via Guantánamo), he would probably be too old to start up a new restaurant—not due to a lack of entrepreneurial ability, which he clearly has, but because he arrived to this community—*el exilio*—too late to really be a member of it.

The literature on ethnic enterprise tells us that solving the problem of capitalization depends on the social resources of entrepreneurs—their ties and social networks to other members of the community. Someone who spent 34 years in Cuba living the revolution will not likely be able to muster the social resources (as sociologists call them) necessary to solve the perennial problem of capitalization that lies at the root of opening up small business enterprises. Too recently arrived to *el exilio,* his fellow Cubans will likely look at him askance, and he is not likely to have very strong ties and networks to other members of the Cuban community, especially the small business community in Miami; nor to receive a very favorable credit rating in the eyes of conservative fellow bankers; nor to attend the same churches where one can meet other like-minded Cuban friends; nor to have an intimate knowledge of American institutions.

With these detailed examples I hope to have shown the difference that only a few years of age can make, for both those who left and remained in Cuba. Being sensitive to these important differences, for short called "political generations," is crucial in making this paper a quality paper, as it has the potential to be. However, these differences cannot be captured by the sample selection and the use of the independent variables presently used. Faced with all the limitations posed by the Census data, I offer the following concrete suggestions:

• Select a sample consisting *only of immigrants,* excluding the native-born from the analysis. The study of the second generation properly belongs with the study of the native-born, whose mother tongue is English, and whose educational credentials are American. Moreover, a consistent finding of the literature on ethnic enterprise is that it is an immigrant phenomena—i.e., although there is substantial variation among the rates of self-employment among the foreign-born, all immigrant groups have higher rates of self-employment in small businesses than the native-born. When the analysis is performed on immigrants only, some of the results may well gain in clarity.

- *Exclude* self-employment in Medicine and Law from the analysis, focusing only on *la petite-bourgeoisie*. While Medicine and Law can be practiced as a form of selfemployment, in truth they are professions, a labor market that requires a different route of access (years of scholastic training, to be exact) than that of small business, the route of access to which consists of solving the problem of capitalization (through lending, borrowing, and inheriting).

- Using the variable on the *year of immigration* as a proxy for the changing stages of the Cuban revolution that people lived through in Cuba seems to me the right choice (there is no other way of doing it, frankly). Given the limitations imposed by the Bureau of the Census' precoding of this variable, the best coding that can be achieved of this variable to approximate the four major waves of the actual Cuban exodus is as follows: 1960-1964; 1965-1979; 1980-1981 (el *Mariel)*; and 1982-1990.

- Let *age* be a variable that is unrecoded, in single years of age, alone, and also one that interacts (still in single years) with the variable on *waves of migration*, so as to better catch the small differences in age that imply large differences in social experience.

I believe that these different choices, in sample selection and recoding of variables, will get you a lot closer to the lives of the young men that I earlier described, both in Cuba and Miami. In my view, that should give a better answer to the very good question this paper posed.

INFORMATION ON THE CUBAN ECONOMY IN DATABASES

During recent years, evolution in the Cuban economy has been witnessed. Reforms aimed at opening the external sector of the economy to foreign investors have been implemented gradually. In 1993 important market oriented reforms, such as the decriminalization of possession of dollars, drastically changed domestic policy as well. Recently, changes such as taxation of self employment point to a reversal of the 1993 internal opening.

As analysts, investors and the general public demand more information on the subject, reliable and timely data continues to be difficult to obtain. As is the case with any subject, no single source is adequate. In the case of the Cuban economy, however, other components such as insufficient official information render the use of diverse and at times unconventional sources particularly vital.

This paper presents an overview of primary information found in a variety of formats and bibliographic sources, and focuses on one of the most important of these sources: online databases. Intended as a tool for researchers of the Cuban economy, it analyzes the contents of a selection of relevant databases. As expected, a great deal of literature was found in business, news, and social sciences databases. Other sources—agricultural and biomedical databases—were not as obvious. The overall arrangement consists of a general discussion of information in various formats followed by a presentation of searching methods and analysis of the contents of a selection of relevant databases grouped by broad subject categories.

OVERVIEW OF PRIMARY AND BIBLIOGRAPHIC SOURCES

The volume of published literature on the Cuban economy and related topics is abundant and diverse, despite of the lack of primary sources. Information supplied by the Cuban government remains the authority for economic policy, the regime's position on issues and other factual information. Such information is published in a variety of formats ranging from serials and monographs to press releases.

Along with government reports providing statistical and other data, the most authoritative primary sources of policy are speeches to Communist Party Congresses and reports presented to the national assemblies. But precisely because of its official character, this type of information at times simply confirms what has long been evident, such as the existence of the black market. Also, many technical and policy reports, primarily published as serials, are published or distributed irregularly. The last statistical yearbook, to cite one example, was published in 1989. Data published in Cuba is supplemented by international publications based on figures provided by the Cuban government such as United Nations and UNESCO reports.

A fair amount of government furnished information, however, is presented in fragmentary fashion. Interviews granted by Cuban officials to the international press are often chosen as a venue to disseminate official announcements. Biographies of appointees give clues to economic forecasts: the nomination of hard liners or moderates to key positions is frequently an indication of the type of reform to expect.

Thorough reviews of print and broadcast media, both domestic and international, are therefore a fundamental source for timely, if not complete, financial information. News items about particular aspects of trade relations and joint venture announcements by some of Cuba's main foreign investors are only found in those countries' newspapers and wire services.

Newsletters are the format of choice for timeliness and economy of information. Some focus on such specific angles as legal or investment aspects. However, because they tend to be schematic and superficial, newsletters are a more adequate format for investors than scholars.

Symposia are also sources of current and unique information and analysis. Some foundations, law firms and think tanks sponsor conferences and symposia about the Cuban economy. While conference proceedings are selectively indexed in a number of databases, relatively few, like the Foreign Broadcast Information Service, index symposia.

ONLINE DATABASES AS INDEXING TOOLS
Given the variety of sources, databases seem the most appropriate indexing tool. They provide flexibility, efficiency and diversity of contents: every topic discussed in the preceding section was represented in at least one of the databases searched.

The basic search strategy for identifying records consisted of the root "Cuba" within five words of the following roots: "econom," "financ," "market," "trade," "trading," and "commerc." The number of "hits" found with the preliminary search was used as a guideline for selecting databases for analysis, since differences in years of coverage, frequency of updating, and overlapping affect the number of hits.

The search was then refined according to the structure and subject of each database. In some cases the search was limited to current years or most important fields such as main subjects. In most cases, it was narrowed or expanded with additional terms, such as: development, forecasting, informal sector, or foreign investments. Databases comprised exclusively of book and serial titles and general press articles were excluded because the type of coverage they provide is common knowledge. The list of general interest newspapers which yielded the highest number of postings on business and investments in Cuba is provided as an appendix.

ANNOTATED BIBLIOGRAPHY
The following list reviews the contents of a selection of the most significant databases on the basis of the extent, uniqueness, and relevance of their contents, and highlights some distinctive and unusual characteristics of the contents. They are grouped in broad subject categories. Analysis of databases in such categories as Social Sciences, and Latin American and International materials is briefer since these are well known and often-used indexes, and researchers are familiar with the type of coverage they provide.

a) Business and Economic Databases
The criterion for inclusion in this group was that the database, or group file, deal exclusively with business and finance topics. Databases included cover a broad spectrum of business and financial information, ranging from scholarly analysis to up-to-date coverage of financial and commodity market events in newspaper articles.

ABI Inform
Provider: University Microfilms International, Ann Arbor, Michigan.
Business information from business journals worldwide, including company news and analysis, market conditions, trade and investments. Also international trade and foreign investments, business conditions, economic planning, futures market and commodity prices. Includes records on small business and entrepreneur ventures.

Business Dateline
Provider: University Microfilms International, Louisville, Kentucky.
Articles from American and Canadian business journals, newspapers and magazines about new products, manufacturing methods, market conditions, etc. Local and regional coverage, such as local industry ventures and future investment plans in Cuba.

Canadian Business and Current Affairs
Provider: Micromedia Ltd., Toronto, Ontario, Canada.
Articles from Canadian business periodicals and

newspapers and corporate filings deposited with the Ontario Securities Commission. Subjects include company, product and industry information, with abundant local coverage.

Economic Literature Index

Provider: The American Economic Association, Pittsburgh, Pennsylvania.

Journal articles and book reviews from 260 economics journals and monographs. Corresponds to the index section of the *Journal of Economic Literature* and to the annual *Index of Economic Articles*. Scholarly, in-depth analysis of such topics as assessments of economic growth and the informal sector. Includes historical research articles.

Infomat International Business (Globalbase)

Provider: Information Access Company, Foster City, California.

English language abstracts of articles from business newspapers and journals from more than 20 countries. Topics include biotechnology, communications, financial services, construction and civil engineering.

Investext

Provider: Thomson Financial Networks, Boston, Massachusetts.

Company, industry and topical analysis; includes reports by experts on competitive analysis, evaluation of companies, market research, etc. One of the most relevant databases because of its full text coverage of reports by companies investing in Cuba. One such report produced by Sherritt Company contained field research on economic reform and forecasts, political risk and historical background.

Journal of Commerce

Provider: Journal of Commerce Inc., New York.

News, columns, editorials, etc., from the world's premiere business daily and *Traffic World*, the transportation weekly, on international trade, transportation, banking, finance, etc.

Knight Ridder/Tribune Business News

Provider: Knight Ridder/Tribune Business News, Washington, D.C. and Knight Ridder Financial Information, New York.

Business and financial news from Knight Ridder newspapers plus the *Journal of Commerce*.

PREDICASTS Databases

Provider: Information Access Company, Foster City, California.

Industry information, including new technologies and products, market conditions, forecasts and projections.

- **PTS Newsletter Database.** Business and trade newsletters covering a variety of industries such as computers, electronics, etc., products, trends, etc. International economic relations and foreign investments, Cuban agricultural production, sugar industry and communications issues. Complements coverage of individual newsletters on Cuba.

- **PTS Prompt (Predicasts' Overview of markets and technology).** International coverage of products, markets, technologies, etc. in various industries. Includes investment analysis reports, corporate news releases, and other publications such as USDA Research Studies from the Department of Agriculture.

- **Trade & Industry ASAP.** Selection of text and indexing of many journals covered in Trade & Industry Index plus news releases from PR Newswire. Coverage of various industries, notably tourism and travel, metals—particularly nickel—and telecommunications.

- **Trade & Industry Index.** Trade, industry and business journals abstracted in Trade and Industry Index. Similar to above, with more newspaper, loose-leaf (such as *Facts on File*) and regional coverage.

- **PTS F&S Index.** Business and economic data including product and industry information, financial activities, government regulations, etc. News and reports of Cuban international trade relations particularly with European nations. Good coverage of the tobacco industry and grains trade.

- **PTS MARS (Marketing and Advertising Reference Service).** Coverage of multi-industry advertising, marketing, market research and new product information. Trade and tourism, health tourism and policy, reports on U.S. companies positioning themselves for post-embargo investments.

b) Databases in the Social Sciences

Mostly online versions of standard print indexes, these sources cited scholarly, materials with an emphasis on analysis of economic subjects, and their social and public affairs implications and historical background.

CIS

Provider: Congressional Information Service, Inc. Washington, D.C.

Online equivalent of the Congressional Information Service's *Index to Publications of the United States Congress.* Cites congressional working papers published by the House, Senate and Joint committees and sub-committees. Also bills and resolutions about economic and international issues, comparative country studies as they relate to Cuba and Cuban Americans, and economic implications of post-embargo investments. Most frequently discussed (in recent reports) were the downing of the Brothers to the Rescue planes and the Helms-Burton law.

Historical Abstracts

Provider: ABC-CLIO, Inc., Santa Barbara, California.

Periodical literature in history and related disciplines, excluding the U.S. and Canada. Includes economic and cultural history, international relations, social and political history, etc.

PAIS International

Provider: Public Affairs Information Service (PAIS), New York.

Index to the public policy aspects of business, economics, finance, banking, law, international relations, etc. Covers various aspects of the Cuban economic crisis, transition and reforms from the perspective of public policy, and implications on other sectors like education.

Social SciSearch

Provider: Institute for Scientific Information (ISI), Philadelphia, Pennsylvania.

Indexing from the most important social science journals worldwide; corresponds to *Social Science Citation Index.* Historical perspectives on such topics as pre-revolutionary class structure. More coverage from an American perspective than most databases, e.g. coverage of Cuban Americans and U.S. sanctions.

Sociological Abstracts

Provider: Sociological Abstracts, Inc., San Diego, California.

Covers the world literature on sociology and related disciplines. Includes reviews, monographs, conference papers, etc. Scholarly analysis of all aspects of the economy, including the informal sector and Cuba in the context of Marxist economics.

U. S. Political Science Documents

Provider: Mid-Atlantic Technology Applications Center, University of Pittsburgh, Pennsylvania.

Abstracts and indexing from scholarly American journals in political science. Includes foreign policy, international relations, economics, law and political science theory. Emphasis on analysis of current topics like the collapsing economy, the transition to market economy, economic implications of Cuban involvement in Africa.

Agricultural, Biomedical and Technological Databases

The number of articles on economic implications or consequences of topics covered in this group was surprising, given the range of coverage: medicine, public health, genetics, agriculture, food production and environmental issues. In some, there was substantial coverage of social and public policy ramifications. Particularly important was the inclusion of Cuban, particularly regional, publications.

Agris International.

Provider: U.S. National Agricultural Library, Beltsville, Maryland.

Worldwide agricultural literature including food production, rural development, administration and legislation, etc. Corresponds in part to the United Nations' Food and Agriculture Organization's AgrIndex. Excellent reporting of agricultural issues, especially livestock and sugar production; best coverage of technical studies of such topics as rice and cassava harvesting and soil evaluation.

Agricola

Provider: U.S. National Agricultural Library, Beltsville, Maryland.

Worldwide journals and monographic literature on agriculture and related subjects such as animal studies, botany, entomology, forestry, soils, etc. Good coverage of agricultural and technological topics and their economic implications: sugar processing, food shortage, rural development and entomology; emphasis on the sugar industry.

Biosis Previews

Provider: Biosis, Philadelphia, Pennsylvania.

Citations from *Biological Abstracts, Biological Abstracts/RRM* and *BioResearch Index*. Includes reports of original research, monograph titles, and citations from media abstracts, reviews, government reports, etc. Clinical studies in virology and epidemiology topics such as the recent neuropathy epidemic, production of pharmacological products, fisheries and natural resources; one of the few databases to include information on biotechnology.

CAB Abstracts

Provider: CAB International, Farnham Royal, Slough, United Kingdom.

Agricultural and biological information from the main abstract journals published by the Commonwealth Agricultural Bureau plus additional journals, books, conference proceedings, thesis, etc. Subjects include agricultural engineering, animal breeding, dairy science, veterinary science, etc. Scholarly studies of agricultural, health and related issues with emphasis on the sugar industry and public health, and including health tourism and biotechnology.

Geobase

Provider: Elsevier Science Publishers, Norwich, United Kingdom.

Worldwide literature on geography, geology, ecology and related disciplines. Covers *Geographical Abstracts, International Development Abstracts, Geological Abstract Series, Mineralogical Abstracts* and *Ecological Abstracts*, plus many additional publications in related disciplines. Best coverage of Cuban ecology and climatology; broad definition of economic and social geography to include articles on the impact of the dissolution of the Soviet Union and Eastern bloc on Cuba, agrarian reform studies, energy and housing policies.

Pascal

Provider: CNRS/INIST, Institut de l'Information Scientifique et Technique, Vandoeuvre-les-Nancy, France.

Index to Pascal journals including literature from international journals, thesis, reports, books, etc. on life sciences, pollution, food and agricultural science, and other subjects. Articles (some from Cuba and Eastern Europe), on public health, clinical and genetic studies, library and information studies.

Lexis-Nexis Libraries and Files

Provider: Reed-Elsevier/Lexis-Nexis, Dayton, Ohio.

The Lexis-Nexis system focuses on legal and financial topics. It features a multitude of arrangements of information, from single title files to comprehensive multi-format topical files, thus allowing for customized searches focusing on specific angles of a topic. The system is updated daily, so it is the best source for current press coverage, and for focusing on an aspect or geographic area—for example, searching the Asia/Pacific Rim Library to focus on Asian investments in Cuba. What follows is a brief selection of the libraries and files that yielded the most pertinent records.

- **NEWS Library.** General press coverage from newspapers, magazines, newsletters, newswires and broadcast transcripts. Individual newspapers can be searched separately. Selected pertinent files: Current news, Non-English News, Business, Legal, Trade & Technical Group.

- **North and South America Library.** Information from and about the Americas from various sources, including newspapers, newswires, etc. Ample information on NAFTA and other trade agreements. Selected pertinent files: Current News, Latin American Newsletters. Of particular importance was the Cuba file, which allows searching information on that country only.

- **Asia/Pacific Rim Library.** Information about every country in the area from a broad variety of sources including press coverage of both Asian countries and Western Press. Selected pertinent files: Current News, Business News Analysis, Company Information.

- **Company Library.** Business and financial information, including research reports from leading banks and brokerage houses, investment banks, company annual reports, profiles and filings, etc. Yielded information on specific companies investing in Cuba. Selected pertinent files: USCO (American and Canadian) Company.

- **Markets and Industry Library.** Information from an extensive variety of sources covering advertising, marketing, market research, sales, consumer information, etc. Selected pertinent files: Current News, Marketing & Public Relations, Industry.

c) Databases of Latin American and International Materials

Databases in this group offered a different outlook. Those comprised solely of materials from or about Latin America present not only a unique perspective but subjects not covered in other databases as well. Emphasis on analysis and historical reviews (such as examinations of the economy in colonial times) rather than current issues, although the subject of economic conditions was extensively discussed in all databases.

Foreign Broadcast Information Service (FBIS)

Provider: Provider: U.S. Department of Commerce, Newsbank-Readex.

Electronic subject index to FBIS Daily Reports, which monitors and translates worldwide news commentary from foreign broadcasts, wire services, government press releases and newspapers.

The best broad picture of international press coverage; numerous articles on current events and specific trade agreements and diplomatic visits. Most complete international press coverage of all databases analyzed.

Hispanic American Periodicals Index (HAPI)

Provider: The University of California, Los Angeles, Latin American Center.

Largest index to journal literature from and about Latin America, dealing with all issues in the social sciences and humanities, plus economic, financial and related topics.

The Handbook of Latin American Studies

Provider: The United States Library of Congress.

Selective annotated guide to publications in the social sciences, the humanities, art and music about Latin America with emphasis on Mexico and Argentina.

UNBIS-Plus

Provider: The United Nations Bibliographic Service in collaboration with Chadwick-Healy.

United Nations official records, agendas and resolutions, including voting records, speech citations and session numbers, U.N. authority and geographic files. Best coverage of human rights in Cuba and discussions on the consequences of the economic crisis.

CONCLUSION

There is no lack of well documented, scholarly literature on the subject of the Cuban economy. Yet because of the relevance of such factors as the exile community and the informal sector of the economy, as well as the incomplete and sporadic nature of Cuban government publications, well balanced coverage requires reliance on both established and unconventional sources. Online databases are one of the foremost indexing sources because they allow for efficient and flexible searching. Many also contain materials unavailable elsewhere, combine various formats on a given topic, and offer unmatched timeliness.

Although the number of "hits" yielded by a preliminary search can be used as a guideline, other factors should be considered when selecting databases. Background and historical perspective are to be gained from more extensive, in-depth analysis usually published as monographs or in scholarly articles indexed in such databases as *Economic Literature Index, Sociology Abstracts, Political Science Documents* and *Historical Abstracts*. Equally scholarly but more focused on Latin American materials are *HAPI* and the *Hand-*

book of Latin American Studies, the fundamental sources when that perspective is preferred.

Currency and timeliness are best served by monitoring databases which cover print and broadcast media. There are numerous databases offering such reporting and the Lexis-Nexis system combines them in a number of group files allowing for customized topical searches. When conciseness is as important as timeliness, newsletters are the format of choice. The contents of such databases as PTS Newsletter complement the growing number of newsletters devoted solely to the Cuban economy. Other relevant factors are regional and political balance, as well as the agenda behind profit making producers. Experience in online searching is a basic consideration. Knowledge of the system's capabilities, careful database or group file selection, and ultimately an examination the database structure can greatly influence the outcome of a search as well as its cost.

Finally, intangibles such as perspective and perception must be considered when reviewing the literature. The number of recent articles in the European and Canadian press, for instance, about the potential consequences of the Helms-Burton Law to the Cuban economy presents a disproportionate picture of its relevance.

New sources of information on the Cuban economy are continually emerging due to the timeliness and widespread interest on the subject. Those seeking balanced information about this topic, both current and historical, will find in online databases an exceptional indexing tool leading to a wide variety of sources.

Appendix. Largest Press Coverage on the Cuban Economy

Name	Total Records
Newspapers	
Miami Herald	2756
Fort Lauderdale Sun Sentinel	734
The Orlando Sentinel	485
Washington Post Online	416
Los Angeles Times	404
Palm Beach Post	369
Chicago Tribune	361
Philadelphia Inquirer	355
(New Orleans) Times Picayune	318
St. Petersburg Times	315
San Francisco Chronicle	293
Atlanta Journal/Constitution	290
San Jose Mercury	288
Newsday/New York Newsday	280
Arizona Republic/Phoenix Gazette	278
The Boston Globe	264
(Portland) The Oregonian	256
(New Jersey) The Record	236
The Seattle Times	228
St. Louis Post-Dispatch	226
Newswires	
Reuters	2388
AP News	1470
Textline Global News	1137
Newspaper and Periodical Abstracts	597
Magazine ASAP	508
AFP English Wire	412
UPI News	410
AFP International French Wire	302
National Newspaper Index	164
Federal News Service	153
Newswire ASAP (1995 only)	125
Newspaper Abstracts	89
PR Newswire	68
Time Publications	63
Japan Economic Newswire	38

CUBAN COMPUTER NETWORKS AND THEIR IMPACT

Larry Press

This paper summarizes the current state of Cuban networks and discusses some of the potential, marginal impacts of those networks. We summarize the state of four networks with international connections. While much smaller and less powerful than networks in developed nations like the United States, they have grown substantially since 1992 and are significant relative to other Caribbean nations. We also discuss the possible marginal impact of improved networks on various policy goals, and conclude that, in spite of costs, the improvement of Cuban networks would be desirable.

CUBAN NETWORKS

There are four Cuban networks with international Internet connectivity: CENIAI, Tinored, CIGBnet, and InfoMed.

- *CENIAI*, the Center for Automated Interchange of Information of the Cuban Academy of Sciences, began networking in 1982, and has had a dial-up link to the Internet since 1991. They currently offer email, database access, mail lists, and programming and consulting services, and maintain a presence on a Gopher server located in Uruguay.

- *Tinored* (Tino Network—Tino, a Cuban cartoon character, is the logo, and "red" means "network") was established by the Cuban Youth Computer Clubs, an organization with explicit support of Fidel Castro, that operates 150 walk-in computer centers throughout the nation [13]. One hundred of these have Tinored email accounts, and approximately 80 have working (2400 bits per second, bps) modems. Tinored is

also a gateway for Red David, which supports at least 31 NGOs.

- *CIGBnet* is the network of the Center for Genetic Engineering and Biotechnology and affiliated institutions [1]. They have a central site in Havana and three remote sites. CIGBnet began in 1991 and has grown to 900 users. They provide email, database access, a biological sequence server, mailing lists, and Gopher and Web servers (accessible only from the main center). CIGB staff have developed their own mail-based database server, off-line mail package, and sequencing server software, and they are continuing such work.

- *InfoMed*, the network of the National System of Health Information of the Cuban Ministry of Health, has been operating since 1992. They have 500 accounts, 80% of which are shared by more than one person within an organization, and provide email, discussion groups, file retrieval, database search, and consultation. While they currently operate a single node in Havana, they are building a distributed network with 13 servers in Cuban medical schools with support from the Pan American Health Organization and UNESCO.

Table 1 summarizes these and the more important subnetworks they serve. For more information on these networks, see [14 and 15].

Note that these networks are not the equivalent of regional or even campus networks in the U.S. or other developed nations. While U.S. networks are perma-

Table 1.   Four International Networks and Selected Sub-Nets

1. CIGBnet (950)

UOnet	Oriente University Network
COMUH	University of Havana network
ICID(280)	Institute for Digital Research
RENACYT	ICIMAF/CIDET Center for Research on Telematics
CNCNet (250)	Network of the National Neurosciences Center
CRC	Center for Clinical Research
IMRE	Reagents and Materials for Electronics Institute
Binanet	The Network of the National Library

2. CENIAI (732)

ISPJAE/CUJAE	Instituto Superior Politécnico José A. Echevarría
REDUNIV	University Network for Scientific and Technological Information of the Ministry of Education
BIOMUNDI (39)	Biological Information Network
UCLV	Las Villas University network, using CENIAI
Red Granma	Center of Documentation and Scientific and Technological Information
Red Yayabo (50)	A regional network based in Ciudad Sancti Spíritus, providing UUCP services to 6 institutions in that province. Has a PC XT with 640 K RAM, a 20 MB hard drive, and a 9600 bps modem.
Red Holguín	A regional network based in Ciudad Holguín, providing services to institutions in that province.
Red Perla (62)	A regional network based in Ciudad Cienfuegos, providing services to institutions in that province.

3. TinoRed (13)

Red David	NGO Network

4. InfoMed (500)

Red Príncipe	Based in Ciudad Camagüey; it provides service for Camagüey University, Camagüey Medical Services Faculty, and some other enterprises and institutions.

Note: The numbers in parenthesis are the number of accounts that have been active at least once per month during the last three months.

Sources: Carlos Armas, CIGBnet; Jesús Martínez, CENIAI; Carlos Valdés, Tinored; and Pedro Urra, InfoMed. Sub-network user counts were obtained by Armas.

nently connected to the Internet, Cuban networks connect temporarily. For example, 4-6 times a day a call is placed from an Internet access provider in Canada to CENIAI in Cuba. When the connection is established, batches of waiting email messages are transferred in both directions, and the connection is dropped. This means that Cubans and outsiders can exchange email with only a few hours delay, but interactive activity like browsing the World Wide Web is not possible. Interactive Internet access to and from Cuba would require permanent international circuits and use of communication software implementing the Internet Protocol (IP).

Most, though not all, intranational traffic is handled in the same manner as international traffic. This means most Cuban users can only exchange email or query databases by emailing commands within the nation. However, technicians at several centers are experimenting with intranational IP connections. As

such, they are gaining experience for the time when Cuba has international IP connectivity.

The computers comprising the Cuban networks are also small by U.S. standards. They are typically 386 or 486-based PCs. Although several years out of date, they are still sufficient for a meaningful email network. A single computer may also be shared by several users.

In spite of difficult economic conditions in recent years, Cuban networks have grown substantially since 1992 [11]. Cuban authorities are well aware of these networks and they require hard currency for hardware, therefore it seems the government supports them.

This support has brought Cuban networks to the point where they are significant by Caribbean standards. It appears that the number of users in Cuba is greater than the rest of the Caribbean nations combined, and international traffic is over 37% of the rest of the Caribbean [15].

Cuba has developed a sizable user community, with networking skills and applications. This has grown out of a long-standing commitment to education throughout the society, and major research, development, and therapy programs in biotechnology and medicine. Cuban networking experts have the expertise to operate an international IP link, and permission of the government to do so. They are missing funding and a working agreement or plan for cooperation between the various networks, but these will be achieved. CENIAI has had a proposal to establish a leased, IP link to the Internet for several years, and a commission was recently established to oversee this process. At the same time, it was announced that users would be registered and access controlled. Cuba, like other repressive nations, faces the dictator's dilemma—they fear the political affects of open access to information and communication (inter and intranationally), but desire the economic benefits of networks.

NETWORK IMPACT

The Cuban Democracy Act sets forth a number of goals for U.S.-Cuban policy. This section delineates these and several other goals, and discusses possible marginal impact of improved communication and networking on each.

Free and Fair Elections

The Cuban Democracy Act calls for "free and fair elections" in which all candidates are permitted "full access to the media." While the Cuban government currently shows no inclination to hold free elections, they will occur at some time, and at that time, an improved communication infrastructure would be an asset for all political parties. In general, one would

expect networks to encourage democracy by providing Cubans with outside information and ideas, and by enabling them to share ideas and coordinate activity, much as the Internet was used for inter and intranational communication during the failed Soviet Coup attempt [12]. The Internet also carried news and discussion of events in Tiananmen Square, Chiapas, etc.

Going beyond anecdote, Kedzie [5, 6] presents multivariate analysis showing that interconnectivity is a better predictor of democracy than schooling, GDP, life expectancy, ethnic homogeneity, or population, particularly in regions of newly emerging democracy. One could speculate that democracy causes interconnectivity or they are spuriously correlated with a third variable like development, but Kedzie's analysis does not support these suggestions. Kedzie suggests that networking policy can encourage democracy:

> To the extent that we as a nation aim to influence the development of democracy world wide, we do so through programs to enhance economic development, education, health, legal reform, etc. The causal connection supporting these programs is no stronger, and in some cases quite a bit weaker, than can be inferred in the case of network communication technology. [6]

INCREASED CIVIL LIBERTIES AND HUMAN RIGHTS

The Cuban Democracy Act calls for the Cuban government to show "respect for the basic civil liberties and human rights of the citizens of Cuba," and authorizes the U.S. Government to "provide assistance, through appropriate NGOs, for the support of individuals and organizations to promote nonviolent democratic change in Cuba."[1] At least 31 NGOs have accounts on Cuban networks (see Table 2).

---

1. The 1995 U.S. State Department report on human rights [17] lists problems in Cuba, including extrajudicial killing of people leaving in boats, routine use of arbitrary arrest and detention, and obtrusive block committees that monitor behavior and attitudes. The government does not allow freedom of critical speech, and the Cuban Constitution states that electronic and print media are state property. As a visitor, one notes propaganda in the electronic media and billboards, and is aware of surveillance. On the other hand, the State Department report acknowledges there were no reports of disappearances, no restriction on domestic travel, an easing of religious repression, and that many blacks have benefited from the social changes of the revolution. As a visitor, one is struck by the willingness of people on the street to speak openly of politics, and of cultural liberalization. For example, the movie "Strawberry and Chocolate," which presents political criticism and a sympathetic portrayal of eccentric behavior and homosexuality, played in theaters and was widely available on video tape.

Table 2. Cuban NGOs with Tinored Accounts

Centro de Estudios de Africa y Medio Oriente
Centro de Estudios Europeos
Casa de las Américas
Centro de Estudios Martianos
Centro de Estudios sobre Estados Unidos
Centro de Estudios sobre Alternativas Políticas
Centro de Investigaciones de la Economía Mundial
Centro de Estudios de la Economía Cubana
Movimiento Cubano por la Paz
Grupo de Desarrollo Integral de la Capital
Memoria de los Movimientos Populares de América Latina
Centro Memorial "Martin Luther King"
Centro "Félix Varela"
Asociacion por la Unidad de Nuestra América
Radio Habana-Cuba
Centro de Estudios sobre Asia y Oceanía
Grupo de Desarrollo de la Bicicleta en Cuba
Cátedra "Pablo de la Torriente Brau"
Consejo de Iglesias de Cuba
Centro de Investigación y Estudios de las Relaciones Interamericanas
Centro de Investigación de la Economía Internacional
Centro de Información para la Prensa
Federación de Mujeres Cubanas
Grupo para la Educación sobre el SIDA
Instituto Superior Latinoamericano de Ajedrez
Asociación Cubana de Esperanto
Alcohólicos Anónimos
Unión de Escritores y Artistas de Cuba
Federación de Mujeres Cubanas
Editorial Jose Martí
Consejo Ecuménico de Cuba

Source: Carlos Valdés, Tinored System Administrator. (Valdés states there are some others, but their names were not available at the time of his message.)

Gillian Gunn has conducted a study of the Cuban NGOs [4], and states that the Cuban Ministry of Justice "reports explosive growth in their number from 1989 to 1993, and a leveling off in 1994." Gunn states that "Approximately 2,200 NGOs are now registered with the government and many others exist underground." She surveys the NGOs and their relation to the Government, and concludes:

> Are Cuba's NGOs government puppets or seeds of civil society? The answer is ideologically and intellectually unsatisfying. They are both, though the latter characteristic is very gradually growing.

In a September, 1995 interview, Gunn stated that since the Spring of 1993, there have been Cuban government memos stating there are too many NGOs, and calling for increased audit and control by the ministry which oversees them. Subsequently, Raúl Castro has commented on Gunn's report, suggesting that NGOs are a threat.

Gunn feels email is a lifeline for the NGOs since fax and telephone are unreliable and expensive. For instance, the Georgetown University Cuba Project, which she directs, is organizing an environmental conference with two Cuban NGOs, which would have been impossible without email. I had the same experience as chairman of the 1994 Conference on The Impact of Informatics on Developing Countries, of the International Federation of Information Processing Societies in Havana, which would have been impossible without the network, as would be the paper you are now reading.

While these examples involve communication between Cuba and the rest of the world, the network also facilitate open communication within a nation. Again, the Soviet Net, Relcom, serves as an illustration. Relcom functioned without interruption throughout the coup attempt, providing reports on the status of troops, protest, strikes, and so forth in various Soviet cities. There was also considerable two way exchange with other nations.[2]

MOVE TOWARD A FREE MARKET ECONOMY

The Cuban Democracy Act calls for movement toward "establishing a free market economic system," and there has been some movement in this direction, including dollar legalization, limited markets, and, most recently, a liberalization of investment laws.

In a communication-poor nation, a computer network can make a meaningful contribution to a market economy. Again, the Relcom Network, which carried commercial traffic from its inception, provides an example of this role. A market economy also

---

2. An archive of this traffic is available to scholars at http://www.cs.oswego.edu/misc/coup/index.html.

Table 3.   Basic Indicators: Chile, Costa Rica, and Cuba

	1993 Population (million)	1993 GNP per capita (U.S. dollars)	1993 Life Expectancy (Years)	1991 Primary School Enrollment (%)	1990 Illiteracy Rate (%)
Chile	13.80	3170	74	87	7
Costa Rica	3.30	2150	76	87	7
Cuba	10.86	1537	76	97	6

Source: World Bank. Cuban GNP is from the International Telecommunications Union.

requires private capital, and a robust communication system is an asset in the eyes of a potential investor.

Maintain the Achievements of the Revolution and Improve Cuban Living Standards

While this is not an explicit goal of U.S. policy, it is consistent with the humanitarian ends our policy seeks to achieve. Cubans point with justified pride to significant gains in racial equality, health care, education and science, and improved life in rural communities, as achievements of the Castro regime. As Table 3 shows, Cuban basic indicators are comparable to successful South and Central American nations Chile and Costa Rica which have reached satisfactory levels of economic growth and addressed the basic needs of their populations. One can argue that historical conditions and policies of pre-Castro Cuba are responsible for some of Cuba's success, or that there were alternative means of reaching the same end, but there have been major accomplishments which should be preserved and extended.

To the extent that improved telecommunications will help the Cuban economy recover from its current crisis, it will help provide the stability and economic surplus necessary to continue social programs. Additionally, improved telecommunications can bring some of the economic, educational, and cultural advantages historically enjoyed in cities to the country side.

Many in the U.S. argue that cutting Cuban living standards destabilizes the government, and will lead to change; however, this is achieved at great humanitarian cost. It also increases the danger of a violent revolution, with attendant loss of life, economic ruin, refugees, and political-economic responsibility for the U.S. [2]. For pragmatic and humanitarian reasons, we would surely prefer a peaceful, democratic

transition as exemplified by the Chilean elections to a violent change.

Provide Investment and Trade Opportunity for U.S. Companies

U.S. policy has been to pressure the Cuban government by stopping foreign investment. While we have slowed foreign investment, we have not stopped it. Pérez-López [9, 10] discusses the quality, quantity, strategic value, and other aspects of foreign joint ventures in Cuba. He reports that the number of joint ventures has grown from fewer than 20 at the end of 1990 to about 60 at the end of 1991, 76 in November 1992, 180 at the end of 1994, and 230 by May 1995 [10]. (On the other hand, he reports that that these investments are often worth less than their reported face value [9].) Further evidence of foreign business and investment is provided by Table 4, showing the number of businesses with Cuban offices by nation.

While designed to precipitate change, our policy has had the undesirable side effect of reducing U.S. business opportunity. Prior to the passage of the Helms-Burton Act it was arguable that network-related investment was consistent with the Cuban Democracy Act. This no longer appears to be the case, but if and when it again becomes legal, it would have destabilizing effects and provide opportunity to U.S. business.

While trade is illegal today, one day trade relations will be established, and good communication infrastructure will be of value.

Find New Forms of Management and State/ Enterprise Relationships

Humanity has experimented broadly during the 20th century. We have learned that a central, planned economy is less efficient than a market economy at the production of goods and services, and can inflict

Table 4. Foreign Firms Registered in Cuba, April 1994

Country	Number	Percent	Country	Number	Percent
Spain	80	24.5	Austria	2	0.6
Panama	52	15.9	Chile	2	0.3
Germany	17	5.2	Belgium	2	0.3
Japan	17	5.2	Dominican Republic	2	0.3
France	14	4.3	Uruguay	2	0.3
Mexico	13	4.0	Gibraltar	1	0.3
Canada	13	4.0	Martinique	1	0.3
Italy	12	3.7	Peru	1	0.3
Argentina	10	3.1	Czech Republic	1	0.3
Switzerland	9	2.8	Portugal	1	0.3
England	9	2.8	Greece	1	0.3
Virgin Islands	8	2.4	Bermuda	1	0.3
Holland	8	2.4	India	1	0.3
Russia	6	1.8	San Bartholomew	1	0.3
Dutch Antilles	5	1.5	Denmark	1	0.3
Venezuela	5	1.5	Singapore	1	0.3
Nicaragua	4	1.2	Costa Rica	1	0.3
Colombia	4	1.2	Cyprus	1	0.3
Lichtenstein	4	1.2	Isle of Jersey	1	0.3
Ecuador	3	0.9	Australia	1	0.3
Brazil	3	0.9	Slovakia	1	0.3
Curacao	3	0.9	TOTAL	327	100.0
Cayman Islands	2	0.6			

Source: Cuban Chamber of Commerce.

catastrophic environmental damage and lead to arbitrary and capricious distribution of income and power. While relatively efficient, market economies also inflict environmental damage and lead to wide variance in the distribution of income and wealth, with attendant human and moral cost. These concerns are widely held, as witnessed, for example, in the NAFTA debates in the U.S. Congress or the Pope's recent U. N. speech.

Transitions like those in Eastern Europe and Cuba may provide the opportunity for further experimentation and variety in management and state/enterprise relationships. For example, the recent law liberalizing foreign investment in Cuba allows the investor to own an enterprise and its capital assets, but the employees work for the state. It will be interesting to see the results of this arrangement over time.

A robust communication infrastructure would help create the environment needed for new forms of organization to evolve and would also be used by these organizations. While only one component of that environment, it is significant.

Protect the Environment and Conserve Natural Resources

The current economic crisis has caused Cuba to cut energy consumption. This has caused hardship, but also conservation, rationing, reengineering and substitution—for example in the large scale use of bicycles. To the extent that communication can be traded for transportation in the economy and education systems, an improved communication infrastructure may be seen as making a contribution to efficiency and preservation of the Cuban environment.

Gain Access to Cuban Information

Discussion of communication networks in developing nations often centers on the advantages to the developing nation of gaining access to information and experts in developed nations; however, this is a two-way street. For example, Cuba has strong biomedical research and therapy programs, and improved communication will facilitate access to Cuban databases and experts. Cuban science will also benefit from contact with colleagues internationally, to the advantage of all mankind. The improvement of Cuban biomedical science and access to its results would be to the humanitarian benefit of Cubans and all others, particularly Latin Americans who make use of Cuban health resources. Cuba also has information resources in other fields, for example, the digitized Havana Art Museum collection or Spanish-language educational software.

CONCLUSION

On balance, I would argue in favor of a policy which facilitates the improvement of Cuban computer networks and the infrastructure needed to support them. Such communication would further a number of U.S. goals, such as free elections and respect for human rights. It would also have economic benefit for Cuba, which would be of humanitarian value, but would be counter to the strategy of trying to force Cuba to capitulate and oust Castro. This is the U.S. policy dilemma.

Fidel Castro and the Cuban Government also face the dictator's dilemma. Communication technology is an important resource for economic growth [18], yet it opens the door for freedom of internal and external expression which could threaten the regime. Some governments have chosen to suppress information technology regardless of the economic cost [3], but as we have seen, Cuba is more positive toward computer networks.

In the current energy and economic crisis, communication is difficult in Cuba. The obsolete telephone infrastructure is deteriorating, paper, copier toner and other supplies are very difficult to find, and television broadcast schedules have been cut. Computer networks may partially fill these voids, making them a low-cost investment with a high marginal return.

REFERENCES

1. Armas, Carlos, "Cuba," in the Eye on Developing Nations section, *OnTheInternet* (July/August 1995), pp 38-39.

2. Gonzalez, Edward and Ronfeldt, David, *Storm Warnings for Cuba*, MR-452-OSD. Santa Monica, CA: RAND Corporation, 1994.

3. Goodman, S., and Green, J. D., "Computing in the Middle East," *Communications of the ACM*, Vol 35, No 8 (August 1992), pp 21-25.

4. Gunn, Gillian, *Cuba's NGOs: Government Puppets or Seeds of Civil Society*, Cuba Briefing Paper Number 7. Washington, D.C.: Georgetown University Haiti-Cuba Project, February 1995.

5. Kedzie, Christopher R., "Democracy and Network Interconnectivity," *Proceedings of INET '95, International Networking Conference, Honolulu, Hawaii*. Reston, VA: Internet Society, August 1995.

6. Kedzie, Christopher R., "Coincident Revolutions," *OnTheInternet*, in press.

7. Martínez Alfonso, Jesús, "Desarrollo de la Iniciativa Cubana Red CENIAI de la Academia de Ciencias de Cuba," III Foro de Redes Académicas de la América Latina y El Caribe, Caracas, Venezuela, October 17-22, 1993.

8. Martínez, Jesús, "Profile of the Cuban Scientific Network Project," email document, February 1995.

9. Pérez-López, Jorge F., "A Critical Look at Cuba's Foreign Investment Program," Meeting of the Latin American Studies Association, Washington, D. C., September 28-30, 1995.

10. Pérez-López, Jorge F., "Islands of Capitalism in an Ocean of Socialism: Joint Ventures in Cuba's Development Strategy," in Pérez-López, Jorge F., ed., *Cuba at a Crossroads*. Gainesville: University of Florida Press, 1994, pp 190-219.

11. Press, L. and Snyder, J., "A Look at Cuban Networks," *Matrix News* 2(6), Matrix Information and Directory Services, Austin (June 1992).

12. Press, L., "Relcom, An Appropriate Technology Network," *Proceedings of INET '92, International Networking Conference, Kobe, Japan*. Reston, VA, Internet Society, 1992. Reprinted in *The Proceedings of the Telecommunications Conference*, Moscow, Russia, June 1992.

13. Press, L., "Technetronic Education: Answers on the Cultural Horizon," *Communications of the ACM*, Vol. 36, No. 5 (May 1993), pp. 17-22.

14. Press, L., and Armas, C., "Cuban Network Update," *OnTheInternet* (January/February 1996), pp 46-49.

15. Press, L., *Cuban Telecommunications, Computer Networking, and U.S. Policy Implications*, DRR-1330-OSD. Santa Monica, CA: RAND Corporation, February 1996.

16. Press, L., "The Role of Computer Networks in Development," *Communications of the ACM*, Vol. 39, No. 2 (February 1996), pp 23-30.

17. United States State Department, *The 1995 Annual Report on Human Rights*, gopher://gopher.gate.net/00/florida/CubaNet/PRESS/mar/amnesty95

18. Wellenuius, Bjorn and others, *Telecommunications: The World Bank Experience and Strategy*, Discussion Paper # 192. Washington, D.C.: The World Bank, March 1993.

TRANSFORMATIONS AND TRANSITIONS: THE CHANGING NATURE OF LABOR ORGANIZATIONS IN POST-COMMUNIST EUROPE AND THE IMPLICATIONS FOR LABOR IN CUBA

Guillermo J. Grenier

The Central and Eastern European region is of critical importance to the world political economy. Many think that the tone of the new world order will be set in the 21st Century by the events occurring in this region. Not surprisingly, interest in the region has grown immensely in the last decade, especially among business people and political analysts. Rarely, however, have labor organizations received serious attention in the transition stories of Central and Eastern European countries. In fact, unions are either ignored as social actors in the process of society creation or seen as anachronistic political institutions responsible for retarding the fall of communism as well as the rebuilding of new social relations of production.

The labor movement in Cuba suffers the same lack of attention when it comes to its role in a possible political and social transition on the island. This is understandable, given the role of the main confederation, the Confederación de Trabajadores Cubanos (CTC), as a transmission belt of party policies in the arena of industrial and labor relations. Still, it is instructive to look at the role of Central and Eastern European unions in the transition process of the region as a way of understanding the potential for organizations of Cuban workers to be agents of change.

This paper presents the experiences of the major confederations of six Central and Eastern European countries in the process of transition and discusses some of the implications that their experiences hold

for Cuban labor in transition. The six countries are the Czech Republic, the Slovak Republic, Hungary, Bulgaria, Romania, and Belarus.

The paper divides the topic in the following manner. First, I will look at the two dominant paradigms guiding the analysis of transition in Central and Eastern Europe, then I will present some of the common characteristics of the regional transition process. The common characteristics of pre-transition unions are then presented followed by the principal changes in the structure of labor relations in the process of transition. Some of the general issues facing labor leaders in all countries because of the transition process are then discussed. Finally, we look at the case of Cuba and how some of the current changes in the economic and social structure are shaking, and establishing, the foundation for the role of unions in the future transition of the country.

TRANSITION AND UNIONS IN CENTRAL AND EASTERN EUROPE: THEMES IN THE LITERATURE

Except for the obvious case of Poland, where the role of Solidarity in the transition process has been well documented, the vast majority of the academic and professional literature on the post-communist transition does not analyze the role of labor organizations in this process. Labor organizations, after all, were but one set of the many institutions attempting to keep viable a bankrupt system. The few studies that have considered unions as players in the process look at unions as either: 1) mediators or obstructors of economic transformation or 2) how labor is developing its relationships with emerging state structures (Thirkell, 1994; Jones, 1992). Most of the massive literature accumulated over the last six years on communist societies in transition has focused on the political or economic factors associated with the collapse and subsequent reconstruction of the societies in question.

In this context, two general paradigms of analysis seem to emerge as most promising for the analysis of the role of unions in the transition process: the "tabula rasa" paradigm and the path dependency paradigm (Stark, 1992).

The paradigm which can be called the "tabula rasa" paradigm associates the collapse of communism with the collapse of all or most of the social structures existing within the old communist regimes, thus creating a social and economic "tabula rasa" where free market gurus can exercise their craft. Indeed, most western social scientists have been preoccupied with the total collapse idea in part because an image of an all-powerful state loomed so large in their portrayal of state socialism before the changes of 1989. It is not surprising that in its absence, the transitional period is viewed as without institutional form and void of social organization.

The path analysis paradigm focuses on the continuation of social relationships from old to new political structures. According to these analysts, some the social relationships which existed in the old system contributed directly to the collapse of communism and now these relationships are determining how specific societies pull themselves together after the collapse. They argue that, while it is clear that the old communist state attempted to dominate all aspects of individual and organizational behavior, it is also evident that it failed to do so uniformly across all levels of society (Bruszt and Stark, 1991).

Ethnographic studies of work environments and survey research, support this view of change and continuity in the former Soviet bloc. There existed a multiplicity of social relations that are less hierarchical and centralized in structure (see Stark and Nee,

1989) than the ideal communist model that we often assume existed before 1989. This literature suggests the existence of parallel structures in the informal and formal labor networks. For our purposes, this means that instead of an institutional vacuum, analysts find routines and practices, organizational forms and ties, informal leadership and followers at the shop floor level that serve as the basis for organizational development and coordinated actions in a post communist social structure. These organizational forms varied across the societies in the region but they existed everywhere and they influenced the development of the current labor movement.

At the shop floor level, research suggests that the production process led to bargaining between supervisors and informal groups; groups that existed with relative independence from the massified labor bureaucracy, and from which some present labor leadership arose. These groups would often see themselves, as a vice president of the Slovak confederation reported, as units that could "correct" some of the orders sent down by the Party.

This view of transition as a continuity of pretransition social processes is presented by David Stark as the "path dependency model." Stark describes that the paths taken by each society to free itself from state socialism determines the choices available to solve the economic, social and political problems of transition. In an elaborate sociological comparison of privatization strategies in Eastern Europe, Stark (1992) develops a typology of the different strategies of privatization adopted by the countries in the region. He concludes that to explain these distinctive strategies of privatization, one must begin by taking into account the social forces propelling each society away from the communist model of organization:

...their distinctive paths of extrication from state socialism-reunification in Germany, capitulation in Czechoslovakia, compromise in Poland, and electoral competition in Hungary... The collapse of communism in East Germany resulted in the colonization of its new political institutions during incorporation into the powerful state of the German Federal Republic. The capitulation of Communist authorities in Czechoslovakia after decades of suppressing almost all institutions of civil society, meanwhile, resulted in the rapid restructuring of its political institutions with relatively few remnants from the earlier period. Communism did not collapse in Hungary and Poland; its demise was negotiated in both countries.

In support of this view, Bruszt (1992) points out that trade unions existing Czechoslovakia in 1990 bore relatively little resemblance to the pre-1989 unions—in contrast to Hungary and the other former communist countries, where the old official union remained the largest and most powerful trade union confederation, and to Poland where both Solidarity and OPZZ are the continued legacy of the 1980s. This pattern of numerical dominance of the pre-1989 trade unions is found in all of the countries studied.

GENERAL CHARACTERISTICS OF THE EASTERN AND CENTRAL EUROPEAN SOCIAL TRANSITION

Given the massive nature of the changes occurring in Eastern Europe, it is worthwhile remembering that even in the apparent balkanization of the monolithic Soviet Bloc there remain strong similarities among countries. Or, at least, the challenges which each confront have common roots and profiles even while solutions are characterized by rediscovered nationalist traditions and processes. This section presents some of the common features of the transition process in the societies studied.

All of the countries share with Cuba features derived from their common organizational legacy based on central planning. The structure and institutions of the labor markets in centrally planned economies developed some distinguishable characteristics.

- They all had extremely high workforce participation rates, especially among women. In the Soviet Union the female participation rate was over 80 percent while Eastern European countries averaged over 70 percent. (Western European rates hover around the 50 percent mark.)

- Countries sharing the legacy of central planning also tend to have large firms, with the average employment per firm being about 200 workers, against 80 workers in Western Europe.

- Wage and income differentials were small. Studies show that the income of two randomly selected workers differed by less than 45 percent in Central and Eastern Europe, while it differed by 65-75 percent in Western Europe and more than that in the U.S.

- School enrollment was high and basic education was considered to be of relatively high quality with literacy rates approaching 100 percent in all countries.

- The traditional socialist labor market also depended a great deal on subtle and sometimes not so subtle admonitions to work, mandatory assignments of graduates, strict control of migration, and involuntary recruitment of labor to carry out specialized tasks.

- The essential elements of the transition process as they are usually described in economic terms, stabilization, liberalization and institutional reforms, created a situation where the uncompetitive nature of the existing sectors became obvious but the emerging sectors remain too weak to alleviate the situation.

- When changes began, an unprecedented fall in GDP and real wages was felt in all countries, the structure of labor demand changed dramatically and nearly 200 million workers had to adjust to new rules of the game while job security for many disappeared. Unemployment emerged for the first time as a political and economic concern.

- Wage differentials increased. For instance, in Poland wages of two randomly selected white collar workers differed by 42 percent in 1987 and by 51 percent in 1992.

- Regional differentials, long a characteristic of developed economies, became evident, even in smaller countries like Hungary, where regional unemployment in 1993 ranged from 7 to 46 percent.

- All societies faced the issues of unemployment, inflation, drop in real wages, political instability and others and there was no easy way out.

- The number of working poor in the former centrally planned economies has risen across the board, especially in the countries where working hours were cut, rather than employment. Overall increases in poverty are most dramatic in the CIS countries in general and Belarus specifically.

- All of the countries of the ex-Soviet Union and Eastern Europe lacked a large labor force not allocated to protected sectors of the economy. This created problems in restructuring strategies. (See *1995 World Development Report*, Barr, 1994.)

These structural similarities gave rise to similar policy issues during the process of transition.

- Destruction of old jobs became unavoidable and how to do it became a political question.

- In general, the governments did not undertake dramatic transition policies until each felt strong enough to survive the political fallout.

- Where the government is successful in establishing its commitment to reform, such as is the case in the Czech Republic, transition processes seem to point in a positive economic direction.

- Although it is difficult to untangle cause from effect in the transition process, there are signs that countries that move rapidly to establish reforms are also the quickest to record gains for labor.

General Characteristics of the Pre-Transition Unions in Socialist Totalitarian Societies

The centralization mentioned above also contributed to the creation of common characteristics among the labor confederations in the different countries. These characteristics are shared by the Cuban official labor movement.

- The one party system which prevailed extended its control over the workforce through a one confederation system. The labor movement, in effect, was the most socially pervasive method of social control.

- The one confederation system in each country served, in the Leninist tradition, as a transmission belt between the party and the workers, pro-

viding incentives and controls to direct the behavior of the enterprise and of the workers.

- Leadership in the confederation was bestowed upon those whose allegiance to the party was beyond reproach (in all countries top leaders had to be members of the party) and who maintained a base among the workers. This legacy explains the divisions, sometimes bitter, that exist today in all countries between those who held positions in the old union system and those who consider themselves representatives of "free labor", e.g., free from any ties to the old communist order.

- Transition economies inherited heavily unionized labor markets with above 90 percent of workers belonging to unions in all countries.

- Unions in pre-transition societies functioned primarily as social, not economic organizations; as the gatekeepers to the socialist welfare state.

In order to understand the nature of labor relations in pre-transition societies one must first understand that the terminology used, although similar to that used in market economies, does not mean the same things.

- wages were not the price of labor negotiated in the process of bargaining between social actors, but a reward for labor provided by the central authorities first to enterprises and then by enterprises to employees, according to their ideological and production "merits";

- unions were not organizations which defend the rights of workers against the interest of employers, but organizations designed to support the fulfillment of the state established production plan in the domain of labor relations;

- supervisors and plant managers are just as much employees as those whose work they supervise, only their position in the hierarchy is higher;

- the government was not an enforcer of labor law and mediator of labor conflict, it was the universal owner and employer;

- enterprises were not (and most still are not) organizations producing profits for their individual owners, but mere organizational units in the state hierarchic system;

- laws governing labor relations were not designed to protect the legitimate expectations of social actors or to prevent conflict among them. They were understood to be orders from the central committee intended to achieve certain production and social control results (Jezek, 1993).

PRINCIPAL CHANGES IN THE STRUCTURE OF LABOR RELATIONS IN THE PROCESS OF TRANSITION

Confederation Structure

The most significant evidence of the changes in industrial relations in transition societies is the development of independent trade unions. This has and continues to come about in two ways. First, through the creation of new organizations and movements that have no connection with the state, and second, through the reform and revival of state controlled trade unions.

The new independent unions were established in all countries before or after the political changes attempting to follow the example of Solidarity in Poland. In Hungary many of the smaller new unions united to form the Democratic League of Independent Trade Unions (LIGA). In a similar way Podkrepa was established in Bulgaria and Fratia emerged in Romania. Other new union confederations have since emerged in these countries. On the other hand, with the exception of the former Czechoslovakia where the traditional unions officially were dissolved, the trade unions of the party state survived. They redefined their functions and made the representation of workers' interests their principle priority. They also declared their independence from all political parties, and democratized their organizational structures.

Despite these reforms, the traditional unions continue to be looked upon with suspicion and even hostility by the some of the new democratic governments, parliamentary parties and foreign support organizations. Regardless of government attitudes and actions, the traditional trade unions have remained, in numerical terms at least, large and strong organiza-

tions. Traditional trade unions have had difficulty, just like new unions, functioning in the murky political environments of transition and have established, just like new unions have attempted to establish, policies fluctuating between confrontations and pragmatic cooperation with emerging political leadership.

However, most trade unions have accepted the inevitability of transformation, and generally speaking have not actively opposed the basic concept of economic reform and greater reliance on market forces. This does not mean that they have accepted all aspects of economic reform. For instance, trade unions like MSZOSZ in Hungary, and CITUB in Bulgaria have opposed various manifestations of economic neo-liberalism and have been prepared to threaten or even abandon the tripartite council as a form of protest against the social consequences of extending privatization to public utilities and cutbacks in government services. Moreover, to varying degrees each assisted the socialist parties in their respective countries to achieve national election victories in 1993-94 hoping to influence the economic development policies of the government.

The relations between competing trade union confederations are complex and far from homogenous across the countries of the region. In Hungary, seven major trade union confederations exist, of which six participate in the tripartite council. Of these, the most significant is the National Confederation of Hungarian Trade Unions (MSZOSZ) which now claims to have about one million members. This compares with a peak membership level which exceeded 2.5 million at the end of 1990. In Bulgaria Podkrepa (Support) and the "successor" Confederation of Independent Trade Unions (CITUB) are in a similar position. Romania has the largest number of trade union confederations, officially numbering around 20 in 1996. More recently there has been some consolidation and the trade union scene is now dominated by four organizations: CNSLR-Fratia, ALFA CARTEL, BNS (National Trade Union) and the recently created Confederation of Democratic Trade Unions of Romania (CSDR). In the former Czechoslovakia the Czech and Slovak Federation of Trade Unions (CSKOS) was the dominant organization prior to the division of the country. Subsequently, CSKOS was formally dissolved and the union structures in the two republics--which had previously been part of the confederation--also split and assumed the role of the dominant national trade union confederation in their respective countries. The Czech and Moravian Labor Confederation (CM-KOS) and the Confederation of Trade Unions of the Slovak Republic (KOZSR) now stand as the dominant confederations in each country.

The co-existence of old and new trade unions engendered division and confrontation in several countries. The example of Poland, where the two major confederations did not talk to each other for years, is relevant, while in Hungary the relations of the large "traditional" MSZOSZ, LIGA and the Workers Councils (another newly formed confederation) were severely strained by conflicts and debates about legitimacy and representativeness between 1990 and 1992.

The thorny issues underlying these conflicts between old and new unions in all countries are the different political perspectives of the organization as well as the disputes over the redistribution of the assets of the state controlled unions. The matter of redistribution was resolved in Czechoslovakia as early as 1990, but in the other countries of the region several years were necessary to reach a compromise. For example, in Hungary a compromise was not reached until late 1992 and in Romania the issue remains a political wedge used by the government to divide the union movement. Discussions have been initiated this year (1996) to expand the function of administering the assets, currently performed by CSLNR/Fratia and Alpha, to include the BNS.

Despite inter-trade union friction, events since 1989 have demonstrated that democratic reform of an existing trade union structure and the establishment of new competitor unions can have a mutually beneficial impact. Not only were the new independent unions a desirable addition in their own right, they also helped to accelerate the pace of reform in the traditional unions.

It is notable that in some countries where the union movement has gone through a period of fission over the last few years there are tentative indications that this trend may be starting to reverse itself. In Romania, as mentioned, the conflictive issue of union patrimony is bringing three major confederations closer together and the movement is also uniting to combat the passage of a new Collective Bargaining Law perceived as being anti-union.

One factor spurring greater unity in the trade union movement is that since 1993 in most countries the traditional reformed trade unions (MSZOSZ in Hungary, CITUB in Bulgaria) had consolidated their positions as the largest and politically most powerful confederation while their rivals seem to have lost ground. For example, in Hungary the new organizations have a small and shrinking membership base and little political influence with the socialist government. Only in Romania, where the CNSLR/Fratia, although still the largest, is facing direct competition from Alfa Cartel, BNS and the newly formed CSDR, has the successor union failed to grow in power.

In general, the trade unions in the countries covered by this study have devoted very little attention to recruiting members from the new and expanding sectors of the economy. In most countries the new private sectors are growing slowly and unions have more pressing problems than to organize this relatively small number of workers. Despite this, by the standards of the OECD countries, trade unions in Central and Eastern Europe remain numerically strong and politically significant.

Tripartism

Perhaps because of the ambivalent nature of political alliances, unions have expressed much of their political voice through the tripartite process at the national level. National tripartite forums have been established in all countries except Romania. In Romania a PHARE project designed to establish such a forum is currently underway. The forums have some similar characteristics, given the nature of the tripartite model, but each country approached the quest for tripartism in its own unique fashion.

Following the tradition of Western industrial countries where tripartism exists, such councils tend to have limited authority to implement policy decisions and really rely on the good will of the government to see the product of their consultations reflected in policy or programs. They merely have the power to "advise" the government on economic and other policy issues. Without exception, this advisory tradition is maintained in the countries with functioning tripartite councils.

Nevertheless, in all countries where they exist, tripartite bodies have exerted direct influence on the establishment of minimum wage limits (Czech and Slovak Republics, Bulgaria, and Hungary) while in Hungary the council's workgroup on labor market issues has the authority to determine the principles and direction of expenditures on training and other employment programs.

In Romania, the failure of the government to quickly commit to the establishment of a tripartite council has created an environment of animosity and competition among the major trade union confederations as the government fails to establish definitive participation criteria and conditions.

Collective Bargaining

Little variety exists in the collective bargaining models being supported by confederations in each country. Most confederations are working hard to establish blanket agreements, through tripartite bodies or national agreements, but enterprise level agreements, although allowed by all labor laws, are reportedly declining. The general decline in local agreements is well documented in Hungary but further research needs to be done to discover the nature of enterprise level collective bargaining in most countries (Héthy, 1995).

The exception to this tendency is Romania where the collective bargaining law requires all state employees to be covered by an enterprise level agreement. In this case, only those employees working in the slowly expanding private sector are not protected by a collective bargaining agreement.

In general, one can identify similar characteristics in the nature of collective bargaining in all countries studied.

- In all countries three levels of bargaining exist although bargaining activity is not shared equally among the three levels.

- The national agreements establish the minimum standards that subsequent branch and local agreements must meet. This agreement is reached among representatives of labor and the government and the emerging employer organizations. The confederations are the labor representatives at this national level of bargaining.

- In all countries, the employer organizations are the weak link in collective bargaining at the national level.

- In all countries unions were active in the creation of employer organizations to that they could have social partners in negotiations.

- The corporatist solution, associated with decades of positive industrial relations and good wages and job security in Western Europe, is the one most commonly preferred by the confederations of each country. Given the desire for tripartism and the tradition of centralized industrial relations, the national level, corporatist bargaining model dominates in all countries studied.

All countries have redrawn the legal framework of labor relations in the last five years. The dominant features of labor legislation in the studied countries are the following:

- Emphasis on the principle of free association or union membership rights;

- Creation of independent labor organizations;

- Defining labor organizations as non-political organizations and restricting direct participation in the political process of these organizations;

- Establishing numerical lower limits on labor organizations.

The representative of the various ministries in the region expressed concern that collective agreements at any level other than the national level would be disruptive to the development strategies of the countries. While minister officials are not going to promote eliminating lower level agreements, they also would like to control the process. In the Czech Republic, for example, while local collective agreements are declining, the ministry can extend branch agreements to the local level after a review process. The ministry officials estimated that about 30 percent of the petitions to extend the branch agreement to a specific work place are granted. It is worth noting that these same officials also insist that unions should stay out of national level policy issues and concentrate on dealing with member grievances at the shop floor level. It seems that they want agreements, but agreements that are signed on their terms with social partners that they can control.

Unions and Politics

The relationship between political institutions and unions has changed since 1989 in all countries. What a high ranking ministry official from the Slovak Republic said about unions in the Slovak Republic can be said about unions throughout the region. "The trade unions are trying to find their niche. They want to influence politics but in a careful way."

The role of workers and their organizations as catalyst for social change in the process of transition varied from country to country. Yet, if we look at the development of independent labor movements in each country studied, we see that there are two dominant organizational models of labor involvement in the process of transition. The Internal Combustion model, characterized by the establishment of strike committees as units of opposition within the monolithic state controlled confederation, was utilized in Czechoslovakia and Belarus. The transformation of the Czech Moravian Labor Confederation and the Labor Confederation of the Slovak Republic represent the success stories of this model. In Belarus, the strike committees were unable to mobilize enough resources to transform the official labor confederation primarily because the political structure of the State remained unchanged and continued to rely upon and support the official confederation as a control mechanism.

The Independent Organization model, which, as the name implies, entails the establishment of organizations outside of the official labor confederation, served to form strong opposition confederations in Hungary, Bulgaria and Romania. The ultimate example of this model is the case of Romania where we find the labor movement fragmented into four major confederations but with an additional sixteen other organizations claiming to be confederations. (This aberration is created by a labor law which allows sixty workers to create a confederation.)

Along with these organizational models, we have to consider the timing of their creation. In Belarus, Czechoslovakia, Hungary, and Bulgaria, the independent and opposition organizations developed to some degree before the political changes occurred. In Romania opposition organizations were formed after the crumbling of the political control structure.

In all cases, the grass roots level served as incubators for the leadership of the newly created or reformed confederations. Whether elected or in a more informal fashion, grass roots leaders have carried their support to the national level in all countries. Even in Romania, where major restructuring of the confederations did not occur until after the death of Ceaucescu, the leaders of the major confederations emerged from the leadership of local unions. In Bulgaria, the leadership of Podkrepa even included a clause in its constitution that no one who ever held any type of position in the pre-transition communist structure could hold leadership position in the labor confederation.

In general, the principal role of trade unions in the process of political change can be described as follows. First, in each country an alternative labor organization emerged early in the process of transition which was identified strongly with the process of socio-political change. This was the case of Podkrepa in Bulgaria in 1990, LIGA in Hungary in 1988, Fratia in Romania in 1990 and of the various strike committees emerging in Czechoslovakia, and Belarus during the same time.

Second, these organizations became instrumental in developing strategies of opposition at the national and regional levels. The union structure was ideally suited for coordinating widespread opposition and mobilizing citizens.

Third, labor unions became critically important because they were relatively well organized representatives of the emerging interests of a broad section of the citizens of each country. They immediately became the largest civic organizations in each country, dwarfing the size of even the largest political party. They were organizations with a truly mass membership and which existed purely to represent the interests of not only workers but pensioners and the unemployed.

Fourth, the very structure of the labor organizations changed because the structures that gave them their primary characteristics of dependency and subordination, the party and the state, changed. That is why even the traditionally unions were forced into some sort of reform process.

Fifth, labor laws were changed that institutionalized the independence and functions of the new labor movement. In all countries strike and dispute resolution statutes were introduced (Hungary, March 1989; Bulgaria, March 1990; Czechoslovakia, 1991; Romania, 1991).

These elements combined to make the alternative and transformed labor organizations into social movements with goals that, in the context of social change sweeping all countries, were as much political as they were related to the specific issues of labor relations. This socio-political character of labor organizations was more pronounced in Bulgaria and Hungary where alternative organizations emerged with strong support from professionals and intellectuals, but even in Romania, where the confederations shunned political activity, they were strongly in opposition to the post Ceaucescu government, which they considered a neo-communist extension of power.

The pressures from alternate organizations and the disintegration of the communist state forced the established labor structures to undergo irreversible change. The confederations serve to unite the political activity of the member unions but no longer control the internal operations of the affiliates.

In the emerging labor legislation in the region, pain is taken to make clear the independence of labor organization from the political process. Given the legacy of party control, this is understandable. A clause is usually included in the statute defining a labor organization which specifies that it is a non-political entity, functioning as a civic organization.

In cases, such as in Bulgaria, where unions have played a significant and direct role in political developments, members have recognized the importance of having a strong, representative voice at the national level. Podkrepa in Bulgaria was an important element of the UDF and its ultimate ascent to power in the 1992 elections. While it received its share of criticism for tying its fortunes, and the fortunes of its members, to one party, it reversed its support for the UDF when the party turned a deaf ear to the union agenda. Similarly, CITUB was always perceived as the old union which supported the socialist ascent to power in the 1994 elections, yet it is a vociferous opponent of the government's wage and unemployment policies.

General Issues Facing Labor Confederations after Transition is Initiated

As the transition process grinds on, labor confederations in Eastern Europe must decide whether to be on the bus of transition or off. All have decided to sit as close to the front as possible.

- No leaders of a major confederation in the region oppose the reform process. They do have specific concerns about the impact of reform on their members and this concern is manifested by demanding a voice in the decision making process, and, sometimes, in the opposition of specific reform strategies.

- In all countries labor sees itself as a partner in the transition process even when specific interests vary from those of capital or government. In all countries, except perhaps Belarus, labor has received some benefits in the restructuring of economic, social and political relations.

- The trade union movement in all countries sees itself as playing a fundamental role in the creation of a national social-economic infrastructure, this includes contributing to: (1) the creation of a legal framework for trade union activity, addressing issues such as representativeness, autonomy, redistribution of trade union assets and, more generally, recognition of the role of the social partners; (2) the promotion of bipartite or tripartite dialogue in order to monitor economic and social developments; (3) the establishment of collective bargaining and possibility of concluding agreements at all levels of economic life (enterprise, branch and nationwide); (4) the development of a system of social security, including compulsory and complementary insurance and unemployment benefits, protection of minimum wages and family rights. This system should be administered by the direct contributors, e.g. the representative organizations of workers and employers; (5) the adaptation of natural legislation to international and European standards and conventions such as the ILO Conventions, The European Social Charter and the European Charter on Social Security.

Similar organizational questions confront the leaders of the confederations studied. Among these are:

- The question of how and to what extent labor should be involved in the political arena is a question that confounds all labor leaders. Given the negative legacy of labor and political party relationships, and the fact that their members span the ideological spectrum, most leaders find themselves unsure of their actions when asked to become involved politically.

- Trade unionists in all countries stress the importance of trade union education and training trade union activists; of independence from political and state structures; of financial independence based on self-supporting mechanisms such as membership fees; of technical and political independence through the development of its own capacity to elaborate legal, economic and social strategies.

- While they recognize the importance of developing concrete services to meet the aspirations of their members, most confederations have prob-

lems extending services to the members, primarily for financial reasons.

- In all countries, most of the money collected in dues stays at the local union level. A varying percentage reaches the federation level and a much smaller portion is remitted to the confederation.

- A major hurdle facing all union leaders is the desire by the membership to the reestablishment of the social service network in place during the communist era. At the base level, most of the money is utilized to provide these "social services" to the members; services attempt to maintain some continuity from the pre-transition era, e.g. day care support, sports teams, vacations.

- The confederation services to the members, when they have something to offer, consist of more general activities such as insurance policies, legal support, and in the case of one confederation in Hungary, credit cards.

- Training or retraining initiatives are seen as activities that belong in the government sphere and for which confederations lobby.

SOME LESSONS FOR CUBAN LABOR TRANSITION

Perhaps it is in the arena of unions and politics that we can draw the most direct implications for the existing situation of workers in Cuba. As mentioned above, in three of the six countries studied, opposition structures arose within the state controlled confederation. In the other three, independent organizations served as forces of social mobilization either before (Hungary and Bulgaria) or after (Romania) the collapse of the Soviet-supported regime. Also of importance is the fact that in all cases, the base organizations (local unions) gave rise to a large number of the labor leaders that rose to prominence after the loosening of political controls.

In recent years, events have contributed to the fragmentation of the monolithic CTC structure as the dominant control mechanism of the Cuban worker. The restructuring of the Cuban economy during the 1990s has had an important impact on the nature of labor relations in the country. Processes such as growth of unemployment and the creation of the class of workers known as "disponibles," the emergence in some sectors of a mixed economy, and the strengthening of foreign investments have created friction within the CTC, which has become accustomed to the harmonious operations of its transmission belt role.

Contributing to the friction has been the redistribution of the labor force into emerging sectors of the economy. Tourism, pharmaceutics and biotechnology are sectors that have received an infusion of labor partly because of the interest of foreign capital in the growth of the associated industries. Similarly, the non-state sector has grown at a rapid rate through the creation of the Unidades Básicas de Producción Co-operativa (UBPC) and the extension of laws permitting small scale entrepreneurial activity (the "cuentapropistas"). These two activities have grown from comprising 5.9 percent of the labor force in 1988 to 30.2 percent of the labor force in 1994. The most recent figures that I have—from November 1994—put the "cuentapropistas" at 208,500 workers with licenses to operate private businesses; 60,000 of these were unemployed or "disponible," 56,000 had other employment, 50,000 were retirees and 38,000 were "housewives." The licenses are approved by individual "municipios" so this contributes to the general process of decentralization of production. These sectors are not under the control of the CTC, a fact that has increased the debate on the role of the confederation in the process of economic restructuring.

In 1993, the National Assembly of Popular Power (Asamblea Nacional del Poder Popular) worked with the Workers Parliament (Parlamento Obrero) at each worksite to analyze the problems of production afflicting the country. The recommendations of the Parlamento Obrero were taken to the CTC, which created a new grouping within the enterprises called the Assemblies of Economic Efficiency (Asambleas de Eficiencia Económica). According to my sources, these Assemblies are an attempt to rejuvenate the labor movement by involving the rank and file in enterprise-level decision making and changing the bureaucratic nature of the CTC structure. It is unlikely that any of these goals are attainable but what does

seem to be occurring is that the rank and file is communicating more at the base level.

There are indications that at the grass roots level within the CTC, leaders are questioning the traditional functions of the organization. Current debates within the CTC manifest growing concerns about the organization's ability to play a role in the current economic transformations being implemented. In the tourism and services sectors, the role of the CTC is increasingly under fire. Issues of representability and protection of employment rights are being discussed more or less openly. Undoubtedly, these types of concerns will serve to create different interest groups within the CTC. How these groups are able to express their disagreement will influence the development of the confederation as a catalyst or retardant of change.

If the voices of reform within the CTC are supported by dynamic changes at the national and international social and political levels, as was the case in Czechoslovakia, then the Internal Combustion model might ignite organizational transformation and maintain the labor movement as a viable agent of change in the ensuing period of transition.

Regardless of the transformation of the CTC, it appears certain that the process of political transition in Cuba will engender a proliferation of small, independent labor organizations. In recent years, the activities of small, independent labor groups have increased in activity in Cuba. While these groups are small and afflicted with much infighting and competition, their very existence presents the potential for the expression of dissenting voices and mobilization. If political changes occur which transform the system and its existing institutions, these "grupúsculos" will be rendered marginal unless they can establish strong coalitions among themselves and with international organizations. The marginalization of opposition labor groups will bring with it competition and conflict and the smaller organizations will find it difficult to compete with the transformed remnant of the CTC. If this fragmentation continues too long (as has been the case in Belarus) and labor laws are created which encourage the fragmentation of the labor movement (as in Romania) the labor movement will be weakened as a force of social change.

A post transition society will present Cuban labor leaders with many of the same challenges being faced today by leaders of the former Soviet Bloc. The social costs of privatization, the organizing of the rapidly growing private sector, unfriendly government policies, recalcitrant labor leadership and a membership that will long for the "good old days" of full employment and bountiful social benefits will burden new leaders with an almost unbearable load. If one adds to this the myriad problems that can arise if labor has to deal with Cuban-American capitalists from Miami, one begins to appreciate the difficulties facing free labor in Cuba.

REFERENCES

Barr, Nicholas (ed.). 1994. *Labor Markets and Social Policy in Central and Eastern Europe.* London: Oxford University Press.

Bruszt, L. 1992. "Transformative Politics in East Central Europe." *East European Politics and Societies* 6:52-70.

Bruszt, L. and Stark, D. 1991. "Remaking the Political Field in Hungary: From the Politics of Confrontation to the Politics of Competition." *Journal of International Affairs,* 45:201-45.

Carranza, Julio. 1992. "Cuba: Los Retos de la Economía." *Cuadernos de Nuestra America.* Julio-Diciembre.

Espina, M. y otros. 1995. *Impactos socio-estructurales del reajuste económico.* CIPS.

Héthy, L. 1995. "Collective Bargaining in Hungary." Unpublished manuscript.

Jezek, Tomas, 1993. "Czechoslovakia," in Miriam Rothman, Dennis R. Briscoe and Raoul C.D. Nacamulli (Eds.), *Industrial Relations Around the World: Labor Relations for Multinational Companies.* New York: Walter de Gruyter, pp. 99-110.

Jones, Derek C. 1992. "The Transformation of Labor Unions in Eastern Europe: The Case of Bulgaria." *Industrial and Labor Relations Review,* v. 45 no. 3, pp. 452-470, April.

MINTRAB-Cuba. 1994. *Situación del empleo a partir del 1990,* Informe.

Stark, D. 1992. "Path Dependence and Privatization Strategies in East Central Europe." *East European Politics and Societies* 6:17-51.

Stark, D. and Nee, V. (Eds) 1989. *Remaking the Economic Institutions of Socialism: China and Eastern Europe.* Stanford: Stanford University Press.

Thirkell, John. 1994. "Labour Relations in Transition in Eastern Europe." *Industrial Relations Journal,* v. 25, no. 2, pp. 84-95, June.

Valdés, Paz Juan. 1994. *La transición socialista en Cuba.* La Habana: Editorial de Ciencias Sociales.

THE SITUATION OF CUBAN WORKERS DURING THE "SPECIAL PERIOD IN PEACETIME"

Efrén Córdova

The purpose of this article is twofold: 1) to examine the extent to which Cuban workers experienced adversity and hardship during the years ensuing the collapse of the Soviet Union; and 2) to ascertain whether economic crisis and deterioration of conditions of work and life are likely to bring about the downfall of a totalitarian regime. I have organized my remarks around the following themes: the overall economic environment, unemployment, mobilization and forced labor, self-employment, hours of work, level and protection of wages, security of employment, freedom of association and social security. These themes will be examined against the backdrop of the so called "special period in peacetime," which, coupled with some limited marked reforms, was instituted by the Castro government as a result of the serious economic decline that followed the breakdown the Soviet Union. A brief conclusion is presented at the end.

THE ECONOMIC ENVIRONMENT

The special period was introduced in March 1990. Events in the USSR and other socialist countries brought about a suspension of the generous subsidies that Castro was receiving, a drop in oil shipments and a sharp decline in foreign trade. For many years the Cuban economy had been dependent on the Soviet Union which in 1989, for instance, provided several forms of aid valued at around five billion dollars.

The dramatic geopolitical changes that had taken place in Europe caught the Castro regime unprepared to deal with the new state of things. All of a sudden the country had to rely on its own resources and on new commercial alliances. Coming on the heels of another difficult stage of the revolution represented by the period of rectification of errors and negative tendencies, the crisis reached alarming proportions. In the circumstances, the special period was intended to find a way to overcome the acute economic crisis and to convey to workers the need to adjust to the strictures of the forthcoming lean years.

In terms of financial measures, the special period signified that priority would be given in the future to export production and that other factories engaged in the production of nonessential goods would be temporarily closed. The program also called for invitations addressed to foreign firms to invest in Cuba under the most favorable and enticing conditions. So desperate was the Castro regime to attract investors, that some of the incentives offered to non-Cuban firms (repatriation of profits, tax exemptions and labor flexibility) smacked of neo-liberal approaches. What foreign investors had not been able to secure in their own countries as regards new forms of employment contracts, low level of wages, tamed unions, no strikes and facilities to discharge workers, Castro was willing to recognize and give away quickly. As far as social projects were concerned, the special period signaled the suspension of a number of welfare projects, the expansion of rationing to cover many basic items, and the chronic shortages of oil affecting the provision of electricity, transportation, the use of modem machinery and a number of amenities. In the area of political programs, the period in question meant that the wave of democratic reforms that was sweeping Eastern Europe in 1989 and early 1990s was not going to be followed in Cuba.

At the time of its inception, the special period was billed as a temporary and belttightening series of measures that had to be accepted by the Cuban population lest a more draconian program—called "zero option"—would have to be imposed. Six years after its introduction the special period was still in force, restrictions and damages caused to the working people were still present, foreign enterprises (particularly Canadian, Mexican and Spanish) were still enjoying their privileges, and the totalitarian structure of the regime was still intact. However, the special period had achieved its ultimate, real purpose, namely, to preserve Castro's hold to power.

UNEMPLOYMENT

Unemployment always existed in revolutionary Cuba, although its rate was low and its existence somehow hidden. With the help of the subsidies furnished by the Soviet Union and other socialist countries, Castro was able to provide a measure of stable employment to a greater number of Cubans. However, useful, productive, freely chosen and full employment, as defined by Conventions of the International Labor Organization (ILO)[1] was never achieved in Cuba. To be sure, the Castro regime asserted on many occasions that full employment was one of the gains of the revolution, but this claim ran counter to the real situation, as Castro himself acknowledged in 1986 when he denounced the artificially swollen payrolls of state enterprises.[2]

Now, during the special period and despite agreements concluded with the Soviet Union and later with Russia, unemployment rates skyrocketed. The agreements guaranteed the continuation of some economic aid and oil exports to Cuba but at reduced levels and conditioned to the selling of a considerable percent of the sugar production to Russia.

Unfulfillment of the agreements by both parties led to a further deterioration of the Cuban economy. By 1995 the industrial sector had experienced a decline of 70 percent vis-a-vis the 1991 figures. The sugar industry registered in 1994-1995 the lowest production in 60 years (3.3 million tons). While government authorities maintained that factories and shops were only temporarily shut down, few were actually able to reopen or to regain normal production figures. According to some conservative estimates, unemployment affected some 35 percent of the labor force. The government refused to disclose the exact statistics, but the Minister of Labor recognized in 1995 that in some municipalities, jobless persons reached 20 percent.[3] Later, speaking at 17th Congress of the Cuban Labor Central (Confederación de Trabajadores de Cuba, CTC), the same minister stated that 120,000 jobs were eliminated between 1991 and 1994 due to the closing of factories and enterprises.[4] Estimates made by the Cuban Association of Independent Economists indicate an unemployment rate of 51 per cent. On its part the ILO Yearbook of Labor Statistics omitted any reference to Cuba, although figures and rates of unemployment concerning other Latin American countries appeared in it. The Cuban Government had obviously failed to communicate the relevant data.

Workers who had lost their jobs were never called unemployed by the government but classified as temporarily interrupted (interruptos), redundant (sobrantes), and available (disponibles). The imagination of the regime has always been rich in finding terms apt to conceal the truth.

The remedies provided by the government to mitigate the sorrow of the jobless were apparently reasonable, given the critical economic situation. Transfer to another job was the first option given to the unemployed. If the workers concerned did not accept the offer, then they were entitled to receive a com-

---

1. See the ILO Employment Policy Convention, 1964 (No. 122).

2. See Efrén Córdova, *Clase trabajadora y movimiento sindical en Cuba* (Miami: Ediciones Universal, 1996), Vol. II, pp. 360-361.

3. *Bohemia* (24 November 1995).

4. "Government Unveils Job Reduction Plan," *Prensa Latina*, in Spanish (30 April 1996), p. 1.

pensation consisting of 100 percent of their salaries during the first month and 60 percent for the subsequent months up to a period of one year.[5] In theory the government's offer could also include an opportunity to register for a retraining program. The problem with these options was that transfer to another job soon became the only real alternative and that the transfer was limited to work in the agricultural sector or in a construction brigade. Workers who rejected the transfer had to show good reason for the rejection and the meaning of this phrase was left to the interpretation of the administrative officials involved. In the context of an authoritarian and impoverished society and for all practical purposes, the choice was reduced to selecting between mobilization and starvation.

It may be noted that the decrease of job opportunities and the need to downsize the staff of state enterprises, were not limited to the first years of the special period. At the 17th Congress of the CTC held in April 1996, the government submitted a plan to further curtail the payroll of the said enterprises and the delegates unanimously approved it.[6] Although Castro affirmed in the same congress that his reforms were not intended to lead to capitalism, some aspects of the plan had the distinctive taste, of a market-oriented program.

MOBILIZATION

Until the advent of the totalitarian regimes, the word mobilization was a military term specifically related to the emergencies created by war, when governments felt compelled to make armed forces bigger and ready for war. It was in this sense that Lenin used it during the civil war and the period of war communism, though he later expanded its meaning to include the mobilization of all the country's resources for defense. Subsequent Soviet leaders resorted to

mobilization with regard to other public purposes and particularly in connection with the economic development of the country. The spread of this practice to other totalitarian regimes and one-party countries and the abuses that were committed under the guise of economic progress, led the ILO to adopt in 1952 Convention 105 calling for the abolition of any form of forced labor including the practice of appealing to it as a method of mobilizing and using labor for purposes of economic development.

In Cuba the reasons invoked for putting workers into massive and intensive motion varied but were mostly related to government exhortations to increase production and to have labor organized and ready to defend the revolution. The massive mobilizations connected with the ten million ton sugar crop in 1969 and the creation since 1959 of popular militias are examples of these two kinds of mobilization. So frequent became these campaigns that by early 1970s the Castro regime was aptly characterized as a mobilization system.[7]

Early mobilization drives were usually combined with rallies, attendance at mass meetings, voluntary work and collective efforts related to pet projects of the Maximum Leader. A cloak of voluntarism, i.e., the willingness of the people to achieve some nationalistic or populist goals, often presided over these mobilization campaigns. As with voluntary work, there were at bottom elements of coercion, but the seemingly wilful character of the mobilization was always stressed by government.

What characterized mobilization during the special period, was that government officials abandoned any pretense of claiming that its drives of the 1990s had the acceptance of the workers, and embarked on the contrary on a clear violation of Convention 105.[8] The leaders of the revolution probably realized that

---

5. Córdova, *Clase trabajadora y movimiento sindical en Cuba*, p. 392.

6. "Government Unveils Job Reduction Plan."

7. Richard Fagen, "Mass Mobilization in Cuba: The Symbolism of Struggle," in Rolando E. Bonachea and Nelson P. Valdés, eds., *Cuba in Revolution* (New York: Anchor Books, 1972), p. 205.

8. See International Labor Conference, 73rd session, 1987. *Report of the Committee of Experts on the Application of Conventions and Recommendations* (Geneva, 1987), p. 91.

the dramatic turn of events in 1989-1991 called for some expedient and appropriate action. Reliance on Soviet supplies and government mismanagement had resulted in a neglect of the agricultural production. The country had a surplus of doctors but not enough capable agricultural workers and motivated peasants. Seventy five percent of the people were concentrated in the urban areas; food supplies were insufficient and the threat of starvation was looming in the horizon. In 1990 it thus became necessary to check this situation and carry out a makeshift return to the countryside. Mobilization under these conditions had indeed a twofold purpose: provide occupation to the unemployed and feed the urban population. Its semi-compulsory design was also determined by the fact that the survival of Castro and his colleagues was at stake.

The choice given to unemployed workers between accepting a transfer to agriculture or the construction sector (where labor intensive methods were still used) or receive unemployment compensation benefits, was in fact more apparent than real. This choice existed at the beginning on paper, but in practice (and in subsequent laws) those who rejected the offer were denied the right to get unemployment compensation. The option actually boiled down to the right to choose between mobilization which gradually meant to work in the countryside or to suffer from great poverty and need. Castro no doubt feared the prospect of unrest and possible turmoil that might be created by having one million people/e idle and therefore decided to condition the granting of benefits to compliance with his favorite recourse to mobilization.

To avoid mobilization many workers tried to obtain medical documents certifying that they were temporarily or permanently unable to work. That a great number of them succeeded is best demonstrated by the dramatic increase in the number of social security beneficiaries (see below) that began by 1992.

Once mobilized, the job performed by the workers concerned was closely monitored by supervisors, CTC officials and Cuban Communist Party (PCC) officials. Although used now in connection with production activities, mobilization has kept some of its military undertones. Oblivious of the inconveniences brought about by relocation as well as the hardships of being forced to switch to a completely different kind of work, the Castro regime was now determined to transform mobilization into a compulsory enrollment of men and women to work in the government projects. Small wonder that it was during these years that the number of rafters and boat people reached incredible figures (35,375 in 1994, for instance).[9]

SELF-EMPLOYMENT

Fearful that the mass of jobless people would not dissipate easily, Castro decided to add a third remedy to the unemployment crisis, namely, the authorization given to the citizens to work on their own. Such authorization was contrary to a long-lasting policy of the revolutionary regime, which in keeping with the Marxist doctrine, has always sought to concentrate all employment opportunities in the state. All forms of self-employment were prohibited, despite that fact the this prohibition violated Article 23 of the U.N. Declaration of Human Rights. So rigid was the prohibition that a special government department was created to uncover and prosecute self-employed people who could then be sentenced by the revolutionary courts to up to three years in jail.[10]

This arbitrary and unnatural provision was kept in force until the Fourth Congress of the PCC, held in October 1991, when one of its resolutions recognized the need to authorize self-employment, but only with regard to minor occupations (servicios menores). The authorization was later expanded to cover a list of 140 different jobs; some of these jobs related to such secondary and minuscule activities as repairer of baby dolls and hair dresser of pets.[11] Yet, the mere fact that permissive measures were adopted

---

9. Córdova, *Clase trabajadora y movimiento sindical en Cuba*, p. 223.

10. Efrén Córdova, *El mundo del trabajo en Cuba Socialista* (Caracas: Fondo Latinoamericano de Ediciones Sociales, 1992), pp. 81-84

11. Córdova, *Clase trabajadora y movimiento sindical en Cuba*, p. 398.

in this respect, was a telling indication of the gravity of the unemployment crisis. Suddenly, the Castro government was willing to open an outlet to the many unemployed who refused to work in the agricultural or construction sectors.

Persons interested in working on their own had to request a government permit which indicated the scope and limits of their self-employment. They were obligated to pay taxes—as much as 50 percent in some cases—and their activities were closely monitored by labor inspectors specifically trained to detect infringements of the existing regulations and to impose fines. Operators of the small restaurants called *paladares,* for instance, were not permitted to sit more than 12 clients. Other self-employed people working as taxi drivers were also restrained by the amount of fuel allowed and the number of passengers and trips they were authorized to make in a given period. Excluded from self-employment were the professional activities, although those who had earned university degrees were allowed to work outside their profession.

While more than 200,000 people registered for self-employment and many of them promised to make donations to the regime or expressed in other ways their allegiance to the revolution, the government never resigned itself to the idea that these independent-minded workers were going to make a living beyond its pale. The prospect of a sizable number of people doing good and perhaps acquiring a middle class mentality was not easy to stomach by Castro and his colleagues; indeed, such a likelihood represented a potential indictment of the whole communist philosophy.

It was thus necessary to make clear to the Cuban people that the existence of this growing number of workers was only grudgingly accepted. Self-employed workers were to be frequently characterized as a bunch of greedy people who had never adapted to the revolution and should consequently be treated as second class citizens. This explains why the 400 labor inspectors appointed in 1995 were instructed to harass the self-employed and why the 1,900 delegates attending the 17th Congress of the CTC were encouraged to demonstrate their hostility to the self-employed.[12] In his speech at the 17th Congress of the CTC Castro frowned upon the farmers' markets and the independent taxi drivers and excoriated the middle men and the "nouveau riche."[13] The Minister of Labor indicated in turn, that self-employed workers who had lost their association with an established enterprise would forfeit their pension rights.[14] In some cases, government authorities confiscated the properties of those enterprising workers who in their view were making too much money in their businesses.

The question of self-employment presents another interesting angle. Once the door of private ownership of businesses was open—albeit in ajar fashion—Cuban workers began to show motivation, initiative and resourcefulness. The quality of services provided by self-employed people was considerably better than those furnished by state enterprises. This behavioral change was particularly apparent in the restaurant business; *paladares,* for instance, gradually became a glaring success and began to attract greater number of clients. The 12 client limit was so repeatedly transgressed that it began to be regarded as a dead letter. On and off the government counterattacked by appointing the above-mentioned labor inspectors and by prohibiting private restaurants in Varadero. But *paladares* proved to be resilient and kept functioning, sometimes gathering 40 or 50 clients, mostly tourists. Soon, the government found itself in the horns of a dilemma: it could close down the *paladares* at the risk of infuriating tourists or pretend not to see, in the understanding that private businesses would continue to prove their superiority over state enterprises.

How could these small restaurants prosper when they had to secure the provision of the meat, vegetables, seafood, beer, wine, etc., that all restaurants require?

---

12. See "Castro Speaks at the 17th Congress of the CTC," Havana Radio and Television Networks (1 May 1996).
13. "Castro Speaks at the 17th Congress of the CTC."
14. "Interview with Salvador Valdés, Minister of Labor," *Bohemia* (24 November 1995).

The answer was found in the growing network created by other self-employed people who anxious to earn dollar little by little developed the capacity to supply goods or acted as middle-men between farmers and *paladares*. The opening that the Castro regime permitted in 1992 was giving rise to a parallel economy that proved to be more efficient than the collectivist one. It was a meaningful manifestation of the vitality of the civil society that for so many years had been suppressed.

HOURS OF WORK

The pattern of having workers laboring in excess of eight hours a day and 44 hours a week continued all along the special period. It was particularly visible and even systematically used in the paramilitary organizations, i.e., in microbrigades, brigades and contingents as well as in the enterprises run by the Armed Forces. It was less predictable in other state enterprises depending on the availability of resources. Hours of work could in fact be fixed above or below the norm at the discretion of supervisors. While lack of energy and scarcity of other inputs brought about a relief in the practice of unpaid voluntary work, it also entailed substantial dislocations in the standard timetable of most enterprises. Workers in some undertakings which had been particularly hit by lack of energy resources saw their hours of work reduced to seven by resolutions of the Labor Ministry. Government decrees also discontinued the established practice of working on alternate Saturdays. However, the Ministry hastened to make clear that the new arrangements were temporary and did not represent a change in government policies. The notion that work was primarily a duty was deeply rooted among the leaders of the revolution. It is noteworthy that work schedules of 10, 12 or 14 hours were frequently mentioned in the Cuban press.[15] In 1990 it was also reported that members of as many as 67 contingents often worked 16 and 18 hours a day;[16] in the case of the Lázaro Peña contingent, weekly and monthly schedules reached 65 and 260 hours respectively.[17] Workers who so glaringly transgressed the Constitutional top were often congratulated by revolutionary leaders.

The imposition of heavier workloads was specially important with regard to workers employed in the sugar industry. Before the revolution, the harvest and grinding season (*zafra*) lasted for about 100 days (7 January to the end of April). The zafra now starts in November and is prolonged until the last days of June in a number of sugar mills. Cane cutters, who perform one of the hardest and most unmerciful kinds of work, are frequently called upon to labor 15 hour days seven days a week. However, their sacrifices and contributions are not always appreciated by Castro, who speaking in December 1995 before the National Assembly of People's Power scolded their performance in the 1994-1995 *zafra*.[18]

Other three aggravations of the conditions of work have arisen in connection with the special period and the deterioration of the economy. Transportation facilities decreased significantly and compounded the workers predicament as they were forced to spend more time away from their homes. Although the government purchased or manufactured around two million bicycles, many workers had to walk to their workplaces or spend lengthy periods of time waiting for the few buses at hand. Eateries or dining facilities (*comedores obreros*) were also eliminated or temporarily discontinued in a large number of enterprises. Finally, several mechanical implements and power driven machines which facilitated work in agriculture, industry and certain building trades gradually disappeared and were substituted by primitive devices. The return to the yoke or team of oxen was a prime example of this regressive tendency.

The worsening of conditions of work was coupled with a deterioration of living conditions. The quality of several public services, including water supply, sewage treatment and health care, declined consider-

---

15. See, e.g., *Granma* (12 August 1995), p. 3.

16. *Trabajadores* (26 January 1990), p. 12.

17. *Trabajadores* (19 January 1991), p. 2.

18. Córdova, *Clase trabajadora y movimiento sindical en Cuba*, p. 425.

ably. Blackouts of several hours were still occurring in 1996 in most cities of the island. Education continued to be thoroughly influenced by the mandatory teaching of Marxism and suffered from a gross mutilation of Cuban history. Services that were provided before free of charge or for a low contribution, such as transportation, attendance to sports events, child care, provision of some medicines and certain aspects of education, now required some payment. The government was following the advice given by the former Minister of Economics of Spain, C. Solchaga, with respect to the need to do away with the huge budget deficit. Solchaga recommended the elimination of all the subsidies given to unprofitable enterprises, the levying of several taxes and the increase of the rates charged by the authorities in connection with water supply, electricity and other items.

However, the fall of living conditions persisted for several years until at least 1995. Nutrition deficiencies and poor sanitation were responsible for the appearances of epidemics of beri beri, optical neuritis and leptospirosis. In 1993 the rate of suicides amounted to 21.7 per one hundred thousand inhabitants; the next year it reached 20.7 and both figures were the highest in Latin America.[19] It should be added that the relevant data on Cuba do not appear in the World Health Statistics published by the WHO, again for the same reason mentioned in regard to unemployment. Sharp increases in the number of abortions (8 for each 10 births), the consumption of alcohol and the crime rate were also salient features of the special period.

A final word must be said about the spread of prostitution during this period. The combination of the lingering economic crisis with the opening of tourism drove thousands of young women and men, into soliciting foreigners to pay a few dollars for sexual favors. They were doing this out of sheer necessity, though Castro stated on one occasion that their real motivation was sexual desire. It was indeed prostitution tolerated and even fomented by Castro and other government authorities eager to attract visitors of all sorts to Cuba. The leader who in 1975 said that tourists would have to come to the island to admire its beauties and the gains of the revolution, was now employing a completely different kind of approach. The ruler who blasted the existence of prostitution in pre-revolutionary Cuba, was now willing to use lust and hunger as a means of procuring hard currency.

LEVEL AND PROTECTION OF WAGES

Nominal wages, which had never been high as a result, inter alia, of the emphasis placed on the so called social wage, became even lower during the special period. Minimum wages were at some point fixed at 80 pesos and the mean salary reached only 200 pesos per month. While these figures were low in themselves they still tell very little about the dramatic situation in which Cuban workers lived during the period under examination. They were in effect doomed to carry a miserable existence and to survive with great effort due to the incredibly low amount of their real wages. As the value of the peso deteriorated and reached a point in which a dollar was worth 150 pesos—as Castro acknowledged at the closing session of the 17th congress[20]—workers had to eke out a living planting vegetables in their gardens, stealing cattle or exchanging food among them. The exchange rate improved later and dollars now equal around 25 pesos, but even this rate means that the great majority of workers are earning some seven or eight dollars a month, which places Cubans at the bottom of all Latin American workers. In 1996 the Minister of Agriculture reported that 52, 000 heads of cattle had been stolen in the previous year.

The workers' income further declined because wage supplements, such as bonuses, overtime and material incentives were abolished or substantially diminished. In 1994, the Minister of Finance and Prices declared that 24 percent of Cuban households could

---

19. See *Anuario Nacional de Estadísticas 1993 y 1994* (La Habana, 1993 and 1994).
20. "Castro Speaks at the Closing of the 17th CTC Congress," p. 9.

be regarded as being of very low income,[21] a rather remarkable understatement.

Apparently seeking to alleviate this dire condition, the Castro regime recently decided to establish three different categories of workers as regards their remuneration: 1) those working in strategic industries (like tourism, mining, ports and the electric and power sector) who are allowed to receive part of their remuneration in dollars; 2) those active in other important but not so critical sectors who, as an incentive, may receive "*convertible*" pesos in specified quantities; 3) the rest of the labor force who continue to receive only Cuban pesos. Clearly, such an approach introduced an element of discrimination among workers who are differentiated in the treatment they receive, not because of their performances but according to the capacity of the sector in which they work to generate hard currency to the government.

Although those working in the tourism industry enjoy a special status, they are also adversely affected by other government measures. Foreign companies operating hotels for instance must pay their workers in dollars through a transfer of the corresponding amount to a government agency called Cubatec. The agency then pays the workers in pesos at the exchange rate fixed by the government. Such an arrangement represents a handsome profit for Castro and an infraction of Convention 95 of the International Labor Organization (ratified by Cuba) which in order to protect wages provides that they should be paid directly to the workers. It also constitutes an infringement of the principle of integrity regarding the amount owed to the workers. Since Cuba has been repeatedly found guilty by the ILO of violating international conventions and has been condemned six times by the U.N. Commission on Human Rights, it is fair to assume that the new infractions will not worry Castro too much. Simply put, the workers will be once again the only losers.

To be sure, Castro's supporters can always argue that the ration book (*libreta de abastecimiento*) always listed its prices in pesos. The problem with this arrangement is that the shortage of food and other basic commodities rendered the book largely irrelevant.

JOB SECURITY

There has never been real security of employment in Cuba. Termination of employment regarding the conduct and efficiency of the worker was always construed in favor of the employer, that is to say, the government. True, just causes for termination were spelled out in the law but the rigor of socialist discipline, the need to increase production at all cost and the urge to discriminate against alleged counterrevolutionary activities, marred any attempt at an objective application of the law.

The first indication that the existing system of labor discipline was going to get stiffer during the special period came with regard to the tourist industry. Eager to please the Spanish entrepreneurs who were going to invest in that area and aware of the chronic difficulties concerning workers' behavior at the workplace—difficulties that were highlighted in almost all union congresses—the Castro regime expanded the list of duties and obligations of hotel employees and created new just causes for disciplinary action. Not only was the probationary period of newly hired employees extended to 180 days, but successive regulations provided for 22 new workers' obligations and 46 prohibitions.[22] Together with 12 just causes for termination included in the labor code, this meant that the staff of hotels and other tourist attractions was going to be subjected to a total of 80 possible infractions.

Similar rigid systems of labor discipline were also established for the railway industry, educational and health care institutions, ports and customhouses and scientific research. Alongside these sectoral systems, heads of government corporations were also authorized to issue specific ad hoc regulations; workers were thus subjected to a three tier web of disciplinary

---

21. *Trabajadores* (2 May 1994), p. 7.

22. See Decree-Law No. 122, of 13 August 1990, and CETSS Resolution of 5 September 1990.

provisions: the general one contained in the labor code, the sectoral system and the enterprise rules and regulations.

The culmination of this process aimed at hardening labor discipline took place in 1992 with the adoption of Law 132 in respect of basic organs for the administration of justice (Ley de Organos de Justicia Laboral de Base, LOJLB). This law, which was general in scope, put together some of the provisions contained in previous legislation and then strengthened the sanctions that were to be applied to those guilty of disciplinary violations.

Instead of the five penalties foreseen in the labor code, the LOJLB provided for eleven disciplinary measures, including fines of up to 25 percent of the salary, the loss of material incentives, suspension of seniority rights and forfeiture of all decorations and honors won by the worker. The law eliminated private reprimand as a sanction and substituted it for public reprimand; it mattered little that while the former might have had some corrective value, the latter was intended to humiliate the accused worker in front of his or her colleagues.

It may be noted that beyond legislative provisions, the practice was on many occasions even harsher. Refusal to join the paramilitary groups called Rapid Response Brigades (BRR), for instance, was regarded as proof of opposition to the government and hence led in many cases to dismissals or loss of benefits. Equipped with iron bars, sticks, machetes or other appropriate tools, the BRR acted as instruments of intimidation and closely resembled goon squads.

FREEDOM OF ASSOCIATION

Violations of freedom of association, another constant feature of the Castro regime, acquired virulent characteristics during this period. Starting in 1991 when efforts were made to create independent unions, i.e., organizations of workers not affiliated to CTC, the government decided to harden its position

contrary to any sign of pluralism. Not less than seven or eight attempts were made to establish organizations of this nature and all of them were aborted by the government. Appropriate submissions made by the organizers to the relevant authorities remained unanswered. The main promoters of some of these unions were prosecuted, jailed or forced into exile. Others were denied permits to assemble or subjected to acts of repudiation. At the 17th Congress of the CTC, Castro stated that independent unions will never be tolerated.[23] The supervisor organs of the ILO and the International Labor Conference have repeatedly disapproved of these actions and in 1994 pointed out the importance of having independent unions in accordance with the principles enshrined in Convention 87, ratified by Cuba.[24]

The absence of independent labor unions and the fragmentation and insufficient relevance within Cuba of the exile workers' organizations do not bode well for the future of the Cuban labor movement. If and when genuine political change takes place in Cuba, there will be no replacement mechanisms to put rapidly in control of the CTC's vast network of workers' organizations. Unlike what happened after the overthrow of Batista, when the formerly clandestine fronts created by the 26 of July Movement were in a position to replace the "Mujalista" leadership, no such a situation is likely to arise after Castro. A period to uncertainty and turmoil will probably follow Castro's demise: the present CTC will not survive and no other organized group will be in place to ensure the normal continuation of labor's activities.

Also objectionable were the methods used by the government to increase union affiliation. Individual workers were not free to join or not to join the organization; they just were automatically affiliated to the CTC as soon as they started to work. Small wonder that the CTC claims that 98 percent of the labor force are members of unions.[25] This extraordinary and unprecedented rate of membership is simply the

23. "Castro Speaks at the Closing of the 17th CTC Congress."

24. Córdova, *Clase trabajadora y movimiento sindical en Cuba*, p. 433.

25. Córdova, *Clase trabajadora y movimiento sindical en Cuba*, Chapter 22.

result of the real compulsory nature of affiliation in Cuba.

Although represented as the unanimous, voluntary and enthusiastic wish of the workers to support the labor movement, payment of union dues and the contributions owed to the so-called Territorial Milicias (MTT), were also made mandatory. Any worker who refused to pay these contributions was immediately denounced as counter-revolutionary and liable to suffer certain reprisals. Small wonder that the CTC collected over 27 million pesos in 1994,[26] notwithstanding the penurious living conditions of the rank and file. Finally, no free and voluntary negotiations leading to the conclusion of a collective agreement has ever taken place, either in the state-run sector of the economy or with private foreign firms.

The increase in the number of entirely foreign or mixed enterprises, which in 1996 reached the figure of 650 (of which 140 were Spanish firms)[27] offered a precious opportunity to develop collective bargaining. Cuban labor unions interested in submitting lists of demands and engaging in negotiations would be dealing here with foreign capitalists who had decided to invest substantial amounts of money for the purpose of securing quick and handsome profits. Some were big multinational corporations; others were motivated by sheer greed or historical resentment (against the United States). Whatever the reasons, it is plain that none of the arguments invoked to deny real negotiations (as distinct from the mere conclusion of agreements) in the area of public enterprises could have been called for in connection with these private entities. However, there was the risk (for the government) that the success of workers and unions in negotiating better conditions of work in the private sector might incite other workers to request real bargaining with state-enterprises. This represented a danger that the Castro regime was not pre-

pared to afford. Terms and conditions of employment in the tourist, mining and communications industries thus continued to be discussed between the Cuban Government and the foreign enterprise or unilaterally determined by the latter. The result was that some 60,000 workers were deprived of the opportunity to improve their lot during the special period.

SOCIAL SECURITY

At the 17th Congress of the CTC, Castro referred to the case of a retired worker who was receiving a monthly pension of 95 pesos, which according to the exchange rate he also mentioned,[28] represented between sixty five cents and some three or four dollars, probably one of the lowest pensions in the Western world. In nominal terms the amount alluded to by the Maximum Leader was not, by any means, the lowest amount paid in Cuba as a retirement benefit, since pensions of 50 to 60 pesos (around two dollars) are not unknown. In 1995 the Minister of Labor recognized that 60 percent of pensioners were receiving less than 100 pesos a month.[29] True, the extent of health care and public assistance would probably prevent the death by malnutrition or despondency of those pensioners. But the said examples represent vivid denials of the claim of social progress constantly made by the Castro regime. Suffice it to indicate that while in 1996 Argentinean pensioners were demanding a minimum pension of 450 dollars per month, in Cuba retired people had to get by with some three or four dollars.

In 1996 the number of people receiving social security benefits was of 1,350,000 of which a growing percentage corresponded to disability benefits.[30] Because pensions are very low in real terms, many pensioners are forced to re-enter the labor market to supplement their meager incomes. Approximately 40 percent of pensioners retire before the normal retirement age of

---

26. *Trabajadores* (27 June 1993), p. 4.

27. See *El País* (Madrid), Suplemento Domingo (21 July 1996), p. 4.

28. "Castro Speaks at the Closing of the CTC Congress," p. 9.

29. "Interview with Salvador Valdés, Minister of Labor," p. 9.

30. Marta Beatriz Roque, "Un 'logro' que tiende a desmoronarse," in this volume.

60 (men) and 55 (women) and look then for another activity in the state sector or as self-employed, thus affecting the job opportunities of new entrants into the labor force. In 1995 the cost of the social security system represented 12.40 per cent of the national budget.[31] Two years earlier, the social security budget showed a deficit of 425 million pesos.[32]

It is quite possible that, as Raúl Castro stated at the latest CTC Congress, the Cuban Government has managed to retain its defense and military capabilities during these difficult years. What is nevertheless absolutely sure is that the ambitious social security system envisaged at the beginning of the revolution, is now another casualty of the special period.

CONCLUSION

The upshot of the above discussion is easy to discern: the special period not only added new sorrows to the Cuban workers but also served to highlight some of the structural problems that had existed through all the previous stages of the revolution. While the Castro-Communist system relied during its first two years on the considerable amount of wealth confiscated from the propertied classes and the high prices of sugar, and later on the subsidies coming from the socialist countries, the special period represented the moment of truth. Left to its own, the revolution floundered in both the economic and social realms. Only the political fabric remained intact.

Two additional lessons can be learned from the experience of the special period. The first is that the dramatic deterioration of the conditions of work and life that occurred after 1996 did not bring about any generalized and lasting signs of protest or dissatisfaction. True, there was a demonstration in Havana on 5 August 1994, but this was an isolated event. There were also some acts of sabotage, "frequent thefts and slaughter of cattle, robbery, and in crease in petty crimes," but no strikes—general or partial—ever ever took place. Either the totalitarian regime had reached a fool-proof perfection or the majority of workers were resigned and willing to conform to the new state of things.

Closely related to the above observation is the realization that economic pressures do not work when confronted with an authoritarian regime led by a charismatic leader capable of combining nationalistic and demagogic exhortations with ruthless repression. The special period was coupled in effect with the adoption by the U.S. Government of the Torricelli Act (1993) and the Helms-Burton Act (1996), both designed to strengthen the embargo imposed in 1962 and to increase the constraints and difficulties of the special period. Neither of them has so far been successful in provoking a serious crisis. Even if the full application of the Helms-Burton Act results in discouraging further investments, there is no reason to believe that it will lead to the downfall of the regime. With the existing revenues coming from tourism, sugar and mining (not to mention drugs), the government has the resources necessary to maintain its two pillars of the army and the state security apparatus. There will always be desperate rafters and boat people but this never ending exodus of the Cuban population—particularly of those of European descent—will probably be the only alternative to organized opposition and confrontation.

---

31. Roque, "Un 'logro' que tiende a desmoronarse." p. 5.
32. See *Trabajadores* (29 August 1994), p. 5.

COMMENTS ON

"The Condition of Cuban Workers During the Special Period in Peacetime" by Córdova

Lorenzo Cañizares

I would have loved to make the emphasis of my response to Mr. Cordova's paper the last point he made: "left to its own, the revolution floundered in both the economic and social realms. Only the political fabric remained intact." This statement fascinates me because there is no doubt that the experiences that Cuba has gone through in the last few years should have toppled the Government.

But I was asked to react as a trade unionist.

1. *On Unemployment*: I have to say that it is amazing that in spite of the economic debacle that the Cuban government is facing, they have been—at least on paper—so incredibly generous. Not only unemployment benefits are double in length to what we receive here. But also unemployed workers do not lose their medical benefits or are in danger of going homeless. Regarding the choices that Mr. Córdova fears between mobilization and starvation, it is also a choice being faced in many different parts of the non-socialist world. And without the benefits of the social net that Cuba provides.

2. *Work as Duty*: This concept definitely has not been invented by Cubans. Anyone who has followed the Welfare Reform debate in the U.S. Congress is aware that work as a duty is a position shared by many. Let's not forget the Protestant ethic. I agree that 65 hours per week is definitely humanly taxing. But I can tell you there are many people out there in the good, old USA who are working double shifts, 5 days per week in order to maintain the life style that they used to have. The victims of downsizing.

3. *Compulsory Trade Unionism*: This is the topic of a major fight in labor contracts in New Jersey since the Reagan days. Labor history tells us that for a period, American workers, at least in the north, could expect that winning union recognition at a worksite would mean that every worker would belong to the union. But since our own special period things have changed. The opposite to compulsory affiliation of workers to their unions is the "right to work" concept that we in the American trade union movement view as measure to weaken the power of labor and ultimately destroy unions.

I believe the point to highlight here is the limitations of the Cuban trade union movement to be able to act as an independent political force on the issues that concern workers. But, again, even on this point, many U.S. trade unionists here will tell you there is not much difference with our experience. But there is no doubt that vibrant, energetic leadership with a mind of its own has room to roam in the U.S. labor movement. I believe the Cuban labor experience calls for degrees of cautiousness unknown here.

4. *On Different Categories of Workers:* Again this is not a Cuban invention. I will like to remind the audience that even in the best days of U.S. capitalism (when we had a large middle class) we had a situation kind of similar. We had the labor aristocracy in high paying jobs like in the automobile industry, airplane manufacturing, unionized construction work, as a first level. Second level were jobs manufacturing minor consumer goods, mining, transportation, hospital work, etc. And the third level was composed of low-skilled service and manual workers. I hate to recognize it, but discrimination among workers—or any other profession for that matter—is part and parcel of any system of belief that rewards people according to status. And to tell you the truth, I don't know that the human race has been able to device anything better yet. That the Cubans reward in the levels indicated is because of their choice of values. The same way we have our own set of values.

5. *Labor Discipline:* It might be that Castro is trying to become like us. The probationary period for most U.S. workers was at one time of three months. Nowadays in most U.S. contracts, employers are calling for six months probationary periods. In terms of discipline I don't think it can be any worse than in the State of New Jersey, the second richest per capita in the U.S., where public workers if they call in sick have to stay home or face disciplinary measures if they get called and are not home.

The concept of progressive discipline which was a major victory won by labor in the U.S. is now under attack. Only those workers with a fighting union behind them have a chance to win an arbitrary disciplinary decision.

6. *Labor Inability to Negotiate Wages:* This is a point where I agree wholeheartedly with Mr. Córdova's indignation. This is an outrage and goes against all labor principles. It is a mechanism of control to keep workers without the ability to bargain for their own well-being. As a trade unionist, I am very conscious of the need to think on behalf of the common good, but the excuse of the common good should not be used to obliterate labor and human rights. Again I ask, where are the Cuban trade unions?

The acceptance of this modus vivendi gives rise to the mentality that excuses the abuses committed against workers for refusing to participate in projects not to their liking. The Cuban trade unions who have clearly expressed that not all Cuban workers are Communists cannot in good conscience stand by and allow these transgressions of labor rights.

Let me also add that I don't see the official Cuban trade unions as a totally useless outfit. I am not an scholar on the Cuban trade unions. But I do know that the Cuban trade unions were the only government controlled organism that defied Fidel Castro and openly requested the reestablishment of the farmers' market.

This leads to another point where I strongly agree with Mr. Córdova—that the move made by the Cuban government towards an economic opening was not easily made. Castro's greatest fear is the development of an independent source of power that will challenge his arbitrary powers. To explain crudely the Cuban dilemma, the Chinese could not have accomplished what they have if Mao Tse-Tung was still in control of China. Cuba still has its Mao Tse-Tung.

In regards to Mr. Córdova's conclusion, I also agree that the special period has been the culmination of past mistakes, like the total servile reliance on a foreign power, the arbitrariness of Castro (as an example the incredible occurrence that during the beginning of the special period, there was serious scarcity of food in Cuba that could have been solved immediately, as it was later done through the reinstatement of the farmers' markets).

But the ability of Castro to survive is not only the result of some good policies that have been structuralized. In the main, Castro owes his survival to his ability to be able to wear the mantle of David fighting Goliath. And the sad part of this is that those who claim to be his most ardent opposition continuously ball him out by providing an objective reality to his claims.

ARE CUBA'S EDUCATIONAL STATISTICS RELIABLE?

Benigno E. Aguirre and Roberto J. Vichot

One of the consequences of the recent collapse of the Soviet Union and the Communist bloc has been a renewed appreciation of the lack of correspondence between the ideology and the practice of socialist revolutionary states. Not surprisingly, this lack of correspondence between the two is nowadays the most serious challenge to the legitimacy of the Cuban state: the central promises of the ideology of the revolution on which the legitimacy of the revolutionary state ultimately rests, the tremendous collective effort of the Cuban people on their prosecution and behalf, and side by side to it the grim reality of widespread inequality, corruption, and impoverishment in the island, aggravated, after years of public administrative mismanagement, by the international isolation of the regime.

This context makes an assessment of the reliability of Cuban educational statistics particularly worthwhile. Marxist societies like Cuba consider ideas weapons in the class struggle, stress the function which education has in facilitating the political indoctrination of the population, and value universal education as a way of bringing about social equality (Hollander 1982). Thus, it is appropriate to examine now, in the twilight of this failed experiment, the reliability of Cuban educational statistics. To what extent are they affected by the generalized tendency of these social systems to exaggerate accomplishments and make untenable claims?

The question is not gratuitous, for there have been widespread and persistent concerns among social scientists about the reliability and validity of Cuban statistics. Carmelo Mesa-Lago (1969; 1979) was the

first to explore these issues for economic statistics. Demographic statistics have been manipulated by the government. Lisandro Pérez (1984) shows how Cuban 1970 Census data on race and education was suppressed by the government for political reasons. Norman Luxenburg (1984) using health statistics, exploited the often-found exaggerations about the achievements of the communist government resulting from the inattention and underestimation of the remarkable progress of pre-1959 Cuban society. Given these uncertainties, we made internal and external reliability checks on Cuba's educational statistics.

METHODS

The primary source of statistical information used in this report are the educational statistics published by the United Nations and by the Cuban government. UNESCO information on Cuba's post-1958 increases in student enrollments, the average number of students per teachers, and the proportion of students repeating their grades are good measures of educational changes available for most countries in the world. The Cuban government has tried to increase the number of students, teachers and graduates. These indices have been used repeatedly by Mr. Fidel Castro and other leading members of the government to document the successes of the Cuban revolution and the continued relevance of socialist ideology (Castro 1990b).

External reliability criteria used in this analysis come from UNESCO reports. Its yearbooks are the most complete, up-to-date source of educational statistics on Cuba. Moreover, UNESCO statistics are collected from official sources in Cuba and throughout the world using uniform definitions, operationalizations, and procedures. Unlike the problems that arose from comparisons of socialist and capitalist economic indices, UNESCO publishes comparable international educational indices appropriate for this analysis.

We did not have access to the procedures used in Cuba to collect educational statistics and lacked the resources to evaluate the accuracy of the educational statistics of the countries in the UNESCO reports. Nor were there sufficient number of reports by independent observers which would provide external validity checks to country-level statistics. Thus, we could not determine the relative accuracy of Cuba's statistics *vis-a-vis* specific countries. Instead, our comparisons are less exact. They are based on Cuba's relative ordinal positions in the distribution of measures of educational achievement by continent (Africa, America, Asia, Europe, Oceania) (see below). Cuba's relative position in these distributions of national scores provides a criterion of internal consistency to evaluate the reliability of the Cuban data: we expect that most European countries would score higher than Cuba in various dimensions of formal education while Cuba would score higher than most of the countries in the other continents.

For reasons of limitations in time and resources, the analysis is restricted to information available from every country included in the UNESCO *Statistical Yearbook*. This information is used to calculate students-per-teacher ratios for the years 1980-1984, inclusive, and percent repeaters in each of the grades of the first and second levels of education for the years 1980, 1983, and 1984. The number of countries with values less than or equal the Cuban values in these distributions are reported in the form of proportions in the figures; years are represented by chronologically-consecutive columns; countries are grouped by continent.

To conduct internal reliability checks we used information on indicators of Cuban formal education published in the Cuban mass media, particularly Mr. Castro's speeches. We also used first-hand published and unpublished accounts such as the educational experiences of some of the authors' acquaintances, an in-depth interview of a defecting journalist from Cu-

ba's Prensa Latina who specialized in educational matters, other documentary qualitative information on educational practices, and mass campaigns that occur in Cuba.

The internal reliability checks compare 1969-1988 UNESCO educational information on Cuba with information presented in Cuban official accounts of the educational system published in *Granma*, *Bohemia*, and *Juventud Rebelde* during 1968-1992 and in radio, television, and other mass media sources collected by the Foreign Broadcast Information Service (FBIS), U.S. Joint Publications Research Service (JPRS) and the U.S. Information Agency's *Quarterly Situation Report on Cuba*.

We stress that the analysis presented in this essay does not ascertain the **validity** of Cuban educational statistics. It does not answer the question of whether there have been improvements in the **quality** of formal education. Such an analysis would require very different information and arguments from the ones presented here (e.g. Carnoy 1981; Badía 1993).

RESULTS

Pre-primary education begins for Cuban children when they are 5 years old. Education for 6 to 11 year-olds is mandatory. The first six grades, corresponding to ages 6 through 11, inclusive, make up the first level of formal education. Before 1977 first level education encompassed seven years of schooling. The second level of education is composed of six grades divided into two three-years stages. It corresponds to ages 12 through 17, inclusive. Third level education corresponds to college, university and technical training (Leiner 1981 and Epstein 1988).

Table 1 presents UNESCO educational information on Cuba's number of teachers, students, and students-per-teacher ratios (STR) for all levels of education for the years 1969-1988, inclusive. Table 2 includes Cuba's percent of grade repeaters by level of education and grade for the years 1975, 1980, 1983, 1984, 1985, 1987 and 1988. These are the most recent years for which these statistics are available.

Internal reliability checks show that UNESCO's statistics in Table 1 are comparable to educational sta-

Table 1. Number of Teachers, Students, and Students per Teacher Ratios By Year and Level of Education: Cuba

| Year | Pre-Primary | | | First Level | | |
	Number of Teachers	Number of Students	Students per Teacher	Number of Teachers	Number of Students	Students per Teacher
1969	3846	130538	34	52008	1427607	27
1970	4037	134258	33	56555	1530376	27
1971	3979	127960	32	57110	1631187	29
1972	—	—	—	—	—	—
1973	4015	118491	30	71906	1778724	25
1974	—	—	—	—	—	—
1975	4358	126565	29	77472	1795752	23
1976	4775	151294	32	80845	1747738	22
1977	—	—	—	—	—	—
1978	5143	134848	26	86738	1626386	19
1979	4796	122637	26	86519	1550323	18
1980	5047	123741	25	84041	1468538	17
1981	5248	123302	23	83113	1409765	17
1982	5258	118072	22	83358	1363078	16
1983	4898	107660	22	82424	1282989	16
1984	4931	109061	22	79610	1174453	15
1985	4847	108881	22	77111	1077213	14
1988	7076	143705	20	73216	899936	12

Sources: UNESCO Statistical Yearbook 1986 Tables 3.3, 3.4., 3.7, 3.11; 1991 Tables 3.3, 3.4. 3.7, 3.11; U.N. Demographic Yearbook 1972, p. 791; U.N. Demographic Yearbook 1973, p. 764; U.N. Demographic Yearbook 1974, p. 825; U.N. Demographic Yearbook 1975, p. 848; U.N. Demographic Yearbook 1976, p. 842; U.N. Demographic Yearbook 1977, p. 896; U.N. Demographic Yearbook 1978, p. 909; U.N. Demographic Yearbook 1981, pp. 326, 338, 357, 383; U.N. Demographic Yearbook 1983/84, pp. 341, 351, 366, 388.

tistics published elsewhere in Cuba. To wit: *Granma* (JPRS #76724, 20 September 1980) gives student enrollment figures in thousands similar to the figures in Table 1 for the 1975-76 and 1979-80 school years, respectively. It shows, for pre-school, 126.6 and 122.6; for primary, 1795.8 and 1550.3; for intermediate, 604 and 1150.3; for advanced, 84 and 200.2; for a total of 3244.4 and 3452.9 for the two years. Likewise, Gil Green (1983:96), writing in the early 1980s, reports a students-per-teacher ratio of 13 for the first and second levels combined. Marvin Leiner (p. 42) reports that "at the start of the 1980-81 school year, Fidel Castro announced that Cuba had close to 213,000 teachers and professors," with 90,000 in the primary schools, 80,000 in the secondary schools, 5,000 in special education, about 24,000 in adult education and nearly 11,000 in university centers. *Bohemia* (JPRS #82231, 15 November 1982) places the number of students at the beginning of the 1982-83 school year at 3,393,800 (1,355,500 in primary schools; 1,152,000 in intermediate

grades; 270,000 in technical and trade schools, and 93,000 in pedagogy and education). L. Margulis and T.H. Kunz (1984, p. 638) place total university enrollment in 1983-84 at about 200,000 students.

There are very few published reports by independent observers which could be used to provide external reliability checks. Lois Mickey (1977) visited a primary school in the Alamar area of Havana. She reported a student enrollment of 969 and a teaching staff of 38, for a student-per-teacher ratio of 25.5. This ratio for this school is a little bit higher than the first level national average ratios of 22 and 19 shown in Table 1 for 1976 and 1978, respectively, the two years for which information is available nearest to 1977. Nevertheless, while UNESCO does not provide information on the variance in the distribution of educational scores which would allow us to estimate the relative statistical significance of the deviation of this school's score from the national mean, it does not seem to depart much from the national average.

Table 1. Number of Teachers, Students, and Students per Teacher Ratios By Year and Level of Education: Cuba *(continued)*

Year	Second Level			Third Level			Overall Students per Teacher Ratio
	Number of Teachers	Number of Students	Students per Teacher	Number of Teachers	Number of Students	Students per Teacher	
1969	19732	266651	14	—	—	—	24[a]
1970	21781	235241	11	—	—	—	23[a]
1971	22614	259160	11	—	—	—	24[a]
1972	—	—	—	—	—	—	—
1973	29260	352946	12	—	55435	—	21[a]
1974	—	—	—	5725	68051	12	—
1975	42306	554365	13	5380	82688	15	20
1976	56347	715807	13	6263	—	—	19[a]
1977	—	—	—	—	—	—	—
1978	—	936088	—	10139	133014	13	19[b]
1979	—	1009441	—	—	146240	—	18[c]
1980	80665	1046884	13	10680	151733	14	15
1981	86578	1056763	12	12068	165496	14	15
1982	88199	1017556	12	12200	173404	14	14
1983	89826	1024113	11	15894	192958	12	13
1984	93704	1031365	11	17717	212155	12	13
1985	100673	1156555	11	19552	235224	12	13
1988	108078	1127035	10	24499	242366	10	11

a. Excludes Third Level

b. Excludes Second Level

c. Excludes Second and Third Levels

Table 1 shows the growth in the numbers of students and teachers during 1969-1988. It documents the enormous efforts of the revolutionary state in making good its promise of educating the nation (similar results obtain when the percentages of age cohorts attending schools are examined). Important differences have occurred since 1959 in the student enrollment patterns at each level of education. The number of students in pre-primary and first level education declined during most of the years under study. The decline reflects the combined effects of cohort aging and the well-known declines in Cuban fertility since the mid 1960s to the present. There were 130,538 pre-primary students in 1969 and 108,881 in 1985; in the first level the corresponding enrollment figures were 1,427,607 in 1969 and 899,936 in 1988. During this time, enrollment shifted dramatically to the second and third levels of education.

Table 1 also presents Cuba's students-per-teacher ratios (STR). Independent confirmation for some of these students-per-teacher ratios and numbers is available (see coverage in *Granma* September 5,

1980; *Bohemia* September 3, 15; November, 1982; Leiner 1982, p. 42; Green 1983, p. 96; Margulis and Kunz 1984, p. 638). The shifts in student enrollments already alluded to occur in the presence of near-monotonic declines in the students per teacher ratios at every level of education. The near-uniform declines in these ratios suggests a high level of bureaucratic resources and responsiveness, for manpower and other resources had to be reallocated to match uneven increases during these years in student enrollments in different grades. Nevertheless, we can not observe temporary increases in the second and third levels ratios, particularly around the years of inflection of the shift in students enrollment. Similarly, there are no increases in the ratios during the late seventies and eighties at the pre-primary and first levels of education.

At almost every level of education the students per teacher ratios have declined significantly during 1969-88. For pre-primary education the ratios decreased from 34 to 20; for primary education they declined for 27 to 12; the ratios for second level education dropped from 14 to 10. The total national ratio of 13 for the 1983-85 school years is quite low in terms of Cuban historical patterns. However, even this very low ratio is surpassed by the statistics announced at the beginning of the 1987-88 school year; close to three million students and 270,000 teachers, for a ratio of 11 (see coverage in *Granma*, September 13, 1987). It is clear from the secular trends in these national statistics, however, that the 1969 and 1970 third level ratios of 7 and 6 (excluded from Table 1) are incorrect. They are also unsupported by international comparisons (see below).

The successes of Cuban education in lowering students per teacher ratios become even more impressive when compared to analogous statistics from other countries (Castro 1990b). The annual positions of Cuba in the pre-primary educational level distributions of this ratio are shown in Figure 1 (as mentioned earlier in this and subsequent figures, the heights of the columns represent the proportions of countries in each of the five continents with values lower than or equal to the Cuban values, for every year for which information is available). Cuba's position in the world improved. In 1980, 62 percent of the 87 countries for which there was information had lower students per teacher ratios at the pre-primary educational level of education. By 1984 only 38 percent of the 49 countries with available information surpassed Cuba in this index. Moreover, there are important differences by continent. Most European countries had lower ratios than Cuba and Cuba fared well when compared to other American countries. These results do not challenge the reliability of the Cuban data.

Figure 1 also shows the international comparative positions of Cuba in the first-level educational level distributions of students per teacher ratios. Cuba's accomplishments in this level are obvious, reflected in proportions varying from .10 to .15 during 1980-84. Very few countries in Africa, America, and Asia match Cuba's low students per teacher ratios. As expected, Cuba's positions drop when compared with European countries, ranging from .38 to .30.

Similar results obtain for the second level (general) education distributions of students per teacher ratios.

As shown in Figure 1, Cuba's worldwide position in this level improved during 1980-84 from .28 to .17. Except for European countries, very few African, American, Asian, and Oceanian countries could match or surpass Cuba's ratios. Even compared with Europe, Cuba's position improved from .62 to .43.

To summarize the results so far, the Cuban students-per-teacher ratios in the pre-primary, first, and second levels of education do not make us question the reliability of Cuban education statistics.

Cuba's achievement in higher education is less noticeable. Eighty one percent of the 90 countries for which information was available equaled or surpassed Cuba's ratio of 14 (third educational level) in 1980. By 1984 this ranking had improved somewhat, for only 64 percent of the countries in the world had equal or lower ratios than Cuba's 12. Nevertheless, it is still the case that most of the countries in the five continents equal or surpass Cuba's students-per-teacher ratios. These findings discredit Cuba's reported ratios of 7 and 6 for 1969 and 1970 previously discussed.

As an aside, despite the unreliability of the ratios for these two years, previous scholars have given credence to them. Thus, Samuel Bowles (1971) using Central Planning Board statistics, presents the following students per teacher ratios for the 1968-69 school year: primary school 29.8; total secondary school (general) 16.5; university education 7.9. He fails to explain the extraordinarily low 7.9 ratio. Instead, he contrasts these 1968-69 ratios to the ratios for 1958-59 and concludes that "the number of teachers relative to students has increased substantially at the primary level and not declined significantly at any level except in teacher training."

The drop in class size after 1958 occurred as the educational system employed as elementary and secondary school teachers, particularly during its first 25 years, individuals who had no teaching training (Castro 1992b). Early on the government began a teachers' aide movement to help solve the shortage of instructors, specially at the university level, caused by the exodus of professional staff. These teaching aides were university students who had the approval of

Figure 1: Percentage of Countries with Students-per-teachers Ratios Lower or Equal to Cuban Ratios, in Pre-primary, First, Second, and Third Levels, By Continent: 1980-1984.

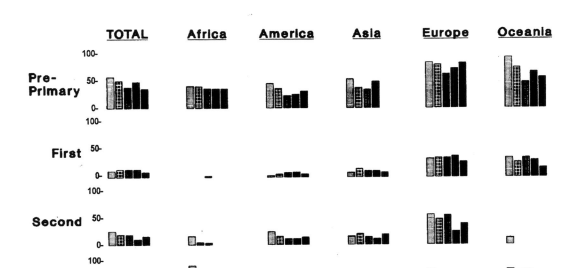

their teachers and the Federation of University Students (FEU) as well as appropriate knowledge of Marxism-Leninism, physics, and mathematics. They worked with professors, prepared laboratory classes, and helped with grading and lower level teaching. Acknowledging such practices, G. Jiménez (1982, p. 4) writes that thousands of students with a 10th grade education also taught classes.

The low STRs shown in this paper are statistical outcomes affected by Cuba's Ministry of Education. The Ministry often counts people twice, first as students and then as teachers. We do not know the extent of this practice, although it has been less common since the mid 1980s. Student-teachers were a very important resource to the state in its drive to make good its promise of universal education.

A drawback to this policy is that, as is typical of other Latin American educational systems, from the very beginning of the revolution to the present one of the most often-mentioned educational problems in Cuba has been the lack of sufficient numbers of well-trained teachers. For example, Paulston (1971a, p. 452; see also Paulston 1971b; 1972) mentioned the lack of training of teachers: "nearly one-half of the 47,690 primary teachers in 1968 were 'maestros populares' with minimal training." Thirteen years later this chronic problem is illustrated in an article in *Juventud Rebelde* (June 9, 1981) about the problems of beginning teachers. The interviewees were experienced teachers. One respondent said that the Union of Communist Youth (UJC) needed to involve itself more deeply with beginning teachers to help them improve their methodological skills. Another respondent complained that several young teachers showed no interest in methodological training and that their lack of aptitude showed that they did not want to be teachers. The respondents opined that young teachers lacked sufficient time at their assigned Technical Teacher Guidance Program. They were hurried through their training. The respondent expressed their concern about the lack of textbooks, other necessary books, chalk, blackboards, and chemical reagents.

Officials at the highest level of the Cuban government, like Mr. Belarmino Castilla Mas, former Minister of Education during the 1960s, repeatedly voiced concern over the poor professional preparation of teachers as well as a host of other problems: too many young and inexperienced teachers, an inadequate supply of professionally trained teachers in part due to the insufficient number and quality of in service training programs for nonprofessional and nongraduate teachers, slow pace in the construction and adaptations of buildings for schools, lack of furniture, instruction material, textbook, school supplies, and laboratory and workshop equipment, insufficient care of educational equipment and property, shortcomings in the organization and control by the Ministry of Education and its provincial offices, deficiencies in study plans and programs, lack of close school and community relations, student absenteeism, especially for youngsters 13 to 16 years old, low academic performance of students, and sizeable numbers of students repeating courses. Years later, as revealed by Mr. José Ramón Fernández, Minister of Education during most of the decade of the 1980s, many of these problems continued to plague the educational institutions (see discussion of these problems in Havana Domestic Service in Spanish February 1980, p. 87; and *Granma*, July 5, 1981, pp. 14-17; April 3, 1981, p. 31; April 24, 1988).

Another indication of the low educational level of some categories of teachers in Cuba is that during the 1978-79 school year 42,000 primary school teachers graduated from "practicing teachers" programs offered to persons with very few years of formal education. That year 25,700 teachers graduated from more advanced training programs in pedagogical schools, although until then entrance requirements to these programs had been less than a ninth grade of education (*Granma* September 5, 1980).

The report to the Fifth National Congress of Education and Science Teachers (*Bohemia* September 10, 1982; *Trabajadores* June 24, 1981: 38), based on extensive nationwide meetings of science teachers, also assigned primary importance to the need to raise the quality of education and pedagogical skills of teachers and professors through conferences, seminars, workshops; the need to increase the level of teachers' activism; the need to emphasize scientific research in higher education; and the need to discover the reason of low promotion rates and rejection of many students in the basic sciences (mathematics, physics, chemistry). Reflecting on these underlying difficulties Maurice R. Berube (1985) writes, partly based on interviews he obtained from officials of Cuba's Ministry of Education, that the need to improve teacher quality and the scarcity of school supplies were two paramount problems of Cuban education in the early 1980s.

In sum, Cuba's success in lowering student per teacher ratios at the pre-university levels is in part the result of deliberate, officially-designed transformations of the educational system which for many years allowed students and others without technical or advanced educational degrees to teach, the accounting procedure used by the Ministry of Education and more generally, the redefinition of the profession of teacher at the pre-university levels. These patterns are important to understand events during the last three decades. They are being superseded rapidly. Greater educational standards for pre-university teachers are being put in place. Mr. Castro (1992b), in a recent address to the Teachers Conference 30 May, announced the stiffening of teaching credentials for primary school teachers. And as we have shown, it should be underscored that in international comparative terms the same successes in lowering students per teacher ratios have not occurred at the third level of formal education. Relatively higher teaching standards have been kept at this level.

Available statistics on the percent of students repeating their grades also provides us the opportunity to look at the reliability of Cuban educational statistics. Maurice R. Berube sets the historical context for the interpretation of the figures in Table 2 when he writes, based on his extensive research of Cuban education, that in the "sixties half of the primary school children were grade repeaters and in the intermediate schools only 13 percent of the students graduated." Other scholars also mentioned these problems. Rolland G. Paulston (1971a) wrote that "the internal efficiency of primary schooling is low, i.e., only some

Table 2. Number and Percent of Repeaters by Year, Level of Education, and Grade: Cuba

	1975	1980	1983	1984	1985	1987	1988
First Level Grades	Percent Repeaters	Percent Repeaters	Percent Repeaters	Percent Repeaters	Percent Repeaters	Percent Repeaters	Percent Repeaters
1	20	0	0	0	0	0	0
2	10	14	15	14	12	12	13
3	6	2	3	3	2	6	3
4	6	8	6	4	3	13	9
5	3	5	3	2	2	9	3
6	2	3	2	1	1	6	2
Total Repeaters	8.12	5.7	4.9	4.1	3.2	7.7	5.2
	145897	83747	62767	48301	34573	73074	46447
Second Level Grades	Percent Repeaters	Percent Repeaters	Percent Repeaters	Percent Repeaters	Percent Repeaters	Percent Repeaters	Percent Repeaters
1	3	7	4	3	4	8	5
2	2	4	3	2	3	5	4
3	1	3	2	2	2	3	2
4	3	3	2	3	3	2	4
5	2	2	1	1	1	1	1
6	2	1	0	0	0	0	0
Total Repeaters	1.74	3.53	2.0	1.7	3.1	4.5	3.3
	9627	36944	20218	17200	22125	35078	25433

Source: UNESCO Statistical Yearbook 1986, Tables 3.6, 3.9; 1990 Tables 3.6, 3.9; 1991 Tables 3.6, 3.9.

40 percent who begin grade one complete grade six." G. Read wrote in the late sixties that "between the first and sixth grades, there are 621,500 school children who have fallen behind one or more grades in school. From the seventh to the tenth grades, the number is 76,506; in the eleventh, twelfth, and thirteenth grades the number is 4,646...some 300,000 children and youngsters within the 6-16 age bracket are now outside the school system."

In light of this situation in which many students repeated grades or dropped from school, the low percents of students repeating their grades less than a decade later is in some cases striking. Incredibly, at least since 1980 there are no first grade repeaters in Cuba. In 1975 20 percent of the 305,278 first graders were repeating the grade. However, only five years later there were no repeaters among the 205,595 first graders throughout the island. This pattern continued during the 1980s.

Figure 2 presents, for the years 1980, 1983, and 1984, the proportions of countries with percents of grade repeaters in the first grade (first level) lower than or equal to Cuba. In 1983 there was only one country in Europe presumably like Cuba, with no re-

peaters in the first grade and there were no European countries with this score in 1980 and 1984. Cuba's reported absence of grade repeaters in the first grade was almost unrivaled in the other continents as well.

In our opinion, these results can only obtain if the Cuban statistics are mistaken or, as it is most likely, if a national educational policy prohibits repeating the first grade irrespective of the students' readiness to advance to the second grade. Relatedly, this pattern is not reflected in most of the other grades, where Cuba occupies more modest positions in the distributions of countries. There has not been a continued nationwide mass mobilization that would make these claims even remotely plausible.

In contrast to the first grade (first level), Cuba's ranking during 1980, 1983, and 1984 among the countries of the world in the percent of repeaters in the second grade (first level) are much more modest. Figure 2 shows that almost all countries in Europe had equal or lower scores, and this is generally true also of the countries in the other continents, except for African countries. Cuba's international position in the third grade (first level) distributions is both advantageous and credible. As shown in Figure 2 most African, American, and Asian countries have higher percents of repeaters in the third grade than Cuba, while most European countries surpass Cuba in this index.

While lack of space prevents the detailed presentation of the international statistical comparisons for the fourth, fifth, and sixth grades of the first level of education, the pattern appears reliable. In each of these grades Cuba's position improved during 1980-84 both in comparison with the world and with most continents. Similarly, the comparative analysis of grades one through four in level 2 indicates a respectable and believable level of achievement. For example, in 1984 only 34 percent of the countries of the world had values lower than or equal to Cuba's three percent repeaters in the first grade (second level). There were important variations by continent, so that, as predicted, Cuba fared much worse when compared to European countries and much better when compared to Asian and African countries. This general pattern of findings hold for grades two, three and four of the second level of education.

By way of contrast, the findings shown in Table 2 for grades 5 and 6 of level 2 (the eleventh and twelve grade in Cuba) do not conform with existing knowledge of Cuban education. The claim that there has not been grade repeaters in the twelve grade since 1983 is not credible. These claims are unsupported by what is known about Cuba's formal educational system and by international comparisons. In terms of internal criterion, it is reasonable to expect a positive correlation between the percent of student dropouts and the percent of students repeating the grade. Indeed, there is evidence that most of the dropout problem in Cuba occurs in these two grades. For instance, during the 1980-81 school year 21 percent of youngsters 13 to 16 years of age nationwide were not attending school. Berube (1985; see also Sendón-Oreiro 1983) estimates that 97 percent of eligible elementary school students attend school, 93 percent graduate, and that the dropout problem occurs in the intermediate school years. He estimates that 27 percent of students sixteen years old drop out of school. Our point is that the opposite patterns would have to occur to justify UNESCO's reported proportions of grade repeaters in these grades.

The relative position of Cuba in the distributions of country values also do not support the reliability of these Cuban statistics. As shown, Cuba's relative position in the eleventh grade (fifth level, Figure 3) is unbelievably low. In 1984 only 15 percent of the countries of the world and none of the countries from Europe and Oceania equaled or surpassed Cuba's value in this index (one percent). By way of contrast, greater percents of the countries from Africa, America, and Asia equaled or surpassed the Cuban value. These patterns are contrary to what could be reasonably expected and put into question the reliability of the Cuban figures.

An even more extreme case occurs in the 12th grade (Sixth level, Figure 3). There are no European and Oceanian countries with values equal to Cuba's zero percent of repeaters. We do not believe the accuracy of these statistics, for they cannot be accounted for despite the efforts by Cuban educators to provide alternative educational programs in technical and vocational fields for grade repeaters (so that they would not be counted as repeaters).

The very low proportions of grade repeaters in Cuba is in large part the result of the ideologically-generated social pressures on teachers to promote students at the pre-university levels. Reminiscent of the grade inflationary practices in the United States, grade promotion at these levels is an important goal of the Cuban educational system. The criterion is used to gauge the success of teachers and administrators; presumably good teachers have very high percentages of promoted students in their classes. Teachers' ability to promote their students affects their career advances, prestige and standing in the teaching profession. According to Cuba's former Minister of Education Mr. Fernández (Havana Domestic Service in Spanish February 1980, p. 87), the promotion of students is a "fundamental indicator" of teaching efficiency. Mr. Fernández stressed "top promotion with top quality," in itself an admirable goal. However, given the vulnerability of Cuban citizens to the claims of the state and its mass organizations and organs of social control (Aguirre, 1984), the goal translates as pressure on teachers to advance their careers by having impressive promotion rates in their classes. Aggregat-

Figure 2: Percentage of Countries with Grade Repeat Percei
Lower or Equal to Cuban Percent in First, Second, ar
Third Grades (First Level), by Continent: 1980, 1983,198

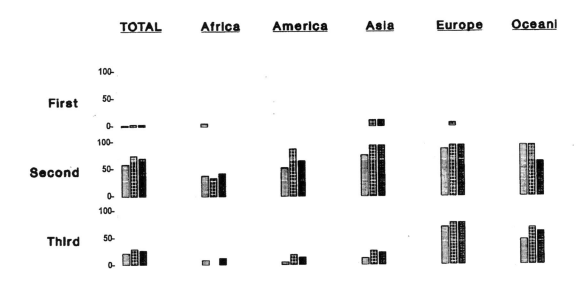

Figure 3: Percentage of Countries with Grade Repeat Percent
Lower or Equal to Cuban Percent, in Fifth and Sixth
Grades (Second Level), By Continent: 1980, 1983, 1984

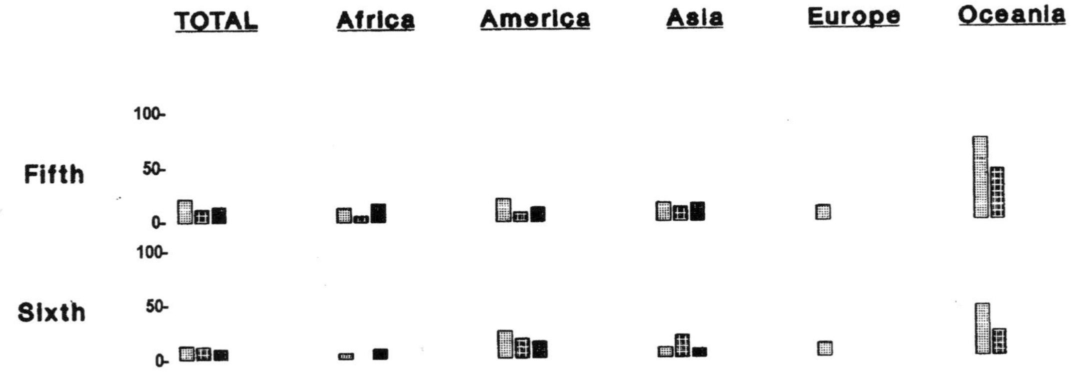

ed nationwide, this pressure is in part responsible for the low percent of grade repeaters.

Marvin Leiner (1981) underscores the importance of student promotion, both on the quarterly and finals exams, for school administrators. Teachers who fail unusually high percent of their students must justify their grading decisions to the director of their school. Their grading decisions, and the students impacted by them, are the focus of investigation by the director, other teachers in the school, and student members of the FEEM in the school. Students contesting their failing grades can request from the school director to retake the exams. Such exams exclude the teachers involved in failing the students and may circumvent their decisions to fail the students entirely.

The emphasis on grade promotion reflects an interest on the part of educational policy planners in late "bloomers." It is a policy which embodies the optimistic view of human nature in classical Marxism, values cooperativeness and mutual help among students, and deemphasizes competition (Allen 1974, p. 52). It is also a principle of educational organization very open to abuse, especially in the absence of independent teachers' professional associations in Cuba which would protect teachers from social pressures to promote students. It becomes easier to measure the percentage of students promoted out of their grades than the quality of their intellect, and in a system which is so highly centralized and bureaucratized, numbers and statistical "proofs" carry the day.

The absence of teachers' professional associations is paired with the predominance of the state bureaucracy and its central planning. In Cuba public education is the only system of formal education available. The national state is the only employer. Workers in the institution of education are grouped by the Cuban state into a syndicate. Their syndicate is not a mechanism of interest politics but is instead part of the socialist state. It has direct representation in and direction from the Central Committee (CC) of the Cuban Communist Party (CCP), as part of its Education, Science, Culture, and Sports directorate.

Educational workers' initiatives to change educational practices must first receive recognition and approval from school directors. Typically, at the pre-university level the director very often must make these decisions with the input and agreement of the CCP member of the staff assigned to represent the CCP in the school and the school' student leaders who are members of the Federation of Middle Level Students. Workers' initiatives that pass this first screening, are then referred to the municipal office of the Ministry of Education, which also must approve the initiative or change it to conform to established policy. If the initiative successfully passes this second screening it is then referred to the Ministry of Education for evaluation. In turn, if it passes this third screening, it is referred by the Ministry to the CC for evaluation and possible approval. Alternatively, the Ministry can advise its Municipal office to present the initiatives to its municipal representatives to the next national congress of educational workers. If the initiative secures the agreement of the municipal representatives to the congress, it is then discussed in the congress and evaluated at the national level. In turn, if the initiative becomes part of the final set of recommendations of the congress, it is then evaluated by the CC and may become official educational policy.

We give this involved explanation of institutional dynamics to show that the closeness of the political and educational institutions of Cuban society and the overwhelming predominance of the former means that only a very narrow range of local-level initiatives to change educational practices ever succeed in becoming policy. These successful claims must "fit" in some fashion within the larger plans of the government before they become policy. Some topics of importance to the teaching profession, such as improvements in teachers' salary, work hours and conditions of work are clearly outside the range of 'appropriate' locally-generated topics of policy discussion. Instead, they may be part of the national development plan devised and executed by the state.

A recent episode illustrates the vulnerabilities of the teaching profession as it tries to maximize both promotion and merit (see coverage in *Granma* January 15, 22, 24, 31; February 1, 5, 26; and March 5, 11, 20, 1985). A 1985-1987 mass campaign to improve educational equality in Cuba generated political pressure on teachers, dramatically decreased grade promotion rates, and was eventually repudiated by the government. In 1985, Mr. Fernández complained about the work of school administrators and called attention to the problem of educational quality and the need to improve teaching methods, testing practices, self-study, and analytical thinking by teachers (*Granma* February 1, 1985, p. 1). In a speech to a Seminar of Higher Education, Mr. Fernández mentioned the need for improvements in disciplinary and educational methods and teachers' skills (*Granma* June 8, 1985). He emphasized "quality teaching," and the value of learning how to teach rather than meeting a numerical goal for the sake of a number, i.e., promoting students to meet a quota (*Granma* September 28, October 3, 8, 1985; *Bohemia* October, 1985). The campaign on teacher quality continued in 1986 (Richmond 1987).

School administrators were urged to visit classes more frequently to detect problems and evaluate teachers (see *Juventud Rebelde* February 19, 25, 1986; *Granma* February 24, 1986, p. 1). Teachers' deficiencies, such as insufficient knowledge of subject matter, preparing simplified study material, reliance on old notes rather than on newer texts, and low standards for promoting students were discussed (*Juventud Rebelde* February 19, 25, 1986; *Granma* February 24, 1986). In April the Ministry of Education announced the creation of a central committee and a special task force attached to the Central Institute for Pedagogical Sciences. Its task was to look at the problem of quality in educational instruction and standards and at the appropriateness of school plans and programs, all in an attempt to improve the skills of teachers and reduce their bureaucratic burdens (*Granma* April 12, 1986, p. 2).

A significant nationwide decline in the rates of grade promotion followed. The decline in the number of students promoted was most pronounced in urban centers, and at the high school and pre-university levels, as reflected in the following promotion percents for the 1984-85 and 1985-86 school years, respectively: primary 96.7 and 95.4; basic secondary 94.9 and 81.4; pre-university 93.3 and 83.1; technical-professional 95.9 and 89.3; teachers' schools 96.7 and 92.7; total, all levels 96.1 and 90.5 (*Granma* August 4, 1986, pp. 1, 3) Some of the most important drops in promotion rates at the basic secondary level occurred in the cities of Havana (65.6 percent promoted), Cienfuegos (77.8 percent), Santiago de Cuba (80), and Villa Clara (80), and in the provinces of Havana (70), Santiago de Cuba (71) and Guantánamo (73).

On July 25 the Ministry of Education reacted to the nationwide decline in grade promotion rates by announcing that it was holding month-long makeup summer school sessions, to be followed by special exams during the last week in August (the special exams have become routine; during the two-semester school year there are two exams and a final exam, and if the final exam is not passed the student must pass a make-up exam to be promoted to the next grade) (*Granma* March 30, April 6, 8, 1987) The special exams were an attempt to improve the grade promotion rates. Mass, professional, party, party-affiliated organizations, and parents, were mobilized to try to ensure that the students who had not passed their exam would attend the special summer school session and study to successfully pass them. The results of this nationwide remedial summer school and special exam effort were not announced. There is only information on one school, the Republica Argentina Democrática Popular; 83 of its students had to take the make-up exam in mathematics, 39 students took it, and 19 passed it. The results in the other exams were equally inauspicious (*Radio Rebelde* August 25, 1986, PM Broadcast). The decline in the rates of grade promotion continued during the 1986-1987 school year. There is information for the City of Havana. During the first semester of the 1986-1987 school year 75 percent of the City of Havana's 96,000 basic secondary students failed the first round of testing, and 39 percent failed the make-up exams. More than 35,000, or about a third of the total student population of the city, had failed one or more courses in the first semester. Of these failing students 15,860 were already repeating the same grade (*Granma* March 30, p. 3, April 6, 1987, p. 4).

This episode was the first collective campaign for the system-wide enforcement of quality standards in the non-university grades. The effort was short-lived. As part of the society-wide rectification campaign begun in 1987 (Díaz-Briquets 1993), the government reverted to the universalist vision of education explicit in its political ideology, denouncing the idea that there was any connection between the toughness of exams and the quality of education. While disclaiming that the new changes were a manifestation of "facilismo" (easy methods), the government lowered, for all educational levels excluding university courses, the minimum passing scores in the exams from 70 (the passing score used since 1962) to 60. It also eliminated the final exams in several academic subjects (*Granma* June 8, 22, 1987).

It is instructive to observe the reactions of the teachers. The 1986 Third Party Congress and 1987 Fifth Congress of the Union of Communist Youth (UJC) repeated the messages of the government's mass campaign about the poor quality of teaching (see *Granma* December 1, 2, 1986; April 4, 6, 1987; Habana Tele-Rebelde December 1, 1986). Teachers participating in the Sixth Congress of the National Syndicate of Workers in Education, Science, and Sports had a different interpretation of the origins of the crisis. The national congress of teachers, held on November 21-22, 1986, convened 451 delegates. During the congress, some of the participants repudiated the accusations that teachers were responsible for the problems besieging the educational system. In a telling response, one of the delegates pointed to the official pressures teachers had felt in years past. He pointed out that,

> the use of easy teaching devices became the reigning method many years ago, and one of its most serious manifestation was promotionism...At the beginning educational policy was incorrectly understood. It was believed that the quality of a teacher's work was demonstrated in the rate of promotion of his students...(and) teachers were demanded to promote more students each year. Teachers did not agree with this and said that it was wrong, but they were not listened to...It was not the teachers who started the race for promotionism (*Granma* November 22, 1986, pp. 1-2; see also *Granma* November 20, 24, 1986).

The educational practices documented so far evidence the promotionist educational practices in Cuba. The foregoing material also documents that these practices had the unintended effect of lowering educational standards in the non university grades.

Perhaps as a way to minimize the negative effects of the lowering of educational standards there has also been a seemingly paradoxical emphasis on educational qualifications and letter grades. Meritocratic achievement is, together with "ideologically-correct" background, the paramount criterion used in Cuba to select those who go on for advanced educational training and who can hope to obtain high-quality education. In fact different educational tracks are used. Marvin Leiner (1981, p. 212) documents the importance of test results for students, their teachers, and their schools. Letter grades are very important for students: "starting especially in grade 5.entrance to the university is determined by scholastic average (Leiner)." Much stress is placed on grades, and only students with the best cumulative grade point average and the appropriate ideological attitude can hope to receive and complete the rigorous university training (e.g., Mickey 1977; Carty 1978). Contrary to what is the case in the lower educational levels, at the highest levels of education grade promotionism is at a minimum. High proportions of university students do not complete their careers. For example, among medical students the dropout rate is close to 50 percent, and in the 1981-82 school year only 48 percent of university students scheduled for completing their university degrees in fact completed them (Carty 1978; Mujal-León 1988, p. 30).

To our knowledge, there has never been an explicit integration of these meritocratic practices into the political ideology of the Cuban state. This is unsurprising, for the traditional meritocratic individualistic policies used in Cuba work against the very essence of socialism. Bowles (1971, p. 498; see also Kahl 1977) identified the implications of meritocratic practices in Cuba. He argued that the establishment of secondary schools for the intellectual elite of the country, begun in the late 1960s, represented the recreation of social inequality in the school and a "sense of hierarchy in the consciousness of the students." Likewise, Paulston (1971a, p. 484) commented that Cuban schools were highly centralized and bureaucratized and pointed to the discrepancy between socialist educational slogans and the presence of bourgeois behaviors in the Ministry of Education and among teachers. He concluded that Cuba had two choices: to "undergo a sweeping radicalization of her educational system or move into a conservative phase."

The hoped-for radicalization did not take place. Years later M. Pastor (1983; see also Carnoy 1981: 10; Richmond 1990), among others, visited elite schools like the Lenin School in Havana, modeled after U.S.S.R. educational criteria and reputedly the best secondary school in the country, and commented on the emphasis on testing and grading of students. These schools epitomize the Soviet hierarchical model of bureaucratic organization that according to Harris (1992) violates socialist principles of bureaucratic organization.

The de facto contradiction between merit and promotion coexists with the centralization of Cuban education and the autonomy of the educational bureaucracy from pressures from parents and students. Paralleling the centralization of the economy and the absence of independent organizations and individual civil rights, the educational system is highly centralized in the Ministry of Education, which sets national educational policy (Berube 1985). Even though parents and students provide a lot of support to school administrators and teachers, they do not have access to the decision-making process, nor can they influence school policy. Parents who are members of school councils cannot criticize the teachers or the instructions they give their children. Mr. Abel Prieto, a high official of the Cuban Ministry of Education, said it most succinctly: parents "cannot tell the teacher that he or she is not doing a good job because it is assumed that the parent knows less about it than the teacher" (Martuza 1981, p. 266). Instead, they can ask the educational inspectors of the Ministry of Education for an inspection of the classrooms.

The rights of the educational bureaucracy are stated in law. The body of laws governing students and the educational system is extensive (*Granma* March 14,

1980; Havana Domestic Service March 14, 1980) and directed to make the institution of education immune to outside pressures. Thus, for example, on March 14, 1980, Cuba's State Council approved a law on student discipline which abolished the right of students to appeal to courts in cases of disciplinary violations. Henceforward, the treatment of disciplinary cases became an entirely internal procedure (Havana Domestic Service March 14, 1980: 42).

People participate in the educational system within the limits and by the rules imposed by the bureaucracy. The government, primarily through its mass organizations, tries very hard to encourage adult continuing education and to train dropouts. Similarly, it provides educational opportunities to military personnel and veterans, and spends considerable resources in increasing the average educational level of the population. In spite of these encouragements, however, at least in two respects the educational institution is a closed system. The concern of parents and the special interests of the local citizenry do not affect tightly centralized educational planning, program, and training. Meetings are held and parents participate, but their involvement is in support of the official vision of education. Moreover, advanced educational training continues to be restricted on the basis of letter grades, other indicators of achievement, and the right ideological identity.

In summary, as is also true for other national educational systems, the very high rates of grade promotion in Cuba are to an important albeit unmeasured extent directly affected by the political climate in which teachers teach, and by the fluctuating pressures on teachers now to pass students, later to improve quality and educational rigor. The inability to maintain high quality standards throughout the educational system strengthens the traditional emphasis on merit and the subsequent uneven application of promotionism in the Cuban educational system.

CONCLUSION

The foregoing analysis shows one general inconsistency worth commenting upon. On the one hand, our tests, limited as they are, nevertheless show that most of the official statistics reported by UNESCO about Cuba are reliable. They give no grounds to challenge the often-repeated claim that the Cuban government has tried very hard to encourage the education of the Cuban people. On the other, however, some official statistics are plainly unreliable and invalid. We have identified these scores and shown the reasons for our incredulity. The puzzle for us is why such systematic errors become part of an otherwise reliable statistical record.

The unreliable statistics can not be explained by assuming that they are the results of accidents, coding mishaps, or other data management problems. Instead, in our opinion they are the result of a generalized tendency to exaggerate real revolutionary achievements to such an implausible extent that in the long term results in the erroneous discredit by outsiders of the entire government effort. This is the paradoxical result of the presence of two distinct and opposed principles of power: rationality and charisma. The first builds the bureaucracy and the programs and practices which produce the achievements; the second, unbounded by principles of logic and human limits, claims the most amazing feats as its own and demand their 'proofs.' Our prediction is that this postulated commingling of rationality and charisma will help social scientists understand the workings of other social institutions in the island.

REFERENCES

Aguirre, B. E. 1984. "The Conventionalization of Collective Behavior in Cuba." *American Journal of Sociology* 90: 541-566.

Allen, Garland E. 1974. "Education in Revolutionary Cuba." *The Education Digest* (October): 51-54.

Badía, Arnhilda, editora. *La Educación en Cuba: Pasado, Presente y Futuro*. Washington, D.C.: The Endowment for Cuban American Studies, Cuban American National Foundation.

Berube, Maurice R. 1985. "Assessing a Revolution." *Commonwealth* 112 (September 6):460-464.

Bowles, Samuel. 1971. "Cuban Education and the Revolutionary Ideology." *Harvard Educational Review* 41 (November): 472-500.

Carnoy, Martin. 1981. "Educational Reform and Economic Development in Cuba: Recent Developments." Unpublished manuscript.

Carty, James W. Jr. 1978. "Communist Ideology Basic to J-Education in Cuba." *Journalism Educator* 33 (3): 4043.

Castro, Fidel. 1992b. "Castro Addresses Teachers Conference 30 May." *FBIS-LAT-92-109*, June 5: 6-18.

Castro, Fidel. 1990b. "Castro Makes Closing Remarks at FEU Meeting." *FBIS-LAT-90-045*, March 7: 3-8.

Díaz-Briquets, Sergio. 1993. "Collision Course: Labor Force and Educational Trends in Cuba." *Cuban Studies* 23.

Epstein, Erwin. 1988. "Cuba." Pp. 262-274, in *World Education Encyclopedia*. New York, New York: Facts on File Publications.

Green, Gil. 1983. *Cuba, the Continuing Revolution*. New York, International Publishers.

Harris, Richard L. 1992. "Bureaucracy Versus Democracy in Contemporary Cuba: An Assessment of Thirty Years of Organizational Development." Pp. 77-96 In Sandor Halebsky and John M. Kirk, editors, *Cuba in Transition: Crisis and Transformation*. Boulder: Westview Press.

Hollander, Paul. 1982. "Research on Marxist Societies: The Relationship Between Theory and Practice." *Annual Review of Sociology* 8: 319-351.

Jiménez, Georgina. 1982. "The Selection, Training of Internationalist Teachers Noted." *Granma* (26 November).

Kahl, Joseph A. 1977. "Cuban Paradox: Stratified Equality." Pp. 241-264, in *Cuban Communism*, edited by Irving L. Horowitz. New Brunswick: Transaction Books.

Leiner, Marvin. 1981. "Two Decades of Educational Change in Cuba." *Journal of Reading* 25(3): 202-214.

Leiner, Marvin. 1982. "Educational Change in Cuba." *The Education Digest* 47 (May): 44-45.

Luxenburg, Norman. 1984. "A Look at Castro's Statistics." *Encounter* 62 (3): 58-62.

Margulis, Lynn and Thomas H. Kunz. 1984. "Glimpses of Biological Research and Education In Cuba." *BioScience* 34 (November):634-35; 638-39.

Martuza, Victor. 1981. "A Conversation with Abel Prieto." *Journal of Reading* 25(3): 261-269.

Mesa Lago, Carmelo. 1969. "Availability and Reliability of Statistics in Socialist Cuba." Part I. *Latin American Research Review* 4:2 (Spring): 53-91.

Mesa Lago, Carmelo. 1979. "Cuban Statistics Revisited" *Cuban Studies/Estudios Cubanos* 9 (2): 14-23.

Mickey, Lois. 1977. "Education in Cuba: An American Report." *Kappa Delta Pi Record* 14 (October): 29.

Mujal-León, Eusebio. 1988. *The Cuban University Under the Revolution*. Washington, D.C.: The Cuban American National Foundation.

Pastor, Manuel, 1983. "Cuba." *Integrated Education* 20 (6): 9-11.

Paulston, Rolland G. 1971a. "Revolutionizing Educational Policy in Cuba." *School and Society* 99 (November): 452-453.

Paulston, Rolland G. 1971b. "Education." Pp. 375-397, in *Revolutionary Change in Cuba*, edited by Carmelo Mesa-Lago. Pittsburgh: University of Pittsburgh Press.

Paulston, Rolland G. 1972. "Cultural Revitalization and Educational Change in Cuba." *Comparative Education Review* 16 (October): 474-485.

Pérez, Lisandro. 1984. "The Political Contexts of Cuban Population Censuses, 1899-1981." *Latin American Research Review* 19:2, pp. 143-161.

Richmond, Mark. 1987. "Educational Change in Postrevolutionary Cuba: A Critical Assessment." *International Journal of Educational Development* 7(3): 191-204.

Richmond, Mark. 1990. "Revolution, Reform and Constant Improvement: 30 Years of Educational Change in Cuba." *Compare* 20(2): 101-113.

Sendón-Oreiro, Olga. 1983. "Problemas del Ausentismo Escolar en el Adolescente/Problems of School Absenteeism in Adolescents." *Boletín de Psicología Cuba* 6(2): 44-54.

COMMENTS ON

"Are Cuba's Educational Statistics Reliable?" by Aguirre and Vichot

Erwin H. Epstein

I like this paper very much and for many reasons, too many to discuss in the time available in this forum. I wish therefore to limit my focus to two of these reasons. First, the paper furnishes the kind of analysis that reduces the opportunities for others with less than scholarly motives to issue wild claims about socioeconomic currents in Cuba. Second, its comparative approach gives us a reasonable standard by which to judge education in that country. In the brief time available, let me quickly go over these points, beginning with how this paper reduces the prospect for egregiously erroneous claims about life and conditions in Cuba.

We all know that it is easy to justify a political argument when data are lacking. Life must go on and policy must be formulated to guide social and economic behavior whether or not pertinent information exists. People must be governed, and in the absence of objective information, policy makers have only their subjective judgment — or coercive powers — with which to justify their actions. Hence, when information is absent, policy makers are prone to resort to some mix of public emotional appeal and naked physical compulsion to gain their objectives.

In countries with very low levels of education and with concomitantly low levels of political sophistication, or where societies have experienced collective trauma due to war, revolution, economic depression, or such, the public will more likely be responsive to emotional appeals bereft of objective substance, and political leaders may find the absence of data convenient in garnering public support. As aggregate educational levels rise, however, purely emotional appeals carry incrementally less influence. When that happens, political leaders are likely to feel compelled to use data—even if manufactured—as a base for their claims. Moreover, those who furnish leaders with such data and those who sympathize with the leaders' political objectives may be more interested in effecting that political agenda than getting the facts straight.

The main point here is that leaders and the researchers who supply them with manufactured data can act with substantial impunity when those data remain inaccessible and unexplored. Aguirre and Vichot discuss the use that Samuel Bowles makes of Cuban Central Board of Planning statistics that show an impossibly low students-per-teacher ratio at the tertiary educational level for 1968-69, but many other examples can be given. Jonathan Kozol, the popular education writer who inspired a strong reformist movement with his book *Death at an Early Age* plays fast and loose with information on Cuban education another book, *Children of the Revolution*. Kozol's book on Cuba is, in fact, a good example of what reporters can get away with when scholars like Aguirre and Vichot are not around to set the parameters of objective information. Let's take a look at what Kozol did.

Children of the Revolution is about Kozol's visits to Cuba in 1976 for 6 weeks and in 1977 "for even fewer weeks." His first visit was absorbed in recording memories of a few individuals who led or otherwise took part in the "Great Campaign" of 1961—the "battle" to eliminate illiteracy—and in touring some schools. The intent of his second visit was "to go to the children, to go into their dorms, into their classroom and . . . into their trust and confidence as well," and to do so unaccompanied by "the experts." Kozol made his visits with little knowledge of Spanish and in the constant company of a government-furnished translator.

Kozol's praise of Cuba's schools is effusive. But even if we grant his claim that the achievements of Cuban education are extraordinary, his report is seriously flawed. It is not simply that he was never without a government functionary to act as his translator—who, if she did not actively distort communication with informants, plausibly had the effect of stifling candor. It is also that his methods incorporated virtually no provision for controlling bias. Much of what he learned about the Great Campaign came from highly placed education officials: his other sources were individuals who were evidently beneficiaries of the program and apparently selected for interview by the government. The schools that Kozol visited during his first tour were chosen "at random"—by the minister of education, no less, in whose company the visit was conducted. Despite the claim of randomness, Kozol makes quite clear that these schools were not ordinary, but "splendid" and "modernistic" models of their kind.

Although the main purpose of his second tour was to observe secondary schools on his own, unimpeded by officials, he failed to conduct his inquiry in a way that would yield an objective picture. Kozol stresses that the schools visited during this tour were those of his own choice. But the sole criterion he used for selection of the school in which he collected his most useful information was his "sentimental fascination" with its **name**—Che Guevara. Besides the obvious importance the government would attach to a school carrying the name of its most illustrious fallen hero, Kozol describes the school as having been "intended to be the first of all the schools *en campo*—a model for the rest." Later we learn that the students are special, having been admitted by examination and evaluated for appropriate "character". As if it were not

enough that the schools Kozol chose to visit could not conceivably be viewed as representative, the students he interviewed were unrepresentative of the children even in those schools. When Kozol wished to converse directly with students, with minimal reliance on his translator (although she remained to assist on "complex" thoughts), he resorted to interviewing students competent in English, who were plausibly (we are not told for certain) chosen by the teacher or principal and quite likely paragons of committed learners and dedicated young socialists.

In the light of Aguirre and Vichot's work, Kozol's book could impress only the most gullible of readers. Clearly, if Kozol's account of Cuba is accurate, we can now see that the result is wholly fortuitous. Indeed, Kozol's clumsy approach casts a shadow of suspicion on what might in fact be real accomplishments. To readers with a knowledge of the nature of Cuban data, *Children of the Revolution* will be seen as fatuous, as orchestrated to a predictable conclusion. Kozol used no sources of information—including documentation—critical of the revolution for balance. When he describes the activities of Cuban revolutionaries, it is entirely in altruistic terms, despite evidence that suggests the ample presence of self-interested motivation. Most important, Kozol fails to consider some potentially profound implications, especially the Orwellian consequences of isolating children from their parents for long periods of time, socially as well as physically, by placing them in country boarding schools and subjecting them to intense politicization. When Kozol lauds the intensity of the children's revolutionary commitment, he fails to acknowledge another picture that he paints—the formation of young minds bereft of spontaneity, a sense of critical judgment, and natural childhood frivolity. Indeed, the submission of will and blind allegiance to Castro displayed by many of these children smacks of cultism.

The kind of analysis done by Aguirre and Vichot is the antidote to Kozol and those like him. It is Aguirre and Vichot's use of comparison that yields a standard by which we can make judgments about data generated by Kozol and others. The authors construct that standard by showing where Cuba fits educationally in the framework of international tendencies. International comparison is an ingenious device to reveal whether Cuban data are "reasonable."

I have nothing but good words to say about this work. Yet there is more that the authors can do using a comparative approach. Comparison, especially when done historically, can plausibly yield important insights in judging Cuban educational accomplishments overall. To make that judgment requires going back to the condition of Cuba just before the revolution. What can comparisons with prerevolutionary data tell us about current conditions? In 1955 the proportion of primary-school-aged children enrolled in school was 51 percent, only 6 percent higher than a half-century earlier when American military forces governed the island, and lower than that claimed by all but three Latin American countries and well under the 64 percent average for Latin America as a

whole. In little more than a decade Castro's government managed to enroll almost 100 percent of 8-year-old children and over 90 percent of all children of primary-school age. And what about efficiency of investments? Aguirre and Vichot discuss bureaucratic disabilities of the current government, but they don't do enough to put those disabilities in their proper context. For example, how do current deficiencies compare to the prerevolutionary period, when Cuba spent nearly one-fifth of the total state expenditure on public education—placing Cuba among the Latin American countries making the largest investment of its resources in schools—but ranked close to last in the proportion of school-age children being educated? In short, Aguirre and Vichot have started us down the right road to having an accurate grasp of Cuban education, but there is much more that needs to be done.

CUBAN CONSTITUTIONALISM AND RIGHTS: AN OVERVIEW OF THE CONSTITUTIONS OF 1901 AND 1940

Rebeca Sánchez-Roig

CONSTITUTIONALISM

Definition

Generally, questions of constitutionalism—ideas, institutions, rights, review and limitations on governmental powers—are addressed in terms of the United States Constitution (the "U.S. Constitution") and the American idea of rights. A constitution serves to protect human rights by establishing the necessary implementation and review procedures. A constitution, fundamental or supreme law, is a written document promulgated by an elected governing body, establishing the structure of the state, fundamental rights, limitations on the scope of governmental powers, and amendment procedures.[1] The term "constitution" can be traced back to ancient Greece and Rome with approximately the same meaning employed today.[2] A constitution is considered the law of the land, and no other dispositions or norms, can contravene the privileges, liberties and rights it guarantees its citizens.[3]

American Constitutionalism

The main focus of the U.S. Constitution and American constitutionalism is in the area of human rights.[4] In the American idea of rights, "[r]ights are not gifts from government."[5] This theory places the fundamental rights of the individual beyond the government's reach.[6] Fundamental rights are protected against legitimate authority and elected representatives of the people, even when these act in good faith and in the public interest.[7] As antecedent to government, fundamental rights are not granted to individuals by a constitution. Rather, a constitution protects fundamental rights from infringement by government.[8]

The structure necessary for protection of fundamental rights is a key element in constitutionalism. In the U.S. Constitution, the most important means provided for protection of human rights is judicial review.[9]

---

1. Leonel-Antonio de la Cuesta, *Constituciones Cubanas.* New York: Ediciones Exilio, 1976, p. 15.

2. De la Cuesta, *Constituciones Cubanas,* p. 15.

3. De la Cuesta, *Constituciones Cubanas,* p. 15.

4. Louis Henkin and Albert J. Rosenthal, *Constitutionalism and Rights: The Influence of the United States Constitution Abroad* (1990), p. 3.

5. Henkin and Rosenthal, *Constitutionalism and Rights.*

6. *American Journal of International Law,* vol. 86 (1992), pp. 192, 194.

7. Henkin and Rosenthal, *Constitutionalism and Rights,* p. 1.

8. Henkin and Rosenthal, *Constitutionalism and Rights,* p. 1.

9. Henkin and Rosenthal, *Constitutionalism and Rights,* p. 1.

The American idea of rights denotes a distinctive relationship between the individual and society.[10] The rights themselves, and the way these are granted, reveal a philosophy of individualism connected to a guarantee of restricted government intervention.[11] This concept of rights is an aspect of a broader political idea.[12] Specifically, the idea of a liberal state and a free economy.[13]

Despite the protection of rights encompassed in the U.S. Constitution, many aspects are not constitutionally recognized or protected in the United States. For example, the U.S. Constitution does not directly, and in many instances, indirectly protect or affect economic, social and/or cultural rights. The U.S. Constitution's silence on social rights (considered traditional rights in most western and non-western societies outside of the U. S.), and its failure to render protection in this area, suggests a marked difference between the American perception of rights and the importance of economic, social and/or cultural rights in Europe and Latin America.

Clearly, cultural, social and economic differences are indicators of the fact that American constitutionalism and its idea of rights, may not be comprehensively adaptable to other countries.[14] While many constitutionally protected American rights have been incorporated into the constitutions of other countries, the scope of the American idea of rights must be tailored to the particular society.[15]

The American idea of rights as fundamental and beyond the government's reach, is achieving recognition in other nations. Scholarly opinions differ, however, on which rights are truly fundamental and the scope thereof. The discrepancy in the variations and perception of rights considered fundamental, is not as noticeable between the United States and Cuba as it is between the United States and other western and non-western countries.

Divergence in attitude as to the breadth and character of fundamental rights, is secondary to the rapidly increasing universal acknowledgment that human rights are fundamental and not gifts from one sector of society to the other. Consequently, human fundamental rights are entitled to constitutional protection through legislative constraints and judicial review.

CUBAN CONSTITUTIONALISM
Generally

Prior to the Constitution of 1940, Cuba was "governed"[16] by eight constitutions and four sets of amendments, reforms, statutes, constitutional laws and dispositions, in its attempt to forge a document amply reflecting the will of the Cuban people and guaranteeing them certain rights and liberties.

Cuban constitutionalism was born with the constitutions of "Joaquín Infante," also known as the Constitution of 1812, and "El Ave María," the Constitution of 1858.[17] Both the Infante and the Ave María constitutions clearly evidenced Spanish, French and North American liberal thoughts and doctrines of the 19th century.[18] Cuba's constitutional history, however, cannot be neatly separated from its turbulent political history.

---

10. *American Journal of International Law*, p. 193.

11. *American Journal of International Law*, p. 193.

12. Henkin and Rosenthal, *Constitutionalism and Rights*, p. 4.

13. Henkin and Rosenthal, *Constitutionalism and Rights*, p. 4.

14. *American Journal of International Law*, p. 194.

15. *American Journal of International Law*, p. 194.

16. It is important to note that all Cuban constitutions promulgated prior to the Constitution of 1940, were born out of the various revolutionary movements advocating Cuba's separation from Spain. De la Cuesta, *Constituciones Cubanas*, p. 13. Despite the Cuban liberators' dauntless attempts at self-governance, constitutions of the Kingdom of Spain, later the Republic of Spain, actually reaped and dictated over the Cuban people until December 10, 1898 when the United States and Spain signed the Treaty of Paris (see below).

17. De la Cuesta, *Constituciones Cubanas*, p. 14.

18. De la Cuesta, *Constituciones Cubanas*, p. 14.

Overview of Cuban Political History

The "War of '68" erupted on October 10, 1868, with Carlos Manuel de Céspedes, an attorney, and his liberation army, proclaiming freedom and liberty for de Céspedes' slaves and the island of Cuba from Spanish rule, at his plantation "La Demajagua."[19] The War of '68 raged on for 10 years with a significant number of casualties to become known as the "Ten Year War."[20] On April 10, 1869, de Céspedes, along with other supporters, assembled a constitutional convention known as the "Asamblea de Guáimaro" which gave birth to the Constitution of Guáimaro.[21] The Constitution of Guáimaro, which called for a republican type of government, precariously governed Cuba until February 8, 1878, when it was dissolved.[22] The Cuban liberators had lost their battle against Spain ending the Ten Year War.

A new struggle against Spain was launched in the early 1890's with the Cuban Revolutionary Party led by José Martí, Máximo Gómez and Antonio Maceo.[23] The War of Independence of 1895, also known as the "War of '95," officially commenced on March 25, 1895 with Martí proclaiming the Party's revolutionary causes in the now famous Montecristi Manifesto.[24] Two constitutions were promulgated during the War of Independence, specifically the Constitution of Jimaguayú[25] and the Constitution of La Yaya.[26]

On February 15, 1898, the United States joined the Cuban struggle against Spain when the warship Maine exploded in Havana harbor. On April 20, 1898, the United States Congress passed a joint resolution proclaiming Cuba's independence from Spain.[27] The United States gave the Spanish an ultimatum "inviting" them to immediately abandon Cuba.[28] Spain, however, refused to peacefully depart the island. Thus, on April 25, 1898, the United States declared war on Spain.[29]

On July 3, 1898, the Hispano-Cuban-American war culminated with the destruction of the Spanish fleet in the port of Santiago de Cuba. The Spanish surrendered on July 16, 1898, and on October 30, 1898, the "Constitution of Santiago"—or of "Leonard Wood"—was implemented.[30] The Constitution of Leonard Wood governed Cuba until December 31, 1898.[31]

On December 10, 1898, the United States and Spain signed the Treaty of Paris, formally terminating the oppressive Spanish rule. Unfortunately, Cuba, and the liberators who had steadfastly battled for its independence, were excluded from representation at the

---

19. Carlos Márquez Sterling and Manuel Márquez Sterling, *Historia de la Isla de Cuba* (1975), p. 90.

20. Márquez Sterling and Márquez Sterling, *Historia de la Isla de Cuba*, pp. 102-114.

21. Márquez Sterling and Márquez Sterling, *Historia de la Isla de Cuba*, pp. 97-100.

22. Márquez Sterling and Márquez Sterling, *Historia de la Isla de Cuba*, pp. 97-101. The Zanjón Pact, signed on February 28, 1878, officially terminated the Ten Year War. Antonio Maceo rebelled against the Pact, briefly continuing his struggle against Spain. Maceo's enduring battle against Spain, gave rise to the promulgation of a new constitution on March 15, 1878, the Constitution of Baraguá. The Constitution of Baraguá is characterized by two prominent features: (a) the document is comprised of only 6 very short articles; and (b) its determinative intent is liberation of Cuba. De la Cuesta, *Constituciones Cubanas*, p. 38.

23. Márquez Sterling and Márquez Sterling, *Historia de la Isla de Cuba*, pp. 120-130.

24. Márquez Sterling and Márquez Sterling, *Historia de la Isla de Cuba*, p. 130.

25. Promulgated on September 16, 1895 and consisted of 24 articles. De la Cuesta, *Constituciones Cubanas*, pp. 42 and 129.

26. Promulgated on October 29, 1897, consisted of 48 articles, and like its predecessors, was named after its place of promulgation. De la Cuesta, *Constituciones Cubanas*, p. 44.

27. De la Cuesta, *Constituciones Cubanas*, p. 44.

28. De la Cuesta, *Constituciones Cubanas*, p. 44.

29. Márquez Sterling and Márquez Sterling, *Historia de la Isla de Cuba*, p. 44.

30. De la Cuesta, *Constituciones Cubanas*, p. 45. The Constitution of Santiago was more of a declaration than a constitution. On this point see also De la Cuesta, *Constituciones Cubanas*, p. 45.

31. De la Cuesta, *Constituciones Cubanas*, p. 45.

signing of the Treaty of Paris.[32] Though now free from Spanish rule, Cuba was once again in the hands of a foreign power, this time, the United States.

The desire to be governed by a document evidencing the will of the people through democratically elected officials, thus, has been demonstrated in Cuba since 1812, only 36 years after promulgation of the U.S. Constitution. Notwithstanding the various constitutions and amendments which governed Cubans between 1812 and 1940, the two fundamental constitutions of Cuba, both modeled after the U.S. Constitution, were the Constitution of 1901 and the Constitution of 1940.

The Constitution of 1901

Cuba's first constitution, labeled as the "constitución individualista" or the individualist constitution, was directly inspired by the U.S. Constitution. This "inspiration" was not necessarily a result of the American occupation of the island at the time of the Constitutional Convention of 1901, but rather a result of the "intelligencia's" captivating fascination with the American document; and because unlike any other constitutional document, the U.S. Constitution has enjoyed the singular privilege of ubiquitous celebrity status in Latin America and Europe.[33]

The Constitution of 1901 consisted of 115 articles, 7 dispositions and was appendixed with the nefarious Platt Amendment.[34] Title IV of the Constitution of 1901 embraced all fundamental rights,[35] the structure for protection thereof, and the mechanism limiting the scope of governmental powers.

Article 32 of Title IV protected private ownership of property. Specifically, Article 32 provided that no one could be deprived of property without competent authority, just cause determined with respect to public need, and indemnification for those whose property had been expropriated.[36]

The Constitution of 1901 established a democratic, presidential and representative form of government.[37] It divided governmental powers into the three traditional branches, to wit, (a) executive, (b) legislative and (c) judicial.[38] Under the Constitution of 1901, the executive powers were identical to those found in the U.S. Constitution.[39] Like the U.S. Constitution, the Constitution of 1901 limited the president's term to four years, and authorized re-election for a second four-year term.[40]

The judiciary was elected by the executive branch based on recommendations from the legislature.[41] Under the Constitution of 1901, Congress was bicameral and the judiciary was comprised of a Supreme Court, provincial courts, and various other lower courts.[42]

Senators served an initial eight-year term, and could seek re-election for another four years; house representatives were elected to serve for a four-year term and could seek reelection for a two-year term.[43] The Constitution of 1901 provided for election of gover-

---

32. Márquez Sterling and Márquez Sterling, *Historia de la Isla de Cuba*, p. 156.

33. De la Cuesta, *Constituciones Cubanas*, p. 48.

34. See Cuban Constitution of 1901, articles 1-115.

35. Cuban Constitution of 1901, title IV, section 1, articles 11-37.

36. Cuban Constitution of 1901, title IV, section 1, article 32.

37. Cuban Constitution of 1901, titles I, V-X.

38. Cuban Constitution of 1901, titles VI-X.

39. Cuban Constitution of 1901, titles VI-X.

40. Cuban Constitution of 1901, title VII, sections 1-2, articles 64-71.

41. Cuban Constitution of 1901, title X, sections 1-3, articles 81-90.

42. Cuban Constitution of 1901, title X, sections 1-3, articles 81-90.

43. Cuban Constitution of 1901, title VI, sections 1-6, articles 44-63.

nors[44] and mayors[45] from all of Cuba's provinces, with each serving four-year terms.[46]

Like the U.S. Constitution, the Constitution of 1901 could not be amended without congressional participation and convening a constitutional assembly to ratify or reject proposed modifications.[47]

The Platt Amendment: The infamous Platt Amendment, imposed on Cuba during William McKinley's presidency,[48] originated as an amendment to a United States budgeting law. The Platt Amendment was introduced by Senator Orville H. Platt of Connecticut and quickly approved by the United States Congress. Immediately after receiving congressional approval, the United States demanded that the Cuban Constitutional Convention of 1901, appendix the Amendment to the Constitution. After a long and onerous battle, the Platt Amendment passed by only one vote.[49] The Platt Amendment provided as follows:

> The President of the United States is hereby authorized to *leave the government in control of the Island of Cuba to its people* so soon as a government shall have been established in said island under a constitution which, either as a part thereof or in an ordinance appended thereto, shall define the future relations of the United States with Cuba, substantially as follows:

> 1. That the Government of Cuba shall never enter into any treaty or other pact with any foreign power or powers which will impair or tend to impair the independence of Cuba, nor in any manner authorize or permit any foreign power or powers to obtain by colonization or for military or naval purposes or otherwise, lodgement in or control over any portion of said island.

> 2. That said government shall not assume or contract any public debt to pay the interest upon which, and to make reasonable sinking fund provision for the ultimate discharge of which the ordinary revenues of the island, after defraying the current expenses of government, shall be inadequate.

> 3. That the Government of Cuba can sense that the United States may exercise the right to intervene for the preservation of Cuban independence, the maintenance of a government adequate for the protection of life, property and individual liberty, and for discharging the obligations with respect to Cuba imposed by the Treaty of Paris on the United States, now to be assumed and undertaken by the Government of Cuba.

> 4. That all acts of the United States and Cuba during its military occupancy thereof, are ratified invalidated and all lawful rights acquired thereunder shall be maintained and protected.

> 5. That the Government of Cuba will execute, and, as far as necessary, extend the plans already devised or other plans to be mutually agreed upon for the sanitation of the cities of the island, to the end that a recurrence of the epidemic and infectious diseases may be prevented, thereby assuring protection to the people and commerce of Cuba, as well as to the commerce of the southern ports of the United States and the people residing therein.

> 6. That the Isle of Pines shall be omitted from the proposed constitutional boundaries of Cuba, the title thereto being left to future adjustment by treaty.

> 7. That to enable the United States to maintain the independence of Cuba, and to protect the people

---

44. Cuban Constitution of 1901, title XI, section 3, articles 99-102.
45. Cuban Constitution of 1901, title XII, section 3, articles 110-113.
46. Cuban Constitution of 1901, title XI, sections 1-3, articles 99-112.
47. Cuban Constitution of 1901, title XIV, articles 115.
48. Márquez Sterling and Márquez Sterling, *Historia de la Isla de Cuba,* p. 161.
49. Márquez Sterling and Márquez Sterling, *Historia de la Isla de Cuba,* p. 161.

thereof, as well as for its defense, the Government of Cuba will sell or lease to the United States lands necessary for coaling, or enable stations at certain specified points, to be agreed upon by the President of the United States.

Thus, commenced 33 years of Cuban protest against, and resentment towards, a document that authorized the United States to intervene in Cuban affairs to protect Cuban national interest and independence, and required the Cuban government to lease certain properties to the United States for military purposes. On March 28, 1934, the United States Senate, at Roosevelt's insistence, abrogated the Platt Amendment.[50]

The Constitution of 1940

The Constitution of 1940, a remarkably progressive document, established some of the most advanced civil rights principles of its time.[51] It guaranteed social, economic, educational and cultural rights and privileges, and facilitated agricultural and industrial development.[52]

The Constitution of 1940 consisted of 19 titles, 286 articles, a transitory and a final disposition.[53] The Constitution of 1940, (a) endorsed the previously established form of government, specifically republican, democratic, representative and centralized; (b) confirmed individual rights and privileges including

private property rights; and (c) substantiated voting as a right, obligation and function of the people.[54]

Under the Constitution of 1940, the separation between the three branches of government remained, but with obvious distinctions. Specifically, (a) Congress' form was changed to one representative in the house to every 35,000 citizens or greater fraction of 17,500, and nine senators per province; (b) the role of the prime minister was introduced;[55] and (c) the executive branch converted to semi-parliamentary form, where half of its ministers could also be congressmen.[56]

The president's role became one of moderator, director and promoter of national solidarity. The president was empowered to freely nominate and remove ministers.[57] A Council of Ministers was created under the president's power which was authorized to: (a) legislate by decree with congressional supervision; and (b) proclaim states of national emergency.[58]

House representatives and senators, elected to four-year terms, comprised the legislative power.[59] Senatorial terms were renewable every four years, while house representative terms were renewable every two years for two-year terms.[60] Despite its progressive character, the Constitution of 1940 proposed inadequate reforms with respect to the form, function and efficiency of provincial and municipal government.[61]

50. Márquez Sterling and Márquez Sterling, *Historia de la Isla de Cuba*, p. 165.

51. See Cuban Constitution of 1940, articles 1-286. The Constitution of 1940 has been called the most progressive constitutional document in the Americas.

52. Márquez Sterling and Márquez Sterling, *Historia de la Isla de Cuba*, pp. 221-222.

53. Cuban Constitution of 1940, titles I-XIX, articles 1-286.

54. Cuban Constitution of 1940. See also De la Cuesta, *Constituciones Cubanas*, p. 59.

55. Cuban Constitution of 1940. It was thought that a prime minister could assist in mediation of governmental disputes and foster national unity.

56. Congress was authorized to interplead the ministers and provoke a crisis situation within the cabinet. De la Cuesta, *Constituciones Cubanas*, p. 59.

57. Cuban Constitution of 1940, title X, sections 1-2, articles 138-146.

58. Cuban Constitution of 1940, title X, sections 1-2, articles 138-146.

59. Cuban Constitution of 1940, title IX, sections 1-6, articles 119-137.

60. Márquez Sterling and Márquez Sterling, *Historia de la Isla de Cuba*, p. 222.

61. Márquez Sterling and Márquez Sterling, *Historia de la Isla de Cuba*, p. 222.

The Constitution of 1940 ratified the power and separation of the judiciary. Specifically, the judicial branch remained autonomous and empowered to nominate judges and magistrates.[62] Like the Constitution of 1901, and the U.S. Constitution, Supreme Court justices were appointed by the president and confirmed by the senate.[63]

In addition, the Constitution of 1940 instituted a Court of Constitutional and Social Guarantees (the "Constitutional Court") under the Supreme Court's jurisdiction.[64] The Constitutional Court was empowered to hear labor and constitutional law matters, and determine remedies for violations thereof.[65]

Under the Constitution of 1940, (a) provincial government was terminated; the provincial counsels, however, endured, but were now comprised of the mayors of various municipalities incorporated into each province; (b) the governor's power to suspend mayors ceased, while the municipalities gained the right to tax locally; (c) public expenses and budgeting at all levels became subject to a ministerial officer under the auspices of a newly created Court of Public Administration; and (d) a Court of Public Works was instituted.[66]

The constitutional amendment clause was very strictly enforced in the Constitution of 1940. Title XIX, article 285 (a)-(b) of the Constitution of 1940, required a constitutional convention to modify the language of the Constitution. Congress, however, was authorized to make minor reforms to the document; *provided, however,* that the following requirements were adhered to: (a) quorum (joint session); (b) two-thirds vote of the total number of legislators; and (c) "doble consideración" or consideration of the proposed amendments at two consecutive legislative sessions.[67] Additionally, the Constitution of 1940 could also be reformed via a referendum clause.[68]

The most notable difference between the Constitution of 1901 and the Constitution of 1940 was the addition of constitutional protection for issues relating to family, culture, property and labor.[69] Without constitutional antecedents and expertise in the area of protection of social rights, the drafters of the Constitution of 1940 sought guidance from Spain's "Constitución de la Segunda República Española" and Germany's "Weimar Constitution."[70]

The Constitution of 1940 was only in effect for 12 years.[71] Its implementation during this short period of time, however, was extremely arduous. Despite its extraordinarily progressive character, the Constitution of 1940 encompassed doctrines that were (a) never totally achieved; (b) at odds with other constitutional doctrines; or (c) never implemented.[72]

---

62. Cuban Constitution of 1940, title XIV, section 1, article 170.

63. Cuban Constitution of 1940, title XIV, section 2, articles 172-181.

64. Cuban Constitution of 1940, title XIV, section 3, articles 182-183. See also De la Cuesta, *Constituciones Cubanas*, p. 59.

65. Cuban Constitution of 1940, title XIV, section 3, articles 182-183.

66. De la Cuesta, *Constituciones Cubanas*, p. 60.

67. Cuban Constitution of 1940, title XIX, article 285.

68. Cuban Constitution of 1940, title XIX, article 285.

69. For example, the Constitution of 1940 provided for collective bargaining agreements negotiated between management and labor specifically providing for (a) unremovability in the workplace after six months and one day of employment, (b) raises, (c) one month's paid vacation annually, (d) 9 paid sick days and 4 paid holidays per year, (e) payment of one and one-half time for overtime work, (f) reinstatement for arbitrary and unjust dismissal of a worker as well as compensation for said dismissal of 55% of the worker's salary, (g) right to strike, and (h) 12-weeks paid maternity leave. See generally, Cuban Constitution of 1940, articles 1-285.

70. De la Cuesta, *Constituciones Cubanas*, p. 60.

71. De la Cuesta, *Constituciones Cubanas*, p. 60.

72. De la Cuesta, *Constituciones Cubanas*, p. 61.

Notwithstanding, the Constitution of 1940 represented an important post-New Deal document.[73] This document, one of the most serious political achievements of the Cuban people, was accomplished as a result of the astonishing collaborative efforts of numerous politicians.[74] Despite the almost enumerated laundry list of constitutional rights ensconced in the Constitution of 1940, the document signaled a veritable endeavor towards social democracy and reform.[75] To implicate controversial legislative ideas in the text of a Constitution, meant, however, that opposition to those measures could lead to discussion, criticism or even denunciation of the Constitution itself.[76]

CONCLUSION

It is difficult to forecast Cuba's constitutional-political future. What is evident, however, is the historical perseverance of the Cuban people to be governed by a system of elected officials under the auspices of a document representing their will. One hundred and seventy two years after implementation of its first constitution, the Cuban nation, once again, desperately seeks its freedom and independence from tyrannical rule. Castro's exodus will not be simple. With his imminent fall, however, the issue of constitutionally protected fundamental rights must be confronted in a new and democratic Cuba. A good beginning embraces reimplementation of the Constitution of 1940.

---

73. Hugh Thomas, *Cuba: The Pursuit of Freedom* (New York: Harper and Row, 1971), p. 719.

74. Thomas, *Cuba: The Pursuit of Freedom*, p. 719.

75. Thomas, *Cuba: The Pursuit of Freedom*, p. 719.

76. Thomas, *Cuba: The Pursuit of Freedom*, p. 720.

CONSTITUTIONAL PROTECTION OF CUBAN PROPERTY RIGHTS

Ignacio E. Sánchez

"The [1940] Constitution is understood to be the basic and supreme law of the land—to define the country's political structure, regulate the functioning of government agencies and determine the boundaries of their activities. It must be *sui generis,* stable, enduring—and to a certain extent inflexible."— Fidel Castro (October 16, 1953)

On January 1, 1959, following the abdication of power by Fulgencio Batista, Fidel Castro entered Havana as the revolutionary leader of the Republic of Cuba. The new year marked the end of the popular uprising against Batista that had begun on March 10, 1952, when Batista executed a military coup d'etat and suspended constitutional guarantees. The declared purpose of Batista's opponents was to restore the 1940 Constitution.[1] This objective became the unifying banner under which Cubans fought and ultimately forced out Batista.

The victory over Batista inspired hope that the Republic of Cuba would once again be governed by a constitution that expressed the will of the people. Unfortunately, history bears witness to the fact that Castro and his ministers betrayed the public trust. Within days of seizing power, Castro began the process of illegally amending the Cuban Constitution. The illegal amendments to the Cuban Constitution were part of a scheme orchestrated by the Castro revolutionary government to illegally confiscate and expropriate assets belonging to Cuban nationals and

foreign companies and individuals. These confiscated properties, worth billions of dollars, ranged from sugar mills and petroleum refineries to small businesses and private residences.

Castro's rule has lasted for more than thirty-five years and one can only speculate as to when his regime will end. Nevertheless, as with the former communist bloc countries of Eastern Europe, Castro's regime will come to an end. On that day, the Cuban people will have to grapple with important constitutional and legal issues arising from the Castro regime's illegal confiscation of private property. The purpose of this paper is to highlight the private property rights guaranteed in the 1940 Constitution and highlight the illegality of the Castro regime's confiscations. The violation of the constitutionally guaranteed private property rights will need to be addressed in a post-Castro Cuba.

HISTORICAL OVERVIEW

The desire to be governed by a Constitution clearly expressing the will of the Cuban people can be traced to the Spanish colonial era. Since as early as 1812, Cubans sought to be governed by a fundamental or supreme law of the land.[2]

From 1812 to the mid 1890's several attempts at independence from Spain and self governance were unsuccessful. In the mid 1890's, José Martí, Máximo Gómez and Antonio Maceo, through the Partido

---

1. International Commission of Jurists, *Cuba and the Rule of Law* (Geneva 1962), p.78.

2. Rebeca Sánchez-Roig, "Cuban Constitutionalism and Rights: An Overview of the Constitutions of 1901 and 1940," in this volume.

Revolucionario Cubano (Cuban Revolutionary Party), began Cuba's ultimate struggle for independence against Spain.[3] In early 1898, the United States entered the conflict between the Cuban revolutionaries and the Spanish government when the U.S. battleship Maine exploded in Havana harbor. By the end of 1898, the conflict was over. On December 10, 1898, the Treaty of Paris was signed between the United States and Spain whereby Spain renounced sovereignty over Cuba. Unfortunately, the Cubans who led the struggle for independence were excluded from participating in negotiations and drafting of the Treaty of Paris. As a result, although Cuba obtained its independence from Spain it was left in the hands of the United States.

As a step towards self-governance, in September of 1900, elections were held in Cuba for delegates to a constitutional convention. The thirty-one delegates to the convention drafted a constitution by February of 1901. This constitution established Cuba as an independent, sovereign state. The constitution, however, contained as an annex the Platt Amendment (named after U.S. Senator Orville H. Platt) which gave the United States the power to intervene in Cuban affairs to preserve Cuba's independence and maintain its government and any other obligation placed on the U. S. under the Treaty of Paris. The constitutional convention agreed to annex the Platt Amendment to the new constitution. The vote, however, was decided by a bare majority of one vote.[4]

Pursuant to the new constitution, the constitutional convention adopted an electoral law for the election of the first president and, thereupon, the convention was dissolved. On December 31, 1901, Tomás Estrada Palma was elected president of the Republic of Cuba. On May 20, 1902, the Republic of Cuba was officially born and governed under a constitution enacted pursuant to the will of the people.

Between 1902 and 1940, political instability fueled by resentment created by the Platt Amendment resulted in uncertain and inconsistent application of the 1901 Constitution. In 1933 Dr. Ramón Grau San Martín, then President of Cuba and an opponent of the Platt Amendment, abrogated the 1901 Constitution and promulgated provisional statutes to govern Cuba while calling for a constitutional convention to be held on April 1, 1934.[5] Political unrest, however, continued and the constitutional convention was not convened until 1939.

In 1939, elections were held for delegates to a constitutional convention that was to put an end to the political unrest and uncertainty with regard to self-governance. The convention was charged with the task of reconciling all of the disparate interests which had led to the instability of the 1920s and 1930s. Toward that end, the constitutional convention was made up of 76 delegates representing 9 political parties (including the Communist party). The convention met and debated for approximately 4 months and on July 8, 1940, the new Constitution was published in the *Gaceta Oficial.*

The period following the enactment of the 1940 Constitution resulted in twelve years of relative stability. During that time, three presidents, Fulgencio Batista (1940-1944), Dr. Ramón Grau San Martín (1944-1948) and Carlos Prío Socarrás (1948-1952) succeeded each other through democratically held elections.

PROPERTY RIGHTS UNDER THE 1940 CONSTITUTION

The right to own and use property, is one of the fundamental or natural rights of free men. It is a right recognized in the Universal Declaration of Human Rights and other international conventions. For example, the American Convention on Human Rights of 1969 states: "No one shall be deprived of his property except upon payment of just compensation, for reasons of public utility or social interest, and in the cases and according to the forms established by law."

---

3. Jaime Suchlicki, *Cuba: From Columbus to Castro*, 3d Ed. Rev. (London: Brassey's 1990), p. 86.

4. Suchlicki, *Cuba: From Columbus to Castro*, p. 82.

5. Suchlicki, *Cuba: From Columbus to Castro*, p. 111.

To secure their property was one of the great ends for which men entered into society. The right to acquire and own property, and to deal with it and use it as the owner chooses, so long as the use harms nobody, is a natural right. It does not owe its origins to constitutions. It existed before then. It is part of a citizen's natural liberty, an expression of his freedom ...

The ancient and established maxims of law ... which protect these fundamental rights in the use, enjoyment and disposal of private property, are but the outgrowth of the long and arduous experience of mankind. They embody a painful, tragic history -- the record of the struggle against tyranny, the overseership of prefects and the overlordship of kings and nobles, when nothing so well bespoke the serfdom of the subject as his incapability to own property. They proclaim the freedom of men from those odious despotisms, their liberty to earn and possess their own, to deal with it, to use it and dispose of it, not at the behest of a master, but in the manner that it benefits free men.[6]

The 1940 Cuban Constitution sought to protect and guarantee the natural right of its citizens to own and use property freely.

The two seminal provisions pertaining to property rights in the 1940 constitution are found in Article 24 and Article 87. Article 24 is found in the section titled "Individual Rights." Within these individuals rights, it states:

Art 24.—Confiscation of property is prohibited. No one can be deprived of his property except by competent judicial authority and for a justified cause of public utility or social interest, and always after payment of the corresponding indemnity in cash, judicially fixed. Non-compliance with these requisites shall determine the right of the person whose property has been expropriated, to be protected by the courts, and if the case calls for it, to have his property restored to him.

The reality of the cause of public utility or social interest, and the need for the expropriation, shall be decided by the courts in case of impugnation.

Significantly, Article 24 establishes an individual's property rights as a fundamental right to be protected under the Constitution. Article 24 prohibits the taking of property without judicial proceedings that establish a justified cause of public utility or social interest. Additionally, adequate payment *in cash* must be made to the person who owned the property. Unless these criteria are complied with, the person whose property is confiscated is permitted access to the court in order to obtain restitution of his property.

Article 87 is found in the section of the Constitution titled "Labor and Property." Article 87 reads:

The Cuban Nation recognizes the existence and legitimacy of private property in its broadest concept as a social function and without other limitations than those which, for reasons of public necessity or social interest, are established by law.

The remaining articles in the property section of the Constitution, Articles 88 through 96, set forth additional property concepts such as the prohibition of "latifundios" (large landholdings), recognition of intellectual property rights, etc.

The prominence of the property rights guarantee provided by the 1940 Constitution is reflected in the articles governing amendment of the Constitution. Articles 285 and 286 set out the process for amendment of the Constitution.

Article 285 sets out the prerequisites for raising an issue with respect to constitutional amendment or revision. Two methods exist: (1) by initiative of the people whereby the corresponding proposition, signed by not less than one hundred thousand voters, is presented to the Congress [see Article 285(a)]; or (2) by initiative of Congress, by means of a corresponding proposition, signed by not less than one-fourth of the members of the colegislative body to which the proponents belong [see Article 285(b)]. If either of these is met, then Article 286 sets forth the manner for consideration of the amendment.

---

6. *Spann v. City of Dallas*, 235 S.W. 513, 515 (Tx. 1921).

Article 286 recognizes that revisions or amendments are of three kinds: 1) specific; 2) partial; or 3) complete. When specific or partial amendment is sought, the approval process for the proposed revision depends upon whether it was brought forward by initiative of the people or whether it was brought on by initiative of the Congress.

In case of initiative by the people, the specific or partial revision must be submitted to a referendum at the next election to be held. If the specific or partial revision is by initiative of Congress, approval may be obtained by a favorable vote of two-thirds of the total members of both the House and Senate, jointly assembled, and the revision cannot become effective until it is ratified in a like manner within the following two regular sessions of the Congress.

In the case of a complete revision of the Constitution, Article 286 calls for an election of delegates to a plebiscitary assembly to address the complete revision of the Constitution. The delegates to the assembly are elected by province (1 delegate for every 50,000 citizens). No sitting congressman is eligible for election as a delegate. Finally, the assembly is required to address the issues at hand within 30 days of the assembly being called to order.

There are four articles of the Constitution which are considered of such magnitude that even if each alone is the subject of revision (which otherwise would classify as a specific or partial amendment) Article 286 of the Constitution calls for the plebiscitary assembly procedure. Two of the four articles of the Constitution which are raised for purposes of amendments to a level as significant as a complete revision of the Constitution are Articles 24 and 87 guaranteeing property rights.[7] Therefore, under the 1940 Constitution amending the property rights sections contained in Articles 24 and 87 required the creation of a quasi-constitutional convention to decide the limited issue of amending those property rights provisions.

THE CONSTITUTIONAL ACT OF 1952

On March 10, 1952, towards the end of Carlos Prio's term as President, Fulgencio Batista executed a military coup d'etat. On April 4, 1952, Batista's government decreed a Constitutional Act which was to govern the country and, in effect, repealed the 1940 Constitution while incorporating most of its terms. At times throughout his tenure, constitutional guarantees were suspended. Batista's coup broke the legal continuity of the political system which was created with the enactment of the 1940 Constitution.[8] As a result, many opposition groups were established, including the 26th of July Movement (named after the Fidel Castro-led assault on the Moncada military barracks in the province of Oriente on July 26, 1953).

Because of the suspension of constitutional guarantees, the restoration of the 1940 Constitution became a unifying factor among the groups which opposed Batista. Although the Constitutional Act of 1952 incorporated verbatim most of the articles of the 1940 Constitution, great dissatisfaction resulted from the fact that under the Constitutional Act of 1952 the Council of Ministers (i.e, the Cabinet), which was appointed by the President, was given the power to amend the Act. Amendment of the Act was possible by merely obtaining a two-thirds quorum vote of the Council of Ministers. This clearly violated Articles 285 and 286 of the Constitution. In his infamous "History Will Absolve Me" recitation, Fidel Castro criticized the Constitutional Act of 1952 by stating:

> Batista's statutes contain an article that has not received much attention but which furnishes the key to the situation and is the one from which we shall derive decisive conclusions. I refer specifically to the modifying clause included in Article 257, which reads: "this constitutional law is open to reform by the Council of Ministers by a two-thirds quorum vote." Here, mockery reached its maximum. Not only did they exercise sovereignty in order to impose upon

---

7. The third article is Article 22, which prescribes the retroactive effect of laws. The fourth article is Article 23, which recognizes the sanctity of private contracts and prohibits their annulment or alteration by the legislature or the executive branch.

8. International Commission of Jurists, *Cuba and the Rule of Law*, p. 78.

the people a Constitution without the people's consent and to install a regime which concentrates all power in its own hands; but also, through Article 257, they assume the most essential attribute of sovereignty -- the power to change the basic and supreme Law of the Land and they have already changed it several times since the tenth of March. Yet, with the greatest gall, they assert in Article II "that sovereignty resides in the will of the people and that the people are the source of all power . . ."

On its face it appears Castro is attacking the usurpation of popular sovereignty. History, however, has shown us that what Castro apparently objected to was the fact that Batista retained this power and not him. Upon seizing power, Castro's regime enacted its own constitutional reforms by also providing its Council of Ministers with the "constituent power."

CASTRO'S CONSTITUTIONAL ABUSES

Following the abdication of power by Batista, Fidel Castro appointed Judge Manuel Urrutia to be the President of Cuba. In a speech to the Cuban people on January 5, 1959, Urrutia recognized it was necessary to "provide for the exercise of the legislative power properly belonging to the Congress of the Republic, in accordance with the 1940 Constitution."[9] As a result, it appeared the 1940 Constitution was once again restored as the supreme law of the land.

This restoration, if there was one, proved to be short-lived. The Cuban Constitution underwent drastic modifications during the early days of the Castro regime.

The first amendment to the 1940 Constitution was published on January 13, 1959. Notwithstanding Castro's prior denouncement of Batista, the Castro regime's very first amendment established the use of "constituent power" by the Council of Ministers. In effect, the Council of Ministers gave itself the right to amend the Constitution in derogation of the requirements set forth in Articles 285 and 286.

Using the constituent power, the Council of Ministers' first amendment also attacked Article 24. The revised article reads as follows:

> Confiscation of property is prohibited. *However, confiscation is authorized in the case of property of natural persons or corporate bodies liable for offenses against the national economy or the public treasury committed during the tyranny which ended on December 31, 1958, as well as in the case of property of the tyrant and his collaborators.* No one can be deprived of his property except by competent judicial authority and for a justified cause of public utility or social interest, and always after payment of the corresponding indemnity in cash, as fixed by a court...[10]

Therefore, within 14 days of taking power, the Castro regime ignored and violated constitutional process and began to chisel at fundamental property rights in the 1940 Constitution. We can now refer to Castro's own words in criticizing the Constitutional Act of 1952 and apply his criticism to him by saying:

> Here mockery reached its maximum. Not only did [the Castro regime] exercise sovereignty in order to impose upon the people a constitution without the people's consent and to install a regime which concentrates all power in its own hands; but also ... they assume the most essential attribute of sovereignty -- the power to change the basic and supreme Law of the Land.

Fundamental property rights once safeguarded under the Constitution were the first to be illegally modified by the Castro regime to punish political foes and to reward friends of the revolution.

CASTRO'S "FUNDAMENTAL LAW"

The property confiscation scheme continued on February 7, 1959, when the 1940 Constitution was repealed and replaced by the Fundamental Law. The new law (like Batista's Constitutional Act of 1952) repeated verbatim most of the articles of the 1940 Constitution.[11] Under the Fundamental Law, the

---

9. International Commission of Jurists, *Cuba and the Rule of Law*, p. 85.

10. International Commission of Jurists, *Cuba and the Rule of Law*, p. 87. In addition, this first amendment authorized the retroactivity of criminal law and introduced the death penalty for political causes.

11. International Commission of Jurists, *Cuba and the Rule of Law*, p. 91.

Council of Ministers (not a popularly elected Congress) officially became the supreme legislative body and under its articles was given authority to amend the Fundamental Law, in whole or in part.[12] The Fundamental Law also carried forward the January 13th amendment to Article 24.

Between February 7, 1959, and August 23, 1961, the Fundamental Law itself was amended sixteen times.[13] Each modification made it increasingly easier for the Castro regime to exercise direct repressive action against broader groups of property owners. The second amendment of the Fundamental Law came through the adoption of the Agrarian Reform Act (ARA) of June 3, 1959.[14]

Under the ARA, large and medium agricultural estates were taken over and converted into state farms. The ARA was challenged before the Court of Constitutional and Social Guarantees on the basis that it violated Articles 24 and 87. The ARA survived "constitutional" scrutiny by the Castro judiciary. The Court of Constitutional and Social Guarantees rejected the argument that Articles 24 and 87 were violated, by finding:

> It is also the doctrine of this Court that such standards regulating the right of property cannot be invoked with regard to property falling under the special system of the agrarian reform, which is subject to special provisions laid down by the ARA which is on equal footing with the Constitution.[15]

The court further held that "the delegates of agrarian development areas may not be denied the power to occupy property affected by the [ARA]; they are not required to apply to the organs of ordinary jurisdiction, nor are there provisions [in the ARA] for prior compensation to the owners."[16] Thus, with one broad pronouncement the Castro regime executed a widespread confiscation plan affecting thousands of acres of privately owned lands, all under the auspices of "agrarian reform."

On November 22, 1959, the Council of Ministers again used the constituent power to amend Article 24. As a result of this amendment, confiscation of property from the following class of persons was permitted:

1. Persons found guilty of offenses defined by law as counter-revolutionary;

2. Persons evading the action of the revolutionary courts by leaving the national territory in any manner whatsoever; and

3. Persons who, having left the national territory, perform conspiratorial acts abroad against the Revolutionary Government.[17]

The second and third provisions were clearly aimed at the ever increasing exile community.

On July 5, 1960, Article 24 was further amended. This amendment substituted the following paragraph for the second part of the original Article 24 text:

> No other natural or juridical person can be deprived of his property except by competent authority and for a cause of public utility or social or national interest. The law shall regulate the procedure for expropriation and shall establish legislation and forms of payment and shall determine the competent authority to declare the case to be of public utility or social or national interest and that expropriation is necessary.[18]

---

12. International Commission of Jurists, *Cuba and the Rule of Law*, p. 93.

13. International Commission of Jurists, *Cuba and the Rule of Law*, p. 98.

14. International Commission of Jurists, *Cuba and the Rule of Law*, p. 98. Citing *Gaceta Oficial*, Special Edition (June 3, 1959).

15. International Commission of Jurists, *Cuba and the Rule of Law*, p. 99, quoting Judgment No. 45 of the Court of Constitutional and Social Guarantees.

16. International Commission of Jurists, *Cuba and the Rule of Law*, p. 99, quoting Judgment No. 45 of the Court of Constitutional and Social Guarantees.

17. International Commission of Jurists, *Cuba and the Rule of Law*, p. 100.

18. International Commission of Jurists, *Cuba and the Rule of Law*, p. 104.

This amendment bears witness to the way in which the Castro regime stripped the right of property of all constitutional protection. Where the original text says "no one can be deprived of his property except by competent *judicial* authority," the amendment merely says "competent authority," which can mean any authority. Also, where the original text says "and always after payment of appropriate compensation in cash," the amendment states that "the law shall regulate the procedure for expropriation and shall establish legislation and forms of payment," which also allows the government to not pay just compensation. Significantly, the amendment adds "national interest" to the causes that may lead to expropriation. Finally, this Amendment deleted the provision of Article 24 that allowed the party whose property was expropriated to appeal to the courts and, if the case justified it, have the property returned.[19]

The Agrarian Reform Act was followed by yet another "reform" labeled the Urban Reform Act. The Urban Reform Act (URA) adversely affected not only the right to property but also the freedom of contract. Article 2 of the URA provides: "Leasing of urban property is prohibited, [and] any contract which implies the use of urban property is also prohibited."[20] This declaration rendered null and void all leases of urban property that existed at the time the URA was decreed. The URA also ordered the compulsory sale of urban houses and apartments. The sales price for such property was fixed by its rental value over a period of from five to twenty years.[21] The URA restricted the free alienability of houses or apartments. In order to sell or transfer a house or apartment, the consent of the Council of Urban Reform was required.

On January 4, 1961, Article 24 was once again rewritten. The category of property subject to confiscation was extended to include "those [cases] deemed necessary by the Government in order to prevent acts of sabotage, terrorism or any other counter-revolutionary activities."[22] This amendment served as the basis for Law No. 989 which caused the confiscation of the real and personal property of Cubans who had left the country for at least one month.

Ultimately, Castro ended the charade by openly proclaiming himself a communist. On February 24, 1976, seventeen years after Castro's revolutionary government came to power, a socialist constitution was proclaimed without the benefit of a freely elected constitutional convention to represent the Cuban people.[23] The new constitution replaced the provisional Fundamental Law of 1959, under which Castro had ruled since suspending the 1940 Constitution in February of 1959. Chapter I, Article 15 of the Castro Constitution defines state property as follows:[24]

> The socialist state property, which is the property of the entire people, becomes irreversibly established over the lands that do not belong to small farmers or to cooperatives formed by the same; over the subsoil, mines, the natural resources and flora and fauna in the marine area over which it has jurisdiction, woods, waters, means of communication; over the sugar mills, factories, chief means of transportation; and over all those enterprises, banks, installations and properties that have been nationalized and expropriated from the imperialists, the landholders and the

---

19. International Commission of Jurists, *Cuba and the Rule of Law*, p. 104.

20. International Commission of Jurists, *Cuba and the Rule of Law*, p. 104. Citing *Gaceta Oficial*, Special Edition No. 23 (October 14, 1960).

21. International Commission of Jurists, *Cuba and the Rule of Law*, p. 104. Citing *Gaceta Oficial*, Special Edition No. 23 (October 14, 1960).

22. International Commission of Jurists, *Cuba and the Rule of Law*, p. 110. Citing *Gaceta Oficial*, Special Edition, No. 1 (January 4, 1961).

23. Albert P. Blaustein and Gisbert H. Flanz, *Constitutions of the Countries of the World: Cuba*, Pamela S. Falk, editor and translator. New York: Oceana Publications, 1993.

24. Blaustein and Flanz, *Constitutions of the Countries of the World: Cuba*, p. 9.

bourgeoisie; as well as over the people's farms, factories, enterprises and economic, social, cultural and sports facilities built, fostered or purchased by the state and those which will be built, fostered or purchased by the state in the future.

This comprehensive declaration of socialist property marked the final blow to the once protected constitutional principle of individual property rights in Cuba. As such, the Castro regime eliminated every legal guarantee for individuals to own property.

CONCLUSION

It is significant that fundamental property rights once safeguarded by the 1940 Constitution were the first to be illegally modified by the Castro regime. Cuba had come full circle. From 1812 to 1901, Cubans had fought to gain independence from Spain. From 1902 to 1933, they fought the Platt Amendment. By enacting the 1940 Constitution, Cubans proclaimed their complete sovereignty and, in doing so, declared fundamental property rights worthy of the greatest degree of protection. The tragic result, however, was that Fidel Castro reestablished a tyranny that immediately subjugated Cubans' rights to own, use and dispose of their property in the manner that befits free men.

Clearly, the issues pertaining to the reprivatization of property will have to be addressed in a democratic Cuba. Resolution of this issue will require a difficult and complex process. Among all of the political and social factors to be considered, it will be important not to lose sight of the constitutional protections afforded fundamental property rights and the subsequent stripping of those fundamental rights.

RIGHTING OLD WRONGS: A SURVEY OF RESTITUTION SCHEMES FOR POSSIBLE APPLICATION TO A DEMOCRATIC CUBA

Nicolás J. Gutiérrez, Jr.

Over the past seven years, the world has witnessed the transformation of a number of communist-controlled countries into democratic regimes. Among the myriad of expectations and questions arising from this trend is the resolution of the status of confiscated private property by the formerly communist governments. By analyzing the treatment of former owners by the newly democratic Central/Eastern European and Latin American governments, Cubans can learn valuable lessons in how to handle this crucial issue, should Cuba follow the lead of its former communist comrades.

THE STATUS OF PRIVATE PROPERTY IN CUBA TODAY

Despite the existence of official corruption, political instability and relative wealth disparities, pre-revolutionary Cuba already ranked at or near the top of all of the Latin American nations in terms of most of the statistical categories indicative of a high standard of living and was continuing to rapidly develop.[1] Beginning shortly after Fidel Castro seized power from President Fulgencio Batista in 1959, the Cuban government has seized an estimated 100 billion dollars worth of assets (in today's dollars) ranging from sugar mills and cattle ranches to small shops and homes

from both Cuban citizens and American investors. Aside from a few cooperative farms and small domestic properties, the overwhelming majority of these confiscated properties remain in the hands of the state to this day.

The U.S. Congress responded by passing the Foreign Assistance Act[2] back in 1961, which provides that, except as may be deemed necessary by the President, any assistance, sugar quota or any other benefit is prohibited from being extended to any government of Cuba, until the President determines that such government has taken significant steps to return the confiscated properties of all of the affected American citizens and corporations, which have certified their claims with the Foreign Claims Settlement Commission (amounting to about 5% of the total confiscations by the communist regime). In addition to the Cuban exiles themselves (who have recently been granted a statutory right-of-action in U.S. federal courts against foreign entities "trafficking" in their confiscated Cuban properties[3]), both American companies seeking to recover confiscated assets, as well as others seeking to invest *de novo* after Castro's fall and the subsequent lifting of the present U.S. embargo, are currently gearing up to set up their operations on

---

1. V. Echerri, "'Gains' of Cuban Revolution Built on Towers of Illusion," *Wall Street Journal* (January 24, 1992), p. A15.

2. 22 U.S.C. § 2370(a)(1) (1990).

3. Cuban Liberty and Democratic Solidarity (LIBERTAD) Act of 1996, 22 U.S.C. 6081, 110 STAT. 815, P.L. 104-114 (Mar. 12, 1996), Title III.

the island in the near future. A still highly speculative market in pre-Castro government securities and defaulted bonds of the old Republic of Cuba has even emerged on Wall Street.[4]

SURVEY OF RESTITUTION SCHEMES
Baltic Republics

Throughout the areas formerly known as the Union of Soviet Socialist Republics, the world's first communist regime, the issue of restitution of private property has only seriously arisen in the Baltic Republics, primarily because of the long period of time that the formerly private property has been held by the state in other regions of the former U.S.S.R. While the Soviet Union was established in 1917, the Baltics were not annexed by it until 1940, when Soviet dictator Josef Stalin launched a military invasion of these three small, independent democracies, pursuant to the notorious Molotov-Ribbentrop Pact signed with Nazi Germany.[5] The passage of 74 years from the Bolshevik Revolution in 1917 to the dissolution of the U.S.S.R. at the end of last year has rendered it extremely difficult to locate the heirs and the corresponding documentation of the former owners of confiscated properties in the non-Baltic republics of the former Soviet Union. Throughout the repressive history of the Soviet Union, and particularly during the Stalinist era, the possession of legal documents purporting to establish ownership of confiscated real or personal property was equivalent to a death warrant in the hands of the communist authorities.[6]

The three Baltic Republics, Lithuania, Estonia and Latvia (none of which opted to join the Commonwealth of Independent States), have each enacted laws providing for the return of nationalized property after over five decades of Soviet rule. Although their individual programs vary, their core principle--that confiscated private property should be returned to its legitimate former owners—is the same in all of the Republics.[7]

This legislation returning property to its former owners in the Baltics is resulting in one of the most sweeping transfers of real estate in history, as heirs re-examine the time period during which Soviet authorities confiscated virtually everything belonging to their parents or grandparents and then either deported them by the hundreds of thousands to gulags in Siberia for forced labor or conscripted them into the expansionist Red Army.[8] This process, however, may create significant short-term economic and political dislocations, as all three Baltic Republics already suffer from severe housing shortages and finding new homes for displaced tenants could take years. Additionally, the conversion of farmland from collective to private cultivation, in some cases under absentee owners, is likely to hamper agricultural productivity in the short run, although it is expected to greatly enhance such productivity in the long run.[9]

The Baltic Republics, whose independence was not fully recognized by Moscow until September 6, 1991, will generally issue government securities to claimants representing an interest in other state assets in cases where nationalized property cannot be returned because it has been de stroyed, lost or irreversibly converted to permanent state use. The expense borne by these new governments is to be quite substantial. In Lithuania, for example, economists estimate that fully 51% of the country's working population, or more than 800,000 individuals, will be eligible for such compensation, as taxpayers must

---

4. P. Falk, "Plan Now for Cuba After Castro," *The Miami Herald* (October 8, 1991), p. 16A; see also A. Chardy and L. Alvarez, "Planning a Post-Castro Bonanza," *The Miami Herald* (September 29, 1991), p. 1A.

5. "The Former Soviet Republics Confront Privatization: A Russian Analysis," *Heritage Foundation Backgrounder*, No. 859 (October 11, 1991), pp. 1-3.

6. "The Former Soviet Republics Confront Privatization: A Russian Analysis," p. 2.

7. M. Hiltzik, "Reclaiming the Past in the Baltics," *Los Angeles Times* (September 16, 1991), p. A1.

8. M. Hiltzik, "Reclaiming the Past in the Baltics."

9. M. Hiltzik, "Reclaiming the Past in the Baltics."

collectively pay for what was confiscated from them individually.[10]

The Baltics' determination to return seized property also stems from their collective preoccupation with what they term "historical continuity," or the notion that present-day Lithuania, Estonia and Latvia should resume their national lives from where they were interrupted by the Soviet takeover of 1940. This concept of honoring pre-Soviet landholdings is driven not only by nationalistic pride, but also because this legal continuity provides the new Baltic governments with stronger claims on national assets, particularly gold bullion, spirited out of the region by the Soviets or still frozen in Western banks since the occupation.[11]

The long Soviet occupation of the Baltics has created a maze of mutually antagonistic rights and obligations, such as the difficult issue of compensating tenants and farmers who moved into nationalized homes or farms in good faith and may have spent their own funds on repairing such homes or cultivating such farmland, which are now being returned to their former owners.[12]

The Lithuanian Parliament adopted its property reclamation law, which is entitled "On the Procedure and Conditions for Restoration of Citizens' Ownership Rights over Real Estate Still in Existence," after several months of debate, although no faction seriously disputed the principle of returning nationalized real estate to its former owners. The new law allows reclaiming owners to raise tenants' rents, but not evict them before alternative living space is found. Housing construction around Vilnius, Lithuania's capital and largest city, dropped by about half over the last two years as the country became preoccupied with its struggle for independence from the Soviet

Union. Eduardas Vilkas, a Lithuanian economist and leading member of its Parliament, estimates that at the current pace of construction, enough adequate housing will be provided for displaced tenants within ten years.[13] The law also limits the amount of farmland that can be reclaimed by any one claimant and requires that such claimant be prepared to farm it or finance its cultivation. Otherwise, the land is placed in a land bank to be redistributed to other claimants.[14]

The property reclamation law's restriction that claims may only be made by current Lithuanian citizens gives rise to an additional caveat to the restitution issue, since many Lithuanian Jews had their property seized by the Nazis and redistributed to non-Jewish Lithuanians, during the period of World War II in which Germany wrested control of the Baltics from the Soviet Union between 1940 and 1944. Most of these Lithuanian Jews have long since emigrated to Israel, the United States or elsewhere and are no longer citizens of Lithuania with valid claims to their former properties.[15] Lithuania recently elected a parliamentary majority of former communists, albeit dramatically moderated ones.

Of the three Baltic countries, Estonia's restitution law is the broadest, applying not only to housing and farmland, but also to securities, machinery and valuables confiscated by the Soviets. These additional categories are generally ignored in the analogous Lithuanian and Latvian statutes, on the grounds of the inherent difficulty in tracing such property and determining its rightful ownership in a cost-effective manner. By contrast, in Lithuania's property reclamation law, the term "property" includes only land, timber and housing, as well as "economic or commercial" buildings.[16] Estonia required all claimants to

10. M. Hiltzik, "Reclaiming the Past in the Baltics."

11. M. Hiltzik, "Reclaiming the Past in the Baltics."

12. M. Hiltzik, "Reclaiming the Past in the Baltics."

13. M. Hiltzik, "Reclaiming the Past in the Baltics."

14. M. Hiltzik, "Reclaiming the Past in the Baltics."

15. Y. Trigor, "Lithuania, the U.S.S.R. and the Jews: Time for Restitution," *The Miami Herald* (September 6, 1991), p. 15A.

16. "Republics and R.S.F.S.R. Pass Foreign Investment Laws," *Soviet Business Law Report*, Vol. 2, No. 3 (July 1991).

file their claims by December 27, 1991, although supporting documentation can be thereafter retroactively added to such claims. In order to establish property ownership, old wills, deeds, mortgages and tax records can be supplemented with witnesses' testimony.[17]

When it is not feasible to return confiscated property to its former Estonian owners, the new government has pledged to issue securities in other state assets to these owners equal to the value of their confiscated property. It is not clear what valuation method is being utilized for these calculations.[18]

The Latvian Parliament has passed a resolution stating that individuals who owned factories, houses and shops in Latvia before June 17, 1940, must be given preference during the ongoing national process of privatization of state property. Former owners or their heirs must either have their property returned or be provided with compensation in the form of securities in other state assets. State property, which remains unclaimed, will be auctioned off to the highest bidder.[19] Municipal authorities in Riga, the capital of Latvia, delayed in auctioning off industrial facilities as part of that country's national privatization program, because of apprehension about selling off factories which may later be claimed by their former owners or the heirs thereof (who had until October 30, 1994 to file such claims). Local authorities estimated that some 16,000 claims were filed.[20] This Latvian legislation also specifically calls for the return of property confiscated from foreigners after the Soviet annexation of 1940.[21]

Bulgaria

Since the Iron Curtain crumbled at the end of 1989, the nations of the former Eastern Bloc have generally evolved into two separate "tiers," distinguished as much by political and economic characteristics as by geography. The "Northern Tier" countries of Poland, the Czech Republic and Slovakia (formerly, the Czech and Slovak Federal Republic and, previously, Czechoslovakia), and Hungary have been able to implement significant legal and economic reforms, thereby attracting the bulk of Western attention and investment. The "Southern Tier" nations of Bulgaria, the former Yugoslav Federation—now consisting of Croatia, Slovenia, Yugoslavia (Serbia and Montenegro), Macedonia and Bosnia-Hercegovina, as independent states—Romania and Albania, however, have struggled with more fundamental issues, such as replacing their former communist leaders with committed democratic reformers and dealing with ideologically/ethnically-inspired violence. As a result, this latter group has acquired a less positive reputation in the West than its northern counterpart.[22]

Nonetheless, Bulgaria, under its new Union of Democratic Forces-led Government, has begun to ascend above the ills plaguing its other Balkan neighbors, in order to join Eastern Europe's "Northern Tier." Bulgaria's bold bid includes the passage of key legal and economic reforms, the adoption of a new constitution, and the recent normalization of trade relations with the United States (a first in the Balkans).[23]

Bulgarian lawmakers have begun to grapple with the key issue of restitution of confiscated private property to its legitimate former owners. In February 1991, the Bulgarian Parliament passed the "Law for Agricultural Land Ownership and Use," with the intent of returning confiscated land to its original owners and their heirs based on the ownership rights created by that country's Agrarian Reform Law of 1946.[24]

---

17. M. Hiltzik, "Reclaiming the Past in the Baltics."

18. "Five Top-Ranked U.S.S.R. Republics for Foreign Investment," *U.S.A. Today* (September 30, 1991), p. 6B.

19. "Defective Conversion," *Ekonomika I Zhizn*, no. 18 (April 29, 1991), p. 2.

20. "Waiting for Former Owners," *Rossiiskaya Gazeta* (January 6, 1992), p. 2.

21. "Latvia to Return Seized Property," *New York Times* (September 5, 1991), p. A16.

22. "Bulgaria Making Strong Bid to Join Region's 'First Tier,'" *BNA International Business Daily* (December 11, 1991), p. 4.

23. "Bulgaria Making Strong Bid to Join Region's 'First Tier.'"

24. "Central Europe: Agriculture in the New Market Economies," *Agricultural Outlook* (December 1991), p. 33.

Land ownership is limited, however, to twenty hectares (49.4 acres) in "intensive" areas of cultivation and thirty hectares (about 74 acres) in hilly or mountainous areas. In order to prevent fragmentation, the land that former owners receive is not necessarily their original holding, but owners are entitled to receive plots which are equivalent in size and quality.[25] The land must be used for agricultural purposes, although an owner may lease the land to a third party under this same condition. The restituted land cannot be sold for three years and foreign ownership is prohibited. As of late September 1991, ten percent of confiscated lands presently either in state hands or set up as cooperative farms had been claimed by their previous owners or their heirs.[26]

The new government is currently in the process of amending this legislation to be even more favorable to the former owners, including an increase in the maximum size of the permitted land holdings following restitution.[27] Elements in the Bulgarian Government, however, are cautioning against an aggressive program of property restitution, particularly in the industrial arena, which they fear will result in lengthy delays in the establishment of clear title to property. These sectors advocate the government issuance of vouchers to all of its citizens, which may be employed to purchase a variety of state assets, as a means of hastening the privatization process in general.[28]

Romania

Despite being saddled with many of the problems afflicting the "Southern Tier" nations, Romania has also initiated serious efforts in the past year to resolve the crucial legal and economic issue of property restitution. Since most of Romania's privately held agricultural land was forcibly collectivized into state or cooperative ownership during the forty-year reign of

Nicolae Ceausescu, after his overthrow the Romanian Parliament enacted legislation in February 1991 seeking to acknowledge the property rights of these former owners.[29]

Based upon an intricate set of guidelines, each former owner-claimant is entitled to be compensated with up to ten hectares (24.7 acres) of land, although certain restrictions apply to the selling, farming foreign ownership and family plot size of such land. Additionally, these former owners may become shareholders in new agricultural joint stock companies replacing the old state farm cooperatives, with unclaimed land being forfeited to the state. This provision induces former landowners to engage in a more individually autonomous version of cooperative farming than under previous communist rule.[30]

At least as far as its agricultural sector and subject to considerable restrictions, Romania has opted to implement a form of restitution to redress the takings perpetrated by the communist regime from private landowners.

Czech Republic and Slovakia

To date, the Czech Republic stands as the Eastern European nation which has been the most generous in redressing communist-era takings by returning confiscated private property to its legitimate former owners. The reforms occurring in this republic may well serve as models for whether property restitution is compatible or inconsistent with efficient economic restructuring.

As its name indicates, Czechoslovakia's post-Iron Curtain successor state, the Czech and Slovak Federal Republic, contained two fairly independent and sometimes antagonistic republics, the Czech Republic and the Slovak Republic. The entire country had a

---

25. "Central Europe: Agriculture in the New Market Economies."

26. "Central Europe: Agriculture in the New Market Economies."

27. "Bulgaria Making Strong Bid to Join Region's 'First Tier.'"

28. "Bulgaria Making Strong Bid to Join Region's 'First Tier.'"

29. C. Steedman, "Recent Developments in Relation to Investment, Privatisation and Economic Restructuring in Romania," *International Business Lawyer*, Vol. 20, No. 1 (January 1992), pp. 21-23.

30. "Central Europe: Agriculture in the New Market Economies."

territorial size comparable to that of Louisiana and a population roughly equivalent to that of Texas (15.6 million inhabitants).[31] Three years ago, these two republics voted to peaceably dissolve their union and currently constitute two separate states (through the so-called "Velvet Divorce").

Prior to World War II, Czechoslovakia was a thriving capitalistic democracy, which had achieved an economic status among the ten most developed industrial nations in the world at that time (a list which did not even include Germany).[32] Czechoslovakia's bloodless "Velvet Revolution," led by imprisoned playwright-turned-President Vaclav Havel in late 1989, was followed by approximately a year of political debate over the nature and pace of economic reform. Actual implementation of the broad range of adopted reform measures, such as price liberalization, limited internal convertibility of Czechoslovakian currency and privatization of state assets did not begin until 1993.

In contrast to East German and Polish communism, which tolerated to a certain extent small, semi-private businesses in the manufacturing and service sectors, the Czechoslovak communists nationalized practically all privately held businesses and set them up as either state enterprises or cooperatives. In fact, the 1960 Czechoslovakian Constitution expressly celebrated this feat as "an astounding victory for socialism."[33]

Contemporary economic thinking in the Czech Republic (and to a lesser degree in Slovakia) is dominated by the Austrian school and monetarism personified by Vaclav Klaus, the influential Federal Minister of Finance, who led a business-oriented group of parliamentarians in designing a speedy transformation to a free market economy. The opposition Civic Forum, a dominant political party in the national legislature, promotes a more Keynesian vision of equitable distribution of income through government intervention.[34]

The First Restitution Act, adopted on October 2, 1990, provides for the return to the original owners or their successors of any property expropriated by the communist state, in accordance with certain laws and decrees adopted in 1955 and 1959.[35] This act covers only a small portion of the private property confiscated by the Czechoslovakian communist regime, consisting mostly of small, individually-owned businesses in the service sector. The First Restitution Act provides for the return of these businesses to their original owners or their successors, with compensation being offered only if physical restitution is not feasible due to the property's destruction, irrevocable alteration or improvement through use.[36] Both citizens and non-citizens were entitled to file claims prior to May 1, 1991 for their confiscated properties, although non-citizens' ability to do so was curtailed by the existence of a relevant bilateral treaty between Czechoslovakia and their domiciliary country.[37] Furthermore, any enterprises or organizations, such as private companies, joint ventures or other entities, which are former owners of the confiscated property must enter into contracts with individual claimants

---

31. R. Sumann, "Investing in Czechoslovakia," *Vanderbilt Journal of Transnational Law* 24 (1991), pp. 369-370.

32. R. Sumann, "Investing in Czechoslovakia," p. 372.

33. V. Pechota, "Privatization and Foreign Investment in Czechoslovakia: The Legal Dimension," *Vanderbilt Journal of Transnational Law* 24 (1991), pp. 305, 308.

34. Pechota, "Privatization and Foreign Investment in Czechoslovakia," p. 307.

35. Pechota, "Privatization and Foreign Investment in Czechoslovakia," pp. 309-310.

36. Pechota, "Privatization and Foreign Investment in Czechoslovakia," p. 310.

37. "Agreement on the Settlement of Certain Outstanding Claims and Financial Issues, United States- Czechoslovakia, Nov. 6, 1981," reprinted in *International Legal Materials* 21 (1982), p. 371; see also "Czechoslovak Claims Settlement Act of 1981," 95 Stat. 1675, Pub. L. No. 97-127 (1981); Pechota, "The 1981 U.S.-Czechoslovak Claims Settlement Agreement: An Epilogue to Postwar Nationalization and Expropriation Disputes," *American Journal of International Law* 76 (1982), p. 639.

in order to prove their titles and consequently recover their assets.[38]

The Second Restitution Act, which was approved on February 21, 1991, allows for the return of or compensation for confiscated property with a total aggregate value in excess of $10.7 billion, which constitutes a transfer of wealth on an historically unprecedented scale.[39] This act authorizes the return of private property nationalized, confiscated or otherwise expropriated during the period from the communist takeover on February 25, 1948 to the end of 1989. Only individuals, however, are entitled to this restitution, with companies and other legal entities specifically excluded.[40] This Act requires that current owners, which are usually state enterprises or municipalities, actually relinquish the appropriate property deeds to the original owners. If a dispute arises, the case is submitted to a court.[41] If property cannot be returned in kind, approximately $750 million will be assigned for cash compensation to the original owners or their heirs, with the balance of such compensation being paid in government-issued bonds. Significantly, only resident citizens of the Czech and Slovak Federal Republic are entitled to benefits under the Second Restitution Act, with Czechoslovaks permanently residing abroad and foreign nationals not qualifying for such restitution.[42] Similarly, this legislation does not apply to property nationalized or confiscated pursuant to any of the various decrees issued between May of 1945 and February of 1948, with certain limited exceptions. Pending future legislative action, this law does not extend either to state-owned agricultural cooperatives or to property confiscated from religious organizations after February 1948.[43]

By law, before a state enterprise is privatized in the Czech and Slovak Federal Republic, the records of the registry of deeds must be examined to determine whether there was a private owner of the business prior to 1948. If one did exist, the privatization action had to be deferred until six months after the effective date of the relevant Restitution Act. Only if no valid claim was filed by a former owner during this time period, was the privatization of the state enterprise allowed to proceed.[44]

In terms of the scope of the restitution programs implemented by the Czech and Slovak Federal Republic, an October 1990 survey by the Czechoslovak State Institute of Public Opinion determined that one out of every four citizens intended to lodge an ownership claim to recover expropriated property. Indeed, an estimated 30% of the country's commercial properties are subject to restitution.[45] Opponents of this restitution legislation claim that it will lead to continuing chaos and delay in the process of national privatization, while courts adjudicate numerous and complicated questions of ownership and valuation. While not unfounded, these concerns have so far been somewhat exaggerated in practice.[46]

Eastern Germany

In late 1989, the East German people staged a series of peaceful, coordinated, mass street demonstrations, which resulted in the destruction of the Berlin Wall, the ouster of their communist rulers, and the evaporation of the artificially created and imposed German Democratic Republic. The result of these events was

---

38. Pechota, "Privatization and Foreign Investment in Czechoslovakia," p. 310.

39. Pechota, *Central & Eastern European Legal Materials* (1990 Ed.).

40. S. Glick and W. Richter, "Legal Framework for Privatization in Czechoslovakia." *International Business Lawyer* (November 1990), pp. 442, 444.

41. Glick and Richter, "Legal Framework for Privatization in Czechoslovakia," p. 444.

42. Pechota, "Privatization and Foreign Investment in Czechoslovakia," p. 311

43. Pechota, "Privatization and Foreign Investment in Czechoslovakia," p. 310.

44. Pechota, "Privatization and Foreign Investment in Czechoslovakia," p. 312.

45. Glick and Richter, "Legal Framework for Privatization in Czechoslovakia," p. 445.

46. Glick and Richter, "Legal Framework for Privatization in Czechoslovakia," p. 445.

the Unification Treaty of August 31, 1991 (Eini-gungsvertrag), which stipulated that as of October 3, 1990 the five states comprising the territory of the former German Democratic Republic would join their western counterparts in the Federal Republic of Germany.[47] The Unification Treaty ended the post-war division imposed on Germany by the victorious Allies as retribution for its Nazi past. The newly reunified Germany is clearly the dominant actor in Europe and, coupled with the recent demise of the Soviet Union, ranks with the United States and Japan as one of the world's economic superpowers. The existence of West Germany's ready-made economic and legal infrastructure, which was in turn transposed to the former German Democratic Republic, facilitates the successful filing of claims for restitution or at least compensation by former owners deprived of their property by the East German communist regime or even by the preceding Third Reich, as a major component of the general privatization plan for eastern Germany.

The Unification Treaty also effectively extended the federal law of the Federal Republic of Germany to the five new states, subject to several significant exceptions contained in the treaty itself.[48] The basis for the statutory guidelines regarding property restitution and compensation claims is the Joint Declaration of the governments of the Federal Republic of Germany and the former German Democratic Republic issued on June 15, 1990, which has been incorporated into the Unification Treaty. Based upon the Joint Declaration, the Unification Treaty provides that the "Law Concerning Regulation of Unre-solved Property Issues" (the "Property Law") and the "Law Relating to Special Investments in the German Democratic Republic" (the "Special Investments Law") became applicable to property claims in eastern Germany.[49]

Unfortunately for some former owners, the Joint Declaration states that confiscations executed on the basis of Soviet occupation law between 1945 and 1949 (including those resulting from the implementation of extensive land reform) are no longer reversible, with the authority to compensate these former owners in any form reserved to the Parliament.[50] The constitutionality of this provision of the Joint Declaration, however, was challenged in the German Constitutional Court (Bundesverfassungsgericht).[51]

According to the Property Law, any property of which a former owner has been deprived by state acts either (i) transferring such property to state ownership (Volkseigentum) (as in the nationalizations carried out by the East German communists); or (ii) transferring ownership to a third party with insufficient or zero compensation to the owner (as in the Nazi-orchestrated redistributions and forced sales of Jewish properties to non-Jews) is to be reconveyed to its former owner or the successors thereof.[52] The Property Law applies to, inter alia, real estate (land and/or buildings), chattels, claims for payment of money, equity interests in companies and ownership in branches of companies having their domicile outside the former German Democratic Republic.[53]

Under the Property Law, German companies and foreign owners are also permitted to file claims for

47. M. Gruson and G. Thoma, "Investments in the Territory of the Former German Democratic Republic," *Fordham International Law Journal* 14 (1990-1991) pp. 540-542.

48. Gruson and Thoma, "Investments in the Territory of the Former German Democratic Republic," p. 542.

49. Gruson and Thoma, "Investments in the Territory of the Former German Democratic Republic," p. 553.

50. K. Brammen, "German Reunification- Privatization of Socialist Property on East Germany's Path to Democracy," *Georgia Journal of International and Comparative Law* 21 (1991), pp. 123-129.

51. N. Doman, "Options for Those Filing Compensation Claims in Germany," *New York Law Journal* (February 11, 1991), p. 1.

52. Doman, "Options for Those Filing Compensation Claims in Germany."

53. Gruson and Thoma, "Investments in the Territory of the Former German Democratic Republic," pp. 555-556; see also "The Compensation and Restitution of Property Confiscated by Communist Governments to Former Owners: The Example of Eastern Europe," *Fundación Sociedad Económica de Amigos del País*, Interim Report 1 (April 8, 1991), pp. 2-4.

restitution and/or compensation. The U.S. Foreign Claims Settlement Commission, the division of the Justice Department responsible for adjudicating private claims against foreign governments, had unsuccessfully attempted since 1981 to retrieve approximately $78 million in cash settlements for 1,900 American citizens and companies who had their properties confiscated by the East German communist regime. That figure was arrived at during a series of hearings before the Commission between 1979 and 1981.[54] The U.S. State Department, however, has been able to recoup lump-sum payments from some other East Bloc nations as compensation for part of what it claims was confiscated from American citizens and companies, including $90 million from Czechoslovakia, $40 million from Poland and $21 million from Hungary.[55]

Former owners may opt to relinquish their claims to reconveyance of their former property and demand compensation instead, if they so decide.[56] The Property Law, however, is silent on the questions of how the compensation will be computed and how the compensation fund to be created will in fact be funded. Proving ownership of title is often complicated by the fact that Germany's title registry (Grundbuch) is riddled with gaps due to documents lost as a result of fires caused by the Allied bombing during World War II and the blacking out of key entries perpetrated by both Nazi and communist revisionists.[57]

In the case of a reconveyance, a former owner may have to pay an adjustment to the state for an increase in the value of his property, which was financed with public funds. Correspondingly, an owner will be compensated for a decrease in the value of his proper-

ty due to its confiscation by the state.[58] In certain cases, former property owners are limited to compensation payments or substitute property and are barred from demanding reconveyance of their own property, such as when a church or non-profit organization has acquired the property in good faith from the state. A lack of good faith is defined as involving some sort of corruption, coercion, deception or undue influence, not as simply having the knowledge that the property was originally owned by someone other than the regime which confiscated it.[59] Similarly, reconveyance of property is excluded if it would not be feasible because the property has been materially altered, dedicated to common use (such as for streets or "complex housing") or inextricably incorporated into a public enterprise.[60] Recent amendments to the Property Law now permit former owners to retain ownership of the fee underlying certain public buildings, which cannot be reconveyed, and then enter into a market-based ground lease with the state.[61]

The most flexible exception to reconveyance at the disposal of the Treuhandanstalt (which was the statutorily-created, Berlin-based public agency entrusted with directing all aspects of the privatization process in the five new federal states), and the one which is the greatest potential obstacle to former owners, is the special investment purpose exception. This somewhat ambiguous exception, which was created by the Special Investments Law, relegates a former owner's claim only to compensation rather than reconveyance, if the subject property is deemed necessary by the government in order to (i) create jobs; (ii) satisfy housing needs; or (iii) develop the infrastructure required for the creation of such jobs and housing.[62]

---

54. R. Sherman, "A Scramble to Retrieve Property," *National Law Journal* (October 15, 1990), pp. 3, 27.

55. Sherman, "A Scramble to Retrieve Property," p. 27.

56. Gruson and Thoma, "Investments in the Territory of the Former German Democratic Republic," p. 556.

57. K. Hafner, "The House We Lived In," *New York Times* (November 10, 1991), p. C32.

58. Gruson and Thoma, "Investments in the Territory of the Former German Democratic Republic," p. 556.

59. Gruson and Thoma, "Investments in the Territory of the Former German Democratic Republic," p. 557.

60. Brammen, "German Reunification," p. 130.

61. Gruson and Thoma, "Investments in the Territory of the Former German Democratic Republic," pp. 1139-1141.

62. K. Herold and S. Taibl, "Trade Law Rewritten in Germany," *National Law Journal* (September 16, 1991), pp. 19-20.

Consequently, the Treuhandanstalt may decide that a former owner's property must remain in government hands or (more likely) be auctioned off to a western German or foreign investor, whose presence is necessary to offset eastern Germany's temporary economic dislocations, such as a relatively high unemployment rate and a lack of adequate housing.[63] The present or prospective owner is required to apply for a certification of a special investment purpose by the Treuhandanstalt, which is subject to review by German courts, and arrangements must then be made to compensate the former owner.[64]

The Treuhandastalt was prohibited from privatizing state property, which is subject to a reconveyance claim by its former owner, if such claim was filed by the filing deadline of October 13, 1990 (there were also certain allowances for late filings). In order to encourage foreign investment by decreasing the liability of new purchasers to reconveyance claims by former owners, the Treuhandanstalt or the present owner (usually either another state enterprise or a foreign investor) are required to investigate the existence of any such claims.[65] Recent amendments to the Special Investment Law have granted further concessions to former owners in obtaining reconveyance of their confiscated properties, notwithstanding state efforts to otherwise privatize such properties.[66]

The Treuhandanstalt sought to set up a somewhat delicate balance between the often competing legal and economic interests of the resolution of reconveyance claims by former owners versus the promotion of speedy privatization efforts in general, by making certain allowances for stepped-up privatization efforts to offset temporary economic dislocations, while still maintaining a relatively high degree of deference to claims by former owners.

Hungary

Even before the Hungarian people were able to oust the reigning communist regime seven years ago and subsequently elect a center-right parliamentary majority, the country enjoyed relatively high levels of Western orientation and economic liberalization by East Bloc standards. This background favors a rapid transition to a free market economy, including the compensation of former owners of property confiscated by a series of totalitarian regimes in Hungary.

On July 11, 1991, the Hungarian Parliament passed the "Law to Provide Partial Compensation for Unjust Damage Caused by the State to the Property of Citizens," which became effective on August 10, 1991.[67] Designed to partially re-establish private property rights in Hungary without delaying the national process of privatization, this legislation does not return confiscated property to its former owners, but does provide for compensation to such owners in the form of interest-bearing certificates that may be used to buy state-owned property, businesses or shares in businesses put up for sale by the State Property Agency or by local governments. These certificates may also be sold or traded to Hungarians and foreigners alike. Former owners have priority, but not exclusive, rights to re-acquire their own properties, either with cash or with their compensation certificates, except in the case of apartments, where current tenants are awarded priority rights.[68]

Passage of the compensation law has been delayed because President Arpad Goncz, after conferring with the Ownership and Privatization Committee affiliated to the Hungarian Government's Economic Cabinet, vetoed a previous version of this statute because of concerns that the proposed compensation for land at higher rates than for other types of prop-

---

63. Herold and Taibl, "Trade Law Rewritten in Germany," p. 20.

64. T. Marshall, "In the Old Bloc, Who Owns What?" *Los Angeles Times* (April 9, 1991), p. A1; see also, "Benefits of Investing Promptly Outlined by Treuhand Official," *BNA International Business Daily* (December 3, 1991).

65. Gruson and Thoma, "Inv[stments in the Territory of the Former German Democratic Rebublic," pp. 1142-1143.

66. Gruson and Thoma, "Investments in the Territory of the Former German Democratic Rebublic," p. 1144.

67. "Property Compensation Law to Take Effect in Hungary," *BNA International Business Daily* (August 9, 1991).

68. "Property Compensation Law to Take Effect in Hungary."

erty would be violative of the Hungarian Constitution. After review by the Constitutional Court, demanded by the opposition party Free Democrats, the measure was revised and enacted.[69]

The final version of the act invalidates 64 laws and decrees permitting the confiscation and nationalization of private property without any compensation from May 1, 1939 to the present. In order to avoid a potentially bitter controversy, however, the act lays down the conditions for actual compensation only for the period from June 8, 1949 (the day the first Hungarian communist regime convened) to the present and only vaguely requires the Parliament to decide how to provide compensation for property confiscated during the tumultuous decade between 1939 and 1949.[70]

The significance of the compensation cut-off dates is heightened because of the ideological and ethnic complexity of Hungary's past confiscations. Between 1938 and 1939, a quasi-fascist government, backed by Nazi Germany, came to power in Hungary and began to enact laws curtailing the property rights of Hungarian Jews, as well as barring them from entering certain professions. Jewish stores, for example, were confiscated and in many cases awarded to Swabian and other ethnic Germans living in Hungary at that time.[71] Next, after the Nazis were driven from Hungary in 1944, many of these ethnic Germans were held collectively accountable for the Nazi occupation and expelled from Hungary. Ethnic Hungarians, in turn, occupied their abandoned shops and offices. Finally, in the late 1940's and early 1950's, virtually all Hungarian property owners had their assets nationalized by the then ruling communist regime.[72]

The dates contained in the compensation act have been hotly debated among ethnic Hungarians, ethnic Germans in Hungary, the surviving Hungarian Jews and even small farmers. The Smallholders, a key member party in the current government's coalition, represents a constituency made up largely of small farmers who obtained land in 1945 under a land reform law and lost it to more hard-line communist-inspired collectivization programs in the 1950's.[73] According to some reliable estimates, 98 million acres, 3,970 small factories and roughly 400,000 dwellings and shops could be covered by the act. Out of these, ethnic Germans estimate that 980,000 acres and about 60,000 homes were seized from them after the World War II, when the ethnic German population in Hungary was about 550,000 people (today it is only about 200,000).[74] Hungary's Jews number only about 80,000, out of a group that was comprised of over half a million persons before the war. An estimated 337,000 properties belonging to Jews exterminated in Nazi concentration camps were turned over to the Hungarian state after World War II (under deeds that showed that the former owners had died of "poisoning"). Much gold and other valuables seized from Jews, in connection with the mass deportations staged by Hungary's Nazi-backed government during World War II, have never been recovered either.[75]

The compensation act provides for compensation of up to 200,000 forints ($2,700) for each small property and compensation not to exceed 5 million forints ($67,500) for each large property. A sliding scale sets the level of partial compensation for values in between: e.g., (i) 50% compensation for values between 201,000 and 300,000 forints ($2,700 - $4,050); (ii) 30% compensation for values between

---

69. "Property Compensation Law to Take Effect in Hungary."

70. "Property Compensation Law to Take Effect in Hungary," p. 774.

71. C. Bohlen, "Hungarians Debate How Far Back to Go to Right Old Wrongs," *New York Times* (April 15, 1991), p. A1.

72. Bohlen, "Hungarians Debate How Far Back to Go to Right Old Wrongs," p. A4.

73. T. Bauer, "Reforming the Planned Economy: The Hungarian Experience," *Privatizing and Marketing Socialism* (January 1990), pp. 103, 106-107.

74. Bauer, "Reforming the Planned Economy: The Hungarian Experience," p. 107.

75. Bohlen, "Hungarians Debate How Far Back to Go to Right Old Wrongs," p. A4.

301,000 and 500,000 forints ($4,050 - $6,700); and (iii) 10% compensation for values between 501,000 and 5,000,000 forints ($6,700 - $67,500).[76]

The value of buildings, apartments, shops, workshops and vacant lots is to be determined according to a sliding scale ranging from 200 - 2,000 forints ($2.70 - $27.00) per square meter. In the case of companies, the number of former employees will determine the value of the compensation. In most cases, former owners can claim only up to 20% of the value of their old commercial properties, which they must purchase either with cash or with their government-issued compensation certificates.[77] Land, however, is to be valued against a fictitious currency, the golden crown, which has traditionally been used to assess the value of land in Hungary. The law stipulates that one golden crown currently is to be valued at 1,000 forints ($13.50). If no such valuation data are available, the average yields of the period between 1982 and 1985 are to be taken as a basis.[78] Hungarian economists first estimated that the cost of compensation, a crucial sticking point on whether this bill would pass, was between 70 and 90 billion forints ($1 - $1.28 billion), but already the estimate has surged to more than 100 billion forints (approximately $1.5 billion).[79]

Hungary has foregone physical restitution to former owners of confiscated property and opted for compensation instead, primarily as a means of trying to prevent the stalling of national privatization efforts (already hampered by the complexity of competing claims by Hungary's various classes of past confiscation victims), without simultaneously being unduly unresponsive to the legitimate claims of former owners.

Poland

Many analysts agree that the initial spark which precipitated the liberation of Central/Eastern Europe and even the Soviet Union occurred in Poland in the early 1980's, as the Solidarity trade union pioneered the concept of organized opposition to communist rule. Since the return of democracy to Poland in 1989, that nation has been attempting to redress the past wrongs perpetrated by its former communist regime, while simultaneously striving to privatize (or more correctly, reprivatize, which is an allusion to its capitalist past prior to communist rule, a past it shares with the other countries of Eastern Europe's "Northern Tier") its economy, rejoin the West and move forward towards the twenty-first century.

Poland's first democratic President, Lech Walesa, and its parliament, the Sejm (which was finally rid of its communist majority), jointly sponsored eagerly awaited reprivatization legislation compensating only those persons or their heirs whose property was taken without legal compensation by the state between 1944 and 1960, but only when this was done in contravention of the laws then in force.[80] Former landowners may still file lawsuits in order to regain land confiscated in accordance with one of the various Polish nationalization decrees, but must do so at their own expense and without any government policies to back them.[81]

Rather than restitution, the government decided that the usual form of compensation would be capital bonds enabling former owners to purchase shares in state enterprises being privatized and guaranteeing them priority in purchasing shares in their own former enterprises.[82] Former owners can only reacquire their property, if they pay the state in cash the market value of real estate or the reproduction value

---

76. "Proposal on Privatization Strategies in Hungary," *MTI Econews* (June 3, 1991).

77. "Proposal on Privatization Strategies in Hungary."

78. "Proposal on Privatization Strategies in Hungary."

79. "Proposal on Privatization Strategies in Hungary."

80. J. Billewicz, "Reprivatization: Government vs. President," *Warsaw Voice* (June 23, 1991).

81. Billewicz, "Reprivatization: Government vs. President."

82. Billewicz, "Reprivatization: Government vs. President."

of other immovable property.[83] In a compromise measure, it was agreed that chemists' shops, forests and estates (as long as outlays on their reconstruction or modernization by the state or state farms were not too large) are to be returned to their former owners. This exception also applies to other property forcibly taken by the state that can be separated from existing state, municipal or cooperative property currently in use.[84] Although the 4.2 million acres of agricultural land redistributed by the communists in their various land reform programs and any land sales made during the first Solidarity-led government of Prime Minister Tadeusz Mazowiecki in 1990 will be honored, some former landowners have been promised 50 to 100 hectares (125-250 acres) each of substitute land, if they agree to live there, cultivate it and finance its cultivation.[85]

This reprivatization statute applies only to individuals of Polish nationality and residence, who can legally prove that they are the former owners or the descendants thereof, of confiscated industrial or agricultural fixed assets in Poland. Poles living abroad are eligible for physical restitution of property or compensation in the form of state bonds, if they adopt Polish citizenship (in cases in which it has been given up) and return to Poland permanently in order to administer the enterprises and/or farm the lands which they regain.[86]

Former owners, who file claims during the one-year filing period terminating in the summer of 1994 (and whose property does not qualify under any of the specific categories guaranteeing physical restitution), will be entitled to compensation in state bonds or vouchers financed by the proceeds of the general reprivatization sales, which began in 1991 and are scheduled to be completed by 1993.[87] The Polish Cabinet is responsible for separately processing the claims of persons whose Warsaw real estate was confiscated pursuant to the communist regime's state administration decree of October 26, 1945, as well as former property owners beyond the Bug River (this former Polish territory was annexed by the Soviet Union after World War II and today is part of Ukraine). Claims concerning war damages and pre-war state bonds are not considered valid and will not be honored.[88] Before reprivatizing any state assets, Polish authorities must prepare a legal analysis investigating the status of the enterprise's assets with regard to any possible claims by former owners subjected to illegal expropriation by the communist regime.[89]

This Polish legislation intends to lure more foreign investment by eliminating the uncertainty generated by the lack of clear title to property and instituting a uniform system of ownership relations.[90] The Polish Privatization Ministry reports that well over 70,000 applications have been filed to reclaim property with an aggregate value of over $1 billion, including 2.4 million acres of land and more than 2,000 factories. In fact, the Privatization Ministry estimates that compensation might eventually cost the state as much as $14 to $23 billion, a sum roughly seven to ten times larger than Poland's 1991 annual budget.[91]

At least 52 private organizations have sprung up in Poland to make the legal and economic case for respecting the private property rights of the scores of thousands of former owners who had their lands, factories and homes seized subsequent to the installation

---

83. C. Banasinski, "Poland," *International Lawyer* (Fall 1991), pp. 771, 773-774.

84. Banasinski, "Poland," p. 774.

85. Banasinski, "Poland," p. 775.

86. "Poland Enacts Reprivatization Initiative to Pay for Communist-Era Losses," *BNA International Finance Daily* (June 18, 1991).

87. "Poland Enacts Reprivatization Initiative to Pay for Communist-Era Losses."

88. "Poland Enacts Reprivatization Initiative to Pay for Communist-Era Losses."

89. Z. Slupinski, "Polish Privatization Law of 1990," *International Business Lawyer* (November 1990), pp. 456-458.

90. Slupinski, "Polish Privatization Law of 1990," p. 458.

91. "Bids to Reclaim Property Increasing," *BNA International Business Daily* (December 3, 1991).

of a communist government in Poland by the Soviet Union in 1944.[92] The communist state took over nearly all industries in Poland following World War II, allowing only a few private businesses to survive in vestigial form as work shops. Jerzy Grohman, heir to Poland's largest pre-war textile factory, is President Walesa's chief advisor on reprivatization issues and has sought to represent the views of the former owners both to the President and Privatization Minister Janusz Lewandowski.[93]

Groups such as the Polish Landowners' Association and the Committee for the Defense of Private Property continue to negotiate with the Privatization Ministry for the return of as many as 150,000 diverse properties to the previous owners, which include brickmaking and other plants, forests, lakes, medieval castles, palaces, mansions, agricultural lands, and state bonds.[94] Al though the current legislation fails to do so, these landowners contest the legality of the various land reform and nationalization acts passed in post-war Poland, especially those passed in 1944, 1946, 1949 and 1958.[95] Some former owners have also even volunteered to actively participate in the management of factory assets once belonging to their families, attempted to restore the traditional logos and names of their family businesses and have demanded that the state at least symbolically recognize their moral right to legally confiscated property.[96]

While the government claims that both restitution and compensation must be limited due to Poland's cash-poor status and need to sell off industries to foreigners in order to bring in revenues, former owners stress that it is in interests of Poland's economy to have former owners managing factories which they: (i) have acquired expertise in running (rather than obtaining vouchers from the government granting

them shares in an industry which they know little about); and (ii) are tied to by tradition and thus will actually invest in for the future (as opposed to spiriting profits out of the country as foreign investors have a tendency to do).[97] The government often responds by asking former owners to write off the balance of their claims as a "patriotic donation" to their cash-strapped nation. Some workers and unions, fearing a return to what they consider to be Poland's inequitable pre-war social order, also claim rights to the state enterprises at which they have toiled for at least 45 years, while demanding job guarantees prior to any restitutions of companies to their former owners.[98]

Although Poland's reprivatization programs do seek to compensate former owners of property confiscated by the communist regime either by restitution in special cases or more typically by partial compensation with capital bonds, the government has placed more emphasis on reprivatizing the state's moribund industries and attracting foreign investment, with an eye towards the concomitant revenues to the struggling state treasury. Poland has recently regressed, after considerable political, economic and social progress, by electing former communists to the presidency and the parliamentary majority, although they now espouse an essentially social democratic philosophy.

Nicaragua

After overthrowing Nicaraguan strongman Anastasio Somoza Debayle on July 19, 1979, the Marxist-Leninist Sandinista National Liberation Front aligned itself with its Soviet and Cuban backers and proceeded to impose a totalitarian system on that Central American nation of roughly three million inhabitants, featuring the confiscation of thousands of

---

92. "Editors' Note," *Warsaw Voice* (January 5, 1992).

93. "Editors' Note."

94. "Editors' Note."

95. "Editors' Note."

96. "Editors' Note."

97. M. Swiecicki, "Against Minister Lewandowski's Mass Privatization Plan," *Gazeta Wyborcza*, No. 184 (August 8, 1991).

98. M. Battiata, "Issue of Seized Property Divides Poles," *Washington Post* (May 5, 1991), p. A35.

factories, farms, mines and homes. Nicaragua's democratic opposition fought an eight-year counter-revolution against the Sandinistas, which culminated in a surprising presidential electoral victory on February 24, 1989 for the Unión Opositora Nacional ("UNO"), a fourteen-party, right-of-center coalition led by Violeta Barrios de Chamorro.

During the month before the president-elect was sworn into office, the Sandinistas initiated what has come to be known as the "piñata" by passing Law Nos. 85 and 86 through the then Sandinista-dominated National Assembly, which deeded to themselves and their supporters approximately 40,000 confiscated homes and 700 acres of land.[99] Last year, UNO, now firmly in control of the National Assembly, passed Law No. 133 seeking to nullify Law Nos. 85 and 86. President Chamorro, however, intimidated by Sandinista-inspired violence in the streets of Managua, Nicaragua's capital and largest city, vetoed Law No. 133 and just recently narrowly avoided having that veto overridden by the required two-thirds vote of the National Assembly.[100] President Chamorro then decreed a compromise requiring the Sandinista occupants of the homes and farms deeded under the "piñata" to pay the market value of those properties to the state, but only if they choose to sell or rent them out.[101]

In an attempt to recover their confiscated properties, over 6,000 former owners have filed petitions with a Nicaraguan government review board assigned to handle their claims. If the board decides that a property was unjustly confiscated, it issues an order awarding such property to the former owner.[102] As of the end of last of year, the Nicaraguan government had either returned to its previous owners, sold or

shut down 86 of the 352 enterprises in state hands when President Chamorro took office in April 1990.[103] Although such an order theoretically represents the last step in the legal process of restitution, many former factory and farm owners have nonetheless been prevented from entering their properties by armed Sandinista union members supported by the national police. Although electoral losers, the Sandinistas demanded that General Humberto Ortega, their own defense minister and brother of unsuccessful Sandinista presidential candidate Daniel Ortega, remain in his office during the Chamorro presidency and that the Sandinistas be given control *de facto* of the national army and police.[104] Given Sandinista control over the armed forces and police, there is no adequate enforcement mechanism to implement Nicaraguan government restitution orders in favor of former owners.

The Nicaraguan Supreme Court's Sandinista majority struck down government decrees awarding hundreds of commercial properties to their former owners. Accordingly, the government re-assumed control of the newly privatized properties and reached a compromise with Sandinista leaders to let some of the previous owners manage the properties, as long as plant workers were collectively issued a 25% interest in each of the affected companies.[105] Under pressure by the Sandinistas, Nicaragua's government has dealt with former owner claimants in a more or less *ad hoc* manner, requiring returning former owners to either grant ownership interests to current workers, guarantee certain job force levels, assume company debts incurred during the period of Sandinista control, pay the government varying amounts of cash or regain one confiscated property at the expense of relinquishing all claims to another.[106] Additionally, certain

---

99. R. Boudreaux, "Whose Factory Is It?," *Los Angeles Times* (December 18, 1991), p. A14.

100. Boudreaux, "Whose Factory Is It?"

101. C. Goldfarb, "Dispossessed Nicaraguans Fight to Recover Businesses," *The Miami Herald*, Dec. 23, 1991, p. 1A, col. 5.

102. Goldfarb, "Dispossessed Nicaraguans Fight to Recover Businesses," p. 11A.

103. Boudreaux, "Whose Factory Is It?," p. 14.

104. Boudreaux, "Whose Factory Is It?," p. 14.

105. S. Christian, "Unrest in Nicaragua as Sugar Harvest Nears," *New York Times* (November 6, 1991), p. A5.

106. Goldfarb, "Dispossessed Nicaraguans Fight to Recover Businesses," p. 11A.

Western governments, such as Finland's, which are ideologically sympathetic to the Sandinistas and provided aid to certain state enterprises during the period of Sandinista rule, have protested to the new Nicaraguan government that returning former owners may benefit from the modernization of plants financed with such aid (much of which, former owners claim, has already been squandered due to Sandinista corruption and ineptness).[107]

Despite the extraction of some concessions from returning former owners in exchange for physical restitution and the lack of state funds with which to compensate other owners, the Nicaraguan government has attempted to implement an enlightened system *de jure* for the legal restoration of private property rights. Nicaragua's experience with restitution is actually the first in Latin America following the demise of a full-fledged communist regime, although in 1973-74 General Pinochet's free market-oriented, military government in Chile sold off assets, which had been previously nationalized by the short-lived Marxist government led by Salvador Allende, at fire sale prices to its former owners. Sandinista control of the Supreme Court, the defense forces, militant labor unions and the infamous "turbas divinas" (violent mobs of sympathizers), how ever, render nearly impossible the enforcement of former owners' restitution orders. Much like in Eastern Europe's "Southern Tier" countries, neither foreign investors nor Nicaraguan exiles (many of whom are former owners and about 150,000 of which now live in South Florida) have ventured back to Nicaragua in great numbers.

The relatively short period of communist control in Nicaragua (a single decade versus four or five decades in Central and Eastern Europe) is certainly advantageous for the return of confiscated property because claims can be brought by the actual former owners, rather than having to rely on claims made by their children or grandchildren as in Central and Eastern Europe (although Nicaraguan exiles have had less time to amass fortunes outside their country to now

invest back home upon their return, as compared to their Central and Eastern European counterparts), and because of the greater availability of documents to prove title of ownership. On the other hand, since the Sandinista revolution has had less time in which to stagnate and lose its ideological fervor than its former role models and benefactors in Central and Eastern Europe, the Sandinistas' continued hostile and obstructionist presence in that country makes the transition to a democracy with a market economy more difficult in Nicaragua than in Europe. The results of this October's electoral contest essentially between former Managua mayor, Arnoldo Alemán of the country's Liberal Party, and slightly recycled Sandinista chieftain, Daniel Ortega, will have a significant impact on Nicaragua's future course, in general, and the resolution of the confiscated property question, in particular.

Summary of Restitution Schemes

Essentially, the governments of formerly communist nations have thus far adopted two basic models of restitution to former owners with regard to their confiscated private property.

The first of these models is based upon actual physical restitution to the former owners of nationalized assets if at all possible, with compensation in cash, bonds or vouchers being reserved as a fall-back measure in special circumstances (which we will refer to as the "Restitution Model"). The Czech Republic has implemented the purest and most well-defined application of the Restitution Model. The Baltic Republics of Lithuania, Estonia and Latvia, although less far along in terms of instituting their own restitution schemes, are also basing these schemes on the Restitution Model. Similarly, in eastern Germany the current system of property restitution is again based on the Restitution Model, albeit with certain significant limitations (which include elements of the second model described below). In Nicaragua, a dangerously divided government has conditionally embraced the Restitution Model at least in theory, but has been largely unable to enforce and implement its corre-

---

107. Goldfarb, "Dispossessed Nicaraguans Fight to Recover Businesses," p. 11A.

sponding decisions and plans in practice. Finally, Bulgaria and Romania, which are still mired in the more embryonic stages of reinstating property rights throughout their respective territories, seem to have adopted, with certain restrictions, significant aspects of the Restitution Model, particularly with regard to agricultural properties.

Generally, the existing applications of the Restitution Model: (i) deal primarily, yet not exclusively, with commercial as opposed to domestic properties; (ii) often impose various conditions on the newly restituted former owners; and (iii) just like the other main competing model mentioned below, is based on a claims deadline and the often difficult process of establishing clear title to the confiscated assets after the passage of many, often turbulent, years (particularly, when there are various competing classes of claimants).

The other major model of re-establishing property rights in formerly communist countries involves varying forms of compensation to former owners, with actual physical restitution reserved only for certain limited cases (which we will refer to as the "Compensation Model"). Both Hungary and Poland have adopted the Compensation Model, each implementing its own distinct variation. While both the Restitution Model and the Compensation Model recognize the property rights of former owners to one extent or another and consequently must grapple with some (although not all) of the same practical problems that arise, the differences are not so much philosophical distinctions as ones of degree and emphasis. For former property owners, however, these differences between the competing schemes can be very substantial, given the new governments' limited compensation funds and the general disposition of most foreign investors to purchase these assets from whomever holds title to them.

APPLICABILITY OF RESTITUTION SCHEMES TO CUBA

In the past several years, Castro has watched while communist regimes in Nicaragua, Central/Eastern Europe, and even in the very cradle of communism, the Soviet Union (his former role models and benefactors), have ceded to democracy and free market capitalism. Consequently, (i) Cuba has lost its geopolitical importance as a Soviet pawn due to the waning of the Cold War; (ii) rationing and shortages have become even more unbearable on the island as its Soviet-bloc subsidies dry up and eventually disappear; (iii) dissident and human rights groups have emerged inside of Cuba; (iv) record numbers of "balseros" (rafters) have fled the island across the shark-infested Florida Straits to freedom in Miami; and (v) diplomats, military officers and entertainment celebrities are defecting in foreign embassies around the world. The formerly less-than-water-tight embargo against Cuba, is now much tighter, due to the: (i) fact that one of its major circumventers, Panamanian dictator Manuel Noriega, was removed by U.S. forces in December 1989; (ii) passage of the Cuban Democracy Act, which prohibits U.S. subsidiaries from trading with Fidel Castro's regime; and (iii) enactment this year of the Cuban Liberty and Democratic Solidarity (LIBERTAD) Act.[108] The Cuban exile community has also intensified its efforts to isolate the Castro regime on all fronts from lobbying U.S., Russian and other government officials to beaming radio news broadcasts into Cuba to training for military raids against the island.

A series of private, exile organizations of the legitimate owners of confiscated Cuban properties have emerged to educate and influence public opinion on the future of private property rights in Cuba, such as the Asociación Nacional de Hacendados de Cuba (sugar mill owners), the Asociación Nacional de Colonos de Cuba (sugar cane growers), the Federación Nacional de Trabajadores Azucareros (sugar industry workers), the Asociación Nacional de Ganaderos de Cuba (cattlemen), the Asociación Nacional de Industriales de Cuba (industrialists), the Asociación de Mineros y Petroleros de Cuba (miners and oilmen), and the Asociación de Bancos de Cuba

---

108. C. Blasier, "Moscow's Retreat from Cuba," *Problems of Communism*, Vol. XL, No. 6 (November-December 1991), pp. 96-99.

(bankers).[109] These organizations support the principle that all existing Cuban state assets, which have been confiscated from individuals and companies that can prove that they are the legitimate owners of such property, should be physically returned by the state to such owners, with compensation being reserved only for cases of dismantled or materially altered property. These groups' emphasis has been on commercial properties, rather than homes, which they believe the legitimate owners have some right to, subject to compensation for improvements paid for by the current occupants and possibly also to their relocation to other adequate housing.[110] They generally favor a restoration of Cuba's 1940 Constitution (still internationally viewed as a model for new Iberian and Latin American democracies), Civil Code and Ley de Coordinación Azucarera (a statute regulating Cuba's paramount sugar industry, which was based on the pegging of profits, rents and wages to the current world market prices for sugar; a three million-ton, preferentially priced U.S. sugar quota; a fixed number of sugar mills; and extensive protection for tenants and industrial/agricultural workers), but modified in order to eliminate some of the more paternalistic and protectionist provisions of these laws.[111] These former owners are firmly opposed, however, to various proposed plans, whereby they would have to bid for, temporarily rent, purchase or merely receive compensation for their (non-materially altered) confiscated assets.

The Cuban-American National Foundation, an influential Cuban exile lobbying group, established a Blue Ribbon Commission on the Economic Reconstruction of Cuba (whose membership includes, among other dignitaries, such prominent U.S. economists as Nobel Prize-winning conservative/libertarian Milton Friedman and renowned supply-sider Arthur Laffer), which initially proposed (although its position now seems to be much closer to that of the legitimate owners) that a massive auction to the highest bidder be held by Cuba's new government of all of its confiscated state assets, with former owners relegated to receiving only long-term, interest-bearing government bonds at 1959 values as compensation and possibly also a right of first refusal to the top bid for their former properties. Such bonds would presumably be financed with the proceeds from the auction.[112] The Foundation once claimed that this approach was necessary to bring badly needed revenues into the new country's treasury, avoid social upheaval and resentment by Cubans on the island against exiles (which can be exploited by Castro to extend his brutal reign), prevent inequities stemming from the return of some materially altered confiscated properties and discriminate against non-property owner victims of the communist dictatorship.[113] Although this approach is intended to attract foreign investment and expedite the reprivatization process in Cuba by avoiding a time-consuming and expensive litigious backlog of claims on Cuba's future court dockets, it has been criticized as an anti-nationalistic selling off of Cuban assets primarily to foreign bidders and some of the wealthier exiles, as well as a repudiation of the rights of all former owners in Cuba, including many American citizens and corporations (most of whom filed claims between 1962 and 1972 with the Foreign Claims Settlement Commission established by the U.S. Department of Justice for this specific purpose) and other foreigners.[114]

Former property owners favor an auction of state assets only for unclaimed state properties, property created by the communist regime (such as the national fishing fleet and certain defense, intelligence, and energy production facilities), and for those hotels, tour-

---

109. "Claim Staked to Cuban Properties," *The Miami Herald*, (October 19, 1991), p. B2; see also, A. Remos, "Three Sectors of Cuban Sugar Industry in Exile Proclaim their Unity," *Diario las Américas* (October 10, 1990), p. 11-A.

110. E. Díaz, G. Escagedo, and R. Sardiña, "For the Respect of Private Property," *El Nuevo Herald* (October 18, 1991), p. 9A.

111. Díaz, Escagedo, and Sardiña, "For the Respect of Private Property."

112. J. Tamayo, "Divining Cuba's Future," *The Miami Herald* (September 29, 1991), p. 1C.

113. Tamayo, "Divining Cuba's Future," p. 6C.

114. L. Esquiroz, "Cuba's Claims: Property Rights and Justice," *International Business Chronicle* (November 25, 1990), p. 1.

ist resorts and other new properties constructed by the Spanish, Mexican, Venezuelan and other investors collaborating with the Castro regime through the formation of joint ventures with a 51% controlling interest issued to the communist state (and from which Cuban citizens are strictly barred).[115] Groups of former owners have also warned the respective consulates of these foreign investors that sugar mills, lands and other confiscated properties recently leased to them or their citizens to operate by the Castro regime, in its desperation to acquire hard currency reserves and boost sagging production, will likely be subject to claims for restitution by their former owners in a future, post-communist Cuba.[116]

The few remaining proponents of the auction approach cite the importance of establishing a more equitable new system of property rights in Cuba, with workers being given a stake in the newly privatized industries, and claim it would be unfair to compensate former property owners yet not similarly reward political prisoners and other ideological dissidents who suffered in different ways at the hands of the repressive communist regime, either through incarceration, torture, beatings, denial of daily living privileges, exile or even executions.[117] Critics counter that compensation to political prisoners and restitution to former owners do not have to be mutually exclusive concerns and point to the examples of Germany (where Jewish victims of the Holocaust throughout the world were compensated for both property and non-property-related offenses perpetrated by the Nazis) and Hungary (where former property owners are receiving compensation in lieu of restitution, alongside of about 15,000 survivors of "malenki rabot," the Russian term for the mass deportation to Siberian gulags by the Soviets of Hungarians and ethnic Germans at the end of World War II - who became eligible for cash supplements to their pensions in 1989).[118]

Although many of the same issues arise as in Central/Eastern Europe and Nicaragua concerning the superficially competing interests of legal property restitution and rapid privatization (such as investor confidence and short-term economic dislocations of workers), Cuba's situation is somewhat more favorable to former owners than that of some of its Central and Eastern European counterparts because there is essentially only one class of confiscation victims (not several mutually antagonistic ideological/ethnic waves of claimants), and because of the existence of nearly two million relatively wealthy Cuban exiles concentrated only ninety miles away in South Florida and closely monitoring the situation in Cuba, a resource not readily available to the Central and Eastern European nations to the same degree (with the notable exception of Germany).

---

115. Esquiroz, "Cuba's Claims: Property Rights and Justice."

116. Díaz, Escagedo and Sardiña, "For the Respect of Private Property."

117. Tamayo, "Divining Cuba's Future."

118. Bohlen, "Hungarians Debate How Far Back to Go to Right Old Wrongs," p. A4.

FORESTRY POLICIES OF CUBA'S SOCIALIST GOVERNMENT: AN APPRAISAL

Sergio Díaz-Briquets[1]

Upon assuming power in 1959, Fidel Castro's revolutionary government began to implement an aggressive national reforestation program. In large measure this program responded to a grave national concern given the country's deforestation trend, but also dovetailed with populist policy objectives to improve rural socioeconomic and employment prospects, particularly in mountainous regions, as well as with national development priorities outlined by Castro as early as 1953 (Castro 1972, p. 190). In the short term, reforestation programs offered a viable, relatively low-cost, option to generate employment among those segments of the rural population that had harbored the revolutionaries during the armed struggle (e.g., the peasantry in the mountainous areas of Eastern Cuba).

The reforestation strategy adopted by Castro's government had been banded about in Cuba for years, with selected elements of the strategy beginning to be implemented in the early- to mid-1950s. Several technical foreign missions sent to Cuba had advocated such an approach to arrest centuries of abuse of the country's natural resource base, begin to reverse serious erosion problems, and curtail the country's extreme dependency on lumber imports (Foreign Policy Association 1935; The World Bank 1951; FAO as cited by Reed 1992, p. 37).

From the time of discovery to 1959, the total amount of land area forested in Cuba had declined from 72 percent (Marrero 1950, pp.107 and 195; Bucek 1986, p. 15) to 14 percent (COMARNA 1992, p. 1992, p. 30). As a result of the reforestation program initiated in 1959, by 1992, according to official estimates, the amount of land area forested had increased to 18.2 percent of the national territory.[2] This 30 percent increase was achieved partly through better management of timber harvesting rates but principally through reforestation (Westoby, 1989, p. 132). Of the total area forested in 1992, natural forests accounted for 84 percent, or two million hectares. Two-thirds (67.6 percent) of national forests were set aside as protected areas, while one-third (32.4 percent) was used for timber production. Between 1959 and 1992, the net annual addition in forested land area approached 14,000 hectares

These gains, particularly considering the experience of other Caribbean and Central American countries, are commendable, Cuba being the only country in the region that reversed secular deforestation trends. In eight Caribbean and Central American countries studied by the World Bank, the forest cover declined

---

1. The comments of Jorge Pérez-López and René Costales on an earlier draft of this paper are gratefully acknowledged.

2. The *Anuario Estadístico de Cuba 1989* (Comité Estatal 1990, Table VIII.4, p. 185), however, shows data suggesting that in 1989, 23.7 percent of the national territory was forested (*forestal*, in Spanish). This figure appears to include small tree stands as well as dispersed trees both within state-owned and in privately held small farms, but excludes fruit tree plantations, including coffee, cacao, citrus, and other fruit trees (see Table VIII.6, p. 186).

between 10 and 24 percent in the period 1981 to 1990 (Current, Lutz, and Scherr 1995, p. 152). However, in only two of these countries—El Salvador (6.2 percent) and Haiti (1.3 percent)—were forests less prevalent than in Cuba. By comparison, Costa Rica (28.8 percent), the Dominican Republic (22.5 percent), Guatemala (39.3 percent), Honduras (41.2 percent), Nicaragua (50.8 percent), and Panama (41.1 percent) had much higher forest covers.

REFORESTATION FRAMEWORK

Although the overall reforestation trend in Cuba since 1959 has been broadly documented, no systematic attempt has been made to evaluate the relative success or difficulties associated with the implementation of the reforestation policies. In doing so, I rely on a broad definition of forestry that includes initiatives to preserve natural forests and restore formerly forested areas, inclusive of national parks, nature preserves, and tree plantations (for commercial purposes). My forestry paradigm also includes agroforestry practices and selected environmental issues related to mangrove areas.

Impetus for the new government's forestry program was provided by the *Ley de Repoblación Forestal* (Reforestation Law) of April 10, 1959. Article 10 created nine new national parks (in addition to the Sierra Cristal National Park), namely Cuchillas de Toa, Gran Piedra, Sierra Maestra, Escambray, Laguna del Tesoro, Los Organos, Guanacahabibes, Ciénaga de Lanier, and Sierra de Cubitas (Núñez Jiménez 1972, pp. 356-357; see also Ministerio de Ciencia 1995, pp. 36-40). The Law specified that the national parks individually should not have an extension of less than 500 *caballerías* (6,700 hectares). With domestic tourism in mind, the parks were to be made accessible to the public and be provided with hotel accommodations, including utilities.

The localization of these national parks was in part dictated by the distribution of remaining forests, which in itself was a function of state land holding patterns prior to 1959. In pre-revolutionary days, the Cuban state claimed ownership to 37,000 *caballerías* (or 495,800 hectares) of forests, 42 percent of which where located in the Easternmost province of Oriente. In 1930, in the Sierra Cristal National Park, in

the Baracoa region, a 2,000-*caballería* (or 26,800 hectares) forest preserve had been established to protect the local flora and fauna, prohibiting hunting and logging (Marrero 1950, p. 309).

Municipal forestry parks were also called for by the 1959 reforestation law. These were to be created with support from the national forestry authorities. Antonio Núñez Jiménez, an influential voice in the conceptualization of the revolutionary government's forestry and ecological initiatives, revived the notion of replanting forests along the banks of the country's major rivers (to a depth of 100 meters), the focus of legislation enacted in 1923 (Foreign Policy Association 1935, p. 466). Núñez Jiménez went further and proposed the development of a "Gran Barrera Forestal" (Great Forestry Barrier)—presumably running all along the spine of the island—to retain humidity, preserve water resources, address the problem of erosion, and moderate the country's climate. Grandiose as it was, his proposal was sensitive to geographic and economic regional variations, and was premised on the use of approaches consistent with local circumstances (Núñez Jiménez 1972, pp. 358-359). The barrier was to consist of rapidly growing tree species (e.g., eucalyptus, teaks), combined with other species, including fruit trees.

By 1991, according to Santana (1991, p. 13):

> The Cuban National System of Protected Areas ... [had] over 200 protected areas that cover 12 percent of the country. However, only 1-2 percent of the country is strictly protected and some reserves appear to be too small to effectively preserve the biota they contain. It is estimated that Cuba has about two million hectares of forests, of which 1.7 million hectares (85 percent) consist of natural forests and the remainder of forestry plantations. Of these forested lands, national parks cover 5.1 percent, wildlife conservation areas 24.3 percent, water-shed protection areas 17.0 percent, coastal protection areas 19.2 percent, production forests 32.7 percent, and other categories 2.7 percent.

ACCOMPLISHMENTS AND PROBLEMS OF THE REFORESTATION PROGRAM

The post-1959 reforestation efforts were initiated in 1960 under the direction of the Instituto Nacional de Desarrollo y Aprovechamiento Forestal (National Institute for Forestry Development and Use, IN-DAF). Between 1960 and 1966, as part of the *Plan de Repoblación Forestal,* 299 tree nurseries were established, and 348 million trees planted (Núñez Jiménez 1972, pp. 355-357). About one third of the trees planted were eucalyptus (122 million), followed by pines (68 million), casuarinas (48 million), and other species (109 million). Seedlings produced in fruit tree nurseries established in the country's (then) six provinces were used to plant 1.6 million fruit trees between 1964 and 1965.

Table 1 presents data on number of trees planted between 1960 and 1989 in the state sector's tree plantations.[3] In the late 1970s, the number of trees planted each year was roughly twice the number planted in 1960. Annual tree planting totals increased rapidly during the 1980s, exceeding over 100 million annually after 1982. Three times as many trees were planted in 1989 as in 1979.

Between 1960 and 1990, as a result of the revolutionary government's reforestation program, 2.5 billion trees were planted in Cuba. By the late 1980s, COMARNA (1992, p. 30) claims that for every hectare of forest harvested, 16.9 hectares of trees were being planted (or 110,000 hectares replanted annually vis-a-vis 6,500 hectares harvested annually) (Reed 1992, p. 38). This pattern is in marked contrast with that observed by the mentioned World Bank study of eight Caribbean and Central American nations, where, on an annualized basis, deforestation exceeded reforestation in all eight (Current, Lutz, and Scherr 1995, p. 152).[4]

A number of observers have voiced special concern about the difficulties of reclaiming the open-pit nickel mining areas found in Eastern Cuba. Open pit mining completely removes the topsoil, thus leaving behind a "lunar landscape," denuded of vegetation (Reed 1993, p. 32). By the late 1980s, after four decades of mining operations, 200 square kilometers of land (or 20,000 hectares) in the Moa-Nicaro area were totally degraded (Bucek 1986, p. 15). Reed (1993. p. 38), using a much lower estimate of amount of land degraded by open-pit mining, claims that by the early 1990s some 3,000 of 11,000 degraded hectares had been reclaimed.

Note that the species distribution of trees planted changed appreciably over the years (see Tables 1 and 2), indicating an improvement in forestry policies. Whereas in 1960 (see Table 1), 92 percent (or 85 percent according to the data in Table 2) of all trees planted were eucalyptus (35 percent between 1960 and 1966), by 1989 eucalyptus accounted for only 3 percent of all seedlings. As Cuba's cadre of professional foresters was trained and experience about Cuba's natural conditions gained, more informed decisions appear to have been made about which species of trees to plant and where. By the early 1990s, Cuba had more than 1,000 forestry engineers and biologists, as well as close to 2,000 forestry technicians (Atienza Ambou et. al. 1992, p. 6).

The early emphasis on planting eucalyptus trees was probably guided by ignorance and the Castro's government tendency to make rushed and wasteful economic decisions, a characteristic not only found in forestry. In support of this interpretation, Westoby (1989, p. 132) notes that "much of the early [reforestation] effort was wasted as the result of elementary errors: seed of poor provenance, species ill-adapted to sites, over-emphasis on the number of trees planted and neglect of subsequent tending." The focus on eucalyptus at the beginning of the reforestation program may have been dictated by the belief that reforestation with this rapidly-growing species would help arrest soil erosion, a widespread problem that was assigned the highest priority (Núñez Jiménez 1968). As noted by FAO (Poore and Fries 1985, pp. 21)

---

3. We assume that these figures are inclusive of all trees planted, including those located in eroded areas as well as in national parks and forests preserves.

4. In Chile, however, where forestry is a vibrant export industry, more than 110,000 hectares are reforested each year, with about 40,000 hectares being felled annually (Prado 1996, p. 8).

Table 1. Reforestation: Number of Trees Planted, by Selected Tree Species, 1960, 1965, 1970, 1975, and 1976-1989 (in millions)

| | Coniferous | Latifolious | | | | | | | Total |
		Caoba	Majagua	Ocuje	Casuarina	Eucalyptus	Other		
1960	0.5	0.1	0.1	0.1	0.3	28.1	1.5		30.7
1965	7.0	5.4	1.5	0.9	10.9	7.3	4.3		37.3
1970	6.5	0.7	0.7	1.2	2.7	0.1	1.1		13.0
1975	24.7	1.9	4.1	5.4	10.8	1.8	3.8		52.5
1976	26.9	3.0	4.0	1.7	13.2	3.8	3.1		85.7
1977	34.9	2.4	4.6	0.8	9.8	3.5	5.6		61.6
1978	41.2	3.5	3.3	0.9	10.6	3.2	5.3		68.0
1979	31.5	2.3	4.1	1.2	7.4	2.3	5.7		54.5
1980	34.7	1.7	4.2	3.2	9.7	2.1	11.5		67.1
1981	32.1	3.7	5.8	4.2	6.9	4.0	18.1		74.8
1982	22.9	3.9	5.3	7.8	7.0	3.0	19.3		69.2
1983	36.9	8.4	5.5	10.6	15.5	12.9	49.3		139.1
1984	40.1	6.6	3.5	11.1	17.0	12.4	50.1		140.8
1985	38.8	4.8	5.1	14.5	24.2	15.2	38.4		141.0
1986	30.5	2.7	4.8	11.1	15.0	12.5	48.3		124.9
1987	31.9	3.3	4.6	8.0	14.7	13.0	52.5		128.0
1988	23.0	3.3	3.8	6.3	7.6	7.5	86.6		138.1
1989	16.6	5.0	6.8	10.6	9.0	5.9	128.4		182.3

Source: Comité Estatal (1990, Table VIII.52, p. 215).

Table 2. Number of Trees Planted, by Type of Tree, 1960-1966 (in millions)

	Eucalyptus	Pines	Casuarinas	Other	Total
1960	25.8	0.1	0.2	4.1	30.5
1961	35.4	2.0	3.5	18.6	54.0
1962	31.9	3.7	8.2	26.2	58.1
1963	12.5	14.1	7.3	20.0	32.5
1964	4.9	8.6	7.3	16.3	37.1
1965	8.0	7.0	12.6	13.9	41.5
1966	3.6	31.9	9.3	10.4	55.2

Source: Núñez Jiménez (1972, Volume 5, pp. 355-356).

most eucalyptus are not good trees for erosion control. When young, they are very susceptible to grass competition, and to obtain good growth, clean weeding is necessary during the establishment period, which is undesirable on steep or eroding terrain. Even mature stands may be ineffective in halting surface run-off.

The problem with the selection of eucalyptus as the main reforestation vehicle was not an isolated phenomenon. There is some evidence of poor species selection in other reforestation, reclamation and agricultural projects. Plantings of casuarina trees in the 1960s for shade and aesthetic reasons in Varadero, Santa María del Mar, and Guanabo, some of Cuba's most renown beaches, were responsible for extensive erosion as their shallow and dense roots—not naturally found in these areas—interfered with normal sand shifts. In the 1970s the government decided to uproot the casuarina trees planted a decade earlier in these beaches (Pagés 1981, p.4). Dumont (1970a, pp. 135 and 137) reported poor planting practices and high tree mortality associated with the large scale development of citrus plantations, as well as with the planting of hard wood trees in coffee areas. Another reported instance of poor reforestation practices is provided by Levins (1993, p. 57). In the mid-1970s, he notes:

> the Institute of Botany refused to work with the Forestry Institute on its plan for terracing mountainsides in Pinar del Río, planting monocultures of teak or hibiscus and clear-cutting of trees. They saw the plan as too vulnerable to pest problems and provoking massive erosion.

The most outlandish example of poor decision-making, however, was a grandiose scheme to plant coffee trees in an agricultural belt around Havana (see below).

ESTIMATES OF THE EFFICACY OF THE REFORESTATION PROGRAM

A gross estimate of the result of Cuba's reforestation program can be made by relating the total number of trees planted between 1959 and 1989, to the increase in number of forested hectares, net of forested area harvested. Our estimating procedure is summarized by the following relationships:

$$FA(t+I) = FA(t) + RA(t+I), \text{ and}$$

$$RA(t+I) = TP/D - HA$$

Where:

FA(t+I) = forested area in 1989 (in hectares);

FA(t) = forested area in 1959 (in hectares);

RA(t+I) = area reforested between 1959 and 1989 (in hectares);

TP = total number of trees planted between 1959 and 1989;

D = density of tree plantings (in trees per hectare); and

HA = number of hectares harvested between 1979 and 1989.

The net gain in forested area is the difference between the land area forested in 1959 and the area in state forest enterprises in 1989 (inclusive of virgin and reclaimed forests), minus an estimate of the forested area harvested between 1979 and 1989.

In 1959, according to COMARNA, 1,540,000 hectares were forested. There are two estimates of forested land area in 1989. The *Anuario Estadístico de Cuba 1989* (Comité Estatal 1990, p. 216) reports that forests in state forestry enterprises accounted for 2,273,300 hectares in 1989. COMARNA (1992), however, provides data suggesting that the increase in forests was considerably smaller, slightly over two million hectares. The differences between the 1959 figure and the two 1989 estimates entail a gain of 730,000 and 500,000 hectares of forest cover, respectively, over the intervening period. For estimating purposes we assume that 65,000 hectares of forests were harvested between 1979 and 1989.[5]

By assuming two different forestry plantation densities of 1,500 and 2,000 trees per hectare,[6] relating these densities to the 2.5 billion trees COMARNA claims have been planted in Cuba, and accounting for the forest area harvested between 1979 and 1989, the reforestation program's success can be calculated as ranging between 27 and 53 percent. In other words, 27 to 53 percent of trees planted survived to maturity, tree mortality rates being in the order of 47 to 73 percent. Both estimates are considerably higher that the only official tree mortality estimate of 40 percent we have been able to identify in the Cuban literature (Gómez 1979, p. 5). Mortality rates of this magnitude are not out of line with international experience, especially in situations where seedling care and early weeding practices are not given the required attention.[7] For a reforestation project to succeed, effective weeding is essential. During the first two to three years of a project, as many as three to four weedings a year are necessary (Committee on Selected 1982, p. 143). That proper seedling care procedures were not followed in Cuba, at least during the initial years of the reforestation program, is consistent with Westoby's observations (cited above) and with what is generally known about the poor follow-up associated with many of Cuba's agricultural practices. These estimates suggest that Cuba's forestry accomplishments have been achieved at a very high economic cost.

---

5. This estimate is based on the assumption that it takes at least 20 years for a tree plantation to mature and be ready for harvesting, and COMARNA figures cited by Reed (1993, p. 38) indicating that, in the early 1990s, 6,500 hectares of trees were being harvested annually.

6. Our hypothetical densities are based on recommended tree plantation densities provided by Poore and Fries (1985, p. 12) for different species. They range from 472 (for tectona grandis) to 1,678 (for shorea robusta) trees per hectare. The recommended density for eucalyptus hybrid is 1,658 trees per hectare. For our purposes, we assume 1,500 trees per hectare as the most likely tree density, although we also consider a higher density of 2,000 trees per hectare.

7. Personal communication with a forestry expert. Preeg (1996, p. 27), in his discussion of reforestation rates in Haiti during the 1980s, considers survival rates of 50 percent as "exceptionally high."

SOCIALIST AGRARIAN DEVELOPMENT POLICIES LEADING TO TREE LOSSES

A balanced assessment of the accomplishments of the reforestation program must evaluate the adverse impact the socialist rural development model implemented since the early 1960s had on the 1959 tree stock. This model was largely premised on the establishment of large scale state farms and agricultural cooperatives. There are ample reasons to believe (see Dumont 1970a and 1970b) that large scale Soviet-style farming led to the destruction of countless trees. A well-known French rural development expert, Dumont described what happened as brutal "because not even a tree that could provide shade or serve other purposes was left" (as cited by Nelson 1972, p. 94).

Land clearing on a vast scale was underway in the 1960s as the government embraced an agricultural development approach based on several pillars, including widespread mechanization, collectivization, and extensive use of land. To ease the mechanization of vast tracts of land, small stands of mature and productive trees were obliterated. Trees were uprooted to permit heavy tractors and combines to operate unobstructed.[8] Also contributing to the destruction of localized tree stands was the consolidation of small farms into agricultural cooperatives. In pre-revolutionary days, Cuban peasants relied on traditional agroforestry practices (Current, Lutz, and Scherr 1995, pp. 153-154), planting trees--for fruit, shade, fencing, wood, cooking fuel and other purposes--for domestic consumption and as cash crops. Fewer and fewer tree groves were left standing, collectivization policies led to the consolidation of small farms into state farms and cooperatives, peasants were relocated to planned urbanized communities, and large scale mechanization was introduced.

The land clearing tasks were assigned to mechanized military brigades, the notorious "Che Guevara columns." The modus operandi of these brigades was to drag a chain between two tractors or army tanks, pulling along the way any vegetation they encountered, be they brushes, *marabú*, or small and large trees. Thirty-six such units were operating throughout the country in December 1969, each equipped with twenty pieces of heavy equipment and manned by 117 men (Nelson 1972, pp. 94-95). One astonishing result of this policy was to nearly obliterate palm trees, Cuba's national symbol, from much of the national countryside, leading some observers to note that in the 1990s "most state farms are devoid of palm trees" (Deere, Pérez, and Gonzalez 1994, p. 225). These same observers note that lack of shade trees is interfering with the implementation of the Voisin grazing system (p. 215). This system is based on feeding a herd primarily in pastures which are fertilized with the cattle's own manure. Pasture productivity is maintained by periodically rotating the herd from one small enclosure to the next through the use of shifting movable electrified fences. Supplementary feeding, transportable water sources, and a relative abundance of strategically distributed shade trees are essential components of the Voisin grazing system. Many shade trees currently lacking fell victim to the Che Guevara Brigades in the 1960s.

Compounding the detrimental effects of this strategy was the extensive use of land and the decision to bring under cultivation marginal agricultural land. To bring them into production, these lands had to be cleared of trees and shrubs (Dumont 1970b, p. 39). Particularly damaging to trees and forest cover were agricultural policies of the mid- to late-1960s, when most agricultural land resources were assigned to the failed goal of producing ten million tons of sugar in the 1970 harvest. Expanding the area under cultivation, however, was a constant of national agricultural policy during nearly three decades. In the absence of foreign subsidies (after 1990), when critical agricultural inputs were no longer available, many of the reclaimed lands were abandoned. This process has been documented with regard to citrus plantations. According to a joint study conducted by researchers from the University of Havana and the University of

---

8. Associated field preparations included the removal of large boulders and stones, and in some instances, even contouring the soils (e.g., by filling small ravines and streams with soil).

Florida, between 1990 and 1993 the land area planted in citrus trees declined by 16,997 hectares, as plantations in the more marginal areas were left to wither or removed (Spreen et. al. 1996, p. 20).

To partially compensate for the destruction of traditional fruit tree groves because of the expansion of sugar production, and as part of the country's development strategy, the government embarked on a program to develop fruit tree, coffee and cacao plantations. Resources were assigned to develop mango and guava tree groves, as well as to expand coffee and cacao plantations in mountain areas, often as part of agroforestry projects. In some cases, ill-advised attempts were made to develop coffee plantations in regions poorly suited for this permanent tree crop. Best known was the directive during the 1970s to develop a "green belt" of coffee plantations in the lowlands surrounding the city of La Habana. This project was eventually abandoned, the coffee trees never having borne fruit. The waste of economic resources on this project alone was colossal.

The performance of planting efforts of fruit bearing trees can be partially judged by analyzing the data in Table 3. The table provides statistics on the number of hectares planted with four fruit trees (mango, guava, coffee, and cacao) for 1970 and 1975, and for 1978 to 1989. Increases in the number of hectares planted with mangoes and guavas during the late 1970s and 1980s can almost definitely be attributed to efforts to reverse the damage done to fruit tree stands during the 1960s. An important characteristic, likely to differ from pre-revolutionary patterns, is that most mango and guava trees were planted in large stands, as opposed to small scale groves, as suggested by differential growth patterns between the state and private sectors. This pattern is consistent with the socialist model of organizing agricultural production on a large scale, in part to facilitate the use of chemical inputs and mechanization in agriculture. Particularly telling are the major fluctuations observed from year to year in number of hectares planted in the state sector. Fluctuations of this magnitude suggest poor planting practices or shifting agricultural priorities. In any event, they are indicative of a vast waste of resources and may also explain (together with exports) the persistent fruit shortages reported in Cuba. The environmental underpinnings of these trends, if any, as well as their consequences, remain to be analyzed.

The trend for coffee is consistent with the gradual depopulation of Cuba's mountain regions (up to the early 1990s) and with the failed attempts to expand coffee production into poorly suited areas close to major urban centers. The area planted with coffee peaked in 1979, gradually diminishing through 1989; the decline amounted to 25 percent over this period. The decline is especially noticeable in the private farming sector, although in 1989 over half of coffee production remained in private hands. Rural flight to urbanized localities is likely to be implicated in the decline of coffee plantations. Former coffee areas were the target of reforestation, given that coffee has traditionally been planted in association with other trees that provide shade and protection to coffee plants and also contribute to soil improvements. The declining trend is certain to have been reversed in the 1990s during the Special Period with the push to increase agricultural production in the mountains as part of the food self-sufficiency program. Cacao plantings remained relatively constant over the 1970-1989 period, except that the share of these plantations in the state sector increased. Cacao plants often are also found in close association with larger trees.

Also harshly criticized by Rene Dumont were projects begun during the 1960s to restructure pastures in livestock farms according to inflexible geometrical designs. To achieve these designs, it was necessary to remove extensive living tree fences (live fenceposts) and, in many instances, trees planted along river banks (Dumont 1970a, pp. 123-127). Some of these trees could well have been planted decades earlier as part of erosion control projects. The number of trees that were destroyed is unknown, but it was probably in the millions.

Although the evidence is only partial, there is reason to conclude that development projects carried out in several of Cuba's mangrove regions also had a detrimental impact on the natural vegetation, trees included. Perhaps the more damaging were projects to

Table 3.   Land Area Planted with Selected Permanent Fruit and Other Edible Crops, 1970, 1975, and 1978-1989 (in thousand hectares)

| | Mango | | | Guava | | | Coffee | | | Cacao | | |
	Total	State	Private	Total	State	Private	Total	State	Private	Total	State	Private
1970	15.1	11.8	3.3	3.8	3.5	0.3	181.5	59.9	121.6	10.5	2.3	8.2
1975	19.2	15.2	4.0	7.0	4.7	2.3	162.5	73.8	88.7	14.1	5.6	8.5
1978	26.6	20.4	6.2	10.5	7.8	2.7	156.2	74.9	81.3	12.2	5.0	7.2
1979	28.4	22.3	6.1	12.3	9.6	2.7	161.1	80.7	80.4	12.2	5.1	7.1
1980	28.8	22.5	6.3	12.5	9.5	3.0	166.1	84.5	91.6	13.1	6.0	7.1
1981	29.0	22.7	6.3	12.6	10.4	2.2	168.0	80.3	87.7	12.2	4.8	7.4
1982	28.4	22.3	6.1	14.2	11.0	3.2	168.5	76.7	91.8	13.1	5.7	7.4
1983	27.3	20.9	6.4	15.0	11.2	3.8	164.6	73.4	91.2	12.8	5.4	7.4
1984	31.0	24.3	6.7	15.8	11.8	4.0	159.7	71.8	87.9	12.1	4.6	7.5
1985	30.4	23.6	6.8	15.0	10.8	4.2	155.3	70.8	84.5	11.5	4.7	6.8
1986	30.4	23.7	6.7	13.6	9.4	4.2	145.2	64.8	80.4	11.1	4.5	6.6
1987	29.3	23.8	5.5	12.7	8.7	4.0	143.3	65.1	78.2	11.0	4.3	6.7
1988	43.0	36.5	6.4	14.4	10.7	3.7	137.1	65.6	71.5	10.7	4.3	6.4
1989	26.6	21.6	5.0	12.1	8.5	3.6	134.3	65.6	68.7	10.6	4.3	6.3

Source: Comité Estatal (1990, Table VIII.17, pp. 195-196).

increase the agricultural and tourism potential of the Zapata Swamp in South Central Cuba. FAO (1994, p. 84) has called attention to the adverse ecological consequences of road construction and other human activities in mangrove areas, an observation also made by Borhidi (1991, p. 453) in connection with the Zapata swamp in his exhaustive study of Cuba's vegetation ecology. Included here are environmentally damaging agricultural activities—such as inappropriate drainage, pollution, grazing, and use of marginal areas—as well as activities related to the production of charcoal and the extraction of peat. The unfavorable effects of these practices are corroborated by data reviewed immediately below.

ECOLOGICAL CONSERVATION STATUS: FINDINGS OF A REGIONAL ASSESSMENT

A 1995 World Bank/World Wildlife Fund (Dinerstein et. al. 1995) conservation assessment of the major ecoregions of Latin America and the Caribbean provides an overview of the conservation status of some of Cuba's natural ecoregions, identifying their degree of vulnerability and protection needs. The study is particularly revealing since it provides an independent evaluation of the status of Cuba's natural regions within a regional comparative framework. An ecoregion is defined as a "geographically distinct assemblage of natural communities that (a) share a large majority of their species and ecological dynamics; (b) share similar environmental conditions; and

(c) interact ecologically in ways that are critical for their long-term persistence" (p. 124).

According to these criteria (see Table 4), of the five ecoregions into which Cuba is divided, two, the tropical broadleaf dry forests (formerly extending across much of Cuba) and the flooded wetlands (the Zapata swamps) were considered to be endangered, while three, the moist broadleaf forests (found in the country's highest altitudes), the coniferous pine forests (Pinar del Río and Isla de la Juventud in the West), and the cactus scrub (in the Southeast) are considered to be vulnerable. The endangered and vulnerable classifications are intermediate between the classifications of extinct (or completely converted from natural habitat) and critical, on the one hand, and relatively stable or relatively intact, on the other (p. xvi).

The study's of taxonomy is based on five indicators (total loss of original habitat; number and size of blocks of original habitat; rate of habitat conversion; degree of fragmentation or degradation; and degree of protection) of landscape integrity related to the maintenance of ecological processes and biological diversity. Most protected at the present time are the broad leaf moist forest (probably because they are the ecoregions of more difficult access), and least are the broad leaf dry forests, pine forests, and cactus scrub. But even in the most protected areas, human activi-

Table 4. Conservation Assessments of Cuba's Ecoregions

Tropical Moist Broadleaf Forests

Moist Forests: Vulnerable - 20,069 square kilometers.

The moist forests of Cuba, and those of the Greater Antilles generally, maintain exceptionally diverse insular biotas with many regional and island endemic species in a wide range of taxa. Cuba, in particular, has a rich moist forest flora. The Greater Antilles are notable for numerous unusual relict species and higher taxa. Expansion of cacao, coffee, and tobacco production are serious threats in some areas.

Tropical Dry Broadleaf Forests

Dry Forests: Endangered - 61,466 square kilometers.

Clearcutting and selective logging, charcoal production, frequent burning, and slash-and-burn agriculture pose threats to the ecoregion.

Tropical and Subtropical Coniferous Forests

Pine Forests: Vulnerable - 6,017 square kilometers.

The pine forests of Cuba and Hispaniola support a number of endemic plant and animal species. Mining, citrus plantations, grazing, and logging severely threaten the ecoregion. Exploitation of threatened parrot population occurs in western portions of the ecoregion

Flooded Grasslands

Wetlands: Endangered - 5,345 square kilometers.

The Zapata Swamp on the southern coast of Cuba is noted for its large size and endemic species. Draining and agricultural expansion, agricultural pollution, charcoal production, grazing, peat extraction, and exotic invasions all pose severe threats to the ecoregion.

Deserts and Xeric Shrublands

Cactus Scrub: Vulnerable - 3,044 square kilometers.

Grazing, woodcutting, and the conversion and resource exploitation associated with increased urbanization pose threats to the ecoregion for the foreseeable future.

Source: Summarized with minor modifications from Dinerstein, *et. al.* (1995, pp. 86, 93, 96, 100, and 103).

ties, including mining and logging operations, as well as the presence of permanent plantations (e.g., coffee, citrus), are having adverse ecological impacts. In relative conservation terms, Cuba is not doing significantly better or worse than other neighboring nations. Nevertheless, the Cuban forests continue to be threatened by human activities, in particular by excessive logging, the expansion of agroforestry activities, and by slash and burn agriculture. The latter is surprising since slash and burn agriculture is usually associated with landless peasants seeking farm land, a problem not expected in a country where most land is government owned.

Not mentioned by the study is that these threats have intensified in recent years as a result of the food self-sufficiency policies being pursued by the Cuban government during the "Special Period," most of all by the drive to increase food production in mountainous areas and more intensively harvest forests to produce domestic fuel and charcoal. Of note in these regards are the widely publicized Turquino and Manatí plans, whereby attempts are underway to relocate farmers to mountain regions by giving them private plots of land to increase production of several com-modities (e.g., coffee and honey) and engage in forestry activities (e.g., reforestation of denuded areas and reclamation of areas affected by mining activities) (Gersper et. al. 1993, p. 22). These plans were conceived in part to address low agricultural production levels in these areas, their success being predicated on expanding the labor supply, introducing seldom used technologies, developing new types of farming arrangements, and granting farmers access to individual plots of land (Cuban Commission 1996, pp. 11-12).

Increased human interventions in these areas, some with only limited agricultural potential, are playing havoc with preservation and reforestation efforts, despite difficulties with plan implementation and the avowed preservation intent of the mountain development initiatives (Ministerio de Ciencia 1995, pp. 38-41). Preservation and development objectives are clearly contradictory. In the Escambray mountains of Central Cuba, for example, targets have not been met due to poor road conditions, water quality, and other factors ("Cuban Official" 1996, pp. 4-5). The nature of the threats varies depending on the ecoregions in question. They are less severe in the more inaccessible mountain regions, but even here they are so in selected areas (see Table 4). Ecological concern has also been raised by the rush to develop tourism poles, including ecotourism, to earn badly needed foreign exchange (Dewar 1993, p. 6A).

The findings of the World Bank/World Wildlife Fund study clash with the nearly idyllic description of conservation and reclamation policies portrayed in official Cuban government documents. Official interpretations are also at variance with the perspective provided by an FAO document with respect to the National Forestry Action Plan elaborated by Cuba in the early 1990s. The findings of this document are reviewed below.

CURRENT FORESTRY PRIORITIES

Despite the apparent reforestation success, Cuba has requested international assistance to broaden the national forestry effort (Reed 1993, p. 38) and, specifically, to implement the National Forestry Action Plan (NFAP). The NFAP was developed on the heels of the 1992 International Conference on the Environment. The objectives of the NFAP (FAO 1993, p. 197) are:

- restitution of the forest cover and reconstruction of degraded natural forests with a view towards protection and production;

- sustainable management of forest resources for the production of wood products and the protection of fragile watersheds and ecosystems;

- increasing production and diversifying it, [including] development of integrated forest industries;

- intensive use of forest biomass to produce charcoal and fuelwood;

- recuperation of degraded ecosystems;

- application of management techniques to protected and special areas for the benefit of local populations and to protect biodiversity; [and]

- strengthening of research and training institutions.

Driving the NFAP is what is judged to be the limited potential of the national forestry industry because of a dearth of raw materials, obsolete technology, and inadequate infrastructure, which results in the fact that the country is forced to import 55 percent of its wood products needs (FAO 1993, p. 196). Implementing the NFAP, which consists of 18 programs, would require a domestic investment of 61.9 million Cuban pesos (US$81.4 million at the then official exchange rate), and external assistance to the tune of US$34.7 million. FAO (1993, p. 197) concluded, however, that "lack of response from potential donors has not made possible to convene an international Round Table ... to discuss the implementation of the NFAP."

The NFAP may in part be seen as a response to the economic crisis engulfing Cuba since 1990. Cuba used to import much of its lumber from the Soviet Union. During the 1980s, the Soviet Union had a shortage of lumberjacks and therefore lumber shipments to Cuba were irregular. To address this problem, in December 1986 Cuba and the Soviet Union created a joint enterprise to exploit Soviet Far Eastern timber resources for export to different countries, including Cuba. As many as 400 Cuban lumberjacks were assigned to these activities (Pérez-López and Díaz-Briquets 1990, pp. 287-288). How this venture ended has not been documented, but we assume that it concluded with the collapse of the Soviet Union, if not before. Greater reliance on, and better management of, national forests could mitigate supply shortfalls and abate the over-exploitation of forest resources during the Special Period.

There is mounting evidence that forestry conservation efforts have experienced a setback as lumbering rates in the 1990s increased in response to the end of wood and fuel shipments from the former Soviet Union. Shortages of home cooking fuels have been partly compensated by increasing supplies of domestically produced charcoal and fuelwood. Government officials ("Officials Urge Measures" 1994, p. 3) have "sharply criticized the indiscriminate chopping down of trees and theft and misappropriation of the wood," as the unavailability of fuels and other supplies leads to unregulated use of forests products.

434

Attempts to increasingly rely on forest products to attain self-sufficiency extends to the planting of "power forests," or stands of rapidly growing trees to produce charcoal. A 1994 report indicates that this program has run into problems: the locations in which planting goals have been met are too far from where charcoal supplies are needed ("Roundup of Economic Developments" 1994, p. 9). There is also concern about intensified logging pressures on regions that have traditionally served as charcoal sources (National Public Radio 1995). Further, tourism construction projects are likely to have sustained (or even increased) demand for domestic lumber, despite a cutback in housing construction, and the end of wood imports from the former Soviet Union.

As a result of these developments and the apparent lack of reforestation inputs, efforts to further increase forested areas are faltering ("Effects of U.S. Blockade" 1995, p. 8), not only due to higher harvesting rates, but also because reforestation rates have declined. In 1992, for example, only 500,000 seedlings were planted although the target was to plant four million trees ("Roundup of Economic Activity" 1992, p. 3).

OVERALL ASSESSMENT

Given Cuba's current economic crisis, we can foresee increasing pressures on Cuba's natural resource base, including its forests, as a consequence of the policies being followed as part of the Special Period. It is apparent that some of the gains of the last four decades are being reversed under pressure from economic events. Some of these policies emanate from the national drive to attain food self-sufficiency and others from the economic difficulties associated with the curtailment of the ability to import. The policy to encourage urban residents to resettle in coffee-growing mountain regions, for example, adds environmental pressures to heretofore relatively undisturbed areas. Even primitive subsistence agricultural activities will continue to damage the forests as peasant families push further into the country's forested areas. The same is true regarding charcoal production, a pursuit that has received renewed emphasis given the national shortage of commercial home-cooking fuels. The housing shortage and the boom in the tourism industry are also of major concern: in the absence of imports, domestic lumber must be used for construction projects. Dearth of inputs, finally, must also be having a deleterious impact on reforestation efforts as even the import of the most basic reforestation inputs has been curtailed.

REFERENCES

Atienza Ambou, Aida, Anicia García Alvarez, and Oscar U. Echevarría Vallejo 1992. "Repercusiones medioambientales de las tendencias de desarrollo socioeconomico en Cuba," mimeo. La Habana: Instituto Nacional de Investigaciones Económicas.

Borhidi, A. 1991. *Phytogeography and Vegetation Ecology of Cuba*. Budapest, Hungary. Akademia Kiado.

Bucek, Antonio 1986. "Aseguramiento territorial de la estabilidad ecológica y sus condiciones en Cuba." In Instituto de Geografía, *Unidad Hombre-Naturaleza*. La Habana. Editora de la Academia de Ciencias de Cuba, pp. 9-24.

Castro, Fidel 1972. "History Will Absolve Me" (October 16, 1953). In Rolando E. Bonachea and Nelson P. Valdes, Editors, *Revolutionary Struggle: The Selected Works of Fidel Castro*. Cambridge, Massachusetts. The MIT Press, pp. 164-221.

COMARNA (Comisión Nacional de Protección del Medio Ambiente y el Uso Racional de los Recursos Naturales) 1992. *Informe nacional a la confer-*

encia de Naciones Unidas sobre medio ambiente y desarrollo Brasil/1992. Resumen. La Habana.

Comité Estatal de Estadísticas 1990. *Anuario Estadístico de Cuba 1989*. La Habana.

Committee on Selected Biological Problems in the Humid Tropics 1982. *Ecological Aspects of Development in the Humid Tropics*. Washington, D.C. National Academy Press.

"Cuban Commission Views Valley, Mountain Municipalities" 1996. *FBIS-LAT-96-024* (5 February), pp. 11-12.

"Cuban Official on Turquino-Manatí Plan Implementation" 1996. *FBIS-LAT-96-023* (2 February), p. 4.

Current, Dean, Ernst Lutz, and Sara J. Scherr 1995. "The Costs and Benefits of Agroforestry to Farmers." *The World Bank Research Observer* 10:2 (August), pp. 151-180.

Deere, Carmen Diana, Niurka Pérez and Ernel González. 1994. "The View from Below: Cuban Agriculture in the 'Special Period in Peacetime.'" *The Journal of Peasant Studies* 21:2, pp. 194-234.

Dewar, Heather 1993. "Unlocking the Mysteries of Cuba's Rare Wildlife." *The Miami Herald* (26 October), pp.1A, 6A, and 12A.

Dinerstein, Eric, David M. Olson, Douglas J. Graham, Avis L.Webster, Steven A. Primm, Marnie P. Bookbinder, and George Ledec 1995. *A Conservation Assessment of the Terrestrial Ecoregions of Latin America and the Caribbean*. Washington, D.C.: The World Bank and the World Wildlife Fund.

Dumont, Rene 1970a. *Cuba ¿Es socialista?* Caracas: Editorial Tiempo Nuevo.

Dumont, Rene 1970b. *Cuba: Socialism and Development*. New York: Grove Press.

"Effects of U.S. Blockade on Environment Noted." 1995. *FBIS-LAT-95-186* (26 September), p. 8.

FAO 1993. *Tropical Forests Action Programme Update*. Rome: Food andAgriculture Organization.

FAO 1994. *Mangrove Forest Management Guidelines*. FAO Forestry Paper No. 117. Rome: Food and Agriculture Organization.

Foreign Policy Association 1935. *Problems of the New Cuba*. New York.

Gersper, Paul L., Carmen S. Rodríguez-Barbosa, and Laura F. Orlando 1993. "Soil Conservation in Cuba: A Key to the New Model for Agriculture." *Agriculture and Human Values* X:3, pp. 16-23.

Gomez, Orlando 1979. "Esos verdes pulmones de Cuba se multiplicaron muchas veces." *Granma* (June 23), p. 5.

Gregerse, H.M. *et. al.* 1995. "Valuing Forests: Context, Issues and Guidelines." *FAO Forestry Paper* 127. Rome: Food and Agriculture Organization.

Grupo Cubano de Investigaciones Económicas. 1963. *Un estudio sobre Cuba*. Miami, Florida: University of Miami Press.

Knox, Paul 1995. "Sherritt Breathes Life Into Cuban Mine." *The Globe and Mail* (Toronto)(31 July).

Levins, Richard 1993. "The Ecological Transformation of Cuba." *Agriculture and Human Values* X:3, pp. 52-60.

Marrero, Leví 1950. *Geografía de Cuba*. La Habana: La Moderna Poesía.

Memorias Inéditas del Censo de 1931. 1978. La Habana: Editorial de Ciencias Sociales.

Ministerio de Ciencia, Tecnología y Medio Ambiente. 1995. *Cuba: Medio Ambiente y Desarrollo*. La Habana.

Moreno Fraginals, Manuel 1964. *El Ingenio: El complejo económico y social cubano del azúcar*. La Habana.

National Public Radio 1995. "Cuba Struggles to Save Economy and Ecology." Transcript of "All Things Considered" Radio Program. Washington, D.C.: National Public Radio (30 May).

Nelson, Lowry 1972. *Cuba: The Measure of a Revolution*. Minneapolis: University of Minnesota Press.

Núñez Jiménez, Antonio 1968. *La erosión desgasta a Cuba*. La Habana: Instituto del Libro.

Núñez Jiménez, Antonio 1972. *Geografía de Cuba*. La Habana: Instituto Cubano del Libro,

"Official Urges Measures to End Deforestation" 1994. *FBIS-LAT-94-066* (6 April), p. 3.

Pagés, Raisa 1981. "Una riqueza natural que debemos preservar." *Granma* (27 February), p. 4.

Pérez-López, Jorge and Sergio Díaz-Briquets 1990. "Labor Migration and Offshore Assembly in the Socialist World: The Cuban Experience." *Population and Development Review* 15:2, pp. 273-299.

Pichs, Ramón 1992. "Cuba ante los desafíos ambientales globales." La Habana. Unpublished.

Poore, M.E.D. and C. Fries 1985. "The Ecological Effects of Eucalyptus." *FAO Forestry Papers* No. 59. Rome: Food and Agricultural Organization.

Prado, José Antonio 1996. "Kindling." *The Economist* (March 16-22), p. 8.

Preeg, Ernest H. 1996. *The Haitian Dilemma*. Washington, D.C.: The Center for Strategic and International Studies.

Reed, Gail 1992. "On the Razor's Edge: Deforestation in Cuba." *Cuba Update* Nos. 1-2 (September), pp. 36-38.

Reed, Gail 1993. "Protecting the Environment in the 'Special Period.'" *Cuba Update* Nos. 1-2 (September), pp. 29, 31-32.

República de Cuba 1988. *Protección del medio ambiente y uso racional de los recursos naturales*. La Habana.

"Roundup of Economic Activity Reported 23-28 Dec." 1992. *FBIS-LAT-92-252* (31 December), pp. 2-3.

"Roundup of Economic Developments." 1994. *FBIS-LAT-94-109* (7 June), pp. 8-9.

Santana, Eduardo 1991. "Nature Conservation and Sustainable Development in Cuba." *Conservation Biology* 5:1, pp. 13-15.

Spreen, Thomas H., Armando Nova González, and Ronald P. Murato 1996. *The Citrus Industries in Cuba and Florida*. International Working Paper Series, IW96-2, International Agricultural Trade and Development Center. Gainesville: University of Florida.

"Surgen los bosques" 1983. *Prisma Latinoamericano* (September), p. 26.

Thomas, Hugh 1971. *Cuba: The Pursuit of Freedom*. New York: Harper & Row Publishers.

War Department 1900. *Report on the Census of Cuba 1899*. Washington, D.C.: U.S. Government Printing Office.

Westoby, Jack 1989. *Introduction to World Forestry*. London. Basil Blackwell.

The World Bank 1951. *Report on Cuba*. Washington, D.C.

The World Bank 1992. "Development and the Environment." *World Development Report*. Washington, D.C.

COMMENTS ON

"Forestry Policies of Cuba's Socialist Government: An Appraisal" by Sergio Díaz-Briquets

René Costales

Díaz-Briquets has done a very good paper, which is part of a series relating to natural resource and environmental issues. This paper deals with forestry, agroforestry and use of trees within agricultural practices. His perspective and scope covers well the historical participation of the forestry sector in Cuba.

These comments will highlight some additional positive and negative aspects that have not been covered. There is a trend in the data presented showing some improvement in forestry policies (i.e., diversification of species). It is extremely difficult to diversify forestry plantations—the data shows improvement in significant volume of plantings in other than the traditional Caribbean pine and eucalyptus. Another very important fact which is highlighted is a very large investment in training forestry engineers, scientists and technicians. On a comparative basis (e.g., per 1,000 hectares), Cuba, in Latin American terms, has a very important human capital endowment. This also may help to explain the fact that there has been a relatively successful protection of virgin/primary/untouched forests due to the advocacy of such a trained cadre.

Highlighting the serious issue of "virtually no reforestation" during the recent Special Period, let me state that this constitutes a serious case of disinvestment in the sector. This brings to mind that when one hears of current high growth of Gross Domestic Product (GDP), one has to start thinking that national accounts data measuring GDP do not cover the fact that the stock of trees is being cut without re-

placement. In a sense, while current forest income may be high, there is disinvestment by not reforesting at this time. As this will show losses in the future and trees take a long time to grow again, this is disinvestment of the worst possible kind.

Another particular example of disinvestment that is also identified is the very critical problem of land reclamation required by open pit nickel ore mining. This is a case of foreign disinvestment which is occurring—most likely Sherritt is simply not doing the same types of land reclamation activities which would be required by the environmental codes of Canada within their own country. This is a very serious concern which should be addressed by the appropriate parties at the appropriate time.

There are two elements which have not been mentioned in the paper: culling and newsprint paper demand. Culling (or judiciously removing weak trees and branches) in any commercial forestry provides anywhere from 10 to 20% of the present value of the economic benefits of forest plantations. Typically, benefits accrue to the nearby population who work in the area and usually covers the operational costs of forest plantations prior to final cutting of the trees. The other element, newsprint demand, will mushroom in a free Cuba and may justify future investments in commercial forestry.

One recommendation for future studies is that detailed ownership patterns by forest types be obtained since the issue of "who owns the forest" is paramount to quality aspects of forest management and investment. Another recommendation for future related studies is the issue of effectiveness of erosion control. Most of the early efforts of reforestation and forest management in Cuba were done and justified in order to improve erosion control. We need to have time series on river sedimentation and soil transport in order to do that. Some references are made to early laws relating to riverbank vegetation *(mata ciliar)* 100 meters to each side of a river. That is also of critical compliance in any current and future environmental management program.

Again, land ownership is critical to conservation efforts for one protects better that for which one feels "ownership." Both the "slash and burn" agriculture and the references made in the paper about recent efforts to resettle urban population and make them coffee farmers point out to the critical issue of legal framework of land tenancy and the actual belief systems of new farmers as to who really owns the land. In the Special Period, a farmer is less likely to feel certain about his ownership of land and it would take many years for broadly accepted legal principles of land possession *(uso capiao)* to provide certainty to land titles granted by a government that may change in the near term.

In conclusion:

- gains achieved in forest cover have occurred at a very high economic cost and low efficiency;

- there has been a learning curve in sector activities, and this means there is a large untapped potential for future investment in the forestry sector, even though there has been significant disinvestment recently which will require special considerations;

- land ownership is a very critical issue since in this sector there is a strong need for private sector participation coupled with very enlightened public sector regulation. In the political situation that we can foresee happening in Cuba, the issue of government regulation has to be very clearly understood because there have been abuses of centralized power and excessive government regulation and intervention. The forestry sector needs to be well regulated by the State, while at the same time you need strong private sector entrepreneurship;

- one final critical issue is the development of free and independent non-governmental organizations (NGOs) which will strive to protect environmental resources and articulate optimum regulation of the private sector participation in forestry activities.

THE QUEST FOR POWER: ANALYZING THE COSTS AND BENEFITS OF CUBA'S NUCLEAR ENERGY POLICY

Jonathan Benjamin-Alvarado

There is no design control, no procurement document control, no controls on materials and purchases, no control equipment (. . .) Who is going to operate this plant? The indispensable international requirement for operation of a nuclear reactor is that the operator be trustworthy that people believe that this person will respect international law and will be capable of operating and maintaining this plant with strict compliance with safety standards (. . .). It is obvious that Fidel Castro does not meet any of these requirements.

> —Nils Díaz, Director of Nuclear Engineering Sciences at the University of Florida in Congressional Testimony on the Cuban Nuclear Project, July 25, 1991

Since the late 1970s, Cuba has pursued a nuclear energy capability by attempting to build two nuclear reactors at Juraguá, in Cienfuegos province. These policies were ambitious by any measure. Originally, Cuba envisioned a network of nuclear reactors across the island. When completed, the nuclear facilities would represent a shining example of the success of the Cuban revolution, highlighting developments in technological and scientific expertise. The plans for nuclear development have undergone numerous changes and reevaluations until 1992 when the project was placed in a state of "suspension" because of the loss of Russian financing for construction. About this same time numerous questions had been raised surrounding the safety of the partially com-

pleted reactors, as well as the competence of the Cuban nuclear bureaucracy that would be left to operate the plants. The quotation above represents the depth of doubts that follow Cuba's attempt to develop a nuclear capability. These doubts, coupled with the suspect economic value of nuclear energy development on the island, pose more questions than they answer.

The purpose of this examination will be to provide a cost and benefit analysis of Cuba's nuclear project that looks at how the economic, political, and nuclear safety issues surrounding development of nuclear energy may affect the environment. This can be viewed as a part of the Cuban "quest for power." It can also be viewed as part of a broader body of research that looks at the relationship between natural resources, economic development and environmental policy in revolutionary Cuba.[1] It is also an attempt to provide an objective analysis of an issue that heretofore has often been the fodder of many of the less than complimentary exchanges between Havana and Washington. Because it has been used in this propagandistic fashion, much of the credible scientific and political analyses needed for sound decision-making has been forsaken for the expediency of accumulating political capital. A sound analysis requires that we remind ourselves that environmental problems deserving our attention do not necessarily exist "today" but are (at least potentially) in prospect for the future,

---

1. For an example see, Sergio Díaz-Briquets and Jorge F. Pérez-López, "Water, Development, and Environment in Cuba: A First Look," in *Cuba in Transition—Volume 5* (Washington: Association for the Study of the Cuban Economy, 1995).

whether near or distant. Moreover, we must take into consideration under the present circumstances that even the most thoughtful opprobrium to Cuban nuclear aspirations from the United States may have little influence on Cuba. Before engaging in analysis it is useful to place Cuba's nuclear ambitions into a proper historical context. The following section provides a brief examination of the historical development of Cuba's nuclear program and its associated policies.

In retrospect, an analysis of Cuban nuclear activities suggests that officials involved in initiating the nuclear program gave primary consideration to political reasons, viewing potential economic dividends as important but less significant.[2] Moreover it bears to reason that little or no emphasis was placed on all of the parallel nuclear bureaucracies and institutions usually associated with the development of a nuclear power industry. Environmental imperatives lay outside these core considerations and would not be emphasized until after the disaster at Chernobyl.

At the start of the program the government attempted to emphasize the economic benefits. Fidel Castro Díaz-Balart the former Executive Secretary of the Cuban Atomic Energy Commission, claimed that the first Juraguá reactor when running at full capacity, would allow the country to save 600,000 tons of oil annually. If all four units were operating, he said,

the savings would be 2.4 million tons of oil annually.[3]

Yet Cuba's actions left little doubt as to the prime motivation for the venture. Two possible forms of nuclear cooperation were available to Cuba: (1) the construction of a "turnkey" project; or (2) the provision of technical assistance, which would be less efficient.[4] Cuba opted for the latter, which was perceived to be "the most flattering for the political ambitions of the Cuban leadership.[5] Moreover, it was not clear that a nuclear energy program was even needed in Cuba. A 1970 monograph by Soviet geologist Boris Semevski did not even discuss nuclear power engineering as a possible alternative for overcoming Cuba's acute shortage of organic fossil fuel. Semevski concluded that the planned construction of two thermo-electric power stations of 1,200 megawatts would "finally solve the shortage of energy and would make Cuba the Latin America leader in energy production per capita."[6] But only a short while later, Cuba launched its ambitious scheme to construct a network of nuclear power facilities on the island. Cuba's nationalism was an important motivation for the project. The country sought out a symbol to prove its increasing international stature and a means of exhibiting the capabilities of its model of revolution and development. Indeed, a nuclear power station built with Cuban hands would become a brilliant propagandistic confirmation of the success of the Cuban Revolution.[7]

---

2. María Dolores Espino clearly elucidates the reasons for concern over environmental deterioration in Cuba. Among the reasons listed production maximization without consideration of costs, an inadequate regulatory environment, the absence of pressure groups. Additionally, Cuba suffers from many of the same factors that also affect of "developing" countries like, chronic external imbalance and debt burdens, the use of inefficient, inappropriate and obsolete technologies, and a lack of adequate funding for an infrastructure. In Espino, "Environmental Deterioration and Protection in Socialist Cuba," *Cuba in Transition—Volume 2* (Miami: Florida International University, 1992).

3. Jonathan Benjamin-Alvarado and Alexander Belkin, "Cuba's Nuclear Power Program and Post-Cold War Pressures," *Nonproliferation Review*, Vol. 1, No. 2 (Winter 1994), p. 20. See also, Fidel Castro Díaz-Balart, *La Energía Nuclear en la Economía Nacional de la República de Cuba* (Moscow:COMECON, 1986), p. 6.

4. This is based on the assumption that a "turnkey" project would take less time to complete and that Cuba could enjoy the benefits of a lessened dependence on fossil fuels.

5. Igor Ivanov, "The Atlantis of the Castro Brothers: Will Fidel's Bulb Light Up in Cuba?," *Literaturnaya Gazeta,* in Joint Publications Research Service, *Proliferation Issues* (June 25, 1992), p. 20.

6. B.N. Semevski, *Economicheskaya geografiya Kuby (The Economic Geography of Cuba)* (Leningrad: Nauka, 1970), p. 67. This monograph is still considered by some to be the most comprehensive study on Cuban geography.

7. Ivanov, *op. cit.*

As a by-product of nuclear ascendancy, Cuba could lessen its dependence on oil imports, thereby developing a stronger bargaining position with the Soviets and diminishing the impact of the U.S. embargo. Cuba's domestic oil production is roughly one and a half million tons annually.[8] The amount required to meet its basic energy needs is eight million tons annually. Under the old trade agreement with the Soviet Union, Cuba received thirteen million tons of oil annually. This arrangement allowed Cuba to resell the five-million-ton excess and to export six and a half million tons of oil annually.[9] During the "special period" Cuba has been able to generate only 30 percent of its energy requirements. The severely diminished output has resulted in blackouts, limited telephone service and the extensive shutdown of factories throughout the island. The peak energy use on the island is estimated at about 1,500 megawatts per hour. The addition of a 417-megawatt reactor to the grid would partially reduce the impact of the loss of Russian oil.

METHODOLOGY

This paper employs a benefit-cost analysis of Cuba's nuclear energy policy that will describe the potential environmental impact of Cuba's efforts to develop nuclear energy on the island, including potential problems that need to be mitigated or solved. It will lay out a few alternative courses of actions that might be taken. This will include the nature and magnitude of the tradeoffs implicit in the different policy choices. This is accomplished by establishing an evaluative criterion for assessing the major environmental considerations confronting Cuba in its attempt to complete the Juraguá venture: nuclear safety, economic constraints and political imperatives. The resulting outcome matrix present's alternatives that are not mutually exclusive in helping to solve or mitigate the nuclear safety and environmental problems in Cuba. It may be the case that one policy option may be employed in conjunction with another "alternative."

Table 1. Cuba's Sources of Energy

Type of Generation	Potential MW	%
Thermo-electric	2,983.5	80.3
Hydroelectric	48.6	1.3
Gas Turbine	100.0	2.7
Sub-Total	3,132.1	84.3
Industrial Plants	584.4	15.7
TOTAL	3,716.5	100.0

Source: Miguel Serradet Acosta, "Programa Nucleoenergético Cubano," a paper presented at the Regional Seminar on Public Information, Havana, Cuba, May 19, 1995, p. 3.

This study employs a benefit-cost (BC) analysis as the evaluative criteria.[10] BC conceptualizes the domain of benefits accrued to a society (valued by the society itself) in terms of their utility. BC views the nuclear policy problem as involving some production relationship between scarce and highly constrained resources (economic and natural) and beneficial outcomes. This type of analysis also allows for those resources and benefits to be variable in scale. The choice of one policy alternative does not necessarily mean that all other considerations impacting the decision-making process are eliminated. Far too often in the debate surrounding Cuba's nuclear ambitions a zero-sum relationship is established muting the possibility of resolving any of the issues at hand.

---

8. Interview by author with Arnaldo Coro Antich, Chief Science and Technology Correspondent, Radio Havana, Havana, Cuba. Information obtained in this interview was verified in subsequent interviews with Cuban officials and a former engineer with Sherritt Ltd., the leading oil producer in Cuba, in January 1996.

9. Recent visits to Cuba by the now former Russian Deputy Prime Minister Oleg Soskovets and Russian Minister of Foreign Affairs Yevgeniy Primakov sparked a renewed interest in the status of Cuban and Russian economic relations. Together they signed bilateral trade and cooperation agreements in the areas of oil and nuclear energy for preferable trade arrangements, financing and technology assistance. There is a suggestion that this is a renewal of the barter of oil for sugar by two cash strapped economies. See Jonathan Benjamin-Alvarado, "Cuban Nuclear Developments," *The Monitor: Nonproliferation, Demilitarization and Arms Control*, Vol. 2, No. 1-2 (Winter-Spring 1996), p. 1. See also, "Russian, Cuban Accord on Completion of Reactor," Agence France Presse, (February 24, 1996); and "Cuba-Nuclear Plant JV Seen by June," *Caribbean Update* (April 1, 1996).

10. Gene Bardach, *Analysis: A Handbook for Practice (Part 1)*, University of Washington Institute for Public Policy and Management, Public Service Curriculum Exchange, 1995.

The most important criterion is that the projected outcome solves the policy problem to an acceptable degree. The present condition of U.S.-Cuban relations requires us to assess the impact with a judgement on our part whether and why a given alternative is thought to be desirable and by whom. This is the difficulty and the challenge of such an analysis.

ENVIRONMENTAL IMPERATIVES—RISKS AND REWARDS

Prior to Cuba's decision to suspend construction of the two reactors at Juraguá, numerous questions had been raised concerning the safety of the reactors, the lack of international scrutiny of the construction site, allegations of shoddy workmanship, and the potential for a "Cuban Chernobyl," a mere two hundred miles from the southern shore of the United States. This section will attempt to clarify the risks and rewards of Cuba's pursuit of a nuclear energy capability, including those related to nuclear safety, reactor design, the potential impact of a nuclear incident, and a summary of assessments of the state and integrity of the Cuban nuclear program. A review of economic constraints will focus on Cuba's search for a legitimate source of financing to complete the project, as well as details surrounding the formation of the empresa mixta (a joint venture), the Juraguá Consortium between Russia and Cuba. Finally, this section will briefly touch upon the "impact" of the Helms-Burton Amendment of 1996, the political implications of Russia's apparent re-commitment to competing Juraguá.

Nuclear Safety

Critics assert that the prevailing economic difficulties have forced the Castro regime to cut corners, approve shoddy workmanship, and compromise safety considerations. The debate over safety at Juraguá raises the possibility of a "Cuban Chernobyl." Critics contend that if a "major" or "serious" incident were to take place, large amounts of radioactive discharge could spew into the atmosphere and surrounding waters. The radioactive fallout would create a "dead-zone" with a 18-mile radius where nothing could survive; a 200-mile where there would be serious health risks and food production would be impossible; pockets of high contamination that could drift as far as 300 miles away; and a radioactive cloud creating serious ecological damage as far north as Tampa, Florida, with a secondary fallout extending to a 900-mile radius (depending on prevailing weather conditions).[11] The prevailing ocean currents would carry the radioactive fallout westward through the Jagua Trough, possibly spreading the contamination to the southern Cuban archipelago, including the Isla de Pinos.[12]

The Cuban reactor was the first Soviet nuclear venture in the Western Hemisphere. The challenges of building the reactor so far from home and in a completely different climate led to extensive delays in the construction schedule.[13] Moreover, defectors familiar with procedures and practices at the reactor construction site label Juraguá "technical disaster."[14] Vladimir Cervera, an engineer working in quality control at the reactor, stated that x-ray analysis showed that the welding pipes in the cooling system were weakened by air pockets, bad soldering, and heat damage. He continued to say, of the pipes that were originally approved, 15 percent were later found to be flawed. Another defector, geologist José Oro, stated that the plant has numerous faulty seals and structural defects, and that the steam system has been left outdoors uncovered since December 1990. This would have exposed the equipment to highly corrosive tropical salt air, inflicting critical damage. The stability of this equipment is essential to reactor safety, because leakage or other structural failure could result in a

---

11. Benjamin-Alvarado and Belkin, p.22.

12. "Industrial Analysis - Oceanography: Critical to Economic Development," *CubaNews,* Vol. 2, No. 8 (August 1995), p. 9.

13. John Shanahan, "Cuba's Potential Chernobyls," *The Wall Street Journal* (August 5, 1992), p. A14.

14. Shanahan, *op. cit.*

meltdown.[15] Russian and Cuban officials responsible for safety, construction and quality control defensively and flatly deny that Juraguá's safety is a legitimate concern. They point to Finland's Loviisa Soviet-designed VVER nuclear reactor as evidence of a safely-operating Soviet-designed nuclear power facility.[16] Cuban specialists who had worked at the Juraguá site are quoted as saying that the Juraguá facility is virtually earthquake and tornado-proof. They also say that the humid climate and the possibility of direct air crash have been taken into consideration into the construction of the containment structure.[17] They do acknowledge that a nuclear incident is possible but contend that the area of fallout would be limited to an area of no more than 30 km (18.6 miles) and would pose a threat to no other countries. Furthermore, they argue that the probabilities for Juraguá are in line with those of other pressurized water cooled reactors.[18] In response to the criticism of Cuba's nuclear policy, a leading Cuban official states that, "Cubans would never build a nuclear plant that isn't safe, we are the ones who have to live here, we are the ones the most concerned with it."[19] Dr. Daniel Codorniú Pujals, President of the Agencia de Energía Nuclear (AEN) contends that even with the prevailing economic difficulties, Cuba has been able to reorient its focus on maintenance and conservation.[20]

Even with these reassurances from Cuban officials the doubts persist. In testimony before the House Subcommittee on the Western Hemisphere, Kenneth O. Fultz of the Resources, Community, and Economic Development Division of the U.S. General Accounting Office stated:

> Furthermore, the assessments of risks from earthquakes and dispersion of radioactive pollutants suggest that an active seismic fault could produce large to moderate earthquakes. In fact, in 1992 this plate produced a 7.0 on the Richter scale. A 1988 assessment estimated that the Cienfuegos area could produce an earthquake with a probable maximum magnitude of 5.0 on the Richter scale.[21]

At a recent seminar in Washington, Thomas Cochran, Senior Scientist, with the Natural Resources Defense Council discussed the safety concerns regarding the Juraguá plant. The potential dangers posed to the United States by the power plant were dismissed by Cochran. Rather than being based on scientific findings, he concludes that these concerns were fueled by anti-Castro sentiments that have prevented pursuit of a policy that could ensure safe operation of the plant.[22] One could not expect a Cherno-

---

15. "Cuban warns of risky reactors," Editorial, *The Washington Times* (May 6, 1992), p. A1. See also José R. Oro-Alfonso, "Some Aspects About Environmental Pollution and Protection of Ecological Systems in Cuba and Its Surroundings," unpublished manuscript (November 1991), p. 21.

16. Press Conference Transcript, NBC Nightly News (July 5, 1991).

17. A comprehensive exposition of the technical attributes of the CEN Juraguá are contained in Miguel Serradet Acosta, "Programa Nucleoenergético Cubano," a paper presented at the Regional Seminar on Public Information, in Havana, Cuba, May 19, 1995. For details see also, proceedings of the congressional hearing "International Commercial Reactor Safety," July 25, 1991 before the Subcommittee on Nuclear Regulation of the Committee on the Environment and Public Works, U.S. Senate, 102d Congress (Washington, D.C.: GPO, 1991); and "Nuclear Safety: Concerns With the Nuclear Power Reactors in Cuba," testimony before the House Subcommittee on the Western Hemisphere, Committee on International Relations (GAO/RCED-92-262, Sept. 24, 1992) and (GAO/T-RCED-95-236, August 1, 1995).

18. Berta García, Tamara Acosta, Elizabeth Caraballo, and Julio Enrique Milián, "Correspondencia con los lectores: Preguntas e inquietudes acerca de la Central Nuclear en Juraguá," *Nucleus,* No 19 (1995), pp. 55-56.

19. Interview by author with Miguel Serradet Acosta, Director, Centrales Electronucleares, MINBAS, Havana, January 15, 1996.

20. Interview by author in Havana, Cuba, January 18, 1996.

21. "Concerns with the Nuclear Power Reactors in Cuba," GAO/T-RCED-95-236 (August 1, 1995), p. 7; see also Jerome L. Heffter and Barbara J.B. Stunder, *Transport and Dispersion for a Potential Accidental Release of Radioactive Pollutants From the Nuclear Reactor at Cienfuegos, Cuba,* NOAA, Air Resources Laboratory (August 1992).

22. For a summary of Cuba's nuclear bureaucracies see Darío Gandarias Cruz and Daniel Codorniú, "El Programa Nuclear Cubano y su Infraestructura Científico-Técnico," (Havana: Agencia de Energía Nuclear de Cuba, 1995).

byl-type accident in Cuba. Unlike the Chernobyl RBMK-type reactor, the VVER reactor design incorporates a second containment structure for preventing the release of radiation in case of an accident. Juraguá is a "one-of-a-kind" reactor design that is similar in design to 27 other Russian-designed reactors currently operating in the former Soviet Union and Eastern Europe. These reactors have operated for 400 reactor-years without a major accident. Cochran emphasizes that if a nuclear accident were to occur, most of the environmental degradation and radiation discharged would be limited to Cuba. He was critical of the Cuban expenditure on nuclear energy, stating that upgrading the power generation capability of the island's 156 sugar mills using co-generation of bagasse is far less expensive and could provide up to one-quarter of Cuba's energy needs.[23]

Economic Constraints

In the search for a legitimate source of financing to complete construction of the Juraguá project it is necessary to discuss the nature of Cuban cooperation with the Russian nuclear firms, Atomoemergoexport and Zarubezhatomenergostroy, and the role that Russian specialists continue to play at the site. Both firms continue to have a limited number of engineers at the site (estimated at about 200) mostly working in a supervisory capacity.

Numerous international firms have been mentioned as potential partners including Ansaldo SpA of Italy, Siemens KWU of Germany and Electricite de France (EdF). Yet, when these firms are queried about their involvement with Cuban nuclear plans, all deny that there are any plans to provide assistance in the reactor construction. Once this firm is found, any association would ensure that the third partner (tercer socio) of the joint venture (empresa mixta) would be first to recoup its investment in the project, the Russians second and the Cuban partner last.[24] The joint venture proposes to sell electrical generation to the Cuban state electrical power firm. From the time that the joint venture nuclear cooperation deal is finalized it would take approximately 36 to 42 months for operation to begin. This places the startup date at fall 1999 at the absolute earliest.

Political Considerations

The Helms-Burton Amendment of 1996 expressly proscribes any assistance to the Cuban nuclear program and seeks to penalize and states or firms with a dollar-for-dollar reduction in foreign assistance from the United States. Because Russia has committed itself to providing Cuba with assistance to finish the construction at Juraguá, and because Russia is receiving aid from the United States for its nuclear program, it is uncertain what this will mean for relations within this policy triangle. Compounding this uncertainty is the provision within this new law that exempts application of the penalties to aid to Russia covered under the Cooperative Threat Reduction (CTR) Act of 1991. Virtually all assistance going to Russia's nuclear infrastructure is covered under the CTR. Moreover, Russia's Ministry of Atomic Energy (MINATOM) operates with a high degree of autonomy that calls into question how effective sanctions emanating from the Helms-Burton legislation will be against the Russians. The uncertain international environment for accepting U.S. law, the increased Russian commitment to cooperating with Cuba, and Cuban resolve to complete Juraguá, set a complex of obstacles and imperatives before a rational resolution of the potential for a nuclear facility of questionable integrity.

SUMMARY

Three factors currently weigh heavily against the safety of Cuba's nuclear programs. First, the fact that no comprehensive technological and scientific assessment of the Cuba's nuclear facilities is readily avail-

---

23. Comments taken from a presentation at the Washington seminar on Juraguá, May 9, 1996; See also Jonathan Benjamin-Alvarado, "The Washington Seminar on the 'Juraguá Power Plant: Threat to U.S. Security?'" *The Monitor: Nonproliferation, Demilitarization, and Arms Control*, Vol. 2, No. 3 (Summer 1996), p. 31.

24. The total investment for the third partner is estimated at $500 million over a three year period, the Russian investment would total about $300 million dollars. The Cuban contribution to the joint venture would be in the form of labor provided in bulk construction. See authors interview with Serradet Acosta; and Serradet Acosta, *Programa Nucleoenergético Cubano*, pp. 12-13.

Table 2.   The State of Construction at the CEN Juraguá - Reactor No. 1 (as of 5/96)

Type of Work	Volume of Project	Completed	%
CIVIL:			
Movement of earth (m³)	4,321,363	3,600,620	83
Concrete (m³)	354,023	270,268	76
Reinforced Steel (Tons)	27,023	23,396	86
Steel Inserts (Tons)	4,870	4,461	92
Metallic Structures (Tons)	9,967	7,799	78
MECHANICAL:			
Thermo-mechanical Equipment (Tons)	2,031	1,174	44
Pressurized Steam Equipment (Tons)	1,039	655	63
Ventilation Equipment (Tons)	990	241	24
Electrical Equipment (Tons)	14,742	2,066	14

Source: M. Serradet Acosta, "Programa Nucleoenergético Cubano" (1995), p. 12, and interview by the author with Serradet Acosta, (January 15, 1996), Havana, Cuba.

able, gives rise to the uncertainty of the safety of its nuclear program. Second, claims and counterclaims about the shoddy construction and poor construction of the reactors at Juraguá suggests that there is a reasonable doubt for concern. Finally, Russia's legacy in nuclear industry leaves much to be desired. Its intimate cooperation with Cuba compounds the already existing fears and opprobrium to the development of nuclear energy on the island. Although, preliminary assessments of the reactor design, the safety record of other similarly designed reactors, and the on-going development of Cuba's nuclear bureaucracy, all suggest a positive movement toward a competent nuclear industry, legitimate doubts remain. Here, in a passing nod to Ronald Reagan's position regarding Soviet compliance on disarmament measures, we can trust the Cubans are doing the right thing, but we must also verify that this is so.

The loss of Cuba's Soviet benefactor has rocked the Cuban economy. Moreover, it has forced the nuclear program to refocus its meager resources toward maintaining what facilities already existed and hoping to be able to conserve its partially constructed reactors until such time as it could secure financing for the completion of the projects at Juraguá. The constraints are considerable and suggest that if Cuba intends to complete Juraguá, many of the procedures

associated with a safely operating nuclear facility will have to be compromised. This is a realistic suggestion when one sees how much difficulty Brazil, a country with a significantly larger economy, has had in completing its own civilian nuclear energy reactors. The economic rationale of nuclear energy development in Cuba has always been questionable. In light of its recent economic difficulties, and its growing inability to maintain energy sufficiency, its decision to continue this pursuit is understandable yet is a high risk for completion. The resources that have applied to this pursuit may have been put to better use in the development of other sources of energy.

When assessing Cuba's continued pursuit of nuclear energy one must seriously consider how much political capital it could earn by completing the project. Domestically, it would be a gold rush of sorts, the ultimate show of defiance in the backyard of Los Señores Imperialistas.[25] Here it matters little how efficient these reactors would be. The idea of such a high technological accomplishment becomes the highlight of the success of the revolution. Internationally, there is little opposition to Cuba's attempts to develop nuclear energy with the exception of the United States.

---

25. This refers to the billboard across the street from the U.S. Interests Section in Havana, Cuba in which a Cuban revolutionary dressed in full combat gear staring across the water to a wart-nosed caricature of Uncle Sam states "*Señores Imperialistas No Tenemos Ningún Miedo de Uds.*"

FUTURE SCENARIOS AND PROJECTED OUTCOMES

Resuming Construction

The potential for environmental disaster because of a nuclear incident exists but will most likely be concentrated in Cuba, devastating the island. The $800 million estimate from the Ansaldo feasibility study is conservative because there remain unanswered concerns about nuclear safety, no means of independent verification of claims and counterclaims regarding the integrity of the CEN Juraguá. It is important to remember that the IAEA is not a regulatory body in the strictest sense of the word. Although it provides services for operational safety and review assessments, its primary function is that of promotion of nuclear power, providing monitoring and verification against proliferation of nuclear weapons capabilities. Moreover, even with the establishment of new agencies within the Cuban government for the environment, nuclear safety, and material control and accounting, questions remain regarding the competence of such agencies and their inherent ability to meet internationally recognized standards of environmental protection and nuclear safety. This is especially relevant in the wake of the Chernobyl experience and because of Cuba's close cooperation with Russia in the area of nuclear energy. Moreover, Espino, Díaz-Briquets, Pérez-López and others, assert that Cuba's over reliance on symbolic undertakings often negate and are in essence immune to the clearly definable environmental considerations.

Continuing the "State of Suspension"

By continuing to keep the project in the state of "suspension" or "conservation," the Cubans keep open the possibility of finding a source of financing the completion of the nuclear project. The negative implication of this alternative is that it does little to assuage the concerns of the international community regarding the integrity of the Juraguá construction site. Russia's renewed commitment without the requisite financial resources, relegates its capacity to assist the Cubans, to a symbolic gesture of friendship. This is by far the least costly of the options presently available to the Cubans. Choosing this option raises the specter that continues to be a source of much of the criticism related to Juraguá, that of inadequate storage and deterioration of mechanical equipment. If at such time that Cuba finds the means to restart construction, its engineers may find that the equipment has been irreparably damaged by the elements. Here the Cuban nuclear program may find that even with financing secured, the cost of repairing damaged equipment may place completion of the reactors at Juraguá out of reach. Pursuing this option also means that no comprehensive technical assessment of the site will be forthcoming. In this absence, there can be no verifiable and internationally recognized nuclear safety regimen that adequately responds to all the concerns regarding CEN Juraguá.

Yet this alternative remains the most acceptable to critics of the program for the time being because its signifies that there will be no movement toward completion of this venture. It remains a credible option for Cuban officials because it keeps a window of opportunity for external financing open. The Ansaldo feasibility study, while optimistic about completing the project, may have underestimated the costs of completing Juraguá because of the potential for the unforseen and hidden costs of back fitting, update and replacing weather damaged and poorly maintained equipment.[26] Maintaining the "state of conservation" does not allow observers of the Cuban nuclear program to get any closer to resolving the potential environmental problems that remain a mystery. Cuba's efforts to institute bureaucratic mechanisms that address environmental concerns are laudable, but they are constrained in their ability to

---

26. Much has been made of the vaunted Ansaldo feasibility study. Since its release in 1995 it has served to verify, more than anything else, that much work remains before the Juraguá reactor can be completed. Moreover, the $800 million price tag for completion places it far outside the reach of either Cuba or Russia. Cuba remains a high-risk economic environment for any potential investor, regardless of political persuasion. Until such time as the Cuban economy demonstrates a measure of economic stability and growth most prudent investor will steer clear from any projects in Cuba that do not possess the potential for a short-term return. Unfortunately for Cuban nuclear aspirations, the Juraguá project does not possess such a potential at this time.

Table 3. Outcomes Matrix

Policy Alternatives	Environmental Risk	Economic Viability	Nuclear Safety Status	International Support	Need for Tech. Assistance
Resuming Construction	Uncertain	Low	Uncertain	Moderate/Low	High
State of Suspension	Low	Neutral	High	High	Low
Abandonment of Project	Low	Neutral	High	High	Moderate
Pursuing Alternatives	Moderate	Moderate	High	High	Moderate

Source: By author.

assiduously pursue and resolve environmental concerns.

Abandoning Juraguá - Burying the "White Elephant"

Abandoning the pursuit of a nuclear energy capability may result in an overwhelming public relations disaster of sorts for the Cuban leadership. While failing to finish construction of the Juraguá project would appear to be devastating setback for Cuba's economic recovery, continuing to pursue a project that may never come to fruition, might prove to be costlier for Cuba's long-term hopes for economic and fiscal stability. Committing almost another billion dollars to a project of questionable return would lend added credibility to the suggestion that centrally- directed command economies place symbolic emphasis first before any sound economic rationale. In the case of the Juraguá project, almost two billion dollars will have to be committed by a rather weak and indebted economy, before operation of questionably safe nuclear reactor could conceivably begin. The economic aspect of Cuba's nuclear ambition is less than convincing. And still, the nagging criticisms regarding nuclear safety and the threat of environmental disaster remain. Addressing these needs might require Cuba to invest substantially more than the $800 million mentioned in the Ansaldo feasibility report before Juraguá-1 comes on-line. For critics of the program, this would be the best alternative and would essentially relegate the project to the "dustbin of history," having been written off as a gross inefficiency and a poor energy policy option. This would not in any way lessen Cuba's dependence on oil. The recovery of the present economic system, and introduction of a market or mixed economy will require fossil fuels for the time being. Cuba will still be forced to develop alternative sources of energy that could help it

meet its energy demands with the least amount of environmental degradation. This is the most important decision that confronts any choice related to energy and energy development on the island. Cuba has the most to gain from the development of energy self-sufficiency, but also has the most to lose from it. Unfortunately, poor execution of an nuclear scheme could have virtually permanent and irreversible consequences.

CONCLUSION

Rather than hold out any policy option as the best option, the purpose of this examination has been to weigh the risks and rewards of some of the potential policy alternatives presently available in the case of Cuba's nuclear energy policy. The overriding concern of this examination has been to provide a clear exposition of the environmental impact of developing nuclear energy in Cuba. This has only been partially accomplished. What is readily apparent from this analysis is that it is not a simplistic choice of one option over another. There exist a multiplicity and overlapping of interests and imperatives that compound the decision-making process. Unfortunately these approaches are often at loggerheads and have had the effect of placing the issue into a zero-sum context. What has often been lost in this equation is the effect that all of these competing interests have on the Cuban population itself. The unreliable sources of energy impact the Cuban society most. The potential for an environmental cataclysm will effect this very same group the most. Presently, the inability of the Cuban government to resolve the energy crisis and to provide adequate and verifiable environmental protection for its people is justifiably reason enough for close scrutiny of its nuclear aspirations. The absence of the constructive confidence-building measures in the Caribbean Basin, especially as they relate to Cuba, exacerbates the problematic relationships in place and only serves place an adequate resolution of this situation beyond reach.

Although it lies outside of the realm of political possibilities for the time being. A resumption of technological and scientific exchanges between the United States and Cuban nuclear communities would provide the most tangible means to assuaging the fears of a nuclear disaster in Cuba. This would not be something new. In the late 1980's, the Nuclear Regulatory Commission and officials from Cuba's Secretariado de Energía Atómica Nacional (SEAN) conducted exchanges and visits to facilities in both the United States and Cuba. The purpose of the visits were mostly for information exchange. Re-institution of the exchange program could provide a means of conducting the proper scientific assessments of Cuba's nuclear facilities that are certainly of great importance to all interested parties. Such a program of education and consultation would seek to make individuals aware of problems and opportunities that lie outside of its sphere of policy alternatives presently available. It also serves to provide additional training and professional education in areas that demand a high level of competence and responsibility. This process involves a full assessment of the present state of affairs at the reactor sites, and all associated bureaucracies. The two most important products of such an undertaking are: (1) a clearly defined set of scientific analyses of Cuba's nuclear program that includes potential for reward and the potential for environmental risks and hazards from the exploitation of nuclear energy; and (2) the potential for changing values about the integrity of nuclear energy, in general, and in the integrity of the reactors at Juraguá. When provided with such information all interested parties can openly discuss the true nature of Cuba's nuclear policy. Until such time, even under the most optimistic of political environments, the discussion of the subject will be an exchange of partially substantiated claims and counter-claims, if that.

COMMENTS ON

"The Quest for Power: Analyzing the Costs and Benefits of Cuba's Nuclear Energy Policy" by Jonathan Benjamin-Alvarado

Osvaldo A. Juvier

I appreciate the opportunity to participate in this conference. I had the pleasure of reading the paper Mr. Benjamin-Alvarado wrote and would recommend that you do the same. It provides an excellent perspective of the current situation of the nuclear industry in Cuba and the real problems it is facing in the future.

The paper focuses on the economic and environmental impact of the current program to complete the nuclear power station at Juraguá and its effects on Cuba and its surrounding neighboring countries.

I would like, however, to focus on some aspects of the paper which I believe are very important and perhaps are not treated in sufficient detail:

1. While I strongly agree that in order for the project to continue there should be strict and concise verification of previous work, I believe that the verification task will be almost impossible to accomplish, according to recognized world nuclear construction standards, and that much of the work may have to be demolished and rebuilt. As a result, my estimate of the capital required for the completion of the plant could reach as high as US$2 billion and not the $800 million claimed by the Cuban Government.

2. There has not been disclosure of a plan to decommission the plant at the end of its useful life. World standards today require nuclear utilities to provide specific plans and capital allocation programs to make certain that once a nuclear unit reaches the end of its useful life, there will be sufficient planning and capital in place to provide an orderly and environmentally secure dismantling. Also, the spent nuclear fuel storage and disposal plans appear not to be up to international standards, thus creating an environmental uncertainty for the island and neighboring countries.

3. As a result, I believe the project economics do no meet the performance expectations of potential foreign investors, thus creating a scenario of project economics based solely on government subsidies and political motives.

4. The lack of a Cuban nuclear regulatory agency which operates in conjunction with other world nuclear regulators is also a key issue. The current plans of the Cuban government do not call for such agency to exist and the inability of the Cuban nuclear industry to participate and benefit from the international exchange of technology, environmental protection and regulatory issues will be a deciding factor on whether Cuba will effectively implement a nuclear program and whether such program will attract international players.

In summary, Mr. Benjamin-Alvarado's paper contains many interesting details and data which supports his conclusions with which I fully agree. Thank you.

TOURISM/ECOTOURISM IN CUBA

David S. Collis[1]

Cuba's economic crisis and the gradual introduction of market-oriented reforms are having a contradictory impact. These events are damaging the island's physical environment, yet simultaneously creating innovation opportunities for Cuba's environmentalists.

The economic crisis—known to Cubans as the "Special Period in Time of Peace"—has increased pressure to sacrifice environmental protection for economic profit at a time when resources to remedy existing problems are scarce. In addition, the crisis has triggered a decentralized and semi-capitalist development that is incompatible with the existing environmental regulation structure designed for a centralized, socialist economy. However, the crisis has also been the impetus for pursuing "sustainable development" in several sectors. While that rhetorical phrase serves the Cuban government's international political purpose, the term also reflects the opening of real maneuvering room for researchers and environmental activists on the island. These individuals are trying to use this space to influence a centralized system which depends on economic growth for survival. Whether the environmentalists' ideas will be incorporated into official policy remains unclear.

ENVIRONMENTAL REGULATION

Cuba has two main environmental regulation problems. Economic needs frequently over-ride environmental concerns, and the centralized structure means bureaucratic units are often responsible for ensuring their own compliance with environmental laws.

Until April 1994 the Comisión Nacional de Protección del Medio Ambiente y del Uso Racional de los Recursos Naturales (COMARNA-National Commission for Protection of the Environment and the Rational Use of Natural Resources) was the central mechanism through which all matters having an environmental impact passed. This special commission of the Council of Ministers was created in 1977. By 1980, COMARNA offices spread to every province and municipality in Cuba. In April 1994, COMARNA was officially replaced by a new Ministry of Science, Technology and Environment. Though COMARNA has been superseded, its history illustrates the challenges the new bureaucracy will face, and therefore warrants exploration.

In 1981 Law 33, titled "Ley de Protección del Medio Ambiente y del Uso Racional de los Recursos Naturales" (Law for the Protection of the Environment and Rational Use of Natural Resources) made COMARNA the governing organ. This law also made the Havana-based National Commission of COMARNA responsible for suggesting new environmental laws, and verifying that existing laws were obeyed. COMARNA was transformed into a coordinator responsible for incorporating over twenty ministries and institutions in the environmental decision making process.

---

1. This paper draws heavily from the author's article "Environmental Implications of Cuba's Economic Crisis," Issue Number 8, *Georgetown University Cuba Briefing Paper Series* (July 1995).

Analysis of COMARNA as a past overseer of new construction and development illustrates the bureaucratic legacy the new Ministry has inherited. Foreign investors wishing to build hotels in Cuba had to present their ideas to the Institute of Physical Planning which suggested a site and, in most cases, had an environmental impact study performed. The proposed location of the site, the environmental impact study and construction plans were then presented to COMARNA, which reviewed the documents in consultation with environmental experts. Finally CO-MARNA called together a meeting of all relevant ministries and institutions to discuss the project. If all groups agreed on the final proposal, it was approved by Physical Planning and work began. If there were any insurmountable disagreements between the parties, the decision was deferred to the Council of Ministers.

In light of Cuba's economic situation, the Council of Ministers at times may have been more concerned with development than with environmental protection. This occurred, for example, in the discussion of a proposed road linking the mainland with a tourism complex in Cayo Coco. Cuban scientists insisted the road be composed mainly of bridges to permit water circulation vital to the survival of numerous species of fish, sponges and coral. The internal waters, between the archipelago and the mainland, house some of the richest bio-diversity in Cuba. The proposed road/bridges were to take an indirect route spanning gaps between naturally existing land masses.

The construction of these bridges was deemed too expensive by the Cuban government. Because an agreement could not be reached in COMARNA's meeting, the decision was deferred to the Council of Ministers. An important official then intervened pointing out that the planned road/bridge structure did not follow a direct route. The official then proceeded to take out a pen and draw a straight line from the Cayo Coco to the nearest point on the mainland. This design was adopted, and a straight, bermed road with intermittent underwater tunnels was constructed. Scientists argued that there were too few underwater tunnels to maintain natural water flows. Through negotiation, they were able to double

the number of passages, a small victory considering their original opposition to the plan.

This example illustrates that while COMARNA was able to settle minor issues, it did not possess the authority to make a final decision involving controversial matters. When a project was deemed highly attractive, the environmental protection system could be manipulated to serve a more important agenda. In this case, development and the need to attract foreign investment prevailed.

In addition to COMARNA's lack of real authority, its capability to enforce and penalize violators of environmental protection laws was dubious. In several interviews, the author was told that most violations were corrected "voluntarily" because Cuba is "a solution oriented, not penalty oriented" country. No one interviewed could cite an example of violators being taken to court and fined. The majority of Cuban enterprises were (and still are) state-operated, and a COMARNA suit against the state was inconceivable. In essence, COMARNA had no enforcement capability and its only recourse was to work through the existing structures and hope disputes could be resolved voluntarily. This obvious flaw in the system became the center of an ongoing debate, which continued after COMARNA was superseded.

When questioned in early 1994 about the apparent lack of enforcement capabilities, the National Commission of COMARNA pointed out that its staff of approximately twenty people was too small to effectively monitor compliance with regulations. Enforcement was left up to the Ministries which had "more personnel and resources." For example, the Ministry of Agriculture, which both supplied food to the population and promoted agricultural exports, was also responsible for enforcing environmental regulations governing cultivators. In effect, the Ministries were judge and jury of their own affairs.

All of these problems were discussed during interviews with Cuban specialists. They noted that, in the past, when the state was virtually the only investor, disputes were settled relatively quickly, if not necessarily equitably, within the system. However, they acknowledged that the process of "settling disputes among ourselves" began to break down as foreign investments grew and the economic crisis intensified competition between development and environment. Many Cuban specialists suggested that the system would probably be reorganized to address these flaws.

In April 1994, the Cuban government announced the creation of the Ministry of Science, Technology, and Environment, which replaced COMARNA. The publicly proclaimed motivation for the change was a government restructuring aimed at consolidating the activities previously performed by many separate bureaucracies into one ministry. This change reduced a large disconnected bureaucracy into a single ministry of 120 employees led by one minister, two vice ministers, eight directors, and four agency heads. It simultaneously sought to address the previous structure's conceptual problems, including COMARNA's obsolescence and the need for information sharing between the scientific institutes and policy makers.

The new Ministry's structure is geared toward policy formulation, and features four agencies which provide information needed to formulate policy, then implement those policies once they are defined. The agencies are:

- Specialized Information: Integrates the knowledge of the scientific institutes into a central data base.

- Science and Technology: Responsible for the management of the scientific institutes previously affiliated with the Academy of Sciences.

- Environment: Incorporates the expertise of the scientific institutes to recommend policies.

- Nuclear: Pursues the Ministry's agenda for nuclear research and power.

Enforcement of environmental regulations will be carried out by special Provincial Delegations which allegedly will serve as independent overseers separate from the government. Exactly how their independence will be protected is unclear. What power they will have in future conflicts with other parts of government also remains to be clarified.

While the creation of the Ministry was announced in April 1994, it was not until January 1995 that the structure was determined. Raising the environmental issue to the ministerial level and employing "independent overseers" for enforcement purposes appears to be an important step. However, it is too early to determine the relative effectiveness of the environmental protection component of the Ministry. Further research will be needed to determine whether the Provincial Delegations are permitted to carry out their enforcement roles.

TOURISM AND ECOTOURISM

Part of Cuba's response to the elimination of Soviet subsidies has been to develop tourism as a foreign exchange generator.

Between 1990 and 1994, Cuba's tourism grew more than 16 percent annually, compared with 4.7 percent for the Caribbean as a whole. By 1995 tourism ranked as Cuba's second highest gross foreign exchange earner ($1 billion for 1995) after sugar ($1.2 billion). Despite a brief downturn following the rafters exodus in mid-1994, tourist numbers grew again—to 745,000—in 1995. Optimistically, the Cuban government announced it expects to have 50,000 hotel rooms (up from 23,255 in 1995), 2.5 million visitors and a gross revenue of 3-plus billion dollars by the year 2000.[2]

The main tourist centers are Havana, Santiago de Cuba, Cayo Largo, Cayo Coco, and Varadero. This growing industry has profoundly affected Cuba's environment.

For example, the Cuban Institute of Physical Planning states that Varadero was not developed in the most environmentally sound manner. While coastal protection regulations existed, no specific laws were in place. Too many hotels were built and many were badly constructed. Hotels were established close to the beach, and inadequate space was left between buildings. In addition, the introduction of non-na-

---

2. This information is from a forthcoming book by Dr. Martha Honey to be published by the Sierra Club in 1997.

tive trees and plants to the area had an adverse environmental impact.

Only in the last several years has an infrastructure been created to deal with environmental issues associated with tourism. The principal motivation for change has been the realization that if Cuba does not preserve its environment, it will lose its attraction to tourists.

The Institute of Physical Planning has created a sub-group to focus on coastal development. In addition, in 1988 the National Commission of CO-MARNA formed a working group of coastal scientists to minimize the negative impacts of tourism development and preserve the natural surroundings. Scientific experts from the Institute of Ecology, Oceanology, and Geology have also developed programs to address beach erosion, beach regeneration and clean-up. Three years ago the Academy of Sciences created the Dirección de Recursos Naturales y Turismo (Directorate of Natural Resources and Tourism), headed by Dr. Gisela Alonso, to address the new development issues related to tourism. At about the same time Cuba also formed a National Commission on Ecotourism designed to draw on the experiences of other countries. Dr. Alonso is in contact with Costa Rican ecotourism experts and hopes to take a group of two to three Cuban scientists to Costa Rica to see their work first hand.

Already the authorities have decided that a percentage of ecotourism revenue must be spent on park infrastructure, management, and protection. Decisions on the limitation of tourist access to ecotourism sites, preparation of the sites, and development of visitor conduct manuals are also underway. As of November 1994, six sites were under consideration for ecotourism development: Ciénaga de Zapata, Sierra del Rosario, Tope de Collantes, Sierra Maestra, Guanacahabibes, and Pinares de Mayarí. To date, however, ecotourism development has been slow. Preparation of sites requires extensive scientific study, determination of pathways, hotel construction, training of guides, and education of the local population. Funding to start up all these processes simultaneously is lacking.

Whether the need to attract foreign capital will cause Cuba to sacrifice its goal of rational development in this area has yet to be determined. Presently, Cuba has neither the financing nor the construction capability to turn itself into an environmental disaster overnight. The number of proposed ecotourism sites remains small and tourist visits are limited. The current prospects for severe environmental degradation appear low. However, this could change if development plans are redesigned to maximize hard currency earnings.

CONCLUSION

Cuba is at a crossroads. The economic crisis has increased pressures to sacrifice environmental preservation for economic profit. However, that crisis has also presented opportunities for inexpensive, environmentally sound development. It is not yet clear which path Cuba will choose, but some preliminary conclusions are possible.

First, regime survival is linked to economic recovery. Therefore, the government's emphasis on economic development currently overshadows environmental protection. The government is likely to pursue environmental preservation when it is low cost and/or profitable in the short to medium term. By the same token, the government is unlikely to support preservation when it requires costly imported technology or greatly reduces the profitability of a venture.

Second, Cuba's transition to a semi-capitalist economy has rendered obsolete the past environmental regulation structure, designed for a centralized socialist economy. The creation of the Ministry of Science, Technology and Environment has addressed some of the conceptual problems inherent in the former structure. However, it has yet to be seen if regulations will be enforced. Without enforcement, it does not matter how many environmental protection laws are enacted.

In sum, Cuba is neither an ecological disaster area nor a paradise. Environmentally destructive decisions have been taken in some instances, while preservation concerns have won in others. Cuban experts working in the field are aware that the most critical profit versus environmental protection decisions have yet to be made. Growing environmental awareness at the grass roots, the population's relatively high level of scientific education, the lower cost of some environmentally sound methods, and the acknowledged importance of environmental protection to long term tourism revenues all provide limited grounds for hope. However, the economic and political forces militating against environmental protection remain formidable and should not be underestimated.

FOREIGN INVESTMENT IN CUBA: THE LIMITS OF COMMERCIAL ENGAGEMENT

María C. Werlau

Since the collapse of the Soviet Bloc, the Cuban government embarked on economic liberalization based on the adoption of capitalist mechanisms which include an opening to foreign investment. This has led to increasing claims abroad that engagement—particularly commercial engagement within the context of constructive engagement[1]—is the policy instrument that will lead to economic and political reform and the eventual collapse of Castro's regime. Engagement, in fact, is the fundamental element of the foreign policy of most countries towards Cuba. The emerging "new consensus" argues that the Communist Cuban regime will not be able to withstand the corrosive practices of liberal capitalism and, for this reason, considers the development of business ties with the current government desirable.[2]

The United States' policy towards Cuba has generally varied in approach; its importance is widely recognized given the two countries' geographic proximity and the historic significance of their relations. With some exceptions—the most notable during the Carter Administration—since the early years of the Castro government, it has been essentially founded on political isolation and a comprehensive economic embargo.[3] For this reason, since Cuba began a decisive opening to foreign capital, U.S. investors have been precluded from potential business opportunities there and Cuba has been unable to access the largest consumer market and source of capital and tourism in the hemisphere. Presently, the issue of U.S. commercial engagement with Cuba is considered settled until a transition to democracy is initiated there or further legislation dictates a change in policy. The Clinton Administration had been committed to encouraging a distinctive policy mechanism, which might be described as "focused engagement," aimed at supporting the emergence of a civil society in Cuba.[4] But after Cuba's February 1996 repression of an

---

1. Although the term commercial engagement generally refers to diverse international commercial and financial transactions, we will use it primarily in reference to foreign investment. The term "constructive engagement" encompasses economic engagement and is normally used within the context of a more comprehensive diplomatic and political relationship.

2. See, for example, Robert Kagan, "Is Castro Convertible? A Skeptic says No," *Standard*, Vol. 1, No. 5 (October 16, 1995).

3. The embargo was declared by President Kennedy in February 1962 as a result of Cuba's subversion of democratic nations in the hemisphere and its confiscation of $1.8 billion in U.S. properties. Formal diplomatic relations do not exist and almost all trade is banned, with exceptions for humanitarian assistance and payment to Cuba for telecommunications.

4. This policy line was codified in the 1992 Cuban Democracy Act, passed by Congress in 1992 during President Bush's tenure but also supported by then presidential candidate Bill Clinton. This law's Track II seeks to increase "people to people" contacts with looser restrictions on academic and cultural exchanges and was intended by the Clinton Administration as a tool to encourage private U.S. organizations to play a more active role in promoting a civil society in Cuba, looking to facilitate a more peaceful transition to democracy. See Richard Nuccio, "Promoting civic culture and support for the Cuban people," remarks at the conference *The United State and Civil Society in Cuba: A Discussion with the NGO Community*, Washington, D.C., December 1995. At the time, Mr. Nuccio was Special Adviser to the President on Cuba.

emerging organized peaceful opposition and its shoot down of two civilian aircraft belonging to the U.S.-based organization Brothers to the Rescue, President Clinton codified and strengthened the embargo by signing into law The Cuban Liberty and Solidarity Act (known as the Helms-Burton law after its Congressional sponsors). Although the Helms-Burton law does not seemingly affect Track II-focused engagement initiatives, these have been seriously curtailed by Cuba since March 1996. Nevertheless, the new law has elicited heated international debate, underscoring the relevance of commercial engagement as a policy prescription.

This paper explores issues related to the reform-generating capabilities of foreign investment as an instrument of commercial engagement by addressing three main themes deemed essential to developing a comprehensive understanding of this issue. The first part recounts Cuba's campaign to attract foreign capital, contrasting optimistic media reports to its generally unsuccessful results. The second part explains Cuba's disappointing performance by looking at the island's high-risk investment climate. The third part analyzes whether the current Cuban regime will be undermined by the influence of capitalist/market mechanisms of foreign investment and explores certain foreign policy implications.

The emerging conclusion is that two primary factors inhibit the workability of foreign investment as an instrument of reform in Cuba, rendering the argument for commercial engagement insupportable. First, the island's poor business prospects limit opportunities for achieving a level of foreign investment that can impact the economy and society in a meaningful way. Second, the existing joint venture framework—Cuba's *mode* of foreign investment—has been designed to secure regime survival by accessing foreign capital while suppressing the impact of socio-economic and political mechanisms. As a result, its most important reform-generating attributes are restrained and its detrimental side-effects actually hinder the eventual establishment of a stable free-market democracy.

I apologize to the readers for delivering a paper that grew far beyond its intended size as a result of my investigation. For this reason, it appears here in a shortened version, some of its sections greatly summarized.[5]

CUBA'S DRIVE TO ATTRACT FOREIGN INVESTMENT

Selling Cuba

With the demise of Soviet Communism, Cuba faced the loss of massive aid from the former Soviet Union. To cope with the devastating effects on its economy, beginning in 1989 the Cuban leadership took an unprecedented step. It opened the door to selective aspects of capitalism, which had been virtually eradicated and bitterly vilified since Fidel Castro declared Cuba a Marxist-Leninist Republic in 1961. Since its inception, the most decisive element of this opening has been a drive to attract foreign capital, essentially in the form of joint venture and economic cooperation agreements between state enterprises and foreign investors.[6] In the early nineties, several constitutional and legal amendments were passed and the commit-

---

5. This paper is a revised and shortened version of a draft presented at the VI Annual Meeting of the Association for the Study of the Cuban Economy, Miami, August of 1996. My deepest appreciation goes to Stuart Lippe for his valuable advice and encouragement in the preparation of this edited version.

6. The foreign investment law defines three forms of foreign investment in Cuba: foreign joint ventures, international economic associations, and companies with 100 percent foreign capital. Our references to joint ventures apply generally to all three forms of investment. A joint venture is defined as "Cuban commercial company which adopts the form of a nominal share corporation, in which one or more national investors and one or more foreign investors participate." An international economic association is: "Joint action by one or more national investors and one or more foreign investors within the national territory for the production of goods, the offering of services or both for profit, in its two forms, which consist of joint ventures and international economic association contracts." See Republic of Cuba, Ministry of Foreign Investment and Economic Cooperation, *Foreign Investment Law*, La Habana: Editora Política, 1995. It appears that economic association or cooperation agreements do not imply the infusion of capital or the acquisition of capital participation by the foreign partner(s). Nevertheless, for simplicity's sake and due to the unavailability of specific data on this type of foreign investment, our references to foreign joint ventures will also include them.

ment and pace of Cuba's campaign to lure foreign investors intensified.[7] Given the less enthusiastic adoption of other measures of market-oriented reform, luring foreign capital has remained a consistent priority of the Cuban government's attempts to foster a desperately needed economic recovery.[8]

Indeed, Cuba has some unique things to offer foreign investors: neglected factories at bargain prices, investors' ability to freely repatriate profits and a potential to obtain fast and/or high returns. A highly educated workforce, desperately in need of employment, and kept under tight State control, is plentiful. In addition, according to John Kavulich, President of the U.S.-Cuba Trade and Economic Council (US-CTEC),[9] and others, the Cuba of 1995 offers "the potential consumption of 11 million inhabitants, the political stability and the familiarity Cubans have with U.S. brands,"[10] "and most tantalizing of all,

Americans are barred from trading there."[11] Primarily, because "the weight of geography is overwhelming," non-U.S. companies and investors are being urged to tie up as much business as they can get their hands on. "They will be first in a market, which, when the embargo goes, will become one big magnet for American tourists and American cash."[12]

Reports of foreign businessmen and business delegations visiting the island abound. Cuba has signed preferential trade and investment promotion and protection agreements with more than a dozen countries. The 1995 Havana International Trade Fair is said to have attracted 1,690 companies from 52 countries.[13] The U.S. business community has also shown interest in scouting Cuba's potential and conferences on "business opportunities in the new Cuba" have proliferated.[14] The Economist reported that from 1994 to 1996 "about 1,500 representatives of

---

7. In 1992 Cuba's National Assembly passed several Constitutional amendments to modify the concept of private property, providing a legal basis for transferring state property to joint ventures with foreign partners while abolishing the state monopoly on foreign trade. In 1982, Cuba's Council of State had approved Decree Law 50 allowing foreign private investment in the form of joint ventures, but it was only when the economy tailspinned into a severe decline that the Cuban government began an increasingly aggressive campaign to attract foreign investment to the island.

8. The Cuban government has staged an energetic campaign to lure foreign investors. Foreign Minister Roberto Robaina has toured several major world cities, including New York, to court the international business community. Castro's highly publicized trip to New York in October 1995 for the 50th Anniversary of the United Nations has perhaps been the highlight of Cuba's efforts. Bolstering Castro's new image, the Rockefellers, bastion of American Capitalism, extended him a dinner invitation, which provoked strong protests, while Mortimer Zuckermann, editor of *U.S. News & World Report*, hosted a lunch for him at this Fifth Avenue apartment; the *U.S.-Cuba Trade and Economic Council* reported to the media that more than 200 influential persons wanted to meet with Castro.

9. The USCTEC's stated objective is to "provide an efficient and sustainable educational structure in which the U.S. business community may access accurate, consistent, and timely information and analysis on matters and issues of interest regarding United States-Cuba commercial, economic, and political relations." Founded in June 1994 as a non-profit organization, its tax status in the U.S. precludes advocacy. As a result, it does not take official positions vis-à-vis Cuba policies. For its part, the Cuban press has reported that Mr. Kavulich is "the main bridge between U.S. businessmen and Fidel Castro's government" and has "a special mission to open avenues, dissipate doubts, show the cracks through which to penetrate the wall of the blockade." Materials provided by the Council offer services which include "fully hosted" visits to Cuba. In July 1996 the Council had 138 members, which were said to include "some of the largest public and private corporations in the U.S. to individual entrepreneurs." Five percent of the members come from seven countries, including England, Canada and Mexico. Mr. Kavulich explains that the secrecy surrounding the Council's membership since its inception is a result of "competitive reasons." Based on telephone conversations of July 1996 with Mr. Kavulich; "Why the Council was established," *U.S.-Cuba Trade and Economic Council*; Homero Campa y Orlando Pérez, "Business are (sic) business" and "Exxon, IBM, ITT, Ford, y General Electric ya desbloquearon a Cuba," *Proceso, Semanario de Información y Análisis*, No. 959 (March 20, 1995); "John Kavulich: no me importa caminar sobre un campo minado..., *Bohemia; Caribbean Update*, Vol. 10, No.11 (December 1994); *Opciones, Semanario Financiero, Comercial y Turístico de Cuba*, Año 1, No. 46 (11-17 December 1994); and Michael Hayes, "New York entrepreneur offers facts, figures, on Cuban market," *Miami Today* (25 August 1995).

10. Elsy Fors, "Empresas norteamericanas negocian con Cuba," *Síntesis* (7 April 1995). Emphasis added.

11. "Heroic illusions: A Survey of Cuba" ("Cuba Survey"), *The Economist* (6 April 1996), p. 12. Emphasis added.

12. "Heroic illusions: A Survey of Cuba," p. 12.

13. *Economic Eye on Cuba* (30 October-5 November 1995).

14. Among some notable examples have been *The Economist Conferences* "Roundtables with The Government of Cuba." One of them, held in Havana in October of 1995, was co-sponsored by Sherritt and Iberia Airlines and titled "Cuba: a tiger in the making?"

American firms have made 'fact-finding' trips, often at the invitation of the Cuban government."[15] In August 1995 Cuban Ambassador to the United Nations, Bruno Rodríguez, stated that more than 100 U.S. companies had signed letters of intent with state-owned businesses in Cuba outlining areas of potential cooperation if trade relations were normalized (i.e., once, or if, the U.S. embargo is lifted).[16]

Cuba's drive to attract investors has also generated ample media attention. Reports of the island's opening to capitalism were spurred by its late 1993 economic reforms and the revised foreign investment law of September 1995. These incited increasingly optimistic accounts on Cuba's "move toward a market economy."[17] In the U.S. the thrust of most of these reports, together with many editorial pronouncements, was that the U.S. was missing out on opportunities in Cuba while others where eagerly gaining a foothold in a new market, taking advantage of the absence of U.S. competitors.[18] Specific investments received wide coverage, particularly the Canadian company Sherritt's mining investments and Cuba's first privatization—the telephone joint venture ETECSA with the Mexican Grupo Domos.[19] The

most consistently cited source in many media reports is John Kavulich, the President of the aforementioned US.-Cuba Trade and Economic Council.[20] He typically accentuates the interest of the business community with statements such as: "There's no question that Cuba is the most exciting developing market in the world;"[21] and "For every day the U.S. business community is precluded from Cuba, it will take a year to catch up with overseas competitors."[22]

Cuba's professed economic potential has captured interest, yet projections of actual opportunities are widely divergent. At a June 1996 conference in New York, experts, however, agreed that in a post-U.S. embargo/free market scenario Cuba would have investment needs of up to around $14 billion.[23] But given the island's paltry economic performance, most claims tend to seem excessively optimistic. Many assessments lack an explanation on how they have been developed and most presume a series of profound changes that have not taken place—namely implementation of structural economic reform and the lifting of the U.S. embargo. In sum, analysts concur that Cuba must be rebuilt and desperately needs just about everything: telecommunications, railroads,

---

15. "Cuba Survey," *The Economist* (April 6, 1996), p. 15.

16. Sam Dillon, "Companies press Clinton to lift embargo on Cuba," *The New York Times* (August 25, 1995).

17. Some examples include: Howard French, "The end has begun: Even Castro sees the possibilities of enterprise in Cuba," *The New York Times* (August 8, 1993); "Still on the sidelines: Hard-line stance on Cuba may mean missed opportunities for U.S. business," *New York Newsday*, Business Section (September 18, 1994); Micheline Maynard, *USA Today* (December 27, 1994) cover story and related articles: "Cuba; open for business U.S. firms ready to tap opportunity;" "Farmers' markets are big success;" "Planning helps ease travel effort;" "Dollars reign supreme in the marketplace; Cuba scouting for investors"; and Douglas Farah, "Foreign investors finding Cuba more comfortable – with U.S. away," *The Washjington Post* (September 12, 1995).

18. See, e.g., Douglas Farah, "Foreign investors finding Cuba more comfortable"; Mireya Navarro, "Cuba passes law to attract greater foreign investment," *The New York Times* (September 6, 1995); José de Córdoba, "Cuba will allow foreigners to own 100% of firms," *The Wall Street Journal* (September 5, 1995); Jack Kelly, "Cuba's logical step looks like capitalism" (cover story) *USA Today* (March 11, 1996); and Dillon, "Companies press Clinton to lift embargo on Cuba."

19. In "Privatización a la cubana," *AmericaEconomía*, No. 86 (August 1994), especially footnote 51, p. 9.

20. Although the Council does not take official positions with respect to U.S.-Cuba relations, Mr. Kavulich has publicly stated his personal advocacy of the easing of economic restrictions on Cuba.

21. "Seeking a toehold in Cuba," *The Miami Herald* (July 23, 1995).

22. George Moffett, "Lunch with Cuba's Castro? U.S. eyes lifting sanctions," *The Christian Science Monitor* (March 10, 1995). The only member of the Council who has recently come forth publicly—Dwayne Andreas, Chairman of Archer Daniel Midland, ADM— has been frequently quoted calling for the removal of the embargo and the establishment of U.S. business in Cuba. Other prominent members of the U.S. business community publicly identified with this position are executives of *Carlson Companies* (which owns *Radisson* hotels) and *Otis* (elevator company), Lee Iaccoca, and Mortimer Zuckermann of *U.S. News and World Report*.

23. Notes taken by the author. Conference sponsored in New York by the Americas Society, the *U.S.-Cuba Business Council* and the Association for the Study of the Cuban Economy.

sewers, utilities, housing, fertilizers, agricultural machinery, elevators, food, medicine, toilet paper, McDonald's...; what no one can answer is how Cuba will generate the means to consume and make the required investments feasible. The seduction of Cuba's "great" or eventual potential for business is, thus, begging a serious examination of present conditions and actual results.

The Results

Although reports coming from Cuba have pervasive discrepancies, for some investors the lure of getting to Cuba first has been tempting and often appears to have been profitable. Companies from Spain, Canada, Mexico, France, Israel, and other countries, have formed joint ventures and signed economic association agreements with the Cuban government, with a typical participation of up to 49 percent.[24] In August 1996 Vice President of the Council of State Carlos Lage, considered as Cuba's "economic czar," was cited as stating that 43 countries are present in 34 economic sectors, with most ventures operating in the areas of tourism and export-oriented products: 28 in mining, 25 in petroleum, 56 in the general industrial sector and 34 in tourism.[25] Some foreign capital enterprises provide supplies of goods and services to other joint ventures.

The tourist sector has proven what is perhaps the most visible aspect of Cuba's push to attract foreign capital—both in terms of a growing number of tourist visits to Cuba each year and probably also in terms

of investment. Since 1990 the number of visitors to Cuba—primarily from Canada, Spain, Italy, Germany, and France—has reportedly increased by 54 percent, and earnings by 75 percent;[26] from January through June of 1996 visitors were said to have risen 46 percent in comparison to 1995.[27] Although projections are showing 2.5 million tourists by the year 2,000,[28] exultant reports have often been subsequently tempered by reality.[29] Statistics on Cuban tourists and earnings from tourism from the USCTEC are given in Table 1.

Table 1. Number of Tourists and Earnings from Tourism, 1990-95

Year	No. of tourists	% change	Earnings US millions	% change
1990	340,300		$ 242.3	
1991	424,400	19.8%	387.4	37.4%
1992	460,600	7.8%	567.0	31.6%
1993	546,000	15.6%	720.0	21.2%
1994	617,000	11.5%	850.0	15.3%
1995	745,000	17.2%	1,000.0	15.0%

Source: *U.S.- Cuba Trade and Economic Council, Inc., Economic Eye on Cuba* (1-7 July 1996).

Conflictive information on tourism investment is common. Despite reports of numerous hotel joint ventures, particularly with Spaniards and Canadians, it is impossible to determine how much represents actual capital inflow, i.e., direct foreign investment. Importantly, joint ventures in hotels "tend to be management contracts: the foreign partner will put

---

24. The Cuban government tends to be the majority shareholder, but there are exceptions. The 1995 Foreign Investment Law contemplates companies comprised with 100 percent foreign capital. Most analysts, however, think this will be authorized in very exceptional cases.

25. Cited in *Negocios en Cuba*, Suplemento del Mundo en Síntesis (19-25 August 1996), p.1.

26. "Cuba Report/Lage...," *The Cuba Report* (August 1996), p. 4. Between 1993 and 1995 tourism in the Caribbean is said to have grown 6.8 percent per annum, while in Cuba growth reached 17 percent.

27. It should, however, be noted that Cuba's tourist season peaks in the first half of each year and it's not clear whether the comparison is made with the same period last year or with the entire year 1995.

28. "Country Report / Lage...," p. 4.

29. For example, Cuba's Deputy Minister of Tourism expressed disappointment with a 15 percent increase in tourism revenues in 1994, short of a projected 30 percent. See Michael Becker, "Tourism misses its goal," *CubaNews*, Vol. 3, No. 2 (February 1995), p. 8. Actually the 15 percent growth rate reported by the Minister is higher than the 11.5 percent growth rate reported by other sources. Also, at least partly as a result of a migration crisis, 1995 was noted to be a "very bad, difficult year" and with the exception of Canada, the number of tourists into Cuba to have been on the decline. In fact, Minister Lage later reported that the first half of 1995 showed no growth compared to the first half of 1994. See "Country Report / Lage...," p.4.

in people and know-how, but hold back the capital."[30] Cuba's Deputy Minister of Tourism reported in late 1995 that "no significant new investments" in the tourist sector had been undertaken for a substantial time period and all the reported new deals were allegedly management arrangements rather than direct or new foreign investment. In July of 1996 this Minister said that the tourism sector had 13 joint ventures covering 8,905 hotel rooms valued at US$728 million.[31] Because the details of this valuation were not offered and the amount is almost as much as Cuba's reported "committed/delivered" figures for total foreign investment as of mid-1996 (see Table 2), direct investment in tourism would have to be lower. Plus, the recent codification of the U.S. embargo in the Helms-Burton law has dampened expectations that its impending lifting would open Cuba to the U.S. tourist market. It could already be affecting realized investment in the tourist sector, as on-going projects based on prospective U.S. tourists are probably being reassessed. The Cuban government, however, continues to claim that more growth is expected in tourist sector investments and from March through May of 1996, immediately after the passage of the Helms-Burton law, the Ministry of Tourism reported four new joint ventures and eight economic associations.[32]

As with the tourist sector, it has been impossible to arrive at actual figures for overall materialized and direct foreign investment in Cuba.[33] This appears to be clouded by smoke screens and manipulated to fit "agendas." The numbers frequently cited both by academics and in the media are those provided by Cuban government officials in speech engagements and interviews, which are then picked up by the media and Cuba-specialized newsletters and reports. In September 1996 Business Tips on Cuba cites Minister of the Economy and Planning, José Luis Rodríguez, informing of 230 joint ventures involving 2,100 million dollars—the same amount of investment cited by Minister of Foreign Investment Ernesto Meléndez one year earlier.[34] Contradictions abound, reports fail to provide data on direct foreign investment, and a distinction is not made between joint ventures and cooperation agreements.[35]

Perhaps the most telling figures are those provided by USCTEC, which has the official collaboration of

---

30. "Cuba Survey," *The Economist*, p. 13.

31. USCTEC, *Economic Eye on Cuba* (1-7 July 1996), p.2. Reportedly, there are 26,000 hotel rooms in the island, "but many do not yet meet international standards."

32. USCTEC, *Economic Eye on Cuba* (24-30 June 1996), p. 3. On July 1, 1996, for example, Canada's Wilton Properties Ltd. formed a joint venture with Cuba's Gran Caribe Tourism Corporation (VANCUBA Holding, S.A.), to purportedly build 11 hotels with 4,200 rooms during the next ten years. The investment calls for both partners to divide the US$400 million cost of the plan. See USCTEC, *Economic Eye on Cuba*, USCTEC, 1 to 7 July, 1996, p.2.)

33. In July of 1996 the author requested in writing and twice by telephone to the Cuban Mission to the United Nations data on foreign investment and/or a meeting with Cuban specialists in this area. Requests went unanswered.

34. *Business Tips on Cuba*, Vol. 3, No. 9 (September 1996), p. 4. *Business Tips on Cuba*, a monthly magazine which promotes business in Cuba, is a project of the *United Nations Program for Development*. It appears in seven languages and is distributed worldwide in more than 40 countries. In the United States the *U.S.-Cuba Trade and Economic Council* is its official distributor.

35. Examples of confusing and contradictory information include: 1) a report by Cuba's Ministry of Economy and Planning for the first semester of 1996 informing that a "total of 240 association agreements have been signed with foreign capital from 43 nations in 34 areas of the economy, while other 143 projects are under negotiation." See, *Cuba: Economic Report, First Semester 1996*, Ministry of Economy and Planning. This report also cites an unemployment rate of 8 percent, "virtually unchanged from 1995," a figure that most analysts consider absurdly low, virtually impossible; 2) the September 1995 issue of the publication *Business Tips on Cuba* stated that Minister of Foreign Investment and Economic Collaboration, Ernesto Meléndez, has reported in May of that year that 212 *economic associations* with firms from 53 countries "have brought in a capital contribution of 2,100 million dollars, which represents a 78 percent growth in relation to the same period of 1994." This $2.1 billion is the same figure reported one year later; 3) in November 1995 Minister Carlos Lage and the *Comisión de Estudios de la Economía Cubana* provided the following information: whereas in 1993 there were 173 joint ventures from 36 countries, by late November 1995 there were 270 from 50 countries. See Magdalys Rodríguez, "Trabas al empresario interesado," *El Nuevo Día* (23 November 1995) and *Negocios en Cuba*, Suplemento del Mundo en Síntesis (19-25 August 1996), p.1.

Table 2. Foreign Investment in Cuba, as of August 1, 1996 (in U.S. dollars)

The following figures represent the amounts of announced, committed, and delivered investments since 1990 by private sector companies and government companies from various countries to enterprises within the Republic of Cuba as of 1 August 1996. Information was compiled through the media, other public sources, individual discussions with company representatives, non-Republic of Cuba government officials, and Republic of Cuba-based enterprise managers and government officials:

Country	Announced	Committed/delivered
Australia	500,000,000	—
Austria	500,000	100,000
Brazil	150,000,000	20,000,000
Canada	41,000,000	100,000,000
Chile	69,000,000	30,000,000
China	10,000,000	5,000,000
Dominican Republic	5,000,000	1,000,000
France	15,000,000	10,000,000
Germany	10,000,000	2,000,000
Greece	2,000,000	500,000
Honduras	7,000,000	1,000,000
Israel	22,000,000	7,000,000
Italy	97,000,000	87,000,000
Jamaica	2,000,000	1,000,000
Japan	2,000,000	500,000
Mexico	2,256,000,000	250,000,000
The Netherlands	300,000,000	40,000,000
Panama	2,000,000	500,000
Russia	25,000,000	2,000,000
South Africa	400,000,000	15,000,000
Spain	350,000,000	125,000,000
Sweden	10,000,000	1,000,000
United Kingdom	75,000,000	50,000,000
Uruguay	500,000	300,000
Venezuela	50,000,000	3,000,000
TOTAL	5,301,000,000	751,900,000

Source: *U.S.- Cuba Trade and Economic Council,* September 28, 1996.

Cuban government entities and representatives. Although contradicting and vague reports have also come from the Council,[36] in mid-July 1996, its President provided the author an updated table (Table 2) on foreign investment in Cuba: $5.3 billion "announced" and $751.9 million "committed/delivered." It should be noted that the USCTEC table does not furnish an explanation of the meaning of "announced" or of "committed/delivered" investment.[37]

Cuba's accounting practices—its reporting of foreign investment and other national accounts, including GDP—do not follow the standards of most countries.[38] The discrepancy in the foreign investment figures provided by the Cuban government is further enhanced by conflicting information obtained elsewhere. Jorge Pérez-López[39] explains:

- The United Nations Conference on Trade and Development, a United Nations organization of which Cuba is an active participant, shows foreign direct investment into Cuba of $1 million in 1990, $10 million in 1991, $13 million in 1992, $21 million in 1993, and $15 million in 1994. It reports cumulative foreign direct investment of $1 million in 1985, $3 million in 1990, $25 million in 1993, and $40 million in 1994.

- Balance of payments data in a 1995 Banco Nacional de Cuba report show foreign direct investment inflows of 54 million pesos in 1993 (US$540,000) and 563 million pesos in 1994 (US$11 million).

---

36. In 1995 Council materials were reporting more than 200 joint ventures valued at US$1.5 billion and total announced investment of US$4 billion. ("Realities of Market Cuba," *U.S.-Cuba Trade and Economic Council,* not dated.) On the other hand, *The Washington Post* quoted Mr. Kavulich stating that by August 1995 there were US$4.9 billion in announced foreign investments, of which $556 million had been formally committed. See Douglas Farah, "Foreign investors finding Cuba more comfortable." Notice that the terminology "formally committed" is vague; by the choice of lexicon it does not appear to mean "actually invested."

37. In a telephone conversation of September 10, 1996 Mr. Kavulich explained that they did not have a figure for materialized direct investment. In July he had indicated that after the passage of the Helms-Burton law, the data on foreign investment would now tend to be politically sensitive, as this posed risks to investors.

38. As per reports of many Cuba analysts, including José Alonso, Research Specialist at the U.S Information Agency's (U.S.I.A.) Radio Martí.

39. Jorge Pérez-López, "Foreign direct investment in the Cuban economy: A critical look," paper for delivery at *Foreign investment in Cuba: past, present, and future,* Workshop sponsored by Shaw, Pittman, Potts & Trowbridge and Oceana Publications, Washington, D.C., January 26, 1996, pp. 9-10.

• A 1994 government of Spain report on Spanish overseas investment cites Cuba as a recipient of $50 million since 1988 and $117 million committed through the year 2000. Furthermore in November of 1995 a high government official of the Spanish government informed the Spanish Congress that Spanish enterprises had invested $28 million (3,350 pesetas) since 1990, mostly in services and tourism,[40] although it has been often said that Spanish investments in Cuba are one of the highest.

In sum, "the Cuban figures do not correspond to the International Monetary Fund's measurement norms and definitions of direct foreign investment."[41] Contrary to standard practice in the calculation of direct foreign investment, the data provided by Cuban sources, in addition to direct capital inflows, appears to include the following: 1) foreign contribution of assets or debt-equity swaps;[42] 2) supplier credits, and other financial agreements; 3) foreign participation in management contracts or production partnership arrangements, defined as international economic association contracts, which are subject to uncertain valuations; 4) "announced" investments which may be contingent on events that do not materialize; 5) in mining investments, exploitation contracts to service or expand deposits already mined (i.e. the component of fresh capital investment is limited); and 6) canceled deals.[43]

The latter is of particular relevance because some of the most publicized investments in Cuba have eventually failed but may still be included in the government's reports. For example, two very large "announced" Mexican investments have fallen through. In September of 1995 Mexican Foreign Minister José Angel Gurría confirmed "the suspension" of a $200 million investment by Mexpetrol and provided no explanation.[44] The Grupo Domos investment was reported to have floundered even before the crisis that led to the passage of the Helms-Burton law by the United States.[45] Another investment gone sour has proven particularly embarrassing for the Cuban

---

40. José Luis Dehesa, Spain's Secretary of State for International and Iberoamerican Cooperation, as cited in Pérez-López, "Foreign direct investment...," p. 9-10.

41. Armando M. Lago, "An economic evaluation of the foreign investment law of Cuba," 1995.

42. Only two debt-equity swaps have been completed under exceptional circumstances. Both were between Mexico and Cuba and were largely dependent on intergovernmental accord. Cuba's debt situation must be resolved before a debt-conversion program can be established. See *The Cuba Report*, Vol. 5, No. 2, (June 1996), p. 5.

43. Information provided by José Alonso and in J. Pérez-López, "Foreign direct investment..., p.10.

44. This consortium of Mexican state and private companies had planned to run a Soviet-built refinery at Cienfuegos, in Cuba's southern coast. Apparently no U.S. properties were involved in the project, so the threat of U.S. sanctions was not considered the cause for the suspension. *Reuters Wire Service* (September 22, 1995).

45. Domos is, on paper, Cuba's "largest joint venture," and was reported to have failed to make a $320 million payment which was due in October 1995 for its share in ETECSA, the telecommunications joint venture with Cuba's Emtel. Apparently, the company had not been successful in its efforts to 'dump' 24 percent of its share of ETECSA. Domos admitted to be on the lookout for a partner to contribute the needed infusion of capital, which it acknowledged not having, in order to proceed with the announced investment project of $750 million. Its President, Javier Garza, explained that the financial difficulties had arisen after the Mexican government refused to extend a loan it was to extend as part of a $300 million debt equity swap agreement. In June 1994, Mexican Grupo Domos, a Monterrey-based family enterprise focused on real estate development and waste management, was reported to have invested US $200 million and promised to invest $500 million in coming years to obtain 49 percent of Cuba's Empresa de Telecomunicaciones de Cuba (ETECSA). At the time of the announcement Domos was said to have used its initial $200 million to buy $300 in face value Cuban debt from the Mexican National Development Bank. As part of the deal, the Development Bank was also to grant Cuba a $300 million credit line for purchases from Mexico during 1995. Former Mexican President Carlos Salinas De Gortari was reported to have helped put the deal together and flew to Havana to celebrate the signing of the agreement. Subsequently Domos was said to have sold 12-25 percent of ECTESA, allegedly for US$291.2 million, to the Dutch wholly-owned subsidiary of the Italian state telephone company, STET. Emtel is reported to operate with the assets of a subsidiary of ITT, which has a $131 million dollar claim against the Cuban government for its confiscated properties. See L. Crawford and P. Fletcher, "Estocada al programa de privatización de Cuba," *El Nuevo Día* (20 de febrero de 1996); *Cuba Bulletin*, U.S. Cuba Business Council, No. 30 (March 29, 1996), p. 6; Kerry Dolan, "Their man in Havana," *Forbes* (September 11, 1995), pp. 60-66; "Privatización a la cubana," *AmericaEconomia*, no. 86 (August 1994); "Scion of a powerful Mexican family jumps into the big time," *Global Finance* (July 1994); J. Pérez-López, *Odd Couples: Joint ventures between foreign capitalists and Cuban socialists*, University of Miami, The North South Agenda Papers, Number Sixteen (November 1995), p. 24; and Larry Press, "Cuban Telecommunications Infrastructure and Investment," in this volume.

government. In May of 1995 the Cuban government canceled its contracts with the Spanish company Endesa's pension fund, which had been managing several hotels in Cuba.[46] There are still other cases of announced investments not materialized or gone sour.[47]

Given the absence of solid data on direct, materialized, and net foreign investment (which is typically available for most countries), in order to strike some comparisons we must use Cuba's figures for "committed/delivered" investment in relation to net direct foreign investment in other developing countries (Table 3). Keeping in mind that the number we have for Cuba is higher than materialized net investment, a brief sample of some developing countries can put even this inflated figure into context.[48] Out of the 19 countries examined, only one—Bulgaria—reported a lower figure than Cuba's "committed/delivered." Moreover, Cuba pales painfully in comparison with the two countries in Latin America that have similar populations, Ecuador and Chile. In a similar 5-year period, Ecuador had around 2.5 times more net foreign investment and Chile more than 7 times that of Cuba's "committed/delivered" foreign investment. To submit foreign investment in Cuba to an even more poignant contrast, between 1990-95 materialized foreign investment from just one South American country in another—Chilean investment in Argentina—was 69 percent higher than incoming

investment from the whole world reported by Cuba.[49]

Table 3. Net Foreign Investment in Selected Developing Countries, 1990-95 (in million U.S. dollars)

Latin America			
Mexico	31,015	Chile	5,498
Argentina	19,259	Venezuela	4,762
Brazil	13,376	Peru	4,567
Colombia	6,562	Ecuador	1,913
Rest of the world			
Malaysia	26,867	Greece	6,042
Indonesia	12,965	South Korea	5,047
Portugal	11,503	Turkey	4,354
Thailand	10,104	Philippines	3,765
Poland	8,073	Morocco	2,414
Bulgaria	391		

Source: J.P. Morgan (July 1996).

Despite the secrecy and contradictions surrounding Cuba's foreign investment, it is clear that results are not to the government's liking. Regarding the level of foreign investment, in mid-1995 Fidel Castro declared: "It's small, too small." He added that he's had to waste his time in meetings with "idiots and swindlers" who come to Cuba "with false offers and documents, and all sort of meaningless proposals."[50] The March 1996 passage of the Helms-Burton law by the United States is expected to chill investment further,

---

46. Thomas Vogel, "Havana headaches," *The Wall Street Journal* (August 25, 1995).

47. For example, at the end of 1994, Total, the French oil company, had withdrawn from offshore oil explorations which resulted in two dry holes. In 1990, Total had signed a production partnership agreement by which the French company was to supply capital, specialized equipment, technology, and personnel for oil exploration activities; production was to be shared with the Cuban *Unión del Petróleo*. See Pérez-López, *Odd couples...*", p. 9. A well-publicized Spanish hotel investment fell apart—the original partner for the Meliá Cohiba hotel dropped out, leaving the government to complete construction on its own. See Teo A. Babun, "Cuba's investment boom that never was, " *The Wall Street Journal* (March 1, 1996).

48. A net investment figure assumes that Cuban capital is not being invested abroad, which would not be the case if illegal outflows are taking place, and excludes revenue or dividend repatriation on realized foreign investment. The numbers provided for other developing countries are for net foreign investment, which accounts for capital outflows; the materialized gross investment in these countries should actually be higher.

49. Materialized investment by Chile in Argentina for 1990-95 totaled $2.416 billion dollars, while the total for committed investment was $5.916 billion. As for trade, Chile's imports for one month are almost equal to Cuba's for the entire year. See *El Mercurio*, Santiago (February 10, 1996). Total Chilean investment overseas *just in the first semester of 1996* amounted to US$464 million, 62 percent of Cuba's total accumulated "committed/delivered" foreign investment through August 1, 1996. Moreover, materialized foreign investment totaling US$1.03 billion in 1995 and US$1.985 billion in just the first six months of 1996 flowed into Chile. See *El Mercurio*, Santiago (August 9, 1996 and July 24, 1996).

50. Quoted in J. de Córdoba, "Burocracia dificulta apertura de Cuba," *The Wall Street Journal Americas* (October 10, 1995).

although Cuba's drive to attract foreign capital by all counts already appeared generally unsuccessful.

PROBLEMS AND RISKS FOR FOREIGN INVESTORS

In light of Cuba's economic and political scenario, it is perplexing to see frequent reports of business opportunities which downplay and oftentimes almost completely disregard the high risks of investing in Cuba.[51] However, more sophisticated risk reports—such as annual rankings in Euromoney and Institutional Investor—systematically classify Cuba as one of the riskiest countries in the world to do business.[52]

Scouting opportunities and actually making them happen are two very different things. For example, in 1993 Creditfinance Securities Inc., a Canadian investment firm opened an office in Havana, looking to be part of the "avalanche" of expected investment into Cuba. After analyzing many projects during two years of negotiations with the Cuban government, it retreated, alleging too many obstacles to completing transactions. A lack of cooperation and constant changes in the investment policy were cited. The Catalan group Guitart, which took options in a large number of hotels, also withdrew from Cuba due to the island's "increasingly frustrating" political climate.[53]

The gap can be wide between potential investors' high expectations and the actual result of due diligence analyses. Vietnam, for example, has a population of approximately 73 million, almost seven times that of Cuba, and has implemented an economic lib-

eralization program which, in depth, consistency and duration, is far-reaching in comparison to Cuba's.[54] (In fact, advocates of engagement with Cuba use Vietnam as an example to be followed.) Despite sustained economic growth as a result of consistent market-oriented reforms, by 1995 media reports began surfacing of businessmen's difficulties doing business there (also commonly in the form of joint ventures): time-consuming bureaucratic procedures, difficulty in finding the right partners and following the right procedures, lack of housing and supplies, high cost of living, a primitive banking system, and poor infrastructure and communications.[55] Today the mood of investors is being described as "a far cry from the optimism of a year ago when Washington improved relations with Hanoi and investors saw Vietnam as Asia's next tiger economy, rich in natural resources, cheap labor and with a big hungry market."[56] Making matters worse, the July 1996 Vietnamese Communist Party Congress disappointed investors with its determination to pace the economic reforms and keep major industries in government hands retain control while reasserting and increasing the authority of the Party over every facet of Vietnamese life.[57]

No matter how high the adrenaline rush at the prospect of an apparently enticing new market, it is undeniable that Cuba presents a highly risky business climate for investors. Even Cuban officials recognize the limitations. Minister of Foreign Investment Octavio Castilla has stated:

"What Havana wants to do is channel foreign investment into the manufacturing sector, as more than 80 percent of our plants are idle. But it has proven diffi-

---

51. For example, *Time*'s 5-page cover story of February 20, 1995, "Open for Business," has only three sentences referring to risks from 31 paragraphs devoted to business opportunities in Cuba. A 1996 5-page *Foreign Affairs* article by scholar Pamela Falk on the issue of business in Cuba mentions the word *risk* only once and only in the following context: "Meanwhile, the pace for non-U.S. foreign investment in Cuba quickens, despite the country's political risks." See Pamela Falk, "Eyes on Cuba: U.S. business and the embargo," *Foreign Affairs* (March-April 1996).

52. For example, *Euromoney*'s 1995 survey of 181 countries ranked Cuba behind Somalia, just ahead of Haiti. See "Cuba Survey," *The Economist*, p. 12.

53. Babún, "Cuba's investment boom that never was."

54. Carlos Quijano, "A comparison of Cuba and Vietnam," presentation at the V *Annual Meeting of the Association for the Study of the Cuban Economy*, Miami, August, 1995; and Julie M. Bunck, "Market Leninism: Vietnam and Cuba in Transition," in this volume.

55. Edward A. Gargan, "For U.S. business, a hard road to Vietnam," *The New York Times* (July 14, 1995).

56. Steth Mydans, "Tiger economy has become a fading vision for Vietnam," *The New York Times* (July 25, 1996).

57. Mydans, "Tiger economy has become a fading vision" and Bunck, "Market Leninism."

cult. First, there is almost no one whom to sell to, the internal market is practically not existent and one cannot sell to the United States, the largest potential market, due to the commercial embargo. ...Then, there's the Cuban peso, ...not convertible, even if the government wishes it to be. On the other hand, the Cuban workforce although highly qualified, is too expensive. We cannot compete with the rest of the Caribbean."[58]

Due to the fierce global competition for a limited, albeit vast, pool of capital funds, Cuba's ability to capture capital investment should be evaluated realistically and with care. Potential investors will develop cost-benefit analyses which will assign different weight to a distinct set of factors depending on their particular industry, line of business, and the characteristics of the investment proposal. The role of specific issues—such as the inability to access the U.S. market—in the evaluation of business potential will depend on the type of project under consideration. Regardless, the overall high level of risk of investing in Cuba will affect every investment and will have to be entered into the analysis. This appears to explain why Cuba has been generally unsuccessful in attracting foreign investment, why the amounts investors are willing to gamble are low, their return/recovery requirements are very high—discouraging capitalization and re-investment—and the sectors favored for investing limit multiplier and dispersion benefits.

Following are some of the major risks and problems associated with investing in Cuba:

1. The abject condition of the Cuban economy and its scant prospects for meaningful recovery.[59]

The severity of Cuba's economic crisis is worth noting, given its importance in determining Cuba's potential for business. It also puts into proper context the Cuban government's acute need to attract capital, get foreign joint ventures to absorb the country's excess workforce, and bring relief to the economy.

With the fall of Communism in the Eastern Bloc, Cuba suffered a dramatic economic collapse due to the loss of Soviet subsidies and assistance.[60] As a result, by 1993 the Cuban economy had contracted by around 70 percent, experiencing a huge drop in both exports and imports; by the end of 1995 it was estimated that 80 percent of the island's productive sector was paralyzed. Topping off an already dire picture, Cuba's debt with Western financial institutions has been in default since 1986 and remains shut out of international credit markets.[61] As a result, in March 1990 a series of austerity measures were announced within the context of what was called the "Special Period in Time of Peace."

To deal with the crisis, beginning in 1989 the government started to actively seek foreign investment, initially presenting it as a temporary measure centered on developing the tourism industry. This was an important step for a country that had decried cap-

---

58. The Minister was quoted in de Córdoba, "Burocracia dificulta apertura de Cuba."

59. A summary of Cuba's economic condition and reform process has been left out this paper since others in this volume of ASCE's *Cuba in Transition* series cover this issue in depth. Primary sources for this section, in its full version, include: issues of *Economic Eye on Cuba, Cuba News, The Cuba Report, Boletín de la Asociación de Economistas Independientes de Cuba*, articles in *The Wall Street Journal* and *El Nuevo Herald, Foreign Affairs*, publications of the *U.S.-Cuba Business Council, Reuters Wire Service*, and papers presented at Annual Meetings of the *Association of the Study of the Cuban Economy*.

60. It has been calculated that the Castro regime received an estimated $100 to $150 billion in aid from the Soviet bloc over three decades, as well as another $1.2 billion or more a year in military assistance -more aid that the U.S. provided to the whole European continent through the Marshall Plan after World War II. In the last years of the of Soviet Communism, Cuba is said to have been receiving Soviet aid of up to $6.7 billion a year. See Adolfo Leyva, *Propaganda and reality: A look at the U.S. Embargo and Castro's Cuba* (Miami: The Endowment for Cuban American Studies of the Cuban American National Foundation, July 1994).

61. Calculations of Cuba's hard currency debt vary, but National Bank President Francisco Soberón recently put the amount at US$10 billion. See USCTEC, *Economic Eye on Cuba* (8-14 July 1996), p.1). In addition, Cuba owes $14.6 billion rubles to the former Soviet Union which is said to equal between US$20 to 25 billion, depending on the exchange rate applied, *The Cuba Report* (October 1994), p.8. Foreign Minister Robaina has explained: "Cuba simply doesn't have the money to pay," *American Banker-Bond Buyer* (October 2, 1995), cited in Gabriel Fernández, "Cuba's Hard Currency Debt," in this volume.

italism for over three decades and in actuality signaled the beginning of a series of changes. A reform process started in earnest in late 1993 with the legalization of the holding of dollars and was followed by number of measures, namely: the authorization of certain categories of self-employment, the reorganization of land usage to allow agricultural cooperatives to sell production in excess of quotas in free markets, the introduction of income taxes, the authorization of free markets for certain scarce consumer and manufactures products, and the introduction of a convertible peso. Deficit-reduction measures were also implemented.[62]

The reforms appear to have produced positive effects, although still leave much to be desired. The decline was detained in 1994, year in which a growth of 0.7 percent was reported, followed by a growth of 2.5 percent in 1995 and 9.6 percent in the first six months of 1996. But after late 1994 the pace of liberalization slowed down considerably amidst signs of the leadership's unwillingness to continue opening up the economy.[63] Additionally, despite Cuba's dire economic situation, substantial spending as a proportion of GDP continues allocated to maintaining the internal security apparatus. For the first half of 1996, Minister Lage recognized that Cuba's financial situation remained strained and reported a decrease of 7 percent in export prices together with a rise of 13 percent in import costs.[64] At the end of 1994 a desolate assessment had been delivered by two Cuba analysts: "The adopted piecemeal measures and reforms are incoherent, inconsistent, and ill-conceived in design, incomplete in scope, incorrect and delayed in

execution and, consequently, inadequate in impact."[65] This has yet to be proven wrong. Presently, the reform process appears to remain stalled as structural change of any consequence seems to have been vetoed for political reasons.

Regardless of the apparent betterment of a critical situation, an economy which has suffered a decline of this magnitude would require decades to return to previous economic levels unless vigorous growth occurs. And the previous economic level left much to be desired. Before Cuba became interested in foreign investment, it had received substantial foreign capital via international bank credits and, even at the height of its advantageous economic relationship with the Soviet Union, the island suffered shortages of food, clothing, appliances, cars, manufactured goods, and many basic products. In fact, Cuba's economy during the revolutionary period has simply been incapable of producing what it needs/wants to consume.[66] The Cuban economy was able to survive an earlier collapse only thanks to massive Soviet support and, actually, defaulted on its external debt even before the cessation of Soviet assistance. The demise of Soviet aid merely made a lacking performance reach critical mass.

In light of Cuba's daunting experience and the recognized failure of socialist command economies, the obvious conclusion is that Cuba's severe economic decay is a result of the failed economic model and ineffective policies adopted by its leadership, together with severe economic mismanagement.[67] The socialist centrally-planned model has been incapable of

---

62. These included the reorganization of the State bureaucracy, subsidy cuts for state enterprises, price increases for certain products and public services, and cuts in subsidies for health and education.

63. During 1996 several reforms were approved which primarily resulted from previously approved measures, namely in the area of increased taxation. The most significant was the June 1996 regulation on free trade zones, offering substantial tax havens but very similar characteristics of the joint venture arrangements.

64. "Country Report/Lage...," pp. 4-5.

65. R. Castañeda and G. Montalván, "Cuba 1990-1994: Political intransigence *versus* economic reform," *Cuba in Transition—Volume 4* (Washington: Association for the Study of the Cuban Economy, 1994) p. 208.

66. Cuban economist Jorge Sanguinetty, a high official of Cuba's Planning Board until his exile in 1967, has indicated that from the very beginning of the Revolution—since 1963—the Soviet Union had to subsidize the Cuban economy.

67. The gross mishandling and irrationality of Cuba's economic management has been extensively documented starting in the early sixties with French socialist Rene Dumont's account *Cuba, est-it socialist?*

generating sustainable growth and material prosperity and has been described as inherently inefficient, characterized by fraud, corruption, theft and privilege, blocking and even penalizing of individual initiative, beset with irrational, rigid and complex regulations and norms, devoid of concepts such as self-responsibility, efficiency, and incentive, and plagued by poor organization, low productivity and inflexible centralized planning disassociated from the forces of supply and demand. As a result, Cuba's economic viability is unrealizable until profound structural changes are implemented on the economic front. This limits business opportunities significantly and affects the risk factor for investing—a situation that will continue affecting Cuba's ability to obtain badly needed foreign capital.

2. The absence of an independent legal system and a rule of law and a weak foreign investment regime.

The United Nations Special Rapporteur for Cuba, Carl Johan Groth,[68] has stated that Cuba's system of administering justice "is mainly at the service of the prevailing political system"[69] and has detailed many of the problems embodied in the Cuban legal system. Most international human rights organizations report similar conclusions.[70] In addition, Cuba's foreign investment regime is direly deficient in comparison to the regulatory framework of most developing countries.

The new Foreign Investment Law—No. 77 of September 5, 1995—had been long awaited by potential investors with great expectation, but mainly codified

practices that had already been taking place, proving generally disappointing.[71] A renown analyst commented that the revised law "leaves a lot to be desired, since it kept intact many of the risks that were responsible for the failure of the earlier Law No. 50."[72] To compensate for the law's shortcomings, it appears that investment authorizations will continue to include enticing inducements such as expedient capital recovery, attractive pricing, tax free repatriation of revenues, tax holidays, and 100 percent repatriation of profits.

Some of the problems associated with the new foreign investment law are: [73]

i. Restricted liquidity of investments: The sale or transfer of investors' capital to third parties is subject to the approval of the government. Article 13.5 reads: "Once the joint venture is created, the partners cannot change except with the consent of the parties and the approval of the authority that granted the authorization." This is a critical restriction on investors' "exit strategy," which is a fundamental consideration in evaluating investments.

ii. High risk of foreign exchange losses: The law stipulates that the transfer abroad of net profits, dividends, proceeds from sale of capital, and the value of expropriated property are to be calculated in "freely convertible currency," a term or formula which is not defined and, thus, remains uncertain. Due to the volatility of the market conversion rate of the peso to hard currencies and because the Cuban peso is officially set at the artificial rate of one peso to the dollar,

---

68. This Swedish diplomat was named to monitor the human rights situation in Cuba as per the United Nation's General Assembly Resolution of March 1992. He has not been allowed entry into Cuba.

69. October 1995 Report of the United Nations Rapporteur for Cuba, p. 4.

70. Among the many described deficiencies are the subordination of the Judiciary and Attorney General to the Executive and Legislative powers, the requisite that judges and magistrates be "actively involved in the Revolution, the absence of due process and the lack of impartiality of trials. (1993 Interim Report of the United Nations Rapporteur.)

71. It did incorporate some welcome changes, namely allowing certain real estate investments in which ownership and property "rights" would be acquired and the possibility of companies with 100 percent foreign ownership.

72. Lago, "An economic evaluation of the foreign investment law of Cuba," p. 1.

73. Vogel, "Havana headaches." Because it is almost impossible to obtain a copy of a foreign joint venture agreement, we can only make general observations based on what is inferred from the Foreign Investment Law and anecdotal accounts. *The Wall Street Journal* has indicated, in reference to joint ventures: "One of the conditions of these arrangements is that you keep your mouth shut." This has also been reported by several sources to the author.

valuations are unpredictable and could be subject to political manipulations. Furthermore, since the foreign investor is not allowed to have peso deposits in foreign banks outside of Cuba, it is impossible to hedge the risk of devaluation.[74]

iii. Risk of reversibility of investment agreements; unreliability of the government's commitment to capitalism: Although the new law offers investors more guarantees than the previous Decree 50, it does not settle fears that joint venture agreements may be reversible. Article 3.3 of the Foreign Investment law reads: "The foreign investors within Cuban national territory enjoy full protection and security and their assets cannot be expropriated, except for reasons of the public good or in the interest of the society..." Depending on how the clause is applied, it has been noted that joint venture investment agreements could be terminated by the Cuban government essentially at will, without due process nor adequate compensation. What's worse, there is "no mention of recourse to the courts to impugn the validity of the declaration,"[75] and the law stipulates that jurisdiction for any litigation belongs to Cuban courts, which are not independent of the state. It has, however, been reported that certain investments have been or could be negotiated to override this disposition.[76]

Cuba has signed investment protection agreements with 19 countries which diminish fears of expropriations, but troubling precedents already exist.[77] But troubling reports have surfaced—two involving investments from Spain, which under the government of Socialist Felipe González had close ties with Castro: 1) hotel investments entered into in 1991 by the Spanish utility company Endesa's pension fund were unilaterally canceled by the Cuban government in May 1995;[78] and 2) in 1992 Castro decreed the nationalization a Spaniard's 49 percent participation in the Comodoro discotheque, unilaterally fixing the amount of economic compensation. Finally, amidst a climate of concern, Cuban government officials for the first time admitted to have canceled the licenses of "dozens" of foreign firms operating in Cuba since 1992 because of "corrupt practices."[79]

Cuba's foreign investment system forces investors to accept riskier business regimes than those common to most markets by precluding the formation of cor-

---

74. Lago, "An economic evaluation..."

75. Alberto Luzárraga, "Castro's self-imposed embargo," *New York Law Journal* (December 20, 1995). Emphasis added.

76. Armando Lago has noted that some agreements with Spanish investors stipulate that expropriations will be resolved by arbitration in France. See Lago, "An economic evaluation ...," p. 3.

77. Italy, Russia, Spain, Colombia, Great Britain, China, Ukraine, Bolivia, Vietnam, Argentina, Lebanon, South Africa, Romania, Chile, Barbados, Germany, Greece, Sweden, and Switzerland. See USCTEC, *Economic Eye on Cuba* (24-30 June 1996), p. 2.

78. Despite the existence of an investment protection agreement with Spain, the Cuban government unilaterally canceled all management contracts this investor had for several hotels in Cuba. Claiming that the Spanish side had failed to live up to its agreements and was in arrears in some contracted payments, Spanish directors were replaced by Cubans and Endesa bank accounts in Cuba were frozen. The Spanish investor—Kawama Caribbean—has taken its dispute with the Cuban government to the International Arbitration Tribunal in Paris, demanding $12 million from Cuba. It claims that it withheld payments because the Cuban partner was not fulfilling its contractual obligations. See Carlos Alberto Montaner, "The risks of investing in Castro's last hurrah," *The Wall Street Journal* (May 22, 1992.) Two other examples are: 1) In 1992 Davidoff was reported to have gone to court "to defend its rights against the unethical tactics of its Cuban partners." (See Montaner, "The risks of investing..."; and 2) In September 1995 *USA Today* published a letter from a former German investor in Cuba with an "eager warning to potential investors from the United States. Parts of the letter read: "I believed in the huge opportunities being offered by the very promising marketplace. I was proud to call among my Cuban friends high-ranking officials, famous athletes. ...all of this did not save me from being taken by four security agents to their headquarters where I was held without questioning from nine in the morning to four in the afternoon—and then put on a plane back to Germany. ...policeman stole my three vintage Harley motorcycles, antique furniture, jewels, and fax machines from my Havana apartment." See Harry Koening, *USA Today* (September 12, 1995).

79. Expressing the need for greater controls against "adventurers, fortune seekers, and troublemakers who conspire with Cubans to defraud the state," Castro himself called for the creation of a corps of 35,000 to go after them. Although this took place before the enactment of the 1995 Foreign Investment Law, it remains to be seen how the government will proceed. Christopher Marquis, "Cuba set to stop bribes, kickbacks in own ranks," *The Miami Herald* (August 18, 1995).

porate structures such as limited liability companies and general partnerships. Among its peculiarities, it institutionalizes concessions for foreigners not generally available to residents of Cuba and requires investors to participate in joint ventures which subject workers to government control and wage confiscation.[80] These business associations could be readily disallowed by a future government of Cuba, which could declare their expropriation, and even the payment of back wages to workers which have been subject to wage confiscation.[81]

Furthermore, the government's erratic commitment to capitalism and foreign investment is cause for concern. Apprehension is fueled by repeated statements against capitalism, continued expressions of commitment to Marxist-Leninism, and the slow pace of reform. While the text of the foreign investment law is free of the typical ideological language of most Cuban laws and regulations, the National Assembly passed an accompanying statement stressing that Cuba's economic opening "is not inspired by neo-liberalism nor does it aim for a transition to capitalism. It is an opening to defend and develop socialism and this is not concealed by our government and is present in the spirit of this law."[82] It is also possible that the government could grow comfortable with the economic improvement. Analysts have pointed to previous successful reforms which were subsequently reversed, demonstrating what appears to be a pattern of implementing reforms until the results

they produce create ideological contradictions deemed intolerable by the leadership.

Foreigners have also expressed concern over Law 149, passed in May 1994, which applies retroactively against "excess profits," albeit one normally applied to Cubans. The law has been severely applied, especially against the new Cuban capitalists – macetas— and successful private restaurants and taxi services. Foreign investors observe with anxiety that the government considers making money a crime.

iv. Inability to hire workers directly: The Cuban government insists that "those who work for foreign capitalists must continue to feel that they owe loyalty and gratitude to the state."[83] Thus, the new law preserves the Cuban state's identity as sole employer by keeping provisions of the former law which prevent Cuban workers from being hired directly by foreign companies, except in authorized "exceptional cases."[84]

Under the foreign joint venture arrangements, the Cuban government "provides" the workforce through a special employment agency of the government (empleadora nacional).[85] It receives payment in hard currency from the joint enterprise, but remunerates the workers in salaries denominated in Cuban pesos at a minimal fraction of the amount received. Allegedly, wages are fixed at equivalent amounts to what workers in state enterprises are earning for the same or similar jobs.[86] In the tourist sector, a portion

80. Due to, among others, the exclusion of the Cuban population from investing in joint ventures or any type of company Canadian Professor Archibald Ritter has remarked: "Still it's socialism for the Cubans and capitalism for foreigners..." de Córdoba, "Burocracia dificulta..." Cuban exiles, however, can invest, a provision probably fashioned after the Chinese experience with the intent of luring the exile community. China has been successful in attracting substantial capital infusions from the Chinese expatriate community.

81. This amount could be subtracted from the compensation due to expropriated joint ventures.

82. Babún, "Cuba's investment boom."

83. "Cuba Survey," *The Economist*, p. 12.

84. The only known exception to this rule is incorporated in the June 1996 regulation of Free Trade Zones, which authorizes direct employment except in enterprises with 100 percent foreign ownership. Its effect is yet to be seen. *The Cuba Report*, Vol. 5, No. 2 (June 1996), p. 6.

85. The Foreign Investment Law defines the employing entities as: "Cuban organizations with legal status, authorized to establish a contract with a joint venture or a totally foreign capital company, through which it supplies, at the company's request, the workers of various skills needed by the company, who are employed by that organization." Republic of Cuba, *Foreign Investment Law*.

86. Marta Beatriz Roque, President of the *Instituto Cubano de Economistas Independientes* explained that the government applies a wage scale which calls for increases as the worker successfully performs in three different stages of approximately two years, each subject to evaluation, with wages reaching a ceiling. In telephone conversation with the author from Havana, August 21, 1996.

of the tips must also be turned over to the Cuban management. Aside from the negative effects this has on the investors' international image, other practical disadvantages arise from this arrangement.

The salary fixed by the Cuban State is not competitive with the rest of the Caribbean and Central America on the basis of labor costs (Table 4). Joint ventures are said to be paying the state around between US$400 and 500 per month per worker.[87] If we use, for example, hourly wages for garment workers as a rough indication, Cuba's workforce is much more expensive, especially when a series of additional benefits are added to basic wages to give workers some incentives. One investor reports: "You can pay $500 for an employee, and he only gets the equivalent of $20. I know they need more than that to live on, and if they don't get it, they steal or simply not work. So we take measures."[88] These—bonuses, gifts, meals, automobiles, hard currency under the table—increase the cost of labor, which already, in the words of this investor, "does not come cheap." Theft is a huge problem,[89] and providing workers with transportation, uniforms and other requirements of their job brings the tab up, all to the detriment of profitability. Meanwhile, the competition to attract investors among countries offering cheap labor is steep. "Worldwide the number of workers in 'export processing zones' has risen from 50,000 in 1970 to more than 4 million today." In the Caribbean, the Dominican Republic alone has 27 free trade zones.[90]

If international pressure on Cuba to cease the wage confiscation scheme was to strengthen, the government would be hard pressed to lower the share of wages it retains or abolish wage retention altogether. Nevertheless, by eliminating the State's most important source of earnings from foreign joint ventures, the current cost-benefit equation for both the government and foreign investors would be considerably distorted; its underlying rationale could even become obsolete.[91] This would likely diminish, if not altogether eliminate, investors' appetite for investing. Hence, it is not likely that significant improvement will be seen in this area.

Another irritating problem for foreign investors is associated with hiring practices in joint ventures. The government employment agency selects employees by screening their "Labor Record" (expediente laboral) and "Cumulative School Record" (expediente acumulativo escolar), which systematically gather personal information to assess revolutionary commitment. Ideas and behavior deemed contrary to official ideology limit access to academic and work centers. Because hiring is also subject to cronyism, the foreign-capital enterprise's access to workers on the basis of merit may be restricted, as the most capable and experienced workers may be banned for political reasons or patronage may be dictating who gets hired.[92]

On the other hand, foreign investors may regard with convenience certain aspects of the State's "control" over the workers. *The Economist* has noted that because Cuba's foreign investment regime is based on establishing joint ventures with the Cuban state, the partnership makes it "easy to hire, fire, and control workers" and "comes in handy in dealing with the

---

87. Cuban economist Marta Beatriz Roque pins the average at US$450.

88. Douglas Farah, "Foreign investors finding Cuba more comfortable – with U.S. away," *The Washington Post* (September 12, 1995).

89. In one big hotel "the entire kitchen staff had to be sacked for thieving. The 'missing' figures for towels and sheets, passes by chambermaids to their friends at the back door, can only be guessed at." See "Cuba Survey," *The Economist*.

90. Steve Chambers, "Low wages tempt U.S firms to Dominican free trade zones," *The Star Ledger* (March 17, 1996).

91. The opportunity cost of allowing foreign investment would increase for the government, already concerned with its inherent dangers. A reduction in incentives for the government would mean that the risk premium for investing in Cuba would go up. Or, in order to compensate for the loss of earnings from wage retention, the government would seek returns through other mechanisms, which under the current scheme may be working as incentives to investors. This would increase costs and/or or decrease advantages for investors.

92. Joint ventures, however, are said to have some level of flexibility in pressing for certain individuals and the law allows foreign enterprises to request the replacement of workers in cases in which the worker "does not meet the requirements of the job."

Table 4. Monthly Salary of Garment Workers, 1993 (in million U.S. dollars)

Honduras	$100.80
Dominican Republic	110.88
El Salvador	120.96
Guatemala	127.68
Jamaica	131.04
Costa Rica	176.40

Note: Wages paid by foreign joint ventures in Cuba to the state employment agencies are said to range between US$400-500 per month.

Source: This calculation is based on hourly wages, multiplied by 40 hours per week and 4.2 weeks per month, relying on data from the National Cotton Council, the U.S. Department of Commerce, Textile Highlights, the U.S. Department of Labor, and the International Labor Organization, as reported in *The Star Ledger* (March 17, 1996).

bureaucracy."[93] The Cuban government declares that the current labor system is "far more convenient" for foreign investors. Importantly, the special labor regime in the international tourist sector—enforced since 1990 and expanded constitutionally in 1992—restricts the rights of these workers more than in other sectors, allowing foreign investors greater flexibility.[94] Workers in this sector are subject to longer probationary periods and work hours, more irregular schedules, shorter periods for challenging disciplinary decisions, and no right of appeal through usual judicial and administrative channels. In addition, there is

a prohibition against conducts that "might tarnish the exemplary moral and social image" such as criticizing the national tourism enterprise or any government agency in the presence of tourists.[95] Raúl Taladrid, Deputy Minister for Foreign Investment and Economic Development, told *The Wall Street Journal:* "we are free from labor conflict; nowhere in the world could you get this tranquillity."[96]

v. Potential claims on confiscated land and properties and the threat of U.S. sanctions: Foreign and native interests lay claim on land and properties confiscated by the revolutionary government which are being made available for business transactions with foreign investors. Because Cuba's violation of international law on this count is virtually undisputed, litigation in national and international courts could continue for decades. Claims of Cuban citizens alone are estimated at around US$7 billion.[97]

The governments of Switzerland, France, United Kingdom, Italy, Canada, and Mexico have negotiated compensation agreements for nationalized properties. The percentage of settlement payout is said to be very low despite the generally small amounts of property confiscated from these countries.[98] United States citizens, however, are particularly affected by this issue; from May 1959 to October 1960 the Castro government seized assets of U.S. citizens and companies in what is "the largest confiscation without com-

93. "Cuba Survey," *The Economist*, p. 13.

94. Article 141 of the Cuban Constitution of 1976 requires that a referendum be held to ratify any amendments. This provision was ignored. See Rolando Castañeda and George Plinio Montalván, "The Arcos Principles," *Cuba in Transition—Volume 4* (Washington: Association for the Study of the Cuban Economy, 1994), p. 365.

95. Castañeda and Montalván, "The Arcos Principles," p. 366.

96. Vogel, "Havana headaches." The President of the Cuban Chamber of Commerce, Carlos Martínez, has also explained: "...due to the characteristics of the Cuban labor market, the fact that a Cuban businessman takes care of labor aspects gives the foreign investor guarantees that any problems of litigation will be handled by the Cuban partner. ...The foreign businessman does not know the labor market. The Cuban partner selects the best employee. The companies in Cuba are satisfied." Rodríguez, "Trabas al empresario interesado."

97. Pérez-López, "Foreign direct investment in the Cuban economy," p. 20 cites Dick Kirschten, "Raising Cain," *National Journal*, 27:26 (1 July 1995), p. 1714, who has stated these claims are estimated to exceed U.S. claims by a factor of four.

98. *The Cuba Report* (August 1996), p. 5. Historically, post-confiscation settlement ratios have varied significantly but tend to be low. Restitution and compensation schemes have also varied widely, particularly in the recent East European experience. Vietnam is an atypical case; it is said to have compensated the U.S. 100 percent of capital for confiscated properties. See "Resolution of Property Claims in Cuba's Transition," Transcript of Proceedings, Cuba Transition Workshop, Shaw, Pittman, Potts & Trowbridge, Washington, D.C., January 26, 1995.

pensation of U.S. properties by a foreign government in the history of the United States."[99] Since 1991 U.S. embassies all over the world have on several occasions warned their host governments that their investors may face legal complications if they invest in confiscated U.S. properties in Cuba. In fact, two certified U.S. claimants—Procter & Gamble and Consolidated Development Corporation—have recently challenged two joint ventures in Cuba outside of the Helms-Burton's law right of action.[100]

The March 1996 enactment of the Helms-Burton Law by the United States further complicates the issue of claims. Its Title III seeks to protect the property rights of U.S. nationals and corporations by giving U.S. citizens which hold valid claims a right of action to U.S. courts against those who knowingly traffic in their confiscated properties.[101] Its Title IV declares the exclusion of "traffickers" and their immediate families from entry into the U.S. Although both provisions are being denounced and contested as extraterritorial in certain international frameworks—

some countries threatening or passing countermeasures—it seems doubtful that they can be unilaterally overridden.[102] But even before its enactment, despite what at the time was considered the unlikelihood of its passage with sections penalizing foreign "traffickers," just the threat of Helms-Burton had an effect.[103] After its passage, foreign investors are said to be "privately and through a series of offshore corporations effectuating their investments in Cuba."[104] But it appears that the law has indeed discouraged investment. Acting U.S. Assistant Secretary for Inter-American Affairs, Jeffrey Davidow, reported to Congress in July 1996 that as a result of enforcement of Title IV of the Helms-Burton Act "a significant number of companies with possible involvement in confiscated U.S. properties have informed the State Department that they are disengaging from those activities."[105] Several firms, including Cemex of Mexico, the South African mining company Gencor and American Express, are said to be reconsidering or to

---

99. "Questions and Answers about U.S. Claims Against Cuba," *Joint Committee on Cuban Claims*, 1977. The *Joint Committee on Cuban Claims* is a voluntary organization composed of U.S. stockholders and companies. Registered claims with the U.S. government total $1,851,358.00 (5911 claims from individuals and corporations), amounting to over $5.2 billion at the end of 1993. Interest is accrued at a 6 percent annual rate. As per the principle of diplomatic protection, these claims were assumed by the U.S. and are administered under the Foreign Claims Commission's Cuba Claims Program, authorized by U.S. Public Law. See *Cuba News,* Vol.1, No. 4 (December 1993), p.8.

100. Procter & Gamble has challenged a joint venture created between Unilever and the Cuban enterprise Suchel for using its confiscated plants. See Pérez-López, "Foreign direct investment...," p. 20. On July 2, 1996, Consolidated Development Corporation, filed a suit in a U.S. District Court against Sherritt Inc. and the Cuban government, demanding a jury trial and seeks compensatory damages in excess of $1 million in addition to punitive damages, interest, and legal fees. See *U.S.-Cuba Policy Report*, Vol. 3, No. 7 (July 29, 1996). Legal difficulties for these complaints to succeed have been reported as significant, allegedly in light of several previous failed attempts to have U.S. courts seek remedies. *The Cuba Report*, Vol. 5, No. 3 (July 1996), p. 3.

101. This is intended to provide a legal vehicle to claim restitution from those investors in Cuba who also hold assets in the United States.

102. Jennifer Hillman, General Counsel of the U.S. Trade Representative, declared at a July 1996 Congressional hearing that the Administration considers the law "fully consistent with U.S. international obligations, and in particular with our commitments under the NAFTA and the various trade agreements overseen by the WTO." *The Cuba Report* (August 1996), p. 6. Title III has been suspended by Presidential waiver incorporated in the law, pending consultations with allies to build support for the promotion of democracy in Cuba. The law, however, was allowed by President Clinton to "come into force." The first nine "letters of determination" have been sent to Sherritt and Grupo Domos directors and officers warning of 45 days to divest of operations in Cuba before their names are entered into visa lookout systems for their exclusion from U.S. territory. *U.S. Cuba-Policy Report*, Vol. 3, No. 7 (July 29, 1996).

103. It was reported to have derailed important investment plans by companies such as BHP, a giant Australian mining company that sells expertise, equipment and supplies to Cuban nickel operations. Despite a rise in worldwide nickel prices, BHP was allegedly concerned that its investments would make use of plants confiscated from the U.S.; given its steel and coal mining interests in the U.S., it feared retaliation. See Ana Radelat, "Cuba's appeal as investment is cooling off," *The Miami Herald* (June 23, 1995).

104. Radelat, "Cuba's appeal as investment is cooling off," p. 3.

105. *The Cuba Report* (August 1996), p. 2.

have put the brakes on investing in Cuba.[106] Grupo Domos, whose telecommunications joint venture ETECSA is subject to claims by ITT, is apparently having trouble syndicating a 25 percent portion of its share.[107] Canadian financial institutions with significant assets in the U.S. are said to be extremely sensitive to the legislation.[108] Reports of stricter due diligence by investors have been received, in many cases with demands that the Cuban government certify that the targeted investment is clear of U.S. claims.[109] Cuban Minister Carlos Lage has acknowledged that Cuba's chances of attracting investment have been reduced,[110] declaring that the law will have to be "abrogated, frozen or broken."[111]

vi. Administrative and infrastructure constraints affecting profitability and efficiency: Many investors complain about the myriad distortions of efficient economic behavior ingrained in every aspect of Cuba's socialist system. Compounding the absence of such concepts as self-responsibility and managerial efficiency, excessive, irrational, rigid, and complex norms and regulations for every activity.[112] A number of problems have been reported which impose frequent and sometimes serious disruptions, restrict the efficiency of operations, increase costs, and lower profitability:

- poor management, auditing, and accounting practices by the Cuban partner;

- constant interference by Cuban officials ignorant of the norms of the market;

- inability of the Cuban economy to supply inputs[113] or a chronic lack of organization on the part of the existing domestic supplying enterprises;

- restrictions on selling to the local market;[114]

- the chaotic state of Cuba's infrastructure: electricity blackouts, power shortages and poor public services – water, sewage, etc.;

- a poor telecommunications infrastructure, lagging behind most of the world;[115]

- extremely deficient public transportation, hindering workers' ability to get to work;

- unavailability of domestic credit.

vii. Uncertainty and hassles surrounding the approval process of foreign investment projects: Aside from restricting investments in several sectors, including sugar production, the law specifically calls for many investment proposals to be subject to case-by-case

---

106. Cemex, the world's fourth largest cement producer terminated its contracts in Cuba; Gencor dropped plans for an operation in Pinar del Río; and American Express severed business links to Cuba. In addition, Occidental Hotels canceled contracts valued at US$900,000 per year to manage four Varadero hotels, Grupo Vitro, a Mexican bottling company canceled plans said to include property confiscated from Owens-Illinois, and two Dutch firms ceased trade with Cuba. See *U.S-Cuba Policy Report, Vol. 3,* No. 6 (June 28, 1996); *The Cuba Report* (August 1996), p.2 and (June 1996), p. 3; and *U.S.-Cuba Business Council.*

107. *The Cuba Report* (June 1996), p. 8.

108. *The Cuba Report* (July 1996), p. 7.

109. See for example, "First Canadian JV....," *The Cuba Report* (August 1996), p. 3.

110. "Admite Lage efectos de la ley," *Diario Las Américas* (9 de agosto de 1996).

111. *Negocios en Cuba,* op.cit., p. 1.

112. Castañeda and Montalván, "Cuba 1990-1994," p. 192.

113. This is particularly costly for the tourist industry, where common supply shortages, especially of food, drive up costs and hinder efficiency, affecting profitability. Hotels report 50-60 percent of their supplies as imports, while overall estimates of the imported component of the tourism product—ranging from furniture, textiles, food, and electrical systems—are 45-60 percent. Pérez-López, "Foreign direct investment...," p. 12.

114. Although private retailing is not allowed, the June 1996 Free Trade Zone regulations authorize businesses to export 25 percent of production to Cuban national territory, which will be levied with normal import tariffs, with reductions depending on input content. José Alonso, "Foreign Trade Zones in Cuba," (September 20, 1996). Foreign companies are also generally unable to compete against state enterprises offering similar goods and services in the domestic market. See Pérez-López, *Odd couples...,"* p. 22.

115. See Press, "Cuban Telecommunications," for a detailed analysis of the Cuban telecommunications industry.

evaluation.[116] Most investment proposals are, therefore, subject to individual negotiation and approval by the government, allowing for much discretion and complexity. Cuban Foreign Investment Minister Octavio Castilla warned: "By having said we are interested in foreign investment does not mean anyone who comes will receive authorization to invest."[117] The bureaucratic process of approvals often involves several government agencies, complicating the negotiation of agreements and resulting in delays and higher opportunity costs/business expenses in comparison with alternatives.[118] Also, it appears to be common practice to pay bribes, wine and dine and/or give gifts to prospective Cuban partners in order to obtain lucrative contracts. If so, the legal and business risks of an accusation and the added cost of the bribes or gifts must be factored into a decision to invest.

viii. Potential claims for environmental restitution: Because "regime survival is linked to economic recovery,"[119] Cuba's emphasis on development over environmental protection is not surprising.[120] As a result, many measures taken during the "Special Period" are said to convey great threats to the environment. Yet, the 1995 Foreign Investment Law calls for investment to be compatible with the protection of the environment and the sustainable use of natural resources. Because Cuba's law on the environment (Law 33) is so vague and many Cuban industries being made available for joint ventures have historically been heavy polluters, "foreign investors could be forced, at the convenience of Cuban authorities, to do extensive clean-up costing millions of dollars."[121] Some environmental experts further believe the Cuban government "plans to use the environment and the Law 33 as a political tool for their convenience and their benefit."[122] Environmental damage could be used as a "legal justification" at the discretion of the Cuban authorities if a joint venture is suddenly deemed undesirable for any reason. An investment deemed to be harmful to the environment could be subject to substantial new capital requirements for remedies and/or penalties. Furthermore, a new government could penalize foreign investors by seeking environmental restitution; in fact, environmental damage could be included in a calculation of compensation payment for decreed expropriations.

3. Political risk: absence of stability and mounting socio-political ferment

Cuba, by all accounts, presents an unstable political climate given the totalitarian nature of its regime and the current government's eradication of a stabilizing

---

116. Authorization must be obtained for investment proposals over US$10 million, those involving construction or exploitation of any public service -including transportation, communications, aqueducts, and electricity, those proposing total foreign ownership, those related to the Armed Forces' commercial system, and those involving transfers of state property or a real right which is the property of the state. Furthermore, it grants the government the power to authorize "foreign investments not mentioned..." (in addition to those listed). Although the 1995 law states that the maximum period for authorization is 60 days, the enforcement of this clause is questionable at this juncture. The unavailability of information does not allow us to assess whether this provision has been complied with since its inclusion in the September 1995 law.

117. de Córdoba, "Burocracia dificulta apertura..."

118. It has, however, been noted that this also allows investors the opportunity to seek provisions which afford special benefits and protections. See "Is Cuba cooling down?" *The Cuba Report* Vol. 4, No. 5 (September 1995), p. 5 and Lago, "An economic evaluation of the foreign investment law of Cuba," p. 2.

119. David S. Collis, "Environmental implications of Cuba's economic crisis," *Georgetown Cuba Briefing Paper Series*, No. 8 (July 1995), p. 8.

120. See Sergio Díaz-Briquets and Jorge Pérez-López, "The special period and the environment," and B. Ralph Barba and Amparo Avella, "Cuba's environmental law," both in *Cuba in Transition—Volume 5* (Washington: Association for the Study of the Cuban Economy, 1995).

121. Barba and Avella, "Cuba's environmental law."

122. They cite the explanation given by Lionel Soto, President of the Cuban Council of Ministers, that Russia had a debt with Cuba of between 20 and 25 million dollars as a result of its natural resources exploitation and environmental contamination in Cuba. This is the estimated amount of Cuba's debt with Russia. See Barba and Avella, "Cuba's environmental law."

civil society. Aside from the losses that social upheaval and even civil war would represent to investors, we have noted the possibility that a future Cuban government could declare a review of the terms and conditions of joint venture agreements, even their annulment, with the potential expropriation of their assets. Two exiled Cuban economists have stated: "...the rights granted to foreigners in many of the current joint venture agreements will likely be declared null by any future government of Cuba bent on developing a competitive market-based economy."[123] The following reasons are cited: 1) inexperienced and/or corrupt government officials and managers are entering into business agreements with foreign investors; 2) information on the assets involved in negotiations is lacking; and 3) not forcing foreign investors to compete transparently and adequately is probably reducing the market value of national assets and concessions.[124] In addition, opponents of the present Cuban regime regarded it as a de facto government and challenge its legitimacy.

Investments in Cuba have limited country and political risk insurance alternatives. Because traditional export coverage is generally not available, the private insurance sector is required for most policy coverage. Political risk and country risk coverage for expropriation, confiscation, and nationalization is provided by a number of entities primarily in London and premiere pricing is said to vary substantially. [125]

4. Social resentment directed against foreigners

A system of economic and social apartheid linked to foreign investment and tourism is strictly enforced by the Cuban government with foreign acquiescence. The granting to foreigners of exclusive ownership of and access to strategic national interests in tantalizing terms while Cuban citizens are denied property rights and excluded from tourist hotels ("tourist apartheid") has created deep social resentment against foreign presence in Cuba both inside the island and within the exile community.[126] Popular anger was put into sobering evidence during August 1994's riot in Havana; a tourist hotel and a dollar store were picked for attack by the angry mob.[127] The terms of some joint venture agreements could be le-

---

123. Castañeda and Montalván, "The Arcos Principles."

124. Castañeda and Montalván, "The Arcos Principles." As an example, the privatization of Emtel Cuba into a joint venture with Mexico's Grupo Domos was formed with an inexperienced company in the area of telecommunications and is said to have granted a 55-year monopoly in the telecommunications industry without a guarantee of efficiency and competitive prices and services. This agreement is considered illegal even within the framework of the current Cuban Socialist Constitution. Castañeda and Montalván, "The Arcos Principles."

125. "Insuring the Cuba risk," *The Cuba Report* (May 1996), p.7. Government export coverage entities of some countries from time to time reportedly provide specific credit coverage for some exports to Cuba such as food and named products. But even U.S. investments in Vietnam do not have access to Overseas Private Investment Corporation (OPIC) or Export-Import Bank financing because Vietnam, despite its far-reaching reforms, does not meet eligibility criteria of compliance with international laws on workers' rights and is still classified as a Marxist-Leninist country. Edward Gargan, "For U.S. business, a hard road to Vietnam," *The New York Times* (July 14, 1995). OPIC is a U.S. federal agency that helps Americans invest abroad; Export-Import Bank financing is oftentimes a key ingredient in large projects that have U.S. involvement.

126. This has been extensively documented by the media and in academic papers. Gillian Gunn remarks: "the degree of citizen outrage is evident... The government is aware that such as exclusion undermines one of its main claims to legitimacy—egalitarianism... The exclusion also flatly contradicts Article 43 of the Cuban Constitution." Gillian Gunn, "The Sociological Impact of Rising Foreign Investment," *Georgetown Cuba Briefing Paper Series*, No. 1 (1993), p. 8.

127. Cuban dissident leader, Leonel Morejón Almagro, has written a bitter account of the Spaniards in Cuba, known as *pepes*: "It's a tough pill to swallow -seeing the happy Spaniards in Havana driving around in their *Havanatur* rented autos while the Cubans exhausted, desperately hungry ...patiently wait for their infrequent and asthmatic buses... They justify their investment in Cuba with the same phrase over and over again: they're here to 'help the Cuban people.' ...it would be prudent for our peninsular friends to proceed with caution, because they're conducting business against the authentic will of the Cuban people and offending our national dignity... it is not inconceivable that at some future date some *different* Cuban government might well nullify these apparently secure contracts." See Leonel Almagro, "Spain: Cuba's Bitter Chalice," *The Miami Herald* (September 17, 1995). (Dr. Morejón Almagro is a Cuban lawyer nominated for the Nobel Peace Prize for his work with dissident lawyers and independent journalists and his advocacy of human rights and environmental causes in Cuba. He is currently in prison.)

gally challenged by a future government for this particular reason.

Other offshoots of the tourist-generated economy elicit the ire of the population. Doctors, educators, and other professionals—"good revolutionaries"—are earning 20 times less than those linked to the dollar economy through the self-employed sector or the tourist/foreign sector. With a few exceptions they are precluded from self-employment so they can pay back the investment the system has made in their education. "Health tourism" (turismo de salud) grants foreigners exclusive access to top of the line medical facilities, efficient service, and the latest drugs while the Cuban population is severely deprived of even essential medical services and the most basic supplies.[128] Discrimination and racism are added to the potentially lethal combination, as "there is evidence that there has been a reduction in the employment of blacks in the enterprises which are now part of joint ventures, situation very evident in the hotels and 'diplotiendas' catering to tourists."[129]

5. Negative impact on international public opinion

The last few years have seen a rapid rise in the international profile of issues related to transnational company ethics.[130] Multinational professional critics—particularly environmental and human rights lobbyists—have become more organized and appear to be gaining ground. Organizations dedicated to researching and evaluating the social and environmental records of corporations assign ratings and organize boycotts.[131] As a result, companies are increasingly sensitive to engaging in business which raise ethical questions and could lead to consumer boycotts, negative effects on staff morale, and the alienation of political contacts. Many big companies now take moral issues so seriously that ethics committees have been appointed and ethics codes drawn up.[132] In Cuba, three areas arouse particular public concern:

i. Human rights: Cuba violates most universally recognized economic and social rights, even by constitutional and legal mandate.[133] The United Nations General Assembly has passed resolutions condemning Cuba and signaling it as one of the most repressive countries in the world and international human rights organizations continue to call for worldwide condemnation of the Castro regime. The European Union recently refused to sign a commercial cooperation agreement with Cuba unless it shows advances in this area.

---

128. In the mid 1980's the government began promoting and in recent years has stepped up "health tourism," to generate hard currency. The State company SERVIMED was formed as a division of Cubanacán, S. A. to offer "sun and medical attention" to foreigners through programs which includes medical treatment, airfare and accommodations. Health tourism is developed through agreements with more than 200 travel agencies in more than 60 countries. It appears that the comparatively low cost of good quality care in Cuba with respect to medical centers in North America and Europe, is particularly attractive especially to Latin Americans. In 1995 health tourism reportedly brought in 3,500 tourists and generated hard currency revenues of US$24 million. See "One thing Cuba does right," *The Economist* (September 7, 1996), p. 42, and Sergio Beltrán, "Cuba: turismo contra salud," *Boletin del Instituto Cubano de Economistas Independientes*, Vol. 1, No. 1 (enero/febrero 1996), pp. 35-36.

129. Lago, "An economic evaluation of the foreign investment law of Cuba," p. 4.

130. Two recent examples are: 1) Shell's Nigerian operations were loudly criticized in the wake of the execution of seven human rights leaders in that country; and 2) Pepsi has been signaled for investments in Myanmar (formerly Burma) as human rights campaigners press for a boycott such as the one on South Africa. See Steth Mydans, "Pepsi courts Myanmar, preferring sales to politics," *The New York Times* (February 23, 1996).

131. "The fun of being a multinational," *The Economist, p. 52* warns: "Campaigners are also using new tactics. One is to take multinationals to court in rich countries for their behavior in poor ones. ...Another tactic it to lobby shareholders."

132. Of particular interest in this area are the Levi Strauss & Co. "Guidelines for country selection and for terms of engagement with business partners." See "The Denim Revolution," Research Report, Council on Economic Priorities (February 1994).

133. The United Nations Special Rapporteur for Cuba in an October 1995 report charges that strong repression is imparted by the state's security forces, indicating: "The excessive control exerted over the population via the institutional machinery ...is applied in the day-to-day life of every citizen -in the workplace, at educational institutions and even at the neighborhood level. ...[T]he deficiencies in respect to the protection of political and civil rights are so extensive and are so imbedded in the political system under the framework of the Constitution... that each case cannot be seen but ...as part of a general absence of pluralism."

In recent years Cuba's dissident movement has gained in strength and worldwide attention.[134] Human rights activists, inside and outside of Cuba, have specifically denounced foreign investors in Cuba for acquiescing or participating in socio-economic apartheid; some have even been signaled for aiding in the repression of peaceful dissident groups and human rights activists. Several groups have denounced a practice labeled "telephone apartheid" by which political dissidents are denied telephone services. The New York-based Committee to Protect Journalists has accused the Mexican Grupo Domos, of allowing its joint venture ETECSA to monitor and interrupt telephone communications of independent journalists.[135]

ii. Labor rights:[136] The advocacy of labor rights has also become more forceful in the international arena[137] while Cuba continues to be condemned by the International Labor Organization (ILO). for systematic violations of labor rights and encouraged to adhere to international human rights standards.[138]

In socialist Cuba, organized labor has been an instrument of the State and collective bargaining is unheard of.[139] The government denies legal recognition and persecutes independent unions and small labor groups which have emerged in recent years. Their leaders are dismissed from their jobs, blacklisted, tortured, incarcerated, and expelled from the government-controlled CTC (Central de Trabajadores de Cuba). United Nations reports cite cases of dismissal from work for citizens who have written slogans contrary to the government, carried foreign newspapers, expressed opinions, or engaged in activities deemed contrary the "construction of socialism."

The institutionalized abuse of ILO Convention 95 on the Protection of Wages, ratified by Cuba, provokes particular outrage. Cuba's unique confiscatory wage system of foreign joint ventures is said to resemble a feudal system of serfdom[140] "unparalleled in the legal tradition of Latin America."[141] In fact, because economic theory defines exploitation as paying a resource less than the value of its marginal product, the Cuban government, as the single buyer of labor, is engaging in a monopsonistic[142] exploitation of the labor force, usurping almost the entire value added of

---

134. In October of 1995 over 130 dissident groups formed an umbrella organization called *Concilio Cubano* to advocate for a peaceful transition to democracy and a rule of law. Its attempt to hold its first national assembly in February 1996 was violently repressed and received international media attention.

135. Sid Balman (United Press International), "Cierran las puertas de EEUU a unos ejecutivos," *El Nuevo Día* (17 de agosto de 1996); press release by the Miami-based *Grupo de Apoyo a Concilio Cubano* (May 27, 1996) with copies of letters of protest to Grupo Domos President Javier Garza and the General Director of the International Telecommunications Union in Geneva.

136. Lourdes Kistler, Program Officer of the American Institute for Free Labor Development (AFL-CIO) and Ernesto Díaz-Rodríguez, International Coordinator for a dissident Cuban labor group, provided valuable information for this section.

137. For example, in the United States there has been a recent popular outcry against child labor in the garment industry and a controversy over Nike's international labor practices, both receiving abundant media coverage. See Bob Herbert, "Nike's pyramid scheme," *The New York Times* (June 10, 1996), and Herbert, "Nike's bad neighborhood," *The New York Times* (June 14, 1996).

138. These rights are enshrined in the Vienna declaration approved by the World Conference on Human Rights in June 1993. The most frequently cited ILO violations are to Conventions 95, on the Protection of Wages; 87, on Freedom of Association and Protection of the Right to Organize; 29, on Forced Labor; 111, on Discrimination in Employment and Occupation; and 89, on The Right to Unionize and Engage in Collective Bargaining.

139. Labor rights have been essentially absent since Castro's rise to power. Upon Castro's victory in 1959 Cuba's independent labor unions were intervened and many of its leaders arrested, executed, or exiled.

140. Carlos Seiglie compares Cuba's labor system to a feudal economy in which the State is lord of the manor, the Cuban workers its serfs. See his "Cuba's Road to Serfdom," opinion piece submitted for publication (September 1996).

141. Sergio A. Leiseca, *Cuba: Rules Specifically Governing Foreign Investors,* Miami (February 15, 1994).

142. Monopsonist is Greek for "single buyer." Carlos Seiglie in his "Cuba's Road to Serfdom" argues that the Cuban government enjoys a monopsony in the labor market because it requires all firms to hire directly from the State.

labor to the production process.[143] Furthermore, employees of the tourist sector are subject to a series of specific duties and obligations, which include the extension to 180 days of the probationary period of new employees as well as 22 new obligations and 46 prohibitions; counting the 12 just causes for termination already incorporated in the Labor Code, these employees are subject to a total of 80 possible infractions. Law 132 of 1992 (Ley de Organos de Justicia Laboral de Base) further provides for eleven disciplinary measures which include fines of up to 25 percent of salary, the loss of material incentives, suspension of seniority rights, forfeiture of decorations and honors won by the workers and the replacement of private sanctions with public reprimand. The practice is even harsher than the text of the law; refusal to join paramilitary groups has been regarded as proof of opposition to the government and has led to dismissals or loss of benefits. [144]

Public objection is mounting against foreign acquiescence with and participation in the abuse of labor rights in joint ventures. An editor of The New Republic responded to Canada's outrage over the U.S. Helms-Burton law by pointing out that Canadians in Cuba participate of a labor system "that no Canadian would tolerate for five minutes."[145] A *Wall Street Journal* editorial on Cuba of August 1996 declares: "...foreign investors are essentially profiting by exploiting the Marxist government's reserve army of nearly slave labor."[146]

iii. Environmental degradation: In Cuba, environmental issues had been widely ignored until recent history. Not until January of 1981 did the Cuban government pass Law 33—Ley de Protección del Medio Ambiente y del Uso Racional de los Recursos Naturales—giving environmental regulations its first official role in the ecology and exploitation of the island's resources. But two environmental experts indicate in a recent study: "The document ...pales in comparison to existing international laws. ...[E]nvironmental regulations are seldom applied and the majority of decisions are taken without consideration of environmental effects."[147] Furthermore, the environmental structure designed for a centralized socialist economy is obsolete for a semi-capitalist economy.[148]

The collapse of the former Soviet bloc brought into evidence the extreme environmental degradation imposed by improper technology, the prioritization of economic goals, and the lack of accountability of an all-powerful State. Experts find Cuba to be no exception and express particular concern over the environmental implications of some recent foreign investments, particularly in tourism and mining.[149] Despite the discouraging state of affairs, awareness of the sig-

---

143. Raúl Asón, "Notas sobre los Principios Arcos para la inversión extranjera en Cuba," Cuba," *Cuba in Transition—Volume 4* (Washington: Association for the Study of the Cuban Economy, 1994), p. 372, states: "We are sure that this phenomenon doesn't occur anywhere in world with the exception of today's Cuba. This situation is too similar to slave labor, endured by humanity for many centuries, which we believed had disappeared."

144. Efrén Córdova, "The condition of Cuban workers under the *'Special Period in Peacetime,'"* in this volume.

145. Charles Lane, "Canada Sly," *The New Republic* (August 6, 1996).

146. *The Wall Street Journal* (August 5, 1996).

147. Barba and Avella, "Cuba's Environmental Law."

148. Collis, "Environmental implications of Cuba's economic crisis," p.8.

149. For example, the Canadian company Sherritt's joint venture with the Cuban government to mine nickel at Moa Bay, is said to present disturbing environmental problems. A special report published in *The Globe and Mail* of Toronto indicates that pollution at Moa is intense, particularly endangering the 60,000 residents of a nearby town. Nevertheless, Sherritt has allegedly committed to a significant environmental clean-up of the already polluted scenario (air and water), which is said to account for much of the $150 million dollars in spending promised for the next five years. But the company has said its aim is to have the Moa plant operating "in line with international practices," meaning "those followed in North America," *in five years"* (emphasis added). See C. Lane, "Canada Sly." Sherritt Inc. established formed in December of 1992 a 50-50 partnership with the Cuban government to mine nickel and cobalt using the Moa complex in Cuba's eastern shore and two Canadian subsidiaries to refine and market the minerals. The Moa plant had been built by the U.S. company in 1952. Paul Knox, "Cuba to share in Sherritt profit," *The Globe and Mail* (July 31, 1995).

nificance of this issue is growing in Cuba and internationally. Several dissident environmental groups have surfaced within Cuba in recent years, although, as with other independent groups, those not co-opted by the regime are facing huge political obstacles.

6. Industry-specific risks in the tourist sector

Aside from the prospect of future claims from former owners of confiscated lands where hotels now stand, the tourist sector is particularly vulnerable to political upheaval. The massive exodus by raft of the summer of 1994 is said by Cuban officials to have resulted in losses of around 100 million in canceled bookings during the last quarter of 1994.[150] In addition, repeat visits are diminished by deficient services resulting from the country's crippled infrastructure, its difficulties in obtaining imports, and lower service standards. Some tourists also experience anguish when confronted with the misery of the population and the system of tourist apartheid, vowing not to return.[151]

FOREIGN INVESTMENT'S IMPACT ON INTERNAL REFORM AND EXTERNAL POLICY FORMULATION

1. What is reform?

Because the reform-generating capacity of commercial engagement is intrinsically tied to the definition of reform we subscribe to, for reform to be qualitatively or quantitatively evaluated in any meaningful way, we must define its objectives. A thoughtful consideration of this fundamental issue is often missing from the debate on commercial engagement and can lead to misunderstandings and conclusions which lack depth and affect the quality of the debate on Cuba. Therefore, for our discussion we will interpret reform as an issue of "empowerment," term which de-

rives its significance from the meaning "to give power or authority to."[152] As a result, the meaning of reform for Cuba will be understood as the attainment by its people of self-determination—the authority to freely decide a system of government and elect an accountable political leadership and the attainment of universally accepted civil, political, and economic rights under the protection of a rule of law. (This may be generally understood as a free market-oriented, pluralistic democracy.)

In order to assess the potential for reform of foreign investment/commercial exchange, we must address its actual and possible impact in the context of Cuba's overall economic needs and how it is leading or could eventually lead to the empowerment of the Cuban people.

2. Commercial engagement as an instrument of economic and socio-political reform in Cuba

Michael Peters, in his book *International Tourism*,[153] advances a theory on the effects of tourism and identifies five potential benefits for a local economy. Given Cuba's almost four decades of isolation from foreign influence and investment, it has been useful to borrow freely from Peter to address the overall impact of foreign investment. Four of these variables have to do with repercussions on the economy: 1) creation of employment; 2) generation of hard currency earnings; 3) multiplier effects; and 4) dispersion of development to other sectors. A fifth—sociological impact—will be analyzed in respect of the other four, all *vis-à-vis* our definition of reform.

i. Creation of employment: Foreign joint ventures are cited as "officially" employing 60,000 workers.[154]

---

150. Michael Becker, "Tourism misses its goal," *CubaNews*, Vol. 3, No. 2 (February 1995), p. 8. Cuba's Deputy Minister of Tourism has expressed disappointment with the 15 percent annual increase in tourism revenues in 1994, short of a projected 30 percent.

151. The author has received several first-hand accounts from visitors not of Cuban origin.

152. *Webster's New World Dictionary of the American Language*, Second College Edition (Cleveland: The World Publishing Company, 1972), p. 459.

153. Michael Peters, *International Tourism* (Hutchinson Publisher, 1969), cited in Gunn, "The Sociological Impact of Rising Foreign Investment," p. 6.

154. "Castro keeps reform on the leash," *Financial Times* (October 27, 1995) and *The Cuba Report* (July 1996), p. 8. Although Minister Lage had reported that tourism alone provided 59,000 jobs in 1992. Gunn, "The Sociological Impact of Rising Foreign Investment," p. 9.

This means that a mere 1.3 percent of the working age population—or 1.87 percent of the estimated employed population—is employed in foreign joint ventures.[155] With the unemployed said to be topping over a million, this is not significant in alleviating Cuba's grave unemployment crisis. In fact, the State is actually blocking opportunities for the creation of more jobs. Due to Cuba's singular labor system, the State is the only "buyer" in the labor market, or in economic terms that the state acts monopsonistically. By refusing to allow other buyers to bid on this important input of the production process, the government has eliminated market forces which would determine the price of labor competitively. Because it fixes a high price for labor in foreign joint ventures irrespective of internal and external competitive market forces, it actually discourages and limits optimal employment by foreign capital firms. That is a level of employment at which, given the conditions of the market, the cost of labor would almost surely be lower. (Cuba, as we have seen, is not close to being competitive on labor costs.)

Furthermore, the limited number of jobs available for a huge pool of workers in the most desirable sector of the economy actually reinforces the need to play by the government's rules. (The State maintains, as we have seen, strict control over these workers.) As a result, notwithstanding the importance these jobs have for those who attain them, as an element of reform or empowerment, the employment aspect of foreign investment seems relatively meaningless and, in important respects, even detrimental.[156]

iii. Generation of hard currency earnings: If we take the US$751.9 million in total stock of "delivered/committed" investment reported by the U.S.-Cuba Trade and Economic Council for August 1996 and round net earnings to 33.3 percent,[157] assuming Cuba receives an average 50 percent share[158] (a 50/50 partnership generating $248 million), it would be obtaining net earnings of $124 million per annum, or roughly 2 percent of the estimated US$6 billion of the missing annual Soviet assistance. Since these figures for foreign investment are probably significantly inflated, we can assume the results would actually be lower unless a higher capital return ratio is factored in. In fact, Minister Lage has indicated that Cuba's net income from foreign joint ventures for 1995 was merely US$114 million (representing 3 percent of the country's net income),[159] which would suppose a higher return ratio on investments amounting to less than the cited US$751.9 million. In addition, this—which must be income from operations typically amounting to around 30 percent of total earnings—would bring the government an additional US$97.5

---

155. For 1995, the estimated workforce was 4.3 million and the estimated employed population was 3.2 million. See Mario Zequeira, "Labor and self-employment: a dilemma for the state," *CubaNews* (September 1996), p.9. Minister Lage, however, has recently indicated that the foreign joint ventures employ 5 percent of the workforce.

156. Its significance, however, could be heightened by the foreign joint ventures' support needs of certain services and goods, which theoretically generate demands on the State to unleash market forces and allow for private enterprise and self-employment. Nevertheless, it is uncertain whether it can actually bring about meaningful changes in the future.

157. An assumed 3-year rate of return of capital is said to be an average minimum return required for high risk cross-border investments. In fact, an expected 3-year capital recovery ratio is said to be characteristic of foreign joint ventures in Cuba. For example, with regard to British American Tobacco's Brazilian subsidiary, Souza Crus, and the Cuban Tobacco Union, which produce cigarettes through a joint venture (the brand Continental for export, and the brand Popular for the domestic market), it was reported that the initial US$10 million investment in the project was expected to be recouped in 3 years. See USCTEC, *Economic Eye on Cuba* (7-23 June 1996), p. 2.

158. The average investment is said to give Cuba at least 51 percent ownership of joint ventures, although this varies. For simplification, we will assume 50/50 partnerships as a norm.

159. Lage revealed this number before year-end 1995 in an address to Central Committee members as an estimated figure. We can deduce that the net income referred to is $3.8 billion. See *Prospects for Development in a Free Cuba*, Executive Summary, U.S. Cuba Business Council, undated. After year-end, it was confirmed by the government. Yet Lage had previously reported that tourism was earning Cuba an estimated $400 million in hard currency just in the year 1992. See Gunn, "The Sociological Impact of Rising Foreign Investment," p. 8. This reference was probably to gross revenues, but "lax" use of data by government officials leads to much confusion.

million in tax revenues.[160] But whether the total is US$114 million net of taxes or US$211.5 million including tax revenues, given the huge gap left by the loss of Soviet assistance, neither sum constitutes a very heartening overall profit for Cuba from foreign joint ventures.

Tourism, as we have seen, has been the fastest growing sector of the Cuban economy. The impact of tourism revenues appears significant; Castro declared in July 1996 that tourism brings in an even larger gross revenue than the sugar industry.[161] But net revenues for this sector are estimated to be low due to its high dependence on imports and hefty promotional discounts and a number of obstacles are said to hurt profitability. Cuba reports that costs per dollar of income dropped in the first half of 1996 to US$0.68 from US$0.73, while income per tourist day increased from US$80 to US$87, but these figures are highly questionable.[162] Shedding doubt on Cuba's numbers, an analyst explains:

"...government statistics just don't add up. If we are to believe the latest published report, Cuba's tourists spend more than twice what a tourist spends in the Dominican Republic, a much more mature and developed tourist market. And what's more amazing, they spend $4 more per visit than do tourists to the U.S. This from an industry that generated almost no revenue seven years ago."[163]

In fact, it has been calculated that for tourism to replace the sugar and nickel earnings that Cuba had in the 1980s, it would have to bring in 3 million tourists per year, a level which would require one billion dollars in additional investment, a highly improbable achievement.[164]

Revenues from a few joint ventures in sectors other than tourism have ostensibly been considerable yet seem relatively insignificant as a solution to the economic crisis.[165] Yet at this time of severe economic crisis, any revenues—those derived from earnings or

---

160. Assuming Cuba had a 50 percent share of every joint venture, earnings before taxes would total US$325 million, as a 30 percent tax would net US$97.5 million for the government. Net income after tax would equal total US$228 million, of which 50 percent represents $114 million in revenues for Cuba, the figure reported by Lage for 1995.

161. "Castro comments," *The Cuba Report*, Vol. 5, No. 4, p.6.

162. *The Cuba Report* (August 1996), p.4. This means that in 1995, 745,000 tourists would have left Cuba US$324 million if the average visit was 5 days or US$453.7 million if the average visit was 7 days. But, this is questionable: in the Bahamas, despite good gross revenues from tourism, 81 cents on the dollar are going overseas via partner corporations. See David Reiff, "Cuba Refrozen," *Foreign Affairs* (July/August 1996), p. 65.) For an idea of the discrepancy in figures, consider the following: For 1994, when the number of tourists increased by 13 percent, Havana Asset Management estimated that gross tourism receipts of around $800 million netted just $250 million. In March of 1994, a Cuban economist on a visit to the United States privately stated that a 30 percent rate of return by Cuba for tourism was too high. Statement by Pedro Monreal, of the *Centro de Estudios de América*, at meeting of the *Cuban American Research Group*, New York, March 16, 1994.

163. T. Babun, "Cuba's investment boom that never was."

164. Ana Julia Jatar-Hausmann, "Through the cracks of socialism: The emerging private sector in Cuba," in this volume.

165. For example, the Sherritt investment in the Moa Bay nickel plant, as of December 1994 was said to be contributing to the Cuban government half the earnings from sales of finished nickel made by Sherritt's refinery in Alberta (half of $26.6 million, or US$13.3 million) in addition to its share (wage and social security confiscation and labor utilization taxes) of the $16 million annual payroll at Moa Bay. See Lane, "Sly Canada." Labor utilization earnings could reach an estimated US$19 million, which is about one third more than earnings from operations. Assuming a 95 percent wage retention rate, salary confiscation equals US$15.2 million, social security conversion would net roughly $12 million and labor utilization taxes would bring in $1.8 million.) Nonetheless, total earnings for Cuba of $29.3 million per annum from Sherritt's Moa operation are relatively low relative to Cuba's needs, especially considering this is presumably Cuba's most visible joint venture investment. Sherritt International Corporation incorporates Cuban holdings as well as oil production facilities in Spain and Italy and exploration properties in a number of countries. Second quarter 1996 earnings totaled Canadian dollars $74.3 million. See *The Cuba Report* (June 1996), p. 4 and (September 1996), p.6. Sherritt International Company was reported by Cuba's *Prensa Latina* to have declared net profits of US$8.47 million during the second quarter of the year. Assuming Cuba represented *all of its business*, which it doesn't, a 50-50 partnership between Cuba and Sherritt, would leave the Cuban government with equivalent annualized net earnings of $33.8 million from operations, plus an additional $20 million in taxes at a 30 percent rate, for a total of US$53.8 million, but the figure is actually lower by an unknown amount, as Sherritt International's business outside of Cuba must be taken into account. That inflated amount would still equal less than 1 percent of the loss of annual Soviet assistance of US$6 billion.

those obtained from the "utilization" of labor—are, doubtless, highly valued by the Cuban government.

To put into perspective Cuba's overall low net earnings from foreign investment and understand its underlying rationale, it is essential to consider what Cuba must be offering as enticement to investors. Given the traditional investment/lending premise that the higher the risk the higher the required return, and in light of the relatively high labor costs, many analysts assume that Cuba's desperate situation is forcing a "fire sale" of available assets.[166] Only this would allow the investor fast capital recovery through the generation of high earnings, which also benefits the Cuban partner, a State in desperate need of revenues.

The wage retention arrangement is a guaranteed and most lucrative source of hard currency earnings for Cuba—irrespective of how profitably joint ventures operate. Earnings from Cuba's unique system of labor in foreign joint ventures could total more than three times the net earnings from operations reported by Minister Lage for 1995.[167] With a reported 60,000 workers in the foreign investment sector, the State could be making in wage conversion alone an estimated US$26.5 million per month, equivalent to around $317.5 million per year.[168] Additionally, so-

cial security contributions (14 percent of wages) paid by the joint ventures in hard currency are registered by the State on behalf of the workers in pesos at the artificial one-to-one exchange rate, would leave the government an additional US$3.6 million per month, or US $43.3 million per annum. Furthermore, a labor utilization tax of 11 percent of gross salaries would net US$2.97 million more per month, US$35.6 million per year. In all, roughly US$33 million per month, US$396.8 million per year, could be going into the government's coffers.[169]

The confiscation of wages is obviously detrimental to joint venture workers, reported to be receiving salaries equivalent to those employed by the State, -currently around nine dollars per month. The government, thus, is appropriating on average almost 98 percent of the total value added of labor in the production process—in some cases even higher;[170] this in effect, imposes an enormous tax on the workers. Workers in the tourist sector are, however, much better off thanks primarily to tips.[171] Although they are required to turn over up to 75 percent of their foreign currency tips to hotel management, receiving an equivalent sum in pesos calculated a the official one-to-one rate, non-compliance with the tips' rules is reported to be high (it does, however, lead to termination of employment).[172]

---

166. Lago, "An economic evaluation of the foreign investment law of Cuba," p. 4.

167. On a monthly basis, the State would be obtaining an annual gross profit of US$5,289 per worker (US$441 per month). At the current peso-dollar exchange rate of 1 US$ equal to 22 pesos, if the employment agency is receiving US$450 per worker and the government pays a salary to each worker of 203 pesos, the State has retained 97.9 percent of each worker's wages.

168. This is a rough estimate based on the average salary of US$450, paid to workers as 203 Cuban pesos (subject to a retention rate of 97.9 percent) times 60,000—the number of workers said to be employed in foreign joint ventures. The number of workers on the average salary is not known, but it is reasonable to assume that the majority would be earning a similar amount.

169. This is equivalent to 66.5 percent of Cuba's entire 1995 estimated GDP of 13.125 million pesos if we converted it to dollars (US$596.5 million) at the current rate of 22 pesos to the dollar. Nevertheless, this is a mere allusion to the proportions involved, as Cuba's GDP figures are not reliable. José Alonso, Research Economist at USIA's Radio Martí, explains that analysts don't know how this calculation is made. It reflects 1981 constant dollars, but that year's basket of goods is no longer available, as it was the period of massive Soviet aid. Furthermore, the components and methodology used to calculate the price deflator are unknown).

170. The Cuban state employment agency, however, is reported to receive US$2,700 per month for a geologist employed in Sherritt, while the geologist receives US$10.00 from the government. See Lane, "Sly Canada." In this employee's case, the wage confiscation provides a 99.6 percent return for the government—US$32,280.00 annually.

171. In 1993, it was reported that at one Varadero hotel that a waiter turned in US$609 in tips in just one month, "bringing his total income for the month to nearly 1,000 pesos, five times the national average." (Gunn, "The Sociological Impact of Rising Foreign Investment," p.10.) *It should be noted, however, that at the time, 1,000 pesos roughly represented just US$10 at the black market rate.*

172. An average confiscation rate of 75 percent was reported to the author, although rules are said to vary by enterprise. Based on personal conversation with specialist in Cuban labor, Professor Efrén Córdova of Florida International University, August 1996. Assuming a 50 percent non-compliance rate on tips of around $300 per month, a worker could take home over US$187.5 per month which is a fortune in Cuba ($37.50 in 25 percent of the reported $150.00 plus the $150.00 not reported).

Despite the poor wages, the material conditions of workers in the foreign enclaves is better than the rest of the population's, which make jobs in this sector the most prized. Foreign enterprises have found many resourceful ways of compensating workers, including bonuses and gifts.[173] Many workers receive transportation to work and meals; in some cases dress is provided. In the tourist sector, aside from tips, some hotel workers are able to eat the food served at the restaurants and are sometimes allowed to convert tips into left-over food from the hotel's restaurants.[174] Emulation prices given to the workers—bicycles, TVs, etc.—are said to be highly valued, although worth less than the hard currency tip earnings of the winner.[175] Some of these benefits have recently carried over to other areas, as the government has started to provide incentives for non-joint venture workers in order to compensate somewhat for the growing inequalities arising from the dollar-peso dual economy. Approximately one million workers, or 25 percent, of the labor force, is estimated to be receiving some form of payment in dollars or convertible pesos, as reward for meeting or exceeding work quotas.[176] Despite this positive side effect, those workers remain dependent on the State.

The informal incentives provided by joint ventures provide a significant measure of relief to the workers, given the impoverished state of their lot. But relative to empowerment, providing basic guarantees available to workers in most developed and developing countries scenario means little more than putting food in hungry stomachs, allowing the favored workers to get by somewhat better than the impoverished rest. Its importance for the favored individuals, from a humane perspective, should not be underestimated, but at a systemic level, its overall impact on empowerment is trivial. Importantly, as we have seen, because these jobs are more precious, those employed by joint ventures also have more incentive to "behave." Therefore, any material improvement in the situation of joint venture workers is at the expense of even greater political compliance and economic dependence.[177]

Clearly the Cuban government is the main beneficiary of the hard currency earnings derived from foreign investment. These are especially valuable for regime security during the "Special Period." Nevertheless, in relation to the huge needs of the country after the loss of Soviet funds, hard currency net earnings derived from non-telecommunication joint venture foreign investment, estimated here to approximate roughly $608.3 million per year (10.1 percent of one year's estimated Soviet assistance[178]) do not come close to enabling a significant improvement in the economy with meaningful trickle down effects.

Despite the peculiarities and deficiencies of existing joint venture arrangements, foreign investors are rationally interested in the survival of the current Cuban government and its investment agreements for

---

173. In testimony given in private by an executive of a Chilean firm investing in Cuba, the investor acknowledged being aware that the peso salaries of workers had virtually no purchasing power. Yet, the workers of one of their operations, adjacent to a similar State-owned operation, were reporting to work while the State's operation was plagued with absenteeism. As he explained, they were being lured to work because "we give them lunch."

174. Gunn, "The Sociological Impact of Rising Foreign Investment," p. 10. At one hotel, those employees with the highest hard currency tips obtained the food surplus.

175. Gunn, "The Sociological Impact of Rising Foreign Investment," p. 10.

176. See Jatar-Hausmann, "Through the cracks of socialism," p. 13.

177. "In order to attract capital the government has promised investors the right to hire and fire as they see fit." See Gunn, "The Sociological Impact of Rising Foreign Investment," p.12.

178. Soviet assistance has been estimated earlier in this paper at more than US$6 billion, a figure rounded down for this calculation to US$6 billion. Earnings were calculated as follows: $114 from operations (Minister Lage's report for 1995), $97.5 million in taxes of 30 percent on $751.9 million foreign investment per Table 2, plus our estimates of $396.8 million in labor utilization earnings. (Tips were not included in this figure, as it is very difficult to estimate a reliable number.) Telecommunications' payments made by U.S. companies to Cuba totaling $76.8 million in 1995 would bring the total to $685.1 million. See *U.S. Cuba Policy Report*, Vol. 3, No. 10 (October 31, 1996), p. 3.

the minimum period required to secure capital recovery, indefinitely to generate a stream of earnings.[179] In fact, due to the nature of foreign investment in Cuba today, the conditions and terms for the generation of earnings seem to actually reinforce the vested interest both of the State and of foreign investors to preserve existing joint venture arrangements. These have been designed to maximize short-term benefits for the partners—foreign investors and the Cuban State—in the context of a command economy and a closed political system.

iii. Multiplier effects: The characteristics of foreign investment in Cuba have prompted the observation: "Hardly any of the companies ...produce consumer goods for Cubans. (...)They concentrate instead on extractive industries such as nickel and petroleum exploration, providing services for foreign tourists, and export-oriented industries that net hard currency for the Castro regime and little for the Cuban people."[180] As a result, foreign joint venture investment has not affected overall domestic production—furnishings, food, supplies, athletic equipment, etc.—in any significant way. In the tourism sector, it has generated support businesses, but mainly in the service sector. A visiting scholar poignantly illustrates this paradoxical situation: "...the Castro government has steadfastly refused to allow Cubans to set up the small or medium-sized businesses, even to supply the tourist sector. The shampoo in hotel bathrooms, the pillow on the bed, even the packets of sugar in the hotel restaurant- all are imported. The last is particularly astonishing: the sugar, packaged mainly in Canada, was produced on the island."[181] Severely restricted multiplier benefits are a poor precursor of reform.

The economic benefits of multiplier effects emanating from worker remuneration are also quite limited in scope due to wage confiscation. Because the estimated number of workers employed by foreign joint ventures is said to be no more than 60,000 and the average size of the Cuban family is four,[182] approximately 240,000 people can be assumed to depend on those jobs, or around 2 percent of the Cuban population. But the possible benefits to those workers and their families are severely constrained by the salary confiscation scheme, which limits their multiplier effects—the most notable exception being workers of the tourist industry with access to tips. But, if we assumed 40,000 workers to be employed in tourist joint ventures and taking home US$187.5 a month in tips, the US$7.5 million per month would have an impact on the economy but cannot materially change its overall condition.

In terms of empowerment, due to wage confiscation in joint ventures, advances are probably most perceived by the population not in the joint venture sector, but in the informal and self-employed sectors. Castro himself has acknowledged the impact on tourism on employment, indicating that tourism supports (rather than employs) 2 million people.[183] But the government has imposed steep taxes and fees to "redistribute" individual gains.[184]

From the Cuban State's standpoint the rationale for foreign investment is the prioritization of political necessities over structural economic reform while extracting immediate economic gains to face a monumental crisis. From the standpoint of the investor, Cuba's high risk scenario imposes an essentially spec-

179. Peter Breese of Latinvest Security Limited of London, speaking at a June 1996 The Economist Conference on Cuba held in London, made recommendations for investing in Cuba which included: "remember particularly to structure the offer recognizing the investors' requirement to combine a limited exposure with a realistic exit strategy." See *The Cuba Report* (June 1996), p. 5.

180. Frank Calzón, "Is Canada aware of evil of cutting deals with Cuba?" *The Miami Herald* (April 15, 1996).

181. Reiff, "Cuba Refrozen," p. 65.

182. Zequeira, "Labor and self-employment."

183. On July 26, 1996 Castro reported that tourism supports 2 million people, not 2 million workers. See "Castro comments," *The Cuba Report*, Vol. 5, No.4, p.6.

184. Given the difficulty of measuring the overall economic impact of tourism -due to the impossibility of assessing the size of the informal sector and its specific effect on it—we can only assume that tourism indeed is of considerable consequence to the economy when tourist related-services such as taxis and *paladares*—are taken into account.

ulative and short term rationale: limited initial capitalization with a focus on recovery instead of reinvestment. This scenario is contrary to the local economy's need for capitalization, which is what enables the creation of domestic savings and spurs internal growth. Thus, the nature of foreign investment in Cuba today is incompatible with stable and long-term economic growth.

iv. Dispersion of development: In Cuba, the people's eager embrace of capitalism has scared the government.[185] As a result, following the success of free markets, vendors have been swept away and many small restaurantsi—ipaladares—shut down. Nevertheless, certain elements of this second economy tied to foreign capital are harder to control and could trigger, through a "dispersion" effect, elements of reform:[186]

- The second economy is regarded as an instrument to create avenues for civil society to manifest itself as distinct from the state. Foreign joint ventures provide a living example of an alternative to the official centralized command system. When juxtaposed with the administrative and inefficient setting of prices, this can underscore the efficacy of decisions based on supply and demand and profit orientation—which could lead to demands to eliminate senseless regulations and administrative restrictions. Additionally, it helps to demonstrate that economic relationships outside of the official sphere can operate efficiently and affirms market worth based on tradeoffs.[187]

- Cuba's capitalist enclaves have required the development of support enterprises that did not exist, particularly in the tourist sector. This, to-

gether with the success of self-employment, can help dispel the myth that decades of socialism have eliminated private initiative and entrepreneurship, demonstrating that the citizens can react positively to the pursuit of private gain.

- Foreign joint ventures carry the seed for the emergence of an entrepreneurial class which would be psychologically prepared for the transition to capitalism.[188]

These three factors, linked to the emergence of foreign joint ventures, lead to the logical question of the role played by state pseudo-technocrats involved in the opening to foreign capital. At present their dual roles as Party apparatchicks and agents of reform mean that they must remain ideologically committed to the system while recognizing that radical economic changes looking too much like the hated capitalism must be implemented. Moreover, because tomorrow they will probably have to survive in the market, to different degrees they're already positioning themselves. Expectations of their psychological transformation and/or political trajectory from socialism to the market are difficult to assess given their precarious situation and the high degree of pretending that permeates all levels of Cuban society. Because survival can be a deceitful game, we can only speculate on how much capitalist influence would actually encourage and strengthen their commitment to reform. The key for reform, however, is their eventual attainment of any degree of significant influence to bring about change. As of today, their actual economic and political empowerment and influence appears to remain resolutely dependent of and

---

185. The leadership realizes that by "creating alternatives for employment outside of the state sector, the second economy empowers workers and makes it more likely that their wage and conditions of work will result from transactive bargaining between workers and managers than imposed from the center, putting pressure on the first economy for change." See Jorge Pérez-López, *Cuba's second economy* (New Brunswick: Transaction Publishers, 1995), p. 22.

186. Applied to situations described in Pérez-López, *Cuba's second economy,* pp. 14-15.

187. Pérez-López, *Cuba's second economy,* p. 17.

188. For example, it has been argued that the very presence of a second economy in the former Soviet camp led the way to, and even necessitated, economic reform. See Jorge Pérez-López, "Cuba's second economy and market transition," draft of March 25, 1995 prepared for the conference *Towards a New Cuba,* Princeton University, April 7-8, 1995. Analysts, however, hold differing views as to what led to perestroika and glasnost.

under the control of the State.[189] It is, thus, questionable whether "technocratic metamorphosis"[190]—the transformation of a select few "enlightened" State technocrats linked to foreign joint ventures—could enable a change in Cuba.

A "make-over" of the technocracy, however, seems more consequential once a transition (i.e. a process of empowerment) is actually underway. These technocrats could add a level of experience, a possible second tier which could quickly turn away from revolutionary rhetoric, fully embracing the ways of the market and benefiting the privatization process. But the development of this new socio-economic segment also breeds the seeds of destructive societal forces, particularly in case of an eventual transition. Cuban managers of foreign joint ventures could be posed to assume undue power and control during the chaotic phase of a transition.[191] Professor Gunn, of Georgetown University, indicates: "The extremely high concentration of resources in the state sector, and the centralized nature of the management system ...place a greater deal of power in the hands of government officials of socialist countries. ... Economic reforms and the transition to a market economy create opportunities for the nomenklatura to ransack what they can from amid the chaos of disintegration

and lack of regulation."[192] In fact: "Many in leadership positions may actually be creating more incentives for themselves to preserve the regime that allows them their privileged position. In Cuba, a system of privilege based on political allegiance has, in fact, been a "subtle weapon of control;"[193] to varying degrees it permeates different levels of the technocracy.[194] As a result, the role of State technocrats must be carefully assessed.

Foreign investment, whether in the tourist sector or beyond, can also be associated with a dispersion effect on the general population such as what Peters labels "demonstration effect on consumption" — foreign consumption patterns, dress style, access to technology, vehicles, restaurants, etc. and accompanying idiosyncrasies. This is linked to the sociological effect of "a widening, new, understanding of foreigners and foreigners' tastes."[195] But, for it to have any meaningful impact, the premise that people can make economic decisions freely seems somehow implied. A prominent expert on Cuba concluded in late September 1992 after a series of visits to Cuba, that the ideologically subversive effects of foreign investment were not at the time severely disrupting Cuba's social fabric."[196] Several years later, although foreign joint ventures appear to not have proliferated, the

---

189. Minister Carlos Lage's words underscore the nature of their role: "In these existing joint enterprises the Cuban managers are not capitalist or the owners of those facilities. They are members of the Revolution performing the task assigned to them by the Revolution." Gunn, "The Sociological Impact of Rising Foreign Investment," p. 3.

190. Term borrowed from James Shinn, "Engaging China: exploiting the fissures in the facade," *Current History*, Vol. 95, No. 602 (September 1996).

191. *The Economist* recently indicated: "The youngish technocrats who make up the second tier of Cuban government include some impressively intelligent and cultivated men." See "Cuba Survey," *The Economist* (April 1996). This terminology, *pseudo-technocrat*, is chosen by the author due to the fact that in Cuba, to reach these heights of becoming a high level technocrat requires proven political commitment in addition to technical or professional qualifications.

192. Gunn, "The Sociological Impact of Rising Foreign Investment," pp. 23 and 25.

193. Gunn, "The Sociological Impact of Rising Foreign Investment."

194. Since the early days of the Revolution the *nomenklatura* has enjoyed exclusive privileges because rational actors will not allow their investments and interests to be ruined, they will seek to protect their privileges. In Juan Clark, "The Cuban new class," *The Miami Herald* (February 25, 1996). In fact, the younger and well-educated technocrats, state enterprise managers and some party bureaucrats may share a similar situation with those outside the elite who benefit from a second economy and are consequently dissuaded from demanding reform: "(...)the individualistic, wheeling-and-dealing oriented, personalized subculture created by the second economy does not encourage the kind of collective action necessary for revolution and the violent overthrow of a regime." Pérez-López, *Cuba's second economy*, p. 15, quoting Sik.

195. Gunn, "The Sociological Impact of Rising Foreign Investment," p. 6, quoting Michael Peters and John Bryden.

196. Gunn, "The Sociological Impact of Rising Foreign Investment," p. 15.

Cuban people are certainly well aware of their existence. Despite their consequential social repercussions, the rivalries and distortions which have surfaced in their wake have remained under strict state control. Undoubtedly the free markets have revived and encouraged the entrepreneurial spirit of the Cuban people,[197] for the first time in over three decades exposed to the ways of the market. Cuban managers and workers employed in joint ventures and the population at large witness the capitalist model and work ethic, supply and demand, competition, marketing, and efficiency. Nonetheless, if a widening of understanding indeed taking place, the crucial issue is: can it, and if so, when does it, actually lead to reform/ empowerment? In fact, although foreign investment may continue to transform the psychology of those who come in contact with Capitalist ways—both managers and workers, not much can change if their capacity to influence or undermine the current system remains suppressed. In a totalitarian or repressive regime, empowerment seems independent of the psychology of any given individual or group as long as they lack the capacity to effectively exercise power.

Meanwhile, the destabilizing distortions of Cuba's unique breed of selective capitalism are obvious. The creation of a worker elite, particularly in the tourist sector, is causing friction with the rest of the population and fueling socio-political tensions.[198] Reports from Cuba describe growing internal anxiety over this problem.[199] Those who have dollars, approximately 40 percent of the population at any given time,[200] can go to state-run shops to buy goods virtually unobtainable in their ration books or in peso stores, although they are wildly expensive. Those who do not must turn to the "informal" economy, which touches most of life and breeds pilferage, corruption, and theft. Common are anecdotes of girls prostituting themselves for a dinner at a dollar-only restaurant or a pair of jeans. The government has attempted to iron out these inequalities by redistributing wealth through taxation, making those who've profited bear the burden for the rest of society, but nationalistic resentment is festering, even among high government officials and those most faithful to Castro.

Another distorting occurrence associated with the advent of foreign investment is the emergence of quasi-private or private Cuban companies involved in foreign joint ventures, manipulated by the party as "a mechanism for maintaining leverage in a market system."[201] Due to the government's fears that the creation of increasingly independent economic agents may dilute the formal power structure, a concentration of "privatized" financial resources and capital has taken place within the ruling elite, particularly within the Cuban Armed Forces (FAR). Since Cuba's opening to foreign investment, several "private" Cuban companies—so-called S.A. firms[202]—have been officially established, especially in the tourist sector, which are professedly run and owned by the

---

197. It should be noted that Cuba pre-Castro was primarily a market economy, and quite successful, despite its political "underdevelopment."

198. Tourism workers have been said to be dressing so well as to be mistaken for foreigners. See Gunn, "The Sociological Impact of Rising Foreign Investment," p. 11.

199. An economist from Cuba explains: "A process of redistribution of income in the hands of the population has been undertaken....This situation of divisive gaps ...has been insulting and has worsened something which had been happening—the separation of ethical and esthetic values." Marta Beatriz Roque, "Una ventana a la sociedad cubana," *Boletín del Instituto Cubano de Economistas Independientes*, Vol. 1, No. 1, (enero/ febrero 1996), p. 37.

200. A large portion of that 40 percent is reported to have only occasional access in small quantities. "Country Report / Lage...," *The Cuba Report* (August 1996), p. 5.) Prior to the legalization of the holding of dollars, in March 1994, Pedro Monreal, an economist visiting the U.S. from Cuba, stated that the government estimated that 15 percent of the population had access to dollars from abroad at a meeting of *the Cuban American Research Group*, New York, March 16, 1994.

201. Gunn, "The Sociological Impact of Rising Foreign Investment."

202. S.A. is the abbreviation of *Sociedad Anónima*, and stands for Inc.

FAR, reportedly with foreign participation.[203] In essence, the military is being used as a vehicle to access the market in a more controlled manner and co-opt the benefits of capitalism. Marinas, hunting lodges, spas, and small hotels built for the military and the Party are used to generate foreign exchange from tourists. The new firms generally seek partnerships with foreign companies as they grow and are also said to be acting as consultants to foreign investors and clearinghouses for counter-trade deals between foreign and Cuban enterprises and providing services for firms marketing visitors.[204] Their shareholders, the origin of their capital, and their earnings are shrouded in secrecy; the vested interest of the Cuban owners is, naturally, to preserve the exclusivity of these privileges. Although this has been labeled "a state-sanctioned capitalist sector,"[205] because this "leadership-contained" mechanism limits empowerment and multiplier effects, it seems begging of a more descriptive label—which might be "captive or co-opted capitalism."

Concurrent with the concentration of resources in the hands of the nomenklatura, Cuba is witnessing the emergence of another troubling phenomenon linked to foreign capital. Similar to the post-Soviet Russian mafias, a new class has been born: Cuban yuppies or "new rich"—the macetas,[206] black marketeers and individuals who, thanks to the liberalization of certain markets, command large amounts of financial resources and consume conspicuously.[207]

The perpetuation of selective capitalism has harvested destructive societal distortions and harbors the seeds of increasing socio-economic aberrations, sabotaging the eventual establishment of an appropriate framework for achieving social order and a rule of law. Cuba's singular arrangement to access foreign capital through leadership-contained, quasi-Capitalist mechanisms, could best be described as "co-opted dispersion of development" or "distorted dispersion of development." Economist Jorge Sanguinetty has warned that the lack of equity in the privatization process taking place with foreign investor participation excludes most of the non-militant population and "may cast serious doubts on the legitimacy of property rights for a long time and is not a desirable outcome of an effort to establish a market economy."[208] The elite could be poised to take over a "reformed" Cuba while the population at large has been denied access to properties and business dealings available only to foreigners and members of the nomenklatura. (The current situation in Russia offers

---

203. Two of the most prominent enterprises are in the tourism sector: Cubanacán, S.A. and Gaviota, S.A., both with extensive joint ventures

204. The apparent strategy is to establish Cuban firms able to compete for "spin off" business from major foreign investments. Jorge Pérez-López notes that other non-military members of the *nomenklatura* are already also going into business. See Gunn, "The Sociological Impact of Rising Foreign Investment," p. 3; Pérez-López, *Cuba's second economy*, p. 33; and *The Cuba Report* (August 1996), p. 8.

205. Gunn, "The Sociological Impact of Rising Foreign Investment," p. 13.

206. The uneven distribution of existing wealth is evidenced by the fact that 59 percent of deposits in the Banco Popular de Ahorro have been reported to be in the hands of 10 percent of the depositors, who held 80 percent of the cash. See "Las finanzas internas y el mercado agropecuario," *Boletín de la Asociación de Economistas Independientes de Cuba*, No. iii (marzo-abril 1995), p.16; Arnaldo Ramos Laurzurique, "La crisis económica cubana: causas y paliativos," *Boletín del Instituto Cubano de Economistas Independientes*, Vol. 1, No.1 (enero-febrero 1996), p. 3; and USCTEC, *Economic Eye on Cuba* (15-21 July 1996), p.3.

207. This special class is said to drive flashy cars and talk on cellular phones on the way to power lunches. See Christopher Marquis, "Cuba set to stop bribes, kickbacks." Haroldo Dilla, sociologist at the Havana *Centro de Estudios de América* cites a study of the *Instituto Nacional de Investigación Económica*, which has detected the seeds of the new "fortunes": "...the accumulation of capital in few hands is already a reality. ... [T]he main beneficiaries of the economic adjustment have been the 'macetas,' a type of mafia with the pretension of becoming bourgeoisie. They are leading the concentration observed in the area of self-employment and free markets. ... [A] free market in Havana in theory has 22 independent vendors. In reality, the vendors are controlled by three individuals who provide them supplies and pay them a salary, even though this is forbidden by the Cuban Constitution." Quoted in Marquis, "Cuba set to stop bribes, kickbacks."

208. Jorge A. Sanguinetty, "Economic education for a market economy: the Cuban case," *Cuba in Transition—Volume 5* (Washington: Association for the Study of the Cuban Economy, 1995).

a striking lesson.[209]) The negative impact on morale results in the perception by the population of the nature of private property as predatory (reinforced by decades of Marxist education and rhetoric), which can actually hinder the eventual and peaceful adoption of a free market democracy.[210]

Furthermore, the enclave system of foreign joint ventures—captive to the leadership, concessionary to foreigners and the ruling elite, and lacking transparency and competitiveness- is contrary to the conceptual configuration of capitalism. As conceived by Adam Smith, capitalism thrives only when restrained by a system of values and a panoply institutions which allow the market to unleash forces of progress while controlling its worst consequences. Cuba's system poses an intrinsic philosophical negation of the theoretical foundation of the capitalism that has been successful—or at least viable—in Western societies.[211] A political constraint inherent to preserving Cuba's current system prevents meaningful socioeconomic and political empowerment and forestalls the release of those forces which can generate economic recovery/viability/prosperity in a proper

framework and a climate of internal peace. In its present form, foreign investment in Cuba is not helping release those forces, but rather appears to assist in their containment.

3. Economic determinism and political reform[212]

Part of the problem in interpreting Cuba's reform process may have to do with the marked contrast between what the government portrays to the outside world compared to what it says and does inside Cuba. To the world, Cuba has depicted its process of liberalization as "working towards an 'achievable utopia' where socialism has adapted to new world conditions with some market elements, but the state retains a key role. In September 1995 the Cuban Foreign Minister, Roberto Robaina, courted the U.S. business community with the concept that Cuba is on it's way to developing "a new and unique model," where political reform is "not excluded."[213] Visiting New York city again in September 1996, he reiterated that Cuba was searching for its own peculiar model and requested patience and understanding.[214] Minister Lage declared in August 1996: "Cuba has taken its own steps without mechanically copying other ex-

---

209. In Russia, amidst reports of a mafia-type anarchy, former government officials now control most of the shares of huge former state conglomerates and companies that were privatized in a process marred by official corruption, bribery, favoritism, and criminal acts. "Money that was supposed to jump-start the private sector has instead enriched the old Communist ruling class. ... As the average citizen lost his stake in Russia, former Communists, who make up less than ten percent of the population, prospered. ... [N]early two-thirds of the country's millionaires had been members of the Soviet Communist Party. The KGB too has profited." J. Michael Waller, "To Russia with cash," *Readers Digest* (June 1996).

210. For example, the editor of *The New Republic* illustrates the dynamics behind a Canadian investment: "Sherritt's example, and that of other Canadians who do business in Cuba, shows that these foreign operations are a caricature of competitive capitalism. Their impact is anything but subversive. ...When Canadian investors come to Havana, they don't shop around for partners amount the Cuban populace at large; the average Cuban can't own private property, much less engage in ventures with foreigners. All deals are negotiated with the government, often with Fidel personally. No competitive bids, no international tender offers in *The Economist*, just a nod from the man in charge..." Lane, "Canada Sly."

211. The thread that runs through Adam Smith's writings on Capitalism is the imperative to design institutions which draw "the passions" towards socially and morally beneficial behavior. Smith believed that commercial society made it possible for the mass of the people to escape the demeaning relations of dependence characteristic of the past. Direct domination by political elites would be replaced by a network of institutions which promoted self-control among politically free citizens and raised the level of material comfort to make possible the expansion of sympathy and concern for others. See, for example, Jerry Z. Muller, *Adam Smith in his time and ours: Designing the decent society* (New York: The Free Press, 1993).

212. An analysis of the concept and debate on economic determinism—the notion that economic development is a natural precursor to political development—has been left out but is incorporated in the full version of this paper.

213. Roberto Robaina, "Cuba & the United States: Is there room for dialogue?," The New York Hilton, September 28, 1994. Notes taken by the author, who was in attendance.

214. The Minister spoke at a luncheon hosted by the *U.S.-Cuba Trade and Economic Council*, New York, September 26, 1996. As per anecdotal account to the author by an attendee.

periences... assimilating all useful practices which can be taken into account in the closest relation with the world while constructing our own socialist path."[215] This sort of discourse characterizes the prevailing theme for external consumption; it provides an eerie allusion of Lenin's mastery of distortion to advance Communist ends through capitalist means.[216] In August of 1995 the President of the State and Ministerial Councils clearly stated the government's intentions:

> "during many years we fought against foreign investment... however, in the current situation we could not do without foreign investment at a higher level, because we needed capital, technology and markets.... we took this path because this was the only alternative ... the key of all this is the issue of power. Who has the power? That is the key.... Transition to capitalism? There will be no transition to capitalism."[217]

For those who can read between the lines and carefully follow what is said by the Cuban leadership, its commitment to avoiding reform, both in words and in practice, is consistent. It is all too clear that economic liberalization is not enticing the ruling elite towards structural economic reform or political reform of any sort, as it is well aware of the threats re-

forms convey.[218] Internally, the government has consistently justified the changes on the economic front as necessary evils to secure economic survival without a loosening of political control. (This is typically packaged as the "need to preserve the 'achievements' of the Revolution.") Its leadership has repeatedly confirmed its resolve to defend the political status quo despite the adoption of certain elements of "the Chinese model"—that is, to preserve the Revolution, whatever it still represents today, the Marxist-Leninist ideology, and the Socialist economic system. Moreover, Castro continues to decry capitalism and has declared emphatically that Cuba cannot take the risk of repeating the mistakes of the former Soviet bloc and has intoned: "The island will sink into the sea before it stops being Communist."[219]

In the final analysis, assumptions and vague generalizations on Cuba's reform process have to be tested with reality. To this day causality has not occurred nor been proven certain. Perhaps the most telling measure of engagement's outcome is that it has failed to produce tangible payoffs despite Cuba's normal commercial and political relations of many years with most countries. Even the countries with most influ-

---

215. *Negocios en Cuba*, op.cit., p. 7.

216. Lenin spent most of his life at the epicenter of an international conspiracy predicated on the idea that an entire world order -capitalism- could be subverted and overthrown by a small cadre of professional conspirators who would bring about world revolution. "Its success would proceed from secrecy, discipline, and deception. The real would be hidden, the false displayed. Opponents would be confused, diverted, and ultimately misled into collaborating in their own destruction." Edward Jay Epstein, *Dossier: The Secret History of Armand Hammer* (New York: Random House, 1996), pp. 58-59. Lenin was convinced that the Communists did not know how to run the economy. His report for the XIth Party Congress of April 1922, states: "The capitalists ...know how to do things. ... The mixed companies that we have begun to form, in which private capitalists, Russian and foreign, and Communists participate, provide one of the means by which we can learn to organize competition properly." Robert C. Tucker, ed., *The Lenin Anthology* (New York: W. W. Norton & Company, Inc., 1975). In 1921 Lenin masterminded the *Trust Operation*, labeled "one of the most elaborate deceptions in modern history." Designed to make Western governments believe they could achieve the overthrow of Communism by giving up their economic sanctions, its ultimate objective was to obtain help from abroad—spare parts, trucks, etc.—to help Russia survive a desperate economic crisis. It achieved its goal by passing along to Western intelligence misinformation through a Russian organization controlled by Cheek agents masquerading as anti-Communist. Portraying Lenin's economic reforms as signaling the eventual abandonment of Communism, it convinced the West that what kept the Bolsheviks in power was Russian antipathy for foreign subversion. Lenin "had to do whatever was necessary to advance the image of a non-threatening Russia—even when the measures deviated from, or contradicted, Marxist ideology. *The end still justified the means where the survival of the revolution was at stake.*" Epstein, *Dossier: The Secret History of Armand Hammer*, pp. 62-63.

217. Speech delivered at the closing ceremonies of a Youth Festival. See *Boletin del ICEI* (enero-febrero 1996), p. 7.

218. Professor Gunn of Georgetown University had explained in early 1993: "Castro has given considerable thought to the ideological "contamination" inherent in collaboration with foreign capitalist enterprises ...and has concluded that despite the risks, Cuba has no choice but to welcome investment." See Gunn, "The Sociological Impact of Rising Foreign Investment," p. 2.

219. Montaner, "The risks...."

ence have declared their failure and frustration. As proof of the leaderships' determination and its effectiveness in containing reform, the Executive Director of Human Rights Watch recently concluded: "...any improvement in the island's economy which may have resulted from the arrival of European investment has not been matched by any greater opportunity for civil society."[220]

Mechanisms of control operate and remain effective at all levels. The U.N. Special Rapporteur for Cuba continues to report "serious violations of civil and political rights."[221] Information remains "exclusive state property" and international journalists' organizations have denounced widespread attacks against Cuban journalists who have in recent years formed the first independent news agencies in socialist Cuba.[222] The government's resolve and enforcement capabilities are demonstrated by the emergence of sophisticated tactics of repression to counter potential erosions of control emanating from the economic crisis and the measures designed to confront it. A mid-1994 broad reform of the Penal Code toughened the laws for economic crimes amidst a crackdown on "abuses of economic reforms" tied to the legalization of small-scale private businesses.[223] New forms of institutionalized violence based on popular mobilization have been unleashed against those who call for change.[224] To break down the growing internal opposition without provoking a worldwide outcry, dissidents are being habitually harassed and pressured to leave the country in lieu of the long jail terms of the past. Aside from the mechanisms of control embodied in the Foreign Investment Law, specific measures have been taken in the foreign sector to curtail the

emergence of an empowered second economy: 1) pre-screening the applicant pool of workers for "revolutionary behavior"; 2) targeting workforce reductions at employees of certain political views and subjecting those who complain to "Actos de Repudio"; 3) passing especially strict regulations for tourism workers, as discussed above; 4) requiring that hotel management commissions have a representative from the Communist Party, the Union of Young Communists and the government controlled workers' union, CTC; 5) giving emulation prizes to those performing voluntary labor and paying union dues; and 6) subjecting workers in the tourism industry to "forced voluntary labor."

Within the context of Cuba's liberalizing measures and its opening to foreign investment, the question of external-sector generated influence or pressure for reform should not miss the crucial point. With respect to Cuba, as with other totalitarian systems, the root issue is: if it does, how can it, or will it, actually lead to change? A factor that compounds the dilemma and contradicts the workability of the cause-effect dynamic must be considered: if reforms bring relief, they could actually discourage the need for more reform; if economic pressure diminishes on a leadership bent on self-preservation, the need to take such a high risk can be eliminated. Indeed, the following argument has been put forth: "In fact, foreign investment has been used as a means to avoid or postpone unavoidable and necessary changes, rather than acting as an agent in support of reforms."[225]

Particularly, in the aftermath of the February 1996 forceful crackdown on the internal dissident move-

220. José M. Vivanco, *European Voice* (19-25 September 1996), p. 14.

221. See, for example, Anthony Goodman, "U.N. says serious violations continue in Cuba," *Reuters Wire Service* (November 15, 1995).

222. *Committee to Protect Journalists*, News Advisory (July, 25, 1995).

223. John Rice, "Cuba toughens laws for economic crimes, illegal demonstrations," *The San Juan Star* (July 4, 1994); and Kenneth Feed, "Impredecible la situación de Cuba, *El Nuevo Día* (5 de diciembre de 1994).

224. Such as Rapid Response Brigades (*Brigadas de Acción Rápida*)—paramilitary groups ready for immediate action—and Popular Acts of Repudiation (*Actos de Repudio*)—the shouting of insults by a mob, often accompanied by the painting of derogatory slogans on victims' properties and, in some cases, entry into their homes and destruction of their belongings; reports of attacks on the victims and/or their families have also been received.

225. Castañeda, and Montalván, "The Arcos Principles."

ment and the downing of two civilian planes of a Cuban-American group, reform in Cuba seems a distant illusion as the leadership's priorities have been forcefully reasserted.[226] This was further confirmed by Raúl Castro's speech of March 1996, which delivered a forceful blow to moderates and reformists within the leadership,[227] and the July 1996 enactment of a Code of Ethics for Party Members.[228] As a result, it looks like little change can be expected short of a dramatic and unexpected turn of events. The people do not have any means to organize an effective opposition movement and are too busy trying to figure out how to get their next meal. The semi-organized dissident movement continues committed solely to peaceful change and has been kept fragmented and repressed by State Security. With the pervasive control of State Security, in allegiance with and dependent on regime survival, it is unlikely that the population, no matter how much it is influenced by market forces, will attain any capacity to demand or impose change.

In this scenario, it seems improbable that foreign investment/commercial engagement—especially with its relatively low significance in the Cuban economy—could foster actual reform. Given the depths of the economic and social crisis that Cuba has already endured without an aftermath of consequence, it seems very improbable that any further internal discontent will make a difference. This was poignantly proven when the regime abandoned Communist orthodoxy, which entailed an enormous loss of legitimacy. All the emerging and powerful

contradictions to the egalitarian socialist ethos—the debacle on the ideological front, the shocking economic failure of the socialist model, the blatant inequalities of selective capitalism, and the severe hardships that have befallen the population—have not been able to generate a change in the repressive nature of the regime. As long as the regime retains the means of control, the instruments of legitimization can be manipulated.

Because in Cuba power is strongly centralized and forcefully exercised, and decision-making is very vertical, market forces, which operate spontaneously and in a decentralized manner, are inherently constrained. This negates the main theoretical argument for engagement and renders it essentially flawed at the core. Foreign investment in Cuba is, in essence, hostage to the prevailing dialectic. A recent analysis on China concludes that economic engagement has also failed to bring about political moderation and a modicum of pluralism there because the three elements that would foster reform—the rule of law, political accountability and a free press—challenge the security of the regime and are, thus, banned. A prominent scholar on Asia declares: "If China is permitted to merely pick and choose which aspects of integration it finds palatable, and to resist those that push change in the direction of moderation and pluralism, them the time scale required by economic engagement will stretch toward infinity."[229] The same selective approach to capitalist mechanisms is the one applied by the Cuban leadership, and it has been effective. A systematically repressive apparatus appears

226. On February 24, 1996 the Cuban government downed two small and unarmed civilian aircraft belonging to *Brothers to the Rescue*, a volunteer organization which for years has carried on humanitarian flights to identify and assist Cuban rafters. Castro acknowledged giving the order to shoot the planes down and the Cuban government alleged the aircraft were operating in Cuban airspace. Witnesses and the U.S. government insist they were flying in international airspace and an international aviation body established that the aircraft were shot down over international waters. The incident came in the wake of a ten day crackdown on *Concilio Cubano* delegates, an umbrella organization of peaceful dissident groups which had requested government permission to hold their first national assembly on the day of the shoot down.

227. Raúl Castro, head of the Cuban Armed Forces, called Communist Party-affiliated study centers "scant elements of internal opposition ... a *de facto* natural ally of the counter-revolution ... caught in the spider's web spun by foreign specialists on Cuba, who are really working for the United States and its strategy to create a fifth column." Raúl Castro Ruz, "Maintaining Revolutionary Purity," report presented by the General of the Army to the Central Committee of the Communist party of Cuba, March 23, 1996, in *Cuba: political pilgrims and cultural wars* (Washington: The Free Cuba Center of Freedom House, 1996).

228. "Aprobado el código de ética de los cuadros del estado cubano," *Granma* (16 de julio de 1996).

229. Shinn, "Engaging China: exploiting the fissures in the facade."

to have tremendous impact on the feasibility and timing of political change regardless of economic reform. The Cuban people simply do not possess the means to exercise self-determination. When the leadership is committed to survival at all costs, regime legitimization is not the issue; the issue is capacity to exercise control.

4. Commercial engagement's impact on policy formulation

Commercial engagement generates the creation of vested business interests rationally bent on self-preservation. Because business concerns tend to have ample financial resources at their disposal, they can secure considerable political clout with relative ease. Therefore, the risk that decision-making will be tilted in their favor is apt to be high.

In looking to advance their standing, business concerns will naturally look to override those objectives which prove irreconcilable to their goals. For instance, prominent proponents in the United States of commercial engagement with Cuba claim detachment to non-business concerns.[230] John Kavulich, President of the U.S. Cuba Trade and Economic Council has stated: "With our focus being informational, politics doesn't come up."[231] Even the savviest investors have failed to establish creditable reputa-

tions in influencing the design of sound foreign policy. In the pursuit of attractive profits, business concerns have historically engaged in decision-making that has overlooked considerable risks and even ultimately hurt their own best interests, sometimes with devastating consequences spilling over to many other areas. Many historic financial crises have demonstrated that overzealous and negligent cross-border profit-seeking has been painfully common, which is particularly eye-opening given the higher level of sophistication expected of the financial industry.[232] Drawing a parallel with equity investments in underdeveloped and high-risk countries such as Cuba, investors are likely to be assuming unmitigated risks which could lead to their exertion of undue influence in the foreign policies of their home governments.

Cuba, in fact, already offers a prime example of capitalists' naiveté.[233] In the early sixties, the revolutionary government repudiated Cuba's international financial obligations and confiscated all foreign properties in the island,[234] yet in less than two decades it had regained access to foreign credit.[235] By 1982 Cuba could not meet its financial obligations and in 1986 it walked out of negotiation talks with the Paris Club. To this day its hard currency debt is in default and its government refuses to enter into reprogramming programs. During the 1980's interna-

---

230. Trevor Armbrister, "Fawning over Fidel," *Readers Digest* (May 1996), p.150.

231. Armbrister, "Fawning over Fidel," p. 149. The powerful Chairman of ADM, Dwayne Andreas, questioned about Castro's human rights record, responded: "I don't think about that. ...That's for the politicians to worry about." Quoted in Armbrister, "Fawning over Fidel," p. 149.

232. A study of the financial industry is particularly relevant because the element of risk is intrinsic to this business. It is well documented that in the last two centuries U.S. banks and institutional and private investors have overlooked risks in assessing international lending and investment opportunities which at one time they considered highly profitable. The added difficulties of accurately assessing cross-border risks are compounded by the vulnerability and imperfections of the international financial system. The author's Masters' thesis dealt with the 1980's international debt crisis and analyzed commercial bank lending and financial crisis in Latin America since its independence. See María C. Werlau, *Los bancos comerciales internacionales y la crisis de deuda externa en América Latina: una perspectiva histórica a la luz de la crisis de los ochenta* (Santiago: Universidad de Chile, Instituto de Estudios Internacionales, 1995.)

233. In fact, in the early 1920's Lenin, looking to secure the economic survival of Russia, bet that "the capitalists' presumed greed could be used to the Soviet advantage concessions to foreign capitalists were part of Lenin's strategy—the 'bait' to help overcome the political hostility of businessmen, who, looking to obtain better terms vis-à-vis their competitors, would pressure their respective governments to lift restrictions" on trade. See Epstein, *Dossier: The Secret History of Armand Hammer*, p. 59.

234. As discussed above, upon assuming power in 1959, Castro's revolutionary government declared a radical repudiation of the international financial obligations of previous Cuban governments and ordered the expropriation of foreign property in Cuba.

235. While the embargo precluded U.S. banks from doing business in Cuba, European, Japanese, Canadian, and Arab commercial banks made voluminous loans to Cuba starting in the second half of the seventies. At the time Cuba came to be regarded as an "attractive borrower" based on credit risk analyses which disregarded very high risk factors. See Werlau, *Los bancos comerciales internacionales.*

tional debt crisis, Castro even attempted to form a debtor's cartel to repudiate debts.

A reductionist application of the logic of commercial engagement could tilt policy-making in favor of narrow, short-term, business considerations which hinder the development of foreign policies based on a balanced convergence of interests which address the overall long-term economic development and political stability of Cuba. That, in essence, is what can provide lasting opportunities for business and converges with the interests of the international community as a whole.

CONCLUSION

Commercial engagement is often brandished as the appropriate foundation for foreign policies towards Cuba—the ultimate solution to "the Cuba problem." But, as we have seen, conditions and characteristics unique to Cuba inhibit the workability of this rationale. Foreign investment has failed to, in its present context, bring about economic recovery and political/economic reform because Cuba' business climate cannot attract a meaningful level of investment and because it operates within a framework which inherently restrains its reform-inducing forces. As a result, in its present form, it is primarily a tool of regime survival. For commercial engagement to work it would have to advance the very practices that threaten regime survival, i.e. become a tool of "conditional engagement."

The severity of Cuba's crisis makes the adoption of market-enabling policies within a proper legal framework imperative to foster an economic recovery. This, in turn, would enable the forces of economic and political empowerment to operate. In the area of foreign investment, liberalization would require, among others, providing access to the domestic market, allowing Cuban citizens ownership of joint ventures, and eliminating wage confiscation and State control over workers. Yet, the single most important element to achieve economic growth and social empowerment seems to be the continued liberalization of self-employment within a context of an emerging private sector.[236] Nevertheless, it is likely that the ruling elite will continue to prevent changes in the system that will provoke its own demise through the loss of State control, no matter what economic gains they may propitiate. Thus, the political imperatives of a regime with the means to impose power by force will likely preclude economic and political development and will continue to dictate the terms of foreign investment and commercial engagement in Cuba.

Formulism[237] and reductionism, often present in policy debates about Cuba, are dangerous instruments of policy manipulation. The quality of the debate on Cuba would greatly benefit if the limits of commercial engagement as a policy prescription are acknowledged and our expectations adjusted accordingly. Cuba's predicament precludes simple answers. Responsible, comprehensive, and effective policy-making must seek to balance a convergence of interests: geostrategic/national security, economic, political, and ethical. In the final analysis, however, we are compelled to recognize that Cuba's problems are more complex and profound than resolving the issue of whether or not commercial engagement or foreign investment are suitable instruments of foreign policy to foster reform. Ultimately, neither pressure nor engagement may be capable of bringing about the desired democratization and economic viability of Cuba; these may remain primarily dependent on internal circumstances.

---

236. It would allow the absorption of the large number of unemployed. The current numbers of self-employed, said to be around 200,000, puts a very minor dent in the pool of over one million estimated to be unemployed, even worse if one takes into accounts reports that only approximately 30 percent of the self-employed were formerly employed, the balance made up of people holding other jobs, some pensioners and former housewives. But, the current framework would also need reform, as self-employment has already stimulated a series of problems: corruption, the sale of stolen goods or goods manufactured with inputs stolen from state enterprises, the accumulation of wealth in the hands of a few, and tax evasion (estimated at around 40 percent).

237. As described by Stanley Hoffman, formulism is "a desire to reduce complicated realities to fixed formulae and analogies, to shorthand, and/or sum up complexities in slogans and solutions." In V. Vaky, "Political change in Latin America: A foreign policy dilemma for the United States," *Journal of Interamerican Studies and World Affairs*, Vol.28, No.2 (Summer 1986).

HELMS-BURTON: CHECKMATE OR CHALLENGE FOR CANADIAN FIRMS DOING BUSINESS IN CUBA?

Beverly L. Campbell[1]

This paper characterizes the situation that Cuba and foreign investors, alike, find themselves as a result of the adoption by the United States of the Helms-Burton Act. In particular, the paper focuses on dilemmas facing Canadians in maintaining stakes in Cuba and launching challenges to Helms-Burton. The paper is divided into three parts: the Canadian foreign policy framework toward Cuba, the effect of Helms-Burton on Canadian commercial interests in Cuba, and concluding remarks.

CANADA'S FOREIGN POLICY FRAMEWORK TOWARD CUBA

The Four Components of Canadian Foreign Policy Toward Cuba

Normal: Canadian policy toward Cuba is normal in the sense that it advocates similar relations with the rest of the Americas. As an expression of its independence from the United States, Canada charts a different course *vis-a-vis* Cuba. It also maintains a tradition of recognizing the "government of the day." In keeping with that tradition, the Canadian Government recognized the legitimacy of the Castro regime in 1959, and has maintained diplomatic relations with Havana to the present day.

Active: The Canadian Government preserves an active and on-going policy towards Cuba. Last year, Canada and Cuba celebrated 50 years of unbroken

diplomatic relations between the two sovereign states. Prior to 1995, Canada-Cuba trade had been minimal. However, with a number of high-level visits promoting several important bilateral trade agreements, two-way trade has increased substantially.

Foreign aid was suspended in protest to Cuban involvement in the Angolan war. After a 16-year hiatus, humanitarian aid was restored in June 1994. Later that year assurances were given to resume direct bilateral assistance. In March 1995, negotiations began. As of October 1996, still there are no clear indications on the nature of aid disbursements or future flows. Where the Canadian Government goes in those negotiations are of critical importance in light of issues addressed in subsequent sections.

Canadian public and private agents provide economic advice to the Cuban Government, specifically, in areas of taxation and central banking. In the area of private sector development, the Canadian Government funds projects such as feasibility studies and training programs through the industrial arm of the Canadian International Development Agency (CIDA Inc.)

Unlike many programs worldwide that concentrate on export development, CIDA Inc. focuses on funding small cooperative projects, requiring Canadian recipients to select projects with Cuban partners, in

---

1. This paper draws heavily from a paper prepared by Julia Sagebien titled "Foreign Trade and Investment in Cuba After February 24, 1996: Life Between a Rock and a Hard Place," delivered in Ottawa on May 17, 1996. However, the views presented here are exclusively those of the author.

key sectors of the Cuban economy. Although the Canadian equivalent of the U.S. Agency for International Development, CIDA Inc., provides some supports for educational projects and small-scale local initiatives by NGOs, CIDA Inc.'s programs are driven by demand from the Canadian commercial sector. Indeed, the ultimate driving force behind the Canadian involvement has been Canadian commercial interests. As a result, trade between Canada and Cuba now stands at $C550 million (about $US380 million). On the investment side, 18 joint venture agreements have been signed, with 19 pending.

Balanced: The Canadian Government remains cognizant of the inherent risks of involvement with Cuba. The Export Development Corporation (EDC) credit lines are frozen, with accumulating debt which now amounts to $C96 million ($US70 million). Until Cuba finds a solution to its debt woes, EDC managers say credit lines will remain frozen.

The Department of Foreign Affairs and International Trade warns Canadians of the political and commercial risks of engaging in business with Cuba. On the one hand, the Canadian Government seeks to protect the right of its citizens to establish commercial ties with any country, including Cuba. On the other, the Government seeks to limit its liability in the extension of credit to Canadian companies for high-risk commercial ventures.

A point most often missed by American critics, Canada condemns human rights abuses and the lack of civil and political rights, while encouraging constructive initiatives to build civil society through organizations such as the Canada-Cuba Inter-Agency Project. Through NGOs and other private section concerns, the project promotes programs such as park landscaping and public works.

Dialogue and "Constructive" Engagement: Through bilateral consultations, both at ministerial and departmental levels, the Canadian Government advocates the fourth prong of its policy, in the belief that both dialogue and constructive engagement remain the best means for facilitating economic and political liberalization in Cuba. On the international level, Canada demonstrates dialogue and constructive engagement through support of U.N. resolutions for halting the United States embargo, and renewal of Cuba's membership in the Organization of American States (OAS).

Canadian Government Response to Helms-Burton

Abroad, within hemisphere, and domestically, Canada seeks to preserve a legal and fair global trading order, allowing legal sovereign states the option of trading where and with whom they will trade, without interference from another country. Therefore, delinking trade with politics remains a concern of Canadian policy in opposing Helms-Burton. In concert with those aims, the Canadian Parliament enacted Foreign Extraterritorial Measures Act (FEMA) amendments forbidding Canadian companies and Canadian-based U.S. subsidiaries, involved with Cuba, from complying with any directive from any U.S. entity attempting to influence or harass any company operating in Canada. Enacted in 1992 in response to ratification of the Torricelli Act, the amended FEMA responded, once again, to infringements on Canadian sovereignty.

Opposition of Helms-Burton receives wide-spread support among the Canadian populace. In an Angust Reid/Southam News poll conducted one week after the ceremonial signing at the White House, an overwhelming 71 percent of respondents favored noncompliance on grounds that tighter U.S. sanctions have onerous repercussions for Canadian interests.

The Canadian Government's stance against Helms-Burton is not an easy one, considering that 80 percent of all Canadian goods are exported to the United States, and 64 percent of all companies in Canada are U.S. subsidiaries. In overall trade terms, i.e., *vis-a-vis* the whole scope of Canadian worldwide trade, trade with Cuba represents 0.11%. For Canadians, Cuba is not a trade issue. Rather, Cuba represents a matter of principle, namely, the right of a sovereign country to conduct an independent foreign policy. That includes the right of a sovereign country to follow whatever policy that country deems appropriate in bringing democracy and open markets to Cuba. Therefore, the Government's fight with the U.S. over Cuba constitutes a disagreement about means, instead of objectives. The Canadian Government dissents from U.S. policy on Helms-Burton based on the following objections:

- First, that U.S. policy diverges from Canadian policy with respect to Cuba;

- Second, that U.S. policy magnifies the U.S.-Cuba problem, instead of solving it;

- Third, that U.S. policy disrupts international trade and investment patterns; and

- Fourth, that U.S. policy violates Canadian sovereignty, and establishes dangerous precedents for unilateral measures undertaken by the United States.

Parenthetically, Canada joins the chorus of international opposition against Libyan-Iranian sanctions based on similar grounds.

Ottawa has voiced its displeasure with Helms-Burton via the World Trade Organization (WTO), the Organization for Economic Cooperation and Development (OECD), and the Organization of American States, joining lobbying efforts with other U.S. trading partners with business interests in Cuba, along with partners from Mexico and the European Union. However, the Government has raised its most vociferous objections through consultations within the framework of the North American Free Trade Agreement (NAFTA). Because Canadian lawyers have given more thought to formalized challenges than any others among the foreign legal community, the task at hand for Canadian lawyers translates into one of structuring extraterritorial challenges into trade dispute resolution settings like NAFTA.

On the home front, the Canadian Government introduced legislation in September 1966 on further FEMA amendments that would issue "blocking" orders, declaring judgments made in U.S. courts nonenforceable in Canadian courts. Second, "clawbacks" were proposed enabling Canadians to recover in Canadian courts amounts imposed by U.S. courts. And third, penalties were updated for Canadians abiding by tenets of the Helms-Burton provisions. Trade Minister Art Eggleton explained that further amendments were introduced as "antidote legislation" or

preventative measures, should President Clinton implement Helms-Burton Title III provisions. The sticking point for Canada will come in making FEMA amendments enforceable, while fulfilling obligations under NAFTA.

EFFECT OF HELMS-BURTON ON CANADIAN COMMERCIAL INTERESTS IN CUBA

Issues Determining Response by Canadian Companies: Risks vs. Rewards

Responses to Helms-Burton are based on a number of factors. For those engaged in business in Cuba, responses depend on whether their strategies are short-term, or whether they are positioning themselves for the end of the U.S. embargo. Opportunities in newly liberalized sectors such as tourism offer the most advantages in the long term. For short-term traders, tourism offers the best prospects until the embargo ends, when they are likely to lose their competitive advantage to the United States.

For long-term investors, the tourism and real estate card offers the greatest opportunities. Wilton Properties and Sherritt International represent two Canadian companies that have adopted such a strategy. For Sherritt International, the foray into the field enhances its presence in Cuba already established in nickel mining. The end of the embargo presents companies such as Wilton Properties and Sherritt two options: cash in or provide American companies with stiff competition in a freely burgeoning market.

Whether long-term or short-term, Helms-Burton increases risk, uncertainty, and legal costs. For firms with little or no U.S. exposure, the longer the embargo lasts, the greater the rewards for those seeking gains either in the long or short term.

Smaller, less risk-averse companies believe that, because of their size, they can avoid scrutiny of Helms-Burton restrictions. Bear in mind that the largest number of Canadian participants in business activities associated with Cuba are exporters, companies whose combined sales total $C1 million ($US666,000) or less. By contrast, large Canadian companies, namely mining and pharmaceutical firms, represent the importing side.

Regardless of length of engagement, other elements must be factored into the mix, elements which include potential for U.S. lawsuits and sentiments among the Cuban-American community toward Cuba. When evaluating business opportunities, Canadians must remain ever mindful that civil war rages on both sides of the Florida Straits.

Protracted civil war means that those with long-term commercial interests should consider which conditions will satisfy terms for an eventual end of the embargo. The longer the embargo, the greater potential for reaping windfall profits. But a delay contains inherent risks for those with long-term interests. Under those circumstances, the challenge lies in calculating how long to hold out, and in matching the appropriate risk with the appropriate opportunity.

Balancing risk and reward remains a chief concern among Canadians with business interests in Cuba. Contrary to the belief of many Americans that Canadians are naive or nonchalant about the risk factors, many Canadians are fearful of being labeled as "traffickers." For the more risk-averse, Cuba exists as a contrarian's paradise, a place—at the risk of sounding politically incorrect—where the men are separated from the boys.

Ultimately, assessing risk depends on where a company places Cuba in relation to its trade or investment portfolio. Companies with substantial sales volume report holding steadily, attempting to conduct "business as usual" in Cuba, exercising due diligence in seeking legal advice, and searching property registries—to the extent that such registries can be searched in Cuba. The same holds true for Canada's main investor, Sherritt International. Recent developments indicate that Sherritt International's stock is on the rise, expressing long-term investor confidence.

For those with lesser stakes or plans to enter the Cuban market, the "chill" of Helms-Burton may prompt some companies to ask "why bother?" Cuba represents just another emerging market, no different than any other. The most visible Canadian public companies fulfilled or terminated contracts over the past 18 months, Redpath, Labatt, JD Irving, and Fracmaster among them. The majority of companies with plans or current operations still in Cuba maintain a low profile or silence about future activities.

The announcement of the Wilton Properties-Gran Caribe venture raises significantly Canada's profile in Cuba. Announced on July 1, Canada Day, the agreement involves plans for building hotels on 11 sites in Cuba. Other than Sherritt International's 25 percent stake in at least one hotel operation, no other Canadian company maintains an equity position in any hotel in Cuba. Whether the Wilton project actually comes to fruition remains to be seen.

Sectoral Responses to Canada-Cuba Trade: Factoring the Mix

With a 130 percent rise in 1995-1996, Canadian-Cuban trade is on an upward trend. Despite increasing trade, Canadian exporters experience difficulties in the shipment of cargo to Cuba due to limited or non-existent financing. Two major Canadian banks pledged earlier this year to supply $C22 million ($US14.5 million) in additional letters of credit. Since Helms-Burton ratification, both banks canceled earlier plans. Also on hold are additional supports from EDC to shore up credits and augment banking services to Canadian firms with operations in Cuba. Furthermore, EDC announced in 1996 $C1.5 billion ($US1 billion) in export financing for 50 high-risk emerging markets. Absent from the list was Cuba.

Advisory services face somewhat limited prospects, now that negotiations between Canada and Cuba seem at a standstill on certain initiatives aimed at key aspects of the Cuban economy. In a field that includes bankers and legal consultants, priority sector initiatives would harness a range of Canadian commercial expertise and talent under the aegis of CIDA Inc. Through CIDA, Inc., fund disbursements would support projects such as banking computerization, energy conservation, and biotechnological research, along with consultations on fiscal and monetary reform, taxation, and health care matters.

From a foreign policy standpoint, these programs are intended as leverage for Canadian pursuits toward further economic and political liberalization. The stumbling block in negotiations relates to the manner of disbursement of funds, speed of their disbursement, and conditionalities attached for disbursement estimates which could run as high as at $C14-20 million ($US9-13 million). However stumbling blocks are resolved, advisory services remains an area poised for rapid growth. While the payoff is immediate for exporters, the big bang comes for service advisors once the embargo ends, with capital from the international financial institutions and financing from other private sources roll in.

In the interim, arrears continue to compound Cuba's financial problems. Cutting back or curtailing lines of credit to clients with services or operations in Cuba, Canadian banks now play, largely, an advisory role in the functions of the National Bank of Cuba. Among Canadian banks, only the National Bank of Canada maintains a Cuban representative office. Encumbered by having U.S. operations, Canadian banks represent the most visible example of the liabilities that third parties confront under Title IV provisions of Helms-Burton.

In tourism, Canadian auxiliaries and intermediaries participate in an industry subject to seasonal fluctuation. Due to over booking problems last season, it is difficult to gauge how many of the 170,000 Canadians that visited Cuba will return for next season. Canadians comprise the second largest contingent of foreign tourists visiting the Caribbean island each year, obviously a boon for Canadian travel agents. On the equity side, the numbers reflect a different picture. With Canadian hoteliers confined largely to service management contracts, none own stakes in any Cuban hotel operation, apart from Wilton Properties or Sherritt International. Although several development projects are under consideration, none have gone forth to date. Based on the figures, the effects of the "chill" remain inconclusive.

Equally inconclusive are the effects of Canadian participation in Cuban biotechnology. Because Canadian pharmaceutical firms and agents "broker" for commercializing Cuban products, it is doubtful that "trafficking"charges involving intellectual property are enforceable under Title IV provisions, given that the sector was non-existent prior to 1959. However, fortunes of those in this industry will vary depending

on how broadly definitions are applied. The same applies for all industry sectors where auxiliaries or intermediaries act as third parties. As scrutiny intensifies in coming months, watch for the creation of new alliances between third parties and principals, as some exit and others move to the sidelines.

In sectors where the shake-out has already occurred, none have felt the impact of Helms-Burton more than the sugar industry. Traditionally, a third of all Canadian sugar imports have come from Cuba, another factor making the Canadian foreign policy stance toward Helms-Burton difficult. Under threat of possible retaliatory actions by Canada, American sugar lobbyists fought for changes in U.S. certification procedures for sugar products from third country origins. Despite the amendments, certification issues linger, which forced Canadian refiner Redpath to end a lucrative and long-standing arrangement with the Cuban Government. As a result, Canadians now pay a few cents more for sugar imported into Canada from other Latin American countries.

Concerns in mining relate to whether leases awarded to Canadian companies prospecting or extracting mineral are located on expropriated lands belonging to the Cuban Government. Generally speaking, world commodity prices dictate outcomes of Canadian and foreign operations more than political risks associated with Cuba.

For the Canadian company with the greatest stake, Sherritt International's well-being depends, partly on U.S. policy, but more importantly, on intrinsic factors, elements related to scarcity and cyclical fluctuation of the commodity, continued stock performance, sectorial competition within the industry including the impact of the Inco acquisition, as well as new and potential alliances between third parties. Whichever way it weathers the storm, Sherritt International's forays in Cuba will attest to the long-term impact of Canadian companies on the island.

The Business Climate in Cuba: Clash Between Business and Political Decisions

As the Castro regime maintains control by closing ranks, externalizing risks, and tightening ideological reigns, foreigners with business interests in Cuba find themselves caught in a civil war which encompasses both sides of the Florida Straits. While vitriol by the most hardline of Cuban exiles colors a Presidential Election season on the mainland, Fidel sends conflicting messages to hard liners, centrists, and reformers on the island. In a CNN world, messages designed for internal consumption receive global exposure. Often times, mixed signals result, leaving foreigners wondering whether Cuba is truly open for business. Gauging from the Canadian responses, the answer still appears to be "yes," but in limited ways.

Frequently, Canadians complain about lengthy delays in negotiations on joint ventures, constant changes in documentation for clearing cargo out of Cuban customs, and lack of cooperation in conducting accurate and timely title searches. For Canadians and other foreigners alike, Cuba remains plagued with problems related to miscommunication or lack of information. In Cuba, two kinds of communication problems exists relative to business decisions *versus* political decisions.

Where foreigners may consult with partners and associates—conferring or reporting to directors, in the case of large companies, and shareholders in the case of public companies—Cubans take directions from political entities ranging from government bureaucrats, other governmental officials, and ministers. No wonder that often times, clashes occur when the foreign partner and the Cuban counterpart interpret each other's bottom line.

At another level, clashes may occur due to different expectations. For foreign investors or traders, Cuba represents just another investment deal or transaction driven by short-term or long-term financial considerations. For Cuban partners and the Cuban Government, deals involve matters related to politics, sovereignty, and economic development. The differences in expectations or priorities imply cognitive dissonance between the bottom line of the foreign investor or trader and the party line.

CONCLUDING REMARKS

Canadian investors and traders are caught in a civil war between Miami and Havana, exposing them to risks and uncertainty. Cuba remains open for business to Canadian entrepreneurs, but partially, and only within certain conditions. Although the conditions are getting increasingly difficult, Canadians stand committed to pursing opportunities, fostering normalized relations, balanced trade, and dialog and constructive engagement.

Furthermore, Canada stands resolute with international allies in opposition to Helms-Burton, and supports initiatives continuing Cuban economic liberalization and advancements toward a democratic civil society. From the Canadian perspective, Helms-Burton has not provided a checkmate to business prospects, only a formidable challenge. Given Canada's long-standing and vital commercial relationship with the United States, Canadians believe with regard to Helms-Burton, that this too shall pass.

ON THE CONTINUED GOOD STANDING OF PRE-CASTRO LEGAL ENTITIES: *UBI LEX NON DISTINGUIT,* ... *NEC NOS DISTINGUERE DEBEMUS*[1]

Agustín de Goytisolo[2]

This paper evaluates the effect of the legislation subsequent to January 1, 1959 regarding the continued viability of legal entities organized or doing business in Cuba then, primarily corporations and limited liability companies (hereinafter referred collectively as the "Entities") as well as its possible utilization presently.[3]

The post-1959 legal measures affecting such Entities, expressed in order of severity—and not chronologically—were of the following nature:

CONFISCATIONS

Following the advent of Fidel Castro and the abrogation of the 1940 Cuban Constitution by the so-called Ley Fundamental de la República of February 7, 1959 (*Gaceta Oficial* of the same day), as amended by Ley de Reforma Constitucional of December 22, 1959 (*Gaceta Oficial* of the same day),[4] although its Article 24 proclaimed that the confiscation of property was prohibited, it immediately excepted from such protection the properties of the following individuals, as well as the Entities that such individuals allegedly controlled:

• President Batista and his collaborators;

• Individuals and Entities responsible for crimes against the national economy or its treasury;

---

1. "Where the Law does not distinguish, neither ought we to distinguish," a well settled Roman law principle, commonly accepted by common and civil law jurisdictions (*Black's Law Dictionary*, Fifth Edition, 1979, page 1363).

2. In the preparation of this paper, the author recognizes the contributions, amongst other friends, of the following professionals: Antonio Alonso Avila, Esq., well-known jurist, who has facilitated the majority of the substantive Cuban legal material (through 1960) mentioned in this paper; Avelino J. González, Esq., a law school graduate of the Havana University and the University of Miami, recently admitted to the Florida Bar. Mr. Gonzalez has provided invaluable information also regarding the post-1959 Cuban legislation, generously cooperated in the research and prepared the first version of the accompanying translation of this paper to Spanish; and Dr. José Domingo Acosta Sotolongo, a Cuban attorney who practiced through 1960 as an expert on tax law with a reputable firm there, participating also in the drafting of Cuba's 1959 Reforma Tributaria. Mr. Acosta has confirmed that the Reforma Tributaria contained no provision penalizing with confiscation, with its effect indicated herein, any Entity which did not file tax returns or paid taxes in Cuba on a timely basis.

3. Regarding the certainty of the research supporting this paper, it must be considered that Cuba ceased publishing around 1964 the *Legislación al Día* and *Jurisprudencia al Día*, two West-like publications that enabled to do serious legal research. After that date, laws, regulations and some court decisions were published somewhat lackadaisically in the *Gaceta Official*. Therefore, in Cuba there is always the possibility of unpublished and unforeseeable "phantom" legislative measures and court decisions. For the last years, Cuban court decision are published, somewhat sporadically, in the *Boletín del Tribunal Supremo Popular*.

4. The 1959 Cuban Constitution as amended is hereinafter referred as the "Ley Fundamental," which later was superseded by a constitution promulgated on February 24, 1976, later reformed by Cuba's Parliament on July 10, 11 and 12, 1992.

- Other individuals or Entities illicitly enriching themselves in the exercise of Public Authority;

- Individuals sanctioned for felonies that the Law qualified as being counterrevolutionary; or

- Individuals who, in order to evade sanctions by Revolutionary Tribunals, abandoned the national territory or, having abandoned it (for any other purpose), may have participated in conspiratory activities against the Revolutionary Government.

Sanctioned by this exceptional constitutional provision, the Cuban government proceeded to confiscate, amongst other, the properties of the following individuals—and in some cases certain Entities—listed in the applicable laws:

1. Those of President Batista and his so-called collaborators, including principally his ministers, senators, representatives, governors, members of his Consultative Council, presidents of the National Bank of Cuba and other state banks, and members of the Supreme Court (Law 112 of February 27, 1959 as amended by Law 151 of March 17, 1959).

Such confiscation comprised "all the assets" of President Batista and, regarding other individuals mentioned above, their assets were confiscated if they had misappropriated public property or had illicitly enriched themselves in the exercise of Public Authority, as determined from time to time by the tribunals or the Ministry for the Recovery of Misappropriated Property (later replaced by the Ministry of Finance and, upon the dissolution of the latter in 1966, as determined by the Ministry of Justice).

Although this law[5] contained no specific provision affecting the good standing of Entities controlled by the individuals mentioned above and, therefore, at first impression it appears that *Ubi Lex Non Distinguit...* may apply, we believe that, in the event that all, or at least a controlling portion,[6] of the shares of stock or units of participation issued by such Entities were registered in the name of any of the individuals named in the applicable measures, that provided no compensation in favor of the respective Entities or their shareholders or unit owners, following its confiscation by these measures the respective Entities by merger of rights de facto became confiscated in favor of the Cuban government, and the remaining shares of stock or units of participation, owned by individuals, other than those named in the applicable measures, for all practical purposes became worthless.

2. Regarding measures applicable to individuals or Entities that may have illicitly enriched themselves in the exercise of Public Authority, Law 438 of July 7, 1959 (*Gaceta Oficial* of July 13, 1959) declared the confiscation of the assets of a group of prominent government contractors and business leaders close to President Batista, together with a multitude of Entities listed after their respective names (supposedly controlled by these individuals).

It is interesting to note that this Law not only confiscated the assets of these individuals and those of their Entities, but its Article 3 specifically ordered that, as a consequence of the accompanying confiscation of its assets and, accordingly, the exhaustion "of its capital that such measure entail, (the listed Entities) (we)re declared dissolved for all legal purposes in conformity to the provisions of paragraph 2 of Arti-

---

5. It must not be forgotten that in most jurisdictions the possibility of organizing legal entities and granting to them legal personality different from its shareholders/members is a privilege or statutory "fiction" which the incorporating state has the quasi-absolute right to give, enlarge or even withhold or deny at its discretion, being commonly said in the United States that legal entities are "creatures of the statute" and are at their mercy.

6. Although according to the Commercial Code persons organizing legal entities were free to determine what constituted control, for corporate action, as a general rule a majority (51 percent) vote of the persons interested in the capital carried all motions unless otherwise expressly provided in their charter (hereinafter referred as "Estatutos").

cle 221 of the Commercial Code[7] or paragraph 2 of article 1700 of the Civil Code, if applicable."[8]

3. As to individuals who were sanctioned for counter-revolutionary felonies as well as to those who abandoned the national territory to evade its sanctions, Law 664 of December 23, 1959 (*Gaceta Oficial* of same date) ordered the "total confiscation of their assets," which were to become the property of the State.

Although this law contained no specific provision affecting the good standing of Entities controlled by the individuals mentioned above and, therefore, at first impression it appears that *Ubi Lex Non Distinguit...* may apply, we believe that, in the event that all, or at least control, of the shares of stock or units of participation issued by such Entities were registered in the name of any of the individuals named in the applicable measures, that provided no compensation in favor of the respective Entities or their shareholders or unit owners, following its confiscation by these measures the respective Entities by merger of rights de facto became confiscated in favor of the Cuban government, and the remaining shares of stock or units of participation, owned by individuals other than those named in the applicable measures, for all practical purposes became worthless.

4. Under Law 688 also of December 23, 1959 (*Gaceta Oficial* of December 24, 1959) it was ordered that, in the event that any of the individuals sanctioned with the confiscation of their assets had passed away, his/her estate were confiscated likewise.

Although this law contained no specific provision affecting the good standing of Entities controlled by

the individuals mentioned above and, therefore, at first impression it appears that *Ubi Lex Non Distinguit...* may apply, we believe that, in the event that all, or at least control, of the shares of stock or units of participation issued by such Entities were registered in the name of any of the individuals named in the applicable measures, that provided no compensation in favor of the respective Entities or their shareholders or unit owners, following its confiscation by these measures the respective Entities by merger of rights de facto became confiscated in favor of the Cuban government, and the remaining shares of stock or units of participation, owned by individuals other than those named in the applicable measures, for all practical purposes became worthless.

5. Based on the above, even if under some measures *Ubi Lex Non Distinguit...* at first impression would appear to apply, considering the penal nature of confiscatory measures and de facto merger in favor of the State of the assets of the individuals comprised with these measures, including any shares of stock or other units of participation in the capital of their Entities, no right to compensation being provided in those measures in favor of the Entities or to the individuals controlling them, it can be conclusively argued that, in the majority of cases, the capital—present or expectant—of the Entities has been exhausted and that, according to Article 221(2) of the Commercial Code, "the total loss of its capital" has occurred and these Entities "shall (have been) totally dissolve(d)."

NATIONALIZATIONS

The Cuban Government, to assure that its Marxist Leninist agenda took root as well as, in some cases, in retaliation for economic measures of the United

---

7.   The great majority of the provisions of this nineteenth century commercial law, as amended through 1959, has continued to be in force through date, having been expressly declared supletorily applicable to joint ventures with foreign investors by Law-Decree 50 of September 15, 1982, including the following important provision regarding the dissolution of Entities organized thereunder (which translated liberally to English reads as follows): "A corporation, whatever its class, shall totally dissolve for the following causes: 1) The expiration of the term expressed in its charter or the conclusion of the enterprise which constitutes its object; 2) The *total loss* (emphasis added) of its capital; 3) The bankruptcy of the Company.

8.   The reference to Article 1700 of the Cuban Civil Code dealing with the dissolution of Entities, appears at first impression superfluous considering that Article 221 of the Commercial Code promulgated subsequently superseded this prior dissolution provision. However, it is possible that the legislator, apprised that Cuban corporate law distinguished between "civil" and "commercial" Entities, may have referred also to Article 1700 of the Civil Code (dealing with dissolution of legal entities organized thereunder), to declare dissolved the civil Entities, in the event Article 221 of the Commercial Code was not deemed applicable to them.

States, proceeded to nationalize the assets of individuals and Entities not covered by the confiscatory measures referred above, as expressly authorized by Article 24 of the Ley Fundamental. To this effect, it must be noted that this constitutional provision regarding nationalizations also provided the following:

> No other natural or juridical person may be deprived of his property but by order of competent court authority, for justified reasons of public utility or social interest, and always prior payment of the corresponding indemnification in cash, determined by the court. The non-compliance with this provision shall determine the right of the expropriated to be protected by the court, and in its case, *his property returned to him*. The certainty of the cause of public utility or social interest and the need of the expropriation shall be decided by the courts on appeal." (emphasis added)

In the majority of the nationalizations, no compensation was ever paid to the Entities themselves or to its shareholders/members. Therefore, we anticipate that a multitude of claims will be filed in a democratic Cuba seeking the restitution of the nationalized assets or their equivalent. The following nationalizations occurred:

1. The assets or enterprises[9] owned by individuals or Entities of the United States of North America or the Entities in which such individuals have any interest or participation, whether or not organized under Cuban law, following Law 851 of June 6, 1960 (*Gaceta Oficial* of same day) and Resolution 3 of October 24, 1960, which further provided the immediate intervention of the respective Entities and that any due compensation for the taking of its assets or enterprises was made contingent upon the restoration to Cuba of its share in the sugar quota allocated to Cuba by the United States, which had been canceled previously.

2. A multitude of sugar mills, distilleries, liquor and beverage producers, soap and perfume manufactures and many others (practically all industrial enterprises in the island) were nationalized by Law 890 of October 15, 1960 (*Gaceta Oficial* of the same day), which: a) ordered that all titles, "rights and interests of the enterprises mentioned..., are adjudicated to the Cuban State, ... together with their assets and liabilities and, therefore, it is declared that the State is subrogated in lieu of the natural or juridical individuals that owned the (above) mentioned enterprises;" b) declared that justified reasons of public utility or social interest of the nationalizations existed; c) set out that "the means and forms of payment of the indemnifications corresponding to the natural or juridical individuals affected by the nationalization" ordered by this Law, shall be provided in a subsequent law" (which were never enacted!). To that effect, "the Central Planning Board[10] shall submit to the Council of Ministers in the most brief period possible, the proposed bill;" and d) further stated that regarding enterprises ... which may be currently intervened and not comprised amongst those listed in the present Law, the Central Planning Board was authorized to nationalize those which it deems that correspond to the principles of this Law or, instead, to order that the interventions cease. This law contained no specific provision affecting the good standing of Entities controlled by the individuals mentioned above. Therefore, *Ubi Lex Non Distinguit...*

3. The provision of banking services was declared exercisable solely by the State and, accordingly, all banks operating in Cuba were nationalized, with the sole exception of the Canadian banks, and the National Bank of Cuba was declared expressly subrogated as to all its assets and liabilities. Law 891 regarding banks contained the following express provision regarding the applicable legal entities engaged before in this business:

> "As a result of ... the assumption by the National Bank of Cuba of all the assets and liabilities of the ju-

---

9. This term does not refer to a type of legal entity owning Cuban assets but to the business (enterprise) that is the object of the legal entity. It is synonymous to the business activity in which the legal entity engages.

10. The powers granted to this Board by Law 890 of October 15, 1960 were extended to the Ministry of Finance by Law 1144 of January 23, 1964, to be exercised concurrently with said Board; and by Law 1188 of April 25, 1966 (*Gaceta Oficial* of April 29, 1966), upon the dissolution of the Ministry of Finance by said Law 1188 of 1966, such power was transferred to the Ministry of Justice.

ridical individuals or companies affected by this Law, the same are declared dissolved and extinguished to all legal effects."

The Law also provided that the members or shareholders of the dissolved Entities were entitled to compensation following Article 24 of the Ley Fundamental, such compensation to be payable by the National Bank of Cuba after the close of 1960 with a maximum down payment of ten thousand Cuban pesos ($10,000 Cuban pesos) and the balance by bonds to be issued by the National Bank payable in 15 years bearing 2 percent annual interest. To the best of the author's knowledge, no such compensation was ever paid disbursed, a ground for the possible challenge of the nationalization of the banking Entities and request its restitution to its owners as it clearly infringes the provisions of Article 24 of the Ley Fundamental.

HYBRIDS

Law 989 of December 5, 1961 (*Gaceta Oficial* of December 9, 1961) granted to the Ministry of the Interior the authority to issue new permits to Cuban citizens to enter or depart from the national territory and ordered conclusively that "if the return does not occur within the period for which the departure has been authorized, it shall be considered that (the Cuban citizen) has abandoned definitively the country" (Article 1).

This Law also provided that, regarding individuals who may have "abandoned definitively the country," that "all their movable and real property of any nature, rights, shares and valuables of any type,[11] shall be considered nationalized by confiscation[12] in favor of the Cuban state ...."

In case of individuals who may have "abandoned the country before September 14, 1961 (day of publication in the *Gaceta Oficial* of the Urban Reform Law) holding permits used by the Superior Council of Urban Reform or any of its officers," the Law authorized that these individuals could request the extension of their exit permits by the Ministry of the Interior to allow them to return to Cuba.

It is debatable whether, the individuals who abandoned the national territory **before** September 14, 1961,[13] when there appeared to be no such legal requirement under Cuban law to enter or leave the national territory, are subject to the above-referred nationalization by confiscation and, of course, that neither their Entities have been dissolved nor the shares of stock of these Entities correspond to the Cuban government. Accordingly, we opine that such Entities remain in "good standing" provided that none has incurred in any of the causes of dissolution mentioned in Article 221 of the Commercial Code. In the case of individuals who may have left **after** September 14, 1961 with a valid permit, following the expiration of its term, although their Entities may continue to be in good standing, following this Law 989, such person's interest in the capital of any Entity may have been confiscated in favor of the Cuban government and these measures, being also in the nature of a confiscation, by merger of rights may have resulted, as expressed above, in the *de facto* dissolution of the pertinent Entities.

INTERVENTIONS

Pursuant to Law 647 of November 24, 1959 (*Gaceta Oficial* of November 25, 1959), the Minister of Labor was authorized to order the intervention of those

---

11. It can be argued that other legal entities like limited liability companies ("sociedades de responsabilidad limitada"), general ("sociedades regulares colectivas") and limited ("sociedades en comandita") partnerships, although none have "shares," the proprietary interests of its members are valuables which may be affected by the provisions of this Law.

12. The Cuban legislator, who in the past did not exhibit much refinement in the selection of the terms used to appropriate property, this time promulgated a measure labeled nationalization *by confiscation*. Since Article 24 of the Ley Fundamental authorizes the confiscation of property in the event of persons "who, in order to evade action by the Revolutionary Tribunals, abandoned in any manner the national territory or, having abandoned it, participated abroad in counter-revolutionary activities against the Revolutionary Government," it can be argued that these hybrid takings may be in the nature of confiscation and the owners thereof may not be entitled to any compensation under the above mentioned Article 24 of the Ley Fundamental.

13. As probably was the case for the majority of the members/shareholders of many Entities operating in Cuba, since a preponderance of the country's entrepreneurial class left the national territory before this date.

Entities or work places that "ostensively alter the normal development of production," in the event of the occurrence of:

- Lock-outs or closings, temporary or permanent, that entail the idling of the work places;

- Grave labor conflicts;

- Non-compliance with Court orders or decisions or resolutions of the Minister of Labor as a result of a labor conflict.

This Law also provided that interventions were to be ordered for a term not to exceed six months, to be extended by an express order of the President of the Republic, at the request of the Minister of Labor; the intervenors being authorized, under its Article 5, to exercise "all powers necessary to administer and govern the enterprise or work places, ... and all those other (powers) which corresponded to its officers, being subrogated in lieu of the employer"; the resolutions designating the intervenors specified the scope of the intervention and powers to be enjoyed by the intervenors.

Although the great majority of the Entities intervened were eventually nationalized following the above mentioned legal measures, exceptionally Entities engaged in the tobacco industry appear to have continued as "intervened" through the date of this paper. By Resolution 20260 of September 15, 1960, certain individuals were designated as intervenors of tobacco industry Entities and as such were expressly vested with the full powers of the board of directors[14] of the respective Entities.[15] This Resolution cited the following reasons justifying the intervention of these Entities: (a) guarantee tobacco supply to Cuba's tra-

ditional markets, producing tobacco of the quality that has characterized Cuban exports; (b) normalize (?) the situation created in the cigarette tobacco industries; and (c) assure stability for their personnel in its work, and production in general.

The anomalous situation of the Entities in the tobacco industry has been perpetuated through the current date by the following legal measures:

1. Under the authority granted by Law 843 of June 30, 1960, the Ministry of Labor was authorized to promulgate resolutions extending the duration of interventions as deemed necessary (without any limit as before) for the fulfillment of its (above-cited) purposes.

2. By Resolution 123 of the Minister of Labor dated May 24, 1966, new intervenors were designated and specifically granted these additional powers: (i) to grant powers of attorney; (ii) to collect any funds due to the intervened Entities and issue receipts in full satisfaction thereof, nationally and abroad; and (iii) to authorize Industrial Property Agents worldwide to extend and protect the cigar brands of the intervened tobacco Entities.

CONTINUED GOOD STANDING OF THESE ENTITIES

Except with regard to Entities that may have been confiscated as expressed above, including those controlled by individuals declared to have illicitly enriched themselves, the nationalized banks, and perhaps the hybrids described above, no other declaration of nationalization or intervention of the Cuban government includes any express provision ordering the dissolution of pertinent legal Entities.

---

14. It is interesting to note that neither Cuba's Commercial Code then in force nor the decisions of its courts had ever determined that boards of directors have *inherent powers*. Following such Code and court decisions, the parties who organized Entities enjoyed almost absolute discretion to determine the terms and conditions of their charter (its "Estatutos") including provisions for meetings of its shareholders, the appointment of officers by the shareholders and the powers enjoyed by such officers. The Estatutos seldom provided for the creation of a board of directors, except in the case of banks, insurance companies and public companies, where in practice the directors were named solely for "show" and enjoyed minimal powers, and the Entities were managed by its officers and shareholders. Therefore, the granting to certain intervenors, for example those of the tobacco industry, the "powers of the board of directors," appears to denote the participation of foreign attorneys, who were not well apprised of the traditional Cuban corporate practice, in the drafting.

15. It is interesting to note that some of the Entities intervened were limited liability companies and, following the Commercial Code then in force, such Entities had no "board of directors" but *of members*, it being questionable what powers, if any, its intervenor enjoyed following applicable Cuban corporate law.

Therefore, it appears certain that these Entities are in good standing, applying the axiom of *Ubi Lex Non Distinguit...*

In support of the good standing of the Entities, the following should be considered:

1. Except in the event that the duration of any such Entities has expired or they have been declared bankrupt, it cannot be argued (except regarding the banking industry) that the capital thereof has been exhausted, and they "shall dissolve" under Article 221 of the Commercial Code,[16] since all measures nationalizing them provided for adequate compensation as required by article 24 of the Ley Fundamental then in force. Such contingent right to compensation is undoubtedly an intangible asset and its possession defeats the possibility that the Entities' capital may have been totally exhausted as required for its dissolution under the Commercial Code.

2. It is highly improbable that the "enterprise" that was the sole purpose for which the Entity was organized may have been terminated (an issue never raised in any of Cuba's measures), another cause of dissolution referred in paragraph 1 of Article 221 of Cuba's Commercial Code.

3. Particular consideration should be given to the traditional Cuban corporate practice to include in the Estatutos of the Entities, even if established with a specific purpose, that they could engage in any other business of legitimate commerce or industry.

4. It is interesting to note that Cuba never required that American-style annual reports be filed with an equivalent of our Secretary of State or any similar supervisory governmental body, with the penalty of the potential Dissolution by Proclamation of the Entity in the event of the non-filing of any such annual report. Likewise, these Entities continue to be in good standing even if they had not timely filed tax returns or paid taxes which may have been due, according to reiterated decisions of Cuban Supreme Court.[17]

5. If these Cuban Entities continue to be in good standing, a careful review of their Estatutos is recommended for various purposes, including but not limited to calling and holding a shareholders/members' special meeting[18] following the applicable Estatutos. The agenda for this meeting should expressly cite, amongst the matters to be discussed and acted, the following: (a) possible updating of the Estatutos; (b) consideration of the "continuation" of the Entity; (c) in the event of shareholders/members who have passed away, ratify and accept the transfer of shares/units of participation to their heirs to the satisfaction of a majority of such shareholders/members at the meeting, avoiding probate of last wills and testaments, intestate proceedings and other expensive and delaying procedures. Of course, it is advisable that the persons recognized as successors of deceased shareholders/members execute appropriate indemnification agreements in favor of the Entity and other shareholders/members in the event that their sworn statements supporting their claim to succession prove to be incorrect or invalid for any reason; (d) by majority vote elect new officers and grant to them such powers as may be required. If the Estatutos of the Entity provide for the designation of directors, consideration may be given to their election; and (e) for Helms-Burton Act[19] purposes, hopefully accomplished before the enactment of the Act with the advice of legal counsel, consideration should have been

---

16. As indicated above, it can be argued that the text of this nineteenth century legal measure, as amended from time to time through 1959, continues to be in full force and effect in Cuba today, having been modified partially as to the legal entities for foreign joint ventures by Law-Decree 50 of September 15, 1982, the text of the latter superseded by the Foreign Investment Law of September 5, 1995, which currently governs such joint ventures.

17. Decisions No. 31 of July 15, 1929, and No. 38 of March 10, 1937, cited by Cuba's renowned legal commentator, Dr. Mariano Sánchez-Roca, in his *Leyes Civiles y su Jurisprudencia*, Vol. II (Commercial Code), page 96.

18. Traditional Cuban corporate law did not require that such shareholders/members meetings be held in Cuba, unless otherwise provided in its Estatutos, and in the majority of cases can be held here in Miami, Florida, for example. A responsible effort should be made to reach all shareholders/members and to call the meeting by certified or registered mail, if possible.

19. Common name of the Cuban Liberty and Democratic Solidarity Act of 1996, signed by President Clinton on March 12, 1996.

given to the following alternatives: (i) filing claims on behalf of the Cuban Entities continued in the United States (i.e., under Delaware's General Corporation Law, Section 388), eliminating the need to contribute the shareholders/members' interests in claims to other national legal entities as they, and even foreign citizens, could have done before the enactment of the Act; (ii) recapitalize the Entity, if possible, by issuing all its common stock to United States citizens and represent the interest of non-United States nationals with debentures or other form of Entity debt, consideration being given to issuance of common or preferred non-voting stock, even convertible to voting common after a number of year (e.g., ten); and (iii) assign all right, title and interest to the Entities' Cuban assets, including any rights to claims under the Act, to individual United States citizens and compensating the non-United States citizens as indicated above.

6. Likewise, in a democratic Cuba, the shareholders/members of these Entities whose assets were nationalized by the Castro regime, can deal through these legal Entities with the government authorities then in force in furtherance of return of the property(ies) of which they have been deprived without due compensation as required by Article 24 of the Ley Fundamental then in force or seek equivalent compensation therefor.

COMMENTS ON

"On the Continued Good Standing of Pre-1959 Cuban Legal Entities 'Ubi Lex non Distinguit, Nec Nos Distinguere Debemus'" by Goytisolo

Juan C. Consuegra-Barquín

Through this paper, Dr. Goytisolo has discovered one more legal controversy caused by the unreasonable and non-planned legislation of the Castro regime. He prepared a well documented and informed study which evaluates the question of whether the revolutionary legislation affected the continued good standing of legal entities organized or doing business in Cuba during the first years of the revolution ("the Entities").

The paper groups all possible causes of dissolution of legal entities found in the Civil Code, the Commercial Code, the General Corporation Law and the "Reforma Tributaria," in order to explain how the laws maintained some of these entities in good standing.

Dr. Goytisolo brings to our attention a list of what I would identify as the "10 Most Wanted List of the Confiscation and Nationalization Laws in the Republic of Cuba." The laws are as follows:

1. The Fundamental Law (Constitution of 1959).

2. The law that confiscated property from those individuals related directly or indirectly to Fulgencio Batista.

3. The law that confiscated property from those persons who illicitly enriched while exercising a public authority.

4. The law that confiscated property from those persons who were sanctioned for counterrevolutionary felonies.

5. The law that confiscated property from those persons who were sanctioned and passed away.

6. The law that nationalized property from U.S. citizens.

7. The law that nationalized property from all U.S. citizens.

8. The law that nationalized the sugar mills, the distilleries and other manufactures.

9. The law that nationalized property from those persons who left Cuba without government authorization.

10. The law that allowed the Minister of Labor to nationalize work places and other related enterprises.

Not only does he analyze each of the laws, but he also searches for every possible scenario where the Entities were to be dissolved.

After analyzing each of the 10 Most Wanted Laws, the paper concludes that a great number of these Entities not only are in good standing but capable of engaging in any business activity authorized by its certificate of incorporation and bylaws.

When interpreting any law in the Civil Legal System (which prevails in Cuba), and such law does not distinguishes, then the General Law shall be observed (the General Law shall be the Civil Code). General law always follows the special law. Article 16 of the Old Cuban Civil Code of 1889 ("the Old Civil Code"), derogated in 1988 by the new Socialist Civil Code ("the New Civil Code"), states:

> "En las materias que se rijan por leyes especiales, la deficiencia de éstas se suplirá con las disposiciones de este Código."[1]

Meanwhile, article 8 of the new Socialist Code states:

> "Las disposiciones de este Código son supletorias respecto a materias civiles u otras reguladas en leyes especiales."[2]

Furthermore, in the event the general law (Civil Code) does not distinguishes either, then the Civil Code provides certain guidelines or general principles to interpret the special law. Article 6 of the Old Civil Code states:

> "El Tribunal que rehuse fallar a pretexto de silencio, obscuridad o insuficiencia de las leyes, incurrirá en responsabilidad.
>
> "Cuando no haya ley exactamente aplicable al punto controvertido, se aplicará la costumbre del lugar, y, en su defecto, los principios generales de derecho."[3]

According to article 6, in order to interpret these special laws (the 10 Most Wanted), customary Cuban principles in its legal system are to be observed on the first instance and, in their absence, the general principles of the Civil Law System are to be adopted.

An in depth analysis of the principles in the Cuban legal system must be performed first before concluding on how they shall be interpreted. However, we found that the *Ubi Lex Non Distinguit, Nec Nos Distinguere Debemus* principle is no stranger for the Cu-

ban Supreme Court. This interpretation was used to decide a case in 1903.[4]

On the other hand, I believe one of the general principles of the Civil Law System which deserves to be observed for purposes of this paper is the principle of *In Pari Materia*,[5] which may be found in many Latin American civil codes. For example, Article 18 of the Puerto Rican Civil Code states:

> "Las leyes que se refieran a la misma materia o cuyo objeto sea el mismo deben ser interpretadas refiriendo las unas a las otras por cuanto a lo que es claro en uno de sus preceptos pueda ser usado para explicar lo que resulte dudoso en otro."

The *In Pari Materia* principle explains that the laws related in topic and in object must be interpreted between one another. For example, if a term is clearly interpreted in Law number 1, contrary to Law number 2 where the term is not clearly defined, then Law number 2 may adopt Law number 1´s definition, complementing one another. Likewise, Law number 1 may adopt a term´s definition well defined in Law number 2.

Applying this principle to our analysis, since the 10 Most Wanted Laws are related in topic (confiscation and nationalization) and in object (properties, government, private owners), perhaps, a well defined term in one of these laws may help to complement the other laws. For example, if one of these laws, when referring to "property confiscated" uses and defines the term "property" to include "corporate shares," then the other laws where the term "property" is not defined, or if defined, not well or ambiguously defined, may adopt the term property´s definition under the principle of *In Pari Materia*.

---

1. The Old Civil Code at article 16.

2. The New Civil Code at article 8.

3. The Old Civil Code at article 6.

4. Decision Number 20 of April 18, 1903. It should be noted that in 1903, the Cuban Supreme Court may have been influenced by the Common Law System since on such period the U.S. had total political and sovereign control over Cuba after the Spanish-American War of 1898.

5. A similar principle to the *In Pari Materia* principle was previously used by the Cuban Supreme Court in a few of its decisions. See Decision Number 16 of July 15, 1907; Decision Number 24 of April 14, 1913; Decision Number 34 of June 1, 1915; and Decision Number 138 of November 29, 1924. The principle reads: "Donde existe la misma razón, debe aplicarse la misma disposición."

The second observation is whether the good standing of the Entities and the Cuban Constitution of 1976 (the Socialist Constitution) are in harmony or in conflict. This Constitution, later amended in 1992, provided for the creation of new types of property ownership. Personal property,[6] state property[7] and small farmer property[8] were the three types of property recognized under the socialist constitution of 1976 before its amendments in 1992.[9]

Cuban scholars, commenting on the 1976 socialist constitution, have said that economic function is the main test to determine whether a good should be considered personal property or State property.[10]

"In a socialist society, goods must be classified according their economic function. Goods are either means of production or they are for use and consumption. Only the latter can be considered as personal property, while the former must be social property given its key social function." [11]

Socialist personal goods may only serve to satisfy an individual's basic needs, and according to some jurists, their only limitation is that they cannot be used for the exploitation of another person's work or to make profit through individual private enterprise. Such a transaction would be contrary to the fundamental principles of socialist law, and therefore invalid.

The Socialist Constitution states that personal property includes: (1) savings and income which are the product of personal labor; (2) housing; (3) every good, object or instrument serving to satisfy their cultural or material necessities; and (4) every good, object or instrument needed to carry out personal or family labor.[12]

Therefore, the only type of individual private ownership authorized by Cuban Law, with the exception of the property of small farmers, was personal property. No other type of ownership not included in the definition of personal property was either authorized or legal.

Under the presumption that these Entities are presently in good standing, how could we harmonize their legal existence under the narrow possibilities of ownership provided by the Constitution of 1976? In other words, an argument must be created in order to support the theory that these Entities were in existence during the time period of the Constitution of 1976, when none of the ownership rights recognized under Cuban Law would authorize a person to be a shareholder of a Cuban Corporation or a member of an Entity.

Therefore, in order to conclude that these Entities are presently in good standing and that they may qualify as claimants under the Helms-Burton Law, Dr. Goytisolo must: (1) interpret the 10 Most Wanted Laws according to the Cuban Legal System; and (2) must create a solid argument that prevails over the theory that these Entities were incompatible with the ownership rights recognized under the Constitution of 1976 since it was impossible for a person to own a corporate share of a Cuban corporation under Cuban Law.

---

6. The 1976 Cuban Constitution at article 21.

7. *Id.* at article 15.

8. *Id.* at articles 15, 20-21.

9. In order to understand the ideological debate regarding the non-socialist concepts of property and these three new types of socialist property, see, J. Consuegra-Barquín, "Cuba's Residential Property Ownership Dilemma: A Human Rights Issue Under International Law," *Rutgers Law Review* 46:2 (1994).

10. F. Alvarez Tabío, *Comentarios a la Constitución Socialista* (1985), p. 109.

11. Alvarez Tabío, *Comentarios a la Constitución Socialista*, p. 109.

12. 1976 Constitution at article 21.

Appendix A:
AUTHORS AND DISCUSSANTS

CHARLES A. ADAMS is a Professor in the Food and Resource Economics Department and Florida Sea Grant College Program at the University of Florida, Gainesville, Florida with emphasis on Marine Economics, Commercial Fisheries Production and Seafood Processing.

BENIGNO E. AGUIRRE is Professor of Sociology at Texas A&M University.

PABLO ALFONSO is a journalist specializing on Cuban affairs. Since 1987 he has been with *El Nuevo Herald*, where he currently writes the thrice-weekly column "Cuba por Dentro." Earlier in his career, he was news editor for Radio Station WQBA and Television Station WSCV, Channel 51. He is the author of three books related to Cuba, *Cuba, Castro y los Católicos*, *Los fieles de Castro*, and *El diálogo ignorado*. He earned a degree in Sociology from St. Thomas University in Miami, Florida.

JOSE ALVAREZ is Professor, Food and Resource Economics Department, University of Florida, where he works as the Area Economist in the Everglades Research and Education Center, Belle Glade, Florida. He has been traveling to Cuba in the past few years as one of the principal investigators in two grants provided by the John D. and Catherine T. MacArthur Foundation to study Cuban agriculture and the potential economic impact on the agricultural economies of Florida and Cuba after the lifting of the U.S. economic embargo. He earned a B.A. in Economics (1971), and an M.S. (1974) and a Ph.D. (1977) in Food and Resource Economics all from the University of Florida.

NELSON AMARO is Dean of the Faculty of Social Sciences at the Universidad del Valle de Guatemala, Guatemala City.

RAMON C. BARQUIN III is President of B&B Importers, Inc., an export/import company located in Boston, Massachusetts, and Director of Public Affairs of the Instituto de Formación Democrática in Guaynabo, Puerto Rico. He has a degree in Politics, Latin American Affairs, and Economics from Brandeis University.

JONATHAN BENJAMIN-ALVARADO is a Ph.D. Candidate in the Department of Political Science, University of Georgia. He is also a research associate of the Center for International Trade and Security at the University of Georgia, specializing in Latin American security and nuclear affairs.

BARTON J. BERNALES is a U.S. Navy Intelligence Officer currently assigned to the U.S. Special Operations Command in Tampa, Florida. He holds a B.S. in Applied Mathematics from the University of Florida, a B.S. in International Affairs from Florida State University and a M.S. in National Security Affairs from the Naval Postgraduate School.

ALFREDO BLANCO, JR., is Vice President of Sugar Producers of Cuba, Inc., an association of former mill owners of Cuba. Earlier in his career, he was Vice President for Sales of Gulf + Western Industries, Sugar Division, and Manager of the Sugar Division of Christman & Company, a New York sugar trading house. In Cuba he was CEO of Blanco's Family Enterprises, comprising the sugar mills Ramona and San Ramón; manager and chief engineer of the mill Corazón de Jesús, and assistant manager and chief engineer of the sugar mill Trinidad. He holds a B.S.

in electrical engineering from the Massachusetts Institute of Technology (1941) and an MBA in Corporation Finance from New York University.

JULIE MARIE BUNCK is Assistant Professor, Department of Political Science, University of Louisville, Louisville, Kentucky. She is the author of *Fidel Castro and the Quest for Revolutionary Culture in Cuba* (Pennsylvania State University Press, 1994) and co-author of *Law, Power, and the Sovereign State* (Pennsylvania State University Press, 1995).

BEVERLY L. CAMPBELL is a journalist and professional writer based in Toronto, Canada. For the last two years she has worked as a financial journalist, writing on issues that pertain to Cuban foreign trade and investment. Her articles have appeared in *The Miami Herald* and *Cuba News* and has been interviewed on CBS Newsworld. She has also written and done research for the *Financial Post* of Canada and, in her current capacity, reports on aspects of global finance as they relate to Cuban economic development for *The Wall Street Journal*.

LORENZO CAÑIZARES is an organizer with the Communications Workers of America, AFL-CIO, Local 1040, in New Jersey. He has been a labor union member since 1973. He is a member of the Board of Directors of New Jersey's Citizens Action and of the Mercer County AFL-CIO Labor Council. He was recently chosen to be on the Board of Directors of the New Jersey Work Environment Council.

ROLANDO H. CASTAÑEDA is currently a Senior Operations Officer working with Chile and Perú at the Inter-American Development Bank (IDB), where he has held different positions since 1974. Before joining the IDB, he worked as an economist at the Organization of American States; the Rockefeller Foundation at the University of Cali, Colombia; the University of Puerto Rico at Río Piedras; and the Puerto Rico Planning Board. He holds an M.A. and is a Ph.D. candidate at Yale University, concentrating in monetary policy and econometrics.

DAVID S. COLLIS, former Deputy Director of the Cuba Project at Georgetown University, is currently a consultant in Washington, D.C.

JUAN C. CONSUEGRA-BARQUIN, Esq., is House Counselor for the Corporación Educativa Ramón Barquín, Guaynabo, Puerto Rico. After receiving a B.A. from the University of Puerto Rico (1989), he earned his J.D. at the Inter-American University Law School of Puerto Rico (1992). He also holds an L.L.M. in International and Comparative Law from the Georgetown University Law Center (1993).

EFREN CORDOVA is Professor, Center for Labor Research and Studies, Florida International University.

SERGIO DIAZ-BRIQUETS is a Vice President of Casals and Associates, a Washington-based consulting firm. He was Research Director of the Congressional Commission for the Study of International Migration and Cooperative Economic Development, and earlier held appointments with the International Development Research Centre, Population Reference Bureau, and Duquesne University. A recipient of a Ph.D. in Demography from the University of Pennsylvania, he has published numerous articles and books dealing with Cuba.

MAIDA DONATE-ARMADA is a Sociologist and Social Psychologist. She earned her Ph.D. at the Universidad de la Habana.

ERWIN H. EPSTEIN is Professor of Educational Policy and Leadership at The Ohio State University, and Editor of the *Comparative Education Review*. In 1985 he received the Lourdes Casal Award for the most outstanding work in the social sciences on Cuba.

ISABEL EZQUERRA is currently Science Bibliographer and Assistant Professor at the University of Miami. She was previously Acquisitions Librarian at the North-South Center, University of Miami, developed the library for the Central American Journalism Program at Florida International University, and was director of the Mount Sinai Medical Center Library. She earned a B.A. in Foreign Languages from the University of South Florida, an M.A. in Language and Literature from the University of Florida (1971), and an M.L.S. in Library and Information Science (1977) from the University of Alabama.

GABRIEL FERNANDEZ is currently working as a financial analyst with JP Morgan's corporate real estate group. Previously, he worked as a researcher with Scudder, Stevens and Clark, covering political and economic conditions in Latin America. He holds an MBA in Finance degree from New York University, which he attended as a fellow of the Consortium for Graduate Study in Management.

GERARDO GONZALEZ is an economist and specialist on economic and international relations of Cuba and the Caribbean. His articles have appeared in specialized journals in Latin America, the United States, and Europe. He is the author of *The Caribbean and the Foreign Policy of Cuba* (Dominican Republic, 1991) and co-author of *Popular Participation and Development in Cuban Municipalities* (Venezuela, 1994). He is currently a professor of economics at the Universidad Interamericana of Puerto Rico.

AGUSTIN DE GOYTISOLO, Esq., is Senior Counsel to Katz Barron Squitero & Faust P.A., Miami, Florida. Previously, he practiced law with several law firms in Florida and held top management positions with private companies. He received law degrees from the Georgetown University Law Center (1968) and the Universidad de la Habana (1947).

GUILLERMO GRENIER is Director, Center for Labor Research and Studies, Florida International University, and Professor of Sociology at the same institution.

NICOLAS J. GUTIERREZ, Jr., Esq., is the Executive Director of the International Law Practice Group of the law firm of Adorno & Zeder, P.A., in Miami, Florida. He is a graduate of the University of Miami (B.A., 1985) and received his law degree from Georgetown University Law Center (J.D., 1988).

ANA JULIA JATAR-HAUSMANN is a Senior Fellow at the Inter-American Dialogue, Washington, D.C. She was previously a full-time researcher and professor at the Instituto de Estudios Superiores de Administración in Venezuela (1986-1992) and headed the anti-trust agency in Venezuela (1992-1994). She earned a Ph.D. in Economics at Warwick University, United Kingdom.

ERNESTO HERNANDEZ-CATA is currently Deputy Director of the Western Hemisphere Department, International Monetary Fund (IMF). Previously, he served as Deputy Director of the IMF's European II Department, in charge of relations with Russia and several other states of the former Soviet Union, and held other positions at the IMF and at the Board of Governors of the Federal Reserve System. He received a Licence from the Graduate Institute of International Studies in Geneva (1967) and M.A. (1970) and Ph.D. (1974) in economics from Yale University.

OSVALDO A. JUVIER is an Engineer and Businessman in the energy industry, currently Vice President of Operations and Technical Resources of Duke Energy Corp., a wholly owned subsidiary of Duke Power Company of Charlotte, North Carolina. He is a graduate of the School of Engineering at the University of Madrid, Spain, and of the School of Business at Rice University. With 25 years experience in the energy and electric utility industry, he has been active in the development and privatization of electric markets in the international arena with emphasis in Latin American countries. Prior to joining Duke Energy Corp., he held senior management positions at Transco Energy Co., and General Electric Company.

SERGIO A. LEISECA, Esq., is a Partner in the Dallas office of the international law firm of Baker & McKenzie. He earned a B.A. degree in political science from Tulane University (1968) and a J.D. Degree from Tulane University School of Law (1971), where he was a member of the Law Review.

LUIS LOCAY is currently Associate Professor of Economics at the University of Miami. He was previously Assistant Professor of Economics at the State University of New York at Binghampton. He received his Ph.D. in economics from the University of Chicago in 1983.

ALBERTO LUZARRAGA is the Chairman of the Amerinvest Group, Inc., a merchant banking concern specialized in equity investments in the Americas. He has more than 30 years of experience in the commercial and investment banking business, with emphasis in Latin America. He holds a Ph.D. in Civil Law from the Universidad de Villanueva (La Habana), a CPA degree from the Universidad de la Habana, and an MBA from the University of Miami.

AMBASSADOR ALBERTO MARTINEZ PIEDRA is Professor of Economics at the Catholic University of America. He was Deputy U.S. Ambassador to the Organization of American States (1982-84), U.S. Ambassador to Guatemala (1984-87), and Special Assistant to the U.S. Mission to the United Nations (1987-88). He earned a degree in Political Economy from the Universidad Complutense de Madrid (1957) and a Ph.D. in economics from Georgetown University (1962).

ANDREW M. MELNYK is a Ph.D. candidate at the Department of Economics, University of Miami. He received a B.A. from the University of Illinois and an M.A. from the University of Miami, both in economics. He has taught at the University of Miami and in 1993 he held the position of visiting instructor at the American Insitute of Business and Economics in Moscow, Russia.

CARMELO MESA-LAGO is Distinguished Service Professor of Economics and Latin American Studies at the University of Pittsburgh. He is the author of numerous books and articles on different aspects of the Cuban economy and on social security issues, among others. His most recent books include *Breve Historia Económica de la Cuba Socialista* (Madrid: Alianza Editorial, 1994) and *Are Economic Reforms Propelling Cuba to the Market?* (Coral Gables: North-South Center, University of Miami, 1995).

WILLIAM A. MESSINA, JR., is the Executive Coordinator of the International Agricultural Trade and Development Center within the Food and Resource Economics Department at the University of Florida, Gainesville, Florida.

GEORGE PLINIO MONTALVAN is currently an international economic and management consultant working principally with the Inter-American Development Bank. He was previously Chief Economist at the the Organization of American States and conducted research at the Brookings Institution. He edited several volumes of *Cuba in Transition*, the Papers and Proceedings of ASCE's annual meeting, and is the author of numerous publications, among them *Latin America: The Hardware and Software Markets* (INTERSOL 1991) and *Promoting Investments and Exports in the Caribbean* (Organization of American States, 1989). He holds a B.A. and M.A., and is a Ph.D. candidate in economics from the George Washington University.

ANNE E. MOSELEY is an Economic Analyst in the Food and Resource Economics Department at the University of Florida, Gainesville, Florida. Her areas of specialization include analyzing and assessing agricultural marketing, production and natural resource data to support economic analyses.

SILVIA PEDRAZA is Associate Professor of Sociology at the University of Michigan. She is the author of *Political and Economic Migrants in America: Cubans and Mexicans* (University of Texas Press, 1985) and co-editor with Rubén Rumbaut of *Origins and Destinies: Immigration, Race and Ethnicity in America* (Wadsworth, 1995).

LORENZO L. PEREZ is Assistant Director of the Western Hemisphere Department, International Monetary Fund (IMF). Previously, he served in the IMF's Exchange and Trade Relations Department and the European Department, and held positions at the U.S. Department of the Treasury and the U.S. Agency for International Development. He received a Ph.D. in economics from the University of Pennsylvania.

JORGE F. PEREZ-LOPEZ is an international economist with the Bureau of International Labor Affairs, U.S. Department of Labor. He is the author of *Cuba's Second Economy: From Behind the Scenes to Center Stage* (Transaction Publishers, 1995) and editor of *Cuba at a Crossroads* (University Press of Florida, 1994). He received his Ph.D. in economics from the State University of New York at Albany.

JOSEPH M. PERRY is Professor of Economics and Chairperson of the Department of Economics and Geography at the University of North Florida, where he has been a faculty member since 1971. He was previously a member of the economics faculty of the University of Florida. Dr. Perry received his Ph.D. in

Economics from Northwestern University in 1966, after completing undergraduate studies at Emory University and Georgia State University. His recent research has focussed on regional economic development, with specific reference to Central American and Caribbean nations, and their trade relationships with the United States.

LARRY PRESS is Professor and Chairman of Computer Information Systems at California State University, Dominguez Hills. He is an editor for the *Communications of the Association for Computing Machinery* and *OntheInternet*, the international publication of the Internet Society. He has written two books and over two hundred articles and reports. He has a long standing interest in computer networks in developing nations, has visited Cuba twice, and has written a report and two articles on Cuban networks.

ENRIQUE S. PUMAR, Ph.D., is an Adjunct Professor in the Graduate Program, Department of Sociology, American University, Washington, D.C., and a Senior Project Manager, Consulting Services, EDS.

ARMANDO RIBAS resides in Buenos Aires, Argentina, where he teaches Political Philosophy and consults on economic issues. He is also a journalist associated with Argentinian and Uruguayan newspapers. He received a law degree from the Universidad de Santo Tomás de Villanueva, La Habana, and studied economics at Columbia University.

JORGE LUIS ROMEU is an Associate Professor in the Department of Mathematics, State University of New York at Cortland, and an Adjunct Professor in the Manufacturing Engineering Program, Syracuse University. He is a Fellow of the Royal Statistical Society and a member of the ASA and INFORMS.

DIEGO R. ROQUE is currently Adjunct Professor of Mathematics at Barry University in Miami Springs, Florida. He was Senior Defense Analyst with the U.S. Army Concepts Analysis Agency (1987-94), an Assistant Professor of Operations Research at George Mason University (1982-87), and a Junior Defese Analyst with the Center for Naval Analysis (1974-77). He earned a Doctorate of Science degree from George Washington University, a Master of Science from the University of California,

Berkeley, and a Bachelor of Science in Industrial and Systems Engineering from the University of Miami, Florida.

MARTA BEATRIZ ROQUE CABELLO is Director, Instituto Cubano de Economistas Independientes (ICEI), La Habana, Cuba.

JAMES E. ROSS is Courtesy Professor and Program Advisor, International Agricultural Trade and Development Center, Food and Resource Economics Department, Institute of Food and Agricultural Sciences, University of Florida, Gainesville, Florida.

IGNACIO E. SANCHEZ, Esq., is a partner with the international law firm Kelley Drye & Warren LLP. He is also a Trustee of the Cuban American National Foundation.

JUAN TOMAS SANCHEZ is a consulting engineer to the pharmaceutical industry and a member of the Board of Directors of the Asociación de Colonos en el Exilio, Inc. From 1976 to the present, He has held senior management positions with Abbott Laboratories, Key Pharmaceuticals, Schering-Plough, Pepsi-Cola USA, John Brown Engineers, Ivax and Andrx Pharmaceuticals, in Ecuador and Puerto Rico, and with the State of Florida. In 1979, he co-founded CHCS Inc. (Cane Harvesters Consultants and Suppliers, Inc.), a sugar cane harvesting contractor and consulting firm that held contracts in Florida and Venezuela. He earned an engineering degree from the University of Miami and is a registered engineer in the State of Florida.

REBECA SANCHEZ-ROIG, Esq., is an Assistant District Counsel with the United States Department of Justice, Immigration and Naturalization Service, in Miami, Florida.

JORGE A. SANGUINETTY is founder and President of DevTech Systems, Inc., a Washington, D.C.-based international and domestic economic consulting firm. He has over 30 years' experience in research, teaching, management, and consulting in economic policy design and implementation at the macro and sectorial levels. He received a Ph.D. in economics from the City University of New York.

JOSEPH L. SCARPACI, Jr., is an Associate Professor of Urban Affairs and Planning at the College of Architecture and Urban Studies, Virginia Tech University, Blacksburg, Virginia. He is co-author (with Roberto Segre and Mario Coyula) of a forthcoming book titled *Havana: Two Faces of an Antillian Metropolis* (Wiley Publishers). He received an M.S. in Geography from the Pennsylvania State University (1978) and a Ph.D. in Geography from the University of Florida (1985).

CARLOS SEIGLIE is a Professor of Economics at Rugers University, Newark, New Jersey.

THOMAS H. SPREEN is a Professor in the Food and Resource Economics Department at the University of Florida, Gainesville, Florida. Areas of specialization are the application of quantitative methods to problems related to the agricultural sector with emphasis on citrus.

JEFFREY W. STEAGALL is Associate Professor of Economics and Director of the International Studies in Business Program at the University of North Florida. Dr. Steagall received his Ph. D. in Economics from the University of Wisconsin at Madison in 1990. His undergraduate studies were completed at St. Norbert College. Dr. Steagall is an international trade and finance specialist, with a particular interest in the trade relationships of developing countries.

RICARDO L. TEJADA is currently Special Assistant to the Chief Economist at the United States Department of Labor. He has also worked with the Organization for Economic Cooperation and Development on matters related to the economic transition of Central and Eastern Europe. He holds an M.A. from the Fletcher School of Law and Diplomacy (1995) and a B.A. in International Economics from the American University of Paris (1990).

ROBERTO VICHOT is Visiting Professor of Political Science at Florida International University.

LOUIS A. WOODS is Professor of Geography and Economics at the University of North Florida, where he has been a faculty member since 1972. Dr. Woods received his Ph. D. in Geography from the University of North Carolina at Chapel Hill in 1972, after completing undergraduate studies in Geography at Jacksonville University. He completed postgraduate work in Economics at East Carolina University. His recent research has focussed on the determinants of regional economic development, and the constraints imposed by environmental concerns.

MARIA C. WERLAU is President of Orbis, S.A., of Santiago Chile, operating as Orbis International in Chatham, New Jersey, a company dedicated to consulting and international relocation in Latin America. Previously, she was a financial analyst and second Vice President of The Chase Manhattan Bank, N.A., holding management positions in Puerto Rico and Venezuela. Some of her recent writings on Cuba include *The Facts About Human Rights in Cuba According to Human Rights Organizations* (1995), *The Cuban Liberty and Solidarity Act (Helms-Burton Bill): Issues Surrounding the Proposed Legislation* (1995), and *Cuba and U.S. Policy: Pertinent Issues and Data* (1994). She holds a B.S. in Foreign Service from Georgetown University and an M.A. in International Affairs from the University of Chile.

Appendix B:
ACKNOWLEDGEMENTS

We want to take this opportunity to acknowledge the continued financial support provided to ASCE's activities by the following sponsoring members:

Acosta, José D.	Law and Economics Consultant	Miami, FL
Alverio, Michael	ALVEMAC Representaciones	Caguas, PR
Arellano, Victor		Coral Gables, FL
Asón, Elías R.	Empresas Fonalledas	San Juan, PR
Batista-Falla, Agustín	Neder Finanz NV	Paris, France
Batista-Falla, Víctor	Publisher-Editor	Madrid, Spain
Belt, Juan A.B.	USAID	Guatemala City, Guatemala
Betancourt, Roger	University of Maryland	College Park, MD
Blamberg, Margaret	Tate & Lyle	New York, NY
Botifoll, Luis J.	Republic National Bank	Coral Gables, FL
Carbonell-Cortina, Néstor	Pepsi-Cola	Somers, NY
Carta, Alvaro L.	Sugar Consultant	West Palm Beach, FL
Cisneros, Frank G.	MARMAN USA, Inc.	Tampa, FL
Craft, Ana R., Esq.	Attorney at Law	Miami, FL
Crews, Eduardo T.	Bristol-Myers Squibb	New York, NY
Cueto, Guillermo	CUBAWORLD SERVICES, Inc.	Miami, FL
de la Hoz, José	United Trading Group	Coral Gables, FL
de Lasa, José M., Esq.	Abbott Laboratories	Abbott Park, IL
Delgado, Natalia, Esq.	Jenner & Block	Chicago, IL
Díaz, Manuel L.	Republic Int'l Bank of NY	Miami, FL
Echevarría, Oscar E.	BM-E INTERFUNDING	Caracas, Venezuela
Falcoff, Mark	American Enterprise Institute	Washington, DC
Falk, Dr. Pamela S.		New York, NY
Fernández, Carlos J.	KPMG Peat Marwick	Miami, FL
Fernández, Emilio A.	Pulse Electronics, Inc.	Rockville, MD
Fernández, Matías A.	Technology Park Group	San Juan, PR
Fernández-Morell, Andrés	Popular Leasing	San Juan, PR
Freer, Robert E., Jr., Esq.	Freer & McGarry	Washington, DC
García, Cristina		Los Angeles, CA
García-Aguilera Hamshaw, Carolina	C & J Investigations	Miami, FL
Gayoso, Antonio	CUNA	Washington, DC
Giral, Juan A.	Consultant	Washington, DC
Gómez-Domínguez, Luis A.	Hialeah-Dade Dev. Inc.	Miami, FL
Gómez Martín, Leopoldo	GMCS Corporation	Miami, FL
Gutiérrez, Alfredo	Morgan Guaranty	Sao Paulo, Brazil
Harper, George R., Esq.	Steel, Hector & Davis	Miami, FL
Hernández-Catá, Ernesto	International Monetary Fund	Washington, DC
Herrera, Jorge R.	Merrill Lynch	Coral Gables, FL
Herrero, José Antonio	Consultant	San Juan, PR

Juvier, Osvaldo A.	Duke Energy Corp.	Charlotte, NC
Kaufman Purcell, Susan	Americas Society	New York, NY
La Sociedad Económica	Economic Research	Paris, France
Lasa, Luis R.	Bacardí Imports, Inc.	Miami, FL
Leiseca, Sergio A., Esq.	Baker & McKenzie	Miami, FL
Linde, Armando	IMF	Washington, DC
Lopez, Albert	The Tandem Group	Washington, DC
López, Roberto I.	Citrus Products, Inc.	Tampa, FL
Loredo, Jorge	Intel Medical Systems	Miami, FL
Luis, Luis R.	Scudder, Stevens & Clark	Boston, MA
Luzárraga, Alberto	Cuban American Research Group	New York, NY
Maidique, Modesto A.	Florida International University	Miami, FL
Martínez, Enrique F.	Rohm and Haas Co.	Coral Gables, FL
Masvidal, Sergio J.	American Express Bank, Ltd.	Miami, FL
Mayer, Alfonso	General Cigar Corp.	New York, NY
Menéndez, Benjamín F.	General Cigar Corp.	Miami, FL
Miranda, José E.	Kelly Tractor Co.	Miami, FL
Montaner, Carlos A.	Union Liberal Cubana	Madrid, Spain
Monto, Edward A.	Houston Industries Energy	Houston, TX
Montoulieu, Carlos F.	U.S. Dept. of Commerce	Washington, DC
Morán, Ricardo J.	Consultant	Washington, DC
Muller, Juan Antonio	INTERFIN, C.A.	Caracas, Venezuela
O'Connell, Richard	Private Investor	Paris, France
Padial, Carlos M.	Padial & Associates, Inc.	Baton Rouge, LA
Palomares, Carlos	CITIBANK, Florida	Miami, FL
Pazos, Felipe	Banco Central de Venezuela	Caracas, Venezuela
Perry, Joseph M.	University of North Florida	Jacksonville, FL
Piedra, Lino	Chrysler Corporation	Washington, DC.
Pino, Jorge E.	META	Miami, FL
Quijano, Carlos N.	World Bank	Washington, DC
Ricardo, José M.	Ricards International Inc.	Chantilly, VA
Rivas, Carlos	Martí, Flores, Prieto & Wachtel	San Juan, PR
Rivero Cervera, José A.	Amerop Sugar Corporation	Miami, FL
Roca, Rubén	The Rouse Company	Columbia, MD
Rodríguez, José Luís	Trans-Tech-Ag Corp.	Ft. Lauderdale, FL
Rodríguez, Ricardo	Smith Barney	New York, NY
Rodríguez-Vázquez, Claudio	Sparrow Trading Corporation	Coral Gables, FL
Sabater, Julio	Universal Communications Enterp.	Elizabeth, NJ
Sánchez, Federico F.	Interlink Group	San Juan, PR
Sánchez, Nicolás	College of The Holy Cross	Worcester, MA
Sanguinetty, Jorge	Development Technologies, Inc.	Miami, FL
Seigle, Carlos & Diana	Rutgers University	Newark, NJ
Travieso-Díaz, Matías F.	Shaw, Pittman, Potts & Trowbridge	Washington, DC
US-Cuba Business Council		Washington, DC
Vallejo, Jorge I.	Vallejo & Vallejo	San Juan, PR
Vega, Sr., Juan Antonio	Latin Finance, Inc.	Coconut Grove, FL
Werlau, Maria Cañizares	Orbis, S.A.	Chatham, NJ.
Zayas-Bazán, Eduardo	East Tennessee State University	Johnson City, TN

ASCE also acknowledges the generous contributions of the following corporate sponsors of the Sixth Annual Meeting:

     CITIBANK Florida
     Freer & McGarry
     Baker & McKenzie